Reading

Grade 3, Unit 2

Smart Solutions

D1469230

PEARSON
Scott Foresman

scottforesman.com

Editorial Offices: Glenview, Illinois • Parsippany, New Jersey • New York, New York
Sales Offices: Boston, Massachusetts • Duluth, Georgia • Glenview, Illinois
Coppell, Texas • Sacramento, California • Mesa, Arizona

We dedicate Reading Street to
Peter Jovanovich.

His wisdom, courage,
and passion for education
are an inspiration to us all.

Cover Mark Buehner

About the Cover Artist

Mark Buehner's sisters say that he was born with a pencil in his hand. While he was growing up, pulling out pencils, paper, and watercolors was part of his daily routine. He loved poring over the pictures in books and even used to staple his pictures together to make books. He had no idea that what he was doing would eventually become his career. He grew up to become an award-winning illustrator of books for children. He believes he has the best job in the world!

ISBN-13: 978-0-328-24374-7

ISBN-10: 0-328-24374-4

Copyright © 2008 Pearson Education, Inc.

All Rights Reserved. Printed in the United States of America. This publication is protected by Copyright, and permission should be obtained from the publisher prior to any prohibited reproduction, storage in a retrieval system, or transmission in any form by any means, electronic, mechanical, photocopying, recording, or likewise. For information regarding permission(s), write to: Permissions Department, Scott Foresman, 1900 East Lake Avenue, Glenview, Illinois 60025.

Many of the designations used by manufacturers and sellers to distinguish their products are claimed as trademarks. Where those designations appear in this book, and Scott Foresman was aware of a trademark claim, the designations have been printed with initial capitals and in cases of multiple usage have also been marked with either ® or ™ where they first appear.

2 3 4 5 6 7 8 9 10 11 V064 16 15 14 13 12 11 10 09 08 07
CC:N1

Reading STREET

Where the Love of Reading Begins

Reading Street Program Authors

Peter Afflerbach, Ph.D.
Professor, Department of
Curriculum and Instruction
University of Maryland at
College Park

Camille L.Z. Blachowicz, Ph.D.
Professor of Education
National-Louis University

Candy Dawson Boyd, Ph.D.
Professor, School of Education
Saint Mary's College of California

Wendy Cheyney, Ed.D.
Professor of Special Education
and Literacy, Florida
International University

Connie Juel, Ph.D.
Professor of Education, School of
Education, Stanford University

Edward J. Kame'enui, Ph.D.
Professor and Director, Institute for
the Development of Educational
Achievement, University of Oregon

Donald J. Leu, Ph.D.
John and Maria Neag Endowed
Chair in Literacy and Technology
University of Connecticut

Jeanne R. Paratore, Ed.D.
Associate Professor of Education
Department of Literacy
and Language Development
Boston University

P. David Pearson, Ph.D.
Professor and Dean,
Graduate School of Education
University of California, Berkeley

Sam L. Sebesta, Ed.D.
Professor Emeritus,
College of Education,
University of Washington, Seattle

Deborah Simmons, Ph.D.
Professor, College of Education
and Human Development
Texas A&M University
(Not pictured)

Sharon Vaughn, Ph.D.
H.E. Hartfelder/Southland
Corporation Regents Professor
University of Texas

Susan Watts-Taffe, Ph.D.
Independent Literacy Researcher
Cincinnati, Ohio

Karen Kring Wixson, Ph.D.
Professor of Education
University of Michigan

Components

Student Editions (1–6)

Teacher's Editions (PreK–6)

Assessment
Assessment Handbook (K–6)
Baseline Group Tests (K–6)
DIBELS™ Assessments (K–6)
ExamView® Test Generator CD-ROM (2–6)
Fresh Reads for Differentiated
Test Practice (1–6)
Online Success Tracker™ (K–6)*
Selection Tests Teacher's Manual (1–6)
Unit and End-of-Year
Benchmark Tests (K–6)

Leveled Readers
Concept Literacy Leveled Readers (K–1)
Independent Leveled Readers (K)
Kindergarten Student Readers (K)
Leveled Reader Teaching Guides (K–6)
Leveled Readers (1–6)
Listen to Me Readers (K)
Online Leveled Reader Database (K–6)*
Take-Home Leveled Readers (K–6)

Trade Books and Big Books
Big Books (PreK–2)
Read Aloud Trade Books (PreK–K)
Sing with Me Big Book (1–2)
Trade Book Library (1–6)

Decodable Readers
Decodable Readers (K–3)
Strategic Intervention
Decodable Readers (1–2)
Take-Home Decodable Readers (K–3)

Phonics and Word Study
Alphabet Cards in English and Spanish
(PreK–K)
Alphabet Chart in English and Spanish
(PreK–K)
Animal ABCs Activity Guide (K)
Finger Tracing Cards (PreK–K)
Patterns Book (PreK–K)
Phonics Activities CD-ROM (PreK–2)*
Phonics Activities Mats (K)
Phonics and Spelling Practice Book (1–3)
Phonics and Word-Building Board and Letters
(PreK–3)
Phonics Songs and Rhymes Audio CD (K–2)
Phonics Songs and Rhymes Flip Chart (K–2)
Picture Word Cards (PreK–K)
Plastic Letter Tiles (K)
Sound-Spelling Cards and Wall Charts (1–2)
Strategies for Word Analysis (4–6)
Word Study and Spelling Practice Book (4–6)

Language Arts
Daily Fix-It Transparencies (K–6)
Grammar & Writing Book and
Teacher's Annotated Edition, The (1–6)
Grammar and Writing Practice Book
and Teacher's Manual (1–6)
Grammar Transparencies (1–6)
Six-Trait Writing Posters (1–6)
Writing Kit (1–6)
Writing Rubrics and Anchor Papers (1–6)
Writing Transparencies (1–6)

Practice and Additional Resources
AlphaBuddy Bear Puppet (K)
Alphasaurus Annie Puppet (PreK)
Amazing Words Posters (K–2)
Centers Survival Kit (PreK–6)
Graphic Organizer Book (2–6)
Graphic Organizer Flip Chart (K–1)
High-Frequency Word Cards (K)
Kindergarten Review (1)
Practice Book and Teacher's Manual (K–6)
Read Aloud Anthology (PreK–2)
Readers' Theater Anthology (K–6)
Research into Practice (K–6)

Retelling Cards (K–6)
Scott Foresman Research Base (K–6)
Skill Transparencies (2–6)
Songs and Rhymes Flip Chart (PreK)
Talk with Me, Sing with Me Chart (PreK–K)
Tested Vocabulary Cards (1–6)
Vocabulary Transparencies (1–2)
Welcome to Reading Street (PreK–1)

ELL
ELL and Transition Handbook (PreK–6)
ELL Comprehensive Kit (1–6)
ELL Posters (K–6)
ELL Readers (1–6)
ELL Teaching Guides (1–6)
Ten Important Sentences (1–6)

Digital Components
AudioText CDs (PreK–6)
Background Building Audio CDs (3–6)
ExamView® Test Generator
CD-ROM (2–6)
Online Lesson Planner (K–6)
Online New Literacies Activities (1–6)*
Online Professional Development (1–6)
Online Story Sort (K–6)*
Online Student Editions (1–6)*
Online Success Tracker™ (K–6)*
Online Teacher's Editions (PreK–6)
Phonics Activities CD-ROM (PreK–2)*
Phonics Songs and Rhymes
Audio CD (K–2)
Sing with Me/Background Building
Audio CDs (PreK–2)
Songs and Rhymes Audio CD (PreK)

My Sidewalks Early Reading Intervention (K)

My Sidewalks Intensive Reading Intervention (Levels A–E)

Reading Street for the Guided Reading Teacher (1–6)

v

Grade 3
Priority Skills

Priority skills are the critical elements of reading—phonemic awareness, phonics, fluency, vocabulary, and text comprehension—as they are developed across and within grades to assure that instructional emphasis is placed on the right skills at the right time and to maintain a systematic sequence of skill instruction.

Key
- ● = Taught/Unit priority
- ◐ = Reviewed and practiced
- ○ = Integrated practice

	UNIT 1		UNIT 2	
	Weeks		Weeks	
	1–2	3–5	1–2	3–5
Phonemic Awareness	Phonemic Awareness for Grade 3 appears in *Scott Foresman Intervention.*			
Phonics				
Blend sounds of letters to decode				
Consonants				
Consonant blends and digraphs				●
Short Vowels	●	○	●	○
Long Vowels	◐	○	●	○
r-Controlled Vowels				
Vowel Digraphs		●	○	○
Diphthongs		●	◐	○
Other vowel patterns				
Decode words with common word parts				
Base words and inflected endings	●	●	○	○
Contractions				
Compounds				●
Suffixes and prefixes				
Blend syllables to decode multisyllabic words	●	●	●	●
Fluency				
Read aloud with accuracy, comprehension, and appropriate rate	●	○	●	○
Read aloud with expression/intonation		●	○	●
Attend to punctuation and use appropriate phrasing		●	○	○
Practice fluency in a variety of ways, including choral reading, paired reading, and repeated oral reading	●	●	●	●
Work toward appropriate fluency goals	80–90 WCPM	80–90 WCPM	85–95 WCPM	85–95 WCPM
Vocabulary				
Read high-frequency words and lesson vocabulary automatically	◐	◐	◐	◐
Develop vocabulary through direct instruction, concrete experiences, reading, and listening to text read aloud	○	○	○	○
Use word structure to figure out word meaning	●	●	○	○
Use context clues to determine word meaning of unfamiliar words, multiple-meaning words, homonyms, homographs	●	●	●	●
Use grade-appropriate reference sources to learn word meanings	●	○	○	●
Use new words in a variety of contexts	○	○	○	○
Create and use graphic organizers to group, study, and retain vocabulary	○	○	○	○
Classify and categorize words	○	○	○	○
Use descriptive words	●	○	○	○

UNIT 3		UNIT 4		UNIT 5		UNIT 6	
Weeks		**Weeks**		**Weeks**		**Weeks**	
1–2	3–5	1–2	3–5	1–2	3–5	1–2	3–5

| 90–100 WCPM | 90–100 WCPM | 95–105 WCPM | 95–105 WCPM | 102–112 WCPM | 102–112 WCPM | 110–120 WCPM | 110–120 WCPM |

Grade 3
Priority Skills

	UNIT 1 Weeks 1–2	UNIT 1 Weeks 3–5	UNIT 2 Weeks 1–2	UNIT 2 Weeks 3–5
Text Comprehension				
Strategies				
Preview the text	○	○	○	○
Set and monitor purpose for reading	○	○	○	○
Activate and use prior knowledge	●	○	○	○
Make, confirm, and modify predictions				●
Monitor comprehension and use fix-up strategies		●	○	●
Use graphic organizers to focus on text structure, to represent relationships in text, or to summarize text			●	○
Answer questions				
Generate questions				●
Recognize text structure: story and informational		●	○	○
Summarize text by retelling stories or identifying main ideas	●	○	○	○
Visualize; use mental imagery		●	●	○
Make connections: text to self, text to text, text to world	○	○	○	○
Skills				
Author's purpose	◑	○	○	●
Cause and effect				
Compare and contrast				
Draw conclusions		◑	○	●
Fact and opinion				
Follow directions			●	○
Generalize				
Graphic sources (charts, diagrams, graphs, maps, tables)			●	●
Main idea and supporting details		●	●	●
Realism/fantasy	●	●	●	○
Sequence of events	●	●	◑	○
Literary Elements				
Character (Recognize characters' traits, actions, feelings, and motives)	◑	●	●	◑
Plot and plot structure				
Setting	◑	●	○	◑
Theme				

UNIT 3 UNIT 4 UNIT 5 UNIT 6

UNIT 3		UNIT 4		UNIT 5		UNIT 6	
Weeks		Weeks		Weeks		Weeks	
1–2	3–5	1–2	3–5	1–2	3–5	1–2	3–5

Unit 4
One of a Kind

Unit 5
Cultures

Unit 6
Freedom

Unit 1
Dollars and Sense

Smart Solutions

What are smart ways that problems are solved?

Penguin Chick

A penguin chick survives in Antarctica.

EXPOSITORY NONFICTION

connect to
SCIENCE

Paired Selection

Plants: Fitting into Their World

PHOTO ESSAY

A Day's Work

A boy learns from his mistake.

REALISTIC FICTION

connect to
SOCIAL STUDIES

Paired Selection

What Is a Weed?

E-MAIL

Prudy's Problem

Prudy collects ideas to solve her problem.

FANTASY

connect to
SOCIAL STUDIES

Paired Selection

Meeting the Challenge of Collecting

INTERVIEW

Tops & Bottoms

Hare solves his problem with a trick.

ANIMAL FANTASY

connect to
SOCIAL STUDIES

Paired Selection

The Hare and the Tortoise

FABLE

William's House

William solves problems in his new country.

HISTORICAL FICTION

connect to
SOCIAL STUDIES

Paired Selection

Log Cabins

EXPOSITORY NONFICTION

Unit 2
Skills Overview

WEEK 1

154–173
Penguin Chick/Plants, Fitting into Their World

How have animals adapted to solve the problems of their environment?

EXPOSITORY NONFICTION

WEEK 2

178–197
A Day's Work/What Is a Weed?

When is a solution the wrong solution?

REALISTIC FICTION

Reading		WEEK 1	WEEK 2
	Comprehension	T ⊙ **Skill** Main Idea and Details T ⊙ **Strategy** Graphic Organizers T REVIEW **Skill** Sequence	T ⊙ **Skill** Character ⊙ **Strategy** Visualize T REVIEW **Skill** Realism/Fantasy
	Vocabulary	T ⊙ **Strategy** Context Clues	T ⊙ **Strategy** Context Clues
	Fluency	Accuracy and Appropriate Pace/Rate	Express Characterization
Word Work	**Phonics**	Syllables V/CV, VC/V	Syllable Pattern C + *le*
	Spelling and Phonics	Syllables Pattern V/CV, VC/V	Words Ending in -*le*
Oral Language	**Speaking/Listening/ Viewing**	Informational Speech View Media Messages	Give Directions Follow Directions
Language Arts	**Grammar, Usage and Mechanics**	T Common and Proper Nouns	T Singular and Plural Nouns
	Weekly Writing	Summary Writing Trait: Organization/Paragraph	Rules Writing Trait: Sentences
	Unit Process Writing	How-to Report	How-to Report
	Research and Study Skills	Dictionary/Glossary	Procedures and Instructions
Integrate Science and Social Studies Standards		**Science** Living Things Habitats Animal Adaptation	**Social Studies** Making Choices Personal Responsibility

⊙ Target Skill   T Tested Skill

WEEK 3	WEEK 4	WEEK 5
202–223 **Prudy's Problem and How She Solved It/Meeting the Challenge of Collecting** FANTASY *How can you get ideas to solve a problem?*	228–249 **Tops and Bottoms/ The Hare and The Tortoise** ANIMAL FANTASY *When are respect and understanding important in solving a problem?*	254–271 **William's House/Log Cabins** HISTORICAL FICTION *When you find yourself in a new place, what problems might you meet?*
T ⊙ **Skill** Main Idea and Details T ⊙ **Strategy** Monitor and Fix Up T REVIEW **Skill** Character	T ⊙ **Skill** Author's Purpose T ⊙ **Strategy** Predict T REVIEW **Skill** Main Idea and Details	T ⊙ **Skill** Draw Conclusions T ⊙ **Strategy** Ask Questions T REVIEW **Skill** Character
T ⊙ **Strategy** Dictionary	T ⊙ **Strategy** Context Clues	T ⊙ **Strategy** Context Clues
Expression/Intonation	Appropriate Phrasing	Read Silently
Compound Words	Words with Consonant Blends	Words with Consonant Digraphs
Compound Words	Words with *spl, thr, squ, str*	Digraphs *sh, th, ph, ch, tch*
Speak to Solve Problems Listen to Solve Problems	Compare and Contrast Identify Common Themes of Pictures	Communicate Needs Distinguish Between Speaker's Opinion and Facts
T Irregular Plural Nouns	T Singular Possessive Nouns	T Plural Possessive Nouns
Problem-Solution Writing Trait: Organization/Paragraphs	Feature Story Writing Trait: Voice	Explanatory Paragraph Writing Trait: Focus/Ideas
How-to Report	How-to Report	How-to Report
Magazine/Periodical	Encyclopedia	Diagram/Scale Drawing

 Time for **SOCIAL STUDIES** — Costs/Benefits of Personal Choices
Civic Life
Helping Others

 Time for **SOCIAL STUDIES** — Costs/Benefits of Personal Choices
Helping Others

 Time for **SOCIAL STUDIES** — Colonial Settlements
Change Over Time
Adapting to Environment

Unit 2
Monitor Progress

Predictors of Reading Success	WEEK 1	WEEK 2	WEEK 3	WEEK 4
Fluency *WCPM*	Read with Accuracy and Appropriate Pace/Rate 85–95 WCPM	Express Characterization 85–95 WCPM	Read with Expression/Intonation 85–95 WCPM	Read with Appropriate Phrasing 85–95 WCPM
Vocabulary/ Concept Development (assessed informally) *Oral Vocabulary*	inhospitable predatory refuge	certainty honestly victims	bulky phonograph portable	bragged humiliated vain
Lesson Vocabulary	**Strategy** Context Clues cuddles flippers frozen hatch pecks preen snuggles	**Strategy** Context Clues excitement gardener motioned sadness shivered shocked slammed	**Strategy** Dictionary collection enormous realize scattered shiny strain	**Strategy** Context Clues bottom cheated clever crops lazy partners wealth
Text Comprehension *Retelling*	**Skill** Main Idea **Strategy** Graphic Organizers	**Skill** Character **Strategy** Visualize	**Skill** Main Idea **Strategy** Monitor and Fix Up	**Skill** Author's Purpose **Strategy** Predict

Smart Solutions   🎯 Target Skill   ✷ SuccessTracker/Unit 2 Benchmark Tested Skills

Make Data–Driven Decisions

Data Management
- Assess
- Diagnose
- Prescribe
- Disaggregate

Classroom Management
- Monitor Progress
- Group
- Differentiate Instruction
- Inform Parents

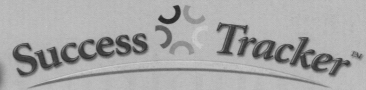

ONLINE CLASSROOM

Read Silently with Fluency

85–95 WCPM

dwellings
gabled
stockade

Strategy
Context Clues

barrels
cellar
clearing
pegs
spoil
steep

Skill Draw Conclusions

Strategy Ask Questions

Manage Data

- Assign the Unit 2 Benchmark Test for students to take online.
- SuccessTracker records results and generates reports by school, grade, classroom, or student.
- Use reports to disaggregate and aggregate Unit 2 skills and standards data to monitor progress.

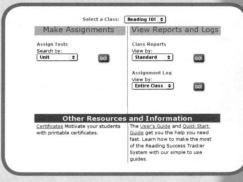

- Based on class lists created to support the categories important for AYP (gender, ethnicity, migrant education, English proficiency, disabilities, economic status), reports let you track adequate yearly progress every five weeks.

Group

- Use results from Unit 2 Benchmark Tests taken online through SuccessTracker to regroup students.
- Reports in SuccessTracker suggest appropriate groups for students based on test results.

Individualize Instruction

- Tests are correlated to Unit 2 tested skills and standards so that prescriptions for individual teaching and learning plans can be created.
- Individualized prescriptions target instruction and accelerate student progress toward learning outcome goals.
- Prescriptions include resources to reteach Unit 2 skills and standards.

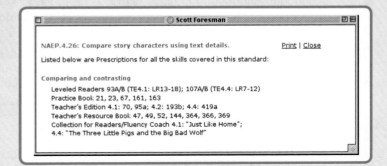

NAEP.4.26: Compare story characters using text details.   Print | Close

Listed below are Prescriptions for all the skills covered in this standard:

Comparing and contrasting
Leveled Readers 93A/B (TE4.1: LR13-18); 107A/B (TE4.4: LR7-12)
Practice Book: 21, 23, 67, 161, 163
Teacher's Edition 4.1: 70, 95a; 4.2: 193b; 4.4: 419a
Teacher's Resource Book: 47, 49, 52, 144, 364, 366, 369
Collection for Readers/Fluency Coach 4.1: "Just Like Home";
4.4: "The Three Little Pigs and the Big Bad Wolf"

Grouping for AYP

STEP 1

Diagnose and Differentiate

Diagnose

To make initial grouping decisions, use the Baseline Group Test or another initial placement test. Depending on students' ability levels, you may have more than one of each group.

Differentiate

If... a student performance is **Below-Level** **then...** use the regular instruction and the daily Strategic Intervention lessons, pp. DI·2–DI·50.

If... a student performance is **On-Level** **then...** use the regular instruction for On-Level learners throughout each selection.

If... a student performance is **Advanced** **then...** use the regular instruction and the daily instruction for Advanced learners, pp. DI·3–DI·51.

Group Time

On-Level

- Explicit instructional routines teach core skills and strategies.

- Independent activities provide practice for core skills and extension and enrichment options.

- Leveled readers (LR1–48) and decodable readers provide additional reading and practice with core skills and vocabulary.

Strategic Intervention

- Daily Strategic Intervention lessons provide more intensive instruction, more scaffolding, more practice with critical skills, and more opportunities to respond.

- Decodable readers practice word reading skills.

- Reteach lessons (DI·52–56) provide additional instructional opportunities with target skills.

- Leveled readers (LR1–48) build background for the selections and practice target skills and vocabulary.

Advanced

- Daily Advanced lessons provide compacted instruction for accelerated learning, options for investigative work, and challenging reading content.

- Leveled readers (LR1–48) provide additional reading tied to lesson concepts.

Additional opportunities to differentiate instruction:
- Reteach Lessons, pp. DI·52–DI·56
- Leveled Reader Instruction and Leveled Practice, LR1–48
- My Sidewalks on Scott Foresman Reading Street Intensive Reading Intervention Program

MY SiDEWALKS ON
SCOTT FORESMAN
READING STREET
Intensive Reading Intervention

4–Step Plan for Assessment

1 **Diagnose and Differentiate**
2 **Monitor Progress**
3 **Assess and Regroup**
4 **Summative Assessment**

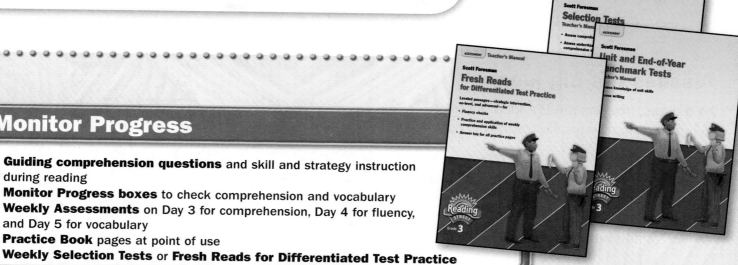

Monitor Progress

STEP 2

- **Guiding comprehension questions** and skill and strategy instruction during reading
- **Monitor Progress boxes** to check comprehension and vocabulary
- **Weekly Assessments** on Day 3 for comprehension, Day 4 for fluency, and Day 5 for vocabulary
- **Practice Book** pages at point of use
- **Weekly Selection Tests** or **Fresh Reads for Differentiated Test Practice**

Assess and Regroup

STEP 3

- **Days 3, 4, and 5 Assessments** Record results of weekly Days 3, 4, and 5 assessments in retelling, fluency, and vocabulary (pp. WA16–17) to track student progress.
- **Unit 2 Benchmark Test** Administer this test to check mastery of unit skills.
- Use weekly assessment information, Unit Benchmark Test performance and the Unit 2 Assess and Regroup (p. WA18) to make regrouping decisions. See the time line below.

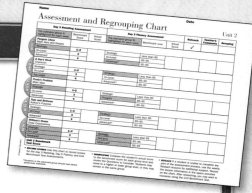

Assessment and Regrouping Chart

YOU ARE HERE
Begin Unit 2

SCOTT FORESMAN ASSESSMENT

Group Baseline Group Test

Regroup Units 1 and 2

Regroup Unit 3

Regroup Unit 4

Regroup Unit 5 (p.175I)

| 1 | 5 | 10 | 15 | 20 | 25 | 30 END OF YEAR |

OUTSIDE ASSESSMENT

Initial placement

Outside assessment for regrouping

Outside assessment for regrouping

Outside assessments (e.g., DIBELS) may recommend regrouping at other times during the year.

Summative Assessment

STEP 4

- **Benchmark Assessment** Use to measure a student's mastery of each unit's skills.
- **End-of-Year Benchmark Assessment** Use to measure a student's mastery of program skills covered in all six units.

Theme Launch

Discuss the Big Idea

As a class, discuss the Big Idea question, *What are smart ways that problems are solved?*

Explain how problem-solving is an important skill to learn in order to live successfully and peacefully in our world, in society, in our school, and in our families.

Ask students how people solve problems among each other. Ask if people can learn how to be good problem-solvers.

Give students one example of effective problem-solving *(wait awhile, smile about it, compromise, and ask for help)*. Explain that any solution will usually require a compromise on both sides.

Theme and Concept Connections

Weekly lesson concepts help students connect the reading selections and the unit theme. Theme-related activities throughout the week provide opportunities to explore the relationships among the selections, the lesson concepts, and the unit theme.

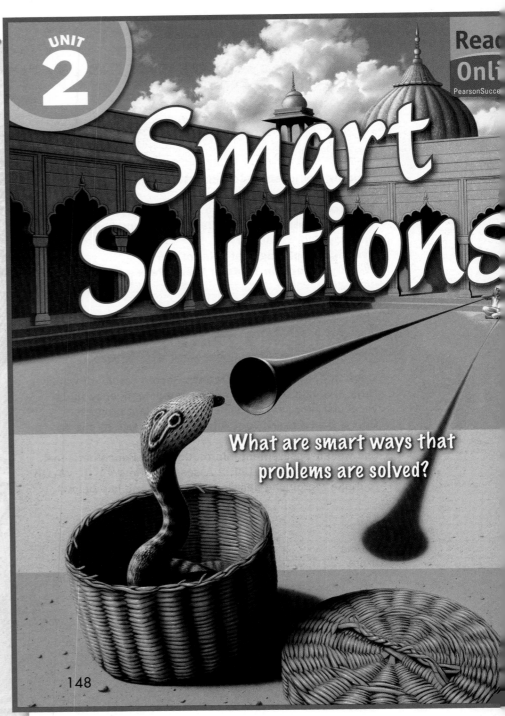

UNIT 2

Smart Solutions

What are smart ways that problems are solved?

148

CONNECTING CULTURES

Help students learn more about how people overcome and solve their problems.

A Day's Work Have students discuss how Francisco attempts to help his grandfather find work but tells a lie in the process. Have them share their ideas about how Francisco not only did not solve the problem, but created a new one by lying.

William's House Have students discuss the different reasons why William's house did not turn out exactly as he had planned. Guide students to arrive at the conclusion that if William had built a home as he planned, he would have had more problems.

Unit Inquiry Project

A Book of Solutions

In the unit inquiry project, students create a Giant Book of Solutions. They can collect riddles, knock-knock jokes, and brain-teasers from brothers and sisters, parents, and so on. They may use print or online resources as available.

The project assessment rubric can be found on p. 272a. Discuss the expectations before students begin the project. [Rubric] [4][3][2][1]

PROJECT TIMETABLE

WEEK	ACTIVITY/SKILL CONNECTION
1	**IDENTIFY QUESTIONS** Students choose a category such as riddles, knock-knock jokes, or brain-teasers and browse a few Web sites or print reference materials to develop an inquiry question about riddles, knock-knock jokes, or brain-teasers.
2	**NAVIGATE/SEARCH** Students conduct effective information searches and look for text and images that can help them answer their questions.
3	**ANALYZE** Students explore Web sites or print materials. They analyze the information they have found to determine whether or not it will be useful to them. Students print or take notes on valid information.
4	**SYNTHESIZE** Students combine relevant information they've collected from different sources to develop an answer to their inquiry questions from Week 1.
	ASSESSMENT OPTIONS
5	**COMMUNICATE** Each student prepares a list of useful resources for other classes who may wish to explore the same topic. Students may also share their Giant Book of Solutions.

CONCEPT DEVELOPMENT

Unit 2
Smart Solutions

CONCEPT QUESTION

What are smart ways that problems are solved?

Week 5

Expand the Concept

When you find yourself in a new place, what problems might you meet?

Connect the Concept

Literature

Develop Language
dwellings, gabled, stockade

Teach Content
Colonial Settlements
Change Over Time
Adapting to Environment

Writing
Explanatory Paragraph

Internet Inquiry
Colonial Times

Week 4

Expand the Concept

When are respect and understanding important in solving a problem?

Connect the Concept

Literature

Develop Language
bragged, humiliated, vain

Teach Content
Costs/Benefits of
Personal Choices
Helping Others

Writing
Feature Story

Internet Inquiry
Good Character

Week 3

Expand the Concept

How can you get ideas to solve a problem?

Connect the Concept

Literature

Develop Language
bulky, phonograph, portable

Teach Content
Costs/Benefits of
Personal Choices
Civic Life
Helping Others

Writing
Problem-Solution
Paragraph

Internet Inquiry
Organizing Collections

Week 1

Expand the Concept

How have animals adapted to solve the problems of their environment?

Connect the Concept

Literature

Develop Language
inhospitable, predatory, refuge

Teach Content
Living Things
Habitats
Animal Adaptation

Writing
Summary

Internet Inquiry
Animal Adaptations

Week 2

Expand the Concept

When is a solution the wrong solution?

Connect the Concept

Literature

Develop Language
certainty, honesty, victims

Teach Content
Making Choices
Personal Responsibility

Writing
List of Rules

Internet Inquiry
Making Good Choices

Illinois

Planning Guide for Performance Descriptors

Penguin Chick

Reading Street Teacher's Edition pages	Grade 3 English Language Arts Performance Descriptors
Oral Language **Speaking/Listening** Build Concept Vocabulary: 150l, 161, 167, 173c Read Aloud: 150m **Viewing** Analyze a Photo: 173d	**1A.Stage C.3.** Discuss the meanings of new words encountered in independent and group activities. **1B.Stage C.13.** Read age-appropriate material aloud with fluency and accuracy. **2A.Stage C.5.** Define unfamiliar vocabulary. **5C.Stage C.1.** Access and use information from a variety of sources.
Word Work Syllable Patterns V/VC, VC/V: 173i, 173k–173l	**1A.Stage C.5.** Use a variety of decoding strategies (e.g., phonics, word patterns, structural analysis, context clues) to recognize new words when reading age-appropriate material.
Reading **Comprehension** Main Idea: 150–151, 154–167, 173b Graphic Organizers: 150–151, 154–167 **Vocabulary** Lesson Vocabulary: 152b, 161, 167, 170 Context Clues: 152–153, 163, 173c **Fluency** Model Reading with Accuracy and Appropriate Pace/Rate: 150l–150m, 173a Choral Reading: 173a **Self-Selected Reading:** LR1–9, TR16–17 **Literature** Genre—Expository Fiction: 154 Reader Response: 168	**1A.Stage C.5.** Use a variety of decoding strategies (e.g., phonics, word patterns, structural analysis, context clues) to recognize new words when reading age-appropriate material. **1B.Stage C.3.** Use a variety of strategies (e.g., K-W-L, anticipation guide, graphic organizer, DR-TA) to connect important ideas in text to prior knowledge and other reading. **1B.Stage C.4.** Identify explicit main ideas. **1B.Stage C.13.** Read age-appropriate material aloud with fluency and accuracy. **1C.Stage C.2.** Use information to generate and respond to questions that reflect higher level thinking skills (e.g., analyzing, synthesizing, inferring, evaluating). **2A.Stage C.5.** Define unfamiliar vocabulary. **2A.Stage C.9.** Classify types of expository text structures (e.g., description, sequence, comparison, cause/effect, problem/solution).
Language Arts **Writing** Summary: 173g–173h **Six-Trait Writing** Organization/Paragraphs: 169, 173g–173h **Grammar, Usage, and Mechanics** Common and Proper Nouns: 173e–173f **Research/Study** Dictionary/Glossary: 173n **Technology** New Literacies: 173m	**1B.Stage C.11.** Summarize or retell information from a text. **3A.Stage C.9.** Demonstrate appropriate use of the various parts of speech (e.g., nouns, pronouns, verbs). **5A.Stage C.4.** Use text aids (e.g., table of contents, glossary, index, alphabetical order) to locate information in a book. **5A.Stage C.5.** Use an organizational system (e.g., media center, classroom resources, available technology) to locate information.
Unit Skills **Writing** How-To Report: WA2–9 **Poetry:** 272–275 **Project/Wrap-Up:** 276–277	**3B.Stage C.4.** Organize around a structure (e.g., paragraph, essay) appropriate to purpose, audience, and context. **3C.Stage C.3.** Experiment with different forms of creative writing (e.g., song, poetry, short fiction, play).

This Week's Leveled Readers

Below-Level

1B.Stage C.4. Identify explicit main ideas.
1B.Stage C.7. Identify genres of fiction and non-fiction.

Nonfiction

On-Level

1B.Stage C.4. Identify explicit main ideas.
2B.Stage C.1. Apply events and situations in both fiction and nonfiction to personal experiences.

Nonfiction

Advanced

1B.Stage C.5. Make connections from text to text, text to self, text to world.
4A.Stage C.2. Distinguish among different kinds of information (e.g., fact, opinion, detail, main idea, fantasy, reality).

Nonfiction

Content-Area Illinois Performance Descriptors in This Lesson

Science

12B.Stage C.2. Apply scientific inquiries or technological designs to examine the interdependence of organisms in ecosystems: identifying adaptations that help animals survive in specific or multiple environments; describing the interaction between living and non-living factors in an ecosystem; predicting what can happen to organisms if they lose different environmental resources or ecologically related groups of organisms.

12C.Stage C.1. Apply scientific inquiries or technological designs to examine the flow of energy: measuring variations of heat absorption or reflection in objects.

12E.Stage C.1. Apply scientific inquiries or technological designs to analyze Earth's land, water and atmosphere as systems: illustrating nature's oxygen and water cycles.

Math

7A.Stage C.4. Describe multiple measurable attributes (e.g., length, mass/weight, time, temperature, area, volume, capacity) of a single object.

7C.Stage C.2. Determine elapsed time between events.

Social Studies

16E.Stage C.8. Tell why knowledge of geography is necessary to understand the history of the people in a place or region.

17A.Stage C.6. Point out the location of the poles, the equator, and the hemispheres on a globe and/or a map.

18C.Stage C.2. Describe the concept of cooperation.

18C.Stage C.3. Describe how individuals work together to obtain food, clothing, and shelter.

18C.Stage C.4. Define division of labor.

Illinois!

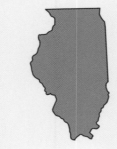

A FAMOUS ILLINOISAN
Carl Sandburg

Carl Sandburg (1878–1967) was born in Galesburg. He wrote several books and poems. In 1940 Sandburg won the Pulitzer Prize in history for the book *Abraham Lincoln: The War Years*. His book of poetry, *Complete Poems*, earned him a second Pulitzer Prize in 1951 for poetry. As a child, Sandburg was very poor. He left school early to earn money to help his parents support the family. After serving in the Spanish-American War, Sandburg put himself through college.

Students can . . .
Read one of Carl Sandburg's poems and draw a picture to illustrate it.

A SPECIAL ILLINOIS PLACE
Glessner House Museum

Architect Henry Hobson Richardson designed the Glessner House, owned by John and Frances Glessner, in 1885. The exterior of the house is granite, giving it a fortress-like appearance. The house has twenty-seven rooms and an enclosed courtyard. It is located on Prairie Avenue in Chicago. A National Historic Landmark, the house is open to the public for tours. The museum includes furniture, pottery, silver, and ceramic vases and tiles.

Students can . . .
Look at pictures of the Glessner House and draw a floor plan for the house.

ILLINOIS FUN FACTS
Did You Know?

- The Sears Tower in Chicago is one of the tallest buildings in the world.

- Illinois became the twenty-first state on December 3, 1818.

- Illinois is the twenty-fourth largest state in the United States. The area of the state is about 58,000 square miles of land and water, including part of Lake Michigan.

Students can . . .
Draw an outline map of Illinois and label three bodies of water in the state.

Unit 2
Smart Solutions

CONCEPT QUESTION
What are smart ways that problems are solved?

Week 1
How have animals adapted to solve the problems of their environment?

Week 2
When is a solution the wrong solution?

Week 3
How can you get ideas to solve a problem?

Week 4
When are respect and understanding important in solving a problem?

Week 5
When you find yourself in a new place, what problems might you meet?

EXPAND THE CONCEPT
How have animals adapted to solve the problems of their environment?

CONNECT THE CONCEPT

▶ **Build Background**
inhospitable, predatory, refuge

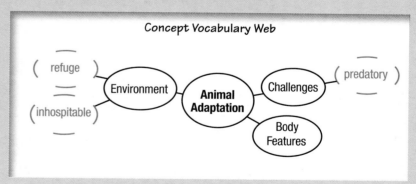

Concept Vocabulary Web

▶ **Science Content**
Habitats, Living Things, Animal Adaptation

▶ **Writing**
Summary

▶ **Internet Inquiry**
Animal Adaptations

Preview Your Week

How have animals adapted to solve the problems of their environment?

Penguin Chick

by Betty Tatham
illustrated by Helen K. Davie

Genre Expository nonfiction gives information about the real world. Read for facts about emperor penguins.

How do emperor penguins protect their chicks from the extreme temperature of Antarctica?

154

155

Audio CD

Student Edition pages 154–167

Genre Expository Nonfiction
Vocabulary Strategy Context Clues
Comprehension Skill Main Idea
Comprehension Strategy Graphic Organizers

Paired Selection

Reading Across Texts
Compare Animals and Plants that Survive Harsh Environments

Genre
Photo Essay

Text Features
Photographs

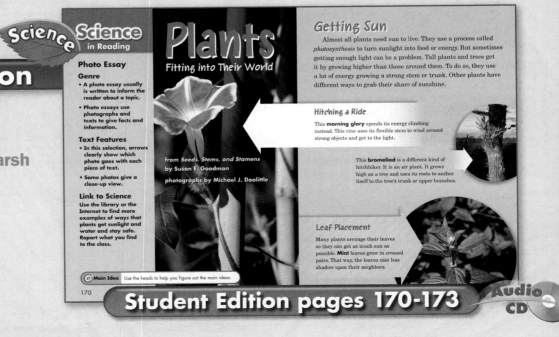

Science in Reading

Photo Essay

Genre
• A photo essay usually is written to inform the reader about a topic.
• Photo essays use photographs and texts to give facts and information.

Text Features
• In this selection, arrows clearly show which photo goes with each piece of text.
• Some photos give a close-up view.

Link to Science
Use the library or the Internet to find more examples of ways that plants get sunlight and water and stay safe. Report what you find to the class.

Plants
Fitting into Their World

from *Seeds, Stems, and Stamens*
by Susan E. Goodman
photographs by Michael J. Doolittle

Getting Sun
Almost all plants need sun to live. They use a process called *photosynthesis* to turn sunlight into food or energy. But sometimes getting enough light can be a problem. Tall plants and trees get it by growing higher than those around them. To do so, they use a lot of energy growing a strong stem or trunk. Other plants have different ways to grab their share of sunshine.

Hitching a Ride
This **morning glory** spends its energy climbing instead. This vine uses its flexible stem to wind around strong objects and get to the light.

This **bromeliad** is a different kind of hitchhiker. It is an air plant. It grows high on a tree and uses its roots to anchor itself to the tree's trunk or upper branches.

Leaf Placement
Many plants arrange their leaves so they can get as much sun as possible. **Mint** leaves grow in crossed pairs. That way, the leaves cast less shadow upon their neighbors.

Main Idea Use the heads to help you figure out the main ideas.

170

Student Edition pages 170–173

Audio CD

Read It
ONLINE
PearsonSuccessNet.com
• Student Edition
• Leveled Readers

Leveled Readers

◉ **Skill** Main Idea
◉ **Strategy** Graphic Organizers
Lesson Vocabulary

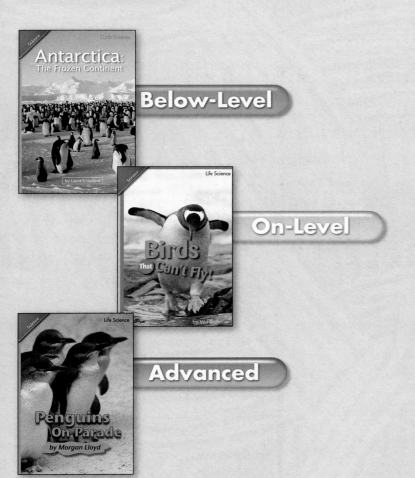

Antarctica: The Frozen Continent

Below-Level

Birds That Can't Fly!

On-Level

Penguins On Parade
by Morgan Lloyd

Advanced

ELL Reader
· Concept Vocabulary
· Text Support
· Language Enrichment

Penguins
by Daniel Petersburg

TIME FOR
Science

Integrate Science Standards
• Habitats
• Living Things
• Animal Adaptation

✓ Read

Penguin Chick pp. 154–167

"Plants: Fitting into Their World" pp. 170–173

Leveled Readers

Below-Level
• Support Concepts

On-Level
• Develop Concepts

Advanced
• Extend Concepts
• Science Extension Activity

ELL Reader

✓ Build
Concept Vocabulary
Animal Adaptation,
pp. 150l–150m

✓ Teach
Science Concepts
Adaptation, p. 159
Life Cycles, p. 163
Ecosystems, p. 165
Wild and Cultivated Plants,
p. 171

✓ Explore
Science Center
Research Local Wildlife,
p. 150k

Weekly Plan

READING

45–90 minutes

TARGET SKILLS OF THE WEEK

⟳ **Comprehension Skill**
Main Idea

⟳ **Comprehension Strategy**
Graphic Organizers

⟳ **Vocabulary Strategy**
Context Clues

DAY 1
PAGES 150l–152b, 173a, 173e–173h, 173k–173m

Oral Language

QUESTION OF THE WEEK *How have animals adapted to solve the problems of their environment?*

Read Aloud: "Swamp Scramblers," 150m
Build Concepts, 150l

Comprehension/Vocabulary

Comprehension Skill/Strategy Lesson, 150–151

⟳ Main Idea and Details **T**

⟳ Graphic Organizers

Build Background, 152a

Introduce Lesson Vocabulary, 152b
cuddles, flippers, frozen, hatch, pecks, preen, snuggles **T**

Read Leveled Readers

Grouping Options 150f–150g

Fluency

Model Accuracy and Appropriate Pace/Rate, 150l–150m, 173a

DAY 2
PAGES 152–161, 173a, 173e–173i, 173k–173m

Oral Language

QUESTION OF THE DAY *How do the mother and father penguin work together to take care of their chick?*

Word Work

Phonics Lesson, 173i
Syllable Patterns V/CV, VC/V

Comprehension/Vocabulary

Vocabulary Strategy Lesson, 152–153

⟳ Context Clues **T**

Read *Penguin Chick,* 154–161

Grouping Options
150f–150g

⟳ Main Idea and Details **T**

⟳ Graphic Organizers

Develop Vocabulary

Fluency

Choral Reading, 173a

LANGUAGE ARTS

30–60 minutes

Trait of the Week

Organization/Paragraphs

Grammar, 173e
Introduce Common and Proper Nouns **T**

Writing Workshop, 173g
Introduce Summary

Model the Trait of the Week: Organization/ Paragraphs

Spelling, 173k
Pretest for Syllable Pattern V/CV, VC/V

Internet Inquiry, 173m
Identify Questions

Grammar, 173e
Develop Common and Proper Nouns **T**

Writing Workshop, 173g
Improve Writing: Include Necessary Information

Spelling, 173k
Teach the Generalization

Internet Inquiry, 173m
Navigate/Search

DAILY WRITING ACTIVITIES	**Day 1** Write to Read, 150	**Day 2** Words to Write, 153 Strategy Response Log, 154, 161
DAILY SCIENCE CONNECTIONS	**Day 1** Animal Adaptation Concept Web, 150l	**Day 2** Time for Science: Adaptation, 159 Revisit the Animal Adaptation Concept Web, 161

DAILY SUCCESS PREDICTORS
for Adequate Yearly Progress

Monitor Progress and Corrective Feedback

Vocabulary	Check Vocabulary, *150l*	

RESOURCES FOR THE WEEK

- Practice Book, pp. 51–60
- Phonics and Spelling Practice Book, pp. 21–24
- Grammar and Writing Practice Book, pp. 21–24

- Selection Test, pp. 21–24
- Fresh Reads for Differentiated Test Practice, pp. 31–36
- The Grammar and Writing Book, pp. 80–85

Grouping Options for Differentiated Instruction

Turn the page for the small group lesson plan.

DAY 3
PAGES 162–169, 173a, 173e–173h, 173k–173m

Oral Language

QUESTION OF THE DAY *Describe a penguin's life cycle.*

Comprehension/Vocabulary

Read *Penguin Chick,* 162–168

Grouping Options 150f–150g

- ⟳ Graphic Organizers
- ⟳ Context Clues **T**
- **REVIEW** Sequence **T**
- Develop Vocabulary

Reader Response

Selection Test

Fluency

Model Accuracy and Appropriate Pace/Rate, 173a

Grammar, 173f
Apply Common and Proper Nouns in Writing **T**

Writing Workshop, 169, 173h
Write Now
Prewrite and Draft

Spelling, 173l
Connect Spelling to Writing

Internet Inquiry, 173m
Analyze Sources

Day 3 Strategy Response Log, 166
Look Back and Write, 168

Day 3 Time for Science: Life Cycles, 163; Ecosystems, 165; Revisit the Animal Adaptation Concept Web, 167

DAY 4
PAGES 170–173a, 173e–173h, 173j–173m

Oral Language

QUESTION OF THE DAY *What challenges do people, like plants and animals, face when trying to adapt to their environment?*

Word Work

Phonics Lesson, 173j
REVIEW Dipthongs **T**

Comprehension/Vocabulary

Read "Plants Fitting into Their World," 170–173

Grouping Options 150f–150g

Photo Essay/Text Features

Reading Across Texts

Content-Area Vocabulary

Fluency

Partner Reading, 173a

Grammar, 173f
Practice Common and Proper Nouns for Standardized Tests **T**

Writing Workshop, 173h
Draft, Revise, and Publish

Spelling, 173l
Provide a Strategy

Internet Inquiry, 173m
Synthesize Information

Day 4 Writing Across Texts, 173

Day 4 Time for Science: Wild and Cultivated Plants, 171

DAY 5
PAGES 173a–173h, 173k–173n

Oral Language

QUESTION OF THE WEEK *To wrap up the week, revisit the Day 1 question.*
Build Concept Vocabulary, 173c

Fluency

Read Leveled Readers

Grouping Options 150f–150g

Assess Reading Rate, 173a

Comprehension/Vocabulary

- ⟳ Reteach Main Idea and Details, 173b **T**
- Graphic Sources, 173b
- ⟳ Review Context Clues, 173c **T**

Speaking and Viewing, 173d
Informational Speech
Analyze a Photo

Grammar, 173f
Cumulative Review

Writing Workshop, 173h
Connect to Unit Writing

Spelling, 173l
Posttest for Syllable Pattern V/CV, VC/V

Internet Inquiry, 173m
Communicate Results

Research/Study Skills, 173n
Dictionary/Glossary

Day 5 Graphic Sources, 173b

Day 5 Revisit the Animal Adaptation Concept Web, 173c

KEY ⟳ = Target Skill **T** = Tested Skill

Check Retelling, *169*

Check Fluency WCPM, *173a*

Check Vocabulary, *173c*

SUCCESS PREDICTOR

Small Group Plan for Differentiated Instruction

Daily Plan AT A GLANCE

Reading
Whole Group
- Oral Language
- Phonics
- Comprehension/Vocabulary

Group Time
Differentiated Instruction
Meet with small groups to provide:
- Skill Support
- Reading Support
- Fluency Practice

Read

This week's lessons for daily group time can be found behind the Differentiated Instruction (DI) tab on pp. DI·2–DI·11.

Whole Group
- Fluency

Language Arts
- Grammar
- Writing
- Spelling
- Research/Inquiry
- Speaking/Listening/Viewing

Use My Sidewalks on Reading Street for Tier III intensive reading intervention.

DAY 1

On-Level	Strategic Intervention	Advanced
Teacher-Led *Page DI · 3*	**Teacher-Led** *Page DI · 2*	**Teacher-Led** *Page DI · 3*
• Develop Concept Vocabulary • **Read** On-Level Reader *Birds That Can't Fly*	• Preteach Syllable Patterns • **Read** Decodable Reader 6 • **Read** Below-Level Reader *Antarctica . . .*	• **Read** Advanced Reader *Penguins on Parade* • Independent Extension Activity

(i) Independent Activities
While you meet with small groups, have the rest of the class...

- Visit the Reading/Library Center
- Listen to the Background Building Audio
- Finish Write to Read, p. 150
- Complete Practice Book 3.1 pp. 53–54
- Visit Cross-Curricular Centers

DAY 2

On-Level	Strategic Intervention	Advanced
Teacher-Led *Pages 156–161*	**Teacher-Led** *Page DI · 4*	**Teacher-Led** *Page DI · 5*
• **Read** *Penguin Chick*	• Practice Lesson Vocabulary • Read Multisyllabic Words • **Read** or Listen to *Penguin Chick*	• Extend Vocabulary • **Read** *Penguin Chick*

(i) Independent Activities
While you meet with small groups, have the rest of the class...

- Visit the Reading/Library Center
- Listen to the AudioText for *Penguin Chick*
- Finish Words to Write, p. 153
- Complete Practice Book 3.1 pp. 55-56, 59
- Write in their Strategy Response Logs, pp. 154, 161
- Visit Cross-Curricular Centers
- Work on inquiry projects

DAY 3

On-Level	Strategic Intervention	Advanced
Teacher-Led *Pages 162-167*	**Teacher-Led** *Page DI · 6*	**Teacher-Led** *Page DI · 7*
• **Read** *Penguin Chick*	• Practice Main Idea and Graphic Organizers • **Read** or Listen to *Penguin Chick*	• Extend Main Idea and Graphic Organizers • **Read** *Penguin Chick*

(i) Independent Activities
While you meet with small groups, have the rest of the class...

- Visit the Reading/Library Center
- Listen to the AudioText for *Penguin Chick*
- Write in their Strategy Response Logs, p. 166
- Finish Look Back and Write, p. 168
- Complete Practice Book 3.1 p. 57
- Visit Cross-Curricular Centers
- Work on inquiry projects

① Begin with whole class skill and strategy instruction.
② Meet with small groups to provide differentiated instruction.
③ Gather the whole class back together for fluency and language arts.

DAY 4

On-Level
Teacher-Led
Pages 170–173

• **Read** "Plants: Fitting into Their World"

Strategic Intervention
Teacher-Led
Page DI · 8

• Practice Retelling
• **Read** or Listen to "Plants: Fitting into Their World"

Advanced
Teacher-Led
Page DI · 9

• **Read** "Plants: Fitting into Their World"
• Genre Study

i Independent Activities

While you meet with small groups, have the rest of the class...

• Visit the Reading/Library Center
• Listen to the AudioText for "Plants: Fitting into Their World"
• Visit the Writing and Vocabulary Centers

• Finish Writing Across Texts, p. 173
• Visit Cross-Curricular Centers
• Work on inquiry projects

DAY 5

On-Level
Teacher-Led
Page DI · 11

Reread Leveled Reader
Birds That Can't Fly

Retell *Birds That Can't Fly*

Strategic Intervention
Teacher-Led
Page DI · 10

• **Reread** Leveled Reader *Antarctica: The Frozen Continent*
• Retell *Antarctica: The Frozen Continent*

Advanced
Teacher-Led
Page DI · 11

• **Reread** Leveled Reader *Penguins on Parade*
• Share Extension Activity

i Independent Activities

While you meet with small groups, have the rest of the class...

Visit the Reading/Library Center
Complete Practice Book 3.1 pp. 58, 60

• Visit Cross-Curricular Centers
• Work on inquiry projects

Grouping Place English language learners in the groups that correspond to their reading abilities in English.

Use the appropriate Leveled Reader or other text at students' instructional level.

TiP Send home the appropriate Multilingual Summary of the main selection on Day 1.

Take It to the NET™ ONLINE
PearsonSuccessNet.com

Peter Afflerbach
For research on prediction strategies, see the article "The Influence of Prior Knowledge and Text Genre on . . . Prediction Strategies" by Scott Foresman author Peter Afflerbach.

TEACHER TALK

A **syllable** is a unit of pronunciation that contains one vowel sound.

Looking Ahead

Be sure to schedule time for students to work on the unit inquiry project, "A Book of Solutions." This week students choose categories and develop inquiry questions about riddles, knock-knock jokes, or brain-teasers.

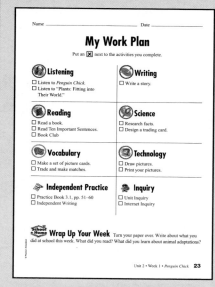

▲ **Group-Time Survival Guide**
p. 23, Weekly Contract

☑ Customize Your Plan *by Strand*

ORAL LANGUAGE

Concept Development

How have animals adapted to solve the problems of their environment?

CONCEPT VOCABULARY

inhospitable   *predatory*   *refuge*

BUILD

❑ **Question of the Week** Introduce and discuss the question of the week. This week students will read a variety of texts and work on projects related to the concept *animal adaptation*. Post the question for students to refer to throughout the week. **DAY 1** *150d*

❑ **Read Aloud** Read aloud "Swamp Scramblers." Then begin a web to build concepts and concept vocabulary related to this week's lesson and the unit theme, Smart Solutions. Introduce the concept words *inhospitable, predatory,* and *refuge* and have students place them on the web. Display the web for use throughout the week. **DAY 1** *150l–150m*

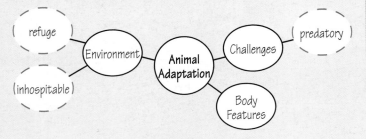

DEVELOP

❑ **Question of the Day** Use the prompts from the Weekly Plan to engage students in conversations related to this week's reading and the unit theme. **EVERY DAY** *150d–150e*

❑ **Concept Vocabulary Web** Revisit the Animal Adaptation Concept Web and encourage students to add concept words from their reading and life experiences. **DAY 2** *161,* **DAY 3** *167*

CONNECT

❑ **Looking Back/Moving Forward** Revisit the Animal Adaptation Concept Web and discuss how it relates to this week's lesson and the unit theme. Then make connections to next week's lesson. **DAY 5** *173c*

CHECK

❑ **Concept Vocabulary Web** Use the Animal Adaptation Concept Web to check students' understanding of the concept vocabulary words *inhospitable, predatory,* and *refuge*. **DAY 1** *150l,* **DAY 5** *173c*

VOCABULARY

🔊 **STRATEGY CONTEXT CLUES**
Context clues are the words and sentences around an unknown word. Sometimes an author uses a synonym as a context clue. A synonym is a word that means the same or almost the same as another word. When you come across a word you don't know, look for a familiar synonym as a context clue. The synonym can help you figure out the meaning of the word you don't know.

LESSON VOCABULARY

cuddles	pecks
flippers	preen
frozen	snuggles
hatch	

TEACH

❑ **Words to Know** Give students the opportunity to tell what they already know about this week's lesson vocabulary words. Then discuss word meaning. **DAY 1** *152b*

❑ **Vocabulary Strategy Lesson** Use the vocabulary strategy lesson in the Student Edition to introduce and model this week's strategy, *context clues*. **DAY 2** *152-153*

Vocabulary Strategy Lesson

PRACTICE/APPLY

❑ **Leveled Text** Read the lesson vocabulary in the context of leveled text. **DAY 1** *LR1–LR9*

❑ **Words in Context** Read the lesson vocabulary and apply *context clues* in the context of *Penguin Chick*. **DAY 2** *154-161,* **DAY 3** *162-168*

Leveled Readers

❑ **Vocabulary Center** Make picture cards to test knowledge of lesson vocabulary. **ANY DAY** *150j*

❑ **Homework** Practice Book 3.1 pp. 54–55. **DAY 1** *152b,* **DAY 2** *153*

Main Selection—Nonfiction

❑ **Word Play** Have partners use reference sources to make lists of words that refer to penguins and their behavior. **ANY DAY** *173c*

ASSESS

❑ **Selection Test** Use the Selection Test to determine students' understanding of the lesson vocabulary words. **DAY 3**

RETEACH/REVIEW

❑ **Reteach Lesson** If necessary, use this lesson to reteach and review *context clues*. **DAY 5** *173c*

Use assessment data to determine your instructional focus.

② Preview this week's instruction by strand.

③ Choose instructional activities that meet the needs of your classroom.

COMPREHENSION

SKILL MAIN IDEA AND DETAILS The topic is what a piece of writing is about. The main idea is the most important idea about the topic. Supporting details are small pieces of information that tell about the main idea.

STRATEGY GRAPHIC ORGANIZERS A graphic organizer is a chart or outline that helps you put information in order, or organize it, as you read. Good readers make graphic organizers to show the main idea and supporting details of a piece of writing.

TEACH

☐ **Skill/Strategy Lesson** Use the skill/strategy lesson in the Student Edition to introduce and model *main idea and details* and *graphic organizers*. DAY 1 150-151

Skill/Strategy Lesson

☐ **Extend Skills** Teach graphic sources. ANY DAY 173b

PRACTICE/APPLY

☐ **Leveled Text** Apply *main idea and details* and *graphic organizers* to read leveled text. DAY 1 LR1-LR9

Leveled Readers

☐ **Skills and Strategies in Context** Read *Penguin Chick*, using the Guiding Comprehension questions to apply *main idea and details* and *graphic organizers*. DAY 2 154-161, DAY 3 162-168

Main Selection—Nonfiction

☐ **Skills and Strategies in Context** Read "Plants Fitting into Their World," guiding students as they apply *main idea and details* and *graphic organizers*. Then have students discuss and write across texts. DAY 4 170-173

☐ **Homework** Practice Book 3.1 pp. 53, 57, 58. DAY 1 151, DAY 3 167, DAY 5 173b

Paired Selection—Nonfiction

☐ **Fresh Reads for Differentiated Test Practice** Have students practice *main idea and details* with a new passage. DAY 3

ASSESS

☐ **Selection Test** Determine students' understanding of the selection and their use of *main idea and details*. DAY 3

☐ **Retell** Have students retell *Penguin Chick*. DAY 3 168-169

RETEACH/REVIEW

☐ **Reteach Lesson** If necessary, reteach and review *main idea and details*. DAY 5 173b

FLUENCY

SKILL ACCURACY AND APPROPRIATE PACE/RATE Accuracy is identifying words correctly as you read, and reading without omitting words or substituting a word. When you read at an appropriate pace and rate, you read at a speed that makes the words and sentences clear and understandable.

TEACH

☐ **Read Aloud** Model fluent reading by rereading "Swamp Scramblers." Focus on this week's fluency skill, accuracy and appropriate pace/rate. DAY 1 150l-150m, 173a

PRACTICE/APPLY

☐ **Choral Reading** Read aloud selected paragraphs from *Penguin Chick*, modeling appropriate rate and accuracy. Then practice as a class, doing three choral readings. DAY 2 173a, DAY 3 173a

☐ **Partner Reading** Have partners practice reading aloud, reading with accuracy and appropriate rate and offering each other feedback. As students reread, monitor their progress toward their individual fluency goals DAY 4 173a

☐ **Listening Center** Have students follow along with the AudioText for this week's selections. ANY DAY 150j

☐ **Reading/Library Center** Have students reread a selection of their choice. ANY DAY 150j

☐ **Fluency Coach** Have students use Fluency Coach to listen to fluent readings or practice reading on their own. ANY DAY

ASSESS

☐ **Check Fluency** WCPM Do a one-minute timed reading, paying special attention to this week's skill—accuracy and appropriate pace/rate. Provide feedback for each student. DAY 5 173a

☑ Customize Your Plan *by Stran*

GRAMMAR

SKILL COMMON AND PROPER NOUNS A common noun names any person, place, or thing. A proper noun names a particular person, place, or thing. Proper nouns begin with capital letters.

TEACH

☐ **Grammar Transparency 6** Use Grammar Transparency 6 to teach common and proper nouns. **DAY 1** *173e*

Grammar Transparency 6

PRACTICE/APPLY

☐ **Develop the Concept** Review the concept of common and proper nouns and provide guided practice. **DAY 2** *173e*

☐ **Apply to Writing** Have students review something they have written and apply what they have learned about common and proper nouns. **DAY 3** *173f*

☐ **Test Preparation** Examine common errors in common and proper nouns to prepare for standardized tests. **DAY 4** *173f*

☐ **Homework** Grammar and Writing Practice Book pp. 21–23. **DAY 2** *173e,* **DAY 3** *173f,* **DAY 4** *173f*

ASSESS

☐ **Cumulative Review** Use Grammar and Writing Practice Book p. 24. **DAY 5** *173f*

RETEACH/REVIEW

☐ **Daily Fix-It** Have students find and correct errors in grammar, spelling, and punctuation. **EVERY DAY** *173e-173f*

☐ **The Grammar and Writing Book** Use pp. 80–83 of The Grammar and Writing Book to extend instruction for common and proper nouns. **ANY DAY**

The Grammar and Writing Book

WRITING

Trait of the Week

ORGANIZATION OF PARAGRAPHS A careful writer tells about events and details in order. Organization is the structure of your story, or how you arrange your information and ideas. The organization keeps your information and ideas in order. For example, when you write a summary, put events in the right time order, the way they happen in the story. Use time words such as *first, next, then,* and *meanwhile* to help your audience know when events happened.

TEACH

☐ **Writing Transparency 6A** Use the model to introduce and discuss the Trait of the Week. **DAY 1** *173g*

☐ **Writing Transparency 6B** Use the transparency to show students how including necessary information can improve their writing. **DAY 2** *173g*

Writing Transparency 6A   **Writing Transparency 6B**

PRACTICE/APPLY

☐ **Write Now** Examine the model on Student Edition p. 169. Then have students write their own summaries. **DAY 3** *169, 173h,* **DAY 4** *173h*

> **Prompt** *Penguin Chick* explains how penguins protect their eggs and their baby chicks. Think about what happens as penguin chicks hatch and grow. Now write a summary of *Penguin Chick.*

Write Now p. 169

☐ **Writing Center** Write a story about "A Day in the Antarctic," from a penguin chick's point of view. **ANY DAY** *150k*

ASSESS

☐ **Writing Trait Rubric** Use the rubric to evaluate students' writing. **DAY 4** *173h*

RETEACH/REVIEW

☐ **The Grammar and Writing Book** Use pp. 80-85 of The Grammar and Writing Book to extend instruction for common and proper nouns, including necessary information, and summaries. **ANY DAY**

The Grammar and Writing Book

❶ Use assessment data to determine your instructional focus.

❷ Preview this week's instruction by strand.

❸ Choose instructional activities that meet the needs of your classroom.

SPELLING

GENERALIZATION SYLLABLE PATTERN V/CV, VC/V When the vowel sound in the first syllable is long, divide the word after the vowel: *pi lot*. When the vowel sound in the first syllable is short, divide the word after the consonant: *fin ish*. The sound of the vowel in the first syllable can determine how the word is divided.

TEACH

❑ **Pretest** Give the pretest for words with syllable pattern V/CV, VC/V. Guide students in self-correcting their pretests and correcting any misspellings. **DAY 1** *173k*

❑ **Think and Practice** Connect spelling to the phonics generalization syllable patterns V/CV, VC/V. **DAY 2** *173k*

PRACTICE/APPLY

❑ **Connect to Writing** Have students use spelling words to write a descriptive paragraph. Then review frequently misspelled words: *before, favorite, pretty.* **DAY 3** *173l*

❑ **Homework** Phonics and Spelling Practice Book pp. 21–24. **EVERY DAY**

RETEACH/REVIEW

❑ **Review** Review spelling words to prepare for the posttest. Then provide students with a spelling strategy—dividing words. **DAY 4** *173l*

ASSESS

❑ **Posttest** Use dictation sentences to give the posttest for words with syllable patterns V/CV, VC/V. **DAY 5** *173l*

Spelling Words

1. finish
2. pilot
3. even
4. wagon
5. music
6. silent
7. rapid
8. female*
9. lemon
10. pupil
11. focus
12. robot
13. tulip
14. camel
15. salad

Challenge Words

16. resident
17. spinach
18. climate
19. tradition
20. innocent

*Word from the selection

PHONICS

SKILL SYLLABLE PATTERNS V/CV, VC/V When a word or a syllable ends with a single vowel, the vowel sound is usually long. When a word or a syllable ends with a consonant, the vowel sound is usually short.

TEACH

❑ **Phonics Lesson** Model how to read words with syllable patterns V/CV, VC/V. Then have students practice by decoding longer words and reading words in context. **DAY 2** *173i*

PRACTICE/APPLY

❑ **Homework** Practice Book 3.1, p. 59. **DAY 2** *173i*

RETEACH/REVIEW

❑ **Review Phonics** Review how to read words with diphthongs. Then have students practice by decoding longer words and reading words in context. **DAY 4** *173j*

RESEARCH AND INQUIRY

❑ **Internet Inquiry** Have students conduct an Internet inquiry on animal adaptations. **EVERY DAY** *173m*

❑ **Dictionary/Glossary** Review the features of a dictionary or glossary, including guide words, entry words, pronunciation, part of speech, and definition. Allow students to find and identify each feature in a dictionary or glossary and then work with a partner to find and learn a new word. **DAY 5** *173n*

❑ **Unit Inquiry** Allow time for students to choose categories and develop inquiry questions about riddles, knock-knock jokes, or brainteasers. **ANY DAY** *149*

SPEAKING AND VIEWING

❑ **Informational Speech** Have students use information from *Penguin Chick* and other resources to prepare and deliver informational speeches about penguins. **DAY 5** *173d*

❑ **Analyze a Photo** Have students look at photographs of adult penguins and then answer questions. **DAY 5** *173d*

Resources for Differentiated Instruction

LEVELED READERS

▶ **Comprehension**
- 🔄 **Skill** Main Idea
- 🔄 **Strategy** Graphic Organizers

▶ **Lesson Vocabulary**
- 🔄 **Context Clues**

flippers cuddles hatch frozen snuggles pecks preen

▶ **Science Standards**
- Habitats
- Living Things
- Animal Adaptation

Leveled Reader Database ONLINE

PearsonSuccessNet.com

Use the Online Database of over 600 books to
- Download and print additional copies of this week's leveled readers.
- Listen to the readers being read online.
- Search for more titles focused on this week's skills, topic, and content.

On-Level

Life Science

Birds That Can't Fly!
by Vita Richman

On-Level Reader

Main Idea
- The **main idea** is the most important idea about a paragraph, passage, or story.
- **Details** are pieces of information that tell more about the main idea.

Directions Read the following passage. Then answer the questions below.

> Birds that cannot fly are called flightless birds. They differ from flying birds in many ways. The bones of flightless birds are heavier than those of flying birds. Flightless birds' feathers are also different from those of flying birds. Like humans, all birds have a breastbone. However, a flightless bird's breastbone is different from that of a flying bird since it has no flight muscles attached.

Possible responses given.

1. In one or two words, what is this paragraph about?
   flightless birds
2. What is the main idea of the paragraph?
   Flightless birds differ from flying birds in many ways.
3. What is one important detail that tells more about the main idea?
   The bones of flightless birds are heavier than those of flying birds.
4. What is another important detail about the main idea?
   The feathers of flightless birds are different from those of flying birds.
5. What is a third detail about the main idea?
   A flightless bird's breastbone is different from that of a flying bird.

On-Level Practice TE p. LR5

Vocabulary
Directions Read each vocabulary word. Find two other words that have almost the same meaning and circle them.

Check the Words You Know
__cuddles __flippers __frozen __hatch
__pecks __preen __snuggles

1. cuddles
   slaps (hugs) throws (snuggles)
2. flippers
   eyes (paddles) (fins) noses
3. frozen
   (chilly) (icy) melted burned
4. hatch
   fall fly (produce) (cause)
5. pecks
   (strikes) walks swims (hits)
6. preen
   see (dress) (groom) laugh
7. snuggles
   (nestles) avoids (holds) kicks

Directions Write a paragraph about penguins using at least four vocabulary words.
Responses will vary.

On-Level Practice TE p. LR6

Strategic Intervention

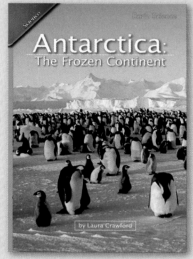

Earth Science

Antarctica: The Frozen Continent
by Laura Crawford

Below-Level Reader

Main Idea
- The **main idea** is the most important idea about a paragraph, passage, article, or book.
- **Details** are pieces of information that support, or tell more about, the main idea.

Directions Read the following passage. What is the main idea of the paragraph? Write it in the box at the top. Then find three details that tell about the main idea. Write one detail in each smaller box.

> Antarctica is very windy and dry. Antarctica is so dry that scientists call it a desert. The small amount of snow that falls there never melts. It is moved around by the wind until it freezes into ice.

Possible responses given.

1. Antarctica is very windy and dry.
2. Scientists call Antarctica a desert.
3. The small amount of snow that falls in Antarctica never melts.
4. Snow is moved around by the wind until it freezes into ice.

Below-Level Practice TE p. LR2

Vocabulary
Directions For each vocabulary word, write the letter of the definition that matches it.

Check the Words You Know
__cuddles __flippers __frozen __hatch
__pecks __preen __snuggles

1. __d__ cuddles
2. __e__ flippers
3. __f__ frozen
4. __c__ hatch
5. __a__ pecks
6. __g__ preen
7. __b__ snuggles

a. strikes at with the beak
b. presses closely against, as for comfort
c. to come out of an egg
d. hugs closely
e. flat body parts that are used for swimming
f. turned into ice
g. to clean and smooth feathers

Directions Write the vocabulary word or words that go best with each clue.
8. This word describes Antarctica. frozen
9. Penguins use these to swim well. flippers
10. A penguin chick does this to its eggshell. pecks
11. This is another word for how a penguin chick is born. hatch

Directions Write a short paragraph. Use at least three of the vocabulary words.
Paragraphs will vary.

Below-Level Practice TE p. LR3

Advanced

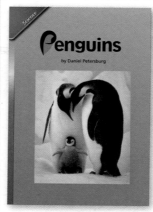

Advanced Reader

Main Idea

- The **main idea** is the most important idea about a paragraph, passage, or story.
- **Supporting details** are pieces of information that tell more about the main idea.

Directions Read each passage. Then answer the questions that follow. *Possible responses given.*

> The Southern Hemisphere is the natural home to the world's penguins. Penguins live on the Galápagos Islands and in Australia, New Zealand, Africa, South America, and the islands that surround Antarctica. They also live on Antarctica itself. All penguins share lives that are tied to the sea and the Southern Hemisphere's marine ecosystems.

1. In a few words, what is this paragraph about?
   penguins and the Southern Hemisphere

2. What is the main idea of the paragraph?
   The Southern Hemisphere is home to the world's penguins.

3. What is an important detail that tells more about the main idea?
   Penguins live on the Galápagos Islands, in Australia, New Zealand, Africa, South America, and islands that surround Antarctica.

> Emperor penguins reduce heat loss through their feet by standing on their heels. This keeps the rest of the foot from touching cold ice.
> Male emperor penguins also huddle to help conserve heat. The temperature in the middle of an emperor penguin huddle can be 95°F! Of course, some penguins must stand on the outside of the huddle. So what do they do to stay warm? They rotate. The penguins on the outside gradually push their way into the middle of the huddle. This way, each penguin gets a chance to become warmed.

4. What is the main idea of the passage?
   There are many things emperor penguins do to stay warm.

5. What is one detail that tells more about the main idea?
   Possible answers: They stand on heels; they huddle together.

Advanced Practice TE p. LR8

Vocabulary

Directions Choose the word from the box that best completes each sentence. Write the word on the line.

Check the Words You Know
blubber	brood patch	crest	down
incubate	molt	rookery	

1. Emperor penguins choose to **incubate** their eggs during the winter.
2. Large groups of penguins gather in a **rookery** to raise their young.
3. A penguin's **blubber** stores energy and helps protect the penguin from cold weather.
4. Fluffy inner feathers known as **down** trap air to keep penguins warm.
5. Penguins **molt** when their old feathers get worn out.
6. Male penguins have a featherless area of skin known as a **brood patch**, which warms their eggs.
7. Some penguins have a **crest** that sticks up from their heads.

Directions Use the context clues in the above sentences to define these words.

8. molt **lose old feathers**

9. rookery **a place where groups of birds gather to raise their young**

10. blubber **a layer that protects animals from the cold**

Advanced Practice TE p. LR9

ELL Reader

ELL Poster 6

Teacher's Edition Notes

ELL notes throughout this lesson support instruction and reference additional resources at point of use.

Teaching Guide
pp. 36–42, 222–223
- Multilingual summaries of the main selection
- Comprehension lesson
- Vocabulary strategies and word cards
- ELL Reader 3.2.1 lesson

ELL and Transition Handbook

Ten Important Sentences
- Key ideas from every selection in the Student Edition
- Activities to build sentence power

More Reading

Readers' Theater Anthology
- Fluency practice
- Five scripts to build fluency
- Poetry for oral interpretation

Leveled Trade Books

- Extended reading tied to the unit concept
- Lessons in the Trade Book Library Teaching Guide

School + Home

Homework
- Family Times Newsletter
- ELL Multilingual Selection Summaries

Take-Home Books
- Leveled Readers

Cross-Curricular Centers

Listen to the Selections

MATERIALS `SINGLES`
CD player, headphones, AudioText CD, Student Edition

Listen to *Penguin Chick* and "Plants: Fitting into Their World" as you follow or read along in your book. Listen for the main ideas in these selections.

If there is anything you don't understand, you can listen again to any section.

Read It Again!

MATERIALS `SINGLES` `PAIRS` `GROUPS`
Collection of books for self-selected reading, reading log

Select a book you have already read. Record the title of the book in your reading log. You may want to read with a partner.

You may choose to read any of the following:

- **Leveled Readers**
- **ELL Readers**
- **Stories written by classmates**
- **Books from the library**
- *Penguin Chick*

TEN IMPORTANT SENTENCES Read the Ten Important Sentences for *Penguin Chick*. Then locate the sentences in the Student Edition.

BOOK CLUB Look at "Meet Authors" on p. 417 of the Student Edition to help you set up an author study of Betty Tatham. Read other books by Tatham and share your favorites.

Classroom Library

Make Matches

MATERIALS `PAIRS`
Pencil, paper, markers, index cards

Make a set of picture cards that matches lesson vocabulary words.

1. **Write the boxed vocabulary words on index cards.**
2. **Draw pictures on other index cards that illustrate the meaning of each word. If you aren't sure of a meaning, use a dictionary.**
3. **Trade cards with your partner and see if you can match his or her cards with the correct pictures.**

moist	frigid	aquatic	iceberg
windswept	hatch	explore	

EARLY FINISHERS Write sentences using the lesson vocabulary words that explain how each card illustrates a word's meaning.

hatch

Scott Foresman Reading Street Centers Survival Kit

Use the *Penguin Chick* materials from the Reading Street Centers Survival Kit to organize this week's centers.

Writing

Write a
Penguin Story

MATERIALS `SINGLES`
Writing and drawing materials

Write a story about a penguin chick.

1. Use the following title or make up your own: "A Day in the Antarctic."
2. Write your story from a penguin chick's point of view.
3. Write in the first person, using words such as *my, I,* and *me.*
4. Use vivid words such as *freezing* instead of *cold.*
5. Include a beginning, middle, and end in your story.

EARLY FINISHERS Draw an illustration for your story.

A Day in the Antarctic

Today was freezing! Of course, every day is cold here. The other young chicks and I decided to go tobogganing on a hill. We had a lot of fun playing together. We were flapping our flippers and running around. Then I was tired, so we went back to the rookery to rest.

Science

Research
Local Wildlife

MATERIALS `GROUPS`
Books about animals, Internet access, writing and art materials

Research facts about animals that live near you.

1. Together, make a list of animals that live in your area.
2. Research facts about two or three of the animals.
3. Design a trading card that can list animal facts along with a picture of the animal.
4. Display your trading card in your classroom.

EARLY FINISHERS Write a list of animals that are not adapted to live in your area.

Chipmunk

1. Chipmunks eat nuts.
2. Chipmunks are small.
3. They live in burrows.
4. They have stripes.

Technology

Draw
Animals

MATERIALS `SINGLES` `PAIRS`
Computer, printer, glue or tape, scissors

Use a computer drawing program to draw the animals you have learned about.

1. Open a drawing program.
2. Use the paint or draw buttons to draw pictures of the animals you researched.
3. Print out your pictures.

EARLY FINISHERS Type and print out the facts about your animal. Glue or tape them to the back of your illustration for a computer-made trading card.

ALL CENTERS

Concept Vocabulary

inhospitable offering no shelter or good conditions for living

predatory living by killing and eating other animals

refuge shelter or protection from danger or trouble

Monitor Progress

Check Vocabulary

If... students are unable to place words on the web,	then... review the lesson concept. Place the words on the web and provide additional words for practice, such as *flourish* and *gills*.

SUCCESS PREDICTOR

DAY 1 Grouping Options

Reading
Whole Group
Introduce and discuss the Question of the Week. Then use pp. 150l–152b.

Group Time
Differentiated Instruction
Read this week's Leveled Readers. See pp. 150f–150g for the small group lesson plan.

Whole Group
Use p. 173a.

Language Arts
Use pp.173e–173h and 173k–173m.

Build Concepts

FLUENCY

MODEL ACCURACY AND APPROPRIATE PACE/RATE As you read "Swamp Scramblers," model appropriate pace. In the first paragraph, you may want to call attention to the punctuation, pausing slightly after each comma and a bit longer after periods and before and after the dashes.

LISTENING COMPREHENSION

After reading "Swamp Scramblers," use the following questions to assess listening comprehension.

1. **Identify the topic, the main idea, and one supporting detail of the selection.** *(Topic: mudskippers; Main Idea: how mudskippers survive on land; Supporting detail: They can keep their gills moist when out of the water.)* **Main Idea**

2. **In what way are mudskippers and other fish similar? In what way are they different?** *(Similar: They have gills and need water to breathe; Different: They can survive outside of water for long periods of time.)* **Compare and Contrast**

BUILD CONCEPT VOCABULARY

Start a web to build concepts and vocabulary related to this week's lesson and the unit theme.

- Draw an Animal Adaptation Concept Web.
- Read the sentence with the word *inhospitable* again. Ask students to pronounce *inhospitable* and discuss its meaning.
- Place *inhospitable* in an oval attached to Environment. Explain that *inhospitable* is related to this concept. Read the sentences in which *refuge* and *predatory* appear. Have students pronounce the words, place them on the web, and provide reasons.
- Brainstorm additional words and categories for the web. Keep the web on display and add words throughout the week.

Concept Vocabulary Web

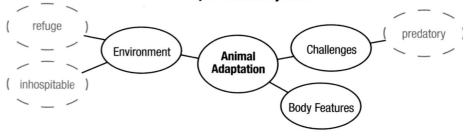

Swamp Scramblers

by Diane Thuna

Running across shoreline sludge, sometimes leaping high into the air, the mudskipper is a fish out of water. But it's definitely not out of place. Though they're truly fish—with fins and gills to prove it—mudskippers are so at home on land, they can not only walk and breathe air, they can also climb trees.

Sound weird? Maybe, but then the world they live in—the mangrove swamps and mud flats of Asia, Africa, and the South Pacific—is a pretty unusual one as well. Covered with water at high tide and a lot of oozing muck when the water goes back down, these areas can seem inhospitable. Yet mangrove trees flourish here. Propped up by their long, stiltlike roots, these trees are able to both rise above the waves and stand firm in the shifting mud. They also provide the climbing mudskippers with the perfect place to snatch a meal of insects or spiders and a safe refuge at high tide, when larger predatory fish patrol the water below.

How do mudskippers move on land? The answer lies in their fins. The sturdy fins near the front of the fish are not only extremely strong, they're also bent to look a lot like arms. Supporting its weight on these fins, the mudskipper lifts its body off the ground and pushes itself forward at the same time, a bit like a seal. The fins at the back of its body are the ones the mudskipper uses when climbing. Shaped like small suckers, they allow the fish to cling to mangrove roots while their front fins find a good grip even farther up the limb. When frightened, the mudskipper can also scurry across the mud or leap into the air with a few powerful lashes from its tail.

Of course, being able to move on land is no good if you can't also breathe. Mudskippers have that problem licked too. Amazingly, they have been known to survive out of water for two and a half days. Most other fish would die in just a fraction of that time. That's because all fish, even mudskippers, use their gills to get oxygen from water. The gills are packed with tiny blood vessels, and, as the water passes over them, the oxygen in the water is absorbed into the fish's bloodstream. Normally when fish leave the water, their gills dry out and become useless. Not a mudskipper's gills, though—they're always moist!

Before leaving the water, mudskippers soak up water into special gill chambers, which are storage pockets located around each gill. Once on land, the fish can absorb oxygen from this stored water by rolling its large, movable eyes back into its eye sockets. This movement swirls the stored water around the pouch and remoistens the gills. It's a great trick, but there's one small catch: eating. As mudskippers swallow insects and other tasty treats, the water stored in the gill chambers floods out, leaving the mudskipper high and dry. Then the fish has to quickly scoot back to a nearby puddle for a refill.

But moist gills are only part of the answer for the land-loving mudskipper. Mudskippers can also soak up oxygen through their skin, as long as it is kept wet. Some scientists think that's why mudskippers roll in mud puddles or lounge on the sun-drenched flats with their tails in the water.

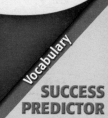

SKILLS ⟷ STRATEGIES IN CONTEXT

Main Idea/Details Graphic Organizers

OBJECTIVES

- Identify main idea and details
- Use graphic organizers to show main idea and details.

Skills Trace	
Main Idea and Details	
Introduce/Teach	**TE: 3.2 150–151, 198–199, 3.6 284–285**
Practice	PB: 3.1 53, 57–58, 73, 77–78, 86; 3.2 103, 107–108, 126, 146
Reteach/Review	TE: 3.2 173b, 223b, 233, 241, DI·54; 3.6 303b, 339, 391, 397, DI·52
Test	Selection Test: Unit 2 Benchmark Tests: Units 2, 6

INTRODUCE

Write the topic "Pets" on the board. Ask students to imagine that this is the main idea of an article they are going to read. Ask what might be some of the details they could expect to find in an article about this topic. *(Possible responses: kinds of pets, caring for pets, where to buy pets, and so on)*

Have students read the information on p. 150. Explain the following:

- When we look for the main idea of a selection, we look for what is implied as the most important idea. Supporting details tell us more about the main idea.

- Graphic organizers, such as charts and graphs, can help us recognize the main idea and tell the difference between it and the supporting details.

Use Skill Transparency 6 to teach main idea and graphic organizers.

 Comprehension

Skill
Main Idea
and Details

Strategy
Graphic
Organizers

Main Idea and Details

- The topic is what a piece of writing is about.

- The main idea is the most important idea about the topic.

- Supporting details are small pieces of information. They tell about the main idea.

Strategy: Graphic Organizers

A graphic organizer will help you organize information as you read. You can make a graphic organizer to show the main idea and supporting details of a piece of writing.

Write to Read

1. Read "The Coldest Continent." Make a graphic organizer to show the main idea and details of the first paragraph.

2. Make two more graphic organizers. Show the main idea of the second paragraph and then the third paragraph.

150

Strategic Intervention

Main Idea and Details Draw a main idea chart, such as Graphic Organizer 16, on the board to help students recognize the main idea and supporting details in the selection. First, ask them to identify the topic, or what the selection is about. Turn their attention to the title of the selection and the other text on the page. Explain that the title often gives clues about the main idea. Write the topic they suggest in the main idea box. As students reread the selection, have them jot down details about the main idea to add to the graphic organizer.

ELL

Access Content

Beginning/Intermediate For a Picture It! lesson on main idea and details, see the ELL Teaching Guide, p. 37.

Advanced Before students read "The Coldest Continent," have them discuss what they know about Antarctica, including the climate and the animal and plant life of the region.

The Coldest Continent

Antarctica is not like any other continent. It is as far south as you can go on Earth. The South Pole is found there. Ice covers the whole land. In some places the ice is almost three miles thick! Beneath the ice are mountains and valleys.

The weather in Antarctica is harsh. It is the coldest place on Earth. The temperature does not get above freezing. It is also one of the windiest places in the world.

Not many living things are found in Antarctica. People go there to study for only a short time. Very few animals can live there. Yet many animals live on nearby islands. Seals and penguins swim in the ocean waters. They build nests on the land. Some birds spend their summers in Antarctica. But most of the continent is just ice, snow, and cold air.

1 Skill Here you can see that the topic of this passage is Antarctica, but the main idea of this paragraph is that Antarctica is covered with thick ice.

2 Strategy The last two sentences contain some supporting details.

151

Available as **Skill Transparency** 6

Main Idea and Details • Graphic Organizers

- The **topic** is what a piece of writing is about. The **main idea** is the most important idea about the **topic**. **Supporting details** are small pieces of information about the **main idea**.
- A **graphic organizer** can help organize information as you read.

Directions Read the following passage. Complete the graphic organizer below.

> What if you wanted to cross Antarctica? What would you need to take along?
> You would need warm clothes, such as a parka and fur-lined boots. You'd also need bulky socks, thick pants, and the warmest mittens you could find!
>
> Don't forget to bring your own food. You could warm frozen casseroles over a fire and eat nuts and snack bars during the day.
> At night you'll need a sleeping bag. Take the warmest one you can find so you are sure to keep warm all night long!

		3. Detail warm clothes
1. Topic Crossing Antarctica	**2. Main Idea** You need to take the right things with you.	**4. Detail** food
		5. Detail sleeping bag

Home Activity Your child found the topic, main idea, and details in a passage. Read a nonfiction book to your child. To find the topic, ask, "In one word, what is the book all about?" To find the main idea, help your child make a sentence that tells the most important part about the topic. Then ask your child to list several details that tell more about the main idea.

Practice Book 3.1 p. 53

TEACH

1 SKILL Use paragraph 1 to model how to identify the topic and the main idea.

Think Aloud **MODEL** I think that this selection is all about Antarctica because all the paragraphs tell about this continent. I decided that the main idea of the first paragraph is that in Antarctica, thick ice covers the continent.

2 STRATEGY Draw a simple graphic organizer and model how to use it to distinguish the main idea in paragraph 1 from supporting details.

Think Aloud **MODEL** A graphic organizer can help me tell the difference between the main idea and supporting details. Writing the main idea helps me remember it. What details in the selection tell me more about the main idea? I can write those in smaller boxes next to or beneath the main idea box.

PRACTICE AND ASSESS

SKILL Students should understand that the topic of the selection is Antarctica. The main idea of the first paragraph is that the continent is covered in thick ice.

STRATEGY The last two sentences explain that Antarctica is covered in ice that is almost three miles thick in places and which covers mountains and valleys.

WRITE Have students complete steps 1 and 2 of the Write to Read activity. You might consider using this as a whole class activity.

Monitor Progress

 Main Idea and Details

If... students are unable to complete **Write to Read** on p. 150,	**then...** use Practice Book 3.1, p. 53, to provide additional practice.

Tech Files ONLINE

Students can find out more about penguins by searching the Internet. Have them use a student-friendly search engine and the keywords *penguins, Emperor penguins,* and *Antarctica.*

Build Background Use ELL Poster 6 to build background and vocabulary for the lesson concept of how animals adapt to their environments.

▲ **ELL Poster** 6

Build Background

ACTIVATE PRIOR KNOWLEDGE

BEGIN A KWL CHART about Emperor penguins.

- Ask students to write as many things as they can about penguins in general and Emperor penguins specifically. Allow them about two to three minutes of writing time.

- Draw a KWL chart on the board, and write what students know in the first column.

- Then have them share two to three questions they have about Emperor penguins. Write some of their questions on the chart in the second column. Add a question of your own if necessary.

- Remind students to look for answers to their questions as they read the selection. Add their new information to the chart.

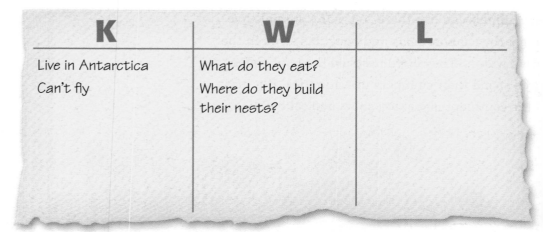

K	W	L
Live in Antarctica Can't fly	What do they eat? Where do they build their nests?	

▲ **Graphic Organizer** 3

BACKGROUND BUILDING AUDIO This week's audio presents information about Antarctica. After students listen, discuss the information on the CD and add any new ideas to the KWL chart.

Audio CD Background Building Audio

Introduce Vocabulary

DISCUSS THE VOCABULARY

Share lesson vocabulary with students. Have students locate each word in their glossaries and note each word's pronunciation and meaning. Ask these questions to help clarify word meanings.

What do flippers help penguins do?

Does your cat purr when it snuggles?

When something is frozen, how does it feel?

How long does it take a bird's egg to hatch?

What is that stuffed animal the baby cuddles with?

Can a monkey preen?

What do you do when something pecks at your window?

Point out that some of this week's words apply specifically to penguins. Ask students what other words they know that might describe penguins.

Activate Prior Knowledge

Explain to students that some of these words are homonyms. Check a dictionary for other meanings for *peck* and *hatch*. **Homonyms**

Have students use these steps for reading any troublesome multisyllabic words. (See the Multisyllabic Word Routine on p. DI·1.)

1 Look for Meaningful Word Parts (base words, endings, prefixes, suffixes, roots) Think about the meaning of each part. Use the parts to read the word. Model: I see *-er* at the end of *flippers.* I know that sometimes final consonants are doubled when a suffix is added. The base word must be *flip. Flip* means "to move something with a snap or jerk," and *-er* means "something or someone who does an action, so *flippers* means "something that moves with a snap or a jerk."

2 Chunk Words with No Recognizable Parts Say each chunk slowly. Then say the chunks fast to make a word. Model: *fro, zen—frozen.*

Continue this activity by having students write their own questions using the vocabulary.

Lesson Vocabulary

WORDS TO KNOW

T **cuddles** lies close and comfortably; curls up

T **flippers** broad, flat body parts used for swimming by animals such as seals and penguins

T **frozen** hardened with cold; turned to ice

T **hatch** to come out of an egg

T **pecks** strikes with a beak

T **preen** to smooth or arrange feathers with a beak

T **snuggles** lies closely and comfortably together; cuddles

---

MORE WORDS TO KNOW

rookery a large group of birds together raising their young; a nesting colony

squid a sea animal that has a pair of tail fins and ten arms

T = Tested Word

Vocabulary

Check the Words You Know

__hatch	__pecks
__snuggles	__preen
__flippers	__frozen
__cuddles	

Directions Choose the vocabulary word from the box and write it next to its meaning.

pecks	1. taps at
frozen	2. turned into solid ice
flippers	3. limbs used for swimming
preen	4. to make yourself clean and neat
cuddles or snuggles	5. curls up comfortably

Directions Write the word on the line that fits the meaning of the sentence.

6. Mother cuddles or snuggles the little baby in her arms.

7. The chick is about to hatch out of its egg.

8. Penguins use their flippers to help them swim.

9. The penguins preen their young until their feathers are clean.

10. It was so cold that we could ice skate on the frozen lake.

Write a News Report

On a separate sheet of paper, tell what happens when a penguin chick hatches. Describe the setting and the sequence of events using as many vocabulary words as possible.

Students should use vocabulary describing an Antarctic setting and sequence of events as a penguin chick hatches.

Home Activity Your child identified and used vocabulary words from *Penguin Chick.* Read a story or a nonfiction article about penguins with your child. Discuss the story using this week's vocabulary words.

▲ **Practice Book 3.1** p. 54

Vocabulary Strategy

OBJECTIVE

 Find synonyms in context clues to determine the meaning of unknown words.

INTRODUCE

Discuss the strategy of context clues to find the meaning of synonyms using the steps on p. 152.

TEACH

- Have students read "Penguins are Birds," paying attention to how vocabulary is used.
- Model using context clues to determine the meaning of *pecks.*

Think Aloud **MODEL** The word *pecks* on p. 153 refers to what the chick does. It says that after the chick *pecks*, the egg breaks open. So *pecks* means "to tap at the egg until it cracks, probably with its beak."

Words to Know

hatch
pecks
snuggles
preen
flippers
frozen
cuddles

Remember

Try the strategy. Then, if you need more help, use your glossary or a dictionary.

Vocabulary Strategy
for Synonyms

Context Clues Sometimes when you are reading, you come across a word you don't know. The author may give you a synonym for the word. A synonym is a word that has the same or almost the same meaning as another word. Look for a word that might be a synonym. It can help you understand the meaning of the word you don't know.

1. Look at the words very near the word you don't know. The author may give a synonym in the same sentence.

2. If not, look in the sentences around the sentence with the unfamiliar word. The author may use a synonym for the word.

3. Try the synonym in place of the word in the sentence. Does it make sense?

As you read "Penguins Are Birds," look for synonyms to help you understand the meanings of the vocabulary words.

152

DAY 2 **Grouping Options**

Reading
Whole Group Discuss the Question of the Day. Then use pp. 152–155.

Group Time Differentiated Instruction
Read *Penguin Chick.* See pp. 150f–150g for the small group lesson plan.

Whole Group Use pp. 173a and 173i.

Language Arts
Use pp.173e–173h and 173k–173m.

Strategic Intervention

 Context Clues Have students work in pairs to follow the steps on p. 152. Encourage them to list clues and synonyms for an unknown word and then decide together the best meaning for it.

ELL

Access Content Use ELL Poster 6 to preteach vocabulary. Choose from the following to meet language proficiency levels.
Beginning Point out clues on p. 153 that show what *cuddles* means.
Intermediate After reading, students can create a three-column chart to show words and a synonym, with the meaning for both.
Advanced Teach the lesson on pp. 152–153. Return to the main idea and supporting details chart used on p. 150 and encourage students to complete it using vocabulary words and their synonyms.

Penguins Are Birds

All birds come from eggs. The mother bird lays the eggs, and then the mother bird or the father bird sits on the eggs until it is time for them to hatch. Each baby bird pecks and hits the shell of its egg with its beak until the shell breaks open. The baby bird cannot fly or get food. It needs its parents to bring it food and keep it warm. When a parent bird sits on the nest, the baby bird snuggles, or presses, into the parent's belly. The parents preen their own feathers. Then they also brush the baby bird's soft feathers. This helps keep the baby bird warm.

Penguins are birds. They have flippers instead of wings, and they swim rather than fly. But they have feathers and lay eggs just as other birds do. Baby penguins hatch from eggs, and they need their parents to give them food and warmth. Some penguins live in Antarctica, where the land and much of the water around it is frozen. Penguins don't have nests, so a penguin parent cuddles, or hugs, the egg or the chick to keep it warm.

Words to Write

Look at the pictures on pages 158–165. Choose a picture to write about. Use words from the Words to Know list.

153

PRACTICE AND ASSESS

- Have students determine the meanings of the remaining words and explain the context clues and synonyms they used.
- Point out that context and/or synonyms do not work with every unfamiliar word. Students may have to use the glossary or a dictionary to find the exact meaning of some words.
- Have students create their own sentences using vocabulary words.
- Have students complete Practice Book 3.1, p. 55.

WRITE Writing should include vocabulary words that describe one of the pictures on pp. 158–165. Students should use as many descriptive words and synonyms as possible in their writing.

Monitor Progress

Context Clues

If... students need more practice with the lesson vocabulary,	**then...** use Tested Vocabulary Cards.

Vocabulary • Context Clues

- Sometimes you come across a word you don't know. The author may give you a clue about its meaning. The clue may be a **synonym**, a word that means the same thing.
- Look for **synonyms** to figure out the meaning of unfamiliar words.

Directions Read the sentences. One word is underlined. Circle the synonym of the underlined word. Write the meaning of the underlined word on the line.

1. The chick pecks at the inside of the egg. After the chick taps a hole in the egg, the chick can leave the egg.

   to strike at something with a beak

2. She made an error in her spelling, so she fixed the mistake.

   something that is done wrong

3. Joe can put on his flippers or his fins to swim quickly.

   broad, flat body parts used for swimming

4. Penguins preen their chicks by cleaning and brushing them with their beaks.

   to smooth with a beak; to dress or groom carefully

5. The penguin chick must stay on its mother's feet to remain warm.

   continue to be

6. Penguins hunt creatures of the sea, such as the tiny animals called krill.

   any living person or animal

7. The newborn chick was very fluffy, with soft and fuzzy feathers all over it.

   covered with soft feathers or hair

8. Like human children who love hugs, penguin chicks love to cuddle.

   to lie close and comfortably

Home Activity Your child used context clues such as synonyms to figure out the meaning of new words. Read a story together and encourage your child to find synonyms in the text that help to figure out the meaning of unfamiliar words.

▲ **Practice Book 3.1** p. 55

Penguin Chick **153**

Prereading Strategies

OBJECTIVES

- Identify main idea and supporting details to improve comprehension.
- Use graphic organizers to identify main idea and supporting details.

GENRE STUDY

Expository Nonfiction

Penguin Chick is expository nonfiction. Explain that expository nonfiction gives us information about the real world. We read expository nonfiction to find out information.

PREVIEW AND PREDICT

Have students preview the selection title and illustrations and discuss the topics or ideas they think this selection will cover. Encourage students to use lesson vocabulary as they talk about what they expect to learn.

Strategy Response Log

Predict Have students write their predictions in their strategy response logs. Students will check their predictions in the Strategy Response Log activity on p. 161.

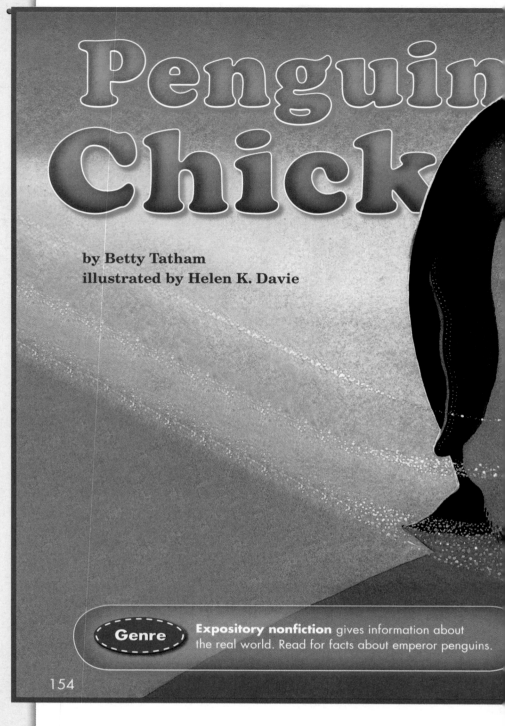

Penguin Chick

by Betty Tatham
illustrated by Helen K. Davie

Genre **Expository nonfiction** gives information about the real world. Read for facts about emperor penguins.

154

ELL

Activate Prior Knowledge Have students share what they know about Antarctica and penguins with their peers. Students can write a short list of their ideas they can refer to as they are reading to help them understand the selection.

Consider having students read the selection summary in English or in students' home languages. See the Multilingual Summaries in the ELL Teaching Guide, pp. 40–42.

How do emperor penguins protect their chicks from the extreme temperature of Antarctica?

155

SET PURPOSE

Discuss with students how we keep ourselves warm and how they think animals keep themselves warm. Point out the question on p. 155. Have them consider their preview discussion and tell what they hope to find out as they read.

Remind students to read for main ideas and supporting details.

STRATEGY RECALL

Students have now used these before-reading strategies:

- preview the selection to be aware of its genre, features, and possible content;
- activate prior knowledge about that content and what to expect of that genre;
- make predictions;
- set a purpose for reading.

Remind students to be aware of and flexibly use the during-reading strategies they have learned:

- link prior knowledge to new information;
- summarize text they have read so far;
- ask clarifying questions;
- answer questions they or others pose;
- check their predictions and either refine them or make new predictions;
- recognize the text structure the author is using, and use that knowledge to make predictions and increase comprehension;
- visualize what the author is describing;
- monitor their comprehension and use fix-up strategies.

After reading, students will use these strategies:

- summarize or retell the text;
- answer questions they or others pose;
- reflect to make new information become part of their prior knowledge.

Audio CD **AudioText**

Guiding Comprehension

1  **Main Idea and Details • Inferential**

Reread pp. 156–157. Find the main idea and one supporting detail.

Main idea: An egg has been laid and must be kept warm. Supporting detail: The father tucks the egg in his brood patch to keep it warm.

Monitor Progress

Main Idea and Details

If... students are unable to find the main idea and one supporting detail,	**then...** use the skill and strategy instruction on p. 157.

---

2 **Use Graphic Organizers • Inferential**

How could a graphic organizer help you identify the main idea and supporting details on pp. 156–157?

Graphic organizers help us organize information so that we can see it and understand it better.

Tech Files
ONLINE

Use the key words *penguins*, *emperor penguins*, and *Antarctica* to find out more about the topic and the region.

A fierce wind howls. It whips snow across the ice. Here, a female emperor penguin has just laid an egg. It is the only egg she will lay this year.

Most birds build nests for their eggs. But on the ice in Antarctica, there are no twigs or leaves. There is no grass or mud. Nothing to build a nest with. Nothing but snow and ice.

The new penguin father uses his beak to scoop the egg onto his webbed feet.

156

He tucks it under his feather-covered skin, into a special place called a *brood patch*. The egg will be as snug and warm there as if it were in a sleeping bag.

One of the penguin parents must stay with the egg to keep it warm. But where penguins lay their eggs, there is no food for them to eat.

The penguin father is bigger and fatter than the mother. He can live longer without food. So the father penguin stays with the egg while the mother travels to the sea to find food.

157

Time for SOCIAL STUDIES

Climate

When you think of Antarctica, your first thought is probably of the cold. Antarctica is indeed cold—in fact, it is the coldest place on earth. The coldest temperature ever recorded there was −128.6°F! It is also windy. Wind has been known to reach speeds of 200 miles per hour. Despite the cold and the wind, Antarctica does not get a lot of snow. In fact, Antarctica is a desert. It gets less than 10 inches of snow a year. What does such a desert look like? You would certainly see lots of ice; in fact, Antarctica doubles in size during the winter because of all the ice that forms along its coasts. You might also see a few rocks here and there, and on the warmer Antarctic Peninsula you would even see some plant life in the form of mosses, lichens, and algae.

 SKILLS ⟷ STRATEGIES IN CONTEXT

Main Idea/Details Graphic Organizers

TEACH

- Explain to students that the main idea helps us see and understand what the selection is about.

- Tell students that when we are looking for the main idea, we first need to think about what the selection implies. Then we look for the most important idea. Finally, we look for details that tell more about the main idea.

- Sometimes, drawing a picture of the information can help us find the main idea and details and better understand what we are reading.

Think Aloud **MODEL** The first thing I want to do when I read an article is ask myself what it is about. What are the first two pages of *Penguin Chick* about? I think they are about the penguin egg. What is the most important idea in these pages? I think the most important idea is that the egg has to be kept warm. One detail that supports this idea is that the father penguin keeps the egg warm.

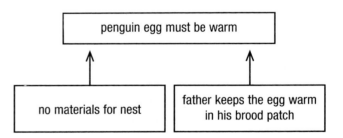

PRACTICE AND ASSESS

Have students identify one or two more details on pp. 156–157 that support the main idea and add one box for each detail to their graphic organizer. To assess, check that details come from the selection and support the main idea.

Guiding Comprehension

 3 **Cause and Effect • Inferential**

The water near shore was frozen for many miles. What caused the water to freeze?

The cold temperatures of the Antarctic winter.

4 **Main Idea and Details • Literal**

The main idea of pp. 158–159 is that the mother penguin leaves the egg in search of food. Find one detail which supports this idea.

Possible response: After three days, the mother penguin comes to the end of the ice.

Monitor Progress

Main Idea and Details

If... students have difficulty identifying finding a detail,	**then...** use the skill and strategy instruction on p. 159.

---

5 **Understand Graphic Sources • Literal**

Often in expository nonfiction, there are photos, illustrations, or graphics (such as charts, graphs, diagrams, and so on) that give us additional information about the article. Look at pp. 158–159. What are the graphics on the pages, and what do they tell you?

Illustrations of fish, squid, and krill; they show what these sea creatures look like.

The two parents sing together before the mother penguin leaves.

Along with many other penguins, the mother penguin leaves the rookery, where she laid her egg.

The mother walks or slides on her belly. This is called *tobogganing*. She uses her flippers and webbed feet to push herself forward over ice and snow.

Context Clues Explain that sometimes we can figure out the meaning of new or difficult words by looking at the words around the word we don' know. Find the word *rookery* on p. 158. Point to the clause *where she laid her egg* and explain that these words are a clue to the meaning of the word *rookery*. They tell us that a rookery is a place where the mother penguin lays her egg. Encourage students to write down new words and their meanings as they come across them in the selection. When possible, help them use context clues to figure out what the words mean.

Because it's winter in Antarctica, water near
the shore is frozen for many miles. After three days
the mother penguin comes to the end of the ice. She
dives into the water to hunt for fish, squid, and tiny
shrimplike creatures called *krill*.

Fish   Squid   Krill

159

Adaptation

Many animals have special features that help
them survive in their environments. These features
have developed over a long period of time; animals
of the same species without these features died. This
is called adaptation. Have you ever seen a chameleon? The
chameleon changes its color to blend in with its environment. If the
chameleon is in a tree surrounded by green leaves, the chameleon is
green. If it is lying on a brown branch, it is brown. It can be very difficult to see. Arctic foxes and hares change color too. They are white
in the winter, so they are difficult to see against snow, and they are
brown in the summer. These adaptations have two purposes. First,
the animals are protected from their enemies, who can't eat them
if they can't see them. It is also easier for them to catch their prey,
since the prey often doesn't see them until it's too late!

 SKILLS ↔ STRATEGIES IN CONTEXT

Main Idea/ Details

TEACH

- Remind students that supporting details are
  small pieces of information that tell more
  about the main idea.

- Explain that, authors will often give us some
  information that is interesting but does not
  help us understand the main idea. These
  details are not supporting details.

- Model finding details that support the main
  idea that the mother penguin must leave her
  egg to look for food.

Think Aloud **MODEL** I read on p. 158 that the
mother penguin walks or slides on
her belly and uses her flippers and
webbed feet to move along. These are interesting details, but they don't help me understand the idea that the mother penguin had
to leave her egg to look for food. I don't think
these are supporting details. On p. 159, I
read that it takes the mother three days to
get to open water. This *does* support the idea
that the mother penguin leaves her egg. This
is a supporting detail.

PRACTICE AND ASSESS

Have students find another supporting detail for
the main idea that the mother penguin leaves
her egg to look for food. (*She dives into the
water to hunt.*) To assess, check that the detail
supports the main idea; otherwise it is not a
supporting detail.

Guiding Comprehension

6 **Summarize • Critical**

In two or three sentences, tell what you have learned about emperor penguins so far.

Responses will vary; check that facts students list are from the selection.

7 **Compare and Contrast • Critical**

Text to World **In what ways are emperor penguins different from other birds you know about? Use your summary to help you answer the question.**

Some facts students may mention: It is the father penguin and not the mother penguin that sits on the egg to keep it warm; penguins don't fly; father penguins huddle together to keep each other warm instead of staying alone.

8 **Use Graphic Organizers • Critical**

Add to your KWL chart for the selection. Think about what you already knew, what you still want to know as you continue to read, and what you have already learned.

Information in charts will vary; check that details in the *L* column come from the selection.

Back at the rookery, the penguin fathers form a group called a *huddle*. They stand close together for warmth. Each keeps his own egg warm.

For two months the penguin father always keeps his egg on his feet. When he walks, he shuffles his feet so the egg doesn't roll away. He sleeps standing up. He has no food to eat, but the fat on his body keeps him alive.

160

ELL

Activate Prior Knowledge Place students in groups according to their abilities in English and have them share and discuss what they know about the life cycle of birds in general and penguins in particular. Using what they have read so far, have them point out the ways in which penguins differ from other birds.

EXTEND SKILLS

Recall and Predict

Have students recall the major points in the text. Discuss what these points have in common, and what other information the students may still want to know. Then, have them predict what information may come next in the selection.

Finally he feels the chick move inside the egg. The chick pecks and pecks and pecks. In about three days the egg cracks open.

The chick is wet. But soon his soft feathers, called *down,* dry and become fluffy and gray. The father still keeps the chick warm in the brood patch. Sometimes the chick pokes his head out. But while he's so little, he must stay covered. And he must stay on his father's feet. Otherwise the cold would kill him.

The father talks to the chick in his trumpet voice. The chick answers with a whistle.

161

Develop Vocabulary

PRACTICE LESSON VOCABULARY

Have students provide oral responses to each question.

1. If something is *frozen*, is it liquid or solid? *(solid)*
2. If humans had *flippers*, which body part would they replace? *(our arms)*
3. What happens when the chick *pecks* at the egg shell? *(The egg cracks open.)*

BUILD CONCEPT VOCABULARY

Review previous concept words with students. Ask if students have met any words today in their reading or elsewhere that they would like to add to the Concept Web.

STRATEGY SELF-CHECK

Use Graphic Organizers

Explain that graphic organizers help us organize information so that we can better understand it. Sometimes, the author or artist creates a graphic organizer for us to complete as we read; other times, we have to create our own.

Remind students that it is important to be able to identify the main idea and supporting details if we want to understand the text. Often, a simple graphic organizer can help us do this.

Have students draw a long rectangle on a separate piece of paper and a line an inch or so from the top. Thinking about the selection title and what they have read, have them write the main idea of the selection in the top part of the box and any supporting details below it.

SELF-CHECK

Students can ask these questions to assess their ability to use the skill and strategy.

- Do I know what the selection is about?
- Have I stated the most important idea of the selection?
- Do the details I have listed support the main idea?

Monitor Progress

Main Idea and Details

If... students have difficulty finding the main idea and supporting details,	then... revisit the skill lesson on p. 150–151. Reteach as necessary.

Strategy Response Log

Check Predictions Provide the following prompt: Was your prediction accurate? Revise your old prediction or make a new prediction about the rest of the selection.

If you want to teach this selection in two sessions, stop here.

Guiding Comprehension

If you are teaching the selection in two days, discuss the story so far, including main ideas, and review the vocabulary.

⑨ Draw Conclusions • Inferential

On p. 162, we read that the father penguin calls across the ice to the mother penguin. Why do you think he does this?

Possible responses: To find out how far away she is; to urge her to hurry home to the chick because it is hungry.

⑩ Facts and Details • Literal

How do the parents feed the penguin chick if there is no food source nearby?

They bring food back up from their own stomachs and feed it to the chick.

⑪ Vocabulary • Context Clues

Reread p. 163. What is the synonym for the word *brush*?

Preen

Monitor Progress

Context Clues

If... students have difficulty finding a synonym,	**then...** use the vocabulary strategy instruction on p. 163.

DAY 3 Grouping Options

Reading
Whole Group Discuss the Question of the Day.

Group Time Differentiated Instruction
Read *Penguin Chick*. See pp. 150f–150g for the small group lesson plan.

Whole Group Discuss the Reader Response questions on p. 168. Then use p. 173a.

Language Arts
Use pp.173e–173h and 173k–173m.

The father's trumpet call echoes across the ice. The penguin mother is on her way back to the rookery, but she can't hear him. She's still too far away. If the mother doesn't come back soon with food, the chick will die.

Two days pass before the mother can hear the father penguin's call.

At last the mother arrives at the rookery. She cuddles close to the chick and trumpets to him. He whistles back. With her beak she brushes his soft gray down.

162

The mother swallowed many fish before she
10 left the ocean. She brings some of this food back
up from her stomach and feeds her chick. She has
enough food to keep him fed for weeks. He stays
on her feet and snuggles into her brood patch.

The father is very hungry, so he travels to open
water. There he dives to hunt for food. Weeks later
11 the father returns with more food for the chick.

Each day the parents preen, or brush, the
chick's downy coat with their beaks. This keeps
the down fluffy and keeps the chick warm.

163

Life Cycles

The life cycle of all species of penguins is quite
similar to that of the emperor penguin. Some lay
two to three eggs, whereas the emperor penguin lays
only one. In all species of penguin, except for the emperor
penguins, both the mother and father sit on the egg; this is probably
because the emperor penguins lay their eggs quite far from the coast,
and the female has a longer distance to travel to the open ocean.
Both parents take care of the chick until it is able to take care of
self; this can be anywhere from two months to a year, depending on
the species of penguin.

  VOCABULARY STRATEGY

Context Clues

TEACH

- Remind students that when we come across
words we don't know, we often can use the
words around it to figure out what it means.

- Explain that sometimes authors use a
synonym to explain a difficult word. A
synonym is a word that means the same
thing, or almost the same thing, as the
unfamiliar word.

- One way we can find out whether a word is a
synonym is to use it in place of the new word
in the sentence. If it makes sense, the two
words are synonyms.

Think Aloud **MODEL** While reading, I came across
the word *preen*. I've never seen or
heard this word before; I don't know
what it means. But then I see that the author
has explained what it means later in the sentence. She says *or* and has used a
synonym between commas. It says *preen*
means "brush." Let me see if that makes
sense. *Each day the parents brush the chick's
downy coat with their beaks.* That makes
sense, so *to preen* means "to brush."

PRACTICE AND ASSESS

Have students find a synonym for *cuddles* on
p. 162 (*snuggles*, p. 163) and use both words
in a sentence of their own.

EXTEND SKILLS

Facts and Details

Explain to students the importance of identifying
facts and details as we read because they help us
understand the text better. Sometimes, we need
simply to remember facts and details to help us
see what we are reading. Facts and details also
point to how a text is organized. If we understand
how a text is organized, we can follow it better.
Have students reread the selection so far and
identify facts and details that help them visualize
the text and see how it is organized.

Guiding Comprehension

If you are teaching the selection in two days, discuss the main ideas so far and review the vocabulary.

12 REVIEW **Sequence • Inferential**

Look back through the selection so far. List the stages in order of the penguin chick's growth from egg to junior penguin.

Possible response: 1. Mother lays egg and then the father keeps the egg on his feet for two months. 2. After two months, chick hatches and stays under father. 3. Mother returns and feeds the chick; chick stays with mother while father goes to get food. 4. Chick leaves parents' brood patch and huddles with other chicks in the crèche for warmth; still needs to eat from parents. 5. Chick starts to play. 6. At five months, chick is old enough to travel to the ocean.

Monitor Progress

REVIEW Sequence

If... students have difficulty identifying the sequence of events,	**then...** use the skill and strategy instruction on p. 165.

13 **Understand Graphic Sources • Inferential**

Look at the time line on pp. 164–165. How does the time line help you understand the selection?

It shows a picture of each stage of the chick's growth in order.

As the chick gets bigger, he and the other chicks no longer need to stay on their parents' feet. Instead they stay together to keep warm.

This group of chicks is called a *crèche,* or a nursery. The chick now spends most of his time here. But he still rushes to his mother or father to be fed when either one comes back from the ocean.

WINTER		SPRING
August	*September*	*October*

164

 E L L

Extend Language Over time, the English language has adopted many words from other languages. You might recognize words such as *spaghetti,* taken from Italian, or, *kindergarten,* taken from German. Point out the word *crèche* on p. 164, taken from French. Have students think of other examples of borrowed words in the English language and discuss their meanings. Encourage students to add such words to their vocabulary notebooks, along with an example using the word in a sentence.

Sometimes the chick and the other young penguins dig their beaks into the ice to help them walk up a slippery hill. They toboggan down fast on their fluffy bellies.

The chick grows and grows. After five months, he has grown into a junior penguin. He is old enough to travel to the ocean. **12**

13

| November | December | SUMMER January |

165

TIME FOR Science

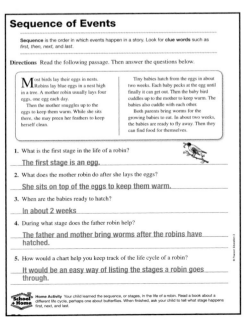

Ecosystems

When we think of the food chain, we think of the bigger animals eating the smaller animals, with the biggest animals (humans) having no natural predators at all. But in the Antarctic, as in every ecosystem, all life actually depends on each other. The smallest link in the Antarctic food chain is the phytoplankton. Krill, small, shrimp-like organisms, eat the phytoplankton. The larger organisms, such as fish and some mammals, eat the krill; these organisms are in turn eaten by even larger predators (except for whales, whose only predators are human). If one animal is affected, all these organisms are affected, resulting in the death of some and the over-population of others.

SKILLS ⟷ STRATEGIES IN CONTEXT

Sequence REVIEW

TEACH

- Explain that the sequence of events in this selection will help students understand the information better.

- Remind students that clue words such as *next* and *later* are not always present; dates and times can be clues to sequence.

- Model looking for the first three stages in the penguin chick's growth.

Think Aloud **MODEL** The very first stage is when the mother lays the egg. We read about this on p. 156. Then the father keeps the egg warm. I think that's the second stage. That's on p. 157. There's no information about the egg on pp. 158–159. I'm looking only for the stages about the penguin chick. Next I see that the father keeps the egg on his feet for two months. That's on p. 160. That's stage three.

PRACTICE AND ASSESS

- Have students find the remaining steps in the penguin chick's growth on their own. To assess, check that the students have recorded stages in sequence and that details come from the selection.

- To assess, use Practice Book 3.1, p. 56.

Sequence of Events

Sequence is the order in which events happen in a story. Look for **clue words** such as *first, then, next,* and *last.*

Directions Read the following passage. Then answer the questions below.

Most birds lay their eggs in nests. Robins lay blue eggs in a nest high in a tree. A mother robin usually lays four eggs, one egg each day.
Then the mother snuggles up to the eggs to keep them warm. While she sits there, she may preen her feathers to keep herself clean.

Tiny babies hatch from the eggs in about two weeks. Each baby pecks at the egg until finally it can get out. Then the baby bird cuddles up to the mother to keep warm. The babies also cuddle with each other.
Both parents bring worms for the growing babies to eat. In about two weeks, the babies are ready to fly away. Then they can find food for themselves.

1. What is the first stage in the life of a robin?
   The first stage is an egg.

2. What does the mother robin do after she lays the eggs?
   She sits on top of the eggs to keep them warm.

3. When are the babies ready to hatch?
   In about 2 weeks

4. During what stage does the father robin help?
   The father and mother bring worms after the robins have hatched.

5. How would a chart help you keep track of the life cycle of a robin?
   It would be an easy way of listing the stages a robin goes through.

School + Home **Home Activity** Your child learned the sequence, or stages, in the life of a robin. Read a book about a different life cycle, perhaps one about butterflies. When finished, ask your child to tell what stage happens first, next, and last.

▲ **Practice Book 3.1** p. 56

Guiding Comprehension

14 **Facts and Details • Literal**

How many years is it before a penguin is ready to have a chick of its own?

Five years.

15 **Author's Purpose • Inferential**

Question the Author **Authors have many reasons for writing. What is one reason you think the author wrote** *Penguin Chick?*

To teach us something about the life cycle of emperor penguins.

16 **Generalize • Critical**

Text to Self **Think about your relationship with the people who take care of you. What do they do for you? What do you need from them? What can you do by yourself? Make a graphic organizer, such as a Venn diagram (Graphic Organizer 17), to show ways in which you and your relationship with your caregivers is similar to the penguin chick and its relationship with its parents. Then make some generalizations about children and parents based on your observations.**

Responses will vary; check that generalizations can be backed up by facts from the selection and the student's experiences.

Strategy Response Log

Summarize When students finish reading the selection, provide this prompt: Imagine that a friend has asked what *Penguin Chick* is about. In four or five sentences, explain its important points.

Now he has a waterproof coat of feathers, instead of fluffy down. He can swim in the icy cold ocean because his feathers keep him dry and warm.

The young penguin spends most of his time in the water. He swims, flapping his flippers as if he were flying underwater. He uses his webbed feet to steer wherever he wants to go.

He catches a fish with his beak and swallows it headfirst.

166

Now the young penguin can catch his own food and take care of himself. In about five years he'll find a mate. Then he'll take care of his own egg until the chick can |hatch.| **14**

15 16

167

STRATEGY SELF-CHECK

Use Graphic Organizers

- Tell students that graphic organizers help us organize and understand what we read.
- Have students fill in any missing information on the KWL chart they started on p. 152a. Then have them think about what they learned.
- Have students write a brief summary of *Penguin Chick* using their KWL chart.

SELF-CHECK

Students can ask these questions to assess their abilities to use the skill and strategy.

- Does my KWL chart help me organize the information from the selection?
- Do I know the most important idea?
- Do the details listed support the main idea?
- To assess, use Practice Book 3.1, p. 57.

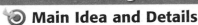

Monitor Progress

Main Idea and Details

If... students have difficulty finding the main idea and details,	**then...** revisit the skill and strategy instruction on pp. 150–151.

Main Idea and Details · Graphic Organizers

- The **topic** is what a piece of writing is about. The **main idea** is the most important idea about the **topic**. Supporting **details** are small pieces of information about the **main idea**.
- A **graphic organizer** can help organize information as you read.

Directions Read the following passage. Then answer the questions below.

Every summer, Jamie's family goes to a beach to swim in the warm waters. Jamie's mom and dad like to snorkel. They breathe through a tube. They wear goggles so they can see the colorful fish. But Jamie does not swim well. He cannot go snorkeling yet.

This summer, Jamie takes snorkeling lessons. He learns how to breathe through a tube. Then Jamie learns how to swim with flippers. The flippers help him kick better and faster. Finally, Jamie's mom and dad help him practice. For the first time, Jamie gets to snorkel and see the colorful fish.

1. What is the topic of the selection?
   snorkeling

2. What is the main idea of the selection?
   Jamie learns how to snorkel.

3. Why can't Jamie go snorkeling at first?
   He doesn't swim well.

4. What three things does Jamie do in order to snorkel?
   learns how to breathe through a tube, learns how to swim with flippers, and practices with Mom and Dad

Home Activity Your child found the topic and main idea of a selection. Then your child answered questions that required understanding the details about the main idea. Write a story with your child about a problem you had and how you solved it. Then ask your child to tell the story's topic and main idea.

▲ **Practice Book 3.1** p. 57

Develop Vocabulary

PRACTICE LESSON VOCABULARY

Have students respond orally *true* or *false* to each question.

1. **Snuggles is a synonym for cuddles.** *(True)*
2. **Mother cats *preen* their kittens with their tongues.** *(False; mother cats lick or clean their kittens with their tongues.)*
3. **All baby animals *hatch* from eggs.** *(False; only baby birds, reptiles, and fish hatch from eggs.)*

BUILD CONCEPT VOCABULARY

Review previous concept words with students. Ask if students have met any words today in their reading or elsewhere that they would like to add to the Concept Web.

Reader Response

Open for Discussion **Personal Response**

MODEL The most important parts of the selection tell about the stages in the penguin's life, from when the egg is laid to when the chick is grown. Some details I might include are how long it takes the chick to hatch and how long it has to stay under its parents for warmth.

Comprehension Check **Critical Response**

1. Responses will vary; help students with pronunciation and fluency. **Author's Purpose**

2. Details: Both parents bring back food for the chick to eat; both parents brush the chick's feathers. **Main Idea and Details**

3. Responses will vary; look for answers that explain how the graphic organizers helped students. **Use Graphic Organizers**

4. Paragraphs will vary; words students may use include *hatch, pecks, snuggles,* and *cuddles.* **Vocabulary**

Look Back and Write For test practice, assign a 10–15 minute time limit. For assessment, see the Scoring Rubric at the right.

Retell

Have students retell *Penguin Chick.*

Monitor Progress

Check Retelling _{Rubric} 4 3 2 1

If... students have difficulty retelling the selection,	then... use the Retelling Cards and Scoring Rubric for Retelling on p. 169 to assist fluent retelling.

SUCCESS PREDICTOR

Check Retelling Have students use illustrations and other text features to guide their retellings. Let students listen to other retellings before attempting their own. See the ELL and Transition Handbook.

Reader Response

Open for Discussion How would you retell the information in this selection to someone who doesn't know much about emperor penguins? What are the most important parts?

1. The author is like a reporter, telling you about the emperor penguins as if you and she were there in Antarctica. Look back at page 156. Read the page aloud as if you are an on-the-scene reporter. **Think Like an Author**

2. Look back at page 163. What details support the idea that the penguin father and mother take care of the chick? **Main Idea and Details**

3. Did you create a graphic organizer to help you as you read? If so, tell how it helped you. If not, what kind of graphic organizer could you have used? Tell why. **Graphic Organizer**

4. This story is about penguin chicks. If you wrote a paragraph about barnyard chicks, which words from the Words to Know list could you use? Try it. **Vocabulary**

Look Back and Write Look back at page 158. What surprising thing do the parent penguins do before the mother penguin leaves? Tell why you think they do it. Use information from the selection to write the answer.

Meet author Betty Tatham on page 417.

168

Scoring Rubric | **Look Back and Write**

Top-Score Response A top-score response will tell what surprising thing the parent penguins do before the mother penguin leaves and will explain why students think this happens.

Example of a Top-Score Response The parents sing before the mother leaves to find food. The mother will be gone for a long time. The father has to stay warm and keep the egg warm. They want to raise their chick together. Maybe they sing to tell each other they will be together again.

For additional rubrics, see p. WA10.

Write Now

Summary

Prompt

Penguin Chick explains how penguins protect their eggs and their baby chicks. Think about what happens as penguin chicks hatch and grow.

Now write a summary of *Penguin Chick*.

Writing Trait

To help readers remember events, **organize** them in time order and in **paragraphs.**

Time-order words help readers follow order of events.

A summary's main ideas are organized into two paragraphs.

Student Model

Summary—Penguin Chick, pages 162–165

After the chick hatches, the father calls and waits for the mother. When she gets back, she holds the chick and brushes its down. She brings up some food she has eaten to feed the chick. It snuggles at her feet. Now the father goes to find food.

After growing a little, the chicks stay together for warmth and go to their parents for food. They use their beaks to help them walk on ice. They slide on their bellies. When they are five months old, they can travel to the ocean.

Last sentence tells last event in time order.

Use the model to help you write your own summary.

169

Write Now

Look at the Prompt Explain that each sentence in the prompt has a purpose.

- Sentence 1 presents a topic.
- Sentence 2 suggests students think about the topic.
- Sentence 3 tells what to write—a summary.

Strategies to Develop Organization/Paragraphs

Have students

- tell the main events in a story to a partner.
- write the steps using time-order words.

NO: Mother penguin lays an egg. The mother leaves. Dad takes over.

YES: Mother penguin lays an egg. Then she leaves. Now Dad takes over.

For additional suggestions and rubric, see pp. 173g–173h.

Writer's Checklist

☑ **Focus** Are only important events included in the summary?

☑ **Organization** Are the events in order? Do transitions, such as *then* and *after*, show time order?

☑ **Support** Do all sentences describe events in the story?

☑ **Conventions** Is the first line of each paragraph indented?

Scoring Rubric — Expository Retelling

Rubric 4 3 2 1	4	3	2	1
Connections	Makes connections and generalizes beyond the text	Makes connections to other events, texts, or experiences	Makes a limited connection to another event, text, or experience	Makes no connection to another event, text, or experience
Author's Purpose	Elaborates on author's purpose	Tells author's purpose with some clarity	Makes some connection to author's purpose	Makes no connection to author's purpose
Topic	Describes the main topic	Identifies the main topic with some details early in retelling	Identifies the main topic	Retelling has no sense of topic
Important Ideas	Gives accurate information about events, steps, and ideas using details and key vocabulary	Gives accurate information about events, steps, and ideas with some detail and key vocabulary	Gives limited or inaccurate information about events, steps, and ideas	Gives no information about events, steps, and ideas
Conclusions	Draws conclusions and makes inferences to generalize beyond the text	Draws conclusions about the text	Is able to draw few conclusions about the text	Is unable to draw conclusions or make inferences about the text

Retelling Plan

☑ **This week** assess Strategic Intervention students.

☐ **Week 2** Assess Advanced students.

☐ **Week 3** Assess Strategic Intervention students.

☐ **Week 4** Assess On-Level students.

☐ **Week 5** Assess any students you have not yet checked during this unit.

Use the Retelling Chart on p. TR17 to record retelling.

Selection Test To assess with *Penguin Chick*, use Selection Tests, pp. 21–24.

Fresh Reads for Differentiated Test Practice For weekly leveled practice, use pp. 31–36.

SUCCESS PREDICTOR

Retelling

Science in Reading

PREVIEW/USE TEXT FEATURES

As students preview "Plants: Fitting into Their World," have them identify each section and tell what they think each will be about. Then ask:

- **How do the arrows help you read and understand the selection?** *(They point to the picture they go with, so there is no confusion about which image goes with which text.)*

Link to Science

Help students use reference materials, such as encyclopedias or online reference sources, to find out more about how plants get sunlight and water. Encourage them to take notes and to organize them before they present their findings.

 **Main Idea**

Students' responses should reflect the wording or main idea in each head and subhead, or title.

DAY 4 Grouping Options

Reading
Whole Group Discuss the Question of the Day.

Group Time Differentiated Instruction
Read "Plants: Fitting into Their World." See pp. 150f–150g for the small group lesson plan.

Whole Group Use p. 173a and 173j.

Language Arts
Use pp.173e–173h and 173k–173m.

Science in Reading

Photo Essay

Genre
- A photo essay usually is written to inform the reader about a topic.
- Photo essays use photographs and text to give information.

Text Features
- In this selection, arrows clearly show which photo goes with each piece of text.
- Some photos give a close-up view.

Link to Science
Use the library or the Internet to find more examples of ways that plants get sunlight and water. Report what you find to the class.

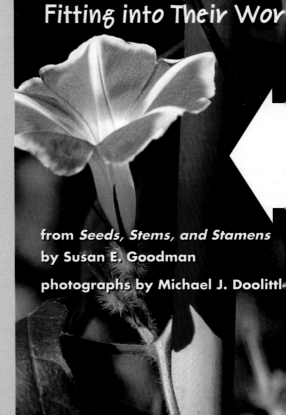

Plants
Fitting into Their Wor

from *Seeds, Stems, and Stamens*
by Susan E. Goodman

photographs by Michael J. Doolittl

Main Idea Use the heads to help you figure out the main ideas.

170

Content-Area Vocabulary · Science

evolved	developed or changed over time
host	a living thing on which another living thing lives
stem	the main supporting part of a plant
trunk	the main supporting part of a tree, similar to the stem of a plant
vine	a plant with a long, slender stem that grows along the ground or climbs something

Getting Sun

Almost all plants need sun to live. They use a process called *photosynthesis* to turn sunlight into food or energy. But sometimes getting enough light can be a problem. Tall plants and trees get by growing higher than those around them. To do so, they use a lot of energy growing a strong stem or trunk. Other plants have different ways to grab their share of sunshine.

Hitching a Ride

This **morning glory** spends its energy climbing instead. This vine uses its flexible stem to wind around strong objects and get to the light.

This **bromeliad** is a different kind of hitchhiker. It is an air plant. It grows high on a tree and uses its roots to anchor itself to the tree's trunk or upper branches.

Leaf Placement

Many plants arrange their leaves so they can get as much sun as possible. **Mint** leaves grow in crossed pairs. That way, the leaves cast less shadow upon their neighbors.

171

Wild and Cultivated Plants

Wildflowers and plants provide seeds, nuts, and fruit for wild animals; prevent soil erosion; and color the landscape. The plants survive and grow when insects carry pollen from one plant to another or when animals and the wind spread seeds. Cultivated plants are those that people grow in a specific place or for a specific purpose. People prepare the land, plant the seeds, and make sure the seeds have enough water and fertilizer to grow.

PHOTO ESSAY

Use the sidebar on p. 170 to guide discussion.

- A photo essay is a collection of photographs on one theme, with written explanations of varying lengths, from short captions to longer expository or narrative writing. The explanations in this photo essay are relatively short.

- Similar to other forms of nonfiction writing, photo essays are often divided into sections. Each section has a title, or subhead. Each caption may have an additional title or subhead as well.

- Discuss with students how they can use the information in the titles and subheads to better understand the selection.

Audio CD AudioText

ELL

Build Background Discuss how plants grow and what elements they need to do so (sun, water, nutrients) with students. Point out the word *photosynthesis* on p. 171 and read the explanation in the selection together. If further explanation is necessary, use a simple drawing of a plant and the sun and the sun's rays hitting the leaves. Look at the photographs in each section and discuss which element each photo relates to.

Strategies for Nonfiction

NAVIGATE A PAGE OF A SELECTION Explain that students may be asked to read photo essays and answer questions about them on standardized tests. A photo essay often follows a specific format. Knowing how to move around the page can help you get the most information out of it and better understand what you are reading. Provide the following strategy.

Use the Strategy

1. Look at the page. Pay attention to the kind of information that is present on the page, such as heads, subheads, captions, and photographs.

2. First, look at the title or head. This will tell you the general topic of that section.

3. Next, look at the photos. Not only are they usually interesting to look at, but they also tell you what the section will be about.

4. Finally, read the captions. Read the caption title, if there is one. This will tell you what that caption will be about. The photograph often is a visual image of the explanation in the caption.

GUIDED PRACTICE Have students discuss how they would use the strategy to answer the following question.

How does a small plant like a morning glory get the sunlight it needs?

INDEPENDENT PRACTICE After students answer the following test question, discuss the process they used to find information.

How can host trees protect themselves from vines like the morning glory or bromeliad?

Getting Nutrients

Most plants get their nutrients from the soil. Some plants have evolved a different way to get their "vitamins."

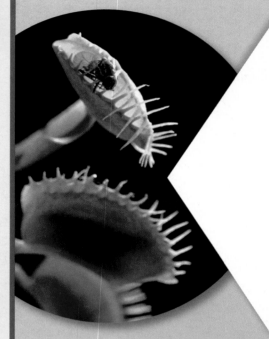

Meat-Eaters

The leaf tips of a **Venus's-flytrap** look very tempting to an insect. They are an easy place to land. They shine with what looks to be food. Mistake! Less than a second after a bug crawls in, the trap springs shut. The bristles on the leaves point outward to keep the insect from escaping as the trap closes. The plant then uses chemicals to digest its meal. In this picture, one leaf tip has just captured a fly, while a bigger leaf tip below is in the middle of digesting another.

The inventor of sticky flypaper might have gotten the idea from a **sundew plant.** A sundew's leaves are covered with hairs. And these hairs are covered with "sundew glue." The insect that lands on a sundew is there for good. It sticks to the hairs, which fold over and trap it.

 Main Idea What details tell about a meat-eating Venus's-flytrap?

172

ELL

Test Practice Tell students that *navigate* means "to move around," and explain that they will be learning to move around the page in order to get the most information from it and understand it better. Model navigating the page as above.

Model navigating the page. Place a photocopy of a page from the selection on the board. Model moving around the page using the instruction to the left. Using sticky notes, put a large number one next to the subhead of the section. Discuss what that section will be about. Put a large number two next to the first photograph and discuss it. Put a large number three next to the caption. Circle the title and discuss the topic of the caption, then read the caption aloud and ask students a question to assess their comprehension of the caption. Have students work in pairs for another page of the selection.

Staying Safe

Plants can't run away from hungry insects and animals. They have developed other ways to protect themselves.

Physical Defenses

Freeloaders like bromeliads and vines don't directly harm their host tree, but they can do damage. They soak up water and sun that the tree could have used. If too many of them pile onto a tree, they can break off its branches. This **terminalia tree** has a great defense. Every so often, it sheds its bark—and with it, most of its unwanted company.

This **floss-silk tree** has what scientists call bark prickles all over its trunk. No matter what you call them, you wouldn't want to run into these things. And that's the point— a lot of painful ones.

Reading Across Texts

Which growing thing do you think has a harder time surviving—penguin chicks or the plants in this selection?

Writing Across Texts Create a chart to explain why you think as you do.

173

CONNECT TEXT TO TEXT

Reading Across Texts

Discuss the difficulties faced by both the chicks and the plants, how they overcome those difficulties (or have adapted to deal with them), and which living thing may have a harder time surviving.

Writing Across Texts Help students set up a chart. Some charts they can use include webs A and B (Graphic Organizers 14 and 5), a Venn diagram (Graphic Organizer 17), and a four-column chart (Graphic Organizer 27).

Main Idea

Possible responses: They are an easy place to land; they shine with what looks to be food; a bug crawls in, and the trap shuts; the bristles point outward to keep the insect from getting out; the plant uses chemicals to digest its meal.

ELL

Access Content Point out that the words *hitchhiker* and *freeloader* are used to describe the bromeliad. Explain that a hitchhiker is someone who asks for free rides and a freeloader is someone who accepts things without paying for them. Help students understand that these words are used to explain that a bromeliad grows on other plants rather than in the ground.

Fluency Assessment Plan

☑ **This week assess Advanced students.**

☐ **Week 2** Assess Strategic Intervention students.

☐ **Week 3** Assess On-Level students.

☐ **Week 4** Assess Strategic Intervention students.

☐ **Week 5** Assess any students you have not yet checked during this unit.

Set individual goals for students to enable them to reach the year-end goal.

• Current Goal: 85–95 WCPM

• Year-End Goal: 120 WCPM

 **Fluency Coach CD** To develop fluent readers, use Fluency Coach.

MORE READING FOR
Fluency

 To practice fluency with text comprised of previously taught phonics elements and irregular words, use Decodable Reader 6.

DAY 5 Grouping Options

Reading
Whole Group
Revisit the Question of the Week.

Group Time
Differentiated Instruction
Reread this week's Leveled Readers. See pp. 150f–150g for the small group lesson plan.

Whole Group
Use pp. 173b–173c.

Language Arts
Use pp.173d–173h and 173k–173n.

ACCURACY AND APPROPRIATE PACE/RATE
Fluency

DAY 1

Model Reread "Swamp Scramblers" on p. 150m. Explain that you will read for accuracy and at a good rate for understanding—not too fast and not too slow. Model for students as you read.

DAY 2

Choral Reading Read aloud p. 156. Have students notice the pace at which you are reading. Tell students that they may want to read a non-fiction selection at slower rate for understanding. Have students practice as a class doing three choral readings of p. 156.

DAY 3

Model Read aloud p. 160. Have students notice that you read with accuracy and appropriate pace. Practice as a class by doing three choral readings.

DAY 4

Partner Reading Partners practice reading aloud p. 160, three times. Students should read with accuracy at an appropriate rate and offer each other feedback.

Monitor Progress | Check Fluency WCPM

As students reread, monitor their progress toward their individual fluency goals. Current Goal: 85–95 words correct per minute. End-of-Year Goal: 120 words correct per minute.

If... students cannot read fluently at a rate of 85–95 words correct per minute,
then... make sure students practice with text at their independent level.
Provide additional fluency practice, pairing nonfluent readers with fluent readers.

If... students already read at 120 words correct per minute,
then... they do not need to reread three to four times.

SUCCESS PREDICTOR

DAY 5

Assessment
Individual Reading Rate Use the Fluency Assessment Plan and do a one-minute timed reading of either selection from this week to assess students in Week 1. Pay special attention to this week's skill, accuracy. Provide corrective feedback for each student.

RETEACH

Main Idea/Details

TEACH

Review the skill instruction for main idea and details on p. 150. Write the following on the board: *Main Idea = the most important idea; Details = little bits of information that support the main idea.* Students can complete Practice Book 3.1, p. 58 on their own, or you can complete it as a class. Point out that the boxes in the main idea and details graphic organizer are empty; students must fill in the boxes with information from the passage.

ASSESS

Have students work in pairs to identify the main idea and one supporting detail on p. 161. *(Main idea: The father penguin takes care of the egg and newly hatched chick; supporting detail: He keeps the chick warm in his brood patch.)*

For additional instruction of main idea and details, see DI·52.

EXTEND SKILLS

Graphic Sources

TEACH

Graphic sources are any graphic—charts, graphs, diagrams, time lines, scale drawings, and so on—that accompanies a selection. They can strengthen our understanding of the text.

- Before reading, scan the selection for graphic sources. Have students read the title of each graphic to determine what it's about and ask themselves what this tells them about the selection they are about to read.

- As they read, use the information in the graphics to help them organize and/or visualize the information and understand it better.

Point to the time line on pp. 164–165. Discuss the information it contains and how it helps them understand the selection better.

ASSESS

Have small groups of students create a time line that shows the growth of a human from 1 month to 5 years.

OBJECTIVES

- Identify main idea and details.
- Understand graphic sources.

Skills Trace
Main Idea and Details

Introduce/Teach	TE: 3.2 150–151, 198–199, 3.6 284–285
Practice	PB: 3.1 53, 57, 58 73, 77, 78, 86; 3.2 103, 107, 108, 126, 146
Reteach/Review	TE: 3.2 173b, 223b, 233, 241, DI•52, DI•54; 3.6 303b, 339, 391, 397
Test	Selection Test: Unit 2 Benchmark Tests: Units 2, 6

ELL

Access Content Reteach the skill by reviewing the Picture It! lesson on main idea and details in the ELL Teaching Guide, pp. 36–37.

▲ **Practice Book 3.1** p. 58

Vocabulary and Word Study

VOCABULARY STRATEGY
Context Clues

SYNONYMS Remind students that they can use context clues to find synonyms for unfamiliar words. Have students list any unknown words and their synonyms that they encountered as they read *Penguin Chick*. They can create a chart showing the unknown word, its synonym, and their definition of the word based on its synonym. Students can confirm word meanings using a dictionary.

Word	Context Clue Synonym	Meaning
snug	warm	warm and comfortable
huddle		
downy		

Penguin Words

Penguin words, such as *brood patch*, refer to birds and their behavior. Have partners use reference sources to make lists of words and their definitions.

Some Penguin Words

rookery:

beak:

colony:

egg tooth:

hatch:

feathers:

mating:

flippers:

waterproof:

fledgling:

BUILD CONCEPT VOCABULARY
Animal Adaptations

LOOKING BACK Remind students of the focus question of the week: How have animals adapted to solve the problems of their environment? Discuss how this week's Concept Web of vocabulary words relates to the theme of animal adaptations. Ask students if they have any words or categories to add. Discuss whether words and categories are appropriately related to the concept.

MOVING FORWARD Preview the title of the next selection, *A Day's Work*. Ask students which Concept Web words might apply to the new selection based on the title alone. Put a star next to these words on the web.

Display the Concept Web and revisit the vocabulary words as you read the next selection to check predictions.

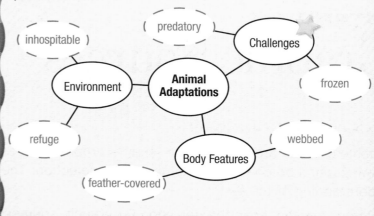

Monitor Progress

Check Vocabulary

If... students suggest words or categories that are not related to the concept,	then... review the words and categories on the Concept Web and discuss how they relate to the lesson concept.

SUCCESS PREDICTOR

Speaking and Viewing

SPEAKING

Informational Speech

SET-UP Have students use information from *Penguin Chick* and other resources to prepare and deliver informational speeches about penguins.

RESEARCH Have students review *Penguin Chick* and outline important information about penguins. Students may also wish to research penguins in the library or on the Internet. Students can use the research and outlines to create note cards.

DELIVERY Provide time for students to rehearse their informational speeches aloud. Share these delivery suggestions:

- Be familiar with your facts.
- Make and keep eye contact with your audience.
- Speak in a loud, clear voice, but don't shout.
- Use note cards only to keep you on target. Don't read from cards.

Listening Tips

- Give the speaker your full attention.
- Identify facts and opinions.
- Think about what you know about the topic.
- Listen for new information and details.

VIEWING

Analyze a Photo

Have students look at photographs of adult penguins. Have students answer these questions orally or in writing. Discuss what the intended use of the photograph may be.

1. **What are the penguins doing in this photograph?** *(Responses will vary, depending on the photo.)*

2. **How would you describe the penguins' appearance?** *(Possible response: black and white, short legs, white belly, long beak)*

3. **What do you think the photographer was thinking when these photographs were taken? Why?** *(Responses will vary.)*

 ELL

Support Vocabulary Use the following to review and extend vocabulary and to explore lesson concepts further:
- ELL Poster 6, Days 3–5 instruction
- Vocabulary Activities and Word Cards in ELL Teaching Guide, pp. 38–39

Assessment For information on assessing students' speaking, listening, and viewing, see the ELL and Transition Handbook.

Check Vocabulary

SUCCESS PREDICTOR

Grammar Common and Proper Nouns

DAY 1 Teach and Model

DAILY FIX-IT

1. Does penguins live in alaska? *(Do; Alaska)*

2. The feemale bird look for food. *(female; looks)*

READING-GRAMMAR CONNECTION

Write this sentence from *Penguin Chick* on the board:

> But on the ice in Antarctica, there are no twigs or leaves.

Explain that *ice, twigs,* and *leaves* are **common nouns.** They name any person, place, or thing. *Antarctica* is a **proper noun.** It names a particular place and begins with a capital letter.

Display Grammar Transparency 6. Read aloud the definitions and sample sentences. Work through the items.

Common and Proper Nouns

A **common noun** names any person, place, or thing. A **proper noun** names a particular person, place, or thing. Proper nouns begin with capital letters.

    Common Nouns These <u>birds</u> live in cold <u>places</u>.
    Proper Nouns It is cold in <u>Antarctica</u> in <u>July</u>.

Capitalize each important word in a proper noun: Fourth of July. The names of days, months, and holidays are proper nouns. They begin with capital letters.

Directions Write *C* if the underlined noun is a common noun. Write *P* if the underlined noun is a proper noun.

1. Penguins have black and white <u>feathers</u>.   **C**
2. Some penguins live in zoos in the <u>United States</u>.   **P**
3. Penguins have webbed <u>feet</u>.   **C**
4. <u>New Zealand</u> has many penguins.   **P**
5. This penguin hatched in <u>July</u>.   **P**

Directions Underline the common nouns and circle the proper nouns in the sentences.

6. Penguins eat fish from the water.
7. There is much food in the Pacific Ocean.
8. Australia has many penguins.
9. Seals and whales also live in Antarctica.
10. Are there penguins at the zoo in Washington?

Unit 2 Penguin Chick   Grammar **6**

▲ **Grammar Transparency** 6

DAY 2 Develop the Concept

DAILY FIX-IT

3. Babys cant get their own food. *(Babies; can't)*

4. It is sillent on the ice of antarctica. *(silent; Antarctica)*

GUIDED PRACTICE

Review the concept of common and proper nouns.

- A **common noun** names any person, place, or thing.

- A **proper noun** names a particular person, place, or thing.

- Proper nouns begin with capital letters. In proper nouns of more than one word, the first word and each important word are capitalized. The names of days, months, and holidays are proper nouns.

HOMEWORK Grammar and Writing Practice Book p. 21. Work through the first two items with the class.

Common and Proper Nouns

A **common noun** names any person, place, or thing. A **proper noun** names a particular person, place, or thing. Proper nouns begin with capital letters.

    Common Nouns You can see <u>penguins</u> at some zoos.
    Proper Nouns In <u>May</u>, <u>Jen</u> saw a penguin from <u>Africa</u>.

Capitalize each important word in a proper noun: Fourth of July. The names of days, months, and holidays are proper nouns. They begin with capital letters.

Directions Write *C* if the underlined noun is a common noun. Write *P* if the underlined noun is a proper noun.

1. There are not many emperor penguins in our <u>country</u>.   **C**
2. A sea park in <u>San Diego</u> has an emperor penguin.   **P**
3. In a zoo in <u>Scotland</u>, penguins stroll around the park each day.   **P**
4. Many people love these unusual <u>animals</u>.   **C**
5. <u>Whales</u> and penguins are popular sea park attractions.   **C**

Directions Underline the common nouns and circle the proper nouns in the sentences.

6. Seals and penguins like the cold Atlantic Ocean.
7. Other animals like cold weather too.
8. Will you find bears near the North Pole?
9. Foxes and hares live in Canada.
10. Which bears live in Alaska?

Home Activity Your child learned about common and proper nouns. Have your child write the names of friends and family members and explain why the names are proper nouns.

▲ **Grammar and Writing Practice Book** p. 21

DAY 3 — Apply to Writing

D·A·I·L·Y F·I·X-I·T

5. A father Penguin cares for a egg. *(penguin; an)*

6. The father wont leave even thogh he is hungry. *(won't; though)*

ADD PROPER NOUNS

Explain that proper nouns can be used to give more detail than common nouns, making writing more vivid.

• Have students review something they have written to see if they can improve it by changing any common nouns to proper nouns.

HOMEWORK Grammar and Writing Practice Book p. 22.

Common and Proper Nouns

Directions Rewrite each sentence. Replace each underlined common noun with a proper noun. **Possible answers:**

1. The <u>city</u> has a zoo with many animals.
   Washington, D.C., has a zoo with many animals.

2. You can get books about animals on a <u>street</u>. **You can get books about animals on Michigan Avenue.**

3. You can see wild animals at a <u>place</u>. **You can see wild animals at Yellowstone National Park.**

4. Fish live in the <u>river</u>.
   Fish live in the Mississippi River.

5. There are many interesting animals in <u>that country</u>.
   There are many interesting animals in South Africa.

Directions Write a description of a place that has interesting animals. Use at least two proper nouns.
The Bronx Zoo is in New York City. It is a very old zoo. It has unusual animals, from anteaters to zebras.

Home Activity Your child learned how to use common and proper nouns in writing. Look at family photos with your child. Have your child write a sentence about a place your family has visited, using at least one proper noun.

▲ **Grammar and Writing Practice Book** p. 22

DAY 4 — Test Preparation

D·A·I·L·Y F·I·X-I·T

7. The birds slide on the ice and they play in the snow *(ice,; snow.)*

8. Isnt the baby's coat soft. *(Isn't; soft?)*

STANDARDIZED TEST PREP

Test Tip

Watch out for proper nouns of more than one word. The first word and each important word should be capitalized.

No: The band played on Independence day.

Yes: The band played on Independence Day.

HOMEWORK Grammar and Writing Practice Book p. 23.

Common and Proper Nouns

Directions Mark the letter of the sentence that is written correctly.

1. A Kelly went to the zoo in San antonio.
   B kelly went to the Zoo in san antonio.
   (C) Kelly went to the zoo in San Antonio.
   D Kelly went to the zoo in san antonio.

2. A Those birds nest in hawaii.
   B Those Birds nest in Hawaii.
   C Those Birds nest in hawaii.
   (D) Those birds nest in Hawaii.

3. A New york city has many pigeons.
   (B) New York City has many pigeons.
   C New York City has many Pigeons.
   D New york City has many pigeons.

4. A My town has many Owls.
   B My Town has many owls.
   (C) My town has many owls.
   D My Town has many Owls.

5. **(A)** The robins sing in April.
   B The Robins sing in April.
   C The robins sing in april.
   D The Robins sing in april.

6. **(A)** Geese and ducks live on the lake.
   B Geese and Ducks live on the Lake.
   C geese and ducks live on the lake.
   D Geese and ducks live on the Lake

7. A An eagle flew on the fourth of july.
   B An Eagle flew on the Fourth of July.
   (C) An eagle flew on the Fourth of July.
   D An eagle flew on the Fourth of july.

8. **(A)** Many seagulls gathered over the ocean.
   B Many Seagulls gathered over the ocean.
   C Many seagulls gathered over the Ocean.
   D Many seagulls gathered over the ocean.

9. A Amy drew a turkey for thanksgiving.
   B amy drew a turkey for thanksgiving.
   C Amy drew a Turkey for Thanksgiving.
   (D) Amy drew a turkey for Thanksgiving.

10. A Can birds fly over the washington monument?
    (B) Can birds fly over the Washington Monument?
    C Can birds fly over the Washington monument?
    D Can Birds fly over the Washington Monument?

Home Activity Your child prepared for taking tests on common and proper nouns. On a drive, say the names of things you pass, such as a street and Spring Creek. Have your child identify which are common nouns and which are proper nouns.

▲ **Grammar and Writing Practice Book** p. 23

DAY 5 — Cumulative Review

D·A·I·L·Y F·I·X-I·T

9. Can birds build they're nests on ice. *(their; ice?)*

10. The mother fish for food and the father watches the egg. *(fishes; food,)*

ADDITIONAL PRACTICE

Assign pp. 80–83 in The Grammar and Writing Book.

EXTRA PRACTICE Grammar and Writing Practice Book p. 127.

TEST PREPARATION Grammar and Writing Practice Book pp. 153–154.

ASSESSMENT

CUMULATIVE REVIEW Grammar and Writing Practice Book p. 24.

Common and Proper Nouns

Directions Write the sentences. Capitalize the proper nouns correctly.

1. We saw the penguins at the zoo on saturday.
   We saw the penguins at the zoo on Saturday.

2. The penguins are from antarctica and south america.
   The penguins are from Antarctica and South America.

3. They are not used to hot summer days in texas.
   They are not used to hot summer days in Texas.

4. Maybe the july sun was too warm for those birds.
   Maybe the July sun was too warm for those birds.

Directions Underline the common nouns and circle the proper nouns in the sentences.

5. Many <u>animals</u> at the zoo come from distant <u>places</u>.

6. <u>Koalas</u> come from (Australia.)

7. <u>Pandas</u> come from (China.)

8. The <u>aquarium</u> brought some <u>whales</u> from the (Pacific Ocean.)

9. That beautiful <u>tiger</u> was born in (India.)

Directions Write a sentence about a wild animal. Use at least one proper noun, and circle it. Underline the common nouns. **Possible answer:**

10. <u>Giraffes</u> live in (Africa.)

Home Activity Your child reviewed common and proper nouns. On a walk in your neighborhood, have your child name some common nouns and some proper nouns that name neighborhood sights.

▲ **Grammar and Writing Practice Book** p. 24

Writing Workshop Summary

OBJECTIVES

- Identify the characteristics of a summary.
- Write a summary of the selection that includes all the necessary information.
- Focus on organization/paragraphs.
- Use a rubric.

Genre Summary
Writer's Craft Include Necessary Information
Writing Trait Organization/Paragraphs

ELL

Organization/Paragraphs Make sure English learners can decode words in the prompt. Work with students to complete a cloze sentence that addresses the prompt and could be used to launch writing (e.g., "Penguin parents protect their chicks by ____.").

Writing Trait

FOCUS/IDEAS Only necessary information is included in the summary.

ORGANIZATION/PARAGRAPHS The summary is in time order. The word *Meanwhile* makes a smooth transition between paragraphs.

VOICE Writing is clear. The writer shows understanding of the selection.

WORD CHOICE The writer uses time-order and transition words (*finally, meanwhile*) and strong verbs (*slides, dives*) to describe actions.

SENTENCES Use of both simple and compound sentences creates clarity and interest.

CONVENTIONS There is excellent control and accuracy.

DAY 1 Model the Trait

READING-WRITING CONNECTION

- *Penguin Chick* tells how emperor penguins cooperate to raise young in the arctic cold.
- The story relates the hatching of the egg and protecting of the baby over a period of months.
- Students will write a **summary** organized in time order using only necessary information.

MODEL ORGANIZATION/ PARAGRAPHS

Discuss Writing Transparency 6A. Then discuss the model and the writing trait of organization/paragraphs.

 Think Aloud The writer has organized the most important information in time order. The summary tells how the mother penguin returns to the sea to feed. A time-order word, *meanwhile*, signals what the father penguin does at the same time. The phrase *after two months* signals what happens next. Through the summary, time passes.

Summary

A **summary** tells the important ideas and information in an article, or it tells what happens in a story.

Summary—Penguin Chick, pages 158–161

Writer repeats only the important details about the mother's journey.
> The mother penguin slides and pushes herself across the ice. She finally gets to the water and dives in. She finds fish and other seafood.

Meanwhile shows that two or more events happen at about the same time.

Strong verbs *slides, huddle,* and *pecks* make the summary clear and vivid.

> Meanwhile, the penguin fathers huddle together. Each father keeps his egg at his feet. He keeps the egg there even when he walks, and he sleeps standing up. After two months, the penguin chick pecks its way out of the egg. The father warms the baby in his brood patch. He talks to the baby with trumpet calls, and the chick whistles back.

Unit 2 Penguin Chick   Writing Model **6A**

▲ **Writing Transparency** 6A

DAY 2 Improve Writing

WRITER'S CRAFT
Include Necessary Information

Display Writing Transparency 6B. Read the directions and work together to summarize the main idea of each paragraph in a sentence or two.

 Think Aloud **CHOOSE THE MOST IMPORTANT INFORMATION** Tomorrow we will write a **summary** of *Penguin Chick*. How could I summarize the main idea of pp. 156–157? I might write, "In the Antarctic, the father penguin warms the egg while the mother travels to the sea to find food." Including details such as how he scoops the egg onto his feet would add too much detail.

GUIDED WRITING Some students may need more help including necessary information. Work with them to summarize parts of another expository nonfiction selection.

Including Necessary Information

In a **summary**, a few sentences tell the main ideas of a story or article. To summarize, include all necessary information that readers need to understand what the article is about. Do not include unnecessary supporting details.

Directions Write one or two sentences summarizing the necessary information in each paragraph.

1. Millions of years ago, penguins could fly. You can see the long black "wings" on the sides of their bodies. But their wings turned into flippers. Now penguins are excellent swimmers. Their flippers are strong paddles. Penguins' webbed feet also help them swim. **Possible answers:**
   <u>Penguins no longer fly. Now they have flippers and webbed feet that make them strong swimmers.</u>

2. Few animals live in the center of Antarctica. But many live in the Antarctic Ocean and along the coast. Many whales go to Antarctica for the summer. The Antarctic fur seal lives on islands near Antarctica. Seals eat fish and squid from the ocean. Many birds, such as gulls and terns, also spend their summers in Antarctica. They nest on land. They get food from the ocean.
   <u>Whales, seals, and birds live in the Antarctic Ocean and along the coast of Antarctica. Many of them eat squid and other fish from the ocean.</u>

3. Antarctica is an unusual continent. About 98% of the continent is covered with an icecap. This is a thick layer of ice and snow. Big sheets of the icecap float in the water off the coast. These are called ice shelves. In summer, parts of the ice shelves break off. They form big, flat icebergs.
   <u>Antarctica is unusual because it is almost totally covered and surrounded by ice and snow.</u>

Unit 2 Penguin Chick   Writer's Craft **6B**

▲ **Writing Transparency** 6B

DAY 3 — Prewrite and Draft

READ THE WRITING PROMPT

on page 169 in the Student Edition.

Penguin Chick explains how penguins protect their eggs and their baby chicks.

Think about what happens as penguin chicks hatch and grow.

Now write a summary of Penguin Chick.

Writing Test Tips

- Explain the important things that happen between the time a female penguin lays an egg and the baby penguin grows up.
- Include all necessary facts. Leave out minor details that describe these facts.
- Use time-order words to make the sequence of events in the penguin's life clear.

GETTING STARTED Students can do any of the following:

- List and number each major event in penguin life in the order in which it happens. Cross out any event that is not necessary.
- Reread each paragraph and summarize it in a sentence.
- Brainstorm vivid verbs to describe penguin actions at each stage of life.

DAY 4 — Draft and Revise

EDITING/REVISING CHECKLIST

- ☑ Are all the important facts included in the summary?
- ☑ Can any unnecessary details be deleted?
- ☑ Do time-order words make the order of events clear?
- ☑ Are V/CV and VC/V words spelled correctly?

See *The Grammar and Writing Book,* pp. 80–85.

Revising Tips

Organization/ Paragraph

- Check whether the events are described in time order, starting with the first event and ending with the last.
- Add time-order words such as *first* and *next* to make the sequence of events clear.

PUBLISHING Students can display their summaries along with drawings of different stages of a penguin's life. Some students may wish to revise their work later.

ASSESSMENT Use the scoring rubric to evaluate students' work.

DAY 5 — Connect to Unit Writing

How-to Report	
Week 1	Summary 173g–173h
Week 2	Rules 197g–197h
Week 3	Problem/Solution 223g–223h
Week 4	Feature Story 249g–249h
Week 5	Explanatory Paragraph 271g–271h

PREVIEW THE UNIT PROMPT

Think of something you learned or figured out how to do that involves a few simple steps. Write the steps in a how-to report. Make sure you provide all the necessary information.

APPLY

- A how-to report explains the steps for making or doing something.
- Provide all the necessary information in a how-to report so that readers can follow the steps.

Writing Trait Rubric

	4	3	2	1
Organization/ Paragraphs	Ideas well developed from beginning to end; strong closure	Ideas that progress from beginning to end; good closure	Some sense of movement from beginning to end; weak closure	No sense of movement from beginning to end or closure
	Summary organized with exceptional logic	Summary organized adequately	Summary not clearly organized	Summary not organized

AFTER READING

OBJECTIVES

- Use word parts to decode words with syllable patterns V/CV, VC/V.
- Review vowel diphthongs *ou*, *ow*/ou/ and *oi*, *oy*/oi/.
- Blend and read V/CV, VC/V words and words that contain vowel diphthongs.
- Apply decoding strategies: blend longer words.

Generalization

Generalization When a word or a syllable ends with a single vowel, the vowel sound is usually long. When a word or a syllable ends with a consonant, the vowel sound is usually short.

Support Phonics The writing systems of languages such as Arabic and Hebrew focus on consonant sounds and long vowels. Short vowels are indicated with separate marks that are often optional. Speakers of these languages may need extra help in spelling words with short vowels or multiple vowel sounds. Play spelling games such as Hangman to give students entertaining opportunities to practice spelling such words.

See the Phonics Transition Lessons in the ELL and Transition Handbook.

Syllables V/CV, VC/V

Directions Circle each word in the box with the **long vowel** sound in the **first syllable**. Underline each word in the box with the **short vowel** sound in the **first syllable**. Then write each word in the correct column.

| (lady) | lemon | finish | (baby) | (robot) |
| panel | (spider) | polish | (moment) | credit |

long vowel		short vowel	
1.	lady	6.	lemon
2.	baby	7.	finish
3.	robot	8.	panel
4.	spider	9.	polish
5.	moment	10.	credit

Directions Circle each word in the box with the **long vowel** sound in the **first syllable**. Underline each word in the box with the **short vowel** sound in the **first syllable**. Then use the words to complete the sentences. Write each word on the line.

| menu | (female) | (motor) | cousin | (zebra) |

female	11. A _____ horse is called a mare.
zebra	12. A _____ has black and white stripes.
menu	13. A _____ is a list of food.
cousin	14. Your _____ is your aunt or uncle's child.
motor	15. A _____ is an engine.

Home Activity Your child identified words that have a long or short vowel sound in the first syllable. Ask your child to read the long and short vowel words he or she circled or underlined on the page above. Help your child use some of these words to write a story.

▲ **Practice Book 3.1** p. 59

Syllable Patterns V/CV, VC/V

TEACH

Remind students that dividing words into syllables can help them read new words. Write *lemon* and *pilot*.

- These words have just one consonant in the middle.
- From looking at the words, we can't tell if the consonant goes with the first syllable or the second syllable.
- If the consonant ends the first syllable (cover *on* in *lemon*), the vowel sound is short.
- If it goes with the second syllable (cover *mon* in *lemon*), the vowel sound is long.

MODEL If I don't know a word like this, I can try saying it with a long *e:* lē mon. That doesn't sound right, so I'll try a short *e* in the first syllable: **lem on.** That's a word I know! The short vowel sound must be correct.

Model blending *pilot.* Try both the long *i* and short *i* sounds. Then have students blend the word with you.

PRACTICE AND ASSESS

DECODE LONGER WORDS Write these words. Have students read them and then identify the vowel sound in the first syllable.

sev/en   la/bor   fi/nest   na/tion

hu/man   div/ide   prov/ince   rap/id

READ WORDS IN CONTEXT Write these sentences. Have individuals read them and identify the vowel sound in the first syllable of the underlined words.

The child stared unhappily at the <u>broken</u> toy. (/ō/)

As soon as the <u>music</u> started, we got quiet. (/ū/)

My mother is a member of the <u>Senate</u>. (/e/)

To assess, have students find and read two words on page 151 of the Student Edition that have just one consonant in the middle. *(cov/ers, liv/ing)*

Review Phonics

REVIEW DIPHTHONGS

CONNECT Write this sentence: *The boy toiled under the hot sun.*

- We studied the sound /oi/ spelled *oi* and *oy*.
- Read the sentence to yourself. Raise your hand when you know which words have the sound /oi/. *(boy, toiled)*
- What letters stand for /oi/ in *boy*? *(oy)*
- What letters stand for /oi/ in *toiled*? *(oi)*

Continue in the same way for the sound /ou/ spelled *ow* and *ou* with the sentence: *He placed the <u>flowers</u> on the <u>counter.</u>*

PRACTICE AND ASSESS

DECODE LONGER WORDS Have individuals read the following words. Provide help chunking and blending the words as needed.

noisy	crowded	hoist	shower
powder	royal	thousand	rowdy
soybean	mouth	chowder	poison

READ WORDS IN CONTEXT Have students read these sentences. Then, to check meaning, have them give their own sentences for the underlined words.

The students cheered <u>loudly</u> for their team.

Grandma placed a handmade lace <u>doily</u> under the vase.

Larry is my oldest sister's <u>boyfriend</u>.

The man <u>scowled</u> and turned away.

To assess, note whether students read the /oi/ and /ou/ words correctly.

Generalization

Generalization Sometimes the letters *ou* and *ow* stand for the diphthong /ou/. The letters *oi* and *oy* stand for the diphthong /oi/. In a diphthong, each vowel contributes to the sound heard.

Vocabulary TIP

You may wish to explain the meanings of these words.

hoist	lift up high
rowdy	noisy and rough
chowder	a thick, creamy soup

Spelling & Phonics   Syllable Pattern V/CV, VC/V

OBJECTIVE

- Spell words with syllable patterns V/CV and VC/V.

Generalization

Connect to Phonics When the vowel sound in the first syllable is long, divide the word after the vowel: *pi lot*. When the vowel sound in the first syllable is short, divide the word after the consonant: *fin ish*. The sound of the vowel in the first syllable can determine how the word is divided.

Spelling Words

1. finish
2. pilot
3. even
4. wagon
5. music
6. silent
7. rapid
8. female*
9. lemon
10. pupil
11. focus
12. robot
13. tulip
14. camel
15. salad

Challenge Words

16. resident
17. spinach
18. climate
19. tradition
20. innocent

*Word from the selection

ELL

Spelling/Phonics Support See the ELL and Transition Handbook for spelling support.

DAY 1 Pretest and Sort

PRETEST

Use the Dictation Sentences from Day 5 to administer the pretest. Read the word, read the sentence, and then read the word again. Guide students in self-correcting their pretests and correcting any misspellings.

Monitor Progress

Spelling

If... students misspell more than 4 pretest words,	**then...** use words 1–8 for Strategic Intervention.
If... students misspell 1–4 pretest words,	**then...** use words 1–15 for On-Level practice.
If... students correctly spell all pretest words,	**then...** use words 1–20 for Advanced Learners.

HOMEWORK Spelling Practice Book, p. 21.

Syllable Pattern V/CV, VC/V

Generalization When the vowel sound in the first syllable is long, divide the word after the vowel: **pi lot**. When the vowel sound in the first syllable is short, divide the word after the consonant: **fin ish**.

Word Sort Sort the list words by long or short vowel.

Spelling Words
1. finish
2. pilot
3. even
4. wagon
5. music
6. silent
7. rapid
8. female
9. lemon
10. pupil
11. focus
12. robot
13. tulip
14. camel
15. salad

long vowel
1. pilot
2. even
3. music
4. silent
5. female
6. pupil
7. focus
8. robot
9. tulip

short vowel
10. finish
11. wagon
12. rapid
13. lemon
14. camel
15. salad

Challenge Words
16. resident
17. spinach
18. climate
19. tradition
20. innocent

long vowel
16. climate

short vowel
17. resident
18. spinach
19. tradition
20. innocent

Home Activity Your child is learning to spell words with long and short vowel sounds. To practice at home, have your child look at the word, pronounce it, and then spell it aloud.

▲ **Spelling Practice Book** p. 21

DAY 2 Think and Practice

TEACH

The vowel sound in the first syllable of a word can be a clue as to how the word is divided. Words with a long vowel sound in the first syllable should be divided after the vowel. Words with a short vowel sound should be divided after the consonant. Write the spelling words on the board. Have students say the words out loud. Then have them identify whether the first vowel sound is long or short, and explain where to divide the word.

    ro bot

FIND THE PATTERN Ask students to group spelling words by the vowel sound in the first syllable.

HOMEWORK Spelling Practice Book, p. 22.

Syllable Pattern V/CV, VC/V

Missing Words Write the missing list word.

Spelling Words
finish
pilot
even
wagon
music
silent
rapid
female
lemon
pupil
focus
robot
tulip
camel
salad

1. It is easy to __focus__ this camera.
2. The __pilot__ of the plane has white hair.
3. My flute teacher has a new __pupil__.
4. The mother cat had two male kittens and one __female__ kitten.
5. This type of __camel__ has two humps on its back.
6. You will be able to swim __even__ better after a little rest.
7. The song had a __rapid__ beat.
8. I pulled the children in a __wagon__.

Syllables Find the list word that fits each word. Write the first syllable, the second syllable, and the complete word.

	First Syllable	Second Syllable	Base Word
9. song	mu	sic	music
10. flower	tu	lip	tulip
11. fruit	lem	on	lemon
12. end	fin	ish	finish
13. vegetables	sal	ad	salad
14. quiet	si	lent	silent
15. machine	ro	bot	robot

Home Activity Your child divided long vowel and short vowel words into syllables and wrote them. Say a list word. Spell the first syllable, and have your child spell the second.

▲ **Spelling Practice Book** p. 22

DAY 3 Connect to Writing

WRITE A DESCRIPTIVE PARAGRAPH

Ask students to write a paragraph describing a place or an event. Students should use at least four spelling words. Encourage children to read their paragraphs aloud to the class or post them on the bulletin board.

Frequently Misspelled Words

favorite   *before*

pretty

These common words are difficult for third-graders to spell. Alert students to these frequently misspelled words.

HOMEWORK Spelling Practice Book, p. 23

Syllable Pattern V/CV, VC/V

Spelling Words				
finish	pilot	even	wagon	music
silent	rapid	female	lemon	pupil
focus	robot	tulip	camel	salad

Proofread an Announcement Circle five misspelled words in this announcement about a special concert. Write the words correctly. Then write the word with a capitalization error.

Don't miss Friday's concert! The (musik) will focus on early (america) You will (evin) hear a jug band. The (femail) group will sing (favorit) songs about (wagen) trains, the gold rush, and California.

Frequently Misspelled Words

favorite
before
pretty

1. __music__   2. __even__   3. __female__
4. __favorite__   5. __wagon__   6. __America__

Proofread Words Fill in the circle to show the correctly spelled word. Write the word.

7. ○ saled ● salad ○ salade   7. __salad__
8. ○ kamel ● camel ○ camal   8. __camel__
9. ● silent ○ silant ○ sylent   9. __silent__
10. ○ leman ○ lemen ● lemon   10. __lemon__
11. ○ finash ● finish ○ fenish   11. __finish__
12. ○ rowbot ○ robat ● robot   12. __robot__

School + Home **Home Activity** Your child identified misspelled multi-syllable words with long and short vowels. Ask your child to explain how to divide a multi-syllable word (immediately after a long vowel; after the consonant that follows a short vowel).

▲ **Spelling Practice Book** p. 23

DAY 4 Review

REVIEW SYLLABLE PATTERN V/CV, VC/V

Write the spelling words on the board and divide each one by syllable. Divide some words correctly and some words incorrectly. Have students identify words that are divided incorrectly, and then write the word correctly.

Spelling Strategy
Dividing Words

The sound of the vowel in the first syllable of a word shows how the word should be divided. Encourage students to sound out words if they are unsure where they should be divided.

HOMEWORK Spelling Practice Book, p. 24

Syllable Pattern V/CV, VC/V

Spelling Words				
finish	pilot	even	wagon	music
silent	rapid	female	lemon	pupil
focus	robot	tulip	camel	salad

Word Clues Read all the directions. Then write list words in the boxes.

- Use three list words that begin with **f**.
- The word with a syllable that rhymes with **sale** is second.
- The word with a **short** vowel in the first syllable is third.
- The word with a **long** vowel in the first syllable is first.

1. __focus__
2. __female__
3. __finish__

- The word with a syllable that rhymes with **hot** is first.
- A list word with a syllable that rhymes with **my** and starts with **s** is third.
- A word with a syllable that rhymes with **few** and starts with **m** is second.

4. __robot__
5. __music__
6. __silent__

Missing Syllables Each underlined word has one missing syllable. Write the complete list word.

7. Nat put the kittens in the wag.   7. __wagon__
8. When I grow up, I want to be a lot.   8. __pilot__
9. Tom is a rap worker.   9. __rapid__
10. Did you see the lip in the garden?   10. __tulip__

School + Home **Home Activity** Your child has been learning to spell words with long and short vowels. Ask your child to identify the three most difficult list words. Have him or her spell these words one syllable at a time.

▲ **Spelling Practice Book** p. 24

DAY 5 Posttest

DICTATION SENTENCES

1. Who will <u>finish</u> the test first?
2. Mel's dad is a <u>pilot</u>.
3. Two is an <u>even</u> number.
4. Put the boxes in the <u>wagon</u>.
5. The <u>music</u> on the radio was loud.
6. We must be <u>silent</u> during a fire drill.
7. Taking the train is a <u>rapid</u> way to get to the airport.
8. I have a <u>female</u> cat.
9. Do you want <u>lemon</u> in your tea?
10. Harry is a good <u>pupil</u>.
11. <u>Focus</u> your eyes on the book.
12. I liked the <u>robot</u> movie.
13. Look at the red <u>tulip</u>!
14. Did you see the <u>camel</u> at the zoo?
15. Dad made a <u>salad</u> for dinner.

CHALLENGE

16. Grandma is a <u>resident</u> of the city.
17. I do not like <u>spinach</u>.
18. The <u>climate</u> in the rain forest is hot and wet.
19. Can you share a family <u>tradition</u>?
20. Nick looks <u>innocent</u>, but I know he broke Mom's vase.

OBJECTIVES

- Formulate an inquiry question that is connected to this week's lesson focus.
- Effectively and efficiently find, evaluate, and communicate information related to an inquiry question using electronic sources.

New Literacies

Day 1	Identify Questions
Day 2	Navigate/Search
Day 3	Analyze
Day 4	Synthesize
Day 5	Communicate

NEW LITERACIES

Internet Inquiry Activity

EXPLORE ANIMAL ADAPTATIONS

Use the following 5-day plan to help students conduct this week's Internet inquiry activity on animal adaptations. Remind students to follow classroom rules when using the Internet.

DAY 1

Identify Questions Discuss the lesson focus question: *How have animals adapted to solve the problems of their environments?* Brainstorm ideas for specific inquiry questions about animal adaptations. For example, students might want to find out how animals change the way they look or where they live when adapting to changes in their environment. Have students work individually, in pairs, or in small groups to write an inquiry question they want to answer.

DAY 2

Navigate/Search Review how to begin a simple Internet search using a student-friendly search engine. Remind students that when they search by keyword, they will get a list of Web sites related to that word. Have students determine appropriate keywords related to their inquiry questions. Students can type keywords and then read the short descriptions of the Web sites to find those that contain information best suited to their inquiry questions.

DAY 3

Analyze Have students explore the Web sites they identified on Day 2. Tell them to scan each site for information that helps answer their inquiry questions. Students may need to do additional searching if more information or different information is needed to answer inquiry questions completely. They can print out or take notes about relevant information.

DAY 4

Synthesize Have students organize the information from Day 3. Remind them that when they organize, they pull information together and arrange it in an orderly functional way. Organizing information helps students develop answers to their inquiry questions.

DAY 5

Communicate Have students share their inquiry results. They can use a word processing program to create a short essay on animal adaptations.

Dictionary/Glossary

TEACH

Ask students how they find the meaning of an unfamiliar word. Students should mention looking up words in a dictionary or glossary. Have all students look at the same word in a dictionary as you define these features.

- **Two guide words** are shown in large dark type and appear at the top of each dictionary page. They show the first and last words on the page. **Entry words** are arranged alphabetically on the page. They are usually in dark type and divided into syllables.

- The **pronunciation** is a group of letters and symbols that appear in parentheses after each word. It shows how to pronounce the word. Syllables with a dark accent get the most force. Syllables with a light accent get less force than one with a dark accent, but more than one with no accent.

- The **part of speech** tells how the word is used. A dictionary uses abbreviations, such as **v,** for verb and **n,** for noun.

- The **definition** tells the meaning. Many words have more than one definition. Some words can be used for different parts of speech. If so, there is a definition for each part of speech.

Give pairs of students a dictionary. Have them find an unknown word and write it on a piece of paper along with the guide words for the page on which they found it. Partners pronounce the word and discuss the definition. Finally, they write the word in a sentence. As a group, discuss these questions:

1. **Would the entry word *attribute* appear before or after *adaptation*?** *(after)*

2. ***Acute* is one of the guide words on the page where *adaptation* is located. Is it the first or last word on the page? Explain.** *(It is the first word since alphabetically it comes before adaptation.)*

ad·ap·ta·tion (ad′ ap tā shən) *n.*
1. an adapting or being adapted
2. something resulting from adapting
3. a change in form, structure, or function that allows an animal to live better in its environment

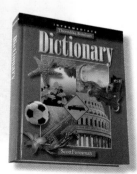

ASSESS

As students use a dictionary, check that they know how to use the pronunciation. Make sure they can identify the parts of speech and find the appropriate definition to match the use of a word.

For more practice or to assess students, use Practice Book 3.1, p. 60.

OBJECTIVES

- Review terms related to a dictionary or glossary.
- Find words in a dictionary or glossary.

Dictionary/Glossary

A **dictionary** is a book of words and their meanings. The words are listed in alphabetical order. **Guide words** are printed in large, dark type at the top of each dictionary page. They show the first and last words printed on the page.

Directions Use the dictionary page to answer the questions.

romp/roost	
rook (rŭk). **1** a bird from Europe that lives in a flock with many other birds. The rook is close in size to a crow. **2** a cheat. **3** to cheat or trick someone.	**rookery** (rŭk′ ər ē), a breeding place for certain animals or birds, such as seals or penguins. **rookie** (rŭk′ ē), a beginner, as on a police force or in a sport.

1. Which word can be used to describe a football player playing his first season?
   rookie

2. Which entry word or words can be used as a verb?
   rook

3. Find the entry word *rook*. Which meaning (1, 2, or 3) of rook is used in this sentence? *The rook flew above the flock.*
   meaning 1

4. What are the guide words for this page?
   romp, roost

5. Which of these words would be found on this dictionary page: *round, roll, roof, rock*?
   roof

Home Activity Your child read entries in a dictionary and used them to answer questions. Read a book with your child, and have him or her identify two or three unfamiliar words. Ask your child to find the meaning of the words in a dictionary.

▲ **Practice Book 3.1** p. 60

Assessment Checkpoints *for the Week*

Selection Assessment

Use pp. 21–24 of Selection Tests **to check:**

 Selection Understanding

 Comprehension Skill *Main Idea*

 Selection Vocabulary

cuddles	pecks
flippers	preen
frozen	snuugles
hatch	

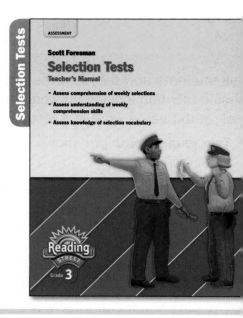

ASSESSMENT

Scott Foresman
Selection Tests
Teacher's Manual

- Assess comprehension of weekly selections
- Assess understanding of weekly comprehension skills
- Assess knowledge of selection vocabulary

Reading STREET Grade **3**

Leveled Assessment

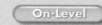
- On-Level
- Strategic Intervention
- Advanced

Use pp. 31–36 of Fresh Reads for Differentiated Test Practice **to check:**

 Comprehension Skill *Main Idea*

 REVIEW Comprehension Skill *Sequence*

 Fluency *Words Correct Per Minute*

ASSESSMENT   Teacher's Manual

Scott Foresman
Fresh Reads
for Differentiated Test Practice

Leveled passages—strategic intervention, on-level, and advanced—for

- Fluency checks
- Practice and application of weekly comprehension skills
- Answer key for all practice pages

Reading STREET Grade **3**

Managing Assessment

Use Assessment Handbook **for:**

 Observation Checklists

 Record-Keeping Forms

 Portfolio Assessment

ASSESSMENT

Scott Foresman
Assessment Handbook

- Suggestions for preparing students for high-stake tests
- Ideas for classroom-based assessment
- Forms in English and Spanish for students to record interests and progress
- Forms in English and Spanish for teachers to record observations of students' reading and writing abilities and progress
- Assessment and Regrouping charts reproduced from *Reading Street* Teacher's Editions

Reading STREET Grades **3–6**

Illinois

Planning Guide for Performance Descriptors

A Day's Work

Reading Street Teacher's Edition pages   **Grade 3 English Language Arts Performance Descriptors**

Oral Language

Speaking/Listening Build Concept Vocabulary: 174l, 185, 191, 197c
Read Aloud: 174m

1A.Stage C.2. Use word analysis (root words, inflections, affixes) to identify words.
1B.Stage C.13. Read age-appropriate material aloud with fluency and accuracy.
2A.Stage C.5. Define unfamiliar vocabulary.

Word Work

Words Ending in *ie*: 197i, 197k–197l

1A.Stage C.2. Use word analysis (root words, inflections, affixes) to identify words.

Reading

Comprehension Character: 174–175, 178–191, 197b
Visualize: 174–175, 178–191

Vocabulary Lesson Vocabulary: 176b, 185, 191
Context Clues: 176–177, 187, 197c

Fluency Model Expressing Characterization: 174l–174m, 197a
Choral Reading: 197a

Self-Selected Reading: LR10–18, TR16–17

Literature Genre—Realistic Fiction: 178
Reader Response: 192

1A.Stage C.5. Use a variety of decoding strategies (e.g., phonics, word patterns, structural analysis, context clues) to recognize new words when reading age-appropriate material.
1B.Stage C.9. Continuously check and clarify for understanding (e.g., reread, read ahead, use visual and context clues) during reading.
1B.Stage C.13. Read age-appropriate material aloud with fluency and accuracy.
2A.Stage C.4. Identify/compare characters' attributes across stories.
2A.Stage C.5. Define unfamiliar vocabulary.
2A.Stage C.7. Classify major types of fiction (e.g., tall tale, fairy tale, fable).
4A.Stage C.6. Respond in an appropriate manner to questions and discussion with relevant and focused comments.

Language Arts

Writing Rules: 197g–197h

Six-Trait Writing Sentences: 193, 197g–197h

Grammar, Usage, and Mechanics Singular and Plural Nouns: 197e–197f

Research/Study Procedures/Instructions: 197n

Technology New Literacies: 197m

3A.Stage C.9. Demonstrate appropriate use of the various parts of speech (e.g., nouns, pronouns, verbs).
3B.Stage C.4. Organize around a structure (e.g., paragraph, essay) appropriate to purpose, audience, and context.
5B.Stage C.2. Discriminate between relevant and irrelevant information.
5C.Stage C.1. Access and use information from a variety of sources.

Unit Skills

Writing How-To Report: WA2–9
Poetry: 272–275
Project/Wrap-Up: 276–277

1B.Stage C.8. Identify genres of poetry.
2A.Stage C.11. Recognize both rhymed and unrhymed poetry.
3B.Stage C.6. Elaborate and support ideas (e.g., pictures, facts, details, description, narration).

This Week's Leveled Readers

Below-Level

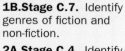

On-Level

Advanced

1B.Stage C.11. Summarize or retell information from a text.
2A.Stage C.4. Identify/ compare characters' attributes across stories.

Fiction

1B.Stage C.7. Identify genres of fiction and non-fiction.
2A.Stage C.4. Identify/ compare characters' attributes across stories.

Fiction

1B.Stage C.10. Ask question to clarify understanding.
2A.Stage C.4. Identify/ compare characters' attributes across stories.

Fiction

Content-Area Illinois Performance Descriptors in This Lesson

Social Studies

14E.Stage C.2. Tell about people who have come from other countries to live in the United States.

15A.Stage C.3. List jobs people do to earn wages.

16A.Stage C.6. Tell why the location of where an event occurred helps to explain why and how it happened.

16D.Stage C.7. Compare how families and other groups of people lived in a past culture with how families and other groups of people in the community live today.

18A.Stage C.4. Explain the significance of the cultural diversity of the United States.

18C.Stage C.1. Describe the concept of conflict.

18C.Stage C.2. Describe the concept of cooperation.

18C.Stage C.3. Describe how individuals work together to obtain food, clothing, and shelter.

18C.Stage C.4. Define division of labor.

Science

12B.Stage C.2. Apply scientific inquiries or technological designs to examine the interdependence of organisms in ecosystems: describing the interaction between living and non-living factors in an ecosystem; predicting what can happen to organisms if they lose different environmental resources or ecologically related groups of organisms.

12E.Stage C.1. Apply scientific inquiries or technological designs to analyze Earth's land, water and atmosphere as systems.

Math

6C.Stage C.2. Select appropriate methods and tools for computing with whole numbers from mental computation, estimation, calculators, and paper/pencil according to the context and nature of the computation and use of the selected method or tool.

Illinois!

A FAMOUS ILLINOISAN
Mary Ann Bickerdyke

Born in Ohio, Mary Ann Bickerdyke (1817–1901) moved to Illinois in 1856. Trained as a nurse, she volunteered to help at an army hospital in Cairo just after the Civil War started. General Ulysses S. Grant gave Bickerdyke free transportation anywhere under his command. She often traveled onto battlefields to help care for wounded soldiers, which earned her the nickname "Mother Bickerdyke."

Students can . . .
Write the words to a memorial for Mary Ann Bickerdyke and share them with their classmates.

A SPECIAL ILLINOIS PLACE
Du Quoin

The town of Du Quoin was named after Jean Baptiste Du Quoin, the son of a Frenchman and a Native American woman. He became a leader of the Tamaroa people, and a small early settlement was named for him. Most of its residents moved away in 1853 to be near a new railroad station. The town that developed near the station was founded as Du Quoin, and the original settlement became known as Old Du Quoin. Today Du Quoin has a population of more than six thousand people.

Students can . . .
Learn more about Du Quoin and write a short paragraph about a typical day in the small town.

ILLINOIS FUN FACTS
Did You Know?

• Prairie Avenue in Chicago is known for its mansions and famous past residents.

• The official state nickname for Illinois is *Land of Lincoln*.

• Illinois is named for a confederation of Native American groups called the Illini, who lived in the Midwest in the 1600s. *Illinois* was a French version of the Native American word *Illiniwek*.

Students can . . .
Look at a map of Illinois and identify communities that have Native American names. Have students create a banner celebrating the Native American heritage of one of these names.

Unit 2
Smart Solutions

Week 2

EXPAND THE CONCEPT

When is a solution the wrong solution?

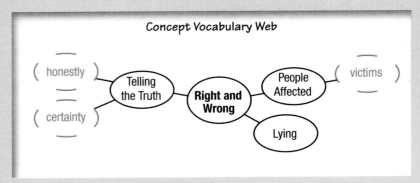

CONCEPT QUESTION

What are smart ways that problems are solved?

Week 1

How have animals adapted to solve the problems of their environment?

Week 2

When is a solution the wrong solution?

Week 3

How can you get ideas to solve a problem?

Week 4

When are respect and understanding important in solving a problem?

Week 5

When you find yourself in a new place, what problems might you meet?

CONNECT THE CONCEPT

▶ **Build Background**
certainty, honesty, victims

Concept Vocabulary Web

(honestly) — Telling the Truth — **Right and Wrong** — People Affected — (victims)

(certainty)

Lying

▶ **Social Studies Content**
Making Choices, Personal Responsibility

▶ **Writing**
List of Rules

▶ **Internet Inquiry**
Making Good Choices

Preview Your Week

When is a solution the wrong solution?

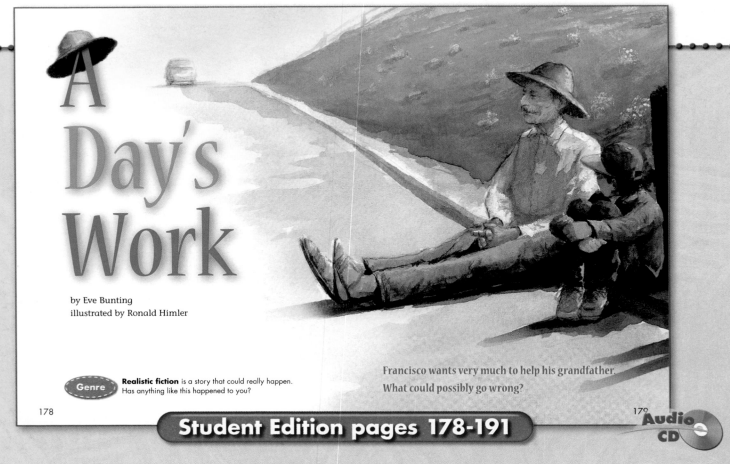

A Day's Work

by Eve Bunting
illustrated by Ronald Himler

Genre **Realistic fiction** is a story that could really happen. Has anything like this happened to you?

Francisco wants very much to help his grandfather. What could possibly go wrong?

178

179

Student Edition pages 178-191

Audio CD

Genre Realistic Fiction

Vocabulary Strategy Context Clues

Comprehension Skill Character

Comprehension Strategy Visualize

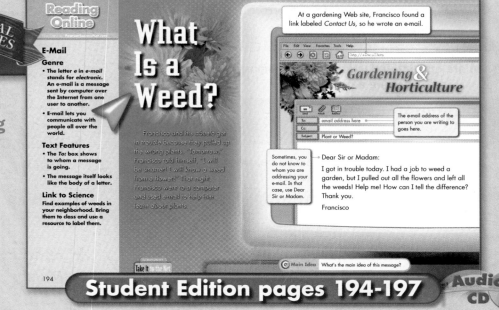

Paired Selection

SOCIAL STUDIES

Reading Across Texts
Learn How to Find Gardening Information

Genre
E-mail

Text Features
Message Box

E-Mail

Genre
- The letter *e* in *e-mail* stands for *electronic.* An e-mail is a message sent by computer over the Internet from one user to another.
- E-mail lets you communicate with people all over the world.

Text Features
- The *To:* box shows to whom a message is going.
- The message itself looks like the body of a letter.

Link to Science
Find examples of weeds in your neighborhood. Bring them to class and use a resource to label them.

Reading Online

What Is a Weed?

Francisco and his abuelo got in trouble because they pulled up the wrong plants. "Tomorrow," Francisco told himself, "I will be smarter! I will know a weed from a flower!" That night Francisco went to a computer and used e-mail to help him learn about plants.

At a gardening Web site, Francisco found a link labeled *Contact Us,* so he wrote an e-mail.

Gardening & Horticulture

The e-mail address of the person you are writing to goes here.

Sometimes, you do not know to whom you are addressing your e-mail. In that case, use Dear Sir or Madam.

Dear Sir or Madam:

I got in trouble today. I had a job to weed a garden, but I pulled out all the flowers and left all the weeds! Help me! How can I tell the difference? Thank you.

Francisco

Main Idea What's the main idea of this message?

194

Student Edition pages 194-197

Audio CD

Read It
ONLINE
PearsonSuccessNet.com
• Student Edition
• Leveled Readers

Leveled Readers

🔵 **Skill** Literary Elements: Character

🔵 **Strategy** Visualize

Lesson Vocabulary

Below-Level

Sarah's Choice
by Ellen Chapman
illustrated by Freddie Levin

On-Level

THE BOY WHO CRIED WOLF
retold by Linda B. Ross
illustrated by Mark Weber

Advanced

The Song Makers Go to Salem
by Sharon Franklin
illustrated by Tony Sansevero

ELL Reader

· Concept Vocabulary
· Text Support
· Language Enrichment

Mamá's Birthday Garden

by Isabella Stefan
Illustrated by Priscilla Burris

Time for
SOCIAL STUDIES

Integrate Social Studies Standards

• **Making Choices**
• **Personal Responsibility**

☑ **Read**

A Day's Work
pp. 178–191

"What Is a Weed?"
pp. 194–197

Leveled Readers

Below-Level   **On-Level**   **Advanced**

• Support Concepts • Develop Concepts • Extend Concepts

ELL Reader

Mamá's Birthday Garden

☑ **Build**
Concept Vocabulary
Right and Wrong,
pp. 174l–174m

☑ **Teach**
Social Studies Concepts
Choices, p. 181
Careers, p. 183

☑ **Explore**
Social Studies Center
Study Costs and Benefits,
p. 174k

Weekly Plan

READING

45–90 minutes

TARGET SKILLS OF THE WEEK

- **Comprehension Skill**
  Character
- **Comprehension Strategy**
  Visualize
- **Vocabulary Strategy**
  Context Clues

DAY 1
PAGES 174l–176b, 197a, 173e–173h, 173k–173m

Oral Language

QUESTION OF THE WEEK   *When is a solution the wrong solution?*

Read Aloud: "The Honest-to-Goodness Truth," 174m
Build Concepts, 174l

Comprehension/Vocabulary

Comprehension Skill/Strategy Lesson, 174–175
- Character **T**
- Visualize

Build Background, 176a

Introduce Lesson Vocabulary, 176b
excitement, gardener, motioned, sadness, shivered, shocked, slammed **T**

Read Leveled Readers

Grouping Options 174f–174g

Fluency

Model Characterization, 174l–174m, 197a

DAY 2
PAGES 176–185, 197a, 173e–173i, 173k–173m

Oral Language

QUESTION OF THE DAY   *Is it ever OK to tell a lie?*

Word Work

Phonics Lesson, 197i
Syllable Pattern C + *le*

Comprehension/Vocabulary

Vocabulary Strategy Lesson, 176–177
- Context Clues **T**

Read *A Day's Work,* 178–185

Grouping Options
174f–174g

- Character **T**
- Visualize
- **REVIEW** Realism and Fantasy **T**
  Develop Vocabulary

Fluency

Choral Reading, 197a

LANGUAGE ARTS

30–60 minutes

Trait of the Week

Sentences

Grammar, 197e
Introduce Singular and Plural Nouns **T**

Writing Workshop, 197g
Introduce Rules
Model the Trait of the Week: Sentences

Spelling, 197k
Pretest for Words Ending in *-le*

Internet Inquiry, 197m
Identify Questions

Grammar, 197e
Develop Singular and Plural Nouns **T**

Writing Workshop, 197g
Improve Writing by Eliminating Wordiness

Spelling, 197k
Teach the Generalization

Internet Inquiry, 197m
Navigate/Search

DAILY WRITING ACTIVITIES

Day 1   Write to Read, 174

Day 2   Words to Write, 177
Strategy Response Log, 178, 185

DAILY SOCIAL STUDIES CONNECTIONS

Day 1   Right and Wrong Concept Web, 174l

Day 2   Time for Social Studies: Choices, 181; Careers, 183
Revisit the Right and Wrong Concept Web, 185

DAILY SUCCESS PREDICTORS
for Adequate Yearly Progress

Monitor Progress and Corrective Feedback

Vocabulary   Check Vocabulary, *174l*

RESOURCES FOR THE WEEK

- Practice Book, *pp. 61–70*
- Phonics and Spelling Practice Book, *pp. 25–28*
- Grammar and Writing Practice Book, *pp. 25–28*
- Selection Test, *pp. 25–28*
- Fresh Reads for Differentiated Test Practice, *pp. 37–42*
- The Grammar and Writing Book, *pp. 86–91*

Grouping Options for Differentiated Instruction

Turn the page for the small group lesson plan.

DAY 3 — PAGES 186–193, 197a, 197e–197m

Oral Language

QUESTION OF THE DAY *What do you think will happen the next time Francisco and his abuelo are looking for work?*

Comprehension/Vocabulary

Read *A Day's Work,* 186–192

Grouping Options 174f–174g

- Character **T**
- Visualize
- Context Clues **T**
- Develop Vocabulary

Reader Response

Selection Test

Fluency

Model Characterization, 197a

Grammar, 197f
Apply Singular and Plural Nouns in Writing **T**

Writing Workshop, 193, 197h
Write Now
Prewrite and Draft

Spelling, 197l
Connect Spelling to Writing

Internet Inquiry, 197m
Analyze Sources

Day 3 Strategy Response Log, 190
Look Back and Write, 192

Day 3 Revisit the Right and Wrong Concept Web, 191

DAY 4 — PAGES 194–197a, 197e–197m

Oral Language

QUESTION OF THE DAY *How would you handle a mistake you might have made in school or at a job?*

Word Work

Phonics Lesson, 197j
REVIEW Syllables V/CV, VC/V **T**

Comprehension/Vocabulary

Read "What Is a Weed?" 194–197

Grouping Options 174f–174g

E-Mail/Text Features
Reading Across Texts

Fluency

Partner Reading, 197a

Grammar, 197f
Practice Singular and Plural Nouns for Standardized Tests **T**

Writing Workshop, 197h
Draft, Revise, and Publish

Spelling, 197l
Provide a Strategy

Internet Inquiry, 197m
Synthesize Information

Day 4 Writing Across Texts, 197

Day 4 Study Costs and Benefits, 174k

DAY 5 — PAGES 173a–173h, 197a–197n

Oral Language

QUESTION OF THE WEEK *To wrap up the week, revisit the Day 1 question.*
Build Concept Vocabulary, 197c

Fluency

Read Leveled Readers

Grouping Options 174f–174g

Assess Reading Rate, 197a

Comprehension/Vocabulary

- Reteach Character, 197b **T**
- Paraphrase, 197b
- Review Context Clues, 197c **T**

Speaking and Listening, 197d
Directions
Listen to Directions

Grammar, 197f
Cumulative Review

Writing Workshop, 197h
Connect to Unit Writing

Spelling, 197l
Posttest for Words Ending in *-le*

Internet Inquiry, 197m
Communicate Results

Research/Study Skills, 197n
Procedures and Instructions

Day 5 Paraphrase, 197b

Day 5 Revisit the Right and Wrong Concept Web, 197c

KEY = Target Skill **T** = Tested Skill

Comprehension Check Retelling, *193*

Fluency Check Fluency WCPM, *197a*

Vocabulary Check Vocabulary, *197c*

SUCCESS PREDICTOR

Small Group Plan *for Differentiated Instruction*

Daily Plan AT A GLANCE

Reading
Whole Group
- Oral Language
- Phonics
- Comprehension/Vocabulary

Group Time

Differentiated Instruction

Meet with small groups to provide:
- Skill Support
- Reading Support
- Fluency Practice

Read

This week's lessons for daily group time can be found behind the Differentiated Instruction (DI) tab on pp. DI·12–DI·21.

Whole Group
- Fluency

Language Arts
- Grammar
- Writing
- Spelling
- Research/Inquiry
- Speaking/Listening/Viewing

Use *My Sidewalks on Reading Street* for Tier III intensive reading intervention.

DAY 1

On-Level	Strategic Intervention	Advanced
Teacher-Led *Page DI · 13*	**Teacher-Led** *Page DI · 12*	**Teacher-Led** *Page DI · 13*
• Develop Concept Vocabulary • Read On-Level Reader *The Boy Who Cried Wolf*	• Preteach Syllable Patterns • Read Decodable Reader 7 • Read Below-Level Reader *Sarah's Choice*	• Read Advanced Reader *The Song Makers Go to Sa...* • Independent Extension Activity

(i) Independent Activities
While you meet with small groups, have the rest of the class...

- Visit the Reading/Library Center
- Listen to the Background Building Audio
- Finish Write to Read, p. 174
- Complete Practice Book 3.1 pp. 63–64
- Visit Cross-Curricular Centers

DAY 2

On-Level	Strategic Intervention	Advanced
Teacher-Led *Pages 180–185*	**Teacher-Led** *Page DI · 14*	**Teacher-Led** *Page DI · 15*
• Read *A Day's Work*	• Practice Lesson Vocabulary • Read Multisyllabic Words • Read or Listen to *A Day's Work*	• Extend Vocabulary • Read *A Day's Work*

(i) Independent Activities
While you meet with small groups, have the rest of the class...

- Visit the Reading/Library Center
- Listen to the AudioText for *A Day's Work*
- Finish Words to Write, p. 177
- Complete Practice Book 3.1 pp. 65–66, 69
- Write in their Strategy Response Logs, pp. 178, 185
- Visit Cross-Curricular Centers
- Work on inquiry projects

DAY 3

On-Level	Strategic Intervention	Advanced
Teacher-Led *Pages 186–191*	**Teacher-Led** *Page DI · 16*	**Teacher-Led** *Page DI · 17*
• Read *A Day's Work*	• Practice Character and Visualize • Read or Listen to *A Day's Work*	• Extend Character and Visualize • Read *A Day's Work*

(i) Independent Activities
While you meet with small groups, have the rest of the class...

- Visit the Reading/Library Center
- Listen to the AudioText for *A Day's Work*
- Write in their Strategy Response Logs, p. 190
- Finish Look Back and Write, p. 192
- Complete Practice Book 3.1 p. 67
- Visit Cross-Curricular Centers
- Work on inquiry projects

① Begin with whole class skill and strategy instruction.

② Meet with small groups to provide differentiated instruction.

③ Gather the whole class back together for fluency and language arts.

DAY 4

On-Level	Strategic Intervention	Advanced
Teacher-Led *Pages 194–197*	**Teacher-Led** *Page DI · 18*	**Teacher-Led** *Page DI · 19*
Read "What Is a Weed?"	• Practice Retelling • **Read** or Listen to "What Is a Weed?"	• **Read** "What Is a Weed?" • Genre Study

(i) Independent Activities

While you meet with small groups, have the rest of the class...

- Visit the Reading/Library Center
- Listen to the AudioText for "What Is a Weed?"
- Visit the Writing and Vocabulary Centers
- Finish Writing Across Texts, p. 197
- Visit Cross-Curricular Centers
- Work on inquiry projects

DAY 5

On-Level	Strategic Intervention	Advanced
Teacher-Led *Page DI · 21*	**Teacher-Led** *Page DI · 20*	**Teacher-Led** *Page DI · 21*
Reread Leveled Reader *The Boy Who Cried Wolf* Retell *The Boy Who Cried Wolf*	• **Reread** Leveled Reader *Sarah's Choice* • Retell *Sarah's Choice*	• **Reread** Leveled Reader *The Song Makers Go to Salem* • Share Extension Activity

(i) Independent Activities

While you meet with small groups, have the rest of the class...

- Visit the Reading/Library Center
- Complete Practice Book 3.1 pp. 68, 70
- Visit Cross-Curricular Centers
- Work on inquiry projects

Grouping Place English language learners in the groups that correspond to their reading abilities in English.

Use the appropriate Leveled Reader or other text at students' instructional level.

TiP Send home the appropriate Multilingual Summary of the main selection on Day 1.

Take It to the NET™
ONLINE
PearsonSuccessNet.com

Sharon Vaughn
For ideas and activities for English-language learners, see the article "Storybook Reading" by P. Hickman, S. Pollard-Durodola, and Scott Foresman author S. Vaughn.

TEACHER TALK

Fluency is the ability to read words and connected text rapidly, accurately, and smoothly. Fluency may be measured in words correct per minute.

Be sure to schedule time for students to work on the unit inquiry project, "A Book of Solutions." This week students look for information that can help them answer their questions.

Looking Ahead

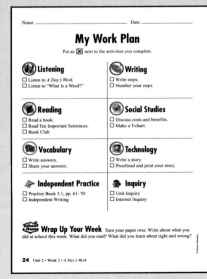

▲ **Group-Time Survival Guide** p. 24, Weekly Contract

☑ Customize Your Plan *by Strand*

ORAL LANGUAGE

SOCIAL STUDIES

Concept Development

When is a solution the wrong solution?

CONCEPT VOCABULARY

certainty   honestly   victims

BUILD

☐ **Question of the Week** Introduce and discuss the question of the week. This week students will read a variety of texts and work on projects related to the concept *right and wrong*. Post the question for students to refer to throughout the week. **DAY 1** *174d*

☐ **Read Aloud** Read aloud "The Honest-to-Goodness Truth." Then begin a web to build concepts and concept vocabulary related to this week's lesson and the unit theme, Smart Solutions. Introduce the concept words *certainty, honestly,* and *victims* and have students place them on the web. Display the web for use throughout the week. **DAY 1** *174l–174m*

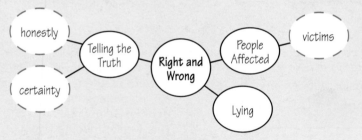

DEVELOP

☐ **Question of the Day** Use the prompts from the Weekly Plan to engage students in conversations related to this week's reading and the unit theme. **EVERY DAY** *174d–174e*

☐ **Concept Vocabulary Web** Revisit the Right and Wrong Concept Web and encourage students to add concept words from their reading and life experiences. **DAY 2** *185*, **DAY 3** *191*

CONNECT

☐ **Looking Back/Moving Forward** Revisit the Right and Wrong Concept Web and discuss how it relates to this week's lesson and the unit theme. Then make connections to next week's lesson. **DAY 5** *197c*

CHECK

☐ **Concept Vocabulary Web** Use the Right and Wrong Concept Web to check students' understanding of the concept vocabulary words *certainty, honestly,* and *victims*. **DAY 1** *174l*, **DAY 5** *197c*

VOCABULARY

STRATEGY CONTEXT CLUES
Context clues are the words and sentences around a word whose meaning you don't know. When you come to a word you don't know, look for clues in the context around the word to help you figure out what the unknown word means.

LESSON VOCABULARY

excitement	shivered
gardener	shocked
motioned	slammed
sadness	

TEACH

☐ **Words to Know** Give students the opportunity to tell what they already know about this week's lesson vocabulary words. Then discuss word meaning. **DAY 1** *176b*

☐ **Vocabulary Strategy Lesson** Use the vocabulary strategy lesson in the Student Edition to introduce and model this week's strategy, *context clues*. **DAY 2** *176-177*

Vocabulary Strategy Lesson

PRACTICE/APPLY

☐ **Leveled Text** Read the lesson vocabulary in the context of leveled text. **DAY 1** *LR10–LR18*

☐ **Words in Context** Read the lesson vocabulary and apply *context clues* in the context of *A Day's Work*. **DAY 2** *178-185*, **DAY 3** *186-192*

Leveled Readers

☐ **Vocabulary Center** Explore the meaning of vocabulary words by answering questions that use them. **ANY DAY** *174j*

Main Selection—Fiction

☐ **Homework** Practice Book 3.1 pp. 64–65. **DAY 1** *176b*, **DAY 2** *177*

☐ **Word Play** Have partners use dictionaries and online reference sources to make lists of words of Spanish and other origins. **ANY DAY** *197c*

ASSESS

☐ **Selection Test** Use the Selection Test to determine students' understanding of the lesson vocabulary words. **DAY 3**

RETEACH/REVIEW

☐ **Reteach Lesson** If necessary, use this lesson to reteach and review *context clues*. **DAY 5** *197c*

COMPREHENSION

👁 **SKILL CHARACTER** Characters are people or animals in a story. To learn what a character is like, look at what he or she says and does.

👁 **STRATEGY VISUALIZE** To understand what a character is like, you can visualize–make a picture in your mind while you are reading. When you read how a character acts, picture it. When you read what a character says, hear it.

TEACH

☐ **Skill/Strategy Lesson** Use the skill/ strategy lesson in the Student Edition to introduce and model *characterization* and *visualization*. **DAY 1** *174-175*

☐ **Extend Skills** Teach paraphrasing. **ANY DAY** *197b*

Skill/Strategy Lesson

PRACTICE/APPLY

☐ **Leveled Text** Apply *characterization* and *visualization* to read leveled text. **DAY 1** *LR10–LR18*

Leveled Readers

☐ **Skills and Strategies in Context** Read *A Day's Work*, using the Guiding Comprehension questions to apply *characterization* and *visualization*. **DAY 2** *178-185*, **DAY 3** *186-192*

Main Selection—Fiction

☐ **Skills and Strategies in Context** Read "What Is a Weed?" guiding students as they apply *characterization* and *visualization*. Then have students discuss and write across texts. **DAY 4** *194-197*

☐ **Homework** Practice Book 3.1 pp. 63, 67, 68. **DAY 1** *175*, **DAY 3** *191*, **DAY 5** *197b*

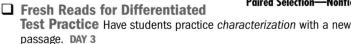

Paired Selection—Nonfiction

☐ **Fresh Reads for Differentiated Test Practice** Have students practice *characterization* with a new passage. **DAY 3**

ASSESS

☐ **Selection Test** Determine students' understanding of the selection and their use of *characterization*. **DAY 3**

☐ **Retell** Have students retell *A Day's Work*. **DAY 3** *192-193*

RETEACH/REVIEW

☐ **Reteach Lesson** If necessary, reteach and review *characterization*. **DAY 5** *197b*

FLUENCY

SKILL CHARACTERIZATION Characterization is the way an author describes or portrays a character. You show characterization by reading as if you are the character, feeling and speaking as the character would.

TEACH

☐ **Read Aloud** Model fluent reading by rereading "The Honest-to-Goodness Truth." Focus on this week's fluency skill, characterization. **DAY 1** *174l-174m, 197a*

PRACTICE/APPLY

☐ **Choral Reading** Read aloud selected paragraphs from *A Day's Work*, modeling voice changes as you read the dialogue of the characters. Then practice as a class, doing three choral readings. **DAY 2** *197a*, **DAY 3** *197a*

☐ **Partner Reading** Have partners practice reading aloud, reading with characterization and offering each other feedback. As students reread, monitor their progress toward their individual fluency goals. **DAY 4** *197a*

☐ **Listening Center** Have students follow along with the AudioText for this week's selections. **ANY DAY** *174j*

☐ **Reading/Library Center** Have students reread a selection of their choice. **ANY DAY** *174j*

☐ **Fluency Coach** Have students use Fluency Coach to listen to fluent readings or practice reading on their own. **ANY DAY**

ASSESS

☐ **Check Fluency** WCPM Do a one-minute timed reading, paying special attention to this week's skill—characterization. Provide feedback for each student. **DAY 5** *197a*

☑ Customize Your Plan *by Strand*

GRAMMAR

SKILL SINGULAR AND PLURAL NOUNS A singular noun names only one person, place, or thing. A plural noun names more than one person, place, or thing.

TEACH

☐ **Grammar Transparency 7** Use Grammar Transparency 7 to teach singular and plural nouns. **DAY 1** *197e*

Grammar Transparency 7

PRACTICE/APPLY

☐ **Develop the Concept** Review the concept of singular and plural nouns and provide guided practice. **DAY 2** *197e*

☐ **Apply to Writing** Have students review something they have written and apply what they have learned about singular and plural nouns. **DAY 3** *197f*

☐ **Test Preparation** Examine common errors in singular and plural nouns to prepare for standardized tests. **DAY 4** *197f*

☐ **Homework** Grammar and Writing Practice Book pp. 25–27. **DAY 2** *197e*, **DAY 3** *197f*, **DAY 4** *197f*

ASSESS

☐ **Cumulative Review** Use Grammar and Writing Practice Book p. 28. **DAY 5** *197f*

RETEACH/REVIEW

☐ **Daily Fix-It** Have students find and correct errors in grammar, spelling, and punctuation. **EVERY DAY** *197e–197f*

☐ **The Grammar and Writing Book** Use pp. 86–89 of The Grammar and Writing Book to extend instruction for singular and plural nouns. **ANY DAY**

The Grammar and Writing Book

WRITING

Trait of the Week

SENTENCES Good writing has a natural flow. Different kinds and lengths of sentences make your writing sound smooth and clear. For example, when you write commands, keep your sentences short and don't use unnecessary words.

TEACH

☐ **Writing Transparency 7A** Use the model to introduce and discuss the Trait of the Week. **DAY 1** *197g*

☐ **Writing Transparency 7B** Use the transparency to show students how eliminating wordiness can improve their writing. **DAY 2** *197g*

Writing Transparency 7A   **Writing Transparency 7B**

PRACTICE/APPLY

☐ **Write Now** Examine the model on Student Edition p. 193. Then have students write their own rules. **DAY 3** *193, 197h*, **DAY 4** *197h*

> **Prompt** *A Day's Work* describes one rule for living and getting along with others. Think about rules for getting along with family members, friends, or neighbors. Now write the rules as commands.

Write Now p. 193

☐ **Writing Center** Write instructions for the back of a seed packet, numbering your instructions. **ANY DAY** *174k*

ASSESS

☐ **Writing Trait Rubric** Use the rubric to evaluate students' writing. **DAY 4** *197h*

RETEACH/REVIEW

☐ **The Grammar and Writing Book** Use pp. 86–91 of The Grammar and Writing Book to extend instruction for singular and plural nouns, eliminating wordiness, and rules. **ANY DAY**

The Grammar and Writing Book

1 Use assessment data to determine your instructional focus.

2 Preview this week's instruction by strand.

3 Choose instructional activities that meet the needs of your classroom.

SPELLING

GENERALIZATION WORDS ENDING IN -LE The final syllable /əl/ is often spelled -le: handle, trouble.

TEACH

☐ **Pretest** Give the pretest for words ending in -le. Guide students in self-correcting their pretests and correcting any misspellings. DAY 1 197k

☐ **Think and Practice** Connect spelling to the phonics generalization for words ending in -le. DAY 2 197k

PRACTICE/APPLY

☐ **Connect to Writing** Have students use spelling words to write a list. Then review frequently misspelled words: little, people. DAY 3 197l

☐ **Homework** Phonics and Spelling Practice Book pp. 25–28. **EVERY DAY**

RETEACH/REVIEW

☐ **Review** Review spelling words to prepare for the posttest. Then provide students with a spelling strategy—spelling schwas. DAY 4 197l

ASSESS

☐ **Posttest** Use dictation sentences to give the posttest for words ending in -le. DAY 5 197l

Spelling Words

1. handle	6. table	11. noodle
2. trouble	7. little*	12. saddle
3. simple	8. gentle	13. juggle
4. people	9. poodle*	14. uncle
5. middle	10. pickle	15. riddle

Challenge Words

16. example	18. obstacle	20. muscle
17. throttle	19. miracle	

*Word from the selection

PHONICS

SKILL SYLLABLE PATTERN C + LE If a word ends in a consonant plus -le, those three letters usually make up the last syllable of the word.

TEACH

☐ **Phonics Lesson** Model how to read words with syllable pattern C + le. Then have students practice by decoding longer words and reading words in context. DAY 2 197i

PRACTICE/APPLY

☐ **Homework** Practice Book 3.1, p. 69. DAY 2 197i

RETEACH/REVIEW

☐ **Review Word Parts** Review how to read words with the syllable patterns V/CV, VC/V. Then have student practice by decoding longer words and reading words in context. DAY 4 197j

RESEARCH AND INQUIRY

☐ **Internet Inquiry** Have students conduct an Internet inquiry on making good choices. **EVERY DAY** 197m

☐ **Procedures and Instructions** Review concepts and features related to procedures and instructions, including numbering, reading through the entire set of instructions, and completing each step before going on to the next step. Have students follow a set of written instructions. DAY 5 197n

☐ **Unit Inquiry** Allow time for students to look for information that can help them answer the questions they formulated last week. **ANY DAY** 149

SPEAKING AND LISTENING

☐ **Directions** Have students give how-to directions for writing an e-mail to a friend, using information from "What Is a Weed?" They can prepare their presentations on a computer. DAY 5 197d

☐ **Listen to Directions** Have students listen as you read aloud directions for a simple gardening project; then answer questions. DAY 5 197d

Resources for Differentiated Instruction

LEVELED READERS

▶ **Comprehension**
- **Skill** Character
- **Strategy** Visualize

▶ **Lesson Vocabulary**
- **Context Clues**

gardener · excitement · sadness · shivered · slammed · shocked · motioned

▶ **Social Studies Standards**
- Making Choices
- Personal Responsibility

Leveled Reader Database

ONLINE
PearsonSuccessNet.com

Use the Online Database of over 600 books to
- Download and print additional copies of this week's leveled readers.
- Listen to the readers being read online.
- Search for more titles focused on this week's skills, topic, and content.

On-Level

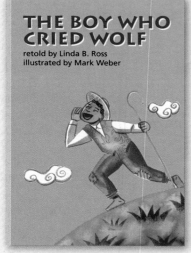

THE BOY WHO CRIED WOLF
retold by Linda B. Ross
illustrated by Mark Weber

On-Level Reader

Character
- A **character** is a person who takes part in the events of a story.
- The qualities of a character are known as **character traits** and usually tell about his or her personality.

Directions Follow the directions below to describe the boy who cried "Wolf!"

1. Name the main character.
   Daniel

2. Write two sentences about Daniel's character traits.
   He is easily bored.
   He is mischievous.

3. Write three sentences about what Daniel wants.
   He wants excitement.
   He wants more responsibility.
   He wants the villagers to notice him.

Directions Write four sentences about what Daniel does and feels during the story.

4. Daniel starts out feeling bored.

5. He acts mischievous and cries "wolf" to get the villagers' attention.

6. He gets scared when a real wolf shows up near his sheep.

7. He promises never to lie again.

On-Level Practice TE p. LR14

Vocabulary
Directions Below each vocabulary word is a list of four words. Find two other words that have almost the same meaning as the vocabulary word. Circle them.

Check the Words You Know
__excitement __gardener __motioned __sadness __shivered __shocked __slammed

1. sadness
   (unhappiness) (sorrow) delight joy
2. slammed
   (smashed) petted (smacked) touched
3. shivered
   sat (trembled) (shook) stood
4. excitement
   boredom (action) dullness (adventure)
5. gardener
   (grower) fisherman shepherd (farmer)
6. motioned
   fell (pointed) stared (signaled)
7. shocked
   (surprised) (jolted) certain confident

Directions What do you think happened after the story ended? Write a paragraph about how Daniel and the farmer worked together. Use as many vocabulary words as you can.

Responses will vary.

On-Level Practice TE p. LR15

Strategic Intervention

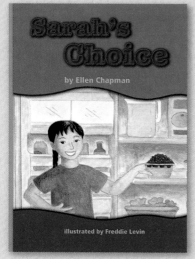

Sarah's Choice
by Ellen Chapman

illustrated by Freddie Levin

Below-Level Reader

Character
- A **character** is a person who takes part in the events of a story.
- The qualities of a character are known as **character traits** and usually tell about his or her personality.

Directions How are Sarah and Julia alike? How are they different? Use the Venn Diagram below to compare the two characters.

Possible responses given.

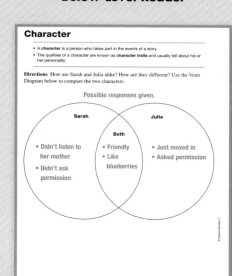

Sarah
- Didn't listen to her mother
- Didn't ask permission

Both
- Friendly
- Like blueberries

Julia
- Just moved in
- Asked permission

Below-Level Practice TE p. LR11

Vocabulary
Directions Draw a line to match each vocabulary word with its definition.

Check the Words You Know
__excitement __gardener __motioned __sadness __shivered __shocked __slammed

1. shivered — a. thrill
2. slammed — b. signaled
3. excitement — c. a person who works outdoors with plants
4. motioned — d. trembled
5. shocked — e. a feeling of unhappiness
6. gardener — f. to be surprised
7. sadness — g. closed with a bang

Directions Write the vocabulary word that completes each sentence.

8. I was _shocked_ when I heard he was joining the circus.

9. The fact that we might never see each other again filled me with _sadness_.

10. She _shivered_ as she stepped out into the cold.

11. He stomped angrily out of the room and _slammed_ the door behind him.

12. I wondered why the _gardener_ planted the bushes so close to the house.

13. When our team won the big game, everyone at school shared the _excitement_.

14. When the new girl walked into the lunchroom, I _motioned_ for her to come over to our table.

Below-Level Practice TE p. LR12

Advanced

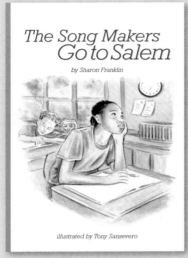

The Song Makers Go to Salem
by Sharon Franklin

illustrated by Tony Sansevero

Advanced Reader

Character

- A *character* is a person who takes part in the events of a story.
- The qualities of a character are known as **character traits** and usually relate to his or her personality.

Directions Fill in the graphic organizers below using details from your reading.
Possible responses given.

| Trait | Tabitha | Trait |
| honest | | thoughtful |

| Clue | Clue |
| told Abbey that she saw her take money | gently convinced Abbey to admit her theft |

| Trait | Abbey | Trait |
| trusting | | strong |

| Clue | Clue |
| believed that Tabitha gave her good advice | stood up and admitted she stole money |

Advanced Practice TE p. LR17

Vocabulary

Directions Choose the word from the box that best completes each sentence. Write the word on the line.

Check the Words You Know
__anxious __concentrate __erupted __frantically
__relieved __solution __suspect

1. Tabitha fought hard to find a **solution** to the problem.
2. Zoe **frantically** waved her hands at Tabitha.
3. People often **concentrate** too much on what others will think.
4. Tabitha didn't just **suspect** that Abbey had taken money— she knew it.
5. Tabitha was **anxious** because she wasn't sure how Abbey would react.
6. Abbey felt **relieved** after she admitted she had taken the money.
7. The crowd **erupted** with applause as Abbey arrived with her delicious cookies.

Directions What do you think happened after the story ended? Write a paragraph about the Song Makers' trip to Salem. Use as many vocabulary words as you can.

Paragraphs will vary.

Advanced Practice TE p. LR18

Mamá's Birthday Garden
by Isabella Stefan
Illustrated by Priscilla Burris

ELL Reader

ELL Poster 7

Teacher's Edition Notes

ELL notes throughout this lesson support instruction and reference additional resources at point of use.

Teaching Guide
pp. 43–49, 224–225

- Multilingual summaries of the main selection
- Comprehension lesson
- Vocabulary strategies and word cards
- ELL Reader 3.2.2 lesson

ELL and Transition Handbook

Ten Important Sentences

- Key ideas from every selection in the Student Edition
- Activities to build sentence power

More Reading

Readers' Theater Anthology
- Fluency practice
- Five scripts to build fluency
- Poetry for oral interpretation

Leveled Trade Books

- Extended reading tied to the unit concept
- Lessons in the Trade Book Library Teaching Guide

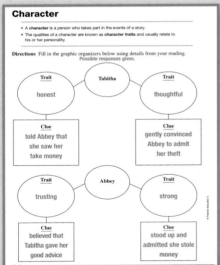

School + Home

Homework
- Family Times Newsletter
- ELL Multilingual Selection Summaries

Take-Home Books
- Leveled Readers

Family Times

Cross-Curricular Centers

Listening

Listen to the Selections

MATERIALS `SINGLES`
CD player, headphones, AudioText CD, Student Edition

Listen to *A Day's Work* and "What Is a Weed?" as you follow or read along in your book. Listen to what the characters in *A Day's Work* say and do.

If there is anything you don't understand, you can listen again to any section.

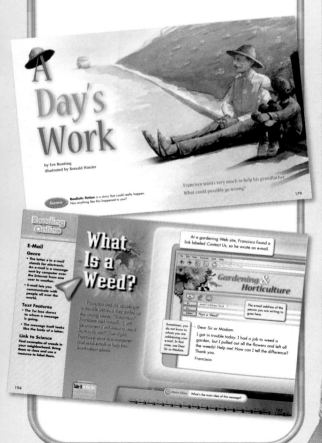

Reading/Library

Read It *Again!*

MATERIALS
Collection of books for self-selected reading, reading log
`SINGLES` `PAIRS` `GROUPS`

Select a book you have already read. Record the title of the book in your reading log. You may want to read with a partner.

You may choose to read any of the following:

- **Leveled Readers**
- **ELL Readers**
- **Stories written by classmates**
- **Books from the library**
- *A Day's Work*

TEN IMPORTANT SENTENCES Read the Ten Important Sentences for *A Day's Work*. Then locate the sentences in the Student Edition.

BOOK CLUB Look at "Meet Authors" on p. 408 of the Student Edition. Write a letter to Eve Bunting, telling her which of her books you have read and which ones you liked best.

Vocabulary

Explore MEANING

MATERIALS `PAIRS`
Pencil, paper, dictionary

Explore the meaning of vocabulary words by answering questions that use them.

1. **Read the questions below.**
2. **Write an answer. Use the underlined word in your answer.**
3. **Use a dictionary for help with meanings.**
4. **Share your answers with a partner.**

- **What <u>emotion</u> might your friend be feeling if she just slammed the door?**
- **If you <u>trembled</u> outside, what would the weather be like?**
- **Who <u>employed</u> a gardener?**
- **When have you <u>experienced</u> sadness?**
- **Would you be <u>startled</u> if you heard a sudden loud noise?**

EARLY FINISHERS Write sentences for each underlined word.

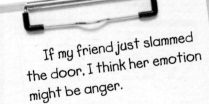

If my friend just slammed the door, I think her emotion might be anger.

Scott Foresman Reading Street Centers Survival Kit

Use the *A Day's Work* materials from the Reading Street
Centers Survival Kit to organize this week's centers.

Writing

How to Garden

MATERIALS `SINGLES`
Gardening books, pens or
pencils, paper, art materials

Write instructions for the back of a
seed packet.

1. Read about how to grow a flower or
   other kind of plant.
2. Write steps telling how to use seeds
   to grow the plant. Be sure to include
   directions for watering and feeding
   the plant after it has sprouted.
3. Number your steps.

EARLY FINISHERS Make a seed
packet out of paper. Draw a picture
of the plant on the front and list
your directions on the back.

Sunflower

1. Plant these seeds in the
   spring in a place with a lot
   of sun.
2. Plant the seeds about 12
   inches apart. They should be
   2 inches below the ground.
3. Remember to water the soil.
4. You can tie really tall
   sunflowers to stakes to
   keep them from falling over.

Social Studies

Study Costs and Benefits

MATERIALS `PAIRS`
Writing materials

What were the costs and benefits
of Francisco's actions?

1. Together, list two other ways
   Francisco might have acted to get
   his grandfather the job.
2. Discuss the costs and benefits of the
   boy's choice in the story.
3. Make a T-chart listing the costs and
   benefits of Francisco's choice.

EARLY FINISHERS Rewrite the
story using one of the ideas you
discussed.

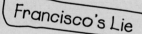

Francisco's Lie

Costs	Benefits
• They pulled the wrong plants.	• Grandfather got the job.
• They had to do the work twice.	• Grandfather got paid.

Technology

Word Processing

MATERIALS `SINGLES`
Computer, printer, printer paper

Compose a story on the computer
and print it out.

1. What happened to Francisco and his
   grandfather the next day? Type a list
   of a few things they did.
2. Type some of these ideas into a
   short description of their Sunday.
3. Proofread and print out your story.

EARLY FINISHERS Draw pictures in
the margins that illustrate scenes
or actions in your story.

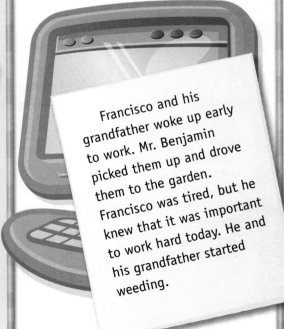

Francisco and his
grandfather woke up early
to work. Mr. Benjamin
picked them up and drove
them to the garden.
Francisco was tired, but he
knew that it was important
to work hard today. He and
his grandfather started
weeding.

ALL CENTERS

OBJECTIVES

- Build vocabulary by finding words related to the lesson concept.
- Listen and visualize.

Concept Vocabulary

certainty freedom from doubt
honestly in a truthful way
victims those badly treated or taken advantage of

Monitor Progress

Check Vocabulary

If... students are unable to place words on the web,	**then...** review the lesson concept. Place the words on the web and provide additional words for practice, such as *harmful* and *honest-to-goodness*.

SUCCESS PREDICTOR

DAY 1 — Grouping Options

Reading
Whole Group
Introduce and discuss the Question of the Week. Then use pp. 174l–176b.

Group Time
Differentiated Instruction
Read this week's Leveled Readers. See pp. 174f–174g for the small group lesson plan.

Whole Group
Use p. 197a.

Language Arts
Use pp.197e–197h and 197k–197m.

Build Concepts

FLUENCY

MODEL CHARACTERIZATION As you read "The Honest-to-Goodness Truth," change your voice for each character. For example, when you read Libby's dialogue, use a young girl's voice, excited and a little hurried (but not so hurried that students can't follow what you are reading).

LISTENING COMPREHENSION

After reading "The Honest-to-Goodness Truth," use the following questions to assess listening comprehension.

1. **What do you think Libby's face must have looked like when her mother caught her in her lie?** (*Possible response: Her mouth was trembling, her face was red, her eyes were full of tears; she looked miserable.*) **Visualize**

2. **Libby decided to tell the truth about everything. What was one effect of her decision?** (*Possible response: She made all her friends mad at her.*) **Cause and Effect**

BUILD CONCEPT VOCABULARY

Start a web to build concepts and vocabulary related to this week's lesson and the unit theme.

- Draw a Right and Wrong Concept Web.

- Read the sentence with the word *certainty* again. Ask students to pronounce *certainty* and discuss its meaning.

- Place *certainty* in an oval attached to Telling the Truth. Explain that *certainty* is related to this concept. Read the sentences in which *honestly* and *victims* appear. Have students pronounce the words, place them on the web, and provide reasons.

- Brainstorm additional words and categories for the web. Keep the web on display and add words throughout the week.

Concept Vocabulary Web

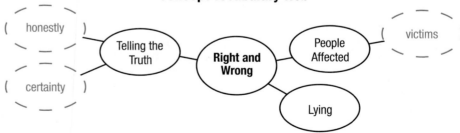

The Honest-to-Goodness Truth

By Patricia C. McKissack

Libby hurried out the door and down the porch steps. "Did you feed and water Ol' Boss?" Mama called from her sewing room window.

Libby stopped at the gate. "Yes, Mama," she answered. She was surprised at how easy the lie slid out of her mouth, like it was greased with warm butter.

Mama stopped sewing Virginia Washington's wedding dress and came outside. Libby dropped her head and wouldn't look in her mother's eyes. "Are you sure?" Mama asked real stern-like.

Libby's stomach felt like she'd swallowed a handful of chicken feathers. Her eyes commenced to fill with water and her bottom lip quivered. Then, taking a deep breath and gulping hard, she owned up to her lie. "I was gon' do it soon as I got back from jumping rope with Ruthie Mae."

Libby felt a lot better, even though Mama punished her double. For not tending to Ol' Boss, Libby couldn't go play with Ruthie Mae. And for lying, she had to stay on the porch the rest of the day. It was the first time Libby had lied to Mama, and as far as she was concerned it was gon' be the last.

"From now on, only the truth," she decided.

The next morning, Libby joined a group of friends on the way to school.

"Did you do your geography homework?" Willie asked Libby.

"It was easy," she answered.

"Not for me." Willie shook his head. "I didn't understand it, so I didn't do it."

First thing in class, Libby started waving her hand. "Me, Miz Jackson, me, me, me, Miz Jackson!" When the teacher called on her, Libby announced, "Willie don't got his geography homework."

"Doesn't have his homework," corrected Miz Jackson.

"No, ma'am, he don't." Libby was pleased with herself.

Willie gave her an ugly look. "Why'd you tell on me?" he whispered as he headed to Miz Jackson's desk to explain.

With certainty she whispered back, "All I did was tell it like it is. So there!" And she folded her hands neatly in her lap.

Before lunchtime, Libby had told a lot of truths. By the time school was out, hardly anyone would talk to her.

"Why are y'all mad at me?" Libby asked as her classmates started home without her.

Before Libby knew it, she was in front of Miz Tusselbury's vine-covered cottage. The woman was in her rocking chair, gliding back and forward and fanning herself with a hand-folded fan. "How-do, Libby Louise," she called in her sing-song voice. "What's that sad look you wearing on such a pretty day?"

continued on TR1

Set Purpose

Have students visualize characters and events in the story as you read. After you read, discuss briefly what they "saw."

Creative Response

Have students work with partners to improvise the conversations they think Libby may have had with her friends when she apologized for being so truthful the day before. ***Drama***

ELL

Activate Prior Knowledge Before students listen to the Read Aloud, have them share their ideas about truths and lies, particularly what is the truth and what is a lie, and what happens when we lie.

Access Content Before reading, share this summary: Libby is a young girl who gets caught in a lie and decides to only tell the truth from then on, but her decision has some effects she didn't expect.

Homework Send home this week's Family Times newsletter.

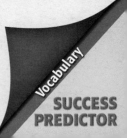

SUCCESS PREDICTOR

SKILLS ⟷ STRATEGIES IN CONTEXT

Character
Visualize

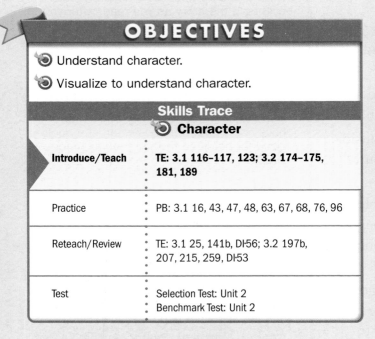

OBJECTIVES

- Understand character.
- Visualize to understand character.

Skills Trace
Character

Introduce/Teach	TE: 3.1 116–117, 123; 3.2 174–175, 181, 189
Practice	PB: 3.1 16, 43, 47, 48, 63, 67, 68, 76, 96
Reteach/Review	TE: 3.1 25, 141b, DI·56; 3.2 197b, 207, 215, 259, DI·53
Test	Selection Test: Unit 2 Benchmark Test: Unit 2

INTRODUCE

Write the topic "Our Favorite Stories" on the board. Ask students to share the titles of their favorite stories. As you add a title to the board, ask who the people in the story are and write their names under the story title. Explain that the people in a story are called characters. As students describe the characters, write down two or three words about each one.

Have students read the information on p. 174. Explain the following:

- What a character says and does helps us understand what the character is like. It also helps us understand the story better and predict what will happen later in the story.

- We can use what a character says and does to visualize, or imagine, what that character looks like. Visualizing helps us understand the character and the story better too.

Use Skill Transparency 7 to teach character and visualize.

A Day's Work

Comprehension

Skill
Character

Strategy
Visualize

Character

- Characters are the people or animals in a story.
- Look at what a character says and does to learn what he or she is like.

| What Character Says | What Character Does |

→ **What Character Is Like**

Strategy: Visualize

Active readers make pictures in their minds of what they are reading. When you read how a character acts, picture it. When you read what a character says, hear it. Visualizing will help you understand what the character is like.

Write to Read

1. Read "The Grasshopper and the Ant." Make a graphic organizer like the one above. Complete it to tell what Grasshopper is like.

2. Use the information in your graphic organizer to write a description of Grasshopper.

174

Strategic Intervention

Character A simple graphic organizer may help students organize details in order to understand a character. Draw a web (Graphic Organizer 14 or 15) on the board. Then write "Grasshopper" in the center. Tell students that sometimes authors tell us directly what a character is like; other times, we have to look for clues in the story that tell what a character is like. Elicit details from "The Grasshopper and the Ant" that apply to the grasshopper. Remind students to think about what the character says and does in the story and add their details to the web. Then have students work together in pairs to write two or three sentences that tell what the grasshopper is like. Repeat for the ant.

ELL

Access Content

Beginning/Intermediate For a Picture It! lesson on character, see the ELL Teaching Guide, p. 44.

Advanced Before students read "The Grasshopper and the Ant," have them share what they know about both insects and fables.

The Grasshopper AND THE Ant

a retelling of an Aesop fable

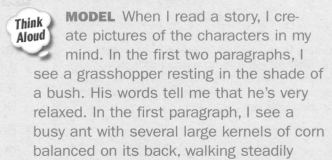

On a warm summer day, Grasshopper sat in the shade and chirped. Ant walked up carrying some corn.

"Ant," said Grasshopper. "What are you doing working in the hot summer sun? Come relax in the shade with me."

"I can't," said Ant. "There is work to be done! I am storing food for the winter, and I suggest you do the same."

"Winter?" said Grasshopper. "That's a long time away. I can't be bothered about winter in the middle of summer! Are you sure you won't sit in this lovely shade with me?"

Ant just picked up the corn and went back to work.

Winter came, and the ground was cold and bare. Grasshopper had no food and lay under a bush. *I'm dying of hunger!* he thought. Nearby, the ants were eating the corn they had stored last summer. When they saw Grasshopper, they dragged some food over to him.

Grasshopper learned an important lesson. Next summer would be different.

1 Strategy Here is a good place to visualize. Picture how Grasshopper looks sitting in the shade. Hear how he talks to Ant.

2 Skill In this paragraph, notice the words that Grasshopper is using. They tell that Grasshopper is not a hard worker.

175

Available as **Skill Transparency** 7

TEACH

1 STRATEGY Use paragraphs 1 and 2 to model how to visualize characters.

Think Aloud **MODEL** When I read a story, I create pictures of the characters in my mind. In the first two paragraphs, I see a grasshopper resting in the shade of a bush. His words tell me that he's very relaxed. In the first paragraph, I see a busy ant with several large kernels of corn balanced on its back, walking steadily toward its nest.

2 SKILL Use paragraphs 1 through 4 to model how to use clues to understand character.

Think Aloud **MODEL** The author doesn't tell directly what Ant and Grasshopper are like, but I can use their words and actions to understand them. Grasshopper relaxes in the shade and tells Ant to rest with him, but Ant is very busy moving corn. I think Grasshopper is lazy, and Ant is hard working.

PRACTICE AND ASSESS

STRATEGY Students should use Grasshopper's words to hear his voice, which might sound slow and lazy.

SKILL Students should recognize how Grasshopper's words reveal that he is a lazy character and not concerned about the future.

WRITE Have students complete the Write to Read activity. You might consider using this as a whole class activity.

Monitor Progress
🔄 **Character**

If... students are unable to complete **Write to Read** on p. 174,	then... use Practice Book 3.1, p. 63, to provide additional practice.

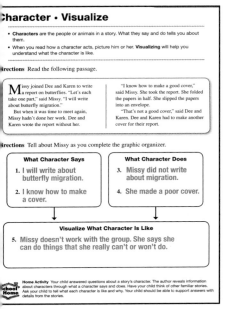

Character • Visualize

- **Characters** are the people or animals in a story. What they say and do tells you about them.
- When you read how a character acts, picture him or her. **Visualizing** will help you understand what the character is like.

Directions Read the following passage.

Missy joined Dee and Karen to write a report on butterflies. "Let's each take one part," said Missy. "I will write about butterfly migration."

But when it was time to meet again, Missy hadn't done her work. Dee and Karen wrote the report without her.

"I know how to make a good cover," said Missy. She took the report. She folded the papers in half. She slipped the papers into an envelope.

"That's not a good cover," said Dee and Karen. Dee and Karen had to make another cover for their report.

Directions Tell about Missy as you complete the graphic organizer.

What Character Says	What Character Does
1. I will write about butterfly migration.	3. Missy did not write about migration.
2. I know how to make a cover.	4. She made a poor cover.

Visualize What Character Is Like

5. Missy doesn't work with the group. She says she can do things that she really can't or won't do.

Home Activity Your child answered questions about a story's character. The author reveals information about characters through what a character says and does. Have your child think of other familiar stories. Ask your child to tell what each character is like and why. Your child should be able to support answers with details from the stories.

Practice Book 3.1 p. 63

Tech Files
ONLINE

Students can find out more about migrant workers in the United States by searching the Internet. Have them use a student-friendly search engine and the keywords *migrant workers, immigrants to America,* and *day laborers.*

Build Background Use ELL Poster 7 to build background and vocabulary for the lesson concept of when a solution turns out to be the wrong solution.

▲ **ELL Poster** 7

Build Background

ACTIVATE PRIOR KNOWLEDGE

BEGIN A T-CHART about gardening (Graphic Organizer 25).

• Write the title "Gardening" above the chart. Label the left column "Things a Gardener Should Do." Label the right column "Things a Gardener Should NOT Do."

• Brainstorm with the class about gardening dos and don'ts. Write their ideas in the appropriate columns of the chart.

• Tell students that, as they read, they should look for details and note new information to add to the chart.

Gardening

Things a Gardener Should Do	Things a Gardener Should NOT Do
water plants	walk on plants
pull weeds	kill earthworms

▲ **Graphic Organizer** 25

BACKGROUND BUILDING AUDIO A discussion about what a landscaper does is featured in this week's audio. After students listen, discuss which aspects of the work they would enjoy and which aspects they would not.

Background Building Audio

Introduce Vocabulary

WORD RATING CHART

Create word rating charts using the categories *Know, Have Seen,* and *Don't Know.*

Word Rating Chart

Word	Know	Have Seen	Don't Know
excitement			✔
gardener		✔	
motioned			
sadness			
shivered			
shocked			
slammed			

▲ **Graphic Organizer** 4

Read each word to students and have them place a check in one of the three columns: *Know* (know and can use); *Have Seen* (have heard or seen the word; don't know meaning); *Don't Know* (don't know the word).

Activate Prior Knowledge

Have students share where they may have seen some of these words. Point out that three of this week's words have a suffix *(excitement, gardener, sadness).* Discuss with students how the suffix changes the meaning of the base word.

Suffixes

Check graphic organizers with students at the end of the week and have them make changes to their ratings.

Use the Multisyllabic Word Routine on p. DI·1 to help students read multisyllabic words.

Lesson Vocabulary

WORDS TO KNOW

T excitement a condition of having strong, lively feelings about something that you like

T gardener someone employed to take care of a garden or lawn

T motioned made a movement, as of the hand or head, to get someone to do something

T sadness unhappiness; sorrow

T shivered shook with cold, fear, or excitement

T shocked caused to feel surprise, horror, or disgust

T slammed threw or hit something with great force

MORE WORDS TO KNOW

coarse rough

convinced made someone believe something

T = Tested Word

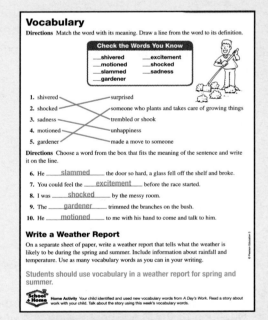

Vocabulary

Directions Match the word with its meaning. Draw a line from the word to its definition.

Check the Words You Know

___shivered ___excitement
___motioned ___shocked
___slammed ___sadness
___gardener

1. shivered — surprised
2. shocked — someone who plants and takes care of growing things
3. sadness — trembled or shook
4. motioned — unhappiness
5. gardener — made a move to someone

Directions Choose a word from the box that fits the meaning of the sentence and write it on the line.

6. He ___slammed___ the door so hard, a glass fell off the shelf and broke.
7. You could feel the ___excitement___ before the race started.
8. I was ___shocked___ by the messy room.
9. The ___gardener___ trimmed the branches on the bush.
10. He ___motioned___ to me with his hand to come and talk to him.

Write a Weather Report

On a separate sheet of paper, write a weather report that tells what the weather is likely to be during the spring and summer. Include information about rainfall and temperature. Use as many vocabulary words as you can in your writing.

Students should use vocabulary in a weather report for spring and summer.

Home Activity Your child identified and used new vocabulary words from *A Day's Work.* Read a story about work with your child. Talk about the story using this week's vocabulary words.

▲ **Practice Book 3.1** p. 64

Vocabulary Strategy

 Use context clues to determine the meaning of unfamiliar words.

INTRODUCE

Discuss the context clues strategy using the steps on p. 176.

TEACH

- Have students read "A Gardening Adventure," paying attention to how vocabulary is used.
- Model using context clues to determine the meaning of *shivered*.

Think Aloud

MODEL The word *shivered* is used on p. 177 to describe what Cecilia did as she dug holes. She mentions that it was cold outside, so that may be the cause. I know that you shake when you are cold, so *shivered* means "shook with cold."

Words to Know

shivered

excitement

motioned

shocked

slammed

sadness

gardener

Remember

Try the strategy. Then, if you need more help, use your glossary or a dictionary.

Vocabulary Strategy
for Unfamiliar Words

Context Clues What do you do when you come across a word you don't know? Sometimes you can figure out what the word means by looking for context clues. Context clues are the words and sentences around the word. They can help you figure out the meaning of the word.

1. Read the words and sentences around the word you don't know. Sometimes the author tells you what the word means.

2. If not, use the words and sentences to predict a meaning for the word.

3. Try that meaning in the sentence. Does it make sense?

As you read "A Gardening Adventure," use context clues to help you understand the meanings of the vocabulary words.

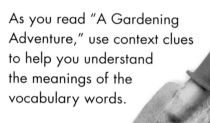

176

DAY 2 **Grouping Options**

Reading
Whole Group Introduce and discuss the Question of the Day. Then use pp. 176–179.

Group Time Differentiated Instruction
Read *A Day's Work.* See pp. 174f–174g for the small group lesson plan.

Whole Group Use pp. 197a and 197i.

Language Arts
Use pp.197e–197h and 197k–197m.

Strategic Intervention

Context Clues Have students work in pairs to follow the steps on p. 176. Encourage them to list clues for an unknown word and then decide together the best meaning for it.

ELL

Access Content Use ELL Poster 7 to preteach vocabulary. Choose from the following to meet language proficiency levels.
Beginning Point out clues on p. 177 that show that *slammed* refers to throwing something with great force.
Intermediate After reading, students can create a two-column list of verbs that describe things people do with their bodies, such as *shiver, motion,* and so on.
Advanced Teach the lesson on pp. 176–177. Students can report on the names of some plants and flowers in their home languages.
Resources for home-language words may include parents, bilingual staff members, bilingual dictionaries, or online translation sources.

A Gardening Adventure

Dear Anna,

This year I decided to plant a flower garden in the backyard. I was in a hurry to get started, so I planted the seeds in late March. It was still cold out, and I shivered as I dug the holes. However, I figured spring would be here soon. A week later, tiny green shoots were poking up out of the ground. Each morning, I rushed outside with great excitement to see how much they had grown.

Then yesterday morning when I came into the kitchen, my mother motioned to me to come to the window.

I was shocked to see that everything outside was coated with ice—including my plants! They looked as if someone had slammed a heavy weight down on them. I felt such sadness.

Later, the sun came out, and the ice began to melt. When I looked at my plants again, they were standing up straight and green. I can't wait for them to flower, but I've learned my lesson. Next year, this gardener will wait until late April to start her garden!

Love,
Cecilia

Words to Write

Look at this picture. Write about what has happened to the flower. Use words from the Words to Know list.

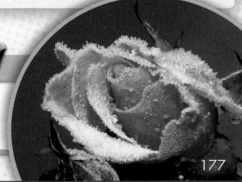

177

PRACTICE AND ASSESS

- Have students determine the meanings of the remaining words and explain the context clues they used.
- Point out that context does not work with every word. Students may have to use the glossary or a dictionary to find the exact meaning of some words.
- Have students revise their word rating charts (p. 176b), reassessing their ratings.
- Have students complete Practice Book 3.1, p. 65.

WRITE Writing should include vocabulary words that describe what happened to the flower. Students should use as many vocabulary words as possible in their descriptive writing.

Monitor Progress

Context Clues

If... students need more practice with the lesson vocabulary,	**then...** use Tested Vocabulary Cards.

Vocabulary • Context Clues

- Sometimes you can figure out the meaning of a word by looking at the words and sentences around it.
- **Context clues** are the words around an unfamiliar word that help you figure out its meaning.

Directions Read the following passage about a garden. Then answer the questions below. Look for context clues as you read.

We used to live in the city. Then we had to move to the country. I was filled with sadness to leave my friends. But I was not unhappy for long. My excitement grew as we drove because I was thrilled to see new things.

It was night when we got to our new house. I got out of the car. It was so cold outside, I shivered. Inside the house, I stopped shaking but was shocked by how dark it was.

"Don't look so surprised," Mom said. "It will look better in the morning."

The next morning, I got up early and went downstairs. Dad was standing by the back door. He raised his arm and motioned for me to follow him outside. There was a beautiful, big garden! It had trees and lots of flowers.

"Can I take care of the garden?" I asked.

"Yes," Dad said, "you can be the family gardener."

I smiled and knew that I would love living in the country.

1. What does *sadness* mean in this passage? What clues help you find out?
   unhappy; Clues: not unhappy for long
2. What does *excitement* mean in this passage? What clues help you find out?
   thrilled; Clues: I was thrilled
3. What does *shivered* mean in this passage? What clues help you find out?
   shook; Clues: I stopped shaking
4. What does *shocked* mean in this passage? What clues help you find out?
   surprised; Clues: "Don't look so surprised."
5. What does *motioned* mean in this passage? What clues help you find out?
   gestured; Clues: raised his arm and motioned to me to follow him
6. What does *gardener* mean in this passage? What clues help you find out?
   someone who gardens; Clues: "Can I take care of the garden?"

School + Home **Home Activity** Your child identified and used context clues to understand new words in a passage. Work with your child to identify unfamiliar words in an article and to find context clues to help with understanding new words. Confirm the meanings with your child.

▲ **Practice Book 3.1** p. 65

Prereading Strategies

OBJECTIVES

◎ Identify and understand character and characterization.

◎ Visualize to understand character and characterization.

GENRE STUDY

Realistic Fiction

A Day's Work is realistic fiction. Explain that in realistic fiction, the characters are like real people, and the events and actions in the story could happen.

PREVIEW AND PREDICT

Have students preview the selection title and illustrations, and discuss the topics or ideas they think this selection will cover. Encourage students to use lesson vocabulary as they talk about what they expect to learn.

Strategy Response Log

Generate Questions Have students write their questions in their strategy response logs. Students will answer their questions in the Strategy Response Log activity on p. 185.

A Day's Work

by Eve Bunting
illustrated by Ronald Himler

Genre **Realistic fiction** is a story that could really happen. Has anything like this happened to you?

178

 ELL

Activate Prior Knowledge Have students talk together about their experiences, or their families' experiences, as immigrants to the United States. They can use this discussion to think about what will happen to the characters in the story.

Consider having students read the selection summary in English or in students' home languages. See the Multilingual Summaries in the ELL Teaching Guide, pp. 47–49.

Francisco wants very much to help his grandfather.

What could possibly go wrong?

179

SET PURPOSE

Read the first page of the selection aloud to students. Have them consider their preview discussion and read on to find out what happens to Francisco and his grandfather.

Remind students to read to understand characters and to visualize as they read.

STRATEGY RECALL

Students have now used these before-reading strategies:

- preview the selection to be aware of its genre, features, and possible content;
- activate prior knowledge about that content and what to expect of that genre;
- make predictions;
- set a purpose for reading.

Remind students that, as they read, they should monitor their own comprehension. If they realize something does not make sense, they can regain their comprehension by using fix-up strategies they have learned, such as:

- use phonics and word structure to decode new words;
- use context clues or a dictionary to figure out meanings of new words;
- adjust their reading rate—slow down for difficult text, speed up for easy or familiar text, or skim and scan just for specific information;
- reread parts of the text;
- read on (continue to read for clarification);
- use text features such as headings, subheadings, charts, illustrations, and so on as visual aids to comprehension;
- make a graphic organizer or a semantic organizer to aid comprehension;
- use reference sources, such as an encyclopedia, dictionary, thesaurus, or synonym finder;
- use another person, such as a teacher, a peer, a librarian, or an outside expert, as a resource.

After reading, students will use these strategies:

- summarize or retell the text;
- answer questions they or others pose;
- reflect to make new information become part of their prior knowledge.

 **AudioText**

Guiding Comprehension

1 Dialogue • Inferential

Look at the dialogue on p. 181. What do Francisco's words tell you about his character?

Possible responses: Francisco's words show that he is helpful (he tries to explain California's weather) and determined (he will help his grandfather find a job).

2 Main Idea and Details • Inferential

Reread pp. 180–181. Find the main idea and one supporting detail.

Main idea: Francisco and his grandfather are looking for work. Supporting detail: No one will hire you with a kid.

3 ↻ Character • Inferential

What kind of person is Francisco? Why do you think so?

Possible responses: Francisco is helpful, hopeful, loving, determined, and generous because he wants to help his grandfather find a job and get warmer clothes.

Monitor Progress
↻ Character

If... students are unable to identify what Francisco is like,	then... use the skill and strategy instruction on p. 181.

Francisco stood in the parking lot with his grandfather and the other men. It was the first time he'd been there.

A truck cruised along, slowed.

The driver held up three fingers. "Bricklaying. I need three men," he called.

Five men jumped in the back.

"Only three," the driver said, and two had to get out.

The workers left in the parking lot grumbled and shuffled around.

Francisco's grandfather shivered. *"Hace frío,"* he said.

180

ⒺⓁⓁ

Extend Language Explain that some words tell how people act, such as *shivered, grumbled,* and *shuffled* on p. 180. Act out the meaning of these words for students. Have students keep a log of words that show actions. Discuss how the words also show how people feel.

"It is cold because it is still early. It will be hot later, you will see," Francisco said in Spanish.

"Why did you bring a kid?" one of the men asked. "No one will hire you with a kid. He belongs in school."

"It's Saturday," Francisco said. "My *abuelo,* my grandfather, does not speak English yet. He came to California only two days ago to live with my mother and me."

Francisco swallowed. "We have been alone—since my father died. I am going to help my *abuelo* get work."

He took his grandfather's cold, rough hand and smiled up at him. Abuelo was tall and skinny as an old tree. Already Francisco loved him. When there was money to spare they'd get him a jacket like Francisco's with sleeves long enough to cover his hands. And an L.A. Lakers cap like Francisco's too. **②** **③**

A van was coming. BENJAMIN'S GARDENING was printed on the side.

181

SKILLS ↔ STRATEGIES IN CONTEXT

Character

TEACH

- Explain that a character is a person or animal in a story. Tell students that characters in a story have personalities, or character traits, just like real people do.

- Authors don't always tell us everything about the characters; sometimes we have to look at the details in the story to understand what characters are like.

- Model using story details to figure out what kind of person Francisco is in *A Day's Work*.

Think Aloud **MODEL** When Francisco explains that it is cold in the morning in California, I can see that he is helpful. I also think he is trying to take care of his grandfather, so he is a caring person. Then Francisco speaks for his grandfather and explains their situation to the other men, so I see that he is protective too.

PRACTICE AND ASSESS

Have students identify details on pp. 180–181 that show some of Francisco's other qualities. To assess, check that the details support their thinking about Francisco.

EXTEND SKILLS

Dialogue

Explain that in writing, conversations are represented as dialogue. In short stories and novels, dialogue is set off by quotation marks. We can learn a lot about characters from their words. Dialogue also makes a story seem more real. This is one reason the author of *A Day's Work* may have used Spanish words in the characters' dialogue. Have students note examples of the characters' dialogue that tells them something about those characters; discuss what they learn about the characters through dialogue.

Time for SOCIAL STUDIES

Choices

The choices we make are important. Sometimes we have to choose between something as simple as what color shirt or socks to wear in the morning; other times the choices we have to make are harder. It's important to think about our choices so we make the right decisions. We have to think about who we choose for friends, what we do with our friends, what we want to do and who we want to be when we grow up. Every choice has consequences, or effects. When we are thinking about what to do or what not to do, we have to think about what will happen as a result of our decisions. Who will be affected? How will we be affected? When we can do this, we make responsible choices.

Guiding Comprehension

4 REVIEW **Realism and Fantasy • Inferential**
In what ways is *A Day's Work* a realistic story so far?

Possible response: The people in the story do and say things like people I know.

Monitor Progress

REVIEW **Realism and Fantasy**

| If... students have difficulty telling how the story is realistic, | then... use the skill and strategy instruction on p. 183. |

5 **Draw Conclusions • Inferential**
How do you think Francisco feels as he jumps into the van after getting the job for his grandfather and himself?

Possible responses: Proud of himself, sure of himself.

6 **Compare and Contrast • Critical**
Text to Text **In what ways is *A Day's Work* like other realistic stories you have read?**

Responses will vary; check that students' responses cite details that support their judgment that these stories are realistic.

Francisco let go of his grandfather's hand. He darted through the swarm of men and was right in front of the van when it stopped.

"One man," the driver said. "For gardening." He was young, with a thick, black mustache. And he was wearing an L.A. Lakers cap, like Francisco's. Maybe cleaner. It must be an omen, Francisco thought.

"Take us, Mr. Benjamin. *Us.*" Francisco pointed back at his grandfather. He tilted his own cap over his eyes. "Look! We love the Lakers, too. And my grandfather is a fine gardener, though he doesn't know English yet. The gardens are the same, right? Mexican and American?"

Francisco waved urgently for his grandfather to come. "Also, you will get two for one," he said. "I don't charge for my work."

4 The man grinned. "OK. I'm convinced. But I'm not Mr. Benjamin. Call me Ben."

He motioned to Francisco. "You and your grandfather jump in back. Sixty dollars for the day."

Francisco nodded. His breath was coming fast. That much for a day's work? Mama would be so happy. Her job didn't pay much. There'd be extra food tonight, maybe *chorizos*.

5 He pulled open the back door, threw in the bag of lunch Mama had packed, and hurried his grandfather into the van ahead of him.

182

A big, tough guy tried to get in too. Francisco pushed him back. *He* was tough. He was a worker.

"It is gardening," he told Abuelo as the van pulled away.

"But I do not know gardening. I am a carpenter. I have always lived in the city."

"It is easy." Francisco waved through the window at the passing cars. "Flowers, roses, things like that." He raised his cap to a lady in a car. "*Señora*," he said politely, though she couldn't hear. **6**

183

Careers

Do you like digging in the dirt and planting flowers and vegetables? Then you might like to be a gardener when you grow up. You can go to school to become a Master Gardener. Master Gardeners often work for their state's government, answering questions about plants, bugs and pests, gardening, and landscaping. They run 4-H Club programs for children and help teachers with gardening programs in the schools. To become a Master Gardener, you have to be a good gardener, of course, but you also have to be comfortable speaking in public and working with all kinds of people; to read and write well; and to give people information they can understand and use. To get your certificate as a Master Gardener, you have to take classes and pass an exam. Then you can get paid for digging in the dirt and planting flowers and vegetables!

Time for
SOCIAL
STUDIES

SKILLS ↔ STRATEGIES IN CONTEXT

Realism and Fantasy REVIEW

TEACH

- Remind students that although realism is fiction, the people and events in the story seem real. A realistic story tells about something that could happen.

- Point out that details in the story show whether or not it is realistic and in what ways.

 MODEL The first thing I want to do is look at the details. Francisco runs through the crowd and starts talking to the driver of the van, a young man with a mustache and a baseball cap. They talk about the work to be done and the pay, and then they drive off. These things could happen, and the characters talk and act like real people. This is a realistic story.

PRACTICE AND ASSESS

- Have students think of some details that would make this story a fantasy. To assess, check that students' ideas could not happen and are not realistic.

- To assess, use Practice Book 3.1, p. 66.

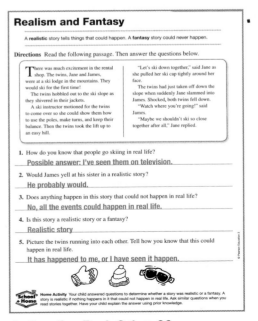

Realism and Fantasy

A **realistic** story tells things that could happen. A **fantasy** story could never happen.

Directions Read the following passage. Then answer the questions below.

There was much excitement in the rental shop. The twins, Jane and James, were at a ski lodge in the mountains. They would ski for the first time!

The twins hobbled out to the ski slope as they shivered in their jackets.

A ski instructor motioned for the twins to come over so she could show them how to use the poles, make turns, and keep their balance. Then the twins took the lift up to an easy hill.

"Let's ski down together," said Jane as she pulled her ski cap tightly around her face.

The twins had just taken off down the slope when suddenly Jane slammed into James. Shocked, both twins fell down.

"Watch where you're going!" said James.

"Maybe we shouldn't ski so close together after all," Jane replied.

1. How do you know that people go skiing in real life?
   Possible answer: I've seen them on television.

2. Would James yell at his sister in a realistic story?
   He probably would.

3. Does anything happen in this story that could not happen in real life?
   No, all the events could happen in real life.

4. Is this story a realistic story or a fantasy?
   Realistic story

5. Picture the twins running into each other. Tell how you know that this could happen in real life.
   It has happened to me, or I have seen it happen.

School + Home Home Activity Your child answered questions to determine whether a story was realistic or a fantasy. A story is realistic if nothing happens in it that could not happen in real life. Ask similar questions when you read stories together. Have your child explain the answer using prior knowledge.

▲ **Practice Book 3.1** p. 66

Guiding Comprehension

7 **Facts and Details • Literal**

Sometimes details help us picture what we are reading. Which details on p. 184 help you picture the place Ben brought Francisco and his grandfather?

Possible responses: The winding road, the sloping bank, new houses, workers on rooftops, the smell of tar.

8 **Visualize • Inferential**

Reread the first paragraph on p. 184. What do you "see"?

Responses will vary; look for responses that reflect the details in the selection.

9 **Sequence • Inferential**

Look back at the most important details in the story and tell what has happened so far. Be sure to keep the details in the order in which they happened.

Possible response: 1. Francisco and his grandfather were looking for a day job. 2. A man arrived in a van, and Francisco convinced him to take himself and his grandfather. 3. The man brought them to a housing development and left them to do some gardening work.

The van turned off the freeway onto a winding road and stopped. A sloping bank led up to the backyards of new houses. Some were not yet finished. Workers climbed **7** **8** high on rooftops, and there was the good smell of tar.

The high bank was dotted with pretty white flowers and overgrown with coarse green spikes. Six big black trash cans waited below.

They all got out of the van but Ben left the motor running.

"I need you to weed this bank," he told Abuelo. "Be sure to get the roots." He pointed to the cans. "Dump them here."

"Good. Fine." It was Francisco who answered.

"I have another job to go to," Ben said. "I'll pick you up at three. It will be hot. Your grandfather will need a hat." He took a straw one from the van.

"*Gracias,*" Abuelo said.

"See you guys then. Work hard. Have a nice day."

"What did he say?" Abuelo asked as the van drove off.

"He said to have a nice day. It is what everyone says up here."

"Your English is very good, my grandson," Abuelo said.

Francisco nodded and smiled. He climbed the bank and hung his jacket on a railing. "Now," he said, "I will show you." He pulled up one of the spiky clumps and shook the dirt from its roots. "These are weeds. Do not touch the flowers." **9**

184

185

 STRATEGY SELF-CHECK

Visualize

Explain to students that often when we read, we make pictures in our minds of what we are reading. Authors use details that help us see, hear, feel, or even smell what we are reading. This helps us understand the selection better.

Have students look back through the selection so far to look for details that show us what Francisco is like. Remind them to look at details such as his actions, his words, and what other characters say to and about him. Then have them write two to three brief sentences describing how they "see" Francisco.

SELF-CHECK

Students can ask themselves these questions to assess their ability to use the skill and strategy.

- Do the details I have chosen show or tell what Francisco is like?
- Do my sentences give a sense of Francisco's character?

Monitor Progress	
Character	
If... students have difficulty visualizing character,	then... revisit the skill lesson on pp. 174–175. Reteach as necessary.

Develop Vocabulary

PRACTICE LESSON VOCABULARY

Have students provide oral responses to each question.

1. **When do you *grumble* about something?** *(Possible response: when doing chores)*
2. **If you *shivered*, were you hot or cold?** *(Cold)*
3. **What is one example of "*motioned*"?** *(Possible responses: to wave, to beckon with your hand, to point)*

BUILD CONCEPT VOCABULARY

Review previous concept words with students. Ask if students have met any words today in their reading or elsewhere that they would like to add to the Concept Web.

Strategy Response Log

Answer Questions Answer the questions you asked about the selection on p. 178, if possible. Leave blank any questions you cannot answer and look for answers as you continue reading.

If you want to teach this selection in two sessions, stop here.

Guiding Comprehension

If you are teaching the selection in two days, discuss the story so far, including characterization and vocabulary.

10 **Draw Conclusions • Inferential**

On p. 186, it says Francisco's shoulders and arms hurt, and on p. 187, it says he had never felt so good. What does it mean that he feels good when his body hurts?

Possible response: It is the first time he has worked for money, so he is proud of himself. He doesn't mind the fact that his body hurts.

11 **Vocabulary • Context Clues**

Use context clues to find the meaning of the word *slammed* in the last paragraph on p. 187.

Clues: Ben is angry; he slammed the cap against the van.

Monitor Progress

 **Context Clues**

If... students have difficulty using context to determine the meaning of *slammed,*	**then...** use vocabulary strategy instruction on p. 187.

DAY 3 Grouping Options

Reading
Whole Group Discuss the Question of the Day.

Group Time Differentiated Instruction
Read *A Day's Work.* See pp. 174f–174g for the small group lesson plan.

Whole Group Discuss the Reader Response questions on p. 192. Then use p. 197a.

Language Arts
Use pp.197e–197h and 197k–197m.

His grandfather smiled. *"Bueno."* Francisco could see his strong white teeth all the way to the back.

They worked through the morning.

A little poodle barked at them through the railings above. "Yap, yap, yap."

An orange cat prowled the bank.

There was a pool in one of the new backyards. Francisco heard splashing and voices. The water sounds made him hotter. His shoulders and arms hurt. He thought about how proud Mama would be tonight.

"Sixty dollars?" she'd say, and she'd hug Francisco and Abuelo. "It is a fortune."

At lunchtime he and Abuelo ate the tortillas and tomatoes and drank the bottle of water she had packed.

In another hour they were finished.

The bank looked so nice with just the brown dirt and the pretty flowers.

186

ELL

Understand Idioms Explain to students that there are many words and phrases in English that we use to express surprise, wonder, amazement, anger, disappointment, and so on. Point out the idiom *Holy Toledo* on p. 187. Explain that this idiom is used when someone is surprised or amazed by something. Francisco misunderstands Ben's amazement, however. He thinks Ben is pleased because he did not expect them to do a good job. Discuss with students what Ben is really amazed about. (*They didn't understand which plants were weeds and pulled up all the good plants.*)

"*Muy bonito,*" Abuelo said.

And Francisco said, "Yes, beautiful!"

He and his grandfather shook hands.

Francisco thought he had never felt so good. He'd helped his grandfather, and he had worked himself.

They sat on the curb to wait for the van, and when it came they stood and brushed the loose dirt from their clothes.

Ben got out and stared up at the bank. "Holy Toledo!" he said.

"You didn't think we could do such a good job?" Francisco wanted to laugh, Ben seemed so shocked.

Francisco gave a little jump and pretended to slam dunk a ball. "Like the Lakers. We work hard."

"I can't believe it!" Ben whispered. "You . . . you took out all the plants and left the weeds."

Francisco stepped closer to Abuelo. "But the flowers . . . ," he began.

Ben pointed. "Those flowers are chickweed. Chickweed! You took out my young ice plants!" He yanked off his Lakers cap and slammed it against the van.

Living Things

What exactly is a weed? Simply put, weeds are plants that grow where you don't want them to. Most weeds can grow just about anywhere. That's part of what makes them weeds. Weeds grow so fast and so well that very often they crowd out other plants. There are several things you can do to control weeds. You can spray them, but if you are growing vegetables, you have to be careful not to use chemicals that can make you sick when you eat the vegetables. You can cover the ground with plastic, but sometimes this stops the good plants from growing too. Or you can pull them out, being careful to get the whole root. That's a backbreaking chore!

 VOCABULARY STRATEGY

Context Clues

TEACH

- Explain to students that they can help themselves understand unfamiliar words by using context clues.
- Tell students to scan for context clues within a sentence, a paragraph, or even among visual elements such as drawings or photographs.
- Reread p. 187, from when Ben gets out of his van, aloud. Model using context clues to determine the meaning of *slammed.*

Think Aloud **MODEL** When I come across the word *slammed* at the end of the page, I have to go back and look for clues that will help me figure out what it means. I know that Ben is angry because Francisco and his grandfather pulled out all his plants and left all the weeds. I'd be angry too! It says he slammed his hat against the van. Since he's angry, I think *slammed* means to hit really hard.

PRACTICE AND ASSESS

Have students use context clues to figure out the meaning of *yanked* in the last paragraph of p. 187. (*pulled hard*)

Guiding Comprehension

12 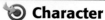 **Visualize • Inferential**

How do you think Francisco's face might have looked when he realized his mistake?

Possible responses: sad, scared, disappointed.

13 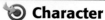 **Character • Inferential**

What kind of person do you think Francisco's *abuelo* is? Why do you think so?

Possible response: Honest; he offers to work an extra day without extra pay to fix their mistake.

Monitor Progress	
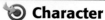 **Character**	
If... students are unable to identify what Francisco's *abuelo* is like,	**then...** use the skill and strategy instruction on p. 189.

14 **Predict • Inferential**

Ben is pretty angry with Francisco and his *abuelo*. How do you think the story will end?

Responses will vary; look for responses that are a logical conclusion based on the events and the characters in the story.

"What is it? Did we do something wrong?" Abuelo whispered in Spanish to Francisco.

Ben's mustache quivered with anger. "I thought you said your grandfather was a fine gardener. He doesn't even know a *chickweed?*"

Abuelo looked from one of them to the other. "Tell me what is happening, Francisco," he said.

"We left the weeds. We took out the plants," Francisco said softly in Spanish. It was hard to look at his grandfather as he spoke.

"He thought we knew about gardening," Abuelo said. His Spanish was fast and angry. "You lied to him. Isn't that so?"

188

"We needed a day's work . . . ."

"We do not lie for work."

Now there was more sadness than anger in Abuelo's voice. "Ah, my grandson." He put a hand on Francisco's shoulder. "Ask him what we can do. Tell him we will come back tomorrow, if he agrees. We will pull out the weeds and put the good plants back." **13**

Francisco felt his heart go weak. "But . . . but Abuelo, that will be twice the work. And tomorrow is Sunday. There is a Lakers game on TV. And there is also church." He hoped the word *church* would perhaps change his grandfather's thinking.

"We will miss them both, then," his grandfather said. "It is the price of the lie. Tell the gentleman what I said, and ask him if the plants will live."

Ben said they would. "The roots are still there. If they're replanted early, they'll be all right."

He rubbed his eyes. "This is partly my fault. I should have stayed to get you started. But tell your grandfather I appreciate his offer, and I'll bring you back in the morning."

The three of them got in the van.

Francisco sat by the window in huddled silence. He didn't wave to passing cars. He didn't raise his cap. He'd helped his grandfather find work. But in the end the lie had spoiled the day. His throat burned with tears.

14

189

Character Visualize

TEACH

- Tell students that if we understand characters in a story, we usually better understand the story as a whole.

- Remind students that often we have to look at the details in the story in order to understand the characters.

- Tell students that active readers look for details that help them see the character, or sense what he or she feels. This gives us information about the character too.

 MODEL Until now, we haven't read much about Francisco's *abuelo*. He offers to fix the mistake by working an extra day without pay. He is also upset with Francisco's lie. I think he must be an honest person.

PRACTICE AND ASSESS

Have students describe how they think Francisco's *abuelo* or Ben looks. To assess, check that their descriptions can be supported by details in the selection.

Living Things

TIME FOR Science

There are several species of chickweed, which gets its name from the fact that chickens like to eat it. Common chickweed grows in most parts of the United States. Chickweed is a low-growing plant that prefers grass and lawns, or open areas, and does well when there are no taller plants blocking its sun. It is easy to confuse with garden flowers if you are not familiar with it because it has small, white flowers and a small, whitish fruit. The leaves are small and light green.

Guiding Comprehension

15 Cause and Effect • Inferential

What was one effect of Francisco's lie?

Possible responses: He missed the Lakers' game; they couldn't get *chorizos*; they had to work an extra day.

16 Author's Purpose • Critical

Question the Author **Why do you think the author wrote the story *A Day's Work*? What are the important things in life the author is talking about? What important things did you learn from reading the story?**

Possible Responses: To teach the importance of honesty and integrity. The author wants to persuade us to learn that it's always important to be honest and to fix any mistakes we make. I learned that if you do the wrong thing, you should admit it and try to solve the mistake.

Strategy Response Log

Summarize When students finish reading the selection, provide this prompt: Imagine that a friend has asked what *A Day's Work* is about. In four or five sentences, explain its important points.

The parking lot was empty. The trash can overflowed with used paper cups and sandwich wrappings.

Ben let them out.

"Look," he said. "If you need money I'll give you half now." He began to pull his wallet from his pocket but Abuelo held up his hand.

190

EXTEND SKILLS

Time

Explain that *six* A.M. as noted on page 191 means six o'clock in the morning. P.M. indicates time after noon. Time is also often expressed in numerals with a colon between the hour and the minutes—6:00 A.M.

"Tell him we take the pay tomorrow, when we finish."

Francisco's grandfather and Ben looked at each other and words seemed to pass between them, though there were no words. Ben slid his wallet back into his pocket.

Francisco sighed. The lie had taken the *chorizos,* too. ⑮

"Tomorrow then. Six A.M.," Ben said. "And tell your grandfather I can always use a good man—for more than just one day's work."

Francisco gave a hop of excitement. More than just a day's work!

Ben was still speaking. "The important things your grandfather knows already. And I can teach him gardening."

Francisco nodded. He understood. He would tell his grandfather, and he would tell him something else. He, Francisco, had begun to learn the important things, too.

Francisco took his grandfather's cold, rough hand in his. "Let's go home, Abuelo," he said. ⑯

191

Develop Vocabulary

PRACTICE LESSON VOCABULARY

Have students respond orally *true* or *false* to each question and make the false statements true.

1. **Happiness is a synonym for *sadness*.** (False, happiness *is an antonym for* sadness.)
2. **To be *shocked* about something is to be surprised.** (True)
3. **We feel *excitement* when we are scared or nervous.** (False; we feel excitement when we are expecting something good to happen.)

BUILD CONCEPT VOCABULARY

Review previous concept words with students. Ask if students have met any words today in their reading or elsewhere that they would like to add to the Concept Web.

STRATEGY SELF-CHECK

Visualize

- Remind students that when we read, we should try to visualize what we are reading.
- Picturing what characters look like in a story helps us understand them and what is happening to them.
- Have students look through the selection and think about what the characters looked like at different points. Encourage them to think about what faces and actions say about character or personality.

SELF-CHECK

Students can ask these questions to assess their ability to use the skill and strategy.

- How do I think the character looked?
- Are there details in the story that support my visualization of the character(s)?
- What do I look like when I'm feeling the same way? Why do I think so?

- To assess, use Practice Book 3.1, p. 67

Monitor Progress
Character

If... students have difficulty visualizing character,	then... use the Reteach lesson on p. 197b.

Character • Visualize

- **Characters** are the people or animals in a story. What they say and do tells you about them.
- When you read how a character acts, picture him or her. **Visualizing** will help you understand what the character is like.

Directions Read the following passage. Then answer the questions below.

Jasmine and Kim play soccer whenever they can. Sometimes they even play on the street in front of their apartment. One Saturday, Jasmine kicked the ball too far, and it went right through a window on the first floor.

"Run!" said Jasmine. "We don't want anyone to find out who did that!"

"But our ball is inside," said Kim. "Everyone will know it was us."

The two girls told the manager what happened. "You must pay for the window," she said, "and then everything will be all right."

1. How do you know that the two girls love soccer?
   They play it whenever they can.

2. What does Jasmine want to do when the ball goes through the window?
   She wants to run away so she doesn't get caught.

3. Tell what each character is like.
   They both love soccer; they do the right thing, even though at first they aren't sure that they will.

4. Do you think the girls will pay for the broken window? Tell why or why not.
   Yes, they went to talk to the manager about it.

5. Picture the girls talking to the manager. Tell how they probably felt.
   They probably felt scared and uncomfortable.

Home Activity Your child answered questions about characters in a story. Read a familiar story together and ask your child to tell about the characters based on their actions in the story.

▲ **Practice Book 3.1** p. 67

Reader Response

Open for Discussion Personal Response

Think Aloud

MODEL I think they continued to work for Ben and earned enough money for the jacket and cap, and the chorizos too!

Comprehension Check Critical Response

1. Students might mention personal experience with immigrants or a story involving her grandfather. **Author's Purpose**

2. Francisco is determined and hard-working. He wants to help his family. 🎯 **Character**

3. Possible response: stooped over the weeds, sweating, stretching. I understood how Francisco felt later when his grandfather told him they would have to do it again. 🎯 **Visualize**

4. Look for actions that accurately show what the words mean. 🎯 **Vocabulary**

Look Back and Write For test practice, assign a 10–15 minute time limit. For assessment, see the Scoring Rubric at the right.

Retell

Have students retell *A Day's Work.*

Monitor Progress

Check Retelling Rubric 4 3 2 1

If... students have difficulty retelling the story,	then... use the Retelling Cards and Scoring Rubric for Retelling on p. 193 to assist fluent retelling.

SUCCESS PREDICTOR

Check Retelling Have students use illustrations and other text features to guide their retellings. Let students listen to other retellings before attempting their own. See the ELL and Transition Handbook.

Reader Response

Open for Discussion What do you think happened to Francisco and his grandfather the next day and the day after that and the day after that?

1. The author, Eve Bunting, has written more than a hundred stories. How do you think she got the idea for *A Day's Work*? **Think Like an Author**

2. What can you say about Francisco? What was he like? What words would you use to describe him? **Character**

3. What picture did you have in your mind of Francisco and his grandfather working in the hot sun? How did that help you as you read? **Visualize**

4. Imagine how Francisco felt at the end of the story. Write a journal entry as Francisco, use words from the Words to Know list. **Vocabulary**

Look Back and Write On page 191 Ben says, "The important things your grandfather knows already." Explain what Ben means when he says that. Use details from the story.

Meet author Eve Bunting on page 408.

Scoring Rubric **Look Back and Write**

Top-Score Response A top-score response will use details from the selection to explain what Ben means when he says, "The important things your grandfather knows already."

Example of a Top-Score Response Francisco and his grandfather get a job gardening, but they pull the ice plants rather than the weeds. Francisco's grandfather says they will work on Sunday to fix the problem. They will miss church and the basketball game. He will not take money from Ben until the work is done. Ben says, "The important things your grandfather knows already." He knows Francisco's grandfather is honest. He knows that he works hard and likes to do a good job.

For additional rubrics, see p. WA10.

Write Now

Rules

Prompt

A Day's Work describes one rule for living and getting along with others.
Think about rules for getting along with family members, friends, or neighbors.
Now write the rules as commands.

Writing Trait

Writing rules calls for using one kind of **sentence**—commands.

Student Model

Rules are written in a numbered list.

Rules may include specific details.

Rules for Living with Your Little Sister

1. Do nice things, such as read her a story.
2. Teach her something, such as how to tie her shoes.
3. Let her play with your toys sometimes.
4. Encourage her instead of teasing her.
5. Be patient even when it seems like she is bothering you.
6. Be pleasant to her when your friends come over.
7. Be friendly when she is playing with other kids.

Each rule is the same kind of <u>sentence</u>— a command.

Use the model to help you write your own rules.

193

Write Now

Look at the Prompt Have students identify and discuss key words and phrases in the prompt. *(rules for getting along, commands)*

Strategies to Develop Sentences

Have students

- find a list of rules and analyze how they are written.
- write some commands that they hear or use every day.
- replace weak verbs in their rules with stronger verbs.

NO: See if your friends can come over.

YES: Invite your friends over.

For additional suggestions and rubric, see pp. 197g–197h.

Hints for Better Writing

- Carefully read the prompt.
- Use a graphic organizer to plan your writing.
- Support your ideas with information and details.
- Use words that help readers understand.
- Proofread and edit your work.

Scoring Rubric | Narrative Retelling

Rubric 4 3 2 1	4	3	2	1
Connections	Makes connections and generalizes beyond the text	Makes connections to other events, stories, or experiences	Makes a limited connection to another event, story, or experience	Makes no connection to another event, story, or experience
Author's Purpose	Elaborates on author's purpose	Tells author's purpose with some clarity	Makes some connection to author's purpose	Makes no connection to author's purpose
Characters	Describes the main character(s) and any character development	Identifies the main character(s) and gives some information about them	Inaccurately identifies some characters or gives little information about them	Inaccurately identifies the characters or gives no information about them
Setting	Describes the time and location	Identifies the time and location	Omits details of time or location	Is unable to identify time or location
Plot	Describes the problem, goal, events, and ending using rich detail	Tells the problem, goal, events, and ending with some errors that do not affect meaning	Tells parts of the problem, goal, events, and ending with gaps that affect meaning	Retelling has no sense of story

Retelling Plan

☑ **Week 1** Assess Strategic Intervention students.

☑ **This week assess Advanced students.**

☐ **Week 3** Assess Strategic Intervention students.

☐ **Week 4** Assess On-Level students.

☐ **Week 5** Assess any students you have not yet checked during this unit.

Use the Retelling Chart on p. TR16 to record retelling.

Selection Test To assess with *A Day's Work*, use Selection Tests, pp. 25–28.

Fresh Reads for Differentiated Test Practice For weekly leveled practice, use pp. 37–42.

Retelling

SUCCESS PREDICTOR

Reading Online

OBJECTIVES

- Examine features of e-mail.
- Compare and contrast across texts.

PREVIEW/USE TEXT FEATURES

As students preview "What Is a Weed?" have them identify who is asking for help and why. After they preview, ask:

- **What kind of information would you put in the "To:" box?** (*Someone's e-mail address*)

- **How would you organize an e-mail letter?** (*Possible response: Just like you would a regular letter, with a salutation or greeting, the body of the letter in correct paragraph form, and a closing.*)

Link to Science

Help students use reference materials such as encyclopedias or gardening books to help them identify weeds. Compare their samples to the pictures in the references to verify.

DAY 4 **Grouping Options**

Reading

Whole Group Discuss the Question of the Day.

Group Time Differentiated Instruction
 "What Is a Weed?" See pp. 174f–174g for the small group lesson plan.

Whole Group Use pp. 197a and 197j.

Language Arts
Use pp.197e–197h and 197k–197m.

Reading Online

New Literacies: **PearsonSuccessNet.com**

E-Mail

Genre

- **The letter *e* in *e-mail* stands for *electronic*.** An e-mail is a message sent by computer over the Internet from one user to another.

- **E-mail lets you communicate with people all over the world.**

Text Features

- **The *To:* box shows to whom a message is going.**

- **The message itself looks like the body of a letter.**

Link to Science

Find examples of weeds in your neighborhood. Bring them to class and use a resource to label them.

What Is a Weed?

Francisco and his *abuelo* got in trouble because they pulled up the wrong plants. "Tomorrow," Francisco told himself, "I will be smarter! I will know a weed from a flower!" That night, Francisco went to a computer and used e-mail to help him learn about plants.

For more practice

Take It to the Net

PearsonSuccessNet.com

194

TECHNOLOGY TOOLS

E-mail

Address Click once to get a screen that shows your personal address book, with the e-mail addresses of people you e-mail frequently.

Attach Click once to attach documents to your message.

Link Click once to get to a related site.

Send Click once to send your e-mail message.

At a gardening Web site, Francisco found a link labeled *Contact Us,* so he wrote an e-mail.

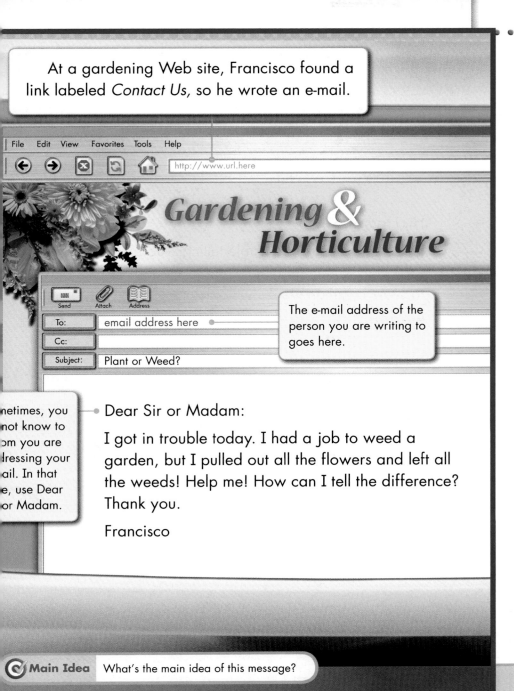

Gardening &
Horticulture

The e-mail address of the person you are writing to goes here.

Subject: Plant or Weed?

...netimes, you ...not know to ...om you are ...dressing your ...ail. In that ...e, use Dear ...or Madam.

Dear Sir or Madam:

I got in trouble today. I had a job to weed a garden, but I pulled out all the flowers and left all the weeds! Help me! How can I tell the difference? Thank you.

Francisco

Main Idea What's the main idea of this message?

195

NEW LITERACIES: E-MAIL

Use the sidebar on p. 194 to guide discussion.

- E-mail, or electronic mail, lets you send letters to people all over the world, just like regular mail, only faster. Generally, when you click "Send," the person to whom you are sending the e-mail will have your letter within minutes. You can have their reply just as quickly!

- Just like regular letters, e-mail letters follow a number of formats, from very formal to very informal. In this example, Francisco is writing a letter to someone he doesn't know to ask for his or her help.

- Discuss with students what kind of response Francisco is likely to get such as a letter in response, links to Web sites, and so on.

 **AudioText**

Main Idea

Francisco wants help telling the difference between weeds and flowers.

Access Content Point out specific terms which may be difficult for non-native English speakers, such as *Chat, Cc,* and *Subject.* Tell students what kind of information appears in the *Cc* and *Subject* fields.

WEB-IQUETTE

E-mail

Tell students that in many ways e-mail is like regular mail, and there are rules of etiquette they should follow, especially when writing to people they don't know or who are in positions of respect, such as teachers or other adults.

- Always address the person to whom you are writing with "Dear," just as in regular mail. For instance, "Dear Sir or Madam:" is the way Francisco addressed his e-mail.

- Use correct paragraph form and indent the first line of each paragraph or double space between paragraphs.

- Always use a proper closing.

Strategies for Navigation

USE FOLDERS Folders for each person or each type of e-mail you receive can help keep you organized and can help you find the information you need quickly and easily.

Use the Strategy

1. Think about from whom you usually receive e-mail—friends, family, newsgroups, and so on. Create a folder for each category, or each person.

2. To create a new folder, look for an "Add" link or an "Add folder" link in your e-mail program and click once on it.

3. Type the name of the new folder in the prompt window and click "OK" or "Add folder."

PRACTICE Think about the ways you use e-mail at home and at school.

- In what ways can e-mail help you with your homework, or with research?

- The next time you access the Internet, compose a brief letter requesting information about something you are studying in school or are simply curious about. Be sure you follow correct letter format in your message.

Write   Reply   Send   Forward   Delete   Address   Print

From: (Sender's e-mail address appears here.)
Sent: Monday, July 22, 2005, 11:15 AM
To: (Receiver's e-mail address appears here.)
Subject: Re: Plant or Weed?

Hi, Francisco,

A lot of people have trouble telling weeds from flowers, especially when the plant is not in bloom. Here is a link to some common weeds with pictures. I hope this helps.

Pat

www.url.here

Francisco was really excited. He clicked on the link and found this information.

Edit   View   Favorites   Tools   Help

http://www.url.here

Common Weeds

Canada Thistle

Canada thistle is a creeping plant that returns every year. The foliage is spiny.

196

Guided Practice If there is time, have students log on to the Internet. Show them how to create and use folders. Help students make connections between the steps they are doing and related vocabulary terms.

Edit   View   Favorites   Tools   Help

http://www.url.here

Dandelion

The dandelion returns every year. It has a long root. Its yellow flowers can bloom anytime between March and November.

File   Edit   View   Favorites   Tools   Help

http://www.url.here

Purslane

Purslane is a summer weed. It has thick leaves and small yellow flowers. The plant is low-growing. It is easily pulled when the soil is wet.

Reading Across Texts

Now that Francisco has this information, what advice would you give him about his next job as a gardener?

Writing Across Texts Write an e-mail to Francisco giving him your advice.

 Visualize Try to visualize the weeds as you read about them.

197

CONNECT TEXT TO TEXT

Reading Across Texts

Discuss Francisco's big mistake and how he could have used this information effectively when he worked for Mr. Benjamin. Then have students share their ideas about how he can use this new information in his next job. Write their ideas on the board.

Writing Across Texts Remind students to use correct letter format when they write their letter. Point out that although they don't need to be very formal because Francisco is young, like they are, they don't want to be too familiar, either, since they don't know him.

 Visualize

Point to the pictures of weeds in the selection to help students visualize the weeds as they read.

Fluency Assessment Plan

☑ **Week 1** Assess Advanced students.

☑ **This week assess Strategic Intervention students.**

☐ **Week 3** Assess On-Level students.

☐ **Week 4** Assess Strategic Intervention students.

☐ **Week 5** Assess any students you have not yet checked during this unit.

Set individual goals for students to enable them to reach the year-end goal.

• Current Goal: 85–95 wcpm
• Year-End Goal: 120 wcpm

To develop fluent readers, use Fluency Coach.

MORE READING FOR
Fluency

To practice fluency with text comprised of previously taught phonics elements and irregular words, use Decodable Reader 7.

DAY 5   Grouping Options

Reading
Whole Group
Revisit the Question of the Week.

Group Time
Differentiated Instruction
ℝeℝead this week's Leveled Readers. See pp. 174f–174g for the small group lesson plan.

Whole Group
Use pp. 197b–197c.

Language Arts
Use pp.197d–197h and 197k–197n.

CHARACTERIZATION
Fluency

DAY 1

Model Reread "The Honest-to-Goodness Truth" on p. 174m. Explain that you will read as if you are Libby and show emotions as you read the selection. Model for students as you read.

DAY 2

Choral Reading Read aloud p. 181. Have students notice voice changes as you read the dialogue of the characters. Have students practice as a class doing three choral readings of p. 181.

DAY 3

Model Read aloud p. 188. Have students notice how you pretend to be the characters as you read what they say. Practice as a class by doing three choral readings.

DAY 4

Partner Reading Partners practice reading aloud p. 188, three times. Students should read with characterization and offer each other feedback.

Monitor Progress   Check Fluency WCPM

As students reread, monitor their progress toward their individual fluency goals. Current Goal: 85–95 words correct per minute. End-of-Year Goal: 120 words correct per minute.

If... students cannot read fluently at a rate of 85–95 words correct per minute,
then... make sure students practice with text at their independent level. Provide additional fluency practice, pairing nonfluent readers with fluent readers.

If... students already read at 120 words correct per minute,
then... they do not need to reread three to four times.

SUCCESS PREDICTOR

DAY 5

Assessment
Individual Reading Rate Use the Fluency Assessment Plan and do a one-minute timed reading of either selection from this week to assess students in Week 2. Provide corrective feedback for each student.

RETEACH

◎ Character

TEACH

Review the skill instruction for character on p. 174. Write the following on the board: *Characters = the people or animals in a story. What do the characters say? What do they do? What does this tell you about them?* Students can complete Practice Book 3.1, p. 68 on their own, or you can complete it as a class. Point out that the boxes in the character graphic organizer are empty, so students must read the passage and fill in the empty boxes with details from the passage.

ASSESS

Have students read the sentences on p. 180 about the first driver who hired workers. Ask pairs of students to review what he says and does. Then tell them to write one sentence about what kind of person they think he is. Remind them to use details about his words and actions to support their ideas. *(The man makes the extra workers get out; he isn't very generous.)*

For additional instruction of character, see DI·53.

EXTEND SKILLS

Paraphrase

TEACH

Paraphrasing is putting the ideas of a story or selection into your own words. Something that is paraphrased has the author's meaning, but it is simpler to read than the original text.

- After you read a difficult sentence or passage, think about what the writer said and retell it in your own words.
- Be sure not to copy the exact words from a sentence or passage.

Read the last paragraph on p. 184, then paraphrase it. *(Francisco showed his grandfather how to weed by pulling up plants and shaking dirt off the roots.)*

ASSESS

Have students pick a sentence from the story and copy it exactly. Then ask them to paraphrase it. *(Responses will vary; check that students have not used the exact words in their paraphrase.)*

OBJECTIVES

◎ Understand character.

● Understand how to paraphrase.

Skills Trace
Character

Introduce/Teach	TE: 3.1 116–117, 123; 3.2 174–175, 181, 189
Practice	PB: 3.1 16, 43, 47, 48, 63, 67, 68, 76, 96
Reteach/Review	**TE: 3.1 25, 141b, DI•56; 3.2 197b, 207, 215, 259, DI•53**
Test	Selection Test: Unit 2 Benchmark Test: Unit 2

ELL

Access Content Reteach the skill by reviewing the Picture It! lesson on character in the ELL Teaching Guide, pp. 43–44.

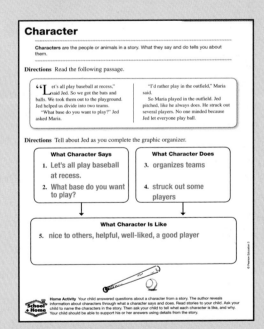

▲ **Practice Book 3.1** p. 68

Vocabulary and Word Study

VOCABULARY STRATEGY
Context Clues

UNFAMILIAR WORDS Remind students that they can use context clues to determine the meaning of unfamiliar words. Have students list any unknown words they encountered as they read *A Day's Work*. They can create a chart showing the unknown word, helpful context clues, and their definition of the word based on its context. Students can confirm word meanings using a dictionary.

Word	Context Clues	Meaning
tilted	cap over his eyes	pushed on an angle
hire		
overgrown		

Word Origins

Many words we use today, such as *canoe* and *hammock*, come from the Spanish language. Have partners use dictionaries and online reference sources to make lists of words of Spanish origin. Students can also include words with origins in different languages.

Words and Their Origins

alligator: Spanish	**cocoa:** Spanish
pretzel: German	**sugar:** Persian
kindergarten: German	**pajamas:** Persian
hurricane: Spanish	**cookie:** Dutch
mosquito: Spanish	**bandana:** Hindi

BUILD CONCEPT VOCABULARY
Right and Wrong

LOOKING BACK Remind students of the question of the week: When is a solution the wrong solution? Discuss how this week's Concept Web of vocabulary words relates to the theme of right and wrong. Ask students if they have any words or categories to add. Discuss whether words and categories are appropriately related to the concept.

MOVING FORWARD Preview the title of the next selection, *Prudy's Problem*. Ask students which Concept Web words might apply to the new selection based on the title alone. Put a star next to these words on the web.

Display the Concept Web and revisit the vocabulary words as you read the next selection to check predictions.

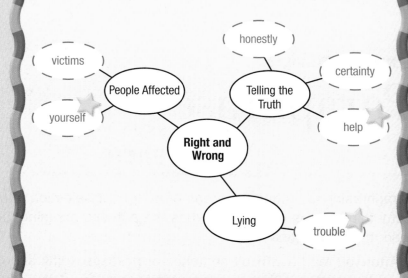

Monitor Progress
Check Vocabulary

If... students suggest words or categories that are not related to the concept,	then... review the words and categories on the Concept Web and discuss how they relate to the lesson concept.

SUCCESS PREDICTOR

Speaking and Listening

Directions

SET-UP Have students give how-to directions for writing an e-mail to a friend. Students can use information from the second selection, "What Is a Weed?" and a computer to help them prepare their presentations.

RESEARCH Have students reread "What Is a Weed?" and practice writing e-mails to review the steps involved. Suggest that students take notes and record each step in sequential order. Students can use note cards to remember the steps in order.

VISUAL AIDS Consider creating a poster of the steps involved in writing an e-mail. You may wish to create a poster that shows the audience what an e-mail screen looks like. Be sure to include the Send to, Copy to, and the Subject line features on the poster.

Delivery Tips

- Speak clearly and fluently.
- Use number words or sequential words, such as first, next, and finally.
- Use visual aids.
- Look at the audience as you speak.

Listen to Directions

Read aloud directions for a simple gardening project while students listen. With partners, students can answer these questions orally or in writing.

1. **What materials do you need for this project?** *(Responses will vary.)*

2. **How long do you think it would take for you to complete this project?** *(Responses will vary.)*

3. **Retell the directions as well as you remember them.** *(Students should retell the directions in order as they remember them.)*

E L L

Support Vocabulary Use the following to review and extend vocabulary and to explore lesson concepts further:
- ELL Poster 7, Days 3–5 instruction
- Vocabulary Activities and Word Cards in ELL Teaching Guide, pp. 45–46

Assessment For information on assessing students' speaking, listening, and viewing, see the ELL and Transition Handbook.

Grammar Singular and Plural Nouns

OBJECTIVES

- Distinguish between singular and plural nouns.
- Spell plural nouns correctly.
- Use singular and plural nouns in writing.
- Become familiar with noun assessment on high-stakes tests.

Monitor Progress

Grammar

If... students	then... see The
have difficulty distinguishing between singular and plural nouns,	Grammar and Writing Book pp. 86–89.

DAILY FIX-IT

This week use Daily Fix-It Transparency 7.

Spiral REVIEW

ELL

Support Grammar See the Grammar Transition lessons in the ELL and Transition Handbook.

▲ **The Grammar and Writing Book**
For more instruction and practice, use pp. 86–89.

DAILY FIX-IT

1. White benchs sat in the middel of the garden. *(benches; middle)*

2. Many colorful rose grow their. *(roses; there)*

READING-GRAMMAR CONNECTION

Write this sentence from *A Day's Work* on the board:

The driver held up three fingers.

Explain that *driver* is a **singular noun.** It names one person, place, or thing. *Fingers* is a **plural noun.** It names more than one.

Display Grammar Transparency 7. Read aloud the definitions and sample sentences. Work through the items.

Singular and Plural Nouns

A **singular noun** names only one person, place, or thing. A **plural noun** names more than one person, place, or thing.

Singular Nouns   A tall <u>weed</u> sprouted beside the <u>creek</u>.
Plural Nouns   <u>Grasses</u> grew among the <u>trees</u>.

Most nouns add -s to form the plural. Add -es to a noun that ends in *ch, sh, s, ss,* or *x: benches, wishes, buses, glasses, foxes.* When a noun ends in a consonant and *y,* change the *y* to *i* and then add -es: *cities.*

Directions Write *S* if the underlined noun is singular. Write *P* if the underlined noun is plural.

1. There are many <u>jobs</u> on the farm. ___P___
2. That <u>job</u> will take you one <u>day</u>. ___S___
3. Daniel picks <u>strawberries</u> with his brother. ___P___
4. The <u>apples</u> are not ripe yet. ___P___
5. Anita plants <u>bushes</u> each fall. ___P___

Directions Underline the singular nouns and circle the plural nouns in the sentences.

6. The farmer planted a garden with many (vegetables)
7. (Foxes) ate the (grapes) off the (vines)
8. (Carrots) grow under the ground.
9. Some (beans) grow on a tall stalk.
10. Many (workers) pick the (crops) each year.

Unit 2 *A Day's Work*   Grammar **7**

▲ **Grammar Transparency** 7

DAILY FIX-IT

3. Can we eat our lunchs in the field. *(lunches; field?)*

4. The workers is puling weeds. *(are; pulling)*

GUIDED PRACTICE

Review the concept of singular and plural nouns.

- A **singular noun** names only one person, place, or thing.

- A **plural noun** names more than one person, place, or thing.

- Most nouns add *-s* to form the plural. Add *-es* to a noun that ends in *ch, sh, s, ss,* or *x.* When a noun ends in a consonant and *y,* change the *y* to *i* and then add *-es.*

HOMEWORK Grammar and Writing Practice Book p. 25. Work through the first two items with the class.

Singular and Plural Nouns

A **singular noun** names only one person, place, or thing. A **plural noun** names more than one person, place, or thing.

Singular Nouns   The <u>carpenter</u> built a <u>table</u>.
Plural Nouns   <u>Workers</u> made <u>desks, chairs,</u> and <u>benches</u>.

Most nouns add *-s* to form the plural. Add *-es* to a noun that ends in *ch, sh, s, ss,* or *x: lunches, dishes, buses, dresses, boxes.* When a noun ends in a consonant and *y,* change the *y* to *i* and then add *-es: bodies.*

Directions Write *S* if the underlined noun is a singular noun. Write *P* if the underlined noun is a plural noun.

1. Tom's father builds <u>houses</u>. ___P___
2. He puts <u>nails</u> in the walls. ___P___
3. Tom made a <u>wagon</u> out of wood. ___S___
4. He put four <u>wheels</u> on the wagon. ___P___
5. Tom's <u>friends</u> played with the wagon. ___P___

Directions Write the plural nouns in each sentence.

6. The workers loaded boxes of grapes.

   workers, boxes, grapes

7. The trees were full of plump cherries.

   trees, cherries

8. Sarah and her mother will make several pies.

   pies

9. George picked pears and peaches at the farm.

   pears, peaches

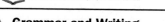 **Home Activity** Your child learned about singular and plural nouns. Say "I see a [something in your house]" and have your child say the plural form of the word.

▲ **Grammar and Writing Practice Book** p. 25

DAY 3 — Apply to Writing

DAILY FIX-IT

5. Most farmers don't work in citys but some gardeners do. *(cities,)*

6. What pritty plants those are. *(pretty; are!)*

USE VIVID NOUNS

Explain that using specific nouns, both singular and plural, makes writing more vivid.

- Have students review something they have written to see if they can improve it by changing general nouns to more vivid, specific ones.

HOMEWORK Grammar and Writing Practice Book p. 26.

Singular and Plural Nouns

Directions Complete each sentence by adding plural nouns. Write the new sentence.

1. The workers planted _____ and _____ in the field. Possible answers:
The workers planted beans and potatoes in the field.

2. Mrs. Thompson made a salad out of _____ and _____.
Mrs. Thompson made a salad out of carrots and tomatoes.

3. _____ and _____ are farm animals.
Horses and cows are farm animals.

4. Workers on a farm use machines such as _____ and _____.
Workers on a farm use machines such as tractors and plows.

5. You can buy fresh farm vegetables at _____ and _____.
You can buy fresh farm vegetables at stores and markets.

Directions Write about workers doing jobs on a farm. Use at least three plural nouns. Possible answer:
Workers pick tomatoes. They feed the pigs and cows. They put boxes of vegetables in wagons.

Home Activity Your child learned how to use singular and plural nouns in writing. Have your child write you a note about his or her favorite meal using at least three plural nouns.

▲ **Grammar and Writing Practice Book** p. 26

DAY 4 — Test Preparation

DAILY FIX-IT

7. There are many pumpkin farmes in california. *(farms; California)*

8. The boy and his uncel picks tomatoes. *(uncle; pick)*

STANDARDIZED TEST PREP

Test Tip

Don't assume that all nouns that end in *s* are plural. Some singular nouns also end in *s*.

Singular Nouns: The <u>class</u> rode on a <u>bus</u>.

Plural Nouns: Three <u>buses</u> picked up the two <u>classes</u>.

HOMEWORK Grammar and Writing Practice Book p. 27.

Singular and Plural Nouns

Directions Mark the letter of the plural form of each underlined noun.

1. The workers saw <u>fox</u> in the field.
   A foxs
   B foxes
   C fox
   D foxies

2. The workers cleaned up their <u>mess</u> each day.
   A mess
   B messs
   C messes
   D messies

3. James planted <u>bush</u> in the new garden.
   A bush
   B bushs
   C bushies
   D bushes

4. The men worked in the garden and told <u>story</u>.
   A stories
   B stores
   C storys
   D storss

5. Some played <u>radio</u> all day long.
   A radioes
   B radies
   C radios
   D radio

6. They planted several different <u>grass</u>.
   A grasss
   B grassies
   C gras
   D grasses

7. The garden was full of roses and <u>daisy</u>.
   A daisys
   B daisies
   C daises
   D daisy

8. The workers ate lunch on the <u>bench</u>.
   A bench
   B benchies
   C benches
   D benchs

9. Some <u>bus</u> picked them up after work.
   A buses
   B bussies
   C buss
   D bus

10. They worked in the garden for three <u>week</u>.
   A weex
   B weekes
   C week
   D weeks

Home Activity Your child prepared for taking tests on singular and plural nouns. With your child, take turns naming kinds of insects. Have your child write the plural form of each word.

▲ **Grammar and Writing Practice Book** p. 27

DAY 5 — Cumulative Review

DAILY FIX-IT

9. Are there pickels on the sandwich. *(pickles; sandwich?)*

10. How hungry the workers is. *(are!)*

ADDITIONAL PRACTICE

Assign pp. 86–89 in The Grammar and Writing Book.

EXTRA PRACTICE Grammar and Writing Practice Book p. 128.

TEST PREPARATION Grammar and Writing Practice Book pp. 153–154.

ASSESSMENT

CUMULATIVE REVIEW Grammar and Writing Practice Book p. 28.

Singular and Plural Nouns

Directions Underline the singular nouns and circle the plural nouns in the sentences.

1. The boy helped his grandfather with odd jobs.

2. An uncle cut branches from bushes and trees.

3. His friend put bricks on an old driveway.

4. The cousins fixed two bicycles and a lamp.

5. Many families hired the good workers.

Directions Write the plural form of the noun in ( ).

6. Where would you like to work for two (day)? days

7. Would you play with Mrs. Tan's (baby)? babies

8. You could water Mr. Johnson's pumpkin (patch). patches

9. Work hard for your (boss). bosses

Directions Write a sentence about a job that could take a day or two to complete. Use at least one singular noun and one plural noun. Possible answer:

10. I could help my neighbors walk their dogs and feed their cat.

Home Activity Your child reviewed singular and plural nouns. Look at a magazine article with your child. Have your child point out three singular nouns and three plural nouns.

▲ **Grammar and Writing Practice Book** p. 28

Writing Workshop Rules

- Identify the characteristics of rules.
- Write a list of rules without wordiness.
- Focus on sentences.
- Use a rubric.

Genre Rules
Writer's Craft Eliminating Wordiness
Writing Trait Sentences

Sentences Read imperative, exclamatory, and interrogative sentences aloud to English learners, using tone to show how these sentences add excitement to writing. Add think-aloud comments to explain how punctuation helps readers understand sentences.

Writing Trait

FOCUS/IDEAS Only essential information for doing a job is included.

ORGANIZATION/PARAGRAPHS Each rule describes a new aspect of the topic.

VOICE Writing is clear. The writer shows understanding of how to do a job.

WORD CHOICE The writer uses strong, precise verbs (*straighten, dust*) to describe actions.

SENTENCES The writer shows understanding of commands.

CONVENTIONS There is excellent control and accuracy, including correct spelling of singular and plural nouns.

DAY 1 Model the Trait

READING-WRITING CONNECTION

- *A Day's Work* tells how a man teaches his grandson the ethics of working with integrity.
- The story uses spare dialogue with commands and questions to establish and resolve conflict.
- Students will write **rules** as brief commands.

MODEL SENTENCES Discuss Writing Transparency 7A. Then discuss the model and the writing trait of sentences.

 Think Aloud Each rule is stated as a command. Each command begins with a strong verb and includes only necessary words. For example, Rule 2 states, "Make your bed." To give complete instructions, important details are clearly stated in few words, such as "Pull up the sheet, blanket, and bedspread smoothly." To add anything else would be too much detail for a rule.

Rules

Rules tell what people should do and shouldn't do. Rules are usually written in a numbered list.

Rules for Cleaning Your Room

The rules are written as commands. The first word or phrase in each rule is a verb that tells readers what to do.

1. Pick up toys, clothes, and books from your floor. Put each item in a drawer, in the closet, or on shelves.
2. Make your bed. Pull up the sheet, blanket, and bedspread smoothly. Fluff up the pillow.
3. Remove trash from your desk, floor, and other areas.

Rules include clear details. For example, #4 includes plural nouns that name specific things in a room.

4. Straighten up the books, papers, and pencils on your desk.
5. Dust the desk, dresser, and night table.
6. Vacuum the floor.
7. Keep your room neat after you clean it.

Each rule is stated briefly and without wordiness.

8. Don't complain!

Unit 2 A Day's Work   Writing Model **7A**

▲ **Writing Transparency** 7A

DAY 2 Improve Writing

WRITER'S CRAFT
Eliminate Wordiness

Display Writing Transparency 7B. Read the directions and work together to revise wordy sentences.

Think Aloud **ELIMINATE WORDINESS** Tomorrow we will write **rules** for getting along. How can I get from a paragraph summarizing how people get along to a command that summarizes the rule it illustrates? A paragraph describing how my sister and I agreed to trade off days using the video game station could be summed up as "Use the station only on days when it is your turn."

GUIDED WRITING Some students may need more help eliminating wordiness. Display some wordy sentences from students' writing and have students suggest revisions.

Eliminating Wordiness

Wordiness means using more words than needed.
Wordy I think the most important thing to remember when you clean your room is to carefully dust each piece of furniture such as the desk, dresser, and night table.
Revised Dust the desk, dresser, and night table.

Follow these steps to eliminate wordiness:
- Use strong one-word verbs instead of phrases (remove instead of take off, slice instead of cut off a piece of).
- State each idea only once in as few words as possible.
- Delete wordy phrases such as kind of and I think that.

Directions Rewrite each sentence to eliminate wordiness.
1. It seems to me that the job of babysitting is one of the hardest jobs in the whole wide world. Possible answers:
   <u>Babysitting is one of the hardest jobs.</u>

2. Little tiny kids run around like crazy some of the time, and it seems like you have to keep your eye on them every single second.
   <u>Sometimes kids run wild, and you have to watch them carefully.</u>

3. I guess taking care of kids is really kind of fun though, because they say cute things and you feel really good when they like you.
   <u>Babysitting can be fun. Kids say cute things that make you feel good.</u>

Directions Write a tip about doing a job. Write it in a sentence that is not wordy.
<u>Possible answer: Pick up as you go.</u>

Unit 2 A Day's Work   Writer's Craft **7B**

▲ **Writing Transparency** 7B

DAY 3 Prewrite and Draft

READ THE WRITING PROMPT

on page 193 in the Student Edition.

A Day's Work *describes one rule for living and getting along with others.*

Think about rules for getting along with family members, friends, or neighbors.

Now write the rules as commands.

Writing Test Tips

- List what actions are most important in getting along with others.
- Add interesting and useful details to each main idea.
- Use a command with a strong verb to describe each rule.

GETTING STARTED Students can do any of the following:

- Take notes about situations that cause people to fight or argue. Then recall how they resolve conflicts.
- Pick the topic—family, friends, or neighbors—and brainstorm ideas for getting along with those people.
- Consider both *do's* and *don'ts* in keeping the peace with others.

DAY 4 Draft and Revise

EDITING/REVISING CHECKLIST

☑ Are unnecessary words included?

☑ Does each rule describe a different idea related to the topic?

☑ Is each rule in the form of a command with a strong verb?

☑ Are words ending in *-le* spelled correctly?

See *The Grammar and Writing Book,* pp. 86–91.

Revising Tips

Sentences

- Make sure sentences present clear directions and are not wordy.
- Use a subject and a verb in each sentence. (The subject of a command is *you* but is not usually stated.)
- Consider using compound as well as simple sentences.

PUBLISHING Students can create comic strips to illustrate their rules and display them together. Some students may wish to revise their work later.

ASSESSMENT Use the scoring rubric to evaluate students' work.

DAY 5 Connect to Unit Writing

	How-to Report
Week 1	Summary 173g–173h
Week 2	Rules 197g–197h
Week 3	Problem/Solution 223g–223h
Week 4	Feature Story 249g–249h
Week 5	Explanatory Paragraph 271g–271h

PREVIEW THE UNIT PROMPT

Think of something you learned or figured out how to do that involves a few simple steps. Write the steps in a how-to report. Make sure you provide all the necessary information.

APPLY

- A how-to report explains the steps for making or doing something.
- Make sure the how-to report is clear and to the point, with no extra words.

Writing Trait Rubric

	4	3	2	1
Sentences	Clear, interesting, unique sentences; excellent variety of sentence structure	Clear sentences; variety of sentence structure	Some sentences clear; limited variety of sentence structure	Most sentences unclear; no variety of sentence structure
	Rules stated as strong commands with effective verbs	Rules stated as commands beginning with action words	Rules sometimes stated as commands	Rules not stated as commands

AFTER READING

OBJECTIVES

- Use word parts to decode words with syllable pattern C+*le*.
- Review syllable patterns V/CV, VC/V.
- Blend and read words that contain the syllable pattern C+*le* and VCV words.
- Apply decoding strategies: blend longer words.

Generalization

Generalization If a word ends in a consonant plus -*le*, those three letters usually make up the last syllable of the word.

Support Phonics Many languages do not have the schwa sound, so English language learners may have difficulty pronouncing and spelling the unstressed syllable in words such as *table* and *apple*. Provide additional practice with such words.

See the Phonics Transition Lessons in the ELL and Transition Handbook

---

Syllables C + *le*

Directions Write the two syllables that make up each word on the lines.

1.	gig	+	gle	=	giggle
2.	mid	+	dle	=	middle
3.	ti	+	tle	=	title
4.	nee	+	dle	=	needle
5.	mar	+	ble	=	marble
6.	ea	+	gle	=	eagle
7.	bub	+	ble	=	bubble
8.	sad	+	dle	=	saddle
9.	can	+	dle	=	candle
10.	tur	+	tle	=	turtle

Directions Choose the word in the box that matches each picture. Write the word on the line. Then draw a line to divide it into its syllables.

| table | poodle | puzzle | rattle | cattle |

11.	cat/tle
12.	poo/dle
13.	ta/ble
14.	rat/tle
15.	puz/zle

Home Activity Your child wrote words that end with the final syllable sound heard in *handle*. Help your child make a list of ten more words that end with -le (such as *little, juggle,* and *nibble*). Work with your child to write a silly poem using some of the -le words from your child's list and from the page above.

▲ **Practice Book 1** p. 69

Syllable Pattern C+*le*

TEACH

Remind students that they have already learned some common syllable patterns. Then write the words *bottle* and *candle.*

- Say *bottle* aloud; then repeat it slowly, with a brief pause between syllables: bot/tle.

- Between which two letters do we divide the word? (between the first *t* and second *t*)

 MODEL When I read the word *candle,* the first thing I notice is a word part I have seen in many words: *le.* I see two vowels, and I will probably hear two syllables. The first syllable is *can,* and the last syllable is *dle.* When a word ends in *le,* the consonant that comes before *le* must be part of the last syllable.

Model blending *candle.* Then have students blend the word with you.

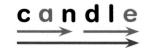

PRACTICE AND ASSESS

DECODE LONGER WORDS Write these words, omitting the slashes. Have students read the words and then draw a line between the two syllables.

bun/dle   ta/ble   cud/dle   strug/gle

whis/tle   cra/dle   a/ble   sim/ple

READ WORDS IN CONTEXT Write these sentences. Have individuals read them, point out words with the syllable pattern C+*le,* and divide the words into syllables. Target words are underlined.

We used a <u>la/dle</u> to scoop out the <u>lit/tle</u> pumpkin seeds.

I grabbed the <u>han/dle</u> to pick up the pitcher from the <u>ta/ble</u>.

We walked around the big <u>pud/dle</u> in the <u>mid/dle</u> of the sidewalk.

To assess, observe how students divide the words.

Review Word Parts

REVIEW SYLLABLE PATTERNS V/CV, VC/V

CONNECT Write this word: *melon*

- We studied the syllable patterns V/CV, VC/V.
- Read the word to yourself. Raise your hand when you know where the word should be divided. *(mel/on)*
- Is the vowel in the first syllable long or short? **(short)**

Continue in the same way with the word *cozy*. *(co/zy,* long)

PRACTICE AND ASSESS

DECODE LONGER WORDS Have individuals read the following words. Provide help blending the words as needed.

liver	rebate	gravel	risen
toxic	atom	axis	cedar
radar	motor	habit	colon

READ WORDS IN CONTEXT Have students read these sentences and divide the underlined words into syllables.

We must <u>fin/ish</u> this lesson.

<u>Phon/ics</u> helps us read words.

I pulled the <u>cov/ers</u> <u>o/ver</u> my head and fell asleep.

The <u>gro/cer</u> put our things in a bag.

To assess, have students do a word hunt for other words with the V/CV and VC/V syllable patterns. They can look in newspapers, magazines, books, or any other available reading materials.

Generalization

Generalization When a word or a syllable ends with a single vowel, the vowel sound is usually long. When it ends with a consonant, the vowel sound is usually short.

Vocabulary TiP

You may wish to explain the meanings of these words.

rebate	a partial refund
gravel	small stones
axis	a line through the center of an object

Spelling & Phonics Words Ending in -le

OBJECTIVE

● Spell words that end in -le.

Generalization

Connect to Phonics The final syllable /əl/ is often spelled -le: handle, trouble.

Spelling Words

1. handle
2. trouble
3. simple
4. people
5. middle
6. table
7. little*
8. gentle
9. poodle*
10. pickle
11. noodle
12. saddle
13. juggle
14. uncle
15. riddle

Challenge Words

16. example
17. throttle
18. obstacle
19. miracle
20. muscle

*Words from the selection

ELL

Spelling/Phonics Support See the ELL and Transition Handbook for spelling support.

PRETEST

Use the Dictation Sentences from Day 5 to administer the pretest. Read the word, read the sentence, and then read the word again. Guide students in self-correcting their pretests and correcting any misspellings.

Monitor Progress

Spelling

If... students misspell more than 4 pretest words,	then... use words 1–8 for Strategic Intervention.
If... students misspell 1–4 pretest words,	then... use words 1–15 for On-Level practice.
If... students correctly spell all pretest words,	then... use words 1–20 for Advanced Learners.

HOMEWORK Spelling Practice Book p. 25

Words Ending in -le

Generalization The final syllable /əl/ is often spelled -le: **handle**, **trouble**.

Word Sort Sort the list words by words you know how to spell and words you are learning to spell. Write every word.

words I know how to spell	words I am learning how to spell
1. Answers will vary.	9. Answers will vary.
2. ___	10. ___
3. ___	11. ___
4. ___	12. ___
5. ___	13. ___
6. ___	14. ___
7. ___	15. ___
8. ___	

Spelling Words
1. handle
2. trouble
3. simple
4. people
5. middle
6. table
7. little
8. gentle
9. poodle
10. pickle
11. noodle
12. saddle
13. juggle
14. uncle
15. riddle

Challenge Words
16. example
17. throttle
18. obstacle
19. miracle
20. muscle

Challenge Words

words I know how to spell	words I am learning how to spell
16. Answers will vary.	18. Answers will vary.
17. ___	19. ___
	20. ___

Home Activity Your child is learning to spell words that end in -le. To practice at home, have your child look at the word, pronounce it, spell it with eyes closed, and then write it.

▲ **Spelling Practice Book** p. 25

TEACH

The /əl/ sound at the end of a word is often spelled -le. Write the spelling words on the board. Ask students what all the words have in common. They should answer that all the words end in -le. Have students say several words out loud and guide them to identify the /əl/ sound in the final syllable of each word.

handle
trouble
simple

FIND THE PATTERN Ask students to come up with other words that end in -le and have the /əl/ sound. Provide a hint by suggesting they think of words that rhyme with the spelling words.

HOMEWORK Spelling Practice Book, p. 26

Words Ending in -le

Spelling Words

handle	trouble	simple	people	middle
table	little	gentle	poodle	pickle
noodle	saddle	juggle	uncle	riddle

Missing Words Write the missing list word.

1. If you tease the dog, you will get in __trouble__ .
2. My uncle bought a new leather __saddle__ for his horse.
3. Would you like a dill __pickle__ on your sandwich?
4. Please set the vase in the __middle__ of the table.
5. She bought some dog shampoo for her __poodle__ .
6. Mom makes chicken __noodle__ soup for me when I am sick.
7. Have you heard the __riddle__ about a chicken crossing the road?
8. The __handle__ on Billy's lunchbox was broken.
9. The clown could __juggle__ five balls at a time.
10. I visited my aunt and __uncle__ last summer.
11. One of my jobs at home is setting the __table__ before dinner.
12. How many __people__ came to the soccer game?

Antonyms Write the list word that means the opposite.

13. big __little__
14. difficult __simple__
15. rough __gentle__

Home Activity Your child wrote words that end in -le. If your child is confident with the list words, have him or her try to use two rhyming list words in a sentence.

▲ **Spelling Practice Book** p. 26

DAY 3 — Connect to Writing

WRITE A LIST

Have students write a list using at least three spelling words. The topic could be a shopping list, a list of things to do, or a list of favorite things.

Frequently Misspelled Words

little   *people*

These words are difficult for third-graders to spell because the /əl/ sound is not spelled like it sounds. Alert students to these frequently misspelled words.

HOMEWORK Spelling Practice Book, p. 27

Words Ending in -le

Proofread a Biography Circle four spelling mistakes in the biography Ned wrote about his uncle. Write the words correctly. Add a comma to the compound sentence.

When my uncle came to America, he had very little money. He had to juggle two jobs to keep food on the table. Some kind people helped him and he never complained about having more trouble than he could handle.

1. uncle   2. juggle
3. people   4. handle

Spelling Words
handle, trouble, simple, people, middle, table, little, gentle, poodle, pickle, noodle, saddle, juggle, uncle, riddle

Proofread Words Circle the word that is spelled correctly. Write the word.

5. (simple) simpel — 5. simple
6. (middle) midle — 6. middle
7. gentol (gentle) — 7. gentle
8. (poodle) poodel — 8. poodle
9. (riddle) ridle — 9. riddle
10. noodel (noodle) — 10. noodle
11. pikle (pickle) — 11. pickle
12. (saddle) saddel — 12. saddle

Frequently Misspelled Words: little, people

▲ **Spelling Practice Book** p. 27

DAY 4 — Review

REVIEW WORDS ENDING IN -le

Have students work in pairs. Ask one partner to say each spelling word aloud. The other partner should spell the word correctly, either by spelling it out loud or writing it on a piece of paper.

Spelling Strategy
Spelling Schwas

The /əl/ sound can be spelled in different ways. At the end of a word, *-le* is a common spelling of this sound.

HOMEWORK Spelling Practice Book, p. 28

Words Ending in -le

Spelling Words: handle, table, noodle, trouble, little, saddle, simple, gentle, juggle, people, poodle, uncle, middle, pickle, riddle

Crossword Puzzle Write list words in the puzzle.

Across
3. cucumber in vinegar
6. a piece of furniture
7. halfway between
8. male relative

Down
1. problems
2. kind
3. a type of dog
4. easy
5. more than one person

Finish the Phrase Write the list word that completes each expression.
9. car door ____ — 9. handle
10. horse's ____ — 10. saddle
11. ____ soup — 11. noodle
12. little by ____ — 12. little

noodle, little, saddle, handle

▲ **Spelling Practice Book** p. 28

DAY 5 — Posttest

DICTATION SENTENCES

1. Handle that box with care!
2. My brother gets into trouble a lot.
3. My sister can spell simple words.
4. Many people live in this town.
5. Joe sits in the middle of the room.
6. Please set the table.
7. Did you see the little wagon?
8. Be gentle with the new kittens.
9. Billy has a pet poodle.
10. May I have a pickle, please?
11. Mom made noodle soup for me when I was sick.
12. Put the saddle on the horse.
13. I can juggle three balls.
14. Uncle Rob is coming to visit.
15. Tell me a riddle.

CHALLENGE

16. Red is an example of a color.
17. Pull back the throttle of the race car.
18. There is an obstacle on the road.
19. If he passes the test, it will be a miracle.
20. The heart is a muscle.

OBJECTIVES

- Formulate an inquiry question that is connected to this week's lesson focus.
- Effectively and efficiently find, evaluate, and communicate information related to an inquiry question using electronic sources.

New Literacies

Day 1	Identify Questions
Day 2	Navigate/Search
Day 3	Analyze
Day 4	Synthesize
Day 5	Communicate

NEW LITERACIES

Internet Inquiry Activity

EXPLORE MAKING GOOD CHOICES

Use the following 5-day plan to help students conduct this week's Internet inquiry activity on making good choices. Remind students to follow classroom rules when using the Internet.

DAY 1

Identify Questions Discuss the topic, making good choices. Brainstorm ideas for specific inquiry questions about making good choices and deciding right from wrong. For example, students might want to find out how to compare options and weigh consequences when making decisions. Have students work individually, in pairs, or in small groups to write an inquiry question they want to answer.

DAY 2

Navigate/Search Explain how to read a Web address and the useful information found in the address. Tell students that the term URL stands for Uniform Resource Locator, an address for documents found on the Web. Knowing how to read a Web address can help students determine if a site will contain relevant information.

DAY 3

Analyze Have students explore and analyze information from the Web sites they identified on Day 2. Tell them to scan and analyze information for credibility, reliability, and usefulness. They can print out and then highlight relevant information.

DAY 4

Synthesize Have students synthesize information from Day 3. Remind them that when they synthesize, they pull together the relevant ideas from different sources to develop answers to their inquiry questions.

DAY 5

Communicate Have students share their inquiry results. They can use a word processing program to create a short article for the school newspaper or class newsletter about making good choices.

RESEARCH/STUDY SKILLS

Procedures and Instructions

OBJECTIVES
- Review concepts related to procedures and instructions.
- Follow a set of instructions.

TEACH

Invite students to tell about a time when they followed a set of directions to do or make something. After a few students have shared their stories, guide them to see that instructions tell what to do in order. Discuss these ideas:

- Instructions are often numbered to tell the order in which things should be done.
- It is helpful to read through the entire set of directions before doing anything. This gives the reader an overall idea of the task.
- Read each individual step and do what it says before going on to the next step.
- As you follow each step, remember what the overall task is.
- Carefully study diagrams and illustrations included with the instructions.

Give students a piece of paper. Tell them that they are going to pretend to apply for a job. Students will follow your instructions to write a few things about themselves. Read the instructions below.

1. Number your paper from 1 to 5.

2. Write your name next to number 1.

3. For number 2, write your address.

4. Write your telephone number next to number 3.

5. On line 4, list three or four things that you like to do.

6. Write four words that describe you next to number 5.

ASSESS

To assess students' work, have them exchange papers with a partner. Read through the directions again and have students check the work done. The information for each number should be complete and in the correct order.

For more practice or to assess students, use Practice Book 3.1, p. 70.

Procedures and Instructions

Procedures and **instructions** tell the reader how to do or make something.

Directions Use the instructions for planting a shrub to answer the questions.

Planting a Shrub
1. Use a shovel to dig a hole. The hole should be as deep as the shrub container and twice as wide.
2. Add peat moss to the soil you dig out.
3. Put the shrub (still in the container) in the hole. The top of the container should match the ground.
4. Remove the shrub from the container and place the shrub in the hole.
5. Fill the hole with soil and peat moss.
6. Water the planted shrub thoroughly.

1. What tool do you need to plant the shrub?
   shovel
2. What do you do with the soil dug from the hole?
   Possible responses: place it beside the hole, add peat moss
3. Why do you put the shrub in the hole when it is still in the container?
   Possible response: to make sure the hole is the right depth
4. What do you do after removing the shrub from the container?
   place the shrub in the hole
5. What is the last thing you do?
   water the shrub thoroughly

School + Home Home Activity Your child answered questions about procedures and instructions. Look through an instruction manual you have and discuss what kind of information it gives the reader.

▲ **Practice Book 3.1** p. 70

Assessment Checkpoints *for the Week*

Selection Assessment

Use pp. 25–28 of Selection Tests to check:

☑ **Selection Understanding**

☑ **Comprehension Skill** *Character*

☑ **Selection Vocabulary**

excitement	shivered
gardener	shocked
motioned	slammed
sadness	

Leveled Assessment

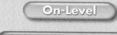
Strategic Intervention
Advanced

Use pp. 37–42 of Fresh Reads for Differentiated Test Practice to check:

☑ **Comprehension Skill** *Character*

☑ **REVIEW** **Comprehension Skill** *Realism and Fantasy*

☑ **Fluency** *Words Correct Per Minute*

Managing Assessment

Use Assessment Handbook for:

☑ **Observation Checklists**

☑ **Record-Keeping Forms**

☑ **Portfolio Assessment**

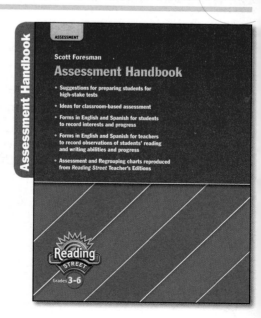

Illinois

Planning Guide for Performance Descriptors

Prudy's Problem and How She Solved It

Reading Street Teacher's Edition pages | **Grade 3 English Language Arts Performance Descriptors**

Oral Language

Speaking/Listening Build Concept Vocabulary: 198l, 209, 217, 223c
Read Aloud: 198m

1A.Stage C.3. Discuss the meanings of new words encountered in independent and group activities.
1B.Stage C.13. Read age-appropriate material aloud with fluency and accuracy.
2A.Stage C.5. Define unfamiliar vocabulary.

Word Work

Compound Words: 223i, 223k–223l

1A.Stage C.5. Use a variety of decoding strategies (e.g., phonics, word patterns, structural analysis, context clues) to recognize new words when reading age-appropriate material.

Reading

Comprehension Main Idea: 198–199, 202–217, 223b
Monitor and Fix Up: 198–199, 202–217
Vocabulary Lesson Vocabulary: 200b, 209, 217, 220
Dictionary/Glossary: 200–201, 211, 223c
Fluency Model Reading with Expression/ Intonation: 198l–198m, 223a
Choral Reading: 223a
Self-Selected Reading: LR19–27, TR16–17
Literature Genre—Fantasy: 202
Reader Response: 218

1A.Stage C.8. Use a variety of resources (e.g., dictionaries, thesauruses, indices, glossaries, internet, interviews, available technology) to clarify meanings of unfamiliar words.
1B.Stage C.9. Continuously check and clarify for understanding (e.g., reread, read ahead, use visual and context clues) during reading.
1B.Stage C.13. Read age-appropriate material aloud with fluency and accuracy.
1C.Stage C.2. Use information to generate and respond to questions that reflect higher level thinking skills (e.g., analyzing, synthesizing, inferring, evaluating).
2A.Stage C.5. Define unfamiliar vocabulary.
2A.Stage C.7. Classify major types of fiction (e.g., tall tale, fairy tale, fable).
4A.Stage C.2. Distinguish among different kinds of information (e.g., fact, opinion, detail, main idea, fantasy, reality).

Language Arts

Writing Problem Solving: 223g–223h
Six-Trait Writing Organization/Paragraphs: 219, 223g–223h
Grammar, Usage, and Mechanics Irregular Plural Nouns: 223e–223f
Research/Study Magazine/Periodical: 223n
Technology New Literacies: 223m

3A.Stage C.9. Demonstrate appropriate use of the various parts of speech (e.g., nouns, pronouns, verbs).
3B.Stage C.3. Use stages of the writing process (e.g., prewriting, drafting, revising, editing, publishing) to develop paragraphs with focus, organization, elaboration, and integration.
5C.Stage C.1. Access and use information from a variety of sources.

Unit Skills

Writing How-To Report: WA2–9
Poetry: 272–275
Project/Wrap-Up: 276–277

3B.Stage C.4. Organize around a structure (e.g., paragraph, essay) appropriate to purpose, audience, and context.
3C.Stage C.3. Experiment with different forms of creative writing (e.g., song, poetry, short fiction, play).

This Week's Leveled Readers

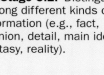
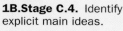

Content-Area Illinois Performance Descriptors in This Lesson

Social Studies

14A.Stage C.1. Distinguish between different kinds of rules and responsibilities as applied in the home, school, and community.

14A.Stage C.3. Explain some reasons for having rules and laws governing the lives of people.

14D.Stage C.1. Explain what is meant by the idea of "the common good of the people."

14D.Stage C.2. Describe a situation wherein the common good supercedes the interests of individuals.

15A.Stage C.2. Analyze the advantages and disadvantages of distributing a good or service in different ways.

15B.Stage C.2. Identify a consumer choice made by families and explain why a choice had to be made.

18C.Stage C.1. Describe the concept of conflict.

18C.Stage C.2. Describe the concept of cooperation.

18C.Stage C.4. Define division of labor.

Math

6C.Stage C.1. Develop and use strategies (i.e. rounding) to estimate the results of whole-number computations and to judge the reasonableness of such results.

6C.Stage C.2. Select appropriate methods and tools for computing with whole numbers from mental computation, estimation, calculators, and paper/pencil according to the context and nature of the computation and use of the selected method or tool.

6C.Stage C.3. Determine whether exact answers or estimates are appropriate for solutions to problems.

Science

12B.Stage C.2. Apply scientific inquiries or technological designs to examine the interdependence of organisms in ecosystems: describing the interaction between living and non-living factors in an ecosystem.

Illinois!

A FAMOUS ILLINOISAN
Mary Todd Lincoln

Mary Todd Lincoln (1818–1882) was the first lady of the United States from 1861 to 1865. She was known as an intelligent, witty person who suffered many tragedies in her life. Mary Todd moved to Springfield when she was twenty-one to live with her sister. There she met Abraham Lincoln, and they married in 1842. They had four sons, only one of whom lived to adulthood.

Students can . . .
Learn more about the first ladies of the United States and write about one of them.

A SPECIAL ILLINOIS PLACE
Chicago Mercantile Exchange

The Chicago Mercantile Exchange was founded in 1898 as the Chicago Butter and Egg Board. It became the Chicago Mercantile Exchange in 1919. At first, futures were traded only on agricultural products, but many other products have been added over the years. In 1961 the first futures contract based on frozen stored meats was introduced. The Exchange established after-hours trading in 1992.

Students can . . .
Learn more about the Chicago Mercantile Exchange and make a list of the products that are traded there.

ILLINOIS FUN FACTS
Did You Know?

• In 1979 Jane Byrne became the first female mayor of Chicago. She ran for re-election in 1983 but lost to Harold Washington, the first African American mayor of Chicago.

• Most of the rivers and streams in Illinois drain into the Mississippi River or the Ohio River.

• The Mississippi River forms the western boundary of Illinois.

Students can . . .
Find the Mississippi River on an outline map and make a list of all the states that border the river or through which the river passes.

Unit 2
Smart Solutions

CONCEPT QUESTION
What are smart ways that problems are solved?

Week 1
How have animals adapted to solve the problems of their environment?

Week 2
When is a solution the wrong solution?

Week 3
How can you get ideas to solve a problem?

Week 4
When are respect and understanding important in solving a problem?

Week 5
When you find yourself in a new place, what problems might you meet?

Week 3

EXPAND THE CONCEPT
How can you get ideas to solve a problem?

CONNECT THE CONCEPT

▶ **Build Background**
bulky, phonograph, portable

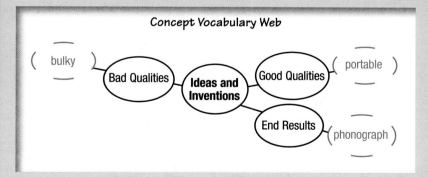

Concept Vocabulary Web

▶ **Social Studies Content**
Costs/Benefits of Personal Choices, Civic Life, Helping Others

▶ **Writing**
Problem Solution Paragraph

▶ **Internet Inquiry**
Organizing Collections

Preview Your Week

How can you get ideas to solve a problem?

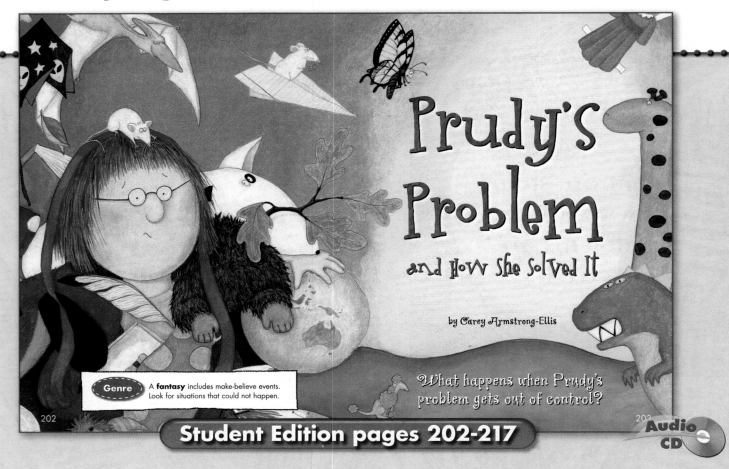

Genre — A **fantasy** includes make-believe events. Look for situations that could not happen.

Prudy's Problem
and How She Solved It

by Carey Armstrong-Ellis

What happens when Prudy's problem gets out of control?

202

Student Edition pages 202–217

Audio CD

Genre	Fantasy
Vocabulary Strategy	Dictionary
Comprehension Skill	Main Idea
Comprehension Strategy	Monitor and Fix Up

Paired Selection

SOCIAL STUDIES

Reading Across Texts
Compare and Contrast Real and Fictional Museums

Genre
Interview

Text Features
Photos

Social Studies in Reading

Overview
...re
...n interview is similar to a conversation.

- An interview usually is written in a question-and-answer format.
- An interview can provide interesting information about a topic.

Text Features
- Photos often illustrate an interview and present a glimpse of the person being interviewed.
- Photos can also provide additional information.

Link to Social Studies
Learn about a museum in your city or state. What do you want to know? Write some questions that you would ask in an interview.

MEETING THE CHALLENGE OF COLLECTING

BY LISA KLOBUCHAR

Dr. Gary Feinman

The Field Museum of Natural History, in Chicago, is one of the world's biggest museums. Dr. Gary Feinman is the head of the Field Museum's anthropology department. Anthropology is the study of how people live. Anthropologists look at how people fit in with the places they live. They study how different groups of people are alike and different. Dr. Feinman explains how the museum puts together its anthropology collections. He also talks about some of the challenges of putting these collections on display and how the museum meets these challenges.

LISA KLOBUCHAR: What kinds of objects does the museum's anthropology department collect?

DR. FEINMAN: We have everything from tapestries to blow guns, from pottery to stone sculpture, from paintings to masks.

LK: That's quite a variety! How many objects does the museum own in all?

DR. F: Our department alone has over one million objects.

LK: Wow! How do you manage to display that many objects?

DR. F: Only a small part of the museum's anthropology collection is on display. We put out about one or two objects out of every one hundred. We don't have the space to display them all.

Incan pottery from Peru

 Monitor and Fix Up — Summarize the facts you've read so far.

220

Student Edition pages 220–223

Audio CD

198b   Smart Solutions • Week 3

Read It
ONLINE
PearsonSuccessNet.com

• Student Edition
• Leveled Readers

Leveled Readers

Skill Main Idea

Strategy Monitor and Fix Up

Lesson Vocabulary

Metal Detector Detective
by Linda Lott
illustrated by Nicole Wong

Below-Level

Katy's Last-Minute Book Report
by Sasha Griffin

On-Level

Collecting Dreams
by Joanna Korba
illustrated by Bradley Clark

Advanced

ELL Reader

· Concept Vocabulary
· Text Support
· Language Enrichment

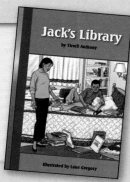

Jack's Library
by Tirrell Anthony

Illustrated by Lane Gregory

Time for SOCIAL STUDIES

Integrate Social Studies Standards

• **Helping Others**

• **Costs/Benefits of Personal Choices**

• **Civic Life**

✓ **Read**

Prudy's Problem pp. 202–217

"Meeting the Challenge of Collecting" pp. 220–223

Leveled Readers

Below-Level | **On-Level** | **Advanced**
• Support Concepts | • Develop Concepts | • Extend Concepts

ELL Reader

Jack's Library

✓ **Build**
Concept Vocabulary
Ideas and Inventions,
pp. 198l–198m

✓ **Teach**
Social Studies Concepts
Choices, p. 205
Civic Life, p. 207
Careers, p. 221

✓ **Explore**
Social Studies Center
Study Community Resources,
p. 198k

Prudy's Problem ⟨ **198c** ⟩

Weekly Plan

READING

45–90 minutes

TARGET SKILLS OF THE WEEK

🎯 **Comprehension Skill**
Main Idea

🎯 **Comprehension Strategy**
Monitor and Fix Up

🎯 **Vocabulary Strategy**
Dictionary

LANGUAGE ARTS

30–60 minutes

Trait of the Week

Organization/Paragraphs

DAY 1
PAGES 198l–200b, 223a, 223e–223h, 223k–223m

Oral Language

QUESTION OF THE WEEK *How can you get ideas to solve a problem?*

Read Aloud: "The Rampanion," 198m
Build Concepts, 198l

Comprehension/Vocabulary

Comprehension Skill/Strategy Lesson, 198–199
🎯 Main Idea **T**
🎯 Monitor and Fix Up
Build Background, 200a
Introduce Lesson Vocabulary, 200b
collection, enormous, realize, scattered, shiny, strain **T**

Read Leveled Readers

Grouping Options 198f–198g

Fluency

Model Expression/Intonation, 198l–198m, 223a

Grammar, 223e
Introduce Irregular Plural Nouns **T**

Writing Workshop, 223g
Introduce Problem-Solution
Model the Trait of the Week: Organization/
Paragraphs

Spelling, 223k
Pretest for Compound Words

Internet Inquiry, 223m
Identify Questions

DAY 2
PAGES 200–209, 223a, 223e–223i, 223k–223m

Oral Language

QUESTION OF THE DAY *How do you know when you have a problem?*

Word Work

Phonics Lesson, 223i
Compound Words

Comprehension/Vocabulary

Vocabulary Strategy Lesson, 200–201
🎯 Dictionary **T**

Read *Prudy's Problem and How She Solved It,* 202–209

Grouping Options 198f–198g

🎯 Main Idea and Details **T**
🎯 Monitor and Fix Up
REVIEW Character **T**
Develop Vocabulary

Fluency

Choral Reading, 223a

Grammar, 223e
Develop Irregular Plural Nouns **T**

Writing Workshop, 223g
Improve Writing: Write Clearly

Spelling, 223k
Teach the Generalization

Internet Inquiry, 223m
Navigate/Search

DAILY WRITING ACTIVITIES

Day 1 Write to Read, 198

Day 2 Words to Write, 201
Strategy Response Log, 202, 209

DAILY SOCIAL STUDIES CONNECTIONS

Day 1 Ideas and Inventions Concept Web, 198l

Day 2 Time for Social Studies: Choices, 205; Civic Life, 207; Revisit the Ideas and Inventions Concept Web, 209

DAILY SUCCESS PREDICTORS
for Adequate Yearly Progress

Monitor Progress and Corrective Feedback

Vocabulary   Check Vocabulary, *198l*

Grouping Options for Differentiated Instruction

Turn the page for the small group lesson plan.

DAY 3
PAGES 210–219, 223a, 223e–223h, 223k–223m

Oral Language

QUESTION OF THE DAY *How does Prudy solve her problem?*

Comprehension/Vocabulary

Read *Prudy's Problem and How She Solved It,* 210–218

Grouping Options 198f–198g

- Main Idea and Details **T**
- Monitor and Fix Up
- Dictionary **T**
- REVIEW Character

Develop Vocabulary

Reader Response

Selection Test

Fluency

Model Expression/Intonation, 223a

Grammar, 223f
Apply Irregular Plural Nouns in Writing **T**

Writing Workshop, 219, 223h
Write Now
Prewrite and Draft

Spelling, 223l
Connect Spelling to Writing

Internet Inquiry, 223m
Analyze Sources

Day 3 Strategy Response Log, 216
Look Back and Write, 218

Day 3 Revisit the Ideas and Inventions Concept Web, 217

DAY 4
PAGES 220–223a, 223e–223h, 223j–223m

Oral Language

QUESTION OF THE DAY *How does correcting a mistake sometimes lead to great inventions?*

Word Work

Phonics Lesson, 223j
REVIEW Syllables C + *le* **T**

Comprehension/Vocabulary

Read "Meeting the Challenge of Collecting," 220–223

Grouping Options 198f–198g

Interview/Text Features
Reading Across Texts
Content-Area Vocabulary

Fluency

Partner Reading, 223a

Grammar, 223f
Practice Irregular Plural Nouns for Standardized Tests **T**

Writing Workshop, 223h
Draft, Revise, and Publish

Spelling, 223l
Provide a Strategy

Internet Inquiry, 223m
Synthesize Information

Day 4 Writing Across Texts, 223

Day 4 Time for Social Studies: Careers, 221

DAY 5
PAGES 223a–223h, 223k–223n

Oral Language

QUESTION OF THE WEEK *To wrap up the week, revisit the Day 1 question.*
Build Concept Vocabulary, 223c

Fluency

Read Leveled Readers

Grouping Options 198f–198g

Assess Reading Rate, 223a

Comprehension/Vocabulary

- Reteach Main Idea, 223b **T**
- Onomatopoeia, 223b
- Review Dictionary, 223c **T**

Speaking and Listening, 223d
Speak with a Purpose
Listen to a Broadcast

Grammar, 223f
Cumulative Review

Writing Workshop, 223h
Connect to Unit Writing

Spelling, 223l
Posttest for Compound Words

Internet Inquiry, 223m
Communicate Results

Research/Study Skills, 223n
Magazine/Periodical

Day 5 Onomatopoeia, 223b

Day 5 Revisit the Ideas and Inventions Concept Web, 223c

KEY = Target Skill **T** = Tested Skill

Check Retelling, *219*

Check Fluency WCPM, *223a*

Check Vocabulary, *223c*

SUCCESS PREDICTOR

Small Group Plan for Differentiated Instruction

Daily Plan AT A GLANCE

Reading
Whole Group
- Oral Language
- Phonics
- Comprehension/Vocabulary

Group Time
Differentiated Instruction

Meet with small groups to provide:
- Skill Support
- Reading Support
- Fluency Practice

Read

This week's lessons for daily group time can be found behind the Differentiated Instruction (DI) tab on pp. DI·22–DI·31.

Whole Group
- Fluency

Language Arts
- Grammar
- Writing
- Spelling
- Research/Inquiry
- Speaking/Listening/Viewing

Use *My Sidewalks on Reading Street* for Tier III intensive reading intervention.

DAY 1

On-Level	Strategic Intervention	Advanced
Teacher-Led Page DI·23	**Teacher-Led** Page DI·22	**Teacher-Led** Page DI·23
• Develop Concept Vocabulary	• Preteach Compound Words	• **Read** Advanced Reader *Collecting Dreams*
• **Read** On-Level Reader *Katy's Last-Minute Book Report*	• **Read** Decodable Reader 8	• Independent Extension Activity
	• **Read** Below-Level Reader *Metal Detector Detective*	

ℹ Independent Activities
While you meet with small groups, have the rest of the class...
- Visit the Reading/Library Center
- Listen to the Background Building Audio
- Finish Write to Read, p. 198
- Complete Practice Book 3.1 pp. 73–74
- Visit Cross-Curricular Centers

DAY 2

On-Level	Strategic Intervention	Advanced
Teacher-Led Pages 204–209	**Teacher-Led** Page DI·24	**Teacher-Led** Page DI·25
• **Read** *Prudy's Problem*	• Practice Lesson Vocabulary	• Extend Vocabulary
	• Read Multisyllabic Words	• **Read** *Prudy's Problem*
	• **Read** or Listen to *Prudy's Problem*	

ℹ Independent Activities
While you meet with small groups, have the rest of the class...
- Visit the Reading/Library Center
- Listen to the AudioText for *Prudy's Problem*
- Finish Words to Write, p. 201
- Complete Practice Book 3.1 pp. 75–76, 79
- Write in their Strategy Response Logs, pp. 202, 209
- Visit Cross-Curricular Centers
- Work on inquiry projects

DAY 3

On-Level	Strategic Intervention	Advanced
Teacher-Led Pages 210–217	**Teacher-Led** Page DI·26	**Teacher-Led** Page DI·27
• **Read** *Prudy's Problem*	• Practice Main Idea and Monitor and Fix Up	• Main Idea and Monitor and Fix Up
	• **Read** or Listen to *Prudy's Problem*	• **Read** *Prudy's Problem*

ℹ Independent Activities
While you meet with small groups, have the rest of the class...
- Visit the Reading/Library Center
- Listen to the AudioText for *Prudy's Problem*
- Write in their Strategy Response Logs, p. 216
- Finish Look Back and Write, p. 218
- Complete Practice Book 3.1 p. 77
- Visit Cross-Curricular Centers
- Work on inquiry projects

---

① Begin with whole class skill and strategy instruction.

② Meet with small groups to provide differentiated instruction.

③ Gather the whole class back together for fluency and language arts.

DAY 4

On-Level	Strategic Intervention	Advanced
Teacher-Led *Pages 220–223*	**Teacher-Led** *Page DI · 28*	**Teacher-Led** *Page DI · 29*
Read "Meeting the Challenge of Collecting"	• Practice Retelling • **Read** or Listen to "Meeting the Challenge of Collecting"	• **Read** "Meeting the Challenge of Collecting" • Genre Study

(i) Independent Activities

While you meet with small groups, have the rest of the class...

• Visit the Reading/Library Center
• Listen to the AudioText for "Meeting the Challenge of Collecting"
• Visit the Writing and Vocabulary Centers

• Finish Writing Across Texts, p. 223
• Visit Cross-Curricular Centers
• Work on inquiry projects

DAY 5

On-Level	Strategic Intervention	Advanced
Teacher-Led *Page DI · 31*	**Teacher-Led** *Page DI · 30*	**Teacher-Led** *Page DI · 31*
• **Reread** Leveled Reader *Katy's Last-Minute Book Report* Retell *Katy's Last-Minute Book Report*	• **Reread** Leveled Reader *Metal Detector Detective* • Retell *Metal Detector Detective*	• **Reread** Leveled Reader *Collecting Dreams* • Share Extension Activity

(i) Independent Activities

While you meet with small groups, have the rest of the class...

• Visit the Reading/Library Center
• Complete Practice Book 3.1 pp. 78, 80

• Visit Cross-Curricular Centers
• Work on inquiry projects

Grouping Place English language learners in the groups that correspond to their reading abilities in English.

Use the appropriate Leveled Reader or other text at students' instructional level.

TIP Send home the appropriate Multilingual Summary of the main selection on Day 1.

Take It to the NET™ ONLINE
PearsonSuccessNet.com

Jeanne Paratore
For ideas on using repeated readings for diverse groups, see the article "Using Repeated Readings to Promote Reading Success..." by J. Turpie and Scott Foresman author J. Paratore.

TEACHER TALK

Generating questions is an effective way for students to engage with and comprehend text. Teach students to ask good questions about important text information as they read.

Be sure to schedule time for students to work on the unit inquiry project, "A Book of Solutions." This week students determine if information is valid, then print or take notes on valid information.

Looking Ahead

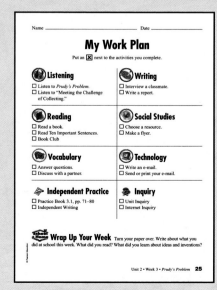

Name _____ Date _____
My Work Plan
Put an ☒ next to the activities you complete.

Listening
☐ Listen to *Prudy's Problem.*
☐ Listen to "Meeting the Challenge of Collecting."

Writing
☐ Interview a classmate.
☐ Write a report.

Reading
☐ Read a book.
☐ Read Ten Important Sentences.
☐ Book Club

Social Studies
☐ Choose a resource.
☐ Make a flyer.

Vocabulary
☐ Answer questions.
☐ Discuss with a partner.

Technology
☐ Write an e-mail.
☐ Send or print your e-mail.

Independent Practice
☐ Practice Book 3.1, pp. 71–80
☐ Independent Writing

Inquiry
☐ Unit Inquiry
☐ Internet Inquiry

Wrap Up Your Week Turn your paper over. Write about what you did at school this week. What did you read? What did you learn about ideas and inventions?

Unit 2 • Week 3 • *Prudy's Problem* **25**

▲ **Group-Time Survival Guide** p. 25, Weekly Contract

ORAL LANGUAGE

SOCIAL STUDIES

Concept Development

How can you get ideas to solve a problem?

CONCEPT VOCABULARY
bulky   phonograph   portable

BUILD

☐ **Question of the Week** Introduce and discuss the question of the week. This week students will read a variety of texts and work on projects related to the concept *ideas and inventions*. Post the question for students to refer to throughout the week. **DAY 1** *198d*

☐ **Read Aloud** Read aloud "The Rampanion." Then begin a web to build concepts and concept vocabulary related to this week's lesson and the unit theme, Smart Solutions. Introduce the concept words *bulky, phonograph,* and *portable* and have students place them on the web. Display the web for use throughout the week. **DAY 1** *198l-198m*

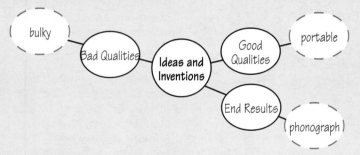

DEVELOP

☐ **Question of the Day** Use the prompts from the Weekly Plan to engage students in conversations related to this week's reading and the unit theme. **EVERY DAY** *198d-198e*

☐ **Concept Vocabulary Web** Revisit the Ideas and Inventions Concept Web and encourage students to add concept words from their reading and life experiences. **DAY 2** *209,* **DAY 3** *217*

CONNECT

☐ **Looking Back/Moving Forward** Revisit the Ideas and Inventions Concept Web and discuss how it relates to this week's lesson and the unit theme. Then make connections to next week's lesson. **DAY 5** *223c*

CHECK

☐ **Concept Vocabulary Web** Use the Ideas and Inventions Concept Web to check students' understanding of the concept vocabulary words *bulky, phonograph,* and *portable.* **DAY 1** *198l,* **DAY 5** *223c*

VOCABULARY

STRATEGY STRATEGY DICTIONARY
A dictionary is a book that tells you the meanings of words and how to say them correctly. You can always use a dictionary to find out the meaning of a word you don't know.

LESSON VOCABULARY
collection   scattered
enormous   shiny
realize   strain

TEACH

☐ **Words to Know** Give students the opportunity to tell what they already know about this week's lesson vocabulary words. Then discuss word meaning. **DAY 1** *200b*

☐ **Vocabulary Strategy Lesson** Use the vocabulary strategy lesson in the Student Edition to introduce and model this week's strategy, using a *dictionary.* **DAY 2** *200-201*

Vocabulary Strategy Lesson

PRACTICE/APPLY

☐ **Leveled Text** Read the lesson vocabulary in the context of leveled text. **DAY 1** *LR19-LR27*

☐ **Words in Context** Read the lesson vocabulary and apply using a *dictionary* in the context of *Prudy's Problem and How She Solved It.* **DAY 2** *202-209,* **DAY 3** *210-218*

Leveled Readers

☐ **Vocabulary Center** Answer questions to show knowledge of vocabulary **ANY DAY** *198j*

Main Selection—Fiction

☐ **Homework** Practice Book 3.1 pp. 74–75. **DAY 1** *200b,* **DAY 2** *201*

☐ **Word Play** Have partners use reference sources to find words that refer to museums and what is inside them. Have students write their words, along with the definitions, on folded index cards to resemble museum labels. **ANY DAY** *223c*

ASSESS

☐ **Selection Test** Use the Selection Test to determine students' understanding of the lesson vocabulary words. **DAY 3**

RETEACH/REVIEW

☐ **Reteach Lesson** If necessary, use this lesson to reteach and review using a dictionary. **DAY 5** *223c*

① Use assessment data to determine your instructional focus.

② Preview this week's instruction by strand.

③ Choose instructional activities that meet the needs of your classroom.

COMPREHENSION

SKILL MAIN IDEA   The main idea of a story is what the story is all about. Details, or little pieces of information, in the story can help you understand what the story's main idea is.

STRATEGY MONITOR AND FIX UP   To monitor means to stop occasionally, and check to be sure you understand what you're reading. Fix up means to do something if you don't understand or are confused. For example, if you're not sure what a story's main idea is, stop and ask yourself, "What are the important details in this story so far?" Summarizing the important details can help you figure out the main idea.

TEACH

❑ **Skill/Strategy Lesson** Use the skill/ strategy lesson in the Student Edition to introduce and model *main idea* and *monitor and fix up*. **DAY 1** 198-199

❑ **Extend Skills** Teach onomatopoeia. **ANY DAY** 223b

Skill/Strategy Lesson

PRACTICE/APPLY

❑ **Leveled Text** Apply *main idea* and *monitor and fix up* to leveled text. **DAY 1** LR19–LR27

❑ **Skills and Strategies in Context** Read *Prudy's Problem and How She Solved It,* using the Guiding Comprehension questions to apply *main idea* and *monitor and fix up.* **DAY 2** 202–209, **DAY 3** 210–218

Leveled Readers

❑ **Skills and Strategies in Context** Read "Meeting the Challenge of Collecting," guiding students as they apply *main idea* and *monitor and fix up.* Then have students discuss and write across texts. **DAY 4** 220–223

Main Selection—Fiction

❑ **Homework** Practice Book 3.1 pp. 73, 77, 78. **DAY 1** 199, **DAY 3** 217, **DAY 5** 223b

❑ **Fresh Reads for Differentiated Test Practice** Have students practice *main idea* with a new passage. **DAY 3**

Paired Selection—Nonfiction

ASSESS

❑ **Selection Test** Determine students' understanding of the selection and their use of *main idea.* **DAY 3**

❑ **Retell** Have students retell *Prudy's Problem and How She Solved It.* **DAY 3** 218–219

RETEACH/REVIEW

❑ **Reteach Lesson** If necessary, reteach and review *main idea.* **DAY 5** 223b

FLUENCY

SKILL EXPRESSION/INTONATION   Reading with expression means reading the words as if you were the character. Intonation means that you use different tones of voice to show surprise, happiness, or other emotions.

TEACH

❑ **Read Aloud** Model fluent reading by rereading " The Rampanion." Focus on this week's fluency skill, expression/intonation. **DAY 1** 198l–198m, 223a

PRACTICE/APPLY

❑ **Choral Reading** Read aloud selected paragraphs from *Prudy's Problem,* reading with dramatic expression and intonations. Then practice as a class, doing three choral readings. **DAY 2** 223a, **DAY 3** 223a

❑ **Partner Reading** Have partners practice reading aloud with proper expression and intonation and offering each other feedback. As students reread, monitor their progress toward their individual fluency goals. **DAY 4** 223a

❑ **Listening Center** Have students follow along with the AudioText for this week's selections. **ANY DAY** 198j

❑ **Reading/Library Center** Have students reread a selection of their choice. **ANY DAY** 198j

❑ **Fluency Coach** Have students use Fluency Coach to listen to fluent readings or practice reading on their own. **ANY DAY**

ASSESS

❑ **Check Fluency** WCPM Do a one-minute timed reading, paying special attention to this week's skill—expression/intonation. Provide feedback for each student. **DAY 5** 223a

GRAMMAR

SKILL IRREGULAR PLURAL NOUNS A plural noun names more than one person, place, or thing. Most nouns add *-s* to form the plural. An irregular plural noun has a special form for the plural. For example, the plural of *child* is *children,* not *childs.*

TEACH

☐ **Grammar Transparency 8** Use Grammar Transparency 8 to teach irregular plural nouns.
DAY 1 *223e*

Grammar Transparency 8

PRACTICE/APPLY

☐ **Develop the Concept** Review the concept of irregular plural nouns and provide guided practice. **DAY 2** *223e*

☐ **Apply to Writing** Have students review something they have written and apply what they have learned about irregular plural nouns. **DAY 3** *223f*

☐ **Test Preparation** Examine common errors in irregular plural nouns to prepare for standardized tests. **DAY 4** *223f*

☐ **Homework** Grammar and Writing Practice Book pp. 29–31.
DAY 2 *223e,* **DAY 3** *223f,* **DAY 4** *223f*

ASSESS

☐ **Cumulative Review** Use Grammar and Writing Practice Book p. 32. **DAY 5** *223f*

RETEACH/REVIEW

☐ **Daily Fix-It** Have students find and correct errors in grammar, spelling, and punctuation.
EVERY DAY *223e-223f*

☐ **The Grammar and Writing Book** Use pp. 92–95 of The Grammar and Writing Book to extend instruction for irregular plural nouns. **ANY DAY**

The Grammar and Writing Book

WRITING

ORGANIZATION/PARAGRAPHS A careful author organizes, or arranges, a main idea and supporting details in order. When an author writes about a problem and solution, for instance, he or she first describes the problem and then the solution. The writer also makes sure that the description of the problem and the description of the solution are clearly connected.

TEACH

☐ **Writing Transparency 8A** Use the model to introduce and discuss the Trait of the Week. **DAY 1** *223g*

☐ **Writing Transparency 8B** Use the transparency to show students how writing clearly can improve their writing.
DAY 2 *223g*

Writing Transparency 8A **Writing Transparency 8B**

PRACTICE/APPLY

☐ **Write Now** Examine the model on Student Edition p. 219. Then have students write their own problem-solution. **DAY 3** *219, 223h,* **DAY 4** *223h*

> **Prompt** *Prudy's Problem* explains how a girl solves a problem. Think about a problem you and your friends have. Now write a paragraph describing the problem and how to solve it.

Write Now p. 219

☐ **Writing Center** Interview a classmate and write a report about his or her collection. **ANY DAY** *198k*

ASSESS

☐ **Writing Trait Rubric** Use the rubric to evaluate students' writing. **DAY 4** *223h*

RETEACH/REVIEW

☐ **The Grammar and Writing Book** Use pp. 92–97 of The Grammar and Writing Book to extend instruction for irregular plural nouns, writing clearly, and problem-solutions. **ANY DAY**

The Grammar and Writing Book

① Use assessment data to determine your instructional focus.

② Preview this week's instruction by strand.

③ Choose instructional activities that meet the needs of your classroom.

SPELLING

GENERALIZATION COMPOUND WORDS A compound word is smaller words joined together. Keep all the letters when spelling compounds: *home + work = homework*. Two words can be joined together to make a new word. In the new word, pronunciation of the smaller words often remains the same.

TEACH

☐ **Pretest** Give the pretest for compound words. Guide students in self-correcting their pretests and correcting any misspellings. **DAY 1** *223k*

☐ **Think and Practice** Connect spelling to the phonics generalization for compound words. **DAY 2** *223k*

PRACTICE/APPLY

☐ **Connect to Writing** Have students use spelling words to write a letter. Then review frequently misspelled words: *everyone, outside, something, sometimes.* **DAY 3** *223l*

☐ **Homework** Phonics and Spelling Practice Book pp. 29–32. **EVERY DAY**

RETEACH/REVIEW

☐ **Review** Review spelling words to prepare for the posttest. Then provide students with a spelling strategy—word combinations. **DAY 4** *223l*

ASSESS

☐ **Posttest** Use dictation sentences to give the posttest for compound words. **DAY 5** *223l*

Spelling Words

1. sunglasses*
2. football
3. homework
4. haircut
5. popcorn
6. railroad
7. snowstorm
8. earring
9. scarecrow
10. blueberry
11. butterflies*
12. lawnmower
13. campground
14. sandbox
15. toothbrush*

Challenge Words

16. thumbtack
17. earthquake
18. scrapbook
19. courthouse
20. whirlpool

*Word from the selection

PHONICS

SKILL COMPOUND WORDS A compound word is a word made up of two or more shorter words.

TEACH

☐ **Phonics Lesson** Model how to read compound words. Then have students practice by decoding longer words and reading words in context. **DAY 2** *223i*

PRACTICE/APPLY

☐ **Homework** Practice Book 3.1, p. 79. **DAY 2** *223i*

RETEACH/REVIEW

☐ **Review Word Parts** Review how to read words with the syllable pattern C + *le*. Then have student practice by decoding longer words and reading words in context. **DAY 4** *223j*

RESEARCH AND INQUIRY

☐ **Internet Inquiry** Have students conduct an Internet inquiry on organizing collections. **EVERY DAY** *223m*

☐ **Magazine/Periodical** Review concepts and features related to magazines, including topic, table of contents, article titles, photographs, and captions. In pairs, have students read children's magazine articles and summarize them for the rest of the class. **DAY 5** *223n*

☐ **Unit Inquiry** Allow time for students to determine whether or not the information they located last week is valid, then take notes on the valid information. **ANY DAY** *149*

SPEAKING AND LISTENING

☐ **Speak with a Purpose** Have students work in small groups to identify and solve problems, then present both problems and solutions to the class. **DAY 5** *223d*

☐ **Listen to a Broadcast** Have students listen to local radio broadcasts about a local or national problem, then answer questions. **DAY 5** *223d*

Resources for Differentiated Instruction

LEVELED READERS

▶ **Comprehension**
  - ◎ **Skill** Main Idea
  - ◎ **Strategy** Monitor and Fix Up

▶ **Lesson Vocabulary**
  - ◎ **Dictionary**

strain
enormous
scattered
realize
collection
shiny

▶ **Social Studies Standards**
  - Helping Others
  - Costs/Benefits of Personal Choices
  - Civic Life

Leveled Reader Database ONLINE

PearsonSuccessNet.com

Use the Online Database of over 600 books to
- Download and print additional copies of this week's leveled readers.
- Listen to the readers being read online.
- Search for more titles focused on this week's skills, topic, and content.

On-Level

Katy's Last-Minute Book Report
by Sasha Griffin

illustrated by Tom Labaff

On-Level Reader

Main Idea
- The **main idea** is the most important idea about a paragraph, passage, or story.
- **Details** are small pieces of information that tell more about the main idea.

Directions Read the following passage. Then answer the questions below.

> Third-grade students have many things to do each day. Homework, sports, and family activities take up a lot of time. It can be hard to decide what to do when. If you don't plan your time well, you might forget to do something important. Sometimes people put off doing things until the last minute. Then they don't have enough time left to do a good job.

Possible responses given.

1. Use one to three words to tell what this paragraph is about.
   planning time well
2. What is the main idea of the paragraph?
   It is important to plan your time well.
3. What is one detail that tells more about the main idea?
   Homework, sports, and family activities take up a lot of time.
4. What is another detail about the main idea?
   If you don't plan your time well, you might forget to do something important.
5. What is a third detail about the main idea?
   You need to plan enough time to do a good job.

On-Level Practice TE p. LR23

Vocabulary
Directions Read each vocabulary word and the four words that follow it. Find two other words that have almost the same meaning and circle them.

Check the Words You Know
___collection ___enormous ___realize
___scattered ___shiny ___strain

1. collection
   (group) (set) scattering book
2. enormous
   (huge) tiny medium (giant)
3. realize
   forget overlook (recognize) (understand)
4. scattered
   grouped (separated) (sprinkled) sorted
5. shiny
   (glossy) dull (sparkly) cloudy
6. strain
   achieve (try) (strive) complete

Directions Write a paragraph that includes at least four of the vocabulary words.
Paragraphs will vary but should use vocabulary words correctly.

On-Level Practice TE p. LR24

Strategic Intervention

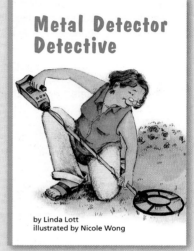

Metal Detector Detective

by Linda Lott
illustrated by Nicole Wong

Below-Level Reader

Main Idea
- The **main idea** is the most important idea about a paragraph, passage, or article.
- **Details** are small pieces of information that tell more about the main idea.

Directions Read the following passage. What is the main idea of the paragraph? Write it in the box on the left. Then find three details that tell about the main idea. Write them in the boxes on the right.

> Using a metal detector can be a fun hobby. But there are rules you must follow before using a metal detector. Metal detectors are not allowed on National Park Service lands. There are also many places, such as public schools, churches, and private lands, where you must ask permission before you use a metal detector. If you are not sure of whether you can use a metal detector, just ask!

Possible responses given.

Main Idea
1. There are rules you must follow before using a metal detector.

Detail
2. Metal detectors are not allowed on National Park Service lands.

Detail
3. Ask permission before you use a metal detector in public places.

Detail
4. If you are not sure whether you can use a metal detector, just ask.

Below-Level Practice TE p. LR20

Vocabulary
Directions Draw a line to connect each vocabulary word with the correct description.

Check the Words You Know
___collection ___enormous ___realize
___scattered ___shiny ___strain

1. collection — a. sprinkled
2. enormous — b. giant
3. realize — c. glossy
4. scattered — d. struggle
5. shiny — e. group
6. strain — f. understand

Directions Write the vocabulary word that completes each clue.

7. This word describes the size of something.
   enormous
8. When you try hard, you do this.
   strain
9. If you sprinkle seeds over a flower bed, you might describe the seeds this way.
   scattered
10. You often use this word to describe a new car.
    shiny
11. People organize seashells, stamps, dolls, and baseball cards into one of these.
    collection

Below-Level Practice TE p. LR21

Advanced

Advanced Reader

Main Idea

- The **main idea** is the most important idea about a paragraph, passage, or story.
- **Supporting details** are small pieces of information that tell more about the main idea.

Directions Read the following passage. Then answer the questions below.

Tina's mother collects teacups made of English bone china. China is another name for porcelain. Porcelain was first made in China, hundreds of years ago. That is why people often call it china. For a long time the Chinese guarded the secret of how porcelain is made. But after a while their secret began to spread to other countries. Then, about two hundred years ago, the English added ash, made from animal bones, to make a special kind of porcelain called bone china.

1. In one or two words, what is this paragraph about? _Possible responses given._
   china; porcelain

2. What is the main idea of the paragraph?
   English bone china is a special kind of porcelain.

3–4. What are the two details that tell more about the main idea?
   Porcelain was first made in China, hundreds of years ago. About two hundred years ago, the English added ash to make a special kind of porcelain called bone china.

5–7. Imagine you are writing a paragraph about one of the characters in *Collecting Dreams*. Write the main idea of your paragraph and two details to support that main idea. Responses will vary.

Main idea _____

Detail _____

Detail _____

Advanced Practice TE p. LR26

Vocabulary

Directions Choose the word from the box that best completes each sentence. Write the word on the line.

Check the Words You Know
__collectibles __credit __fond
__kaleidoscope __porcelain __propped
__rim __specialize __suspiciously

1. The spoon was resting on the ___rim___ of the teacup.
2. Tina worked hard to find the perfect present, so she deserves the ___credit___ for finding such a nice gift.
3. You can see beautiful colors and patterns if you look through a ___kaleidoscope___.
4. An antiques market is a great place for buyers to find ___collectibles___.
5. The teacher looked at the boy ___suspiciously___ when he tried to hide candy in his desk.
6. She was especially ___fond___ of long walks on warm summer nights.
7. Please handle the ___porcelain___ dishes carefully, because they break easily.
8. The broom is ___propped___ against the closet door.
9. I brought my broken antique doll to people who ___specialize___ in repairing toys.

Advanced Practice TE p. LR9

ELL Reader

ELL Poster 8

Teacher's Edition Notes

ELL notes throughout this lesson support instruction and reference additional resources at point of use.

Teaching Guide pp. 50–56, 226–227

- Multilingual summaries of the main selection
- Comprehension lesson
- Vocabulary strategies and word cards
- ELL Reader 3.2.3 lesson

ELL and Transition Handbook

-

Ten Important Sentences

- Key ideas from every selection in the Student Edition
- Activities to build sentence power

More Reading

Readers' Theater Anthology

- Fluency practice
- Five scripts to build fluency
- Poetry for oral interpretation

Leveled Trade Books

- Extended reading tied to the unit concept
- Lessons in the Trade Book Library Teaching Guide

Homework

- Family Times Newsletter
- ELL Multilingual Selection Summaries

Take-Home Books

- Leveled Readers

Cross-Curricular Centers

Listen to the Selections

MATERIALS SINGLES
CD player, headphones, AudioText CD, Student Edition

Listen to *Prudy's Problem* and "Meeting the Challenge of Collecting" as you follow or read along in your book. Listen for the main idea and supporting details in each selection.

If there is anything you don't understand, you can listen again to any section.

Read It Again!

MATERIALS SINGLES PAIRS GROUPS
Collection of books for self-selected reading, reading log

Select a book you have already read. Record the title of the book in your reading log. You may want to read with a partner.

You may choose any of the following:

- **Leveled Readers**
- **ELL Readers**
- **Stories written by classmates**
- **Books from the library**
- ***Prudy's Problem***

TEN IMPORTANT SENTENCES Read the Ten Important Sentences for *Prudy's Problem*. Then locate the sentences in the Student Edition.

BOOK CLUB The theme is the "big idea" of a story. Find a partner who read the same book you did. Discuss the book and figure out what the theme is.

Answer QUESTIONS

MATERIALS SINGLES PAIRS
Copy of sentences below, pencil, paper

Record the answers to the questions below.

1. **Explain why you think as you do. Use complete sentences and the underlined words in your answers.**
2. **Discuss your answers with a partner.**

- **Which object <u>glitters</u>: tin foil or a wooden wall?**
- **If toys were <u>strewn</u> across the playground, were they scattered or organized?**
- **What is something you could <u>investigate</u>?**
- **If you want to know <u>scientific</u> information about dinosaurs, where could you look?**

EARLY FINISHERS Write sentences for the underlined words.

You could investigate the loss of a book.

Investigate means to search for answers carefully.

Scott Foresman Reading Street Centers Survival Kit
Use the *Prudy's Problem* materials from the Reading Street
Centers Survival Kit to organize this week's centers.

Writing

Social Studies

Technology

Report on
Collecting

MATERIALS `PAIRS`
Writing and drawing materials

Interview a classmate about his or her collection.

1. Ask a classmate to describe his or her collection to you. Take notes.
2. Ask questions such as the following: *When did you start collecting? Why? How big is your collection?* Write the answers.
3. Use what you learned to write a report about the collection.
4. Illustrate with a picture of the collection.

EARLY FINISHERS Write about what you collect—or want to collect.

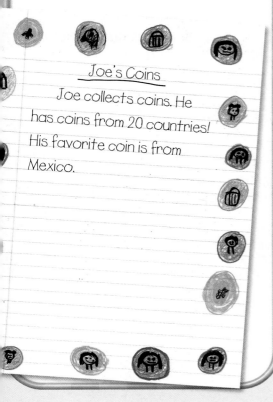

Joe's Coins

Joe collects coins. He has coins from 20 countries! His favorite coin is from Mexico.

Study Community
Resources

MATERIALS `SINGLES` `PAIRS`
Internet access, local directories such as phone books, writing and art materials

Create an advertisement for a place in your community.

1. Choose a community resource for information such as the local library or a nearby museum.
2. List ways the resource can help you.
3. Create an advertisement or flier for the resource. Make sure you write about the kinds of information available there.

EARLY FINISHERS Write a short radio ad convincing people to come visit the resource you chose.

Visit Peytonville Museum
• Learn about the town's history.
• See old photographs of Peytonville.
• Read old newspapers.
• Sit at a 1920s school desk.

Write an
E-mail

MATERIALS `SINGLES`
Computer, printer

Write an e-mail about Prudy on the computer and send or print it.

1. Use the mouse to click on the e-mail program icon. This opens it.
2. Click on "Create Mail" on the toolbar.
3. In the "To" box, type the e-mail address of the person who will get the message.
4. Type the subject of your message in the subject line.
5. Type your message in the message window.
6. Click on the "send" icon.

EARLY FINISHERS Forward the message to another person.

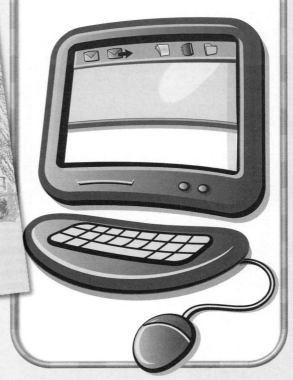

ALL CENTERS

- Build vocabulary by finding words related to the lesson concept.
- Listen for main idea and details.

Concept Vocabulary

bulky large; hard to handle
phonograph an old-style machine for playing recorded music
portable able to be carried or moved

Monitor Progress

Check Vocabulary

If... students are unable to place words on the web,	then... review the lesson concept. Place the words on the web and provide additional words for practice, such as *inflatable* and *lightweight*.

SUCCESS PREDICTOR

DAY 1   Grouping Options

Reading
Whole Group
Introduce and discuss the Question of the Week. Then use pp. 198l–200b.

Group Time
Differentiated Instruction
Read this week's Leveled Readers. See pp. 198f–198g for the small group lesson plan.

Whole Group
Use p. 223a.

Language Arts
Use pp.223e–223h and 223k–223m.

Build Concepts

FLUENCY

MODEL EXPRESSION/INTONATION As you read "The Rampanion," try to use different tones of voice at appropriate times in the selection. For example, when you read the line "But Alison did it" after paragraph three, let your tone of voice suggest surprise or amazement.

LISTENING COMPREHENSION

After reading "The Rampanion," use the following questions to assess listening comprehension.

1. **Find the main idea and one supporting detail of the selection.** *(Main Idea: The Rampanion is a portable ramp people in wheelchairs can use to get over curbs; Supporting detail: It is made of lightweight metal.)* **Main Idea**

2. **Why do you think the author wrote this article about Alison DeSmyter?** *(Possible response: To inform the reader of this girl's invention to help people in wheelchairs get around easier.)* **Author's Purpose**

BUILD CONCEPT VOCABULARY

Start a web to build concepts and vocabulary related to this week's lesson and the unit theme.

- Draw an Ideas and Inventions Concept Web.
- Read the sentence with the word *bulky* again. Ask students to pronounce *bulky* and discuss its meaning.
- Place *bulky* in an oval attached to Bad Qualities. Explain that *bulky* is related to this concept. Read the sentences in which *portable* and *phonograph* appear. Have students pronounce the words, place them on the web, and provide reasons.
- Brainstorm additional words and categories for the web. Keep the web on display and add words throughout the week.

Concept Vocabulary Web

```
( bulky )----Bad Qualities----Ideas and----Good Qualities----( portable )
                                 Inventions
                                    |
                                End Results----( phonograph )
```

The Rampanion

by Arlene Erlbach

Alison DeSmyter knows about the problems people have in wheelchairs. Alison was born with cerebral palsy, a condition that makes it difficult to control muscles. So Alison has used a wheelchair most of her life.

One common problem for wheelchair users is crossing streets with curbs. To get her chair over a curb, Alison needed somebody to push or lift her chair. She wanted more independence. So Alison invented the Rampanion—a portable ramp that allows a wheelchair to move easily over a curb.

Alison first thought of the Rampanion when she was asked to do an invention project for school. She had just two weeks. That wasn't much time to design something as complicated as the Rampanion.

But Alison did it.

First Alison thought about making a rubber ramp, but she decided it would be too bulky to carry around. Next she considered an inflatable ramp. That wouldn't do, either—it would always need to be blown up. Finally Alison decided to make a ramp out of lightweight metal. This type of ramp could easily be folded and carried.

Alison began by building a small model of her ramp from Popsicle sticks. Once she had built the model, she thought about the type of metal she'd use for the real thing. The Rampanion needed to be light yet strong, so Alison decided on aluminum. Her father found some aluminum where he works, and he helped Alison put the ramp together. To build the ramp, they needed a lot of exact measurements, which Alison took herself.

As Alison and her father built the Rampanion, they thought of improvements they could make to its design. They added an edge to the Rampanion's sides, to keep a chair's wheels on track. They put sticky tape on the bottom, to help secure the Rampanion to any surface—even in the rain.

The completed Rampanion weighs only four pounds. When it's folded, it can be carried in its own cloth bag. The bag can be attached to a wheelchair.

Alison's Rampanion won the fifth-grade grand prize for the third annual Houston Inventors' Showcase Exposition. Her prize was a trip to Florida. The trip included visits to Disneyworld, the Kennedy Space Center, and Thomas Edison's estate. Thomas Edison was a great inventor who created many electrical devices, such as the light bulb and the phonograph.

Alison hasn't stopped inventing things for wheelchair users. She's working on a Handy Helper, which is a tray that attaches to a wheelchair. The Handy Helper allows people in wheelchairs to be served more easily in cafeterias and fast-food restaurants.

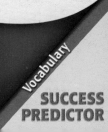

SKILLS ⟷ STRATEGIES IN CONTEXT

Main Idea Monitor and Fix Up

OBJECTIVES

 Recognize main idea and supporting details.

 Use monitor and fix up reading comprehension to identify main ideas and details.

Skills Trace
Main Idea and Details

Introduce/Teach	TE: 3.2 150–151, 198–199, 3.6 284–285
Practice	PB: 3.1 53, 57, 58, 73, 77, 78, 86; 3.2 103, 107, 108, 126, 146
Reteach/Review	TE: 3.2 173b, 223b, 233, 241, DI·52, DI·54; 3.6, 303b, 339, 391, 397, DI·52
Test	Selection Test: Unit 2 Benchmark Tests: Units 2, 6

INTRODUCE

Write the topic "Sports" on the board, and add the following details: *Baseball is played on a diamond-shaped field. Football is played on a large rectangular field. A soccer field is similar to a football field.* Ask what might be the main idea of a selection with this topic and details. *(Possible response: Some sports are played on fields.)*

Have students read the information on p. 198. Explain the following:

• When we read, we want to know what the story or article is about. Little pieces of information, or the details, can help us understand what it is about.

• As we read, we should stop and ask ourselves if we understand what we are reading and fix what we don't understand. Looking for details and thinking about what a story is about can help us do this.

Use Skill Transparency 8 to teach main idea and monitor and fix up.

 Prudy's Problem and how she solved it

Comprehension

Skill
Main Idea

Strategy
Monitor and Fix Up

 ## Main Idea

• When you read a story, ask yourself, "What is this story all about?"

• Details are small pieces of information. Look for details in the story that help tell what it is about.

Detail	Detail	Detail

↓ ↓ ↓

What the story is all about

Strategy: Monitor and Fix Up

Good readers stop when they are confused and figure out what's wrong. Summing up can help. As you read, ask yourself, "What are the important details in this story so far?" That will help you make sure you understand what is happening. It will also help you tell what the story is all about.

Write to Read

1. Read "The Stamp Collector." Make a chart like the one above. Write details and then a statement of what the story is about.

2. Use your chart to write a short summary of the story "The Stamp Collector."

198

Strategic Intervention

 Main Idea Tell students that when we read and talk about stories, the first thing we want to know and understand is what they are about. Details in the story help us figure this out. Write down the name of a story everyone is likely to know, such as a story you've recently read in class. Draw a rectangular box under the title and ask students what the story is about. Then have them call out details that tell what the story is about. If students are unable to identify what the story is about, work backward—elicit details from the story and write them down; then ask students to write a sentence that tells what the story is about.

ELL

Access Content

Beginning/Intermediate For a Picture It! lesson on main idea, see the ELL Teaching Guide, p. 51.

Advanced Before students read "The Stamp Collector," have them discuss the different kinds of things people collect and why. Encourage students to tell about any collections they have.

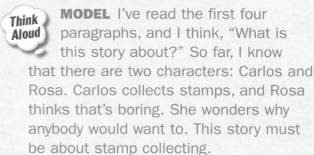

The Stamp Collector

Carlos grabbed the envelope from Rosa's hand.

"Don't tell me," said Rosa. "You want the stamp. Is there anything more boring than collecting stamps? You put them in a book and then what? You can't even play with them."

"What do *you* know?" replied Carlos. "You collect beads."

"I don't collect them. I make beautiful bead jewelry," Rosa said. "People can wear my jewelry. What good is a book of stamps?" •

That evening Carlos cut a stamp from a postcard he had bought at a yard sale. It was a 30¢ stamp with a picture of George Washington on it. He looked it up in a stamp catalog. Carlos carefully matched his stamp with the picture in the catalog. Suddenly he began jumping around. "One of my stamps is worth between 100 and 300 dollars!" Carlos exclaimed. •

"Let me see that!" Rosa demanded.

"No," Carlos laughed. "You said looking at stamps is boring."

1 **Strategy** If you're having trouble, this would be a good place to stop and do something about it. Sum up the story so far. That might help.

2 **Skill** You've read several details so far. What would you say is the main idea of this story?

199

Available as **Skill Transparency** 8

Main Idea • Monitor and Fix Up

- The **main idea** answers the question, "What is this story all about?" **Details** are small pieces of information that help tell what the story is about.
- As you read, ask yourself, "What are the important details in this story so far?" **Sum up** to help you understand what is happening and to help you tell what the story is about.

Directions Read the following passage.

> Kendra saw all sorts of colorful rocks at the beach. She had been looking for something to collect. Kendra decided she would collect rocks.
> Kendra loaded her backpack with red rocks, yellow rocks, black rocks, and speckled rocks. Then she lugged them home.
>
> Once home, Kendra looked for a place to keep her rocks. She couldn't keep them in her backpack.
> Kendra found a pretty box. She set the colorful rocks in the box and put them on the porch.
> Kendra showed her beautiful rock collection to everyone who came to visit.

Directions Complete the graphic organizer to tell what the story is all about.

Detail	**Detail**	**Detail**
1. Kendra puts rocks in her backpack.	2. Kendra finds a pretty box to keep the rocks in.	3. Kendra puts the rocks on the porch.

What the Story Is All About
4. Kendra collects rocks.

 **Home Activity** Your child found the main idea of a story. The main idea is a sentence that sums up what the story is all about. Read a story like the one above, and ask your child to name some of the details in the story and then write one sentence to tell what the story is all about.

Practice Book 3.1 p. 73

TEACH

1 **STRATEGY** Model monitoring reading comprehension and using details to fix problems with comprehension.

Think Aloud **MODEL** I've read the first four paragraphs, and I think, "What is this story about?" So far, I know that there are two characters: Carlos and Rosa. Carlos collects stamps, and Rosa thinks that's boring. She wonders why anybody would want to. This story must be about stamp collecting.

2 **SKILL** Model identifying several details from the story that point to the main idea.

Think Aloud **MODEL** The first important detail is that Carlos collects stamps. Later in the story, I learn how he gets the stamps and what he does with them. Then I read how he and Rosa are excited about a certain stamp. I think this story is about how Rosa discovers that collecting stamps can be interesting.

PRACTICE AND ASSESS

STRATEGY Summary of the fourth paragraph: Carlos collects stamps. Rosa thinks that's boring. She wonders why anybody would want to collect stamps.

SKILL Students should point out details that help them frame the main idea in the story so far.

WRITE Have students complete steps 1 and 2 of the Write to Read activity. You might consider using this as a whole class activity.

Monitor Progress

↻ Main Idea

If... students are unable to complete **Write to Read** on p. 198,	**then...** use Practice Book 3.1, p. 73, to provide additional practice.

Tech Files
ONLINE

Students can find out more about collecting by searching the Internet. Have them use a student-friendly search engine and the keywords *collecting* and *collections*.

ELL

Build Background Use ELL Poster 8 to build background and vocabulary for the lesson concept of how to get ideas to solve a problem.

▲ **ELL Poster** 8

Build Background

ACTIVATE PRIOR KNOWLEDGE

BEGIN A WEB about collecting.
- Write the word "Collecting" in the center oval.
- Give students two to three minutes to think of as many things as they can that people collect. Write their ideas on the web.
- Encourage students to share something they like to collect. Share some ideas of your own.
- As they read, have students jot down things Prudy collected that they can add to the web.

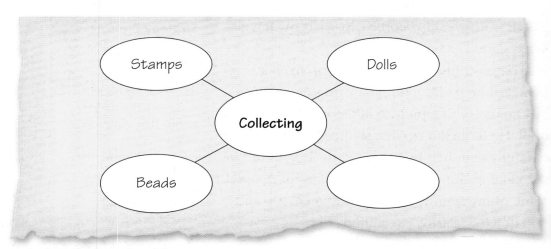

▲ **Graphic Organizer** 15

BACKGROUND BUILDING AUDIO This week's audio spotlights third graders who are collectors. After students listen, discuss how they think they are similar and different from the third graders on the CD.

Background Building Audio

Introduce Vocabulary

DISCUSS THE VOCABULARY

Share lesson vocabulary with students. Have students locate each word in their glossaries and note each word's pronunciation and meaning. Ask these questions to help clarify word meanings.

How big does something have to be to be *enormous*?

Would you add a snail shell to a rock *collection*?

What do you do when you *realize* you are wrong?

How do you keep your shoes so *shiny*?

Will a vacation *strain* our budget?

Did you find all of the papers that the wind *scattered* across the park?

Point out that some of this week's words could describe a collection—*enormous, shiny, scattered.* Ask students what other words they know that might describe a collection. **Activate Prior Knowledge**

Enormous is a synonym for *huge.* What other words are synonyms for *huge*? (Possible responses: *immense, large, gigantic*) **Synonyms**

Continue this activity by having students write their own questions using the vocabulary.

Use the Multisyllabic Word Routine on p. DI·1 to help students read multisyllabic words.

Lesson Vocabulary

WORDS TO KNOW

T **collection** a group of things gathered from many places and belonging together

T **enormous** very, very large; huge

T **realize** to understand something clearly

T **scattered** separated and going in different directions

T **shiny** giving off or reflecting a bright light; bright

T **strain** to draw tightly; to stretch too much

MORE WORDS TO KNOW

clutter filled with objects in a messy way

indescribable not able to be told about in words; beyond description

inspiration a sudden, good idea that solves a problem

T = Tested Word

▲ **Practice Book 3.1** p. 74

Vocabulary Strategy

Prudy's Problem
and how she solved it

Words to Know

- enormous
- scattered
- strain
- realize
- collection
- shiny

Vocabulary Strategy
for Unfamiliar Words

Dictionary You can always use a dictionary to find out the meaning of a word you don't know. A dictionary tells you the word's meaning and how to say the word. The words in a dictionary are listed in alphabetical order.

1. Look at the first letter in the word and turn in the dictionary to the section for that letter.

2. Use the guide words at the top of each page and what you know about the alphabet to help you find the word.

3. Read the definitions. If the word has more than one meaning, decide which meaning you think fits in the sentence.

4. Try that meaning in the sentence to see if it makes sense.

Read "Get Organized." Use a dictionary to find out the meanings of the vocabulary words.

200

OBJECTIVE

Use reference sources, such as dictionaries, to find the meaning of unfamiliar words.

INTRODUCE

Discuss the dictionary strategy for unfamiliar words using the steps on p. 200.

TEACH

- Have students read "Get Organized," paying attention to how vocabulary is used.
- Model using context clues to determine the meaning of *collection*.

Think Aloud

MODEL The word *collection* is on a page that describes things people collect. So *collection* must name the group of things that are collected.

DAY 2 — Grouping Options

Reading

Whole Group Discuss the Question of the Day. Then use pp. 200–203.

Group Time Differentiated Instruction
Read *Prudy's Problem.* See pp. 198f–198g for the small group lesson plan.

Whole Group Use pp. 223a and 223i.

Language Arts
Use pp. 223e–223h and 223k–223m.

Strategic Intervention

Reference Sources Have students work in pairs to follow the steps on p. 200. Encourage them to use the alphabet, guide words, and meanings that make sense in context when looking up a word in a dictionary.

ELL

Access Content Use ELL Poster 8 to preteach vocabulary. Choose from the following to meet language proficiency levels.

Beginning Point out that *enormous* and *shiny* are both adjectives, or words that describe things. Have students use the words in sentences to describe things that are huge and bright.

Intermediate After reading, students can make a list of some of the things that they would like to collect.

Advanced Teach the lesson on pp. 200–201. Students can report on the names of some of the things they or others have collected in their home languages.

Resources for home-language words may include parents, bilingual staff members, bilingual dictionaries, or online translation sources.

Get Organized

Are there enormous piles of stuff in your room? Are your things scattered everywhere? Is your closet clutter putting a strain on the door? Then it's time to take action!

First, realize that this will take time and work. Look at each thing. Ask yourself, "Do I use this? Will I ever use this?" This information will help you decide what to get rid of and what to keep. Take the things you are getting rid of. Put them in large trash bags. Are they in good shape? Give them away to a charity. If not, throw them out.

Next, take the things you are keeping. Put them into groups. Put each group together in one place. Put all the books on a shelf or table. Hang the clothes in the closet or put them in drawers. Do you have a collection of objects, such as rocks, postcards, or stamps? Display them together on a shelf, table, or wall.

Now vacuum and dust your room. Congratulations! You have a shiny, clean, and well-organized room.

Words to Write

What do you collect? Write about your collection. Tell why you like to collect. Use as many words from the Words to Know list as you can.

201

PRACTICE AND ASSESS

- Have students determine the meanings of the remaining words and explain the context clues they used.
- Point out that dictionaries may contain more than one meaning for a particular word. Students should try each meaning in the context of the sentence to see which meaning works best.
- Have students complete Practice Book 3.1, p. 75.

WRITE Writing should include vocabulary words that name and describe the items that students collect. They should also explain why they like or dislike collecting things.

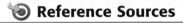

Monitor Progress

⟳ Reference Sources

If... students need more practice with the lesson vocabulary,	then... use Tested Vocabulary Cards.

Vocabulary · Dictionary

- Sometimes when you are reading, you come across a word you don't know. You can use a **dictionary** to find the meaning of the word.
- A **dictionary** has word meanings. The words are listed in alphabetical order.

clutter *n.* mess
collection *n.* a group of similar things one gets and keeps
organize *v.* to put in order

realize *v.* to come to see; to understand
scrutinize *v.* to look very closely at; to study
vacuum *n.* machine used to take dirt from floors, rugs, and carpets

Directions Each sentence has one underlined word. Use the dictionary entries above to find the meaning.

1. Mom told me to <u>organize</u> all the things in my room.

   to put in order

2. Every Saturday morning, Dad uses a <u>vacuum</u> on the rugs in the house.

   machine used to take dirt from floors, rugs, and carpets

3. There is so much <u>clutter</u> in my closet, I can't find anything.

   mess

4. My room looks clean as long as you don't <u>scrutinize</u> it.

   to look very closely at; to study

5. Now I keep each of my <u>collections</u> in a separate box.

   group of similar things one gets and keeps

6. I <u>realize</u> that having too many things can sometimes make life difficult.

   to come to see; to understand

Home Activity Your child used sample dictionary entries to find the meaning of unfamiliar words. Read a story or newspaper article together and look up unfamiliar words. Encourage your child to identify unfamiliar words while reading and then look up their definitions in a dictionary.

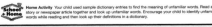
▲ **Practice Book 3.1** p. 75

Prereading Strategies

OBJECTIVES

- Identify main idea and supporting details to improve comprehension.
- Use main idea to monitor and fix up.

GENRE STUDY

Fantasy

Prudy's Problem is a fantasy. Explain that a fantasy is a fictional story in which at least one element in the story is not possible.

PREVIEW AND PREDICT

Have students preview the selection title and illustrations and discuss the topics or ideas they think this selection will cover. Encourage students to use lesson vocabulary as they talk about what they expect to learn.

Strategy Response Log

Predict Have students write their predictions in their strategy response logs. Students will check their predictions in the Strategy Response Log activity on p. 209.

Genre A **fantasy** includes make-believe events. Look for situations that could not happen.

202

ELL

Access Content Lead a picture walk to reinforce vocabulary, such as *collect* (p. 204), *collections* (p. 204), *clutter* (p. 207), *stuff* (p. 207), and *avalanche* (p. 210).

Consider having students read the selection summary in English or in students' home languages. See the Multilingual Summaries in the ELL Teaching Guide, pp. 54–56.

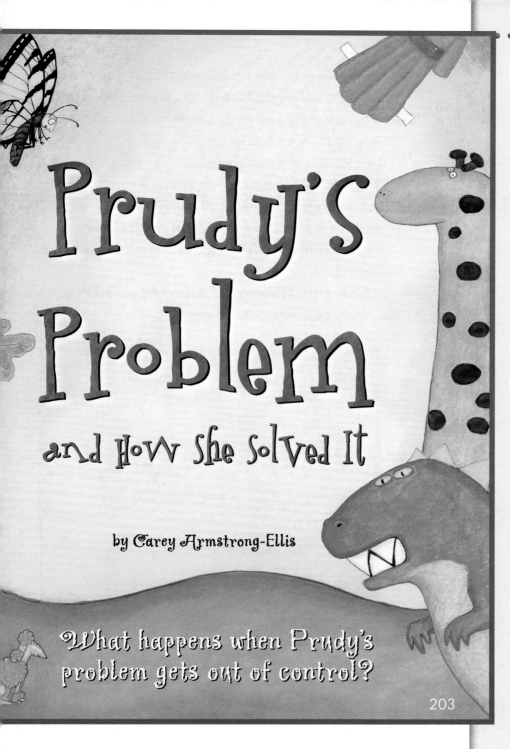

Prudy's Problem

and How She Solved It

by Carey Armstrong-Ellis

What happens when Prudy's problem gets out of control?

203

SET PURPOSE

Read the title aloud to students and look at the illustrations as a group. Have students read to find out what Prudy's problem is and how she solves it.

Remind students to look for main ideas and supporting details as they read.

STRATEGY RECALL

Students have now used these before-reading strategies:

- preview the selection to be aware of its genre, features, and possible content;
- activate prior knowledge about that content and what to expect of that genre;
- make predictions;
- set a purpose for reading.

Remind students to be aware of and flexibly use the during-reading strategies they have learned:

- link prior knowledge to new information;
- summarize text they have read so far;
- ask clarifying questions;
- answer questions they or others pose;
- check their predictions and either refine them or make new predictions;
- recognize the text structure the author is using, and use that knowledge to make predictions and increase comprehension;
- visualize what the author is describing;
- monitor their comprehension and use fix-up strategies.

After reading, students will use these strategies:

- summarize or retell the text;
- answer questions they or others pose;
- reflect to make new information become part of their prior knowledge.

 AudioText

Guiding Comprehension

1 🎯 **Main Idea and Details • Inferential**

Reread pp. 204–205. What are they about? Find one detail that supports your answer.

These pages are about a girl who has a problem collecting too many things. Detail: Prudy collects everything.

Monitor Progress	
🎯 **Main Idea and Details**	
If... students are unable to determine what the story is about,	**then...** use the skill and strategy instruction on p. 205.

2 **Visualize • Inferential**

Prudy collects a lot of things. Picture what her room must look like and write what you see in your mind. Be sure to use details from the story in your answer.

Responses will vary; check that details from the story support students' answers.

Tech Files
ONLINE

Use the key words *collecting, collections* and *hobbies-collecting* to find out more about collecting as a hobby.

Prudy seemed like a normal little girl. She had a sister. She had a dog. She had two white mice. She had a mom and a dad and her own room at home.

Yes, Prudy seemed normal.

But Prudy collected things.

Now most kids collect something. Prudy's friend Egbert collected butterflies. So did Prudy.

Belinda had a stamp collection. So did Prudy.

Harold collected tin foil and made it into a big ball. So did Prudy.

All her friends had collections. And so did Prudy—but Prudy collected *everything*.

204

Activate Prior Knowledge Discuss the examples of collections mentioned on p. 204 to clarify the idea of collections. Ask students, "How many objects make up a collection?" Discuss the idea of collecting things with students. Tell students about something you collect, or collected as a child, and encourage them to tell about something they collect. Have students brainstorm a list of possible problems that could come up with collecting things.

She saved rocks, feathers, leaves, twigs, dead bugs, and old flowers. She kept a box full of interesting fungi in the bottom drawer of her dresser. She saved every picture she had ever drawn and every valentine she had ever gotten. She saved pretty paper napkins from parties and kept them in her desk drawer. She had six hundred and fourteen stuffed animals in different unnatural colors.

205

Choices

As we get older, we are faced with more—and more complicated—decisions. Right now, you might have to decide what clothes you want to wear or whom to invite to a birthday party, but in a few years, you'll have to make decisions about some tougher topics. One thing you can do is decide now how you want to respond—that way, if someone you thought was a friend asks you to try something, you know beforehand how you feel about it and can be firm in your decision. You might also want to think about how some people might try to change your mind, and prepare for that too. Get together with your family and act out a few scenarios in which you always make decisions about tough topics. That way, if and when the time comes, you'll know what to say!

Main Idea/Details Monitor/Fix Up

TEACH

- Explain to students that when we read fiction, it is important to know what the story is about in order to understand it.

- When we are reading, it's a good idea to stop periodically and make sure we have understood what we have read. If we have any questions, we can go back to try to find the answer.

- To check that we have understood what something is about, we can look for details from the selection that support our ideas.

Think Aloud **MODEL** When I finish reading the first two pages of the story, I stop a minute to see if I have understood what I just read. I ask myself, "What is the first page about?" It's about a girl named Prudy who collects too many things. To make sure I am right, I look for a detail in the story that supports my idea. I find a sentence that says that Prudy collects everything. That supports my idea that this story is about a girl who collects too much.

PRACTICE AND ASSESS

Have students summarize the details they see on p. 205. To assess, check that the details they have identified support the main idea that Prudy collects too many things.

Guiding Comprehension

3 REVIEW **Character • Inferential**

Write one adjective that describes Prudy.

Possible response: messy

Monitor Progress

REVIEW **Character**

If... students have difficulty thinking of an adjective to describe Prudy,	**then...** use the skill and strategy instruction on p. 207.

---

4 **Generalize • Critical**

What is one generalization we can make about Prudy? Find at least one detail from the story that supports your generalization.

Possible responses: She never throws anything away. Detail: (any of the things she collects)

5 **Facts and Details • Critical**

The author tells us the different kinds of things Prudy collects. Why is this important information?

Possible response: It shows that Prudy collects too much, including useless things, and it helps us understand how Prudy's collections are a problem.

She had collections of ribbons, shoela souvenir postcards, flowered fabric scraps pencils with fancy ends, pink scarves with orange polka dots, old calendars, salt and pepper shakers with faces, dried-out eras plastic lizards, pointy sunglasses, china animals, heart-shaped candy boxes with the paper candy cups still inside, tufts of hair from different breeds of dogs . . . .

She just could not throw anything awa

It drove her dad to distraction. He was a very tidy person who did not like clutter. He started saying unpleasant things as he tried to mow the lawn.

"Prudy, you have a problem," he said.

"What do you mean?" she asked, baffled.

"You just have too much stuff. Why don't we haul it all to the dump?" he suggested hopefully.

"I don't have too much stuff, Dad," Prudy said.

3 4 5

207

SKILLS ⟷ STRATEGIES IN CONTEXT

Character REVIEW

TEACH

- Remind students that characters are the people or animals in stories.

- Sometimes, authors do not tell us everything about their characters; we have to use clues from the story, such as a character's words and actions, to understand them. We can also learn about characters from the things other characters say about them.

- Model looking at Prudy's actions and the other characters' words to understand her character and come up with an adjective to describe her.

Think Aloud **MODEL** I read in the first two pages that Prudy collects too many things. Then I read a list of the kinds of things she collects. Finally, her father says that she has too much stuff, and it is making him upset. I think Prudy must be a very messy person!

PRACTICE AND ASSESS

- Have students write a sentence describing Prudy. To assess, check that sentences are an accurate representation of the character.

- To assess, use Practice Book 3.1, p. 76.

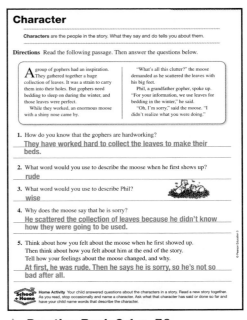

Character

Characters are the people in the story. What they say and do tells you about them.

Directions Read the following passage. Then answer the questions below.

A group of gophers had an inspiration. They gathered together a huge collection of leaves. It was a strain to carry them into their holes. But gophers need bedding to sleep on during the winter, and those leaves were perfect.

While they worked, an enormous moose with a shiny nose came by.

"What's all this clutter?" the moose demanded as he scattered the leaves with his big feet.

Phil, a grandfather gopher, spoke up. "For your information, we use leaves for bedding in the winter," he said.

"Oh, I'm sorry," said the moose. "I didn't realize what you were doing."

1. How do you know that the gophers are hardworking?
   They have worked hard to collect the leaves to make their beds.

2. What word would you use to describe the moose when he first shows up?
   rude

3. What word would you use to describe Phil?
   wise

4. Why does the moose say that he is sorry?
   He scattered the collection of leaves because he didn't know how they were going to be used.

5. Think about how you felt about the moose when he first showed up. Then think about how you felt about him at the end of the story. Tell how your feelings about the moose changed, and why.
   At first, he was rude. Then he says he is sorry, so he's not so bad after all.

School + Home **Home Activity** Your child answered questions about the characters in a story. Read a new story together. As you read, stop occasionally and name a character. Ask what that character has said or done so far and have your child name words that describe the character.

▲ **Practice Book 3.1** p. 76

Civic Life

Have you ever wondered what you could do to help out in your community? Volunteers are involved in everything, from local homeless shelters and food banks, to the Special Olympics. Volunteers help build homes; visit senior citizens confined to retirement homes; help people learn to read; distribute blankets, food, and first aid to victims of natural disasters; and help clean up parks and beaches. Volunteering is good for you too. It makes you feel good about yourself and gives you training that you may use one day to get into college or get a good job.

Time for
SOCIAL
STUDIES

Guiding Comprehension

6 **Cause and Effect • Inferential**

Prudy's little sister starts collections of her own. Why do you think she does this?

Possible response: Prudy's little sister starts collecting things because her sister does. She might want to be like her sister.

7 **Categorize • Inferential**

Look through the selection so far. How many different categories can you make for the things Prudy collects?

Responses will vary; check that details in the story support the categories students have chosen.

8 **Monitor and Fix Up • Critical**

In two or three sentences, tell what the story is about so far. Make sure you include at least one detail that supports your summary.

Responses will vary; check that students have understood what the story is about and that they have identified at least one detail to support their ideas.

It even got to be too much for her mom, who did not mind clutter but could no longer navigate the living room.

"Maybe you could take all this to the thrift shop," she said. "Surely someone could use this old mushroom . . . ."

"I *like* that mushroom," Prudy said.

"Prudy, you have to face your problem," said her mother.

"I do not have a problem," said Prudy.

208

ELL

Understand Idioms Point out the idiom *to (not) mind* on p. 208. Another way to say *to mind about something* is *to care about something*. For example, Prudy's mother did not care about clutter. Use the idiom in another sentence. (For example, I don't mind if you have to leave the room to get a drink of water, but I do mind if you leave without asking me first.) Give each student an opportunity to use the idiom in a sentence of their own. To assess, ask them if they care or not. (For example, Do I care if you have to leave the room? Do I care if you ask me first?)

Prudy's little sister started putting together collections of her own.

"Uh–oh," said Egbert, eyeing Evie's little piles of pine twigs and used toothbrushes. "Prudy, how about if you packed everything all up and stuffed it into a rocket and sent it to Neptune?"

"Yeah, that would solve your problem!" agreed Harold and Belinda.

"There is no problem!" shouted Prudy.

But Prudy herself found that she could barely get to her desk to feed her mice.

6

7 **8**

209

Monitor/Fix Up

- Explain to students that active readers stop and reread if they do not understand something they are reading.
- Understanding what a story is about is the first step to understanding the story. If you're not sure what a story is about, look for the important details.
- Go back through the selection and make a list of the important details. Then look at all the details together to see what they tell you about the story.

SELF-CHECK

Students can ask themselves these questions to assess ability to use the skill and strategy.

- Do the details I have chosen show or tell what the story is about?
- Have I included only details that help me understand what the story is about?

Monitor Progress
Main Idea and Details
If... students have difficulty identifying the main idea and supporting details,   **then...** revisit the skill lesson on pp. 198–199. Reteach as necessary.

Strategy Response Log

Check Predictions Provide the following prompt: Was your prediction accurate? Revise your old prediction or make a new prediction about the rest of the selection.

If you want to teach this selection in two sessions, stop here.

Develop Vocabulary

PRACTICE LESSON VOCABULARY

Have students respond orally *yes* or *no* to each question.

1. **Is there more than one object in a *collection*?** *(Yes)*
2. **Does Prudy *realize* she has a problem?** *(No)*

BUILD CONCEPT VOCABULARY

Review previous concept words with students. Ask if students have met any words today in their reading or elsewhere that they would like to add to the Concept Web.

Guiding Comprehension

If you are teaching the selection in two days, discuss the story so far, including main idea and details, and review the vocabulary.

9 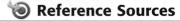 **Vocabulary • Reference Sources**

Find the word *strain* on p. 210. Note how it is used. Then look it up in the dictionary. What does it mean?

To stretch tightly

Monitor Progress

Reference Sources

If... students have difficulty using a dictionary,	**then...** use the vocabulary strategy instruction on p. 211.

---

10 Predict • Inferential

What do you think happens next?

Possible responses: The door will burst open; the door will not close.

DAY 3 **Grouping Options**

Reading
Whole Group Discuss the Question of the Day.

Group Time Differentiated Instruction
Read *Prudy's Problem.* See pp. 198f–198g for the small group lesson plan.

Whole Group Discuss the Reader Response questions on p. 218. Then use p. 223a.

Language Arts
Use pp. 223e–223h and 223k–223m.

She could not even get out of her room without setting off an avalanche of one thing or another.

And then one day while Prudy was walking home from school, something shiny caught her eye. It was a silver gum wrapper.

"I must take this home for my shiny things collection!" she thought.

She ran home and tried to squeeze it into her room.

Something started to happen. The walls started to bulge.

9 The door started to strain at the hinges.

The pressure was building higher . . . and higher . . . .

210

ELL

Extend Language Explain to students that we can also use dictionaries to help with syllabication and pronunciation of words. Look up the word *strain* together. Point out the pronunciation of the word in parentheses next to the word itself. Have students practice saying the word aloud using the pronunciation key. Direct them to a longer word on the same page. Point out the dot(s) in the word that tells them where to divide the word. Have them practice saying the longer word too. Finally, have them use both words in a sentence of their own.

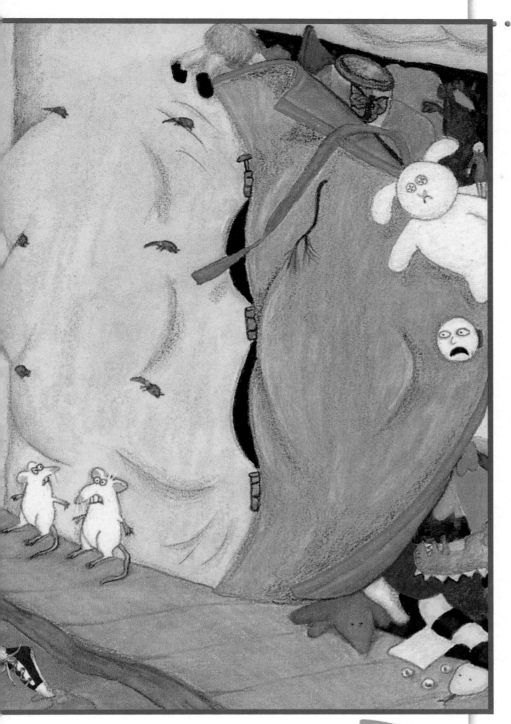

VOCABULARY STRATEGY

Reference Sources

TEACH

- Explain to students that a dictionary is a book that lists words and tells what they mean. Some dictionaries, especially dictionaries for children, use pictures to explain words too.

- Dictionaries list words in alphabetical order.

- At the top of the outer corner of each two pages are two words called guide words. These are the first and last words on those two pages. Students can use these words to figure out on which page to look for the unfamiliar word.

- Once they have found the word, they should try the definition or a synonym in the sentence to make sure they have the correct meaning of the word.

- Model using a dictionary to find the meaning of the word *strain* on p. 210.

Think Aloud

MODEL When I come to a word I don't know, I try to figure out what it means, but sometimes this doesn't work. Then I check a dictionary. Right now I want to find the meaning of *strain*, so I open the dictionary to the *s* words. Then I start looking for *st* words, and then *str* words. I use the guide words to tell me where I should look. When I find the right page, I look until I find the word *strain*. One definition says it is a verb which means "to stretch tightly." Does this make sense in the sentence? *The door started to stretch tightly at the hinges.* That makes sense, so that must be what it means!

PRACTICE AND ASSESS

Have students use a dictionary to find the meaning of *shiny* on p. 210. (*glossy, brilliant, reflective*) To assess, check that the definition they have found makes sense in the context of the sentence.

TIME FOR Science

Museum Collections

f you've ever been to a museum, you may have noticed a small mechanism in each room or display case. These mechanisms are computers that monitor things such as temperature and humidity in the room or the case in which artifacts are stored. Temperatures that are too high can dry out an object, while temperatures that are too low can cause an object to swell or even split. Too much moisture or not enough moisture in the air can have a similar effect. Often, museums won't let you take photographs either. That is because light can harm objects, especially textiles, such as tapestries or old clothes, which can fade and dry out from too much light.

Guiding Comprehension

11 🎯 **Main Idea and Details • Inferential**

Look at pp. 212–213. What are these two pages about?

Prudy's room explodes because she has too much stuff in it.

Monitor Progress

🎯 **Main Idea and Details**

If... students are unable to tell what pp. 212–213 are about,	**then...** use the skill and strategy instruction on p. 213.

---

12 **Author's Craft • Literal**

Question the Author **Sometimes authors use humor to move things along in their stories. Find one detail on pp. 212–213 that is funny.**

Responses will vary; students can mention the text or the illustrations.

13 **Realism and Fantasy • Inferential**

Name a way in which the story is a fantasy.

Possible response: Someone's room would not explode if it had too much stuff in it.

EXTEND SKILLS

Warning Label
Categorize Words

Discuss what kind of warning label Prudy could put on her door. Why does Prudy need to warn people before they enter her room? What other kinds of things have warning labels? Bring in examples of warning labels, or empty containers that have warnings. Have children read the warning labels and sort the products into categories (For example, food, cleaners, yard products).

The room exploded with an enormous BANG!

Bits and pieces of stuff flew everywhere.

11 **12** **13**

213

DURING READING

SKILLS ↔ STRATEGIES IN CONTEXT

Main Idea/ Details

TEACH

- Understanding what each page in a story is about can help us understand the whole story. As we are reading, we should look for details that tell us what each page is about.

- When we are finished reading, we can think back about what each page is about and see what this tells us about the story as a whole.

- Model figuring out what pp. 212–213 are about.

Think Aloud **MODEL** These two pages say the room exploded, and stuff flew everywhere. I think they're about Prudy's room exploding because she had too much stuff in it. The details support the idea that this story is about Prudy's collecting problem.

PRACTICE AND ASSESS

Have students go back through the selection and figure out what the other pages are about. Discuss how this helps them understand what the story as a whole is about. To assess, have them check that details from the story support their ideas.

Careers

TIME FOR Science

Did you know that there are over one million types of insects in the world? Insects are found in almost all climates and are some of the few organisms that were around when the dinosaurs were. You might think insects are yucky or scary, but they're actually very interesting, and you can learn a lot from studying them. There are even people called entomologists who make a living studying them. Entomologists study bugs, where they live, and how they are both good and bad for humans. Some entomologists, called forensic entomologists, even help detectives solve crimes. So if bugs don't bug you, you might have found your perfect job!

EXTEND SKILLS

Humor

Explain to students that writing that makes them laugh is called humor. Usually, we can recognize humor in jokes or funny things a character says or does. The events in the story itself can also be humorous. Point out that sometimes authors will use pictures to add to the humor as well. Discuss what is funny about pp. 212–213. (*both the idea of Prudy's room exploding and the pictures of Prudy and her family, flying through the air*) Have students go back and find other examples of humor.

Prudy's Problem **213**

Guiding Comprehension

14 REVIEW **Character • Critical**

Text to Self **Sometimes it can be difficult admitting we are wrong. What does this tell us about Prudy's character? Do you ever have trouble admitting your mistakes?**

Possible responses: She is strong enough to admit her mistakes. Students should mention a time when they admitted a mistake or had trouble doing so.

Monitor Progress

REVIEW **Character**

If... students are unable to make an inference about Prudy's character,	then... use the skill and strategy instruction on p. 215.

15 Cause and Effect • Inferential

Why does Prudy finally admit she has a problem?

Her room explodes.

16 Predict • Inferential

What do you think Prudy's plan is?

Responses will vary; look for answers that follow logically with the details on p. 214 and what we know about collections.

"Holy smokes," said Prudy. "I guess maybe I do have **14** a little problem."

For six weeks, everyone pitched in to gather Prudy's **15** scattered collections.

"Now what, Prudy?" said her family.

"Now what, Prudy?" said her friends.

"I'm working on it!" said Prudy.

Prudy looked around for inspiration. She visited an art collection. She visited a fish collection. She visited a rock collection. She went to the library to find ideas.

At last, after many hours of scrutinizing stacks of books, she came up with a brilliant plan! **16**

214

Understand Idioms Point out the idiom *pitched in* on p. 214 and read the sentence. Ask students if Prudy picked up her things all by herself or if she got help. Explain that *to pitch in* means to help someone do something. Have students think of at least one time they pitched in to help someone else, or someone else pitched in to help them.

With saws whirring and hammers pounding, everyone set to work.

215

SKILLS ↔ STRATEGIES IN CONTEXT

Character REVIEW

TEACH

- Remind students that authors don't always tell us everything about a character. Sometimes we have to use clues in the story to tell us.
- Model using clues in the story to make an inference about Prudy's character.

Think Aloud **MODEL** Right from the beginning, Prudy refused to see that she had a problem collecting things. She kept telling people she did not have a problem. But then her room exploded, and she admitted that she had a problem. That's hard to do sometimes! This tells me she will admit she's wrong.

PRACTICE AND ASSESS

Prudy tries to find a solution to the problem she created. Discuss with students what else this tells us about Prudy. (*Possible response: She is responsible.*)

Guiding Comprehension

17 **Summarize • Inferential**

In one sentence, tell what *Prudy's Problem* is about. Then tell what happened in the story in the correct order.

Possible response: The story is about a little girl who collects too much stuff. First everyone tries to tell her she has too much stuff, but she disagrees. Then she tries to stuff one last thing into her room, so it explodes. Finally, she decides to set up a museum for all her collections.

18 **Compare and Contrast • Critical**

Text to Text **Think about the character of Prudy in *Prudy's Problem* and the character of Francisco in *A Day's Work*. How are they similar? How are they different? What can we learn from both characters?**

Possible response: Prudy is a character in a fantasy, and Francisco is a character in a realistic story. They are both quick thinkers and both make a mistake, and they both work hard to correct their mistake. From Francisco, we learn to always be honest. From Prudy, we learn to share things with others.

Strategy Response Log

Summarize When students finish reading the selection, provide this prompt: Imagine that you want to tell a friend what *Prudy's Problem* is about. In four or five sentences, explain its important points.

The Prudy Museum of Indescribable Wonderment was an amazing sight to behold.

Everyone wanted to go visit!

Within a year, it was the biggest tourist attraction in Prudy's town.

"Look at that, Egbert," said Belinda. "Did you ever realize how many kinds of gym socks there are?"

"I had no idea cheese rinds could be so fascinating!" said Prudy's mother.

"Can I go to the gift shop?" said Evie.

At last Prudy's collections were neat and orderly and appreciated by everyone. Now she could sit back and enjoy the museum and all her happy visitors . . . .

But she could never *really* stop collecting!

17 **18**

217

Monitor/Fix Up

- Tell students that after finishing a story, it's a good idea to tell what it was about. If we can't do that, then we need to figure out what we are confused about and fix it.

- If we are confused, we should look at the details in the story again.

- Have students think about questions they may have about the story and go back to find answers. Then have them write a summary.

SELF-CHECK

Students can ask themselves these questions to assess ability to use the skill and strategy.

- Does my summary tell what the story is about?

- Do I need to go back and find details that tell me what the story is about?

- To assess, use Practice Book 3.1 p. 77.

Monitor Progress

Main Idea and Details

If... students have difficulty stating main idea and supporting details,	then... use the Reteach lesson on p. 223b.

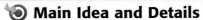

Main Idea · Monitor and Fix Up

- The **main idea** can be found by asking, "What is this story all about? **Details** are small pieces of information that help tell what the story is about.
- As you read, ask yourself, "What are the important details so far?" **Sum up** to help you understand what is happening and to help you tell what the story is about.

Directions Read the following passage. Then answer the questions below.

Jermaine's bedroom was so full of books that they covered the bed, and Jermaine had nowhere to sleep.
"I need to do something about this," thought Jermaine. So he found some old bricks and boards in the garden.
Jermaine took all the books out of his bedroom. He laid bricks on the floor up against the walls and stacked a board on top.

Then Jermaine put down more bricks and stacked another board on top. Jermaine repeated the steps many more times. Soon Jermaine had bookshelves that went to the ceiling, and all of Jermaine's books fit on the shelves.

1. What details in the first paragraph will help you tell what this story is all about?
   Books cover the bed; Jermaine can't sleep in the bed.

2. Jermaine decides he needs to do something about the books. How does this detail help you understand what this story is all about?
   It lets you know that this story will be about how Jermaine solves his problem.

3. The bookshelves went to the ceiling. Is this an important detail? Explain.
   Possible response: No; the important detail is that he built bookshelves to solve his problem.

4. Use the details to sum up. Tell what this story is all about.
   Building bookshelves is a good way to keep books out of the way.

School + Home Home Activity Your child used details in a story to determine its main idea, or what the story is all about. Have your child recall familiar stories. Discuss the important details. Then help your child write a sentence to tell what the story is about.

▲ **Practice Book 3.1** p. 77

Develop Vocabulary

PRACTICE LESSON VOCABULARY

Have students answer each question.

1. Is tin foil *shiny*? (Yes)
2. If you discover *information* about something, what have you discovered? (Facts)
3. What is another way to say *scattered*? (Spread out)

BUILD CONCEPT VOCABULARY

Review previous concept words with students. Ask if students have met any words today in their reading or elsewhere that they would like to add to the Concept Web.

Reader Response

Open for Discussion **Personal Response**

MODEL Prudy's museum is getting full. What could she do? Well, she could add on to it to make it bigger. Or she could sell some of her things to make room for new things.

Comprehension Check **Critical Response**

1. Possible response: The author might use lists to make it clear what kinds of objects Prudy is collecting. **Author's Purpose**

2. Prudy learned the importance of solving her own problems. **Main Idea**

3. Possible response: Stopping to summarize helped me understand the story. **Monitor and Fix Up**

4. Prudy's enormous collection of things scattered all over the room. **Vocabulary**

Look Back and Write For test practice, assign a 10–15 minute time limit. For assessment, see the Scoring Rubric at the right.

Retell

Have students retell *Prudy's Problem.*

Monitor Progress

Check Retelling (Rubric 4 3 2 1)

If... students have difficulty retelling the story,	then... use the Retelling Cards and the Scoring Rubric for Retelling on p. 219 to assist fluent retelling.

SUCCESS PREDICTOR

Check Retelling Have students use illustrations and other text features to guide their retellings. Let students listen to other retellings before attempting their own. See the ELL and Transition Handbook.

Reader Response

Open for Discussion The museum is getting full. Soon Prudy may need a new solution to her problem. Think of two solutions from which Prudy can choose.

1. This author seems to like lists. Why do you think the author uses lists? **Think Like an Author**

2. At the end of the story, Prudy learned something important. What did she learn? **Main Idea and Details**

3. Did anything in this story confuse you? Did you stop to sum up? How did that help you? **Monitor and Fix Up**

4. Prudy's <u>huge</u> <u>group of things</u> <u>flew</u> all over the room. Rewrite this sentence using the Words to Know list in place of the underlined words. **Vocabulary**

Look Back and Write Something shows Prudy that she has a problem. Look at page 213 to find that thing. Write about what it is and how it changes Prudy's mind. Use details from the story in your answer.

Meet author **and illustrator Carey Armstrong-Ellis on page 414.**

218

Scoring Rubric **Look Back and Write**

Top-Score Response A top-score response will use details from the story to identify what the problem is, what Prudy thinks and what event changes Prudy's mind.

Example of a Top-Score Response Prudy's room is packed full of her collections. Her parents tell her she has too many things. Prudy disagrees. She does not think she has a problem. One day her room gets so full it explodes. This changes Prudy's mind, and she realizes she does have a problem.

For additional rubrics, see p. WA10.

Write Now
Problem-Solution

DURING READING

Prompt

Prudy's Problem explains how a girl solves a problem.

Think about a problem you and your friends have.

Now write a paragraph describing the problem and how to solve it.

Writing Trait

Organize your **paragraph** by explaining the problem first and then the solution.

Student Model

First two sentences explain problem.

> I know homework can be helpful. But I have a problem finding time to do homework. So I made a homework plan. First, I cut out some after-school activities. Once a week I have soccer practice. On the other days, I do my homework right after school. After a snack, I get to work. It's amazing how quickly I finish. I usually have time to go outside before dinner. After dinner, I can spend time with my family. All kids should try this solution. Then they can finish their homework and still have time for fun.

Paragraph has two-part organization: problem followed by solution. Word *So* signals change.

Last sentence explains why solution is good idea.

Use the model to help you write your own problem-solution paragraph.

219

Write Now

Look at the Prompt Explain that each sentence in the prompt has a purpose.

- Sentence 1 presents a topic.
- Sentence 2 suggests students think about the topic.
- Sentence 3 tells what to write—a problem-solution paragraph.

Strategies to Develop Organization/Paragraphs

Have students

- state their problem at the beginning of their paragraph and describe their solution.
- use words such as *so* or *but* as transitions.

NO: I couldn't get up in the morning. I started going to bed earlier.

YES: I couldn't get up in the morning, so I started going to bed earlier.

For additional suggestions and rubric, see pp. 223g–223h.

Writer's Checklist

☑ **Focus** Are all sentences about a problem and its solution?

☑ **Organization** Is the problem described first and then the solution? Does a transition word signal the change?

☑ **Support** Do details help make the problem clear and the solution logical?

☑ **Conventions** Are grammar, punctuation, and spelling correct?

Scoring Rubric   Narrative Retelling

Rubric 4 3 2 1	4	3	2	1
Connections	Makes connections and generalizes beyond the text	Makes connections to other events, stories, or experiences	Makes a limited connection to another event, story, or experience	Makes no connection to another event, story, or experience
Author's Purpose	Elaborates on author's purpose	Tells author's purpose with some clarity	Makes some connection to author's purpose	Makes no connection to author's purpose
Characters	Describes the main character(s) and any character development	Identifies the main character(s) and gives some information about them	Inaccurately identifies some characters or gives little information about them	Inaccurately identifies the characters or gives no information about them
Setting	Describes the time and location	Identifies the time and location	Omits details of time or location	Is unable to identify time or location
Plot	Describes the problem, goal, events, and ending using rich detail	Tells the problem, goal, events, and ending with some errors that do not affect meaning	Tells parts of the problem, goal, events, and ending with gaps that affect meaning	Retelling has no sense of story

Retelling Plan

☑ **Week 1** Assess Strategic Intervention students.

☑ **Week 2** Assess Advanced students.

☑ **This week assess Strategic Intervention students.**

☐ **Week 4** Assess On-Level students.

☐ **Week 5** Assess any students you have not yet checked during this unit.

Use the Retelling Chart on p. TR16 to record retelling.

Selection Test To assess with *Prudy's Problem*, use Selection Tests, pp. 29–32.

Fresh Reads for Differentiated Test Practice For weekly leveled practice, use pp. 97–102.

Retelling

SUCCESS PREDICTOR

Social Studies in Reading

PREVIEW/USE TEXT FEATURES

As students preview "Meeting the Challenge of Collecting," have them identify what the man who was interviewed does for a job and where he might work or have worked in the past. After they preview, ask:

- **What do the photographs tell us about Dr. Feinman's work?** *(They tell us he collects and studies objects.)*

Link to Social Studies

Brainstorm a list of questions students might ask, then help them use print reference sources—such as a telephone book or tourist information book—and the Internet to locate information about museums in your area.

DAY 4 Grouping Options

Reading
Whole Group Discuss the Question of the Day.

Group Time Differentiated Instruction
Read "Meeting the Challenge of Collecting." See pp. 198f–198g for the small group lesson plan.

Whole Group Use pp. 223a and 223j.

Language Arts
Use pp. 223e–223h and 223k–223m.

Social Studies in Reading

MEETING THE CHALLENGE OF COLLECTING

BY LISA KLOBUCHAR

Interview

Genre

- An interview is similar to a conversation.
- An interview usually is written in a question-and-answer format.
- An interview can provide interesting information about a topic.

Text Features

- Photos often illustrate an interview.
- Photos can also provide additional information.

Link to Social Studies

Learn about a museum in your city or state. What do you want to know? Write some questions that you would ask in an interview.

The Field Museum of Natural History, in Chicago, is one of the world's biggest museums. Dr. Gary Feinman is the head of the Field Museum's anthropology department. Anthropology is the study of how people live. Anthropologists look at how people fit in with the places they live. They study how different groups of people are alike and different. Dr. Feinman explains how the museum puts together its anthropology collections. He also talks about some of the challenges of putting these collections on display and how the museum meets these challenges.

220

Content-Area Vocabulary Social Studies

pottery	objects made of baked clay
tapestries	pieces of fabric with pictures or designs woven into them

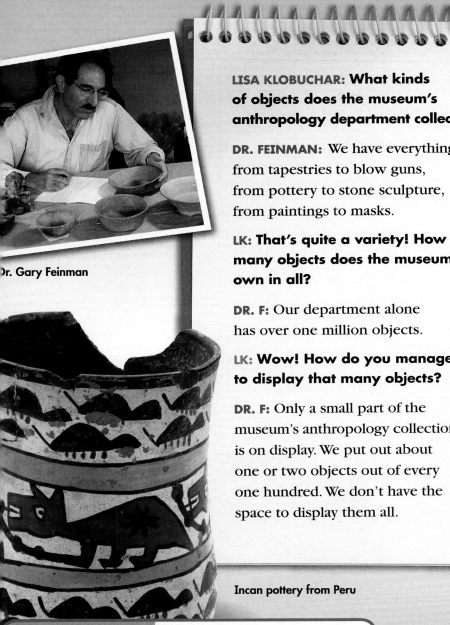

LISA KLOBUCHAR: **What kinds of objects does the museum's anthropology department collect?**

DR. FEINMAN: We have everything from tapestries to blow guns, from pottery to stone sculpture, from paintings to masks.

LK: **That's quite a variety! How many objects does the museum own in all?**

DR. F: Our department alone has over one million objects.

LK: **Wow! How do you manage to display that many objects?**

DR. F: Only a small part of the museum's anthropology collection is on display. We put out about one or two objects out of every one hundred. We don't have the space to display them all.

Incan pottery from Peru

Dr. Gary Feinman

⊘ Monitor and Fix Up Summarize the facts you've read so far.

221

Careers

Time for **SOCIAL STUDIES**

Anthropologists study the physical, social, and cultural development of humans. They may study groups that live around the world or close to home. Archaeologists also study human life. They specialize in past societies and cultures by investigating fossils, burial sites, ancient cities, and other material remains.

DURING READING

INTERVIEW

Use the sidebar on p. 220 to guide discussion.

- An interview is a written record of a conversation between people, usually two—a reporter and a person who has interesting or useful information. The words are exactly what was said in the interview.

- Look at p. 221. There are two kinds of text: bold text and light text. The questions are in bold text, and the answers are in light text. Notice that there are no quotation marks. Instead, the questions and answers are preceded by the speaker's name, either the interviewer or the interviewee (the person being interviewed), and a colon.

- Discuss the kinds of people who are most often interviewed and why. Share the name of someone you would like to interview and encourage students to do the same.

Audio CD AudioText

⊘ Monitor and Fix Up

Students' summaries should tell some or all of the following: who is being interviewed, what he does, where he works, the kinds of objects he collects, how many objects the museum has, and how they display them all.

Activate Prior Knowledge Have students share what they know about museums. Prompt them to think about the kinds of things that are collected. Encourage them to tell about museums they have been to or those that are famous in their home country.

Prudy's Problem **221**

Strategies for Nonfiction

USE QUESTIONS AND ANSWERS Explain that students may be asked to read interviews and answer questions about them on standardized tests. They can use the question-and-answer format to find information quickly and answer the test questions correctly. Provide the following strategy.

Use the Strategy

1. Read the test question and make sure you understand what it is asking.
2. Scan the selection for an interview question that relates to the information being asked in the test question.
3. Read the interviewee's response. Look for details in the response that will help you answer the test question.

GUIDED PRACTICE Have students discuss how they would use the strategy to answer the following question.

What does the museum do with the artifacts it cannot display?

INDEPENDENT PRACTICE After students answer the following test question, discuss the process they used to find information.

Dr. Feinman states that artifacts can get damaged. What is one cause of damage to artifacts?

LK: With so many interesting and unusual objects, how do you decide which to put on display?

DR. F: Our permanent displays all have certain themes. If an object fits in with that theme, we try to put it on display.

LK: Are there any objects that you would like to display but can't?

DR. F: Yes. Some objects are just too easily damaged. Some can be harmed by getting too hot or too cold. Others may be harmed by bright light or by air that is too moist or too dry. Moths or other insects can ruin cloth items and baskets.

Tapa bark cloth from Papua New Guinea

Woven basket of the Wappo Indians

222

ELL

Test Practice Direct students' attention to one page of the interview. Show them how they can identify the interviewer's questions by the bold text. Explain that the questions work like a title—they tell what the answer will be about. Read the Guided Practice question aloud. Go through the selection with students, stopping at each of the interviewer's questions and asking if that question asks about information asked in the practice question. When they successfully identify the correct interview question, have them read the answer and point out details that help them answer the question. Then have them write a short response to the question.

Mask from Cameroon

LK: Sounds like a real problem. How do you protect these objects?

DR. F: We have a full-time staff to care for our collection. They make sure the objects are stored properly. The Field Museum is building an underground collections center. This center will allow the museum to store objects safely. Caring for the collection is like caring for one's health. It is better to avoid problems than to look for a cure after big problems arise.

Reading Across Texts

How are Prudy's Museum and the Field Museum of Natural History alike? How are they different?

Writing Across Texts Make a chart in which you show how the two museums are alike and different.

⊘ Main Idea What is this selection mostly about?

223

CONNECT TEXT TO TEXT

Reading Across Texts

Discuss the kinds of things Prudy collected in her museum and the kinds of things Dr. Feinman collects in his museum. Write their ideas on the board for students to organize into a chart.

Writing Across Texts Help students set up a chart. Some charts they can use include a Venn diagram (Graphic Organizer 17) or a three-column chart (Graphic Organizer 26).

⊘ Main Idea

This selection is mostly about how the museum chooses what to display and how it takes care of its objects.

Fluency Assessment Plan

- ☑ **Week 1** Assess Advanced students.
- ☑ **Week 2** Assess Strategic Intervention students.
- ☑ **This week assess On-Level students.**
- ☐ **Week 4** Assess Strategic Intervention students.
- ☐ **Week 5** Assess any students you have not yet checked during this unit.

Set individual goals for students to enable them to reach the year-end goal.
- Current Goal: 85–95 WCPM
- Year-End Goal: 120 WCPM

Fluency Coach CD To develop fluent readers, use Fluency Coach.

MORE READING FOR
Fluency

Decodable Reader 8
The Scarecrow
Written by Sheldon Cline
Illustrated by Anne Brown

Phonics Skill
Compound Words

To practice fluency with text comprised of previously taught phonics elements and irregular words, use Decodable Reader 8.

DAY 5 Grouping Options

Reading
Whole Group
Revisit the Question of the Week.

Group Time
Differentiated Instruction
Reread this week's Leveled Readers. See pp. 198f–198g for the small group lesson plan.

Whole Group
Use pp. 223b–223c

Language Arts
Use pp. 223d–223h and 223k–223n.

EXPRESSION/INTONATION

Fluency

DAY 1

Model Reread "The Rampanion" on p. 198m. Explain that you will use different tones of voice to show surprise, happiness, or other emotions as you read the selection. Model for students as you read.

DAY 2

Choral Reading Read aloud p. 208. Have students notice how your voice changes as you read *surely* and the italicized word *like*. Have students practice as a class doing three choral readings of p. 208.

DAY 3

Model Read aloud p. 209. Have students notice how you pause as you read "*Uh-oh*" and how you read the italicized words in a louder voice. Practice as a class by doing three choral readings.

DAY 4

Partner Reading Partners practice reading aloud p. 209, three times. Students should read with proper expression and intonation and offer each other feedback.

Monitor Progress   Check Fluency WCPM

As students reread, monitor their progress toward their individual fluency goals. Current Goal: 85–95 words correct per minute. End-of-Year Goal: 120 words correct per minute.

If... students cannot read fluently at a rate of 85–95 words correct per minute,
then... make sure students practice with text at their independent level. Provide additional fluency practice, pairing nonfluent readers with fluent readers.

If... students already read at 120 words correct per minute,
then... they do not need to reread three to four times.

SUCCESS PREDICTOR

DAY 5

Assessment
Individual Reading Rate Use the Fluency Assessment Plan and do a one-minute timed reading of either selection from this week to assess students in Week 3. Pay special attention to this week's skill, intonation. Provide corrective feedback for each student.

RETEACH

 Main Idea

TEACH

Review the skill instruction for main idea on p. 198. Write the following on the board: *What is the story about? What details, or bits of information, tell me what the story is about?* Students can complete Practice Book 3.1, p. 78 on their own, or you can complete it as a class. Point out that the boxes in the main idea graphic organizer are empty; students must fill in the empty boxes with information from the selection.

ASSESS

Have students work together to find the main idea on p. 207. (*Main idea: Prudy's father wanted to get rid of some of Prudy's collections.*)

For additional instruction of main idea, see DI·54.

EXTEND SKILLS

Onomatopoeia

TEACH

A word that sounds like its meaning is an example of onomatopoeia.

• Authors use onomatopoeia to reinforce meaning. Onomatopoeia can also add drama and make writing more lively and interesting.

• Words like *splat, shush,* and *zip* are examples of onomatopoeia.

Point out the word *Bang!* on p. 212, and discuss how it is used. (*It reinforces meaning, showing how big the explosion was; it dramatizes the event in the story, showing how the explosion sounded.*)

ASSESS

Have pairs of students find other examples of onomatopoeia and explain how the words are used. (*Possible response: p. 215, whirring*)

OBJECTIVES

• Recognize the main idea.
• Recognize onomatopoeia.

Skills Trace
Main Idea

Introduce/Teach	TE: 3.2 150–151, 198–199, 3.6 284–285
Practice	PB: 3.1 53, 57, 58, 73, 77, 78, 86; 3.2 103, 107, 108, 126, 146
Reteach/Review	**TE: 3.2 173b, 223b, 233, 241, DI•52, DI•54; 3.6 303b, 339, 391, 397,**
Test	Selection Test: Unit 2 Benchmark Tests: Units 2, 6

ELL

Access Content Reteach the skill by reviewing the Picture It! lesson on main idea in the ELL Teaching Guide, pp. 50–51.

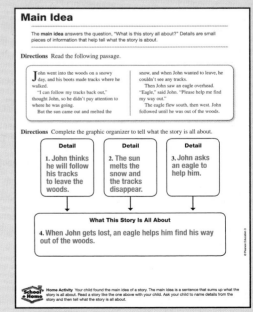

▲ **Practice Book 3.1** p. 78

Vocabulary and Word Study

VOCABULARY STRATEGY
◎Dictionary

UNFAMILIAR WORDS Remind students that they can use a dictionary to determine the meaning of unfamiliar words. Have students list any unknown words they encountered as they read *Prudy's Problem.* They can create a chart showing the unknown word and its dictionary definition.

Word	Dictionary Definition
normal	usual, everyday
unnatural	
baffled	

Museum Words

Museum words, such as *collection*, refer to museums and what is inside them. Have partners use reference sources to find museum words. They should then write them, along with their definitions, on folded index cards, to resemble labels from museums.

Some Museum Words

display case	ancient
curator	valuable
historian	exhibit
docent	gallery

BUILD CONCEPT VOCABULARY
Ideas and Inventions

LOOKING BACK Remind students of the focus question of the week: How can you get ideas to solve a problem? Discuss how this week's Concept Web of vocabulary words relates to the theme of ideas and inventions. Ask students if they have any words or categories to add. Discuss whether words and categories are appropriately related to the concept.

MOVING FORWARD Preview the title of the next selection, *Tops and Bottoms.* Ask students which Concept Web words might apply to the new selection based on the title alone. Put a star next to these words on the web.

Display the Concept Web and revisit the vocabulary words as you read the next selection to check predictions.

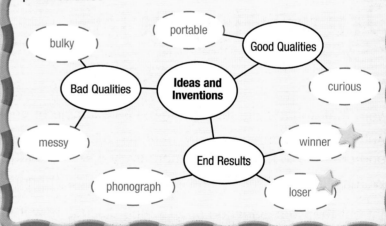

Monitor Progress
Check Vocabulary

If... students suggest words or categories that are not related to the concept,	then... review the words and categories on the Concept Web and discuss how they relate to the lesson concept.

SUCCESS PREDICTOR

Speaking and Listening

SPEAKING

Speak with a Purpose

SET-UP Have students work in small groups to solve problems. Groups will identify and solve problems, then present their problem and solutions to the class.

TOPICS Brainstorm a list of problems if students have trouble identifying one. Possible ideas are: accidentally hitting a ball through a neighbor's window, or receiving more than the correct amount of change at a store check-out.

TEAM PRESENTATION Provide time for groups to rehearse their presentations. Share these group presentation suggestions:

- Decide what each person will talk about.
- Offer several possible solutions to the problem.
- Conclude with the agreed-upon solution.
- Use note cards only to remind you of key words. Speak without reading the cards.

Listening Tips
- Give speakers your full attention.
- Think about what you would do in that situation.
- Listen for alternative solutions.
- Try to summarize the solution in your own words.

LISTENING

Listen to a Broadcast

Have students listen to local radio broadcasts about a local or national problem. Working in small groups, students can answer these questions orally or in writing.

1. **What problem is being discussed in this broadcast?** *(Responses will vary depending on the broadcast.)*

2. **Are the broadcasters offering suggestions to help solve the problem? If yes, what are they suggesting?** *(Responses will vary.)*

3. **Can you think of other ways to help with this problem? What would you suggest?** *(Responses will vary.)*

Support Vocabulary Use the following to review and extend vocabulary and to explore lesson concepts further:
- ELL Poster 8, Days 3–5 instruction
- Vocabulary Activities and Word Cards in ELL Teaching Guide, pp. 52–53

Assessment For information on assessing students' speaking, listening, and viewing, see the ELL and Transition Handbook.

Check Vocabulary

SUCCESS PREDICTOR

Grammar Irregular Plural Nouns

OBJECTIVES

- Define and identify irregular plural nouns.
- Spell irregular plural nouns correctly.
- Use irregular plural nouns in writing.
- Become familiar with irregular plural noun assessment on high-stakes tests.

Monitor Progress

Grammar

If... students have difficulty identifying irregular plural nouns,	then... see The Grammar and Writing Book pp. 92–95.

DAILY FIX-IT

This week use Daily Fix-It Transparency 8.

Spiral REVIEW

Support Grammar See the Grammar Transition lessons in the ELL and Transition Handbook.

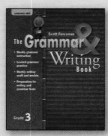

▲ **The Grammar and Writing Book** For more instruction and practice, use pp. 92–97.

DAY 1 — Teach and Model

DAILY FIX-IT

1. Those children has a big collection of butter flies. *(have; butterflies)*

2. Kim collects shells and Maya collects earings. *(shells,; earrings)*

READING-GRAMMAR CONNECTION

Write this sentence from *Prudy's Problem* on the board:

> *But Prudy herself found that she could barely get to her desk to feed her mice.*

Explain that *mice* is an **irregular plural noun.** The singular noun, *mouse,* does not add -*s* or -*es* to form the plural. Instead, it has a special form: *mice.*

Display Grammar Transparency 8. Read aloud the definitions and sample sentences. Work through the items.

Irregular Plural Nouns

A plural noun names more than one person, place, or thing. Most nouns add -*s* to form the plural. An **irregular plural noun** has a special form for the plural.

  Singular Nouns   An <u>ox</u> and a <u>sheep</u> live on the farm.
  Irregular Plural Nouns Three <u>oxen</u> and some <u>sheep</u> live on the farm.

Some nouns and their irregular plural forms are child/children, deer/deer, foot/feet, goose/geese, leaf/leaves, life/lives, man/men, mouse/mice, ox/oxen, sheep/sheep, tooth/teeth, and woman/women.

Directions Write *S* if the underlined noun is singular. Write *P* if the underlined noun is plural.

1. Some <u>children</u> collect pets.   **P**
2. Carrie has four <u>mice</u>.   **P**
3. She has a pet <u>goose</u> in her yard.   **S**
4. Carrie wants some woolly <u>sheep</u>.   **P**
5. She even wants a <u>deer</u>.   **S**

Directions Underline the singular nouns and circle the plural nouns in the sentences.

6. The ⟨children⟩ told the <u>woman</u> about their <u>problem</u>.
7. They could not rake all the ⟨leaves⟩ on the <u>playground</u>.
8. They could not run fast with ⟨leaves⟩ under their ⟨feet⟩.
9. Some ⟨men⟩ brought ⟨machines⟩ to school.
10. The <u>woman</u> and the ⟨men⟩ solved the <u>problem</u> together.

Unit 2 *Prudy's Problem*   **Grammar 8**

▲ **Grammar Transparency** 8

DAY 2 — Develop the Concept

DAILY FIX-IT

3. My friend jody has boxs all over her room. *(Jody; boxes)*

4. How can you do home work in this room. *(homework; room?)*

GUIDED PRACTICE

Review the concept of irregular plural nouns.

- A **plural noun** names more than one person, place, or thing. Most nouns add -*s* to form the plural.

- An **irregular plural noun** has a special form for the plural. Some nouns and their irregular plural forms are child/children, deer/deer, foot/feet, goose/geese, leaf/leaves, life/lives, man/men, mouse/mice, ox/oxen, sheep/sheep, and tooth/teeth.

HOMEWORK Grammar and Writing Practice Book p. 29. Work through the first two items with the class.

Irregular Plural Nouns

A plural noun names more than one person, place, or thing. Most nouns add -*s* to form the plural. An **irregular plural noun** has a special form for the plural.

  Singular Nouns   A <u>goose</u> and a <u>deer</u> ate a leaf.
  Irregular Plural Nouns Some <u>geese</u> and some <u>deer</u> ate some <u>leaves</u>.

Some nouns and their irregular plural forms are child/children, deer/deer, foot/feet, goose/geese, leaf/leaves, life/lives, man/men, mouse/mice, ox/oxen, sheep/sheep, tooth/teeth, and woman/women.

Directions Write *S* if the underlined noun is singular. Write *P* if the underlined noun is plural.

1. The <u>children</u> had a messy room. **P**
2. Aunt Rose would not put a <u>foot</u> into the room. **S**
3. There were <u>leaves</u> on the floor. **P**
4. I've never seen such a sight in my <u>life</u>! **S**
5. <u>Mice</u> could make a nest in there. **P**

Directions Write the plural nouns in each sentence.

6. The men on the farm had a problem.

  men

7. Deer were eating vegetables from their fields.

  deer, vegetables, fields

8. The farmers found holes in the lettuce leaves.

  farmers, holes, leaves

9. The women tried to think of clever solutions.

  women, solutions

 Home Activity Your child learned about irregular plural nouns. Say the words goose, mouse, and child and have your child say the plural form of each word.

▲ **Grammar and Writing Practice Book** p. 29

DAY 3   Apply to Writing

DAILY FIX-IT

5. Many people collects pennys and other coins. *(collect; pennies)*

6. Tim displaied his collection in springfield. *(displayed; Springfield)*

USE CORRECT PLURAL NOUNS

Use the correct plural forms so that readers will not get confused or distracted.

- Have students review something they have written to see if they can improve it by using the correct plural forms of nouns.

HOMEWORK Grammar and Writing Practice Book p. 30.

Irregular Plural Nouns

Directions Write sentences using the plural forms of the nouns.

1. child, tooth **Possible answers:**
   Young children lose their baby teeth.

2. woman, leaf
   Many women enjoyed the colorful autumn leaves.

3. sheep, deer
   Sheep and deer lived in the meadow.

4. goose, mouse
   We saw geese and field mice near the lake.

5. man, foot
   Men have two feet.

Directions Write about a problem you might have in a forest. Use at least two irregular plural nouns. **Possible answers:**
   There were many leaves on the ground. I
   couldn't see where I was walking. I almost
   stepped on two mice.

 Home Activity Your child learned how to use irregular plural nouns in writing. Have your child write a letter or e-mail to a family member about animals he or she has seen. Have your child use at least two irregular plural nouns in the letter or e-mail.

▲ **Grammar and Writing Practice Book** p. 30

DAY 4   Test Preparation

DAILY FIX-IT

7. On saturday, Kate shoped for a doll for her collection. *(Saturday; shopped)*

8. Jay has more then a thowsand stamps. *(than; thousand)*

STANDARDIZED TEST PREP

Test Tip

You will need to memorize the nouns that have irregular plurals. Some nouns have plurals that may not seem logical.

No: James saw two *mooses* in Montana.
James saw two *meese* in Montana.

Yes: James saw two *moose* in Montana.

HOMEWORK Grammar and Writing Practice Book p. 31.

Irregular Plural Nouns

Directions Mark the letter of the plural form of each underlined noun.

1. All the child collect something different.
   A childs
   B childes
   C children
   D child

2. Carlo has 20 foot of string.
   A foots
   B feet
   C foot
   D footes

3. Jo has 8 stuffed mouse.
   A mouses
   B meese
   C mouse
   D mice

4. Nick has all his baby tooth.
   A teeth
   B teeths
   C tooth
   D tooths

5. Jake has 100 toy army man.
   A mans
   B man
   C men
   D manes

6. Maria has 20 plastic sheep.
   A sheep
   B sheeps
   C sheepes
   D sheepe

7. Nan has 15 pictures of fall leaf.
   A leafs
   B leavs
   C leaves
   D leafes

8. Charlie collects toy deer.
   A deere
   B deer
   C deers
   D deeres

 Home Activity Your child prepared for taking tests on irregular plural nouns. Have a discussion with your child about the families in your neighborhood. Ask your child to use the singular and plural forms of man, woman, and child.

▲ **Grammar and Writing Practice Book** p. 31

DAY 5   Cumulative Review

DAILY FIX-IT

9. Julie collected some pretty leafs at the Park. *(leaves; park)*

10. She droped them in the middel of her room. *(dropped; middle)*

ADDITIONAL PRACTICE

Assign pp. 92–95 in The Grammar and Writing Book.

EXTRA PRACTICE Grammar and Writing Practice Book p. 129.

TEST PREPARATION Grammar and Writing Practice Book pp. 153–154.

ASSESSMENT

CUMULATIVE REVIEW Grammar and Writing Practice Book p. 32.

Irregular Plural Nouns

Directions Underline the singular nouns and circle the plural nouns in the sentences.

1. (Neighbors) thought the dirty park was a problem.

2. (Men) cut (branches) and raked (leaves).

3. The (children) picked up (papers).

4. The (workers) saw several (deer) and (geese) during the day.

5. Their (feet) were muddy, but the park was clean.

Directions Write the plural form of the noun in ( ).

6. A big problem was solved by those (woman). **women**

7. The family's garage was full of (mouse). **mice**

8. The ladies brought in cats and (child). **children**

9. Soon the mice ran for their (life). **lives**

Directions Write one or two sentences about a clean-up problem and how it was solved. Use the plural forms of at least two of these nouns: *child, foot, leaf, man*. **Possible answer:**

10. The children tracked their muddy feet all over the rug, but the men washed away the dirt.

 **Home Activity** Your child reviewed irregular plural nouns. Look at a newspaper article with your child. Have your child point out three irregular plural nouns.

▲ **Grammar and Writing Practice Book** p. 32

Writing Workshop   Problem-Solution

OBJECTIVES

- Identify the characteristics of a problem-solution paragraph.
- Compose a problem-solution paragraph that is clearly written.
- Focus on organization/paragraphs.
- Use a rubric.

Genre Problem-Solution
Writer's Craft Write Clearly
Writing Trait Organization/Paragraphs

ELL

Organization/Paragraphs Explain that transition words make order clear in writing. Write *first, next, then, after, before, also,* and *but* on index cards, one to a card, and model their meaning and use. Help language learners use these transition words in their writing.

Writing Trait

FOCUS/IDEAS A problem is clearly stated, and a logical solution is described.

ORGANIZATION/PARAGRAPHS A description of the solution follows the description of the problem, with a clear connection between the two.

VOICE Writing is clear and shows careful consideration of how to solve a problem.

WORD CHOICE The writer uses transitions such as *so* and *because* to indicate a problem-solution structure.

SENTENCES Varying sentence kinds and structures creates interest.

CONVENTIONS There is excellent control and accuracy, including correct spelling of an irregular plural noun.

DAY 1   Model the Trait

READING-WRITING CONNECTION

- *Prudy's Problem* describes a girl's problem with collecting and how she solved it.
- The story presents the girl's problem, her recognition of it, and her solution.
- Students will write a **problem-solution paragraph** clearly organized and explained.

MODEL ORGANIZATION/ PARAGRAPHS
Discuss Writing Transparency 8A. Then discuss the model and the writing trait of organization/paragraphs.

 Think Aloud The writer first names the problem (a messy closet, making it hard to find things) and why this is a problem (the closet made her late for school). Then the writer explains her step-by-step solution. The transition words *first, next,* and *finally* signal each step.

Problem-Solution

A **problem-solution** paragraph describes a problem. Then it tells how the problem was solved or how it could be solved.

My Closet Problem

First part of paragraph describes problem.
My closet was a mess! I couldn't find anything in it. I was late for school three times because I couldn't find a matching pair of shoes. Toys, games, shoes, T-shirts, pants, and jackets were jumbled together. So I called the best organizer I know: my cousin Beth. First, we took everything out of the closet. We gave away all my old clothes. Next, we hung the rest of my clothes on the racks. I put each pair of shoes together on the shelves. Finally, we sorted all my toys and games. I put my books on shelves. Now I can actually see what I have!

Second part of paragraph describes solution. So signals change. First, next, and finally tell order of steps.

Conclusion tells how solution helped writer and looks to future.
From now on, I am keeping my closet neat. I don't want to have to solve this problem again!

Unit 2 Prudy's Problem   Writing Model **8A**

▲ **Writing Transparency** 8A

DAY 2   Improve Writing

WRITER'S CRAFT
Write Clearly

Display Writing Transparency 8B. Read the directions and work together to point out unclear writing and suggest revisions.

 MAKE MEANING CLEAR Tomorrow we will write a **problem-solution paragraph.** I could write about the trouble I have with math homework. How could I state my problem clearly? To be specific, I could write, "I think I understand math problems when the teacher explains them, but when I get home, I can't remember how to do them." This sentence gives enough detail to make the problem clear.

GUIDED WRITING Some students may need more help writing clearly. Point out some writing that is unclear and have them suggest ways to revise it.

The Lincoln Memorial

The Lincoln Memorial in Washington, D.C., is one of our country's great monuments. It stands for freedom because it honors Abraham Lincoln. Lincoln, the United States president during the Civil War, helped bring freedom to all Americans.

The Lincoln Memorial is built of white marble. It is rectangular and has 36 columns. It looks like an ancient Greek building. The 36 columns stand for the 36 states in the United States when Lincoln was president.

Inside the Lincoln Memorial are three rooms. A statue of Lincoln sitting in a chair is in the center room. It is 19 feet tall! The other rooms display paintings and two of Lincoln's most famous speeches. They are the Gettysburg Address and the Second Inaugural Address.

The Lincoln Memorial was dedicated in 1922. It has the Potomac River on one side. The Washington Monument can be seen on the other side. The Lincoln Memorial is beautiful. It overlooks Washington and honors a great president. For all these reasons, the Lincoln Memorial is one of Americans' favorite monuments.

Unit 6 Research Report • PREWRITE   Writing Process **36**

▲ **Writing Transparency** 8B

DAY 3 Prewrite and Draft

READ THE WRITING PROMPT

on page 219 in the Student Edition.

Prudy's Problem *explains how a girl solves a problem.*

Think about a problem you and your friends have.

Now write a paragraph describing the problem and how to solve it.

Writing Test Tips

- List details about the problem and why it causes difficulty.
- List the steps involved in solving the problem.
- Use time-order words to make the steps in solving the problem clear.

GETTING STARTED Students can do any of the following:

- Use a concept web with *Problems I have solved* or *Problems in my school* in the center to list possible topics.
- With a group, discuss a school problem and why it needs to be solved.
- Make a T-chart with the headings *Problem* and *Solution*. Add details about the chosen topic.

DAY 4 Draft and Revise

EDITING/REVISING CHECKLIST

☑ Is the problem described clearly?

☑ Are the steps of the solution described clearly?

☑ Did I use irregular plural nouns correctly?

☑ Are compound words spelled correctly?

See *The Grammar and Writing Book,* pp. 92–97.

Revising Tips

Organization/ Paragraph

- Make sure the problem is stated clearly at the beginning.
- Make sure the solution is described clearly. Use a word such as *so* or *then* to move from the problem to the solution.
- Add time-order words to show the order of the steps in the solution.

PUBLISHING Students can read their paragraphs aloud in small groups. Some students may wish to revise their work later.

ASSESSMENT Use the scoring rubric to evaluate students' work.

DAY 5 Connect to Unit Writing

How-to Report	
Week 1	Summary 173g–173h
Week 2	Rules 197g–197h
Week 3	Problem/Solution 223g–223h
Week 4	Feature Story 249g–249h
Week 5	Explanatory Paragraph 271g–271h

PREVIEW THE UNIT PROMPT

Think of something you learned or figured out how to do that involves a few simple steps. Write the steps in a how-to report. Make sure you provide all the necessary information.

APPLY

- A how-to report explains the steps for making or doing something.
- A how-to report may tell how to solve a problem. Make sure the steps and explanations are clear.

Writing Trait Rubric

	4	3	2	1
Organization/ Paragraphs	Ideas well developed from beginning to end; strong closure	Ideas that progress from beginning to end; good closure	Some sense of movement from beginning to end; weak closure	No sense of movement from beginning to end or closure
	Paragraph organized with exceptional logic	Paragraph organized adequately	Paragraph not clearly organized	Paragraph not organized

OBJECTIVES

- Use word parts to decode compound words.
- Review the syllable pattern C+*le*.
- Blend and read compound words and words with syllable pattern C+*le*.
- Apply decoding strategies: blend longer words.

Generalization

Generalization A compound word is a word made up of two or more shorter words.

Support Phonics In many Asian languages, words are only one syllable. Speakers of these languages may need extra practice with the concept of compound words. Point out examples of compound words as you are reading and encourage students to bring in examples they find in their daily reading. For Spanish speakers, offer examples of compound words in Spanish, such as *rascacielos (skyscraper), abrelatas (can opener),* and *espantapajaros (scarecrow).*

See the Phonics Transition Lessons in the ELL and Transition Handbook.

Compound Words

Directions Identify the two words that make up each compound word. Write the words on the lines.

1.	__sun__	+	__glasses__	= sunglasses
2.	__rail__	+	__road__	= railroad
3.	__hair__	+	__cut__	= haircut
4.	__fire__	+	__house__	= firehouse
5.	__pop__	+	__corn__	= popcorn
6.	__my__	+	__self__	= myself
7.	__green__	+	__house__	= greenhouse
8.	__back__	+	__yard__	= backyard
9.	__rain__	+	__water__	= rainwater
10.	__sun__	+	__flower__	= sunflower

Directions Choose the compound word to complete each sentence. Write the word on the line. Draw a line between the two words that make up each compound word.

__grand/father__ **11.** My (grandfather/uncle) lives on a farm.

__when/ever__ **12.** I help him take care of his animals (whenever/when) I visit.

__snow/storm__ **13.** Last winter I was with him during a terrible (snowstorm/blizzard).

__out/side__ **14.** We had to work (outside/quickly) in the cold and snow.

__some/times__ **15.** It's (sometimes/often) difficult to be a farmer.

School + Home **Home Activity** Your child wrote compound words—words formed by joining two shorter words—such as homework. With your child, read advertisements to find compound words (such as everyday, something, and everyone). Have your child identify the two words that make up each compound word.

▲ **Practice Book 3.1** p. 79

Compound Words

TEACH

Write the words *homework* and *earthquake*.

- What two short words make up the longer word *homework*? (*home* and *work*)
- What is the meaning of each shorter word? (*Home* means "the place where you live," and *work* means "a task or job.")
- What do you think the longer word *homework* means? (A task that you do in the place where you live)

 MODEL A long word like *earthquake* seems hard at first, but when I look more closely, I see that *earthquake* is a compound word. That means it is made up of two shorter words, *earth* and *quake*. I know *earth* and I think *quake* means "shake," so it's easy to figure out that an *earthquake* is a movement of the ground.

Model blending *earthquake*. Then have students blend the word with you.

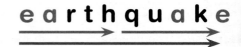

PRACTICE AND ASSESS

DECODE LONGER WORDS Write these words. Have students read them and draw lines between the two shorter words that make up the compound word.

playground   classmate   placemat   doorstop

housefly   raindrop   eyelid   thunderstorm

READ WORDS IN CONTEXT Write these sentences. Have individuals read them, point out the compound words, and define the compound words by defining the shorter words that make up the compound.

The peddler was pushing a <u>handcart</u> filled with fruit. (*hand and cart ; a cart pushed by hand*)

He tripped on his own <u>shoelace</u>. (*shoe and lace; the string you use to lace your shoes*)

I like the <u>outdoor</u>, swimming pool. (*out and door; not inside*)

To assess, have students look through the selection and find at least 3 examples of compound words. (*everything, sunglasses, anything*)

Phonics

Review Word Parts

REVIEW SYLLABLE PATTERN C+*le*

CONNECT Write this sentence: *The bugle sounded the wake-up call.*

- Last week, we studied the syllable pattern C+*le*.
- Read the sentence to yourself. Raise your hand when you know where to divide the word *bugle*. *(bu/gle)*

PRACTICE AND ASSESS

DECODE LONGER WORDS Have individuals read the following words. Provide help chunking and blending the words as needed.

article	spectacle	cubicle	cuticle
giggle	scuttle	paddle	griddle
wriggle	puddle	noodle	struggle

READ WORDS IN CONTEXT Have students read these sentences. Then, to check meaning, have them give their own sentences for the underlined words.

The turkeys <u>gobble</u> softly every morning.

We took a <u>shuttle</u> from the parking lot to the stadium.

I carried a <u>bottle</u> of water in case I got thirsty.

To assess, listen for correct pronunciation of the underlined words.

Generalization

Generalization If a word ends in a consonant plus –*le*, those three letters usually make up the last syllable of the word.

Vocabulary Tip

You may wish to explain the meanings of these words.

griddle	heavy, flat pan on which to cook food
scuttle	to hurry away
cubicle	a private work space surrounded by short walls
cuticle	the hard skin around the sides and base of a fingernail or toenail

Spelling & Phonics Compound Words

OBJECTIVE

● Spell compound words.

Generalization

Connect to Phonics A compound word is smaller words joined together. Keep all the letters when spelling compounds: *home + work = homework*. Two words can be joined together to make a new word. In the new word, pronunciation of the smaller words often remains the same.

Spelling Words

1. sunglasses*
2. football
3. homework
4. haircut
5. popcorn
6. railroad
7. snowstorm
8. earring
9. scarecrow
10. blueberry
11. butterflies*
12. lawnmower
13. campground
14. sandbox
15. toothbrush*

Challenge Words

16. thumbtack
17. earthquake
18. scrapbook
19. courthouse
20. whirlpool

*Words from the selection

ELL

Spelling/Phonics Support See the ELL and Transition Handbook for spelling support.

DAY 1 Pretest and Sort

PRETEST

Use the Dictation Sentences from Day 5 to administer the pretest. Read the word, read the sentence, and then read the word again. Guide students in self-correcting their pretests and correcting any misspellings.

Monitor Progress

Spelling

If... students misspell more than 4 pretest words,	**then...** use words 1–8 for Strategic Intervention.
If... students misspell 1–4 pretest words,	**then...** use words 1–15 for On-Level practice.
If... students correctly spell all pretest words,	**then...** use words 1–20 for Advanced Learners.

HOMEWORK Spelling Practice Book p. 29

Compound Words

Generalization A compound word is smaller words joined together. Keep all the letters when spelling compounds: **home + work = homework.**

Word Sort Sort the list words by words you know how to spell and words you are learning to spell. Write every word.

words I know how to spell	words I am learning how to spell
1. Answers will vary.	9. Answers will vary.
2.	10.
3.	11.
4.	12.
5.	13.
6.	14.
7.	15.
8.	

Spelling Words
1. sunglasses
2. football
3. homework
4. haircut
5. popcorn
6. railroad
7. snowstorm
8. earring
9. scarecrow
10. blueberry
11. butterflies
12. lawnmower
13. campground
14. sandbox
15. toothbrush

Challenge Words
16. thumbtack
17. earthquake
18. scrapbook
19. courthouse
20. whirlpool

Challenge Words

words I know how to spell	words I am learning how to spell
16. Answers will vary.	18. Answers will vary.
17.	19.
	20.

Home Activity Your child is learning to spell compound words. To practice at home, have your child study the words in the second column, write them, and then check the spelling.

▲ **Spelling Practice Book** p. 29

DAY 2 Think and Practice

TEACH

Compound words are formed by joining two smaller words together. Write several spelling words on the board, breaking them into their smaller parts. Have students put the words together and say and spell the new compound word aloud.

> foot + ball = football

FIND THE PATTERN Guide students to see how each smaller word provides part of the meaning for the compound word. For example, a railroad is a road made of rails. Have students define the meaning of other compound words.

HOMEWORK Spelling Practice Book p. 30

Compound Words

Missing Words Write the missing list word.

1. I squeezed toothpaste onto my __toothbrush__ .
2. Do you like __blueberry__ muffins?
3. School was cancelled because of the __snowstorm__ .
4. Our teacher asked us to turn in __homework__ .
5. She felt her ear and discovered she had lost an __earring__ .
6. A good pair of __sunglasses__ will protect your eyes.
7. The __scarecrow__ wore an old straw hat.

Spelling Words
sunglasses
football
homework
haircut
popcorn
railroad
snowstorm
earring
scarecrow
blueberry
butterflies
lawnmower
campground
sandbox
toothbrush

Combinations Underline the two words in the sentence that should be combined into a compound word. Write the compound word.

8. Carrie's mom gave her a <u>hair cut</u>. 8. __haircut__
9. I ate <u>pop corn</u> at the theater. 9. __popcorn__
10. The <u>lawn mower</u> needs to be fixed. 10. __lawnmower__
11. Look at the big blue <u>butter flies</u>! 11. __butterflies__
12. We should take <u>our pails</u> out of the sand box. 12. __sandbox__
13. Do you want to play <u>foot ball</u> after school? 13. __football__
14. A train blocked the <u>rail road</u> crossing. 14. __railroad__
15. We set up our tent at a great <u>camp ground</u>. 15. __campground__

Home Activity Your child wrote compound words. Remind your child that no letters are dropped from the two words that are combined to make a compound word.

▲ **Spelling Practice Book** p. 30

DAY 3 Connect to Writing

WRITE A LETTER

Have students write a letter to a friend or family member, using at least four spelling words.

Frequently Misspelled Words

outside	everyone
something	sometimes

These words are difficult for third-graders to spell. Alert students to these frequently misspelled words and encourage them to break down each word into its smaller parts before spelling.

HOMEWORK Spelling Practice Book p. 31

Compound Words

Proofread a Description Ann wrote about a family reunion. Underline two words that should have been a compound word. Circle three other spelling mistakes. Write the words correctly. Add the missing comma.

Spelling Words
sunglasses
football
homework
haircut
popcorn
railroad
snowstorm
earring

scarecrow
blueberry
butterflies
lawnmower
campground
sandbox
toothbrush

All my relatives met at a camp ground. The grownups talked while the kids played football and chased butterflys. Then everyone ate chicken popcorn, bluebery pie, and other good food. Nobody wanted to say goodnight.

1. campground   2. butterflies
3. everyone   4. blueberry

Frequently Misspelled Words
outside
everyone
something
sometimes

Proofread Words Fill in the circle to show the correctly spelled word.

5. Our family always has ____ on Sunday night.
   ● popcorn   ○ pop korn   ○ pop corn
6. Manuel's grandma has a ____ in her garden.
   ● scarecrow   ○ scarcrow   ○ scare crow
7. I do my ____ right after school.
   ○ homwork   ○ home work   ● homework
8. Let's build a castle in the ____.
   ● sandbox   ○ sand box   ○ sandbocks

Home Activity Your child identified misspelled compound words. Have your child draw a line to divide each list word into its two parts.

▲ **Spelling Practice Book** p. 31

DAY 4 Review

REVIEW COMPOUND WORDS

Have students work in pairs to create a crossword puzzle featuring the list words. Students can exchange their puzzles with other groups to solve each puzzle.

Spelling Strategy
Word Combinations

Have students focus on the spelling of the smaller words in a compound word. If students can spell the smaller words in a compound word, they can spell the bigger word too.

HOMEWORK Spelling Practice Book p. 32

Compound Words

Spelling Words

sunglasses	football	homework	haircut	popcorn
railroad	snowstorm	earring	scarecrow	blueberry
butterflies	lawnmower	campground	sandbox	toothbrush

Joining Words Write the compound word that is made from the two smaller words.

1. rail + road   1. railroad
2. blue + berry   2. blueberry
3. snow + storm   3. snowstorm
4. lawn + mower   4. lawnmower
5. ear + ring   5. earring
6. sand + box   6. sandbox
7. pop + corn   7. popcorn
8. hair + cut   8. haircut

Scramble Unscramble the list words and write them on the lines.

9. tallfoob   9. football
10. ttseelfubri   10. butterflies
11. hthtoosurb   11. toothbrush
12. rowkehmo   12. homework
13. awrrccsoe   13. scarecrow
14. enussslga   14. sunglasses
15. dugnapcmor   15. campground

Home Activity Your child has been learning to spell compound words. Say the two words from a compound word in reverse order (for example, brush and tooth). Have your child pronounce and spell the compound word.

▲ **Spelling Practice Book** p. 32

DAY 5 Posttest

DICTATION SENTENCES

1. Sarah lost her sunglasses.
2. Do you want to play football?
3. I have homework tonight.
4. My sister needs a haircut.
5. I like to eat popcorn.
6. The railroad tracks cross the road.
7. We will have a big snowstorm today.
8. Kim lost an earring.
9. There is a scarecrow on the hill.
10. Mom made blueberry pie.
11. Butterflies are so pretty!
12. The lawnmower is broken.
13. How far is it to the campground?
14. There is a sandbox at the park.
15. Where is my toothbrush?

CHALLENGE

16. I need a thumbtack to hang the picture.
17. The earthquake was very strong.
18. My mom made a scrapbook about our trip.
19. Dad works in the courthouse.
20. The water spins in a whirlpool.

OBJECTIVES

- Formulate an inquiry question that is connected to this week's lesson focus.
- Effectively and efficiently find, evaluate, and communicate information related to an inquiry question using electronic sources.

New Literacies

Day 1	Identify Questions
Day 2	Navigate/Search
Day 3	Analyze
Day 4	Synthesize
Day 5	Communicate

NEW LITERACIES

Internet Inquiry Activity

EXPLORE ORGANIZING COLLECTIONS

Use the following 5-day plan to help students conduct this week's Internet inquiry activity on organizing collections. Remind students to follow classroom rules when using the Internet.

DAY 1

Identify Questions Discuss the topic, organizing and displaying collections. Brainstorm ideas for specific inquiry questions about ways to organize. For example, students might want to find out the best way to organize sports cards or display stuffed animals. Have students work individually, in pairs, or in small groups to write an inquiry question they want to answer.

DAY 2

Navigate/Search Review how to begin a simple Internet search using a student-friendly search engine. Have students type keywords related to their inquiry questions. Explain to students the meanings of endings in URLs. Tell students that addresses ending with .gov are government sites, with .edu are education sites, with .mil are military sites, and with .com are commercial sites which offer current news as well as people trying to sell products. Point out that knowing what these URL endings mean will help determine the credibility of the Web site.

DAY 3

Analyze Students will explore the Web sites they identified on Day 2. Tell them to explore each site for information that helps answer their inquiry questions. Students should analyze information for usefulness. They can print out and then highlight relevant information, or take notes about it.

DAY 4

Synthesize Have students synthesize information from Day 3. Remind them that when they synthesize, they combine relevant ideas and information from different sources to develop an answer to their questions.

DAY 5

Communicate Have students share their inquiry results. They can use a drawing or design program to create a diagram that shows how to organize a collection.

RESEARCH/STUDY SKILLS
Magazine/Periodical

TEACH

OBJECTIVES
- Review terms and ideas relating to magazines.
- Understand information in a magazine.

Ask students what kinds of magazines they have read. Guide them to understand that many magazines are devoted to a topic, such as fashion, sports, or news. Distribute magazines to students as you discuss these ideas.

- Most magazines have a **table of contents** located near the front. It tells where the **articles,** or stories are located. Often, high-interest articles are highlighted in some way in the contents.

- Articles have **titles,** usually followed by the writer's name. In most articles the questions *who, what, where, when, why,* and *how* are answered in the first few paragraphs.

- Many articles include photographs, usually with **captions.** The caption describes the photograph. Articles can include other graphics, such as graphs, charts, and tables.

- Magazines are good sources for current events.

Have students work in pairs or small groups to read a children's magazine article, which they will briefly summarize for the class. Suggest that they use *who, what, where, when, why* and *how* in the summary. Before students begin the activity, provide some questions they should think about.

1. **What kind of article is it? Who would be interested in reading it?**

2. **Are there graphics with the article that include important information?**

Table of Contents

18 Baseball's Top 10

Meet the game's best. Learn about their training methods.

36 Winter's Wonders

Winter will be here soon. Get tips about preparing for your favorite cold-weather sport.

ASSESS

As students work on the summaries, make sure they find the most important ideas. Check that they can interpret captions and graphics.

For more practice or to assess students, use Practice Book 3.1, p. 80.

Magazine or Periodical

Directions Read the magazine article. Use it to answer the questions below.

Collector's Monthly

How to Manage Your Collectibles
By Sara Vega

We all love our collectibles, but often there are too many items to manage. Here are some suggestions:
- Set a goal or purpose for your collection. Get rid of items that don't meet this goal or purpose.
- Buy or make storage containers. You want to be able to view each item.
- Make a list of each item in your collection. Add and remove items from the list as needed. You may want to keep your list on a computer.

FOR SALE

Action Figures
More than 100 favorites.
Call Mike 430-1874.

Rare Coins
Many hard-to-find
U.S. coins.
555-7372 Ask for Marcia.

1. What is the title of the magazine?
   Collector's Monthly
2. What is the title of the article?
   How to Manage Your Collectibles
3. What is the article about?
   The article gives suggestions for organizing a collection of items.
4. Who might buy this magazine?
   Possible response: someone who wants to buy or sell items for a collection
5. If you were looking for a rare coin or sports card, how might you use this magazine?
   I would look at the For Sale section to see what coins or cards are being sold.

Home Activity Your child read a magazine page and answered questions about it. Look through a children's magazine. Ask your child to point out the different parts. Have him or her suggest other articles or materials that might be found in a magazine like this.

▲ **Practice Book 3.1** p. 80

AFTER READING

Selection Assessment

Use pp. 29–32 of Selection Tests to check:

 Selection Understanding

 Comprehension Skill *Main Idea*

 Selection Vocabulary
collection
enormous
realize
scattered
shiny
strain

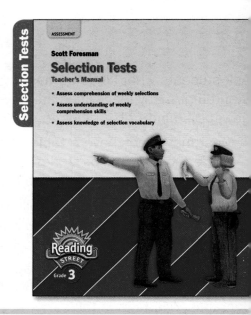

Leveled Assessment

On-Level

Strategic Intervention

Advanced

Use pp. 43–48 of Fresh Reads for Differentiated Test Practice to check:

 Comprehension Skill *Main Idea*

 REVIEW **Comprehension Skill** *Character*

 Fluency *Words Correct Per Minute*

Managing Assessment

Use Assessment Handbook for:

 Observation Checklists

 Record-Keeping Forms

 Portfolio Assessment

Illinois

Planning Guide for Performance Descriptors

Tops & Bottoms

Reading Street Teacher's Edition pages | **Grade 3 English Language Arts Performance Descriptors**

Oral Language

Speaking/Listening Build Concept Vocabulary: 224l, 237, 245, 249c
Read Aloud: 224m

Viewing Analyze a Picture: 249d

1A.Stage C.2. Use word analysis (root words, inflections, affixes) to identify words.
1B.Stage C.13. Read age-appropriate material aloud with fluency and accuracy.
1C.Stage C.8. Explain how authors and illustrators express their ideas.
2A.Stage C.5. Define unfamiliar vocabulary.

Word Work

Words with *spi, thr, squ, str:* 249i, 249k–249l

1A.Stage C.1. Use phonics to decode new words in age-appropriate material.

Reading

Comprehension Author's Purpose: 224–225, 228–245, 249b
Predict: 224–225, 228–245

Vocabulary Lesson Vocabulary: 226b, 237, 245
Context Clues: 226–227, 235, 249c

Fluency Model Reading with Appropriate Phrasing: 224l–224m, 249a
Reader's Theater: 249a

Self-Selected Reading: LR28–36, TR16–17

Literature Genre—Animal Fantasy: 228
Reader Response: 246

1A.Stage C.5. Use a variety of decoding strategies (e.g., phonics, word patterns, structural analysis, context clues) to recognize new words when reading age-appropriate material.
1B.Stage C.2. Make predictions about text events before and during reading and confirm, modify, or reject predictions after reading.
1C.Stage C.2. Use information to generate and respond to questions that reflect higher level thinking skills (e.g., analyzing, synthesizing, inferring, evaluating).
1C.Stage C.4. Identify the message the author conveys in the text.
2A.Stage C.5. Define unfamiliar vocabulary.
2B.Stage C.5. Re-enact/role play/retell (e.g., stories, songs, poems, plays).
4A.Stage C.2. Distinguish among different kinds of information (e.g., fact, opinion, detail, main idea, fantasy, reality).

Language Arts

Writing Feature Story: 249g–249h
Six-Trait Writing Voice: 247, 249g–249h
Grammar, Usage, and Mechanics Singular Possessive Nouns: 249e–249f
Research/Study Encyclopedia: 249n
Technology New Literacies: 249m

3A.Stage C.9. Demonstrate appropriate use of the various parts of speech (e.g., nouns, pronouns, verbs).
3C.Stage C.1. Use the writing process for a variety of purposes (e.g., narration, exposition, persuasion).
5A.Stage C.5. Use an organizational system (e.g., media center, classroom resources, available technology) to locate information.

Unit Skills

Writing How-To Report: WA2–9
Poetry: 272–275
Project/Wrap-Up: 276–277

2A.Stage C.12. Discover poetic devices (e.g., rhyme, rhythm, alliteration, onomatopoeia, repetition, simile, metaphor).
3A.Stage C.1. Develop a paragraph using proper form (e.g., topic sentence, details, summary/conclusion sentence).

This Week's Leveled Readers

Below-Level

1C.Stage C.1. Use evidence in text to form questions and verify predictions.
1C.Stage C.4. Identify the message the author conveys in the text.

Nonfiction

On-Level

1C.Stage C.7. Use text structure (e.g., sequential order, chronological order, problem/solution) to determine most important information.
1C.Stage C.8. Explain how authors and illustrators express their ideas.

Fiction

Advanced

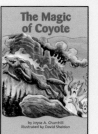

1C.Stage C.4. Identify the message the author conveys in the text.
2A.Stage C.7. Classify major types of fiction (e.g., tall tale, fairy tale, fable).

Fiction

Content-Area Illinois Performance Descriptors in This Lesson

Social Studies

15B.Stage C.1. Match a list of wants with an example of a good, service, or leisure activity that satisfies each want.

15B.Stage C.2. Identify a consumer choice made by families and explain why a choice had to be made.

15C.Stage C.1. List examples of producers in the economy and identify what they produce.

15C.Stage C.2. Classify productive resources as human, natural, and capital.

15D.Stage C.2. List examples of exchanges families make, with and without money.

15D.Stage C.3. Describe how money makes exchange easier.

18C.Stage C.1. Describe the concept of conflict.

18C.Stage C.2. Describe the concept of cooperation.

18C.Stage C.3. Describe how individuals work together to obtain food, clothing, and shelter.

18C.Stage C.4. Define division of labor.

Science

12B.Stage C.2. Apply scientific inquiries or technological designs to examine the interdependence of organisms in ecosystems: identifying adaptations that help animals survive in specific or multiple environments; describing the interaction between living and non-living factors in an ecosystem; predicting what can happen to organisms if they lose different environmental resources or ecologically related groups of organisms.

Math

6A.Stage C.4. Represent, order, label, and compare familiar fractions.

7A.Stage C.4. Describe multiple measurable attributes (e.g., length, mass/weight, time, temperature, area, volume, capacity) of a single object.

7C.Stage C.2. Determine elapsed time between events.

Illinois!

A FAMOUS ILLINOISAN
Harriet Monroe

Chicago-born poet Harriet Monroe (1860–1936) was the founder and longtime editor of *Poetry* magazine. She began writing poetry in the 1880s. One of her poems, "Cantata," was sung at the dedication of the Auditorium Building in Chicago. Monroe wanted to find a way for other poets to get their work published, so she started her magazine in 1912.

Students can . . .
Suppose they are editing a poetry magazine. Ask students to pick a favorite poem that they would want to publish in the magazine. Have them read the poem to the class.

A SPECIAL ILLINOIS PLACE
Chicago

Chicago has the largest population in Illinois and the third-largest population in the United States. The city was built around the transportation industry. In the 1800s it was a hub for transporting food from the Midwest to the East Coast. The city is made up of many different ethnic neighborhoods. Most of Chicago is built on a plain; however, much of downtown Chicago was built on landfill along Lake Michigan. The city has many skyscrapers, including the Sears Tower, which is one of the tallest buildings in the world.

Students can . . .
Draw a picture of the Chicago skyline, including the tallest skyscrapers in the city.

ILLINOIS FUN FACTS
Did You Know?

- The Illinois River, which only flows within the state limits, is 273 miles long.

- The largest human-made lakes in Illinois are Rend Lake and Carlyle Lake.

- Illinois typically has warm to hot summers and cool to cold winters. Cold air comes down from Canada in the winter, and warm air comes up from the Gulf of Mexico in the summer.

Students can . . .
Look up the record high and low temperatures in Illinois and create a bar graph to show the difference in the temperatures.

Unit 2
Smart Solutions

CONCEPT QUESTION
What are smart ways that problems are solved?

Week 1

How have animals adapted to solve the problems of their environment?

Week 2

When is a solution the wrong solution?

Week 3

How can you get ideas to solve a problem?

Week 4

When are respect and understanding important in solving a problem?

Week 5

When you find yourself in a new place, what problems might you meet?

Week 4

EXPAND THE CONCEPT
When are respect and understanding important in solving a problem?

CONNECT THE CONCEPT

▶ **Build Background**
bragged, humiliated, vain

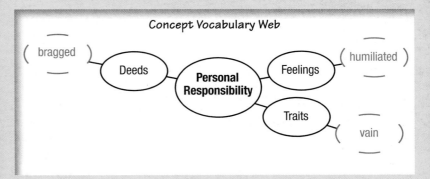

Concept Vocabulary Web

bragged — Deeds — Personal Responsibility — Feelings — humiliated

Personal Responsibility — Traits — vain

▶ **Social Studies Content**
Costs/Benefits of Personal Choices, Helping Others

▶ **Writing**
Feature Story

▶ **Internet Inquiry**
Good Character

Preview Your Week

When are respect and understanding important in solving a problem?

Tops & Bottoms
adapted and illustrated by Janet Stevens

In this story, Hare tries to trick Bear. Does Bear deserve it?

Genre An **animal fantasy** is a story with animal characters that behave like people. Look for ways that Bear and Hare act like people.

228

Student Edition pages 228-245

Audio CD

Genre	Animal Fantasy
Vocabulary Strategy	Context Clues
Comprehension Skill	Author's Purpose
Comprehension Strategy	Predict

SOCIAL STUDIES

Paired Selection

Reading Across Texts
Compare and Contrast Characters in Two Stories

Genre
Fable

Text Features
Moral/Lesson

Folk Literature

Fable
Genre
- Animals are often the main characters in a fable.
- The author tells a very brief story that clearly points to a moral or a lesson.
- The moral is usually stated at the end of the story, highlighting its importance.

Link to Reading
Find other fables in the library. Report other morals or lessons you find to your class.

The Hare and the Tortoise
by Aesop
illustrated by Michael Hague

One day a quick-footed Hare was making fun of a slow-moving Tortoise. Much to the Hare's surprise, the Tortoise began to laugh. "I challenge you to a race," said the Tortoise, "and I bet that I will win."

"Very well," said the Hare, "I will dance rings around you all the way."

It was soon agreed that the Fox would set the course and be the judge. The race began and the Hare ran so quickly that he soon left the Tortoise far behind. Once he reached the middle of the course, the Hare decided to take a nap.

While the Hare slept, the Tortoise plodded on and on, straight toward the finish line. When the Hare awoke from his nap, he was surprised that the Tortoise was nowhere in sight. Racing to the finish line as fast as he could, the Hare was shocked to find the Tortoise waiting for him with a smile on his face.

Slow and steady wins the race.

Reading Across Texts
Who were the winner and the loser in this story and in *Tops and Bottoms*? Why did the loser lose each time?

Writing Across Texts Write a short paragraph comparing the losers.

Author's Purpose What lesson is the author trying to teach?

248

Student Edition pages 248-249

Audio CD

Read It
ONLINE
PearsonSuccessNet.com

- Student Edition
- Leveled Readers

Leveled Readers

Skill Author's Purpose

Strategy Predict

Lesson Vocabulary

Below-Level

On-Level

Advanced

ELL Reader

- Concept Vocabulary
- Text Support
- Language Enrichment

Integrate Social Studies Standards

- **Helping Others**
- **Costs/Benefits of Personal Choices**

✓ Read

Tops and Bottoms
pp. 228–245

"The Hare and the Tortoise"
pp. 248–249

Leveled Readers

Below-Level — • Support Concepts

On-Level — • Develop Concepts

Advanced — • Extend Concepts

ELL Reader

✓ Build
Concept Vocabulary
Personal Responsibility,
pp. 224l–224m

✓ Teach
Social Studies Concepts
Climate, p. 231
Personal Responsibility,
p. 233

✓ Explore
Social Studies Center
**Recognize Personal
Responsibility,** p. 224k

Tops and Bottoms **224c**

Weekly Plan

READING

45-90 minutes

TARGET SKILLS OF THE WEEK

- **Comprehension Skill**
  Author's Purpose
- **Comprehension Strategy**
  Predict
- **Vocabulary Strategy**
  Context Clues

LANGUAGE ARTS

30-60 minutes

Trait of the Week

Voice

DAY 1
PAGES 224l-226b, 249a, 249e-249h, 249k-249m

Oral Language

QUESTION OF THE WEEK *When are respect and understanding important in solving a problem?*

Read Aloud: "Why Possum's Tail Is Bare," 224m
Build Concepts, 224l

Comprehension/Vocabulary

Comprehension Skill/Strategy Lesson, 224-225
- Author's Purpose **T**
- Predict

Build Background, 226a

Introduce Lesson Vocabulary, 226b
bottom, cheated, clever, crops, lazy, partners, wealth **T**

Read Leveled Readers

Grouping Options 224f-224g

Fluency

Model Appropriate Phrasing, 224l-224m, 249a

Grammar, 249e
Introduce Singular Possessive Nouns **T**

Writing Workshop, 249g
Introduce Feature Story
Model the Trait of the Week: Voice

Spelling, 249k
Pretest for Words with *spl, thr, squ, str*

Internet Inquiry, 249m
Identify Questions

Day 1 Write to Read, 224

Day 1 Personal Responsibility Concept Web, 224l

DAY 2
PAGES 226-237, 249a, 249e-249i, 249k-249m

Oral Language

QUESTION OF THE DAY *What other animals, besides a possum and a rabbit, could the author have chosen for this story?*

Word Work

Phonics Lesson, 249i
Consonant Blends

Comprehension/Vocabulary

Vocabulary Strategy Lesson, 226-227
- Context Clues **T**

Read *Tops & Bottoms,* 228-237

Grouping Options 224f-224g

- Author's Purpose **T**
- Predict
- Context Clues **T**
- **REVIEW** Main Idea and Details **T**

Fluency

Readers' Theater, 249a

Develop Vocabulary

Grammar, 249e
Develop Singular Possessive Nouns **T**

Writing Workshop, 249g
Improve Writing: Know Your Purpose

Spelling, 249k
Teach the Generalization

Internet Inquiry, 249m
Navigate/Search

Day 2 Words to Write, 227
Strategy Response Log, 228, 237

Day 2 Time for Social Studies: Climate, 231; Personal Responsibility, 233; Revisit the Personal Responsibility Concept Web, 237

DAILY WRITING ACTIVITIES

DAILY SOCIAL STUDIES CONNECTIONS

DAILY SUCCESS PREDICTORS
for Adequate Yearly Progress

Monitor Progress and Corrective Feedback

Vocabulary — Check Vocabulary, *224l*

RESOURCES FOR THE WEEK

- Practice Book, *pp. 81–90*
- Phonics and Spelling Practice Book, *pp. 33–36*
- Grammar and Writing Practice Book, *pp. 33–36*

- Selection Test, *pp. 33–36*
- Fresh Reads for Differentiated Test Practice, *pp. 49–54*
- The Grammar and Writing Book, *pp. 98–103*

Grouping Options for Differentiated Instruction

Turn the page for the small group lesson plan.

DAY 3 — PAGES 238-247, 249a, 249e-249h, 249k-249m

Oral Language

QUESTION OF THE DAY *How do you think Bear felt after Hare tricked him?*

Comprehension/Vocabulary

Read *Tops & Bottoms, 238–246*

Grouping Options 224f–224g

- Author's Purpose **T**
- Predict
- **REVIEW** Main Idea and Details **T**
- Develop Vocabulary

Reader Response
Selection Test

Fluency

Model Appropriate Phrasing, 249a

Grammar, 249f
Apply Singular Possessive Nouns in Writing **T**

Writing Workshop, 247, 249h
Write Now
Prewrite and Draft

Spelling, 249l
Connect Spelling to Writing

Internet Inquiry, 249m
Analyze Sources

Day 3 Strategy Response Log, 244
Look Back and Write, 246

Day 3 Revisit the Personal Responsibility Concept Web, 245

DAY 4 — PAGES 248-249a, 249e-249h, 249j-249m

Oral Language

QUESTION OF THE DAY *In what way can taking personal responsibility help people achieve their goals?*

Word Work

Phonics Lesson, 249j
REVIEW Compound Words **T**

Comprehension/Vocabulary

Read "The Hare and the Tortoise," 248–249

Grouping Options 224f–224g

Fable

Reading Across Texts

Content-Area Vocabulary

Fluency

Readers' Theater, 249a

Grammar, 249f
Practice Singular Possessive Nouns for Standardized Tests **T**

Writing Workshop, 249h
Draft, Revise, and Publish

Spelling, 249l
Provide a Strategy

Internet Inquiry, 249m
Synthesize Information

Day 4 Writing Across Texts, 249

Day 4 Time for Social Studies: Recognize Personal Responsibility, 224k

---

DAY 5 — PAGES 249a-249h, 249k-249m

Oral Language

QUESTION OF THE WEEK *To wrap up the week, revisit the Day 1 question.*
Build Concept Vocabulary, 249c

Fluency

Read Leveled Readers

Grouping Options 224f–224g

Assess Reading Rate, 249a

Comprehension/Vocabulary

- Reteach Author's Purpose, 249b **T**
Idioms, 249b
- Review Context Clues, 249c **T**

Speaking and Viewing, 249d
Compare and Contrast
Analyze a Picture

Grammar, 249f
Cumulative Review

Writing Workshop, 249h
Connect to Unit Writing

Spelling, 249l
Posttest for Words with *spl, thr, squ, str*

Internet Inquiry, 249m
Communicate Results

Research/Study Skills, 249n
Encyclopedia

Day 5 Idioms, 249b

Day 5 Revisit the Personal Responsibility Concept Web, 249c

KEY = Target Skill **T** = Tested Skill

Comprehension — Check Retelling, *247*

Fluency — Check Fluency WCPM, *249a*

Vocabulary — Check Vocabulary, *249c*

SUCCESS PREDICTOR

Small Group Plan for Differentiated Instruction

Daily Plan AT A GLANCE

Reading
Whole Group
- Oral Language
- Phonics
- Comprehension/Vocabulary

Group Time
Differentiated Instruction

Meet with small groups to provide:
- Skill Support
- Reading Support
- Fluency Practice

Read

This week's lessons for daily group time can be found behind the Differentiated Instruction (DI) tab on pp. DI·32–DI·41.

Whole Group
- Fluency

Language Arts
- Grammar
- Writing
- Spelling
- Research/Inquiry
- Speaking/Listening/Viewing

Use *My Sidewalks on Reading Street* for Tier III intensive reading intervention.

DAY 1

On-Level
Teacher-Led
Page DI · 33
- Develop Concept Vocabulary
- **Read** On-Level Reader *Our Garden*

Strategic Intervention
Teacher-Led
Page DI · 32
- Preteach Consonant Blends
- **Read** Decodable Reader 9
- **Read** Below-Level Reader *Growing Vegetables*

Advanced
Teacher-Led
Page DI · 33
- **Read** Advanced Reader *The Magic of Coyote*
- Independent Extension Activity

ⓘ Independent Activities
While you meet with small groups, have the rest of the class...

- Visit the Reading/Library Center
- Listen to the Background Building Audio
- Finish Write to Read, p. 224
- Complete Practice Book 3.1 pp. 83–84
- Visit Cross-Curricular Centers

DAY 2

On-Level
Teacher-Led
Pages 230–237
- **Read** *Tops and Bottoms*

Strategic Intervention
Teacher-Led
Page DI · 34
- Practice Lesson Vocabulary
- Read Multisyllabic Words
- **Read** or Listen to *Tops and Bottoms*

Advanced
Teacher-Led
Page DI · 35
- Extend Vocabulary
- **Read** *Tops and Bottoms*

ⓘ Independent Activities
While you meet with small groups, have the rest of the class...

- Visit the Reading/Library Center
- Listen to the AudioText for *Tops and Bottoms*
- Finish Words to Write, p. 227
- Complete Practice Book 3.1 pp. 85–86, 89
- Write in their Strategy Response Logs, pp. 228, 237
- Visit Cross-Curricular Centers
- Work on inquiry projects

DAY 3

On-Level
Teacher-Led
Pages 238–245
- **Read** *Tops and Bottoms*

Strategic Intervention
Teacher-Led
Page DI · 36
- Practice Author's Purpose and Predict
- **Read** or Listen to *Tops and Bottoms*

Advanced
Teacher-Led
Page DI · 37
- Extend Author's Purpose and Predict
- **Read** *Tops and Bottoms*

ⓘ Independent Activities
While you meet with small groups, have the rest of the class...

- Visit the Reading/Library Center
- Listen to the AudioText for *Tops and Bottoms*
- Write in their Strategy Response Logs, p. 244
- Finish Look Back and Write, p. 246
- Complete Practice Book 3.1 p. 87
- Visit Cross-Curricular Centers
- Work on inquiry projects

① Begin with whole class skill and strategy instruction.

② Meet with small groups to provide differentiated instruction.

③ Gather the whole class back together for fluency and language arts.

On-Level
Teacher-Led
Pages 248–249
- **Read** "The Hare and the Tortoise"

Strategic Intervention
Teacher-Led
Page DI · 38
- Practice Retelling
- **Read** or Listen to "The Hare and the Tortoise"

Advanced
Teacher-Led
Page DI · 39
- **Read** "The Hare and the Tortoise"
- Genre Study

DAY 4

(i) Independent Activities

While you meet with small groups, have the rest of the class...

- Visit the Reading/Library Center
- Listen to the AudioText for "The Hare and the Tortoise"
- Visit the Writing and Vocabulary Centers
- Finish Writing Across Texts, p. 249
- Visit Cross-Curricular Centers
- Work on inquiry projects

On-Level
Teacher-Led
Page DI · 41
- **Reread** Leveled Reader *Our Garden*
- Retell *Our Garden*

Strategic Intervention
Teacher-Led
Page DI · 40
- **Reread** Leveled Reader *Growing Vegetables*
- Retell *Growing Vegetables*

Advanced
Teacher-Led
Page DI · 41
- **Reread** Leveled Reader *The Magic of Coyote*
- Share Extension Activity

DAY 5

(i) Independent Activities

While you meet with small groups, have the rest of the class...

- Visit the Reading/Library Center
- Complete Practice Book 3.1 pp. 88, 90
- Visit Cross-Curricular Centers
- Work on inquiry projects

Grouping Place English language learners in the groups that correspond to their reading abilities in English.

Use the appropriate Leveled Reader or other text at students' instructional level.

TiP Send home the appropriate Multilingual Summary of the main selection on Day 1.

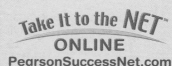

ONLINE
PearsonSuccessNet.com

Connie Juel
For activities to build oral vocabulary, see the article "Walking with Rosie" by Scott Foresman author Connie Juel and others.

TEACHER TALK

An **affix** is a prefix, suffix, or inflected ending attached to a base word.

Be sure to schedule time for students to work on the unit inquiry project, "A Book of Solutions." This week students combine information to develop answers to their inquiry questions.

Looking Ahead

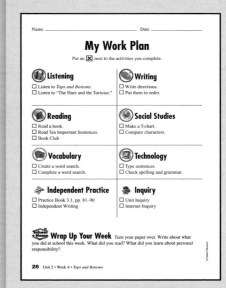

▲ **Group-Time Survival Guide** p. 26, Weekly Contract

Tops and Bottoms **224g**

ORAL LANGUAGE

SOCIAL STUDIES

Concept Development

When are respect and understanding important in solving a problem?

CONCEPT VOCABULARY

bragged   humiliated   vain

BUILD

❏ **Question of the Week** Introduce and discuss the question of the week. This week students will read a variety of texts and work on projects related to the concept *personal responsibility*. Post the question for students to refer to throughout the week. **DAY 1** *224d*

❏ **Read Aloud** Read aloud "Why Possum's Tail Is Bare." Then begin a web to build concepts and concept vocabulary related to this week's lesson and the unit theme, Smart Solutions. Introduce the concept words *bragged, humiliated,* and *vain* and have students place them on the web. Display the web for use throughout the week. **DAY 1** *224l–224m*

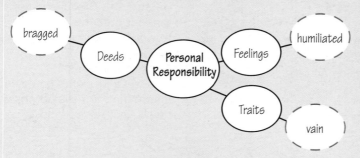

DEVELOP

❏ **Question of the Day** Use the prompts from the Weekly Plan to engage students in conversations related to this week's reading and the unit theme. **EVERY DAY** *224d–224e*

❏ **Concept Vocabulary Web** Revisit the Personal Responsibility Concept Web and encourage students to add concept words from their reading and life experiences. **DAY 2** *237,* **DAY 3** *245*

CONNECT

❏ **Looking Back/Moving Forward** Revisit the Personal Responsibility Concept Web and discuss how it relates to this week's lesson and the unit theme. Then make connections to next week's lesson. **DAY 5** *249c*

CHECK

❏ **Concept Vocabulary Web** Use the Personal Responsibility Concept Web to check students' understanding of the concept vocabulary words *bragged, humiliated,* and *vain.* **DAY 1** *224l,* **DAY 5** *249c*

VOCABULARY

STRATEGY CONTEXT CLUES Context clues are the words and sentences around an unknown word. Sometimes an author uses an antonym as a context clue. An antonym is a word that means the opposite of another word. When you come across a word you don't know, look for an antonym as a context clue. The antonym can help you figure out the meaning of an unfamiliar word.

LESSON VOCABULARY

bottom	lazy
cheated	partners
clever	wealth
crops	

TEACH

❏ **Words to Know** Give students the opportunity to tell what they already know about this week's lesson vocabulary words. Then discuss word meaning. **DAY 1** *226b*

❏ **Vocabulary Strategy Lesson** Use the vocabulary strategy lesson in the Student Edition to introduce and model this week's strategy, *context clues.* **DAY 2** *226–227*

Vocabulary Strategy Lesson

PRACTICE/APPLY

❏ **Leveled Text** Read the lesson vocabulary in the context of leveled text. **DAY 1** *LR28–LR36*

❏ **Words in Context** Read the lesson vocabulary and apply context clues in the context of *Tops and Bottoms.* **DAY 2** *228–237,* **DAY 3** *238–246*

Leveled Readers

❏ **Vocabulary Center** Create a word search using words about gardening. **ANY DAY** *224j*

Main Selection—Fiction

❏ **Homework** Practice Book 3.1 pp. 84–85. **DAY 1** *226b,* **DAY 2** *227*

❏ **Word Play** Have partners use reference sources to make lists of nouns that name vegetables that people eat. Students can illustrate their favorite vegetable nouns. **ANY DAY** *249c*

ASSESS

❏ **Selection Test** Use the Selection Test to determine students' understanding of the lesson vocabulary words. **DAY 3**

RETEACH/REVIEW

❏ **Reteach Lesson** If necessary, use this lesson to reteach and review *context clues.* **DAY 5** *249c*

① Use assessment data to determine your instructional focus.

② Preview this week's instruction by strand.

③ Choose instructional activities that meet the needs of your classroom.

COMPREHENSION

SKILL AUTHOR'S PURPOSE The author's purpose is the reason an author writes something. Authors write for many reasons—to persuade, to inform, to entertain, or to express ideas and feelings.

STRATEGY PREDICT To predict means to guess what you think will happen in a story and why it will happen. Often, you can also predict what the author's purpose is. Read the selection's title, look at the illustrations or photographs, glance at any charts and graphs, and read the captions. All these things give you clues about the author's purpose.

TEACH

☐ **Skill/Strategy Lesson** Use the skill/strategy lesson in the Student Edition to introduce and model *author's purpose* and *predicting*. **DAY 1** 224–225

☐ **Extend Skills** Teach idioms. **ANY DAY** 249b

Skill/Strategy Lesson

PRACTICE/APPLY

☐ **Leveled Text** Apply *author's purpose* and *predicting* to read leveled text. **DAY 1** LR28–LR36

☐ **Skills and Strategies in Context** Read *Tops and Bottoms*, using the Guiding Comprehension questions to apply *author's purpose* and *predicting*. **DAY 2** 228–237, **DAY 3** 238–246

Leveled Readers

☐ **Skills and Strategies in Context** Read "The Hare and the Tortoise," guiding students as they apply *author's purpose* and *predicting*. Then have students discuss and write across texts. **DAY 4** 248–249

Main Selection—Fiction

☐ **Homework** Practice Book 3.1 pp. 83, 87, 88. **DAY 1** 225, **DAY 3** 245, **DAY 5** 249b

☐ **Fresh Reads for Differentiated Test Practice** Have students practice *author's purpose* with a new passage. **DAY 3**

Paired Selection—Fiction

ASSESS

☐ **Selection Test** Determine students' understanding of the selection and their use of *author's purpose*. **DAY 3**

☐ **Retell** Have students retell *Tops and Bottoms*. **DAY 3** 246–247

RETEACH/REVIEW

☐ **Reteach Lesson** If necessary, reteach and review *author's purpose*. **DAY 5** 249b

FLUENCY

SKILL APPROPRIATE PHRASING Appropriate phrasing means pausing at the right places when you read. Punctuation marks, such as commas and periods, signal the right places to pause.

TEACH

☐ **Read Aloud** Model fluent reading by rereading "Why Possum's Tail Is Bare." Focus on this week's fluency skill, appropriate phrasing. **DAY 1** 224l–224m, 249a

PRACTICE/APPLY

☐ **Readers' Theater** Read aloud selected paragraphs from *Tops & Bottoms*, modeling how to use your voice to bring the characters to life. Then practice in groups of three doing readers' theater readings. **DAY 2** 249a, **DAY 3** 249a

☐ **Readers' Theater** Have groups of three practice reading aloud, reading with appropriate phrasing and offering each other feedback. As students reread, monitor their progress toward their individual fluency goals. **DAY 4** 249a

☐ **Listening Center** Have students follow along with the AudioText for this week's selections. **ANY DAY** 224j

☐ **Reading/Library Center** Have students reread a selection of their choice. **ANY DAY** 224j

☐ **Fluency Coach** Have students use Fluency Coach to listen to fluent readings or practice reading on their own. **ANY DAY**

ASSESS

☐ **Check Fluency** WCPM Do a one-minute timed reading, paying special attention to this week's skill—appropriate phrasing. Provide feedback for each student. **DAY 5** 249a

☑ Customize Your Plan *by Strand*

GRAMMAR

SKILL SINGULAR POSSESSIVE NOUNS A singular possessive noun is a noun that shows that one person, animal, or thing owns something. To make a singular possessive noun, add an apostrophe and the letter s to the noun. For example, to show that a boy owns a shirt, add an apostrophe and an s to boy: *the boy's shirts.*

TEACH

☐ **Grammar Transparency 9** Use Grammar Transparency 9 to teach singular possessive nouns. DAY 1 *249e*

Grammar Transparency 9

PRACTICE/APPLY

☐ **Develop the Concept** Review the concept of singular possessive nouns and provide guided practice. DAY 2 *249e*

☐ **Apply to Writing** Have students review something they have written and apply what they have learned about singular possessive nouns. DAY 3 *249f*

☐ **Test Preparation** Examine common errors in singular possessive nouns to prepare for standardized tests. DAY 4 *249f*

☐ **Homework** Grammar and Writing Practice Book pp. 33–35. DAY 2 *249e,* DAY 3 *249f,* DAY 4 *249f*

ASSESS

☐ **Cumulative Review** Use Grammar and Writing Practice Book p. 36. DAY 5 *249f*

RETEACH/REVIEW

☐ **Daily Fix-It** Have students find and correct errors in grammar, spelling, and punctuation. **EVERY DAY** *249e–249f*

☐ **The Grammar and Writing Book** Use pp. 98–101 of The Grammar and Writing Book to extend instruction for singular possessive nouns. **ANY DAY**

The Grammar and Writing Book

WRITING

Trait of the Week

VOICE A writer's voice shows the writer's style and personality. Use your writer's voice to shape your writing. A writer's voice may be funny or serious. It can be friendly or formal. When your writing voice is strong and clear, readers pay attention to what you have to say.

TEACH

☐ **Writing Transparency 9A** Use the model to introduce and discuss the Trait of the Week. DAY 1 *249g*

☐ **Writing Transparency 9B** Use the transparency to show students how knowing their purpose can improve their writing. DAY 2 *249g*

Writing Transparency 9A **Writing Transparency 9B**

PRACTICE/APPLY

☐ **Write Now** Examine the model on Student Edition p. 247. Then have students write their own feature stories. DAY 3 *247, 249h,* DAY 4 *249h*

> **Prompt** In *Tops and Bottoms,* a character uses his creativity to get ahead. Think about an event that happened because of one or more creative people. Now write a feature story about the event and the person.

Write Now p. 247

☐ **Writing Center** Write directions for doing your chores in the order you normally complete them. **ANY DAY** *224k*

ASSESS

☐ **Writing Trait Rubric** Use the rubric to evaluate students' writing. DAY 4 *249h*

RETEACH/REVIEW

☐ **The Grammar and Writing Book** Use pp. 98–103 of The Grammar and Writing Book to extend instruction for singular possessive nouns, knowing your purpose, and feature stories **ANY DAY**

The Grammar and Writing Book

SPELLING

GENERALIZATION WORDS WITH *SPL, THR, SQU, STR* Some words have three letters pronounced together: <u>spl</u>ash, <u>thr</u>ow, <u>squ</u>are, <u>str</u>ike. The letters are spoken together, but each letter can be heard.

TEACH

☐ **Pretest** Give the pretest for words with *spl, thr, squ, str*. Guide students in self-correcting their pretests and correcting any misspellings. **DAY 1** *249k*

☐ **Think and Practice** Connect spelling to the phonics generalization with words with *spl, thr, squ, str*. **DAY 2** *249k*

PRACTICE/APPLY

☐ **Connect to Writing** Have students use spelling words to write a story. Then review frequently misspelled words: *brother, scared*. **DAY 3** *249l*

☐ **Homework** Phonics and Spelling Practice Book pp. 33–36. **EVERY DAY**

RETEACH/REVIEW

☐ **Review** Review spelling words to prepare for the posttest. Then provide students with a spelling strategy—letter sounds. **DAY 4** *249l*

ASSESS

☐ **Posttest** Use dictation sentences to give the posttest for words with *spl, thr, squ, str*. **DAY 5** *249l*

Spelling Words

1. splash
2. throw
3. three
4. square
5. throat
6. strike
7. street
8. split*
9. splurge
10. thrill
11. strength
12. squeak
13. throne
14. strawberry
15. squeeze

Challenge Words

16. squid
17. squander
18. arthritis
19. instrument
20. strategy

*Word from the selection

PHONICS

SKILL CONSONANT BLENDS Consonant blends consist of two or more letters whose sounds are blended together when pronouncing a word.

TEACH

☐ **Phonics Lesson** Model how to read words with consonant blends. Then have students practice by decoding longer words and reading words in context. **DAY 2** *249i*

PRACTICE/APPLY

☐ **Homework** Practice Book 3.1, p. 89. **DAY 2** *249i*

RETEACH/REVIEW

☐ **Review Word Parts** Review how to read compound words. Then have student practice by decoding longer words and reading words in context. **DAY 4** *249j*

RESEARCH AND INQUIRY

☐ **Internet Inquiry** Have students conduct an Internet inquiry on good character. **EVERY DAY** *249m*

☐ **Encyclopedia** Review the features of an encyclopedia, including volume, entry, entry words, and guide words. Give groups of students encyclopedia volumes and have them locate information about an animal that can be found in their volumes. **DAY 5** *249n*

☐ **Unit Inquiry** Allow time for students to combine valid information and develop answers to their inquiry questions. **ANY DAY** *149*

SPEAKING AND VIEWING

☐ **Compare and Contrast** Have students give short speeches that compare and contrast Hare in *Tops and Bottoms* with the hare in *The Hare and the Tortoise*. **DAY 5** *249d*

☐ **Analyze a Picture** Have students view the picture on p. 237 of *Tops and Bottoms*. With partners, have students answer questions. **DAY 5** *249d*

Resources for
Differentiated Instruction

LEVELED READERS

▶ **Comprehension**
- 🎯 **Skill** Author's Purpose
- 🎯 **Strategy** Predict

▶ **Lesson Vocabulary**
- 🎯 **Context Clues**

lazy • crops • partners • cheated • clever • wealth • bottom

▶ **Social Studies Standards**
- **Helping Others**
- **Costs/Benefits of Personal Choices**

Leveled Reader Database
ONLINE
PearsonSuccessNet.com

Use the Online Database of over 600 books to
- Download and print additional copies of this week's leveled readers.
- Listen to the readers being read online.
- Search for more titles focused on this week's skills, topic, and content.

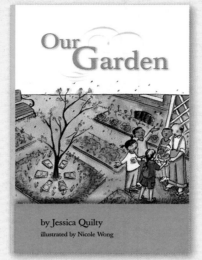

Our Garden
by Jessica Quilty
illustrated by Nicole Wong

On-Level Reader

Author's Purpose
- The **author's purpose** is the reason or reasons the author has for writing.
- To *inform*, *persuade*, *entertain*, or *express* are common reasons for writing.

Directions Answer the questions.   Possible responses given.

1. Why do you think the author gave so many details about how everyone cleaned up the empty lot?
to show how much work is involved

2. Why do you think the author wrote a book about a group of people building a garden rather than just one person?
to show that people working together can do great things

3. Explain why one of the purposes the author may have had was to inform.
The author tells what they can accomplish by working together.

4. How did the author show she also wanted to entertain?
the heartwarming way the author shows how people improve their community

5. In what way did the author try to persuade?
by trying to convince people that good things come from working together

🎯 **On-Level Practice** TE p. LR32

Vocabulary
Directions Find the vocabulary word that matches each clue below.

Check the Words You Know
__bottom __cheat
__clever __crops
__lazy __partners
__wealth

1. It means a large amount of something, usually money. — **wealth**
2. It means the opposite of hardworking. — **lazy**
3. It means the opposite of top. — **bottom**
4. If someone is dishonest, he or she might do this. — **cheat**
5. We use this word to describe a person who likes to lie around all day. — **lazy**
6. We use this word to describe kinds of plants you grow to eat. — **crops**
7. This word is used to describe someone who is smart. — **clever**
8. If you and somebody else are these, you work together toward a goal. — **partners**

Directions Write a sentence that uses two of the vocabulary words.
Sentences will vary but should use vocabulary words correctly.

🎯 **On-Level Practice** TE p. LR33

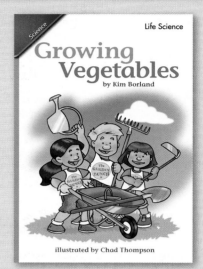

Life Science
Growing Vegetables
by Kim Borland
illustrated by Chad Thompson

Below-Level Reader

Author's Purpose
- The **author's purpose** is the reason or reasons the author has for writing.
- An author may have one or more reasons for writing. To *inform*, *persuade*, *entertain*, or *express* are common reasons.

Directions Answer the questions.   Possible responses given.

1. Why do you think the author wrote about the time Miranda forgot to water the plants?
to show that when you don't water plants, they wilt

2. Why do you think the author told about the special job each person had?
to tell about the different things you need to do to grow vegetables

3. Why do you think the author wrote a book about growing vegetables?
to inform the reader how to grow a vegetable garden

4. What do you think the author wanted you to learn about plants?
They need water, weeding, and sunlight.

5. What do you think the author wanted you to learn about working together?
It's more fun for everyone, and the end result is better.

🎯 **Below-Level Practice** TE p. LR29

Vocabulary
Directions Circle the letter of the correct definition below each vocabulary word.

Check the Words You Know
__bottom __cheated __clever __crops
__lazy __partners __wealth

1. lazy
   a. quick   (b) not wanting to do any work   c. simple to do
2. crops
   a. big hairy dogs   b. clothing   (c) plants or fruits
3. partners
   a. wooden fences   (b) people who work together   c. enemies
4. cheated
   (a) not playing fairly   b. dressed for dinner   c. destroyed
5. clever
   a. hungry   b. silly   (c) smart
6. wealth
   a. dirt   (b) money   c. talent
7. bottom
   (a) lowest part   b. highest part   c. middle

Directions Unscramble the letters to form a vocabulary word.

8. TAEEHCD — **cheated**
9. CREVEL — **clever**
10. TOMBOT — **bottom**
11. PRCOS — **crops**
12. PTNSERAR — **partners**
13. ZALY — **lazy**
14. HTWEAL — **wealth**

🎯 **Below-Level Practice** TE p. LR30

Advanced

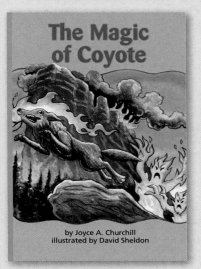

The Magic of Coyote

by Joyce A. Churchill
illustrated by David Sheldon

Advanced Reader

Author's Purpose

- The **author's purpose** is the reason or reasons the author has for writing.
- An author may have one or more reasons for writing. Common reasons are to *inform*, *persuade*, *entertain*, or *express*.

Directions Answer the questions.   Possible responses given.

1. What do you think is the author's purpose for writing this story?
to entertain with a story of how a boy conquered his fear of dogs

2. What do you think is the author's purpose for including the story about Coyote?
This story informs, or explains, how humans got fire.

3. How does the story about Coyote stealing fire help Henry?
Henry likes the story about the coyote, which is similar to a dog, and it makes him less afraid of dogs.

4. What do you think the author wants you to learn about Navajo culture?
She wants to inform readers about their rich tradition of storytelling.

5. Why do you think the author had Henry meet a coydog?
Henry already liked coyotes, so it was easier to like the dog part of the coydog.

Advanced Practice TE p. LR35

Vocabulary

Directions Complete each sentence in the story with one of the vocabulary words.

Check the Words You Know

_artifacts _breakthrough _cunning _descendant
_retreated _scampered _yelping

Henry was afraid of the (1) ___yelping___ dogs. Every time he saw them, he (2) ___retreated___ to the back of the room.

One day, Henry and his class visited a Native American museum. First they studied ancient (3) ___artifacts___, such as pieces of pottery. Then it was time for a story.

The story was told by Mr. Gordon, who was a (4) ___descendant___ of a Navajo storyteller. Mr. Gordon told tales about the coyote, a (5) ___cunning___ creature who often played tricks on the Navajo people. Henry discovered that his interest in coyotes made him feel less afraid about dogs. When Mr. Gordon's coydog, Ranger, (6) ___scampered___ over to Henry, Henry actually petted Ranger. Henry was excited, because he knew this was a real (7) ___breakthrough___.

Directions Write the definition of each word based on its context above. Use a dictionary if necessary. Possible responses given.

8. retreated ___withdrew___

9. breakthrough ___a significant advance___

10. yelping ___making sharp, shrill cries or barks___

Advanced Practice TE p. LR35

ELL

ELL Reader

ELL Poster 9

Teacher's Edition Notes

ELL notes throughout this lesson support instruction and reference additional resources at point of use.

Teaching Guide pp. 57–63, 228–229
- Multilingual summaries of the main selection
- Comprehension lesson
- Vocabulary strategies and word cards
- ELL Reader 3.2.4 lesson

ELL and Transition Handbook

Ten Important Sentences
- Key ideas from every selection in the Student Edition
- Activities to build sentence power

More Reading

Readers' Theater Anthology
- Fluency practice
- Five scripts to build fluency
- Poetry for oral interpretation

Leveled Trade Books

- Extended reading tied to the unit concept
- Lessons in the Trade Book Library Teaching Guide

School + Home

Homework
- Family Times Newsletter
- ELL Multilingual Selection Summaries

Take-Home Books
- Leveled Readers

Cross-Curricular Centers

Listening

Listen to the
Selections

MATERIALS	SINGLES

CD player, headphones, AudioText CD, Student Edition

Listen to *Tops and Bottoms* and "The Hare and the Tortoise" as you follow or read along in your book. Listen for clues about each author's purpose for writing.

If there is anything you don't understand, you can listen again to any section.

Reading/Library

Read It
Again!

MATERIALS	SINGLES
	PAIRS
	GROUPS

Collection of books for self-selected reading, reading log

Select a book you have already read. Record the title of the book in your reading log. You may want to read with a partner.

You may choose to read any of the following:

- Leveled Readers
- ELL Readers
- Stories written by classmates
- Books from the library
- *Tops and Bottoms*

TEN IMPORTANT SENTENCES Read the Ten Important Sentences for *Tops and Bottoms*. Then locate the sentences in the Student Edition.

BOOK CLUB Write a two-paragraph book review of the book you just read. Summarize the story. Include the author's purpose and why you liked or disliked the book.

Vocabulary

Word
Search

MATERIALS	SINGLES
	PAIRS

Writing and drawing materials, ruler

Use the words about gardening to create a word search.

1. **First, use a ruler to draw horizontal (across) and vertical (down) lines on a plain piece of paper.**
2. **Print a letter of each gardening word in a box.**
3. **Print some words down and some across. Leave lots of empty boxes.**
4. **Now, go back and fill in each empty box with a letter. Your word search is complete!**
5. **Complete a classmate's word search by circling the "hidden" words.**

Words About Gardening		
fertile	cultivate	harvest
irrigation	insects	topsoil

EARLY FINISHERS Use a dictionary to find out what each gardening word means.

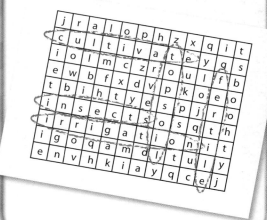

Scott Foresman Reading Street Centers Survival Kit

Use the *Tops and Bottoms* materials from the Reading Street
Centers Survival Kit to organize this week's centers.

Writing

Describe
Chores

MATERIALS | **SINGLES**
Paper, pens or pencils

Tell someone how to complete
your chores.

1. **Recall that Hare did all of Bear's work for him. What if someone else was responsible for your chores?**
2. **Write directions for doing your chores around the house. Write them in the order that you would complete them.**

EARLY FINISHERS Exchange
directions with a partner. Write
sentences telling whether you
would rather do your chores or
your partner's chores.

My Chores
1. First, help my parents clear the dinner dishes.
2. Then, pick up my toys in the living room.
3. Next, put my dirty clothes in the hamper.
4. Finally, walk my dog.

Social Studies

Recognize Personal
Responsibility

MATERIALS | **SINGLES**
Writing and art materials

Compare how Hare and Bear are
different when it comes to work.

1. **Draw a T-chart with the left side labeled *Hare* and the right side *Bear*.**
2. **On each side, describe the character's habits and accomplishments.**

EARLY FINISHERS Write two
paragraphs, one for Hare and
one for Bear. Describe why each
accomplished what he did.

Hare	Bear
works hard	sleeps
tricks Bear	gets tricked
gets the food	gets the scraps

Technology

Check
Your Work

MATERIALS | **SINGLES**
Computer, printer

Your word processing program can
check for errors by proofreading.

1. **Type two or three sentences from the Writing activity.**
2. **Use the mouse to click on the Tools icon at the top of the screen.**
3. **Click on "Spelling and Grammar."**
4. **Spelling and grammar errors, along with extra or missing spaces, will be highlighted and suggested corrections given.**
5. **Proofread and print out.**

EARLY FINISHERS Click on the Help
icon. Then type: "How do I check
grammar and spelling?" You will
learn other ways to check work.

ALL CENTERS

Tops and Bottoms

OBJECTIVES

- Build vocabulary by finding words related to the lesson concept.
- Listen for author's purpose.

Concept Vocabulary

bragged boasted

humiliated lowered someone's pride, dignity, or self-respect

vain having too much pride in your looks, ability, or achievements

Monitor Progress

Check Vocabulary

If... students are unable to place words on the web,	then... review the lesson concept. Place the words on the web and provide additional words for practice, such as *bushy* and *jealous*.

SUCCESS PREDICTOR

DAY 1 Grouping Options

Reading
Whole Group
Introduce and discuss the Question of the Week. Then use pp. 224l–226b.

Group Time
Differentiated Instruction
Read this week's Leveled Readers. See pp. 224f–224g for the small group lesson plan.

Whole Group
Use p. 249a.

Language Arts
Use pp.249e–249h and 249k-249m.

Build Concepts

FLUENCY

MODEL APPROPRIATE PHRASING As you read "Why Possum's Tail Is Bare," be sure to pause at appropriate places and to group words appropriately. For example, in the first paragraph, be sure to pause slightly before the start of the words in the parentheses, and read the words in the parentheses as one phrase.

LISTENING COMPREHENSION

After reading "Why Possum's Tale Is Bare," use the following questions to assess listening comprehension.

1. **Why do you think the author wrote this story?** *(Possible response: To entertain; to teach a lesson)* **Author's Purpose**

2. **What lesson was the author trying to teach?** *(Possible response: Don't be too vain or proud of your appearance.)* **Author's Purpose**

BUILD CONCEPT VOCABULARY

Start a web to build concepts and vocabulary related to this week's lesson and the unit theme.

- Draw a Personal Responsibility Concept Web.

- Read the sentence with the word *vain* again. Ask students to pronounce *vain* and discuss its meaning.

- Place *vain* in an oval attached to Traits. Explain that *vain* is related to this concept. Read the sentences in which *bragged* and *humiliated* appear. Have students pronounce the words, place them on the web, and provide reasons.

- Brainstorm additional words and categories for the web. Keep the web on display and add words throughout the week.

Concept Vocabulary Web

(bragged) — Deeds — **Personal Responsibility** — Feelings — (humiliated)

Traits — (vain)

Why Possum's Tail Is Bare

by Gayle Ross

Long ago in the beginning days of the world, Possum didn't look the way he does now. Creator gave Possum a beautiful, bushy, furry tail, and Possum was vain about this tail. He bragged about it all the time and sang about it at every dance, until Rabbit (who didn't have much of a tail left since Bear had pulled his off) became jealous and decided to play a trick on Possum.

Rabbit went to the other animals and said, "Let's have an honor dance for Possum's tail." But all the other animals said, "We are tired of hearing Possum sing about his tail."

"If we have an honor dance for Possum," said Rabbit, "and we let him sing about his tail all night, perhaps he will not talk about it so much from now on." Well, the other animals said they had never thought about it quite like that, and maybe Rabbit was right. And so they agreed to have an honor dance for Possum's tail.

Rabbit traveled to Possum's house and gave him the news. "You mean I can sit where everyone can see me?" said Possum.

"Oh, yes," said Rabbit. "You will have a special seat of honor right next to the council fire."

"Do you mean I can sing and dance and talk about my tail all night?" asked Possum.

"Oh, yes," said Rabbit. "That's what the dance is for, to honor your beautiful tail!"

Well, of course this pleased Possum very much, and he said that he would come. Rabbit said, "I will send Cricket to you on the day of the dance to comb and brush the fur on your tail so it will look its best." Possum liked this idea as well.

So Rabbit went to Cricket, who is such an expert haircutter that the Cherokee word for him means "the barber." Rabbit told him exactly how to fix the hair on Possum's tail.

On the day of the dance, Cricket went to Possum's house. Possum stretched out and closed his eyes and Cricket began to comb and brush the fur on Possum's tail, until it was its silkiest and shiniest. "Possum," said Cricket, "I'm going to wind a red string around the fur of your tail, very very tight, all the way to the tip. It will keep the hair smooth until it is time for you to dance. Remember, Possum, don't take the string off until just before you dance!"

That night, when the sun went down, the drums began to play and the singers to call. Everyone gathered at the council house. Possum sat in a special seat of honor, right next to the council fire, where the light was brightest.

continued on TR1

Set Purpose

Read the title and have students predict what the selection will be about. Have them listen for author's purpose.

Creative Response

Divide the class into several small groups. Have each group write a short play script for the story. If time permits, have them act out their plays in front of the class. ***Drama***

ELL

Activate Prior Knowledge Before students listen to the Read Aloud, explain that many early Native American tribes told stories to explain events in nature they did not understand. Point out that these stories often used animals as characters and that each animal character was a general example of all animals of that kind. Tell students that possums are small, light-haired animals with long faces and long, skinny tails that play dead when they are surprised or frightened.

Access Content Before reading, explain that they are going to hear a Native American tale that explains why possums have bare, skinny tales.

 Homework Send home this week's Family Times newsletter.

Vocabulary

SUCCESS PREDICTOR

SKILLS ⟷ STRATEGIES IN CONTEXT

Author's Purpose Predict

OBJECTIVES

- Identify author's purpose.
- Make predictions about the author's purpose.

Skills Trace

Author's Purpose	
Introduce/Teach	TE: 3.2 224–225, 3.3 304–305, 3.5 244–245
Practice	PB: 3.1 16, 83, 87, 88, 113, 117, 118, 126, 146; 3.2 93, 97, 98
Reteach/Review	TE: 3.1 51; 3.2 249b, DI·55; 3.3 329b, 347, 391, DI·53; 3.5 275b, DI·56
Test	Selection Test: Unit 2 Benchmark Test: Unit 3

INTRODUCE

Write the following on the board: *Instructions, Joke, Informational Article.* Ask students why they think an author would write each of them. *(Possible responses: To tell how to do something; to make people laugh; to explain something or give information about something)*

Have students read the information on p. 224. Explain the following:

- The reason an author has for writing something is called the author's purpose.
- Authors write for many reasons. Sometimes, an author has more than one reason for writing. Often, you can predict why an author wrote something by previewing the selection and then checking your prediction as you read.

Use Skill Transparency 9 to teach author's purpose and predict.

Comprehension

Skill
Author's Purpose

Strategy
Predict

 # Author's Purpose

- The author's purpose is the reason an author writes something.
- There are many reasons for writing: to persuade, to inform, to entertain, or to express ideas and feelings.

> **Before You Read:** Read the title. For which reason might the author write a piece with this title?
>
> ↓
>
> **As You Read:** Think about the author's purpose.
>
> ↓
>
> **After You Read:** Now what do you think the author's purpose was?

Strategy: Predict

Good readers try to predict what will happen and why. You can also predict why an author might have written something. As you read, check your prediction. Were you right?

 ## Write to Read

1. Read "Salsa Garden." Make a chart like the one above. Fill in each box as you read.

2. The top box shows your prediction. After reading, tell why you made your prediction and whether it was correct.

224

Strategic Intervention

Author's Purpose Tell students that before they read, they should always preview the selection—read the title; look at the illustrations or photographs; glance at any charts, graphs, or other graphic sources; and read the captions. This will tell what the selection is about. Then they should think about why the author wrote the selection. Was it to entertain, inform, persuade, or express an idea? As they read, they should look for details that show author's purpose. Do the details support their original ideas about why the author wrote the selection? When students finish reading, they should write a sentence that tells why the author wrote the selection and include details that support their idea.

ELL

Access Content

Beginning/Intermediate For a Picture It! lesson on author's purpose, see the ELL Teaching Guide, p. 58.

Advanced Before students read "Salsa Garden," discuss the kinds of things people grow in their gardens and what they do with their harvests.

SALSA GARDEN

David saw the sign his father put on the garden fence. It said Salsa Garden.

"Salsa?" David read aloud. "Can you grow salsa?"

Dad replied, "Just watch and see what comes up."

Each time David helped by watering and pulling weeds, he looked at the green plants. They all looked different. Not one looked like salsa.

Finally, harvest time came. First, Dad dug in the ground and pulled out round white things that looked a lot like onions. Then, he pulled off pods hanging from a plant. They looked a lot like hot peppers. Next, he cut a green leafy plant that smelled spicy. Finally, Dad pulled round, red balls from a fat vine. They sure looked a lot like tomatoes.

"Where's the salsa, Dad?" David asked as he followed his father to the kitchen.

Dad washed and cut everything up. He dumped his harvest into a machine with a sharp blade and turned it on. When he opened the lid, it was full of salsa!

1 Strategy Make a prediction here. What do you think this story will be about? Why would an author write a story with this title? Maybe it will tell about making salsa.

2 Skill Now we can determine the author's purpose. What do you think? Perhaps he wanted to inform us that good salsa needs good garden-grown vegetables.

225

Available as **Skill Transparency** 9

Author's Purpose • Predict

- The **author's purpose** is the reason an author writes something. Some reasons are to inform or teach, to entertain, to persuade, or to express ideas and feelings.
- Good readers try to **predict** what will happen and why. You can also **predict** the **author's purpose**.

Directions Read the passage and follow the directions to complete the graphic organizer.

Planting Bushes

STOP and answer Question 1 below.
The Lopez family had just built a nice house in the desert. The only problem was that the hot sun shone through the huge windows on the south side.

Early one morning, Dad and Grandpa planted bushes along the south side of the house.

"I wonder why they did that," thought Lupe.

STOP and answer Question 2 below.
Every day, Dad or Grandpa watered the bushes. They began to grow. Soon the bushes got so tall they blocked the sun from coming in the windows.

"Now I know why they did that!" thought Lupe.

1. Before You Read: Read the title. For which reason might the author write a passage with this title?
Possible answer: to inform the reader how to plant bushes

2. As You Read: Predict the author's purpose. Why do you think the author is telling this story?
Possible answer: to inform

3. After You Read: Give the author's purpose. Why did the author most likely write this selection? Explain.
to teach us that bushes can be a good way to keep out the sun

Home Activity Your child determined the author's purpose for writing a story. Purposes include to inform, to persuade, to entertain, or to express feelings or ideas. Talk about the author's purpose for writing tales your child is familiar with. Ask your child to give reasons for his or her answers.

Practice Book 3.1 p. 83

TEACH

1 STRATEGY Use the title to model making a prediction about author's purpose.

 MODEL The title of the selection is "Salsa Garden." What is a salsa garden? Why would the author write about that? I think maybe the author is going to write about how to grow things to make salsa.

2 SKILL At the end of the selection, model checking your predictions about author's purpose.

 MODEL Before I started reading, I thought the author was going to write about salsa and maybe tell us how to grow a salsa garden. I think I was right—the story was about a family vegetable garden, and the father used the vegetables he grew to make fresh salsa. I think the author was telling us how to make good salsa.

PRACTICE AND ASSESS

STRATEGY Using the title and the illustrations, students can predict that the author wants to explain how to make good salsa.

SKILL When students are finished reading, they can check their predictions. They should use details that support their ideas, such as the descriptions of the vegetables the father harvested and what he did with them to make the salsa.

WRITE Have students complete steps 1 and 2 of the Write to Read activity. You might consider using this as a whole class activity.

Monitor Progress
🎯 Author's Purpose

If... students are unable to complete **Write to Read** on p. 224,	**then...** use Practice Book 3.1, p. 83, to provide additional practice.

Build Background

E L L

Build Background Use ELL Poster 9 to build background and vocabulary for the lesson concept of when respect and understanding are important in solving a problem.

▲ **ELL Poster** 9

ACTIVATE PRIOR KNOWLEDGE

BEGIN A STEPS IN A PROCESS CHART about gardening and growing vegetables.

- On the board, draw a chart that has five boxes. (You may have to add boxes as you discuss the topic.) Write the title "Growing Vegetables" above the chart.

- Ask small groups of students to brainstorm the steps in growing a vegetable garden. Allow about five minutes for the process. Then write their ideas on the chart. Emphasize the importance of placing the information in the correct sequence.

- When the chart is complete, discuss different things people can do with vegetables they harvest from their gardens.

Growing Vegetables

Step 1	Prepare the soil.

↓

Step 2	Plant the seeds or plants.

↓

Step 3	

↓

Step 4	

↓

Step 5	

▲ **Graphic Organizer** 24

BACKGROUND BUILDING AUDIO In this week's audio, Cherokee storyteller Gayle Ross tells another story with a trickster rabbit character. After students listen, discuss why they think the trickster character in tales is often a rabbit.

Background Building Audio

Introduce Vocabulary

DEFINITION CARDS

Write each of the Words to Know on an index card. On separate cards, write a definition of each word. Read each word aloud to students, and then read the definitions. Have students think about where they may have seen or heard some of these words. ***Activate Prior Knowledge***

Distribute the definition and word cards to students. Have one student hold up and read a definition card. The student with the correct word match stands up and says the word. Repeat with reading the word first and then the matching definition.

Point out that the title of this week's story is *Tops and Bottoms,* and that the word *tops* is an antonym for the word *bottoms.* Have students think of antonyms for some of this week's words, such as *lazy (hard-working)* and *wealth (poverty).* As they come up with antonyms, write these words on index cards as well. When a definition is read, first have the students with the correct word match stand, then have students with the word's antonym stand. ***Antonyms***

Students can write sentences using the words from the list. Have them circle words whose meanings they did not previously know but now do.

Use the Multisyllabic Word Routine on p. DI•1 to help students read multisyllabic words.

Lesson Vocabulary

WORDS TO KNOW

T **bottom** the lowest part
T **cheated** tricked someone; acted in a way that is not honest
T **clever** bright; intelligent
T **crops** plants grown for food
T **lazy** not willing to work or move fast
T **partners** members of a company who share the risks and profits of the business
T **wealth** riches

MORE WORDS TO KNOW

cornstalk the main stem of a corn plant
debt something owed to someone else
T = Tested Word

Vocabulary

Directions Each sentence has an underlined word. Circle the word at the end of the sentence with the same meaning as the underlined word.

Check the Words You Know	
__lazy	__bottom
__crops	__clever
__cheated	__partners
__wealth	

1. My lazy brother hates to do his chores. (idle) young
2. Jill put the cookies on the bottom shelf. (lowest) long
3. Juan and I are partners in a lawn mowing business. (co-workers) a class
4. Jim does well in school because he is very clever. lazy (smart)
5. A person with lots of money has lots of wealth. (riches) need

Directions Write a word from the box to complete each sentence below.

6. The farmer plants many ___crops___ , including corn and wheat.
7. A farmer cannot be ___lazy___ because farming takes lots of work.
8. Ann is an honest student, so I don't think she ___cheated___ on the test.
9. The rich man had so much ___wealth___ , he owned five houses.
10. We will work together as ___partners___ to build a business.

Write a Story

On a separate sheet of paper, write about two farmers working together on something special. Describe them and what happens. Use as many vocabulary words as possible.

Students should use vocabulary to describe partners, what they do, and what happens.

Home Activity Your child identified and used vocabulary words from *Tops and Bottoms.* Visit the supermarket produce aisle together and have your child identify the vegetables whose tops or bottoms we eat. Encourage using as many vocabulary words as possible.

▲ **Practice Book 3.1** p. 84

Vocabulary Strategy

INTRODUCE

Discuss the context clues strategy for antonyms using the steps on p. 226.

TEACH

- Have students read "Farming," paying attention to how vocabulary is used.
- Model using context clues to determine the meaning of *bottom.*

Think Aloud **MODEL** The seeds are put in the *bottom* of each hole and are covered with soil on p. 227. So *bottom* must mean "the lowest part."

Words to Know

lazy
bottom
crops
clever
cheated
partners
wealth

Remember

Try the strategy. Then, if you need more help, use your glossary or a dictionary.

Vocabulary Strategy
for Antonyms

Context Clues Sometimes when you are reading you come across a word you don't know. The author may give you an antonym for the word. An antonym is a word that means the opposite of a word. For example, *empty* is the opposite of *full.* Look for a word that might be an antonym. It can help you understand the meaning of a word you don't know.

1. Look at the words around the word you don't know. The author may have used an antonym.

2. Look for words that seem to have opposite meanings. Think about the word you know.

3. Use that word to help you figure out the meaning of its antonym.

As you read "Farming," look for antonyms to help you understand the meanings of the vocabulary words.

DAY 2 Grouping Options

Reading
Whole Group Discuss the Question of the Day. Then use pp. 226–229.

Group Time Differentiated Instruction
Read *Tops and Bottoms.* See pp. 224f–224g for the small group lesson plan.

Whole Group Use pp. 249a and 249i.

Language Arts
Use pp. 249e–249h and 249k–249m.

ELL

Access Content Use ELL Poster 9 to preteach vocabulary. Choose from the following to meet language proficiency levels.

Beginning Point out the text on p. 227. Point out the context clues that tell you what *lazy* means (*not busy*) and what *crops* means (*things that grow*). Have students use each word in a sentence.

Intermediate After reading, students can create a two-column list of vocabulary and other words from the story, then write an antonym for each.

Advanced Teach the lesson on pp. 226–227. Students can report on vocabulary words and their antonyms in their home languages.

Resources for home-language words may include parents, bilingual staff members, bilingual dictionaries, or online translation sources.

Farming

Farming is not an occupation for lazy people. Farmers are always busy. In the spring they till, or turn up, the soil to prepare it for planting. Then they dig holes, put the seeds in the bottom of each hole, and cover them with soil. In the summer, farmers water and weed the growing crops. In the fall, it is time for harvesting. Then they cut or dig up the crops in the fields. In some countries, farmers use machines to do these things. In many countries, however, farmers still do many jobs by hand.

The weather can make any farmer look clever or foolish. Too much rain and the crops wash away; not enough rain and the crops die. The weather has often cheated farmers and ruined their crops. So farmers must be partners with the weather.

Most farmers do not make a lot of money. So why do they farm? Some farm to get the food they need. Many choose to be farmers because to them wealth is not as important as working with the land.

Words to Write

Would you like to be a farmer? Why or why not? Write about your ideas. Use words from the Words to Know list.

227

PRACTICE AND ASSESS

- Have students determine the meanings of the remaining words and explain the context clues they used.
- Point out that not all words have antonyms, nor are antonyms always used in the text. Explain that students may have to use a glossary or a dictionary to find the exact meaning of some words.
- Have students complete Practice Book 3.1, p. 85.

WRITE Writing should include vocabulary words that give reasons why students do or do not want to be a farmer.

Monitor Progress

Context Clues

| If... students need more practice with the lesson vocabulary, | then... use Tested Vocabulary Cards. |

Vocabulary • Context Clues

- Sometimes you come across a word you don't know. The author may use a word with the opposite meaning—an **antonym**—as a clue to the word's meaning.
- Use antonyms as **context clues** to figure out the meaning of unfamiliar words.

Directions Read each sentence. One word is underlined. Circle the antonym of the underlined word. Write the meaning of the underlined word on the line.

1. Sue is always so busy that no one can say she is lazy.
   not willing to work or move fast

2. Put the glass on the top shelf because your sister may break it if it's on the bottom.
   lowest or last

3. Danny is so clever, he would never do a silly thing like that.
   bright; intelligent; having a quick mind

4. The cat was asleep, but the dog was awake.
   not awake; sleeping

5. Months after planting the seeds, the farmer can harvest the corn.
   to gather crops

6. Do not scatter the papers, but gather them into one pile.
   to bring or come together in one place; collect

7. You look so nice when you smile that you should never scowl.
   to look at someone in an angry way; frown

8. Whisper the secret in my ear, don't holler it out loud.
   to cry or shout loudly

Home Activity Your child identified and used new words by understanding antonyms used in context. Read a story together and encourage identifying unfamiliar words. Then help look for antonyms in the text that might help figure out the words' meanings.

▲ **Practice Book 3.1** p. 85

Prereading Strategies

OBJECTIVES

- Identify author's purpose to improve comprehension.
- Use author's purpose to predict.

GENRE STUDY

Animal Fantasy

Tops and Bottoms is an animal fantasy. Explain that an animal fantasy is a made-up story in which the characters are animals that talk and act like people.

PREVIEW AND PREDICT

Have students preview the selection title and illustrations and discuss the topics or ideas they think this selection will cover. Encourage students to use lesson vocabulary as they talk about what they expect to learn.

Strategy Response Log

Generate Questions Have students write their questions in their strategy response logs. Students will answer their questions in the Strategy Response Log activity on p. 237.

Genre An **animal fantasy** is a story with animal characters that behave like people. Look for ways that Bear and Hare act like people.

228

ELL

Activate Prior Knowledge Put students in groups according to their abilities in English and have them discuss what they know about animal fantasies. If there are specific fantasies from their own countries, they can share them with the group. Have them come up with a short list of features common to fantasies. Introduce the idea of an animal fantasy, and have them consider what will happen in *Tops and Bottoms.*

Consider having students read the selection summary in English or in students' home languages. See the Multilingual Summaries in the ELL Teaching Guide, pp. 61–63.

Tops & Bottoms

adapted and illustrated by Janet Stevens

*In this story, Hare tries to trick Bear.
Does Bear deserve it?*

229

SET PURPOSE

Read the first page of the selection aloud to students. Have them consider their preview discussion and tell what they hope to find out as they read.

Remind students to think about the author's purpose as they read.

STRATEGY RECALL

Students have now used these before-reading strategies:

- preview the selection to be aware of its genre, features, and possible content;
- activate prior knowledge about that content and what to expect of that genre;
- make predictions;
- set a purpose for reading.

Remind students that, as they read, they should monitor their own comprehension. If they realize something does not make sense, they can regain their comprehension by using fix-up strategies they have learned, such as:

- use phonics and word structure to decode new words;
- use context clues or a dictionary to figure out meanings of new words;
- adjust their reading rate—slow down for difficult text, speed up for easy or familiar text, or skim and scan just for specific information;
- reread parts of the text;
- read on (continue to read for clarification);
- use text features such as headings, subheadings, charts, illustrations, and so on as visual aids to comprehension;
- make a graphic organizer or a semantic organizer to aid comprehension;
- use reference sources, such as an encyclopedia, dictionary, thesaurus, or synonym finder;
- use another person, such as a teacher, a peer, a librarian, or an outside expert, as a resource.

After reading, students will use these strategies:

- summarize or retell the text;
- answer questions they or others pose;
- reflect to make new information become part of their prior knowledge.

AudioText

Tops and Bottoms **229**

Guiding Comprehension

1  **Author's Purpose • Inferential**

Question the Author **Preview the story. Why do you think the author wrote it? What clues tell you this?**

To entertain. I know this story is a fantasy, and it is about animals. The pictures make the story funny.

Monitor Progress

Author's Purpose

If... students are unable to determine why the author wrote the story,	then... use the skill and strategy instruction on p. 231.

---

2 **Allusion • Critical**

Text to Text **On p. 231, the author refers to a bet between Hare and a tortoise. What story does this remind you of? What kind of story is it? In one or two sentences, tell what happens in that story.**

The Tortoise and the Hare; a fable; the hare bets a tortoise he can beat him in a race and decides he can take his time running the race because the tortoise is so slow. The hare loses because he falls asleep and is too far behind to catch up.

3 **Character • Inferential**

What is Hare like?

Possible responses: clever; bad with money.

---

1 nce upon a time there lived a very lazy bear who had lots of money and lots of land. His father had been a hard worker and a smart business bear, and he had given all of his wealth to his son.

But all Bear wanted to do was sleep.

ELL

Understand Idioms Point out the idiom *to be in bad shape* at the bottom of p. 231. Explain that it means that things are not going well. Point out the context in which it is used to illustrate the meaning. *(The Hare family lost their land and money, so now they are poor.)* Read students these examples: Mr. Bene owns a home and a business. Mr. Dowde lost his job and had to move out of his house. Ask students, Which person is *in bad shape*? *(Mr. Dowde)*

Not far down the road lived a hare. Although Hare was clever, he sometimes got into trouble. He had once owned land, too, but now he had nothing. He had lost a risky bet with a tortoise and had sold all of his land to Bear to pay off the debt. ❷ ❸

Hare and his family were in very bad shape.

SKILLS ⟷ STRATEGIES IN CONTEXT

Author's Purpose Predict

TEACH

- Explain to students that before we read, it is a good idea to look through the selection and try to figure out what it will be about and what the author's purpose for writing was.

- Tell students that understanding author's purpose, or the reason an author has for writing, helps us figure out which reading strategies we should use to understand the selection better.

- The four main reasons an author has for writing are to persuade, to inform, to entertain, and to express ideas and feelings.

Think Aloud **MODEL** Before I read, I looked at the title and the illustrations. I know this is an animal fantasy, and the drawings are funny. I think the author wrote this story to entertain. It will be a funny story.

PRACTICE AND ASSESS

Have students predict a message they will read about in this story. Remind them to use details from pp. 230–231 to support their ideas. To assess, check that their ideas make sense and are supported by details from the story.

Climate

Time for SOCIAL STUDIES

Some crops do better in certain climates than others. Oranges, for example, do well in regions such as Florida or Southern California, where temperatures rarely fall below freezing, and there is a lot of sun and rain. (Orange growers in California often have to irrigate, or water, their orange groves because there is not enough water naturally for oranges to do well.) Corn, on the other hand, does well in the Midwestern United States, where summer nights are warm and summer days are hot, and there is consistent rainfall. Many of the crops mentioned in the story, such as potatoes, lettuce, broccoli, and squash, will do well just about anywhere, with little care.

Guiding Comprehension

4 REVIEW **Main Idea and Details •**
Inferential

Reread pp. 232–233. What are they about?

Hare has a problem. He decides to solve his problem by working with Bear.

Monitor Progress

REVIEW **Main Idea and Details**

If... students have difficulty identifying the main idea,	**then...** use the skill and strategy instruction on p. 233.

---

5 **Realism and Fantasy • Inferential**
In what ways is *Tops and Bottoms* a fantasy?

The characters in the story are animals, and they talk and act like people.

6 **Personification • Inferential**
In what ways are the characters in the story like people? Give examples.

Possible response: They talk and behave like people do. For example, Mrs. Hare is worried about food for her family, just like a human mother would be in a similar situation. Hare and Bear agree to work together.

"The children are so hungry, Father Hare! We must think of something!" Mrs. Hare cried one day. So Hare and Mrs. Hare put their heads together and cooked up a plan.

The next day Hare hopped down the road to Bear's house. Bear, of course, was asleep.

"Hello, Bear, wake up! It's your neighbor, Hare, and I have an idea!"

232

Understand Idioms Point out the idiom *to cook up a plan* on p. 232. Explain that *to cook up* means to invent, or think up. Have students think of a time when they cooked up a plan or an idea and share it with the group. To assess, check that students are using the word correctly.

Bear opened one eye and grunted.

"We can be business partners!" Hare said. "All we need is this field right here in front of your house. I'll do the hard work of planting and harvesting, and we can split the profit right down the middle. Yes, sir, Bear, we're in this together. I'll work and you sleep."

"Huh?" said Bear.

"So, what will it be, Bear?" asked Hare. "The top half or the bottom half? It's up to you—tops or bottoms." **4 5 6**

233

Personal Responsibility

Time for
SOCIAL STUDIES

How many times have you said or heard someone else say, "Hey! That isn't fair!" Maybe someone cut in front of you in line, or your older brother or sister got to stay up later than you one night, to see a movie that you couldn't see, and you protested—loudly! Have you ever stopped to think about what fair is? More importantly, have you ever stopped to think what you can do to be fair towards others? Generally, when we protest that something is unfair, we are upset because someone did something that goes against the rules, whether those be the rules of the house, the rules of the playground, or the rules of society. What are some simple things you can do that show others you can be fair? Give others a turn, be polite, say excuse me, don't cheat, be honest, and apologize when you realize you have been wrong.

SKILLS ⬌ STRATEGIES IN CONTEXT

Main Idea and Details (REVIEW)

TEACH

- Remind students that when we read a story, we try to understand what it is about. We use details from the story to help us and to support our ideas.

- Model thinking what the story is about and using details to support your ideas.

Think Aloud **MODEL** I read that Hare is in trouble and comes up with a plan to get out of trouble. One detail that supports this idea is when Hare goes over to Bear and tells him they can work together.

PRACTICE AND ASSESS

- Have students find another detail that tells what the story is about.

- To assess, use Practice Book 3.1, p. 86.

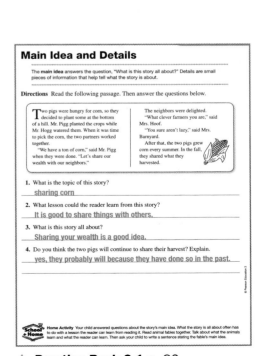

Main Idea and Details

The **main idea** answers the question, "What is this story all about?" Details are small pieces of information that help tell what the story is about.

Directions Read the following passage. Then answer the questions below.

Two pigs were hungry for corn, so they decided to plant some at the bottom of a hill. Mr. Pigg planted the crops while Mr. Hogg watered them. When it was time to pick the corn, the two partners worked together.

"We have a ton of corn," said Mr. Pigg when they were done. "Let's share our wealth with our neighbors."

The neighbors were delighted. "What clever farmers you are," said Mrs. Hoof.

"You sure aren't lazy," said Mrs. Barnyard.

After that, the two pigs grew corn every summer. In the fall, they shared what they harvested.

1. What is the topic of this story?
   sharing corn

2. What lesson could the reader learn from this story?
   It is good to share things with others.

3. What is this story all about?
   Sharing your wealth is a good idea.

4. Do you think the two pigs will continue to share their harvest? Explain.
   yes, they probably will because they have done so in the past.

Home Activity Your child answered questions about the story's main idea. What the story is all about often has to do with a lesson the reader can learn from reading it. Read animal fables together. Talk about what the animals learn and what the reader can learn. Then ask your child to write a sentence stating the fable's main idea.

▲ **Practice Book 3.1** p. 86

Guiding Comprehension

7  **Vocabulary • Context Clues**

Use context clues to figure out the meaning of the word *tops* on p. 235.

Clues: antonym—*bottoms*. Meaning: the upper half.

Monitor Progress

 Context Clues

If... students have difficulty using context clues to determine the meaning of *tops*,	then... use vocabulary strategy instruction on p. 235.

---

8 **Facts and Details • Literal**

What does Bear do while Hare and his family plant, water, and weed?

He sleeps.

Tech Files
ONLINE

Use the keywords *fables, fantasy,* and *animal stories* to look up similar stories. Students can read another story and summarize it for the class.

"Uh, let's see," Bear said with a yawn. "I'll take the top half, Hare. Right—tops." **7**
Hare smiled. "It's a done deal, Bear."
8 So Bear went back to sleep, and Hare and his family went to work. Hare planted, Mrs. Hare watered, and everyone weeded.

ELL

Fluency Non-native speakers of English may have difficulty with consonant blends, depending on their native languages. Spanish speakers, for example, may try to add a short *e* sound before words starting with *s* (*snake, spirit*). Help students practice blending the sounds in words with consonant blends that they have difficulty with by having them read short passages aloud. Listen and correct their pronunciation as necessary.

Bear slept as the crops grew.

When it was time for the harvest, Hare called out, "Wake up, Bear! You get the tops and I get the bottoms."

235

VOCABULARY STRATEGY

Context Clues

TEACH

- Explain to students that when we come across a word we don't know, we can sometimes use context clues to help us figure out what it means. Context clues are words and sentences around the word we don't know which can tell us what it means.

- Sometimes the author uses an antonym for a difficult word. This helps us figure out the meaning of the word we don't know.

- Model using an antonym to figure out the meaning of *tops* on p. 235.

Think Aloud **MODEL** I'm not sure what the author means by *tops* here. I've seen the word before, but it has different meanings. If I continue reading, I see the word *bottoms*. *Bottoms* is an antonym for *tops*. This tells me that *tops* means the top part of something.

PRACTICE AND ASSESS

Have students use context clues to figure out what *crops* on p. 235 means. *(Possible response: plants)*

Guiding Comprehension

9 Sequence • Literal

When did Bear choose tops or bottoms—before or after Hare planted the crops and dug them up?

Before.

10 Generalize • Inferential

Look through the story and identify some of the character traits of either Bear or Hare. What generalizations can we make about bears or hares based on the characters' traits?

Possible response: Bear: lazy, bossy; Hare: hard-working, clever. Bears sleep a lot; hares are smart animals.

11 ⏺ Predict • Inferential

What do you think will happen the second time Hare plants the garden?

Possible response: He will trick Bear again.

EXTEND SKILLS

Comparing Stories

Explain to students that there are some fantasy stories, tales, and fables that are different versions of the same story from other cultures. The story from another culture may have the same or different characters, setting, or moral. Have students compare and contrast *Tops & Bottoms* with the same story from another culture.

Hare and his family dug up the carrots, the radishes, and the beets. Hare plucked off all the tops, tossed them into a pile for Bear, and put the bottoms aside for himself.

236

ELL

Access Content Students may not know what radishes and beets are. Explain that radishes are small, round, red vegetables with a slightly spicy taste. Beets are large, round, purple vegetables with a slightly sweet taste. Ask them what carrots, radishes, and beets have in common *(they are root vegetables; they grow underground)*. Discuss how Hare tricks Bear *(He plants vegetables that grow underground so that he gets the better part of the vegetable.)*

Bear stared at his pile. "But, Hare, all the best parts are in your half!"

9 "You chose the tops, Bear," Hare said.

"Now, Hare, you've tricked me. You plant this field again—and this season I want the bottoms!"

Hare agreed. "It's a done deal, Bear." **10** **11**

STRATEGY SELF-CHECK

Predict

Explain to students that when we make a prediction, we are looking at the facts and details and telling what we think will happen in the future. If we can make a prediction about what we are reading and we are correct, then we have understood what we are reading.

Sometimes the facts and details let us make predictions about why the author wrote a selection.

Have students look through the story at the facts and details and tell what they think the author's purpose for writing this story was. Have them make a prediction about what lesson, if any, the author wants to teach with this story.

SELF-CHECK

Students can ask these questions to assess their ability to use the skill and strategy.

- Do the facts and details in the story support my prediction?
- Do the facts and details tell me why the author wrote this story?

Monitor Progress
🔄 **Author's Purpose**

If... students have difficulty identifying author's purpose,	**then...** revisit the skill lesson on p. 224–225. Reteach as necessary.

Strategy Response Log

Answer Questions Look at the questions you asked on p. 228 before you started reading the story. Answer the questions you can here. Continue reading to answer any remaining questions. If you have answered all your questions, write one or two more and look for the answers as you finish the story.

If you want to teach this selection in two sessions, stop here.

Develop Vocabulary

PRACTICE LESSON VOCABULARY

Have students provide oral responses to each question.

1. **Does someone who is *lazy* like to work a lot or sleep a lot?** *(Sleep a lot)*
2. **What are *partners*?** *(People who work together and share the work and the rewards)*
3. **If someone has *wealth,* does he or she have a lot of money or little money?** *(A lot of money)*

BUILD CONCEPT VOCABULARY

Review previous concept words with students. Ask if students have met any words today in their reading or elsewhere that they would like to add to the Concept Web.

Guiding Comprehension

If you are teaching the selection in two days, discuss the story so far, including the author's purpose, and review the vocabulary.

12 ○ **Author's Purpose • Inferential**
Question the Author **What is another reason the author may have written this story?**

To teach a lesson

So Bear went back to sleep, and Hare and his family went to work. They planted, watered, and weeded.

Monitor Progress
○ **Author's Purpose**

If... students are unable to determine the author's purpose,	**then...** use the skill and strategy instruction on p. 239.

13 ○ **Predict • Inferential**
What do you think will happen next?

Possible response: Hare and his family will trick Bear again.

DAY 3 Grouping Options

Reading
Whole Group Discuss the Question of the Day.

Group Time Differentiated Instruction
Read *Tops and Bottoms*. See pp. 224f–224g for the small group lesson plan.

Whole Group Discuss the Reader Response questions on p. 246. Then use p. 249a.

Language Arts
Use pp.249e–249h and 249k–249m.

Bear slept as the crops grew.

When it was time for the harvest, Hare called out, "Wake up, Bear! You get the bottoms and I get the tops." **12** **13**

239

SKILLS ↔ STRATEGIES IN CONTEXT

Author's Purpose
Predict

TEACH

- Active readers rethink their prediction about the topic and the author's purpose while they are reading. This helps them monitor their own understanding. They also go back and reread if they have not understood.

- Remind students that often an author has more than one reason for writing. The facts and details in the story can help us figure out the author's purpose.

- Model rethinking why the author wrote *Tops and Bottoms* and predicting another reason the author may have written the story.

Think Aloud **MODEL** Before I started reading the story, I thought the author's purpose for writing was to entertain. The pictures are funny, and the characters are animals that talk and act like people do. Now I'm halfway through the story, though, and I think the author had another reason for writing. I think she wanted to teach a lesson too. I'm not sure yet what the lesson is, but I think it has something to do with Bear being lazy and always losing out.

PRACTICE AND ASSESS

Have students predict how the story will end. *(Responses will vary.)*

Guiding Comprehension

Hare and his family gathered up the lettuce, the broccoli, and the celery. Hare pulled off the bottoms for Bear and put the tops in his own pile.

Bear looked at his pile and scowled. "Hare, you have cheated me again."

"But, Bear," Hare said, "you wanted the bottoms this time."

14 **Categorize • Inferential**

What two categories of vegetables are mentioned in the story so far?

Categories: Bottom vegetables: carrots, radishes, beets/Top vegetables: lettuce, broccoli, celery

15 (REVIEW) **Main Idea and Details • Inferential**

Reread pp. 240–241. What are these two pages about?

Hare has tricked Bear again.

Monitor Progress

(REVIEW) Main Idea and Details

If... students have difficulty identifying main idea and details,	**then...** use the skill and strategy instruction on p. 241.

---

16 **Illustrator's Craft • Critical**

Look at the illustrations in the story. What humorous details does the author use in her pictures? What do they tell you about the characters or the story?

Possible response: Bear wears a tie and formal shoes, like a businessman, but the tie is loose around his neck and the shoes are untied, like a businessman who is relaxing. These details are funny, but they also show me how lazy Bear is.

Bear growled, "You plant this field again, Hare. You've tricked me twice, and you owe me one season of both tops and bottoms!"

"You're right, poor old Bear," sighed Hare. "It's only fair that you get both tops and bottoms this time. It's a done deal, Bear."

So Bear went back to sleep, and Hare and his family went to work. They planted, watered, and weeded, then watered and weeded some more.

Bear slept as the crops grew.

When it was time for the harvest, Hare called out, "Wake up, Bear! This time you get the tops and the bottoms!" **14** **15**

16

241

Main Idea and Details REVIEW

TEACH

- Remind students that in order to understand what the whole story is about, we have to understand what each page is about. The facts and details help us do this.

- Model using facts and details to tell what pp. 240–241 are about.

 MODEL What are these two pages about? I think they're about Hare tricking Bear again. Bear says that Hare tricked him, so that supports my idea.

PRACTICE AND ASSESS

Have students identify at least one detail that tells more about what pp. 240–241 are about. To assess, check that the detail students have identified supports the main idea of the pages.

EXTEND SKILLS

Humorous Detail

Tell students that sometimes authors who illustrate their own stories use details in the illustrations that are funny to tell us more about the characters and the story. We can use these details to better understand the story. Point out details, such as the tie and shoes on Bear, that tell us more about Bear or support the idea that he is lazy. Have students look for details in the illustrations that tell us more about Hare and his family.

Guiding Comprehension

17 🎯 **Author's Purpose • Inferential**
Question the Author **What lesson do you think the author is trying to teach us in** *Tops and Bottoms***?**

Possible response: If you work hard, you will do well. If you are lazy, you will lose out.

Monitor Progress

🎯 Author's Purpose

If... students are unable to determine the author's purpose,	**then...** use the skill and strategy instruction on p. 243.

---

18 **Draw Conclusions • Inferential**
How do you think Bear feels now?

Possible responses: Angry, foolish

19 **Cause and Effect • Inferential**
What happens to Bear and why?

Hare takes advantage of Bear because Bear is lazy.

There in front of Bear's house lay a high field of corn. Hare and his family yanked up every cornstalk. Hare tugged off the roots at the bottom and the tassels at the top and put them in a pile for Bear. Then he carefully collected the ears of corn in the middle and placed them in his own pile.

242

Bear rubbed his eyes and watched.

"See, Bear? You get the tops and the bottoms. I get the middles. Yes, sir, Bear. It's a done deal!"

By now Bear was wide awake. "That's it, Hare!" he hollered. "From now on I'll plant my own crops and take the tops, bottoms, and middles!"

Hare and his family scooped up the corn and hopped down the road toward home. **17** **18** **19**

243

Author's Purpose

TEACH

- Point out that understanding why an author wrote a story helps us understand and appreciate what we read.

- When you finish reading, it is a good idea to think again about why the author may have written a story. If you haven't understood the reason for writing, then you probably haven't understood the selection. Think again about why the author wrote the story and look back for details that support your ideas.

 Think Aloud **MODEL** I thought the author wrote the story to entertain, and the story was funny, so I still think that was one reason she wrote it. Later I started to think that maybe she wanted to teach a lesson too. By the end of the story, Bear is really mad and finally awake, so he tells Hare he won't plant crops with him again. I think he learned that he can't sleep and trust others to do all the work for him. I think that's the lesson the author wanted to teach.

PRACTICE AND ASSESS

Have students find another detail that indicates what lesson the author was trying to teach. To assess, check that the detail students have chosen supports their ideas.

Guiding Comprehension

20 **Confirm Predictions • Inferential**

Did the story end as you predicted it?

Responses will vary.

21 **Summarize • Critical**

What was Hare's problem? How did he solve it?

Hare and his family had no land or money, and his children were hungry. He and his wife tricked Bear into sharing his land to allow them to grow crops that they could sell. They used the money they made to buy back their land and open a vegetable stand.

22 **Realism and Fantasy • Critical**

Text to Text **Think of other examples of fantasy you have read and examples of realistic fiction you have read. List some features of both. How are they similar? How are they different?**

Responses will vary. Students should be able to recognize that fantasies are about things that cannot happen, such as animals that talk, while realistic fiction is about things that could happen, or people who could be real. Students should also recognize that even though a fantasy could never happen, it can still, like realistic fiction, entertain or teach a lesson.

Strategy Response Log

Summarize When students finish reading the selection, provide this prompt: Imagine that you want to tell a friend what *Tops and Bottoms* is about. In four or five sentences, explain its important points.

Bear never again slept through a season of planting and harvesting. Hare bought back his land with the profit from the crops, and he and Mrs. Hare opened a vegetable stand.

And although Hare and Bear learned to live happily as neighbors, they never became business partners again! **20 21 22**

245

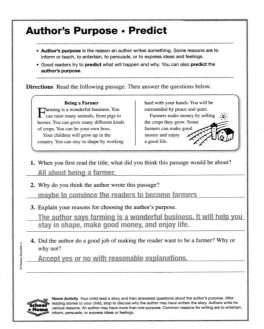

STRATEGY SELF-CHECK

Predict

- Remind students that good readers preview a selection before they read and think about the author's purpose for writing.
- When they finish reading, have them check their predictions and, if necessary, rethink their ideas.
- Ask students to think what they thought the author's purpose for writing was and to consider when they started to think she might have another reason for writing.

SELF-CHECK

Students can ask these questions to assess their ability to use the skill and strategy.

- What did I think the author's purpose was before I read?
- What do I think the author's purpose is now?
- Can I support my ideas with details?
- To assess, use Practice Book 3.1, p. 87.

Monitor Progress

Author's Purpose

If... students have difficulty identifying author's purpose,	**then...** use the Reteach lesson on p. 249b.

Develop Vocabulary

PRACTICE LESSON VOCABULARY

Have students answer *true* or *false* to each statement below and change the false statements to true statements.

1. **Someone who *cheated* got something by working hard.** *(False; someone who cheated got something by acting dishonestly.)*
2. **Smart is an antonym for clever.** *(False; smart is a synonym for clever.)*
3. **Partners work against each other.** *(False; they work together.)*

BUILD CONCEPT VOCABULARY

Review previous concept words with students. Ask if students have met any words today in their reading or elsewhere that they would like to add to the Concept Web.

Author's Purpose • Predict

- **Author's purpose** is the reason an author writes something. Some reasons are to inform or teach, to entertain, to persuade, or to express ideas and feelings.
- Good readers try to **predict** what will happen and why. You can also **predict** the author's purpose.

Directions Read the following passage. Then answer the questions below.

Being a Farmer

Farming is a wonderful business. You can raise many animals, from pigs to horses. You can grow many different kinds of crops. You can be your own boss.

Your children will grow up in the country. You can stay in shape by working hard with your hands. You will be surrounded by peace and quiet.

Farmers make money by selling the crops they grow. Some farmers can make good money and enjoy a good life.

1. When you first read the title, what did you think this passage would be about?
   All about being a farmer.

2. Why do you think the author wrote this passage?
   maybe to convince the readers to become farmers

3. Explain your reasons for choosing the author's purpose.
   The author says farming is a wonderful business. It will help you stay in shape, make good money, and enjoy life.

4. Did the author do a good job of making the reader want to be a farmer? Why or why not?
   Accept yes or no with reasonable explanations.

School + Home **Home Activity** Your child read a story and then answered questions about the author's purpose. After reading stories to your child, stop to discuss why the author may have written the story. Authors write for various reasons. An author may have more than one purpose. Common reasons for writing are to entertain, inform, persuade, or express ideas or feelings.

▲ **Practice Book 3.1** p. 87

Reader Response

Open for Discussion **Personal Response**

 MODEL I'll be Hare because he has more speaking parts, and I like to act in front of people. We'll have to figure out which parts are necessary, and which parts we can cut out, so it isn't too long. This'll be fun!

Comprehension Check **Critical Response**

1. Responses will vary; for accuracy, check the students' details against the page they are describing. ***Author's Purpose***

2. Possible response: Hares are thought to be tricky, wily, smart creatures who must be quick on their feet in order to survive. ***Author's Purpose***

3. Responses will vary. ***Predict***

4. Responses will vary; check that students have used details from the story as well as words from the word list in their comparisons. ***Vocabulary***

 **Look Back and Write** For test practice, assign a 10–15 minute time limit. For assessment, see the Scoring Rubric at the right.

Retell

Have students retell *Tops and Bottoms*.

Monitor Progress

Check Retelling 4 3 2 1 (Rubric)

If... students have difficulty retelling the story,	**then...** use the Retelling Cards and the Scoring Rubric for Retelling on p. 247 to assist fluent retelling.

SUCCESS PREDICTOR

ELL

Check Retelling Have students use illustrations and other text features to guide their retellings. Let students listen to other retellings before attempting their own. See the ELL and Transition Handbook.

Reader Response

Open for Discussion Bear and Hare—what a pair! Get together with a partner and act out the story to retell it. Act out the story twice, until it's a done deal!

1. Janet Stevens must have had fun making the pictures. Pretend you can step into one of the pictures. Look around. Tell everything you see, smell, and hear. **Think Like an Author**

2. Why do you think the author chose to use the hare as the main character in this story? **Author's Purpose**

3. Did you predict that Bear would get nothing after the first harvest? How did that prediction help you with your next prediction? **Predict**

4. Bear and Hare are very different from each other. Make a Venn diagram to show how they are alike and different. Label the circles Bear and Hare. Label the middle section Both. Use words from the Words to Know list and from the story to fill in your diagram. **Vocabulary**

 Look Back and Write Bear and Hare both had problems. Were their problems solved at the end of the story? How? Look back to the end of the selection. Use details from the selection to write your answer.

Meet author **and illustrator** **Janet Stevens on page 415.**

Scoring Rubric **Look Back and Write**

Top-Score Response A top-score response will use details from the selection to tell whether Bear and Hare's problems were solved.

Example of a Top-Score Response Hare's problem is solved after he buys back all his land. He gets money by tricking Bear out of his vegetables and selling them. Bear's problem is also solved. He learns that he can't sleep through the whole growing season. He has to work to grow his own crops.

For additional rubrics, see p. WA10.

Write Now

Feature Story

Prompt

In *Tops and Bottoms,* a character uses his creativity to get ahead.

Think about an event that happened because of one or more creative people.

Now write a feature story about the event and the person.

Student Model

Question at beginning engages readers.

Are you an artist or art lover? Then meet nine-year-old Clark Peterson. Clark and his friends are artists. He had a brilliant idea—open an art gallery in a vacant shop. But who would pay the rent? Clark contacted artists who wanted to display their work. Twenty people chipped in rent money. When the gallery opened, many people came to view and buy the artwork. The artists use some of the money to keep the gallery going. Thanks to Clark Peterson, Milltown's artists and art lovers are happy.

Details and word choice contribute to lively, interested voice.

Last sentence echoes first sentence to emphasize main idea.

Use the model to help you write your own feature story.

247

Write Now

Look at the Prompt Have students identify and discuss key words and phrases in the prompt. *(event, creative people, feature story)*

Strategies to Develop Voice

Have students

- read and discuss feature stories and identify the author's voice in each.
- list voices a feature story writer might use, such as amusing, serious, or lighthearted.
- brainstorm images and figures of speech.

NO: Matt wanted to be an actor.

YES: Matt was a budding Tom Hanks.

For additional suggestions and rubric, see pp. 249g–249h.

Hints for Better Writing

- Carefully read the prompt.
- Use a graphic organizer to plan your writing.
- Support your ideas with information and details.
- Use words that help readers understand.
- Proofread and edit your work.

Scoring Rubric — Narrative Retelling

Rubric 4 3 2 1	4	3	2	1
Connections	Makes connections and generalizes beyond the text	Makes connections to other events, stories, or experiences	Makes a limited connection to another event, story, or experience	Makes no connection to another event, story, or experience
Author's Purpose	Elaborates on author's purpose	Tells author's purpose with some clarity	Makes some connection to author's purpose	Makes no connection to author's purpose
Characters	Describes the main character(s) and any character development	Identifies the main character(s) and gives some information about them	Inaccurately identifies some characters or gives little information about them	Inaccurately identifies the characters or gives no information about them
Setting	Describes the time and location	Identifies the time and location	Omits details of time or location	Is unable to identify time or location
Plot	Describes the problem, goal, events, and ending using rich detail	Tells the problem, goal, events, and ending with some errors that do not affect meaning	Tells parts of the problem, goal, events, and ending with gaps that affect meaning	Retelling has no sense of story

Retelling Plan

- ☑ **Week 1** Assess Strategic Intervention students.
- ☑ **Week 2** Assess Advanced students.
- ☑ **Week 3** Assess Strategic Intervention students.
- ☑ **This week assess On-Level students.**
- ☐ **Week 5** Assess any students you have not yet checked during this unit.

Use the Retelling Chart on p. TR16 to record retelling.

Selection Test To assess with *Tops and Bottoms,* use Selection Tests, pp. 33–36.

Fresh Reads for Differentiated Test Practice For weekly leveled practice, use pp. 49–54.

Retelling

SUCCESS PREDICTOR

Literature in Reading

OBJECTIVES

- Examine features of a fable.
- Practice a test-taking strategy.
- Compare and contrast across texts.

PREVIEW

As students preview "The Hare and the Tortoise," have them identify the animal characters in the story. After they preview, ask:

- **As you look at the illustration, what can you say about the hare and the tortoise?** (They are facing each other and Hare's arms (or front legs) are crossed. They may be confronting each other.)

Link to Reading

Help students use the online library catalog to find other fables or the same fable from different cultures, in the library.

Folk Literature

Fable

Genre

- **Animals are often the main characters in a fable.**
- **The author tells a very brief story that clearly points to a moral or a lesson.**
- **The moral is usually stated at the end of the story, highlighting its importance.**

Link to Reading

Find other fables in the library. Report other morals or lessons you find to your class.

248

The Hare and the Tortoise

by Aesop
illustrated by Michael Hague

One day a quick-footed Hare was making fun of a slow-moving Tortoise. Much to the Hare's surprise, the Tortoise began to laugh. "I challenge you to a race," said the Tortoise, "and I bet that I will win."

"Very well," said the Hare, "I will dance rings around you all the way."

It was soon agreed that the Fox would set the course and be the judge. The race began and the Hare ran so quickly that he soon left the Tortoise far behind. Once he reached the middle of the course, the Hare decided to take a nap.

While the Hare slept, the Tortoise plodded on and on, straight toward the finish line. When the Hare awoke from his nap, he was surprised that the Tortoise was nowhere in sight. Racing to the finish line as fast as he could, the Hare was shocked to find the Tortoise waiting for him with a smile on his face.

Slow and steady wins the race.

Content-Area Vocabulary · Science

hare	an animal with long ears, a short tail, and long hind legs, a little bit larger than a rabbit
tortoise	a turtle

DAY 4 · Grouping Options

Reading
Whole Group Discuss the Question of the Day.

Group Time Differentiated Instruction
Read "The Hare and the Tortoise." See pp. 224f–224g for the small group lesson plan.

Whole Group Use pp. 249a and 249j.

Language Arts
Use pp.249e–249h and 249k–249m.

Reading Across Texts

Who were the winner and the loser in this story and in *Tops and Bottoms*? Why did the loser lose each time?

Writing Across Texts Write a short paragraph comparing the losers.

Author's Purpose What lesson is the author trying to teach?

249

FABLE

Use the sidebar on p. 248 to guide discussion.

- A fable is a short story, usually with animal characters, that has a clearly stated lesson.
- Animal characters in fables are personified and often have one character trait that relates to the lesson being taught.

Audio CD AudioText

Author's Purpose

Possible response: It is more important to be persistent than to be fast.

CONNECT TEXT TO TEXT

Reading Across Texts

Write the characters' names from each story as students name them. Put a star next to winners and a sad face next to losers. Discuss what happened in each story and why the winners won and the losers lost.

Writing Across Texts Students may find it helpful to use a chart, such as a Venn diagram, a compare-contrast chart, and a four-column chart (Graphic Organizers 17, 18, and 27).

ELL

Test Practice Call attention to the words *quick-footed* and *slow-moving* in the first line of the story, and make sure students can explain the contrast between the two characters. To clarify the story ending, ask students which character would most likely win the race (Hare) and why he didn't (he took a nap).

Fluency Assessment Plan

- ☑ **Week 1** Assess Advanced students.
- ☑ **Week 2** Assess Strategic Intervention students.
- ☑ **Week 3** Assess On-Level students.
- ☑ **This week assess Strategic Intervention students.**
- ☐ **Week 5** Assess any students you have not yet checked during this unit.

Set individual goals for students to enable them to reach the year-end goal.
- Current Goal: 85–95 WCPM
- Year-End Goal: 120 WCPM

 To develop fluent readers, use Fluency Coach.

MORE READING FOR
Fluency

 To practice fluency with text comprised of previously taught phonics elements and irregular words, use Decodable Reader 9.

DAY 5 Grouping Options

Reading
Whole Group
Revisit the Question of the Week.

Group Time
Differentiated Instruction
Reread this week's Leveled Readers. See pp. 224f–224g for the small group lesson plan.

Whole Group
Use pp. 249b–249c.

Language Arts
Use pp. 249d–249h and 249k–249n.

APPROPRIATE PHRASING
Fluency

DAY 1

Model Reread "Why Possum's Tail Is Bare" on p. 224m. Explain that you will pause to show appropriate phrasing as you read the selection. Model for students as you read.

DAY 2

Readers' Theater Read aloud p. 237. Have students notice how you use your voice to bring the characters to life. Have students practice in groups of three doing Readers' Theater readings of p. 237.

DAY 3

Model Read aloud p. 243. Have students notice how your voice changes as you read what Bear and Hare say. Practice in small groups by doing three Readers' Theater readings.

DAY 4

Readers' Theater Groups of three practice reading aloud p. 243, three times. Students should read with appropriate phrasing and offer each other feedback.

Monitor Progress | Check Fluency WCPM

As students reread, monitor their progress toward their individual fluency goals. Current Goal: 85–95 words correct per minute. End-of-Year Goal: 120 words correct per minute.

If... students cannot read fluently at a rate of 85–95 words correct per minute,
then... make sure students practice with text at their independent level. Provide additional fluency practice, pairing nonfluent readers with fluent readers.

If... students already read at 120 words correct per minute,
then... they do not need to reread three to four times.

 SUCCESS PREDICTOR

DAY 5

Assessment
Individual Reading Rate Use the Fluency Assessment Plan and do a one-minute timed reading of either selection from this week to assess students in Week 4. Pay special attention to this week's skills, appropriate phrasing. Provide corrective feedback for each student.

RETEACH

Author's Purpose

TEACH

Write the following on the board: *author's purpose = the reason(s) the author had for writing something.* Review the skill instruction for author's purpose and the four main reasons an author has for writing on p. 224. Students can complete Practice Book 3.1, p. 88 on their own, or you can complete it as a class. Explain that they will have to read the selection and answer the questions about author's purpose in the graphic organizer.

ASSESS

Work with the class to summarize the story. Have students discuss why the author may have chosen to feature a bear and a hare in the story. They should support their ideas with details from the story. *(Possible response: Bears sleep through the winter, so they seem slow and lazy, like the bear in the story; hares have to be fast in order to get away from predators, which makes them seem smart.)*

For additional instruction of author's purpose, see DI • 55.

EXTEND SKILLS

Idioms

TEACH

An idiom is an expression whose meaning cannot be determined by looking at the usual meaning of the words that form it. Idioms are a type of figurative language.

• *Cat's got your tongue, his bark is worse than his bite,* and *cut off your nose to spite your face* are examples of idioms.

Point out the idiom *put their heads together* on p. 232, and help students use context clues to figure out its meaning.

ASSESS

Have small groups work together to identify an idiom in "The Hare and the Tortoise" and then use context clues to figure out what it means. *(Possible response: dance rings around on p. 248; meaning: do better than; context clues: Hare thinks he is better than Tortoise.)*

OBJECTIVES

• Understand author's purpose.

• Recognize idioms.

Skills Trace	
Author's Purpose	
Introduce/Teach	TE: 3.2 224–225, 3.3 304–305, 3.5 244–245
Practice	PB: 3.1 16, 83, 87, 88, 113, 117, 118, 126, 146; 3.2 93, 97, 98
Reteach/Review	**TE: 3.1 51; 3.2 249b, DI•55; 3.3 329b, 347, 391, DI•53; 3.5 275b, DI•56**
Test	Selection Test: Unit 2 Benchmark Test: Unit 3

ELL

Access Content Reteach the skill by reviewing the Picture It! lesson on author's purpose in the ELL Teaching Guide, pp. 57–58.

Author's Purpose

Author's purpose is the reason an author writes something. Some reasons are to inform or teach, to entertain, to persuade, or to express ideas and feelings.

Directions Read the title and answer question 1. Read the first part, and answer question 2. Then finish the passage and complete the graphic organizer.

The Cat and the Cherries

Cat loved cherries on the trees in the orchard. Bird helped Cat by dropping cherries onto the ground so she could eat them. But today Bird was nowhere in sight. Cat just had to have a cherry!

Cat clawed her way up the tiny tree. After she feasted on several cherries, she tried to go down. But she couldn't get out of the tree.

Then Bird flew by. "Why are you in the tree?" he asked.

"I wanted a cherry," said Cat. "But now I can't get down."

"You should have waited for your friend to help you," said Bird.

1. **Before You Read:** Read the title. For which reason might the author write a story with this title?
   Possible answer: to entertain us about a cat that loves cherries

2. **As You Read:** Predict the author's purpose. Why do you think the author is telling this story?
   to entertain

3. **After You Read:** Now what do you think the author's purpose was?
   to teach the reader to ask for help when it is needed

Home Activity Your child read a story and then determined the author's purpose. Read a fairy tale or fable to your child. Discuss reasons why the author may have written the story. If your child needs help, ask if the story teaches, entertains, persuades, or expresses ideas or feelings.

▲ **Practice Book 3.1** p. 88

Vocabulary and Word Study

Context Clues

ANTONYMS Remind students that they can use context clues to determine the meaning of unfamiliar words that are antonyms for other words. Have students list any unknown words they encountered as they read *Tops and Bottoms*. They can create a chart showing the unknown word, antonym context clues, and their definition of the word based on the antonym. Students can confirm word meanings using a dictionary.

Word	Antonym	Meaning
risky	certain	something that has an uncertain outcome
asleep		
scowl		

Vegetable Nouns

Some nouns, such as *carrot*, name a vegetable, or plant, that people eat. Have partners use reference sources to make lists of nouns that refer to vegetables that people eat. Students can illustrate their favorite vegetable nouns.

Some Vegetable Nouns

radishes	pumpkins
broccoli	spinach
corn	soybeans
onions	potatoes

Personal Responsibility

LOOKING BACK Remind students of the focus question of the week: When are respect and understanding important in solving a problem? Discuss how this week's Concept Web of vocabulary words relates to the theme of personal responsibility. Ask students if they have any words or categories to add. Discuss whether words and categories are appropriately related to the concept.

MOVING FORWARD Preview the title of the next selection, *William's House*. Ask students which Concept Web words might apply to the new selection based on the title alone. Put a star next to these words on the web.

Display the Concept Web and revisit the vocabulary words as you read the next selection to check predictions.

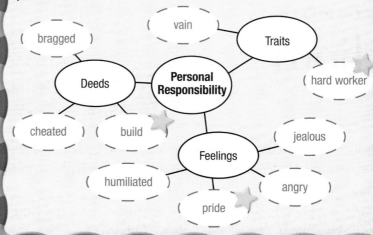

Monitor Progress

Check Vocabulary

If... students suggest words or categories that are not related to the concept,	then... review the words and categories on the Concept Web and discuss how they relate to the lesson concept.

SUCCESS PREDICTOR

Speaking and Viewing

SPEAKING

Compare and Contrast

SET-UP Have students orally compare and contrast Hare in *Tops and Bottoms* with the hare in *The Hare and the Tortoise*.

ORGANIZATION Have students begin their speeches with an interesting similarity about the two hares. Then they can continue describing similarities. After all the similar characteristics have been shared, students can discuss differences. Encourage students to conclude their speeches with a one-sentence summary.

ADAPTATION Provide time for students to rehearse their compare and contrast speeches. Offer these adaptation suggestions:

- If you find yourself running low on time, focus on the most important similarities.
- If you need to fill more time, describe more details about each character.
- Use a visual, such as a two-column chart or Venn diagram, to illustrate similarities and differences.

Rehearsal Tips
- Face the audience when speaking.
- Record your speech, then listen to it.
- Don't speak too fast or too slowly.
- Practice in front of a classmate and ask for feedback.

VIEWING

Analyze a Picture

Have students view the picture on p. 237 of *Tops and Bottoms*. With partners, they can answer these questions orally or in writing.

1. **How can illustrations help you understand a story?** (Possible response: Illustrations offer additional details and give us a better understanding of what the characters look like.)

2. **What is the main idea of this picture?** (Bear gets the tops, and Hare gets the bottoms.)

3. **How did the illustrator depict or characterize Bear?** (Responses will vary but might include lazy, grumpy, not very intelligent.)

ELL

Support Vocabulary Use the following to review and extend vocabulary and to explore lesson concepts further:
- ELL Poster 9, Days 3–5 instruction
- Vocabulary Activities and Word Cards in ELL Teaching Guide, pp. 59–60

Assessment For information on assessing students' speaking, listening, and viewing, see the ELL and Transition Handbook.

Check Vocabulary

SUCCESS PREDICTOR

Grammar **Singular Possessive Nouns**

OBJECTIVES

- Define and identify singular possessive nouns.
- Spell singular possessive nouns correctly.
- Use singular possessive nouns in writing.
- Become familiar with possessive noun assessment on high-stakes tests.

Monitor Progress

Grammar

If... students have difficulty identifying singular possessive nouns,	then... see The Grammar and Writing Book pp. 98–101.

DAILY FIX-IT

This week use Daily Fix-It Transparency 9.

Spiral **REVIEW**

ELL

Support Grammar See the Grammar Transition lessons in the ELL and Transition Handbook.

▲ **The Grammar and Writing Book**
For more instruction and practice, use pp. 98–103.

DAILY FIX-IT

1. Hares family gave Bear two or thee crops. *(Hare's; three)*

2. Hare used his strenth in the field and Bear rested. *(strength; field,)*

READING-GRAMMAR CONNECTION

Write this sentence from *Tops and Bottoms* on the board:

The next day Hare hopped down the road to Bear's house.

Explain that *Bear's* is a **singular possessive noun.** The *'s* shows that Bear owns the house.

Display Grammar Transparency 9. Read aloud the definition and sample sentences. Work through the items.

Singular Possessive Nouns

To show that one person, animal, or thing owns something, use a **singular possessive noun.** Add an apostrophe (') and the letter *s* to a singular noun to make it possessive.

| **Singular Noun** | The <u>bear</u> slept all day. |
| **Singular Possessive Noun** | The hare did not like the <u>bear's</u> laziness. |

Directions Write the possessive noun in each sentence.

1. The class talked about each person's favorite vegetable. **person's**
2. Edward likes the carrot's bright color. **carrot's**
3. Olivia likes broccoli's leafy tops. **broccoli's**
4. Terrell likes his mom's bean soup. **mom's**
5. Everyone enjoys the farm's good foods. **farm's**

Directions Write the possessive form of the underlined noun in each sentence.

6. The market sells the <u>farmer</u> freshest vegetables. **farmer's**
7. The <u>corn</u> sweet flavor makes that soup delicious. **corn's**
8. What vegetable will be good with <u>tonight</u> dinner? **tonight's**
9. The <u>cook</u> recipes for potatoes are wonderful. **cook's**
10. <u>Tracy</u> favorite salad includes lettuce and celery. **Tracy's**
11. The most important thing is a <u>vegetable</u> freshness. **vegetable's**
12. I can almost taste my <u>dad</u> homemade squash casserole. **dad's**

Unit 2 Tops and Bottoms   Grammar **9**

▲ **Grammar Transparency** 9

DAILY FIX-IT

3. Is that Mr. Bears field. *(Bear's; field?)*

4. They planted strawberrys on tuesday. *(strawberries; Tuesday)*

GUIDED PRACTICE

Review the concept of singular possessive nouns.

- To show that one person owns something, use a **singular possessive noun.**

- Add an apostrophe and the letter *s* to a singular noun to make it possessive.

HOMEWORK Grammar and Writing Practice Book p. 33. Work through the first two items with the class.

Singular Possessive Nouns

To show that one person, animal, or thing owns something, use a **singular possessive noun.** Add an apostrophe (') and the letter *s* to a singular noun to make it possessive.

| **Singular Noun** | The <u>hare</u> planted corn. |
| **Singular Possessive Noun** | The bear wanted the <u>hare's</u> corn. |

Directions Write the possessive noun in each sentence.

1. Aesop's fables tell stories about people and animals. **Aesop's**
2. A fox takes a crow's cheese. **crow's**
3. A mouse frees a lion's paw. **lion's**
4. A wolf wears a sheep's fur. **sheep's**
5. People enjoy each story's lesson. **story's**

Directions Write the possessive form of the underlined noun in each sentence.

6. <u>Jeff</u> favorite fable is about the wind and the sun. **Jeff's**
7. The wind challenges the <u>sun</u> power. **sun's**
8. Which one can remove a <u>man</u> coat? **man's**
9. The man feels the <u>wind</u> chill, and he buttons his coat. **wind's**
10. He pulls up his <u>coat</u> collar. **coat's**
11. The <u>sun</u> heat makes the man warm, and he takes off his coat. **sun's**
12. What do you think is the <u>fable</u> lesson? **fable's**

Home Activity Your child learned about singular possessive nouns. Have your child name objects in your home and use a possessive phrase to tell who they belong to, for example, *Dad's book.*

▲ **Grammar and Writing Practice Book** p. 33

DAY 3 Apply to Writing

DAILY FIX-IT

5. That farmers crops are on the wagen. *(farmer's; wagon)*

6. Does that streat go to the market. *(street; market?)*

USE POSSESSIVE NOUNS

Explain that using possessive nouns makes writing less wordy.

Wordy: The house of Mr. Bear is on the corner.

Not Wordy: Mr. Bear's house is on the corner.

- Have students review something they have written to see if they can make it less wordy by using possessive nouns.

HOMEWORK Grammar and Writing Practice Book p. 34.

Singular Possessive Nouns

Directions Write sentences about animal stories you know. Use the singular possessive form of each noun shown.

1. animal Possible answers:

   The animal's nose is cold.

2. forest

   All the forest's animals are friends.

3. wolf

   A little girl is fooled by a wolf's trick.

4. lion

   The lion's roar is the loudest of all.

5. pig

   One pig's house is made of bricks.

Directions Write two sentences about animal characters. Use at least two singular possessive nouns.

Answers will vary. Possible answer: In the book *Charlotte's Web*, Charlotte is a spider. The spider's best friend is a pig.

Home Activity Your child learned how to use singular possessive nouns in writing. Read a story with your child. Have your child write a sentence about the story using at least one singular possessive noun.

▲ **Grammar and Writing Practice Book** p. 34

DAY 4 Test Preparation

DAILY FIX-IT

7. Bear sqweezed the tomato and juice splashed out. *(squeezed; tomato,)*

8. What great blueberrys these are. *(blueberries; are!)*

STANDARDIZED TEST PREP

Test Tip

Don't confuse possessive nouns with plural nouns. Like a possessive noun, a plural noun may end in *s*. But it does not have an apostrophe unless it is possessive.

Plural Noun: The <u>hares</u> ate food from Bear's field.

Singular Possessive Noun: The <u>hare's</u> food tasted good.

HOMEWORK Grammar and Writing Practice Book p. 35.

Singular Possessive Nouns

Directions Mark the letter of the correct possessive noun to complete each sentence.

1. The ____ field needs water.
   - A farmer
   - B farmers
   - (C) farmer's
   - D farmers's

2. The ____ sunlight helps the crops.
   - A day
   - (B) day's
   - C days
   - D days'

3. The ____ family will help out.
   - (A) man's
   - B mans
   - C mens
   - D mans'

4. The ____ soil looks rich.
   - A cornfields
   - (B) cornfield's
   - C cornfields's
   - D cornfield

5. The ____ leaves seem healthy.
   - (A) lettuce's
   - B lettuces
   - C lettuces's
   - D lettuce'

6. These tomatoes grow in a big ____ shade.
   - A tree
   - B trees's
   - C trees
   - (D) tree's

7. The carrots grow near the ____ farm.
   - A neighbor
   - B neighbors
   - (C) neighbor's
   - D neighbors's

8. There will be many crops in this ____ harvest.
   - A falls
   - (B) fall's
   - C falls's
   - D fall'

9. The family will sell them at the ____ market.
   - (A) town's
   - B towns
   - C towns's
   - D town'

10. Then they will plan next ____ crops.
    - A year
    - B years
    - (C) year's
    - D year'

Home Activity Your child prepared for taking tests on singular possessive nouns. Have your child think of a friend's name and something that friend owns and make up a sentence using the possessive form of the friend's name.

▲ **Grammar and Writing Practice Book** p. 35

DAY 5 Cumulative Review

DAILY FIX-IT

9. Mrs. hare raked leafs in the yard. *(Hare; leaves)*

10. She put them in boxs and she took them to the dump. *(boxes,)*

ADDITIONAL PRACTICE

Assign pp. 98–101 in The Grammar and Writing Book.

EXTRA PRACTICE Grammar and Writing Practice Book p. 130.

TEST PREPARATION Grammar and Writing Practice Book pp. 153–154.

ASSESSMENT

CUMULATIVE REVIEW Grammar and Writing Practice Book p. 36.

Singular Possessive Nouns

Directions Write the correct possessive noun in ( ) to complete each sentence.

1. Rob played a trick on his (friends, friend's) brother. ____ **friend's**
2. He put his jacket on (Daves, Dave's) chair. ____ **Dave's**
3. It looked just like the older (boy's, boys's) jacket. ____ **boy's**
4. The (jackets, jacket's) sleeves were too short for Dave. ____ **jacket's**
5. Dave couldn't believe his (bodys, body's) amazing growth. ____ **body's**

Directions Write each sentence. Use the singular possessive form of the underlined noun.

6. Tom put a toy mouse in his <u>sister</u> room.

   Tom put a toy mouse in his sister's room.

7. His parents heard <u>Annie</u> shouts.

   His parents heard Annie's shouts.

8. <u>Tom</u> parents didn't like his tricks.

   Tom's parents didn't like his tricks.

9. His next trick would cost a <u>week</u> allowance.

   His next trick would cost a week's allowance.

Directions Should people play tricks on others? Answer in a complete sentence. Use at least one singular possessive noun. Possible answer:

10. People should not play tricks because they can hurt a person's feelings.

Home Activity Your child reviewed singular possessive nouns. Say the name of a family member. Have your child write a sentence using the singular possessive form of the name.

▲ **Grammar and Writing Practice Book** p. 36

Writing Workshop Feature Story

OBJECTIVES

- Identify the characteristics of a feature story.
- Compose a feature story with a clear purpose.
- Focus on voice.
- Use a rubric.

Genre Feature Story
Writer's Craft Know Your Purpose
Writing Trait Voice

ELL

Voice Show pictures that convey people's feelings, such as being proud or frightened. Model discussion of these feelings: "The girl is proud of her drawing." Explain that *proud* tells a feeling. Remind language learners to show their feelings when they write.

Writing Trait

FOCUS/IDEAS An interesting event and characters are described.

ORGANIZATION/PARAGRAPHS The event is narrated in time order.

VOICE Writing is lively and indicates a clear purpose—to amuse readers.

WORD CHOICE The writer uses quotations and vivid words to engage readers. Time-order words make sequence clear.

SENTENCES Varying sentence lengths and kinds create interest and clarity.

CONVENTIONS There is excellent control and accuracy.

DAY 1 Model the Trait

READING-WRITING CONNECTION

- *Tops and Bottoms* tells the story of a lazy bear and a clever, industrious rabbit.
- The story uses a humorous voice to amuse and instruct readers.
- Students will write a **feature story** in a humorous voice to entertain readers.

MODEL VOICE Discuss Writing Transparency 9A. Then discuss the model and the writing trait of voice.

 Think Aloud The writer has used informal language like *ok* and *awesome* to make his voice informal. He made the feature story lively with words such as *big break* and *bright lights and cameras.* Including Jay's words ("It was fun!") helped keep the voice exciting and interesting.

Feature Story

A **feature story** tells about something interesting that happened to real people. It usually appears in a magazine or newspaper to entertain or inform readers.

Lights! Camera! Action!

Introduction gets readers' attention with hints about what will happen → At 9 years old, Jay Jensen is a movie star. OK, maybe he's not a star. But he has been in a movie with stars.

Informal language helps author accomplish purpose. → Last weekend Jay went to the dinosaur museum. He left with his family, thinking about awesome dinosaurs. Outside were bright lights and cameras. A man said

Direct quotes add interest. → to Jay, "Would you like to be an extra in our movie?" Jay's big break would take only an hour. His parents said sure. Jay just had to run up the museum steps behind actors. "It was fun!" said Jay.

Jay's film, *Dinosaur Danger,* hits theaters next summer. Jay doesn't want

Conclusion lets readers know how Jay's experience changed him. → to become an actor, though. He said, "The director's job looked cooler."

Unit 2 Tops & Bottoms   Writing Model **9A**

▲ **Writing Transparency** 9A

DAY 2 Improve Writing

WRITER'S CRAFT
Know Your Purpose

Display Writing Transparency 9B. Work together to identify the writer's purpose in each paragraph.

 Think Aloud **SUPPORTING YOUR PURPOSE FOR WRITING** Tomorrow we will write a **feature story**. I might write about my aunt's creative plan to get rich by trading. My purpose will be to entertain and inform. I could write, "Aunt Rosa used the Internet to trade small things for bigger, more expensive things." This sentence tells who, what, and how. I could write, "From a pen and pencil set, she traded up to a stuffed owl." This detail is interesting and entertaining.

GUIDED WRITING Some students may need more help knowing their purpose. Point out something that students have previously read and help them identify the author's purpose.

Know Your Purpose

The **purpose** of an article or story is the writer's reason for writing it. A writer's purpose may be to inform, to persuade, or to entertain readers. Knowing your purpose helps you make choices about voice, word choice, and organization. Here are some kinds of writing that could be done for each purpose:

To inform:	newspaper article, how-to article, compare and contrast essay, research report
To entertain:	personal narrative, feature article, story, poem
To persuade:	editorial, letter to the editor, ad

Directions Read each paragraph. Decide whether its purpose is to inform, to entertain, or to persuade readers.

1. Everyone should sign up for the park clean-up day next weekend. No one likes a park full of litter. The park is for everyone to enjoy, so everyone should help keep it beautiful.

   <u>to persuade</u>

2. A fox played a trick. She told the raccoon there were delicious apples under the maple tree. He just had to clear away the fallen leaves. The raccoon raked leaves all day with his paws. But there were no apples. "Thanks," said the fox. And she disappeared into the cozy hole that the raccoon had uncovered for her.

   <u>to entertain</u>

3. People have told stories about animal characters for thousands of years. Some are very old and teach lessons, such as "The Tortoise and the Hare." Some are new and have characters that seem almost like people, such as *Charlotte's Web*.

   <u>to inform</u>

Unit 2 Tops & Bottoms   Writer's Craft **9B**

▲ **Writing Transparency** 9B

DAY 3 Prewrite and Draft

READ THE WRITING PROMPT
on page 247 in the Student Edition.

In Tops and Bottoms, *a character uses his creativity to get ahead.*

Think about an event that happened because of one or more creative people.

Now write a feature story about the event and the person.

Writing Test Tips

- Describe the traits of the main characters of the event.
- Describe the events in order.
- Use time-order words to make the order of events clear.
- Consider using a quotation.

GETTING STARTED Students can do any of the following:

- Make a concept web with *Creative people that made things happen* in the center.
- In a small group, share stories about people who are creative or original.
- Look through magazine articles and newspaper features for stories about creative people.

DAY 4 Draft and Revise

EDITING/REVISING CHECKLIST

- ☑ Is the purpose of the story clear?
- ☑ Are the characters and events of the story described vividly?
- ☑ Are singular possessive nouns used correctly?
- ☑ Are words with consonant blends *spl, thr, squ,* and *str* spelled correctly?

See *The Grammar and Writing Book,* pp. 98–103.

Revising Tips

Voice

- Support your story using words that fit your personality and purpose.
- Choose details about the characters and events that bring them to life and fit your purpose.
- Show your feelings about the characters and events.

PUBLISHING Students can illustrate their stories and collect them in a class magazine. Some students may wish to revise their work later.

ASSESSMENT Use the scoring rubric to evaluate students' work.

DAY 5 Connect to Unit Writing

How-to Report	
Week 1	Summary 173g–173h
Week 2	Rules 197g–197h
Week 3	Problem/Solution 223g–223h
Week 4	Feature Story 249g–249h
Week 5	Explanatory Paragraph 271g–271h

PREVIEW THE UNIT PROMPT

Think of something you learned or figured out how to do that involves a few simple steps. Write the steps in a how-to report. Make sure you provide all the necessary information.

APPLY

- A how-to report explains the steps for making or doing something.
- Remember that the purpose for writing a how-to report is to explain the steps in the process clearly.

Writing Trait Rubric

	4	3	2	1
Voice	Excellent sense of writer's attitude toward topic; strongly engages audience and speaks directly to them	Clear sense of how writer feels and thinks; engages audience	Some sense of how writer feels and thinks; weak attempt to engage audience	No sense of how writer feels and thinks about topic; no attempt to engage audience
	Uses well-chosen words in feature story to clearly show feelings toward topic	Uses words in feature story that show some feelings about topic	Needs to use more words in feature story that show feelings about topic	Uses no words in feature story that show feelings about topic

Consonant Blends

TEACH

Write the words *clever* and *stripe*.

- Say *clever* aloud.
- What are the first two letters of *clever*? What is the sound of each letter? (*c*/k/, */l/*)
- Say the first two letters, first individually and then blended together, so students can hear the difference.
- Do we hear both sounds when we say the word *clever*? (yes)

 MODEL When I see two or three consonants at the beginning or end of a word, I try blending them together as I say the word. I say all the sounds without pausing between them. If the word sounds right, I know it begins or ends with a consonant blend.

Model blending *stripe*. Then have students blend the word with you.

$$s\ t\ r\ i\ p\ e$$

PRACTICE AND ASSESS

DECODE LONGER WORDS Write these words. Have students read them and then underline the two- or three-letter consonant blends.

<u>thr</u>ash   comment   <u>str</u>etchy   <u>spl</u>ashing

<u>tr</u>adition   <u>st</u>argazing   <u>dr</u>agon   <u>squ</u>iggle

READ WORDS IN CONTEXT Write these sentences. Have individuals read them, point out words with consonant blends, and name the letters that spell the consonant blend. Words with a consonant blend are underlined.

The <u>principal</u> <u>spoke</u> to the <u>class</u>.

The <u>splendid</u> <u>throne</u> <u>glittered</u> in the light.

The <u>stray</u> cat <u>climbed</u> the <u>tallest</u> <u>tree</u>.

To assess, check that students are pronouncing all the consonants in each blend clearly.

OBJECTIVES

- Associate consonant blends, including three-letter blends, with the letters that spell them.
- Review compound words.
- Blend and read words that contain consonant blends and are compound words.
- Apply decoding strategies: blend longer words.

Generalization

Generalization Consonant blends consist of two or more letters whose sounds are blended together when pronouncing a word.

Support Phonics Since consonant blends do not exist in many languages, English language learners may hesitate or drop letters when saying them. Spanish speakers may add a short *e* sound at the beginning of words such as *spring, strike,* and *splash.* Help students practice blending the sounds in words with three-letter consonant blends.

See the Phonics Transition Lessons in the ELL and Transition Handbook.

Consonant Blends

Directions Read the story. Underline the words with the three-letter blends **spl, squ, str,** and **thr.** Then write the underlined words on the lines.

Emily <u>threw</u> on her coat and ran down the <u>street</u>. As she got to the town <u>square</u>, she saw <u>three</u> friends <u>throwing</u> water balloons at one another. Each time a balloon <u>struck</u> the ground, it <u>split</u> open. Water <u>splashed</u> everywhere. Then someone tossed a balloon with such <u>strength</u> that it flew <u>through</u> an open car window. Emily knew they had to find the owner and tell what they had done.

1.	threw
2.	street
3.	square
4.	three
5.	throwing
6.	struck
7.	split
8.	splashed
9.	strength
10.	through

Directions Read each word and listen for the three-letter blend. Then write two more words that start with the same blend. Underline the three-letter blend in each word you write. Students' answers will vary.

11. straw	stripe	strong
12. splurge	splint	splendid
13. squeak	squint	squash
14. thread	throat	throne
15. straight	strict	strange

Home Activity Your child wrote words that begin with the three-letter blends *spl* (as in splash), *squ* (as in square), *str* (as in strike), and *thr* (as in throw). Challenge your child to name additional words that begin with these three-letter blends. For help in identifying words with these starting letters, you can use a dictionary.

▲ **Practice Book 3.1** p.89

249i   Smart Solutions • Week 4

Review Word Structure

REVIEW COMPOUND WORDS

CONNECT Write this sentence: *The quarterback leads the football team.*

- We studied compound words.
- Read the sentence to yourself. Raise your hand when you know which words are compound words. *(quarterback, football)*
- What smaller words make up each compound word? *(quarterback: quarter, back; football: foot, ball)*

Continue in the same way with the sentence *The bluebird pecked at the strawberry.*

PRACTICE AND ASSESS

DECODE LONGER WORDS Have individuals read the following words. Provide help chunking and blending the words as needed.

handlebars	schoolbooks	bricklayer	starlight
handwriting	chalkboard	roughhouse	applesauce
clipboard	grapevine	loudspeaker	milkshake

READ WORDS IN CONTEXT Have students read these sentences. Then, to check meaning, have them give their own sentence for the underlined word.

We followed the <u>snowplow</u> down the road.

Dad found the <u>newspaper</u> at the end of the <u>driveway</u>.

We put <u>placemats</u> on the table instead of a <u>tablecloth</u>.

To assess, note whether students use the meanings of the shorter words to understand the compound words.

Generalization

Generalization A compound word is a word made up of two or more shorter words.

Vocabulary Tip

You may wish to explain the meanings of these words.

bricklayer	a person who builds with bricks
loudspeaker	a device that makes voices louder
roughhouse	to act in a rough, noisy way

Spelling & Phonics · Words with *spl, thr, squ, str*

OBJECTIVE

● Spell words with *spl, thr, squ,* and *str.*

Generalization

Connect to Phonics Some words have three letters pronounced together: *splash, throw, square, strike.* The letters are spoken together, but each letter can be heard.

Spelling Words

1. splash	9. splurge
2. throw	10. thrill
3. three	11. strength
4. square	12. squeak
5. throat	13. throne
6. strike	14. strawberry
7. street	15. squeeze
8. split*	

Challenge Words

16. squid	19. instrument
17. squander	20. strategy
18. arthritis	

*Word from the selection

Spelling/Phonics Support See the ELL and Transition Handbook for spelling support.

DAY 1 · Pretest and Sort

PRETEST

Use the Dictation Sentences from Day 5 to administer the pretest. Read the word, read the sentence, and then read the word again. Guide students in self-correcting their pretests and correcting any misspellings.

Monitor Progress

Spelling

If... students misspell more than 4 pretest words,	**then...** use words 1–8 for Strategic Intervention.
If... students misspell 1–4 pretest words,	**then...** use words 1–15 for On-Level practice.
If... students correctly spell all pretest words,	**then...** use words 1–20 for Advanced Learners.

HOMEWORK Spelling Practice Book, p. 33.

Words with *spl, thr, squ, str*

Generalization Some words have three letters pronounced together: splash, throw, square, strike.

Word Sort Sort the list words according to the three-letter blend.

spl
1. splash
2. split
3. splurge

squ
9. square
10. squeak
11. squeeze

thr
4. throw
5. three
6. throat
7. thrill
8. throne

str
12. strike
13. street
14. strength
15. strawberry

Spelling Words
1. splash
2. throw
3. three
4. square
5. throat
6. strike
7. street
8. split
9. splurge
10. thrill
11. strength
12. squeak
13. throne
14. strawberry
15. squeeze

Challenge Words
16. squid
17. squander
18. arthritis
19. instrument
20. strategy

Challenge Words

str
16. instrument
17. strategy

thr
18. arthritis

squ
19. squid
20. squander

Home Activity Your child is learning to spell words with three-letter blends (spl, thr, squ, and str). To practice at home, have your child say each word, write it, and circle the three letter blend.

▲ **Spelling Practice Book** p. 33

DAY 2 · Think and Practice

TEACH

Write the letters *spl, thr, squ,* and *str* on the board. Have students say each of the three letter combinations. Then have them come up to the board and write each spelling word under the appropriate heading.

> str
> street

FIND THE PATTERN Guide students to hear how the three letters *spl, thr, squ,* and *str* are pronounced together by saying and then spelling each word aloud.

HOMEWORK Spelling Practice Book, p. 34.

Words with *spl, thr, squ, str*

Spelling Words				
splash	throw	three	square	throat
strike	street	split	splurge	thrill
strength	squeak	throne	strawberry	squeeze

Rhyming Pairs Finish the sentence with a list word that rhymes with the underlined word.

1. Would you like <u>cherry</u> or __strawberry__ ice cream?
2. Skiing down that <u>hill</u> was a __thrill__ !
3. I don't think he has the __strength__ to swim the <u>length</u> of the pool.
4. See if you can __throw__ the ball to the <u>row</u> of trees.
5. The town __square__ was <u>bare</u>.
6. The __throne__ has been occupied by six men and a <u>lone</u> woman.
7. There are __three__ squirrels playing in the <u>tree</u>.
8. Let's <u>dash</u> into the water and make a big __splash__ .

Missing Blends Add a three-letter blend to finish the list word. Write the word.

9. The officer cleared his __ __ __ oat.   9. __throat__
10. The pitcher threw a __ __ __ ike.   10. __strike__
11. Don't play in the __ __ __ eet.   11. __street__
12. I'd love to __ __ __ urge on an expensive gift.   12. __splurge__
13. Let's __ __ __ it the last piece of pizza.   13. __split__
14. Mom gave my hand a big __ __ __ eeze.   14. __squeeze__
15. We heard the hinges __ __ __ eak.   15. __squeak__

Home Activity Your child wrote words with three-letter blends (spl, thr, squ, and str). Have your child circle and pronounce the three-letter blends in the list words.

▲ **Spelling Practice Book** p. 34

DAY 3 · Connect to Writing

WRITE A STORY

Have students write a story using at least five spelling words. Students can share their stories by reading them aloud, or you can post them on the bulletin board.

Frequently Misspelled Words

scared   brother

These words are difficult for third-graders to spell. Alert students to these frequently misspelled words and encourage them to sound out each word slowly and carefully before spelling it.

HOMEWORK Spelling Practice Book, p. 35.

Words with spl, thr, squ, str

Proofread a Report Circle four spelling mistakes in this report about the gray fox. Write the words correctly. Write the word that should be used instead of **don't** in the last sentence.

A gray fox has a white troat and belly. It can run fast and climb trees. It may splash into the water and swim if it is skared and needs to escape. When hunting, it listens for the sqeak of a mouse. If it sees movement, it strikes quickly. Sometimes in bad weather a gray fox don't leave its den for three or four days.

Spelling Words
splash
throw
three
square
throat
strike
street
split
splurge
thrill
strength
squeak
throne
strawberry
squeeze

1. throat   2. scared
3. squeak   4. strikes
5. doesn't

Proofread Words Fill in the circle to show the correctly spelled word.

6. ○ thril   ● thrill   ○ thill
7. ○ squeze   ○ sqeeze   ● squeeze
8. ○ stawberry   ● strawberry   ○ srawberry
9. ● throne   ○ trone   ○ throan
10. ○ stength   ○ strentgh   ● strength
11. ○ streat   ○ steet   ● street
12. ○ sqare   ● square   ○ squar

Frequently Misspelled Words
scared
brother

School-Home **Home Activity** Your child identified misspelled words with three-letter blends (spl, thr, squ, and str). Ask your child to use some of the list words to tell a story about a mouse.

▲ **Spelling Practice Book** p. 35

DAY 4 · Review

REVIEW WORDS WITH spl, thr, squ, AND str

Have students list other words that begin with spl, thr, squ, and str. Have students exchange lists with a partner and circle the letter combinations in each word on the list.

Spelling Strategy
Letter Sounds

Sounding out each letter will help students correctly spell words with spl, thr, squ, and str.

HOMEWORK Spelling Practice Book, p. 36.

Words with spl, thr, squ, str

Spelling Words				
splash	throw	three	square	throat
strike	street	split	splurge	thrill
strength	squeak	throne	strawberry	squeeze

Words in Context Add the missing list words to the recipe.

Tasty Treat
1. Peel half a banana. Then s p l i t it lengthwise in a dish.
2. Spoon on one-half cup of s t r a w b e r r y yogurt.
3. Crumble a graham cracker s q u a r e on top.

Classifying Write one more word in each category. Use list words.

4. Things to do with a ball: bat, catch, throw
5. Numbers: seven, nine, three
6. Parts of the body: elbow, eardrum, throat
7. Places to ride a bike: driveway, path, street
8. Things to do with water: sprinkle, pour, splash
9. Animal sounds: chirp, bark, squeak
10. Places to sit: chair, bench, throne
11. Things to do with an orange: peel, eat, squeeze
12. Things to do in baseball: bat, run, strike out

School-Home **Home Activity** Your child has been learning to spell words with three-letter blends (spl, thr, squ, and str). Have your child reread the recipe on this page. Then help your child try out the recipe.

▲ **Spelling Practice Book** p. 36

DAY 5 · Posttest

DICTATION SENTENCES

1. Did you see the fish splash in the water?
2. Throw the ball to me!
3. My brother is three years old.
4. A square has four sides.
5. My throat hurts today.
6. Try not to strike out this time.
7. Jake lives on this street.
8. Can you do a split?
9. Dan wants to splurge on a new bike.
10. I feel a thrill when we go to the circus.
11. Bob has the strength to lift that box.
12. The door will squeak when you open it.
13. The king sits on a throne.
14. Do you want strawberry ice cream?
15. Squeeze all the water out.

CHALLENGE

16. Squid live in the ocean.
17. Do not squander all your money.
18. My grandmother has arthritis.
19. What instrument do you play?
20. Ned has a strategy to win the game.

OBJECTIVES

- Formulate an inquiry question that is connected to this week's lesson focus.
- Effectively and efficiently find, evaluate, and communicate information related to an inquiry question using electronic sources.

New Literacies

Day 1	Identify Questions
Day 2	Navigate/Search
Day 3	Analyze
Day 4	Synthesize
Day 5	Communicate

NEW LITERACIES

Internet Inquiry Activity

EXPLORE GOOD CHARACTER

Use the following 5-day plan to help students conduct this week's Internet inquiry activity on good character. Remind students to follow classroom rules when using the Internet.

DAY 1

Identify Questions Discuss the lesson focus question: *When are respect and understanding important in solving a problem?* Brainstorm ideas for specific inquiry questions about personal responsibility and character. For example, students might want to find out how to handle difficult situations or how to get along with others who look at an issue in a different way. Have students work individually, in pairs, or in small groups to write an inquiry question they want to answer.

DAY 2

Navigate/Search Remind students how to begin a simple Internet search using a student-friendly search engine. Have students determine keywords related to their inquiry questions. Tell students to try to spell keywords correctly. Misspelling keywords may not provide the best search results. Point out that some search engines offer other spellings that can be selected. Students can read descriptions of sites to determine if a site will be helpful in answering their inquiry question.

DAY 3

Analyze Have students explore the Web sites they identified on Day 2. Have them scan the sites for information that will help answer their inquiry questions. Remind students to analyze the information to see if it is relevant to their questions. Students can print pages that contain useful information and then highlight relevant details.

DAY 4

Synthesize Have students synthesize information from Day 3. Remind them that when they synthesize, they integrate important and relevant ideas from various sources to create an answer to their inquiry questions.

DAY 5

Communicate Have students share their inquiry results. They can use a word processing program to create a short poem about getting along with others or having good character.

RESEARCH/STUDY SKILLS

Encyclopedia

TEACH

Discuss with students when to use an encyclopedia. Invite volunteers to name topics that might be found in an encyclopedia. Use an encyclopedia to show and define these features.

- A **volume** is one book in an encyclopedia set. Volumes in the set are organized alphabetically.

- An **entry** is one article in an encyclopedia.

- An **entry word** is the word or phrase that begins an entry. It describes the subject or topic of the entry.

- **Guide words** appear in dark type at the top of the page. They tell the first and last entry words on the page.

Put students into small groups, and give each group an encyclopedia volume. Ask groups to find the name of an animal that can be found in their volume. Have them write the entry word and guide words on the page where the animal name is located. After this activity, discuss these questions with the class. If online or electronic encyclopedias are available, demonstrate how the computer makes finding an entry easier.

1. **In what order would you find the entry words *rhinoceros*, *rabbit*, and *robin*?** (rabbit, rhinoceros, robin)

2. **What animal name might you find in volume E–G?** (Sample answer: fox)

Fort   **Fossil**

FORT was, in historical times, a fortified building or structure that gave protection and defense against attack. On the American frontier, many forts were also trading posts. Many American cities that developed around forts still have the fort's names, such as Fort Lauderdale, Florida, and Fort Gratiot, Michigan. Important

term fort is now used to describe permanent Army posts.

FORUM was, in the early days of Rome, a swamp which people of nearby vilages used as a cemetery. The Etruscans turned these villages into the city of Rome, whose people built shops and temples.

E-G Vol. 4

ASSESS

As students look through the encyclopedia, make sure that they understand the difference between entry words and guide words. Mention some simple subjects and ask students to locate them in the encyclopedia.

For more practice or to assess students, use Practice Book 3.1, p. 90.

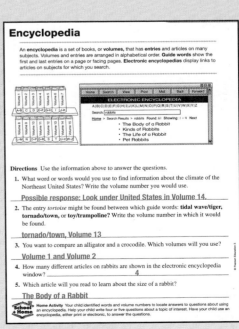

▲ **Practice Book 3.1** p. 90

Assessment Checkpoints *for the Week*

Selection Assessment

Use pp. 33–36 of Selection Tests **to check:**

 Selection Understanding

  Comprehension Skill *Author's Purpose*

Selection Vocabulary

bottom	lazy
cheated	partners
clever	wealth
crops	

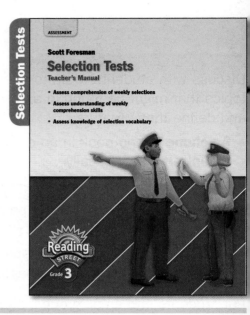

Leveled Assessment

- On-Level
- Strategic Intervention
- Advanced

Use pp. 49–54 of Fresh Reads for Differentiated Test Practice **to check:**

 Comprehension Skill *Author's Purpose*

 REVIEW **Comprehension Skill** *Main Idea*

 Fluency *Words Correct Per Minute*

Managing Assessment

Use Assessment Handbook **for:**

 Observation Checklists

 Record-Keeping Forms

 Portfolio Assessment

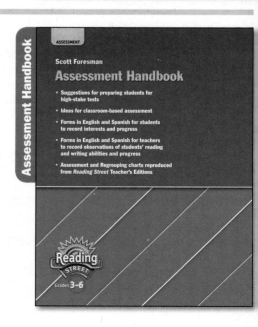

Illinois

Planning Guide for Performance Descriptors

William's House

Reading Street Teacher's Edition pages	**Grade 3 English Language Arts Performance Descriptors**
Oral Language **Speaking/Listening** Build Concept Vocabulary: 250l, 265, 271c Read Aloud: 250m **Viewing** Recognize Opinion: 271d	**1A.Stage C.3.** Discuss the meanings of new words encountered in independent and group activities. **1B.Stage C.13.** Read age-appropriate material aloud with fluency and accuracy. **2A.Stage C.5.** Define unfamiliar vocabulary.
Word Work Digraphs *sh, th, ph, ch, tch:* 271i, 271k–271l	**3A.Stage C.8.** Use knowledge of letter-sound relationships to spell unfamiliar words.
Reading **Comprehension** Draw Conclusions: 250–251, 254–265, 271b Ask Questions: 250–251, 254–265 **Vocabulary** Lesson Vocabulary: 252b, 265, 268 Context Clues: 252–253, 263, 271c **Fluency** Model Reading Silently; Self-Correct When Reading: 250l–250m, 271a Silent Reading Routine: 271a **Self-Selected Reading:** LR37–45, TR16–17 **Literature** Genre—Historical Fiction: 254 Reader Response: 266	**1A.Stage C.5.** Use a variety of decoding strategies (e.g., phonics, word patterns, structural analysis, context clues) to recognize new words when reading age-appropriate material. **1A.Stage C.6.** Self-monitor reading and use decoding strategies to self-correct miscues. **1B.Stage C.10.** Ask questions to clarify understanding. **1C.Stage C.6.** Interpret concepts or make connections through analysis, evaluation, inference, and/or comparison. **2A.Stage C.5.** Define unfamiliar vocabulary. **2A.Stage C.6.** Name several characteristics that distinguish fiction from nonfiction. **2A.Stage C.7.** Classify major types of fiction (e.g., tall tale, fairy tale, fable). **4A.Stage C.6.** Respond in an appropriate manner to questions and discussion with relevant and focused comments.
Language Arts **Writing** Explanatory Paragraph: 271g–271h **Six-Trait Writing** Focus/Ideas: 267, 271g–271h **Grammar, Usage, and Mechanics** Plural Possessive Nouns: 271e–271f **Research/Study** Diagram/Scale Drawing: 271n **Technology** New Literacies: 271m	**1C.Stage C.9.** Use information from simple tables, maps, and charts to increase comprehension of a variety of age-appropriate materials, both fiction and nonfiction. **3A.Stage C.1.** Develop a paragraph using proper form (e.g., topic sentence, details, summary/conclusion sentence). **3A.Stage C.9.** Demonstrate appropriate use of the various parts of speech (e.g., nouns, pronouns, verbs). **5C.Stage C.1.** Access and use information from a variety of sources.
Unit Skills **Writing** How-To Report: WA2–9 **Poetry:** 272–275 **Project/Wrap-Up:** 276–277	**1B.Stage C.8.** Identify genres of poetry. **2A.Stage C.11.** Recognize both rhymed and unrhymed poetry. **3B.Stage C.4.** Organize around a structure (e.g., paragraph, essay) appropriate to purpose, audience, and context.

This Week's Leveled Readers

Below-Level

Colonial New England

1B.Stage C.2. Make predictions about text events before and during reading and confirm, modify, or reject predictions after reading.

1B.Stage C.5. Make connections from text to text, text to self, text to world.

Nonfiction

On-Level

The Colonial Adventure

1B.Stage C.10. Ask questions to clarify understanding.

1C.Stage C.6. Interpret concepts or make connections through analysis, evaluation, inference, and/or comparison.

Fiction

Advanced

Houses Past and Present

1B.Stage C.7. Identify genres of fiction and non-fiction.

1C.Stage C.2. Use information to generate and respond to questions that reflect higher level thinking skills (e.g., analyzing, synthesizing, inferring, evaluating).

Nonfiction

Content-Area Illinois Performance Descriptors in This Lesson

Social Studies

14E.Stage C.2. Tell about people who have come from other countries to live in the United States.

15B.Stage C.2. Identify a consumer choice made by families and explain why a choice had to be made.

16A.Stage C.4. Draw a general conclusion about life during a specific period in a specific region or place using a combination of historical sources (e.g., images, artifacts, texts).

16A.Stage C.6. Tell why the location of where an event occurred helps to explain why and how it happened.

17D.Stage C.4. Arrange in chronological order pictures of house types and explain the changes that have occurred over time (e.g., log cabin, southern colonial, contemporary ranch).

18C.Stage C.3. Describe how individuals work together to obtain food, clothing, and shelter.

Science

12B.Stage C.2. Apply scientific inquiries or technological designs to examine the interdependence of organisms in ecosystems: identifying adaptations that help animals survive in specific or multiple environments; describing the interaction between living and non-living factors in an ecosystem.

12C.Stage C.1. Apply scientific inquiries or technological designs to examine the flow of energy: measuring variations of heat absorption or reflection in objects.

12E.Stage C.2. Apply scientific inquiries or technological designs to examine weather patterns: observing local, state, regional or national weather patterns.

Math

7A.Stage C.6. Show and explain the area of an object by counting square units.

Illinois!

A FAMOUS ILLINOISAN
Frank Lloyd Wright

Frank Lloyd Wright (1867–1959) was a well-known architect. He attended the University of Wisconsin at Madison. Wright moved to Chicago in 1887, where he worked with prominent architects. In 1893 he opened his own firm and became known for creating unusual designs for homes. He also designed apartments, churches, businesses, and recreation centers. One of the most famous buildings Wright designed is the Guggenheim Museum in New York City.

Students can . . .
Look at photographs of Frank Lloyd Wright's buildings and houses. Have students pick one and write a description of it.

A SPECIAL ILLINOIS PLACE
Apple River Fort

The Apple River Fort was built near Galena in 1832 during the Black Hawk War. Settlers in the Apple River area used this fort to protect themselves from an attack by hundreds of Sauk and Fox warriors. The fort was torn down in 1847. An archaeologist discovered the site in 1995. Volunteers began rebuilding the fort in 1996, working with the same kinds of tools and materials that would have been used to build the original fort.

Students can . . .
Find out more about the kinds of tools and materials needed to rebuild the Apple River Fort in 1996 and make a list of them.

ILLINOIS FUN FACTS
Did You Know?

• In northern Illinois, temperatures below freezing (32°F, 0°C) occur about 140 days each year. The temperatures in southern Illinois usually are higher than the temperatures in northern Illinois.

• Illinois gets about thirty-seven inches of precipitation per year, with more rain falling in the south than in the north.

• The growing season ranges from about 150 days in far northern Illinois to about 200 days in far southern Illinois.

Students can . . .
Write a report about the types of crops that can grow in southern Illinois due to the longer growing season and the warmer climate.

Unit 2
Smart Solutions

EXPAND THE CONCEPT

When you find yourself in a new place, what problems might you meet?

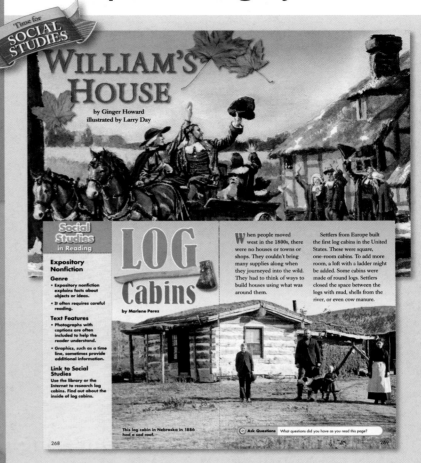

CONCEPT QUESTION
What are smart ways that problems are solved?

Week 1

How have animals adapted to solve the problems of their environment?

Week 2

When is a solution the wrong solution?

Week 3

How can you get ideas to solve a problem?

Week 4

When are respect and understanding important in solving a problem?

Week 5

When you find yourself in a new place, what problems might you meet?

CONNECT THE CONCEPT

▶ **Build Background**
dwellings, gabled, stockade

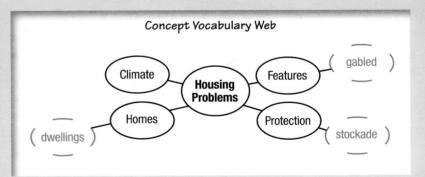

Concept Vocabulary Web

▶ **Social Studies Content**
Colonial Settlements, Change Over Time, Adapting to Environment

▶ **Writing**
Explanatory Paragraph

▶ **Internet Inquiry**
Colonial

Preview Your Week

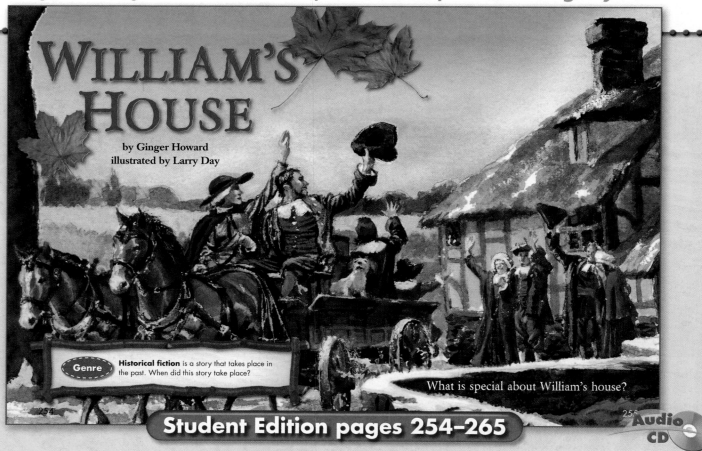

WILLIAM'S HOUSE

by Ginger Howard
illustrated by Larry Day

Genre Historical fiction is a story that takes place in the past. When did this story take place?

What is special about William's house?

254

255

Student Edition pages 254–265

Audio CD

Genre	Historical Fiction
Vocabulary Strategy	Context Clues
Comprehension Skill	Draw Conclusions
Comprehension Strategy	Ask Questions

Paired Selection

SOCIAL STUDIES

Reading Across Texts

Compare and Contrast Two
Log Cabins

Genre

Expository Nonfiction

Text Features

Photographs with Captions
Graphics

Social Studies in Reading

LOG Cabins

by Marlene Perez

Expository Nonfiction

Genre
- Expository nonfiction explains facts about objects or ideas.
- Expository nonfiction often requires careful reading and rereading.

Text Features
- Photographs with captions are often included in a nonfiction article to help the reader better understand the facts.
- Graphics, such as a time line, are sometimes provided to give the reader additional information.

Link to Social Studies
Use the library or the Internet to research log cabins. Find out more about the inside of log cabins. Report your findings to the class.

When people moved west in the 1800s, there were no houses or towns or shops. They couldn't bring many supplies along when they journeyed into the wild. They had to think of ways to build houses using what was around them.

Settlers from Europe built the first log cabins in the United States. These were square, one-room cabins. To add more room, a loft with a ladder might be added. Some cabins were made of round logs. Settlers closed the space between the logs with mud, shells from the river, or even cow manure.

This log cabin in Nebraska in 1886 had a sod roof.

Ask Questions What questions did you have as you read this page?

268

269

Student Edition pages 268–271

Audio CD

Read It
ONLINE
PearsonSuccessNet.com
- **Student Edition**
- **Leveled Readers**

Leveled Readers

Skill Draw Conclusions

Strategy Ask Questions

Lesson Vocabulary

Colonial New England
by Barbara Wood

Below-Level

The Colonial Adventure
by J. Matteson Claus • illustrated by Burgandy Beam

On-Level

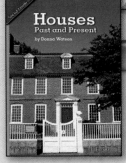

Houses Past and Present
by Donna Watson

Advanced

ELL Reader
- Concept Vocabulary
- Text Support
- Language Enrichment

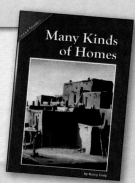

Many Kinds of Homes

Time for **SOCIAL STUDIES**

Integrate Social Studies Standards
- **Colonial Settlements**
- **Change Over Time**
- **Adapting to Environment**

☑ **Read**

William's House
pp. 254–265

"Log Cabins"
pp. 268–271

Leveled Readers

Below-Level | **On-Level** | **Advanced**

- Support Concepts
- Develop Concepts
- Extend Concepts
- Social Studies Extension Activity

ELL Reader

☑ **Build**
Concept Vocabulary
Housing Problems,
pp. 250l–250m

☑ **Teach**
Social Studies Concepts
Housing, p. 257
Climate, p. 261
Opportunity Cost, p. 263
Natural Resources, p. 269

☑ **Explore**
Social Studies Center
Research Homes, p. 250k

William's House **250c**

Weekly Plan

READING

45–90 minutes

TARGET SKILLS OF THE WEEK

- **Comprehension Skill**
  Draw Conclusions
- **Comprehension Strategy**
  Ask Questions
- **Vocabulary Strategy**
  Context Clues

LANGUAGE ARTS

30–60 minutes

Trait of the Week

Focus/Ideas

DAY 1
PAGES 250l–252b, 271a, 271e–271h, 271k–271m

Oral Language

QUESTION OF THE WEEK *When you find yourself in a new place, what problems might you meet?*

Read Aloud: "Colonial Homes," 250m
Build Concepts, 250l

Comprehension/Vocabulary

Comprehension Skill/Strategy Lesson, 250–251
- Draw Conclusions **T**
- Ask Questions

Build Background, 252a

Introduce Lesson Vocabulary, 252b
barrels, cellar, clearing, pegs, spoil, steep **T**

Read Leveled Readers

Grouping Options 250f–250g

Fluency

Model Reading Silently,
250l–250m, 271a

Grammar, 271e
Introduce Plural Possessive Nouns **T**

Writing Workshop, 271g
Introduce Explanatory Paragraph
Model the Trait of the Week: Focus/Ideas

Spelling, 271k
Pretest for Digraphs *sh, th, ph, ch, tch*

Internet Inquiry, 271m
Identify Questions

DAY 2
PAGES 252–261, 271a, 271e–271i, 271k–271m

Oral Language

QUESTION OF THE DAY *What do you think William's father's house in England looked like?*

Word Work

Phonics Lesson, 271i
Consonant Digraphs

Comprehension/Vocabulary

Vocabulary Strategy Lesson, 252–253
- Context Clues **T**

Read *William's House,* 254–261

Grouping Options
250f–250g

- Draw Conclusions **T**
- Ask Questions
- **REVIEW** Character **T**
Develop Vocabulary

Fluency

Silent Reading, 271a

Grammar, 271e
Develop Plural Possessive Nouns **T**

Writing Workshop, 271g
Improve Writing: Use Precise Words

Spelling, 271k
Teach the Generalization

Internet Inquiry, 271m
Navigate/Search

	DAY 1	DAY 2
DAILY WRITING ACTIVITIES	**Day 1** Write to Read, 250	**Day 2** Words to Write, 253 Strategy Response Log, 254, 261
DAILY SOCIAL STUDIES CONNECTIONS	**Day 1** Housing Problems Concept Web, 250l	**Day 2** Time for Social Studies: Housing, 257; Climate, 261; Revisit the Housing Problems Concept Web, 259

DAILY SUCCESS PREDICTORS
for Adequate Yearly Progress

Monitor Progress and Corrective Feedback

Vocabulary   Check Vocabulary, *250l*

250d

RESOURCES FOR THE WEEK

- Practice Book, *pp. 91–100*
- Phonics and Spelling Practice Book, *pp. 37–40*
- Grammar and Writing Practice Book, *pp. 37–40*

- Selection Test, *pp. 37–40*
- Fresh Reads for Differentiated Test Practice, *pp. 55–60*
- The Grammar and Writing Book, *pp. 104–109*

Grouping Options for Differentiated Instruction

Turn the page for the small group lesson plan.

DAY 3
PAGES 262–267, 271a, 271e–271h, 271k–271m

Oral Language

QUESTION OF THE DAY *How did the environment of New England force the colonists to change?*

Comprehension/Vocabulary

Read *William's House, 262–266*

Grouping Options
250f–250g

 Ask Questions

 Context Clues **T**

Develop Vocabulary

Reader Response

Selection Test

Fluency

Model Reading Silently, 271a

Grammar, 271f
Apply Plural Possessive Nouns in Writing **T**

Writing Workshop, 267, 271h
Write Now
Prewrite and Draft

Spelling, 271l
Connect Spelling to Writing

Internet Inquiry, 271m
Analyze Sources

Day 3 Strategy Response Log, 264
Look Back and Write, 266

Day 3 Time for Social Studies: Opportunity Cost, 263
Revisit the Housing Problems Concept Web, 265

DAY 4
PAGES 268–271a, 271e–271h, 271j–271m

Oral Language

QUESTION OF THE DAY *What solutions have we found today to build better homes for our environment?*

Word Work

Phonics Lesson, 271j
REVIEW Consonant Blends **T**

Comprehension/Vocabulary

Read "Log Cabins," 268–271

Grouping Options
250f–250g

Expository Nonfiction/
Text Features

Reading Across Texts

Content-Area Vocabulary

Fluency

Choral Reading (Poetry), 271a

Grammar, 271f
Practice Plural Possessive Nouns for
Standardized Tests **T**

Writing Workshop, 271h
Draft, Revise, and Publish

Spelling, 271l
Provide a Strategy

Internet Inquiry, 271m
Synthesize Information

Day 4 Writing Across Texts, 271

Day 4 Time for Social Studies: Natural
Resources, 269

DAY 5
PAGES 271a–271h, 271k–271n

Oral Language

QUESTION OF THE WEEK *To wrap up the week, revisit the Day 1 question.*

Build Concept Vocabulary, 271c

Fluency

Read Leveled Readers

Grouping Options 250f–250g

Assess Reading Rate, 271a

Comprehension/Vocabulary

 Reteach Draw Conclusions, 271b **T**

Facts and Details, 271b

 Review Context Clues, 271c **T**

Speaking and Viewing, 271d
Speak to Communicate Needs
Recognize Opinion

Grammar, 271f
Cumulative Review

Writing Workshop, 271h
Connect to Unit Writing

Spelling, 271l
Posttest for Digraphs *sh, th, ph, ch, tch*

Internet Inquiry, 271m
Communicate Results

Research/Study Skills, 271n
Diagram/Scale Drawing

Day 5 Facts and Details, 271b

Day 5 Revisit the Housing Problems Concept
Web, 271c

KEY = Target Skill **T** = Tested Skill

Comprehension Check Retelling, *266*

Fluency Check Fluency WCPM, *271a*

Vocabulary Check Vocabulary, *271c*

SUCCESS PREDICTOR

Small Group Plan *for Differentiated Instruction*

Daily Plan AT A GLANCE

Reading
Whole Group
- Oral Language
- Phonics
- Comprehension/Vocabulary

Group Time
Differentiated Instruction

Meet with small groups to provide:
- Skill Support
- Reading Support
- Fluency Practice

Read

This week's lessons for daily group time can be found behind the Differentiated Instruction (DI) tab on pp. DI·42–DI·51.

Whole Group
- Fluency

Language Arts
- Grammar
- Writing
- Spelling
- Research/Inquiry
- Speaking/Listening/Viewing

Use *My Sidewalks on Reading Street* for Tier III intensive reading intervention.

DAY 1

On-Level
Teacher-Led
Page DI·43
- Develop Concept Vocabulary
- **Read** On-Level Reader *The Colonial Adventure*

Strategic Intervention
Teacher-Led
Page DI·42
- Preteach Consonant Digraphs
- **Read** Decodable Reader 10
- **Read** Below-Level Reader *Colonial New England*

Advanced
Teacher-Led
Page DI·43
- **Read** Advanced Reader *Houses Past and Present*
- Independent Extension Activity

(i) Independent Activities
While you meet with small groups, have the rest of the class...

- Visit the Reading/Library Center
- Listen to the Background Building Audio
- Finish Write to Read, p. 250
- Complete Practice Book 3.1 pp. 93–94
- Visit Cross-Curricular Centers

DAY 2

On-Level
Teacher-Led
Pages 256–261
- **Read** *William's House*

Strategic Intervention
Teacher-Led
Page DI·44
- Practice Lesson Vocabulary
- Read Multisyllabic Words
- **Read** or Listen to *William's House*

Advanced
Teacher-Led
Page DI·45
- Extend Vocabulary
- **Read** *William's House*

(i) Independent Activities
While you meet with small groups, have the rest of the class...

- Visit the Reading/Library Center
- Listen to the AudioText for *William's House*
- Finish Words to Write, p. 253
- Complete Practice Book 3.1 pp. 95–96, 99
- Write in their Strategy Response Logs, pp. 254, 261
- Visit Cross-Curricular Centers
- Work on inquiry projects

DAY 3

On-Level
Teacher-Led
Pages 262–265
- **Read** *William's House*

Strategic Intervention
Teacher-Led
Page DI·46
- Practice Draw Conclusions and Ask Questions
- **Read** or Listen to *William's House*

Advanced
Teacher-Led
Page DI·47
- Extend Draw Conclusions and Ask Questions
- **Read** *William's House*

(i) Independent Activities
While you meet with small groups, have the rest of the class...

- Visit the Reading/Library Center
- Listen to the AudioText for *William's House*
- Write in their Strategy Response Logs, p. 264
- Finish Look Back and Write, p. 266
- Complete Practice Book 3.1 p. 97
- Visit Cross-Curricular Centers
- Work on inquiry projects

① Begin with whole class skill and strategy instruction.

② Meet with small groups to provide differentiated instruction.

③ Gather the whole class back together for fluency and language arts.

On-Level
Teacher-Led
Pages 268–271
- **Read** "Log Cabins"

Strategic Intervention
Teacher-Led
Page DI • 48
- Practice Retelling
- **Read** or Listen to "Log Cabins"

Advanced
Teacher-Led
Page DI • 49
- **Read** "Log Cabins"
- Genre Study

DAY 4

ⓘ Independent Activities

While you meet with small groups, have the rest of the class...

- Visit the Reading/Library Center
- Listen to the AudioText for "Log Cabins"
- Visit the Writing and Vocabulary Centers
- Finish Writing Across Texts, p. 271
- Visit Cross-Curricular Centers
- Work on inquiry projects

On-Level
Teacher-Led
Page DI • 51
- **Reread** Leveled Reader *The Colonial Adventure*
- Retell *The Colonial Adventure*

Strategic Intervention
Teacher-Led
Page DI • 50
- **Reread** Leveled Reader *Colonial New England*
- Retell *Colonial New England*

Advanced
Teacher-Led
Page DI • 51
- **Reread** Leveled Reader *Houses Past and Present*
- Share Extension Activity

DAY 5

ⓘ Independent Activities

While you meet with small groups, have the rest of the class...

- Visit the Reading/Library Center
- Complete Practice Book 3.1 pp. 98, 100
- Visit Cross-Curricular Centers
- Work on inquiry projects

Grouping Place English language learners in the groups that correspond to their reading abilities in English.

Use the appropriate Leveled Reader or other text at students' instructional level.

TIP Send home the appropriate Multilingual Summary of the main selection on Day 1.

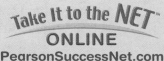
ONLINE
PearsonSuccessNet.com

Donald Leu
For ideas and activities to build new literacies, see the article "The New Literacies" by Scott Foresman author Donald Leu.

TEACHER TALK

New literacies are skills and strategies needed to successfully use information technologies, such as CD-ROMs, the Internet, and e-mail.

Be sure to schedule time for students to work on the unit inquiry project, "A Book of Solutions."
This week students prepare a list of resources for other classes who may wish to explore the same topic.

Looking Ahead

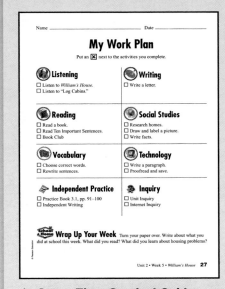

▲ **Group-Time Survival Guide** p. 27, Weekly Contract

William's House 250g

ORAL LANGUAGE

SOCIAL STUDIES

Concept Development

When you find yourself in a new place, what problems might you meet?

CONCEPT VOCABULARY

dwellings gabled stockade

BUILD

❑ **Question of the Week** Introduce and discuss the question of the week. This week students will read a variety of texts and work on projects related to the concept *housing problems*. Post the question for students to refer to throughout the week. **DAY 1** *250d*

❑ **Read Aloud** Read aloud "Colonial Homes." Then begin a web to build concepts and concept vocabulary related to this week's lesson and the unit theme, Smart Solutions. Introduce the concept words *dwellings, gabled,* and *stockade* and have students place them on the web. Display the web for use throughout the week. **DAY 1** *250l–250m*

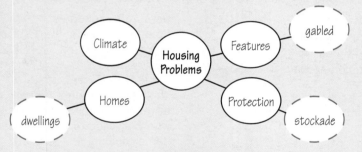

DEVELOP

❑ **Question of the Day** Use the prompts from the Weekly Plan to engage students in conversations related to this week's reading and the unit theme. **EVERY DAY** *250d–250e*

❑ **Concept Vocabulary Web** Revisit the Housing Problems Concept Web and encourage students to add concept words from their reading and life experiences. **DAY 2** *259*, **DAY 3** *265*

CONNECT

❑ **Looking Back/Moving Forward** Revisit the Housing Problems Concept Web and discuss how it relates to this week's lesson and the unit theme. Then make connections to next week's lesson. **DAY 5** *271c*

CHECK

❑ **Concept Vocabulary Web** Use the Housing Problems Concept Web to check students' understanding of the concept vocabulary words *dwellings, gabled,* and *stockade*. **DAY 1** *250l*, **DAY 5** *271c*

VOCABULARY

STRATEGY CONTEXT CLUES Context clues are the words and sentences around a word whose meaning you don't know. When you come to a word you don't know, look for clues in the context around the word to help you figure out what the unknown word means.

LESSON VOCABULARY

barrels pegs
cellar spoil
clearing steep

TEACH

❑ **Words to Know** Give students the opportunity to tell what they already know about this week's lesson vocabulary words. Then discuss word meaning. **DAY 1** *252b*

❑ **Vocabulary Strategy Lesson** Use the vocabulary strategy lesson in the Student Edition to introduce and model this week's strategy, *context clues*. **DAY 2** *252–253*

Vocabulary Strategy Lesson

PRACTICE/APPLY

❑ **Leveled Text** Read the lesson vocabulary in the context of leveled text. **DAY 1** *LR37–LR45*

❑ **Words in Context** Read the lesson vocabulary and apply *context clues* in the context of *William's House*. **DAY 2** *254–261*, **DAY 3** *262–266*

Leveled Readers

❑ **Vocabulary Center** Use context clues to choose the correct word to finish a sentence. **ANY DAY** *250j*

Main Selection—Fiction

❑ **Homework** Practice Book 3.1 pp. 94–95. **DAY 1** *252b*, **DAY 2** *253*

❑ **Word Play** Have partners draw pictures of houses they would like to live in. Then have them use reference sources to label the parts of the house. **ANY DAY** *271c*

ASSESS

❑ **Selection Test** Use the Selection Test to determine students' understanding of the lesson vocabulary words. **DAY 3**

RETEACH/REVIEW

❑ **Reteach Lesson** If necessary, use this lesson to reteach and review *context clues*. **DAY 5** *271c*

COMPREHENSION

🔍 **SKILL DRAW CONCLUSIONS** To draw a conclusion means to make a decision after reading and thinking about details and facts.

🔍 **STRATEGY ASK QUESTIONS** To draw conclusions, ask yourself questions as you read. Ask why certain things happen or why characters act as they do. Asking questions will help you to draw conclusions about the story's characters or events.

TEACH

☐ **Skill/Strategy Lesson** Use the skill/strategy lesson in the Student Edition to introduce and model *drawing conclusions* and *asking questions.* DAY 1 *250-251*

☐ **Extend Skills** Teach facts and details. **ANY DAY** *271b*

Skill/Strategy Lesson

PRACTICE/APPLY

☐ **Leveled Text** Apply *drawing conclusions* and *asking questions* to read leveled text. DAY 1 *LR37–LR45*

☐ **Skills and Strategies in Context** Read *William's House,* using the Guiding Comprehension questions to apply *drawing conclusions* and *asking questions.* DAY 2 *254–261*, DAY 3 *262–266*

Leveled Readers

☐ **Skills and Strategies in Context** Read "Log Cabins," guiding students as they apply *drawing conclusions* and *asking questions.* Then have students discuss and write across texts. DAY 4 *268–271*

Main Selection—Fiction

☐ **Homework** Practice Book 3.1 pp. 93, 97, 98. DAY 1 *251*, DAY 3 *265*, DAY 5 *271b*

☐ **Fresh Reads for Differentiated Test Practice** Have students practice *drawing conclusions* with a new passage. DAY 3

Paired Selection—Nonfiction

ASSESS

☐ **Selection Test** Determine students' understanding of the selection and their use of *drawing conclusions.* DAY 3

☐ **Retell** Have students retell *William's House.* DAY 3 *266–267*

RETEACH/REVIEW

☐ **Reteach Lesson** If necessary, reteach and review *drawing conclusions.* DAY 5 *271b*

FLUENCY

SKILL READING SILENTLY Reading silently means reading only to yourself. When you read silently, you correct yourself when you make a mistake, or reread if something doesn't make sense.

TEACH

☐ **Read Aloud** Model fluent reading by rereading " Colonial Homes." Focus on this week's fluency skill, reading silently. DAY 1 *250l–250m, 271A*

PRACTICE/APPLY

☐ **Silent Reading** Read aloud selected paragraphs from *William's House,* modeling how to self-correct if something does not make sense the first time. Have students practice reading silently. DAY 2 *271a*, DAY 3 *271a*

☐ **Choral Reading** Practice choral reading "The Sure-Footed Shoe Finder" three times. As students reread, monitor their progress toward their individual fluency goals. DAY 4 *271a*

☐ **Listening Center** Have students follow along with the AudioText for this week's selections. **ANY DAY** *250j*

☐ **Reading/Library Center** Have students reread a selection of their choice. **ANY DAY** *250j*

☐ **Fluency Coach** Have students use Fluency Coach to listen to fluent readings or practice reading on their own. **ANY DAY**

ASSESS

☐ **Check Fluency** WCPM Do a one-minute timed reading, paying special attention to this week's skill—reading silently. Provide feedback for each student. DAY 5 *271a*

GRAMMAR

SKILL PLURAL POSSESSIVE NOUNS A plural possessive noun is a noun that shows that two or more people share or own something. To make plural possessive nouns, add an apostrophe to plural nouns that end in *-s, -es,* or *-ies.* If a plural noun does not end in *-s, -es,* or *-ies,* add an apostrophe and an *s.*

TEACH

☐ **Grammar Transparency 10** Use Grammar Transparency 10 to teach plural possessive nouns.
DAY 1 *271e*

Grammar Transparency 10

PRACTICE/APPLY

☐ **Develop the Concept** Review the concept of plural possessive nouns and provide guided practice. DAY 2 *271e*

☐ **Apply to Writing** Have students review something they have written and apply what they have learned about plural possessive nouns. DAY 3 *271f*

☐ **Test Preparation** Examine common errors in plural possessive nouns to prepare for standardized tests. DAY 4 *271f*

☐ **Homework** Grammar and Writing Practice Book pp. 37–39.
DAY 2 *271e,* DAY 3 *271f,* DAY 4 *271f*

ASSESS

☐ **Cumulative Review** Use Grammar and Writing Practice Book p. 40. DAY 5 *271f*

RETEACH/REVIEW

☐ **Daily Fix-It** Have students find and correct errors in grammar, spelling, and punctuation.
EVERY DAY *271e–271f*

☐ **The Grammar and Writing Book** Use pp. 104–107 of The Grammar and Writing Book to extend instruction for plural possessive nouns.
ANY DAY

The Grammar and Writing Book

WRITING

Trait of the Week

FOCUS/IDEAS Good writers focus, or concentrate, on a main idea and develop this idea with strong, supporting details. They also know their purpose for writing. This purpose may be to persuade, to inform, to describe, or just to entertain. Your purpose is important because it helps you focus your main idea.

TEACH

☐ **Writing Transparency 10A** Use the model to introduce and discuss the Trait of the Week. DAY 1 *271g*

☐ **Writing Transparency 10B** Use the transparency to show students how using precise words can improve their writing.
DAY 2 *271g*

Writing Transparency 10A **Writing Transparency 10B**

PRACTICE/APPLY

☐ **Write Now** Examine the model on Student Edition p. 267. Then have students write their own explanatory paragraph. DAY 3 *267, 271h,* DAY 4 *271h*

Prompt In *William's House,* special features make a house suitable for its environment. Think about the features that help your home fit into its environment. Now write an explanatory paragraph about those features.

Write Now p. 267

☐ **Writing Center** Write a friendly letter to the characters in *William's House,* discussing differences and similarities between homes then and now. ANY DAY *250k*

ASSESS

☐ **Writing Trait Rubric** Use the rubric to evaluate students' writing. DAY 4 *271h*

RETEACH/REVIEW

☐ **The Grammar and Writing Book** Use pp. 104–109 of The Grammar and Writing Book to extend instruction for plural possessive nouns, using precise words, and explanatory paragraphs.
ANY DAY

The Grammar and Writing Book

SPELLING

GENERALIZATION DIGRAPHS *SH, TH, PH, CH, TCH* Words can have two or three consonants together that are pronounced as one sound: *English, father, trophy, chapter, watch.*

TEACH

☐ **Pretest** Give the pretest for words with digraphs *sh, th, ph, ch, tch*. Guide students in self-correcting their pretests and correcting any misspellings. DAY 1 *271k*

☐ **Think and Practice** Connect spelling to the phonics generalization for digraphs *sh, th, ph, ch, tch*. DAY 2 *271k*

PRACTICE/APPLY

☐ **Connect to Writing** Have students use spelling words to write a news report. Then review frequently misspelled words: *their, there, they.* DAY 3 *271l*

☐ **Homework** Phonics and Spelling Practice Book pp. 37–40. **EVERY DAY**

RETEACH/REVIEW

☐ **Review** Review spelling words to prepare for the posttest. Then provide students with a spelling strategy—consonants together. DAY 4 *271l*

ASSESS

☐ **Posttest** Use dictation sentences to give the posttest for words with digraphs *sh, th, ph, ch, tch*. DAY 5 *271l*

Spelling Words

1. father*
2. chapter
3. other
4. alphabet
5. watch
6. English
7. weather
8. catch
9. fashion*
10. shrink
11. pitcher
12. flash
13. athlete
14. trophy
15. nephew

Challenge Words

16. northern
17. establish
18. emphasis
19. hyphen
20. challenge

*Word from the selection

PHONICS

SKILL CONSONANT DIGRAPHS Consonant digraphs consist of two or three consonants that stand for a single sound.

TEACH

☐ **Phonics Lesson** Model how to read words with consonant digraphs. Then have students practice by decoding longer words and reading words in context. DAY 2 *271i*

PRACTICE/APPLY

☐ **Homework** Practice Book 3.1, p. 99. DAY 2 *271i*

RETEACH/REVIEW

☐ **Review Phonics** Review how to read words with consonant blends. Then have student practice by decoding longer words and reading words in context. DAY 4 *271j*

RESEARCH AND INQUIRY

☐ **Internet Inquiry** Have students conduct an Internet inquiry on life during colonial times. **EVERY DAY** *271m*

☐ **Diagram/Scale Drawing** Review the terms and ideas related to a diagram. Have students make a diagram to show a part of the school. DAY 5 *271n*

☐ **Unit Inquiry** Allow time for students to prepare a list of resources for other classes who may wish to explore the same topic. **ANY DAY** *149*

SPEAKING AND VIEWING

☐ **Speak to Communicate Needs** Have students use information in *William's House* to prepare and give short speeches about the things that William's family needed to build their house. Encourage students to also include facts about how the family met their needs. DAY 5 *271d*

☐ **Recognize Opinion** Have students watch a video excerpt of *Little House on the Prairie* or another dramatized work of fiction about pioneer life. Then, with partners, have them answer questions. DAY 5 *271d*

Resources for Differentiated Instruction

LEVELED READERS

▶ **Comprehension**
- 🔊 **Skill** Draw Conclusions
- 🔊 **Strategy** Ask Questions

▶ **Lesson Vocabulary**
- 🔊 Context Clues

spoil
barrels
cellar
steep
pegs
clearing

▶ **Social Studies Standards**
- Colonial Settlements
- Change over Time
- Adapting to Environment

Leveled Reader Database

ONLINE
PearsonSuccessNet.com

Use the Online Database of over 600 books to
- Download and print additional copies of this week's leveled readers.
- Listen to the readers being read online.
- Search for more titles focused on this week's skills, topic, and content.

On-Level

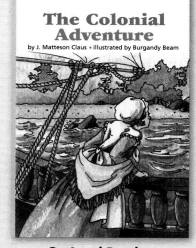

The Colonial Adventure
by J. Matteson Claus • illustrated by Burgandy Beam

On-Level Reader

Draw Conclusions

- To **draw a conclusion** means to use what you already know and what you have read to make reasonable decisions about characters or events.

Directions Read the following message written by a fictional person from England who has settled in colonial Jamestown. Then fill in the charts with facts from the passage and things you know that are related to the facts. Finally, write conclusions based on the facts and what you know.

Sometimes life in New World can be difficult. The land here is very different from England. Jamestown is filled with swamps. Because the land is swampy, the water that we drink is brown, muddy, and not at all fresh. Also, the people of our settlement are trying to make friends with the native people. But there is little that they understand about us or that we understand about them. Papa says that we should still try to work with them and respect their ways.

Possible responses given.

Fact	What I Already Know	My Conclusion
Colonists are drinking brown, muddy water that is not fresh.	Drinking water that is not fresh can make you sick.	The brown, muddy water may be making the colonists sick.
Colonists try to make friends with native people, but they do not understand each other.	Making friends with other people is hard when you do not understand them.	The colonists may find it hard to make friends with the native people.

🔊 **On-Level Practice** TE p. LR41

Vocabulary
Directions Read each list of words. Write a vocabulary word that relates to each group.

Check the Words You Know
__barrels __cellar __clearing
__peg __spoil __steep

1. _peg_
hanger
hook
rod

2. _steep_
sharp
sudden
raised

3. _spoil_
ruin
rot
decay

4. _barrels_
cans
buckets
containers

5. _clearing_
empty space
gap
opening

6. _cellar_
basement
underground room
vault

Directions Write a paragraph about life in colonial New England. Use as many vocabulary words as you can.

Paragraphs will vary but should include some correctly used vocabulary words.

🔊 **On-Level Practice** TE p. LR42

Strategic Intervention

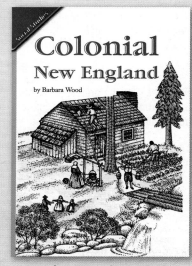

Social Studies

Colonial New England
by Barbara Wood

Below-Level Reader

Character

- A **character** is a person who takes part in the events of a story.
- The qualities of a character are known as **character traits** and usually tell about his or her personality.

Directions How are Sarah and Julia alike? How are they different? Use the Venn Diagram below to compare the two characters.

Possible responses given.

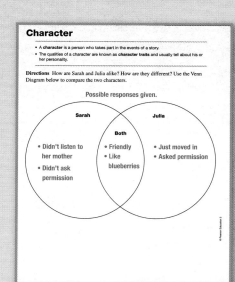

Sarah
- Didn't listen to her mother
- Didn't ask permission

Both
- Friendly
- Like blueberries

Julia
- Just moved in
- Asked permission

🔊 **Below-Level Practice** TE p. LR38

Vocabulary
Directions Draw a line to match each vocabulary word with its definition.

Check the Words You Know
__excitement __gardener __motioned __sadness
__shivered __shocked __slammed

1. shivered — a. thrill
2. slammed — b. signaled
3. excitement — c. a person who works outdoors with plants
4. motioned — d. trembled
5. shocked — e. a feeling of unhappiness
6. gardener — f. to be surprised
7. sadness — g. closed with a bang

Directions Write the vocabulary word that completes each sentence.

8. I was _shocked_ when I heard he was joining the circus.
9. The fact that we might never see each other again filled me with _sadness_.
10. She _shivered_ as she stepped out into the cold.
11. He stomped angrily out of the room and _slammed_ the door behind him.
12. I wondered why the _gardener_ planted the bushes so close to the house.
13. When our team won the big game, everyone at school shared the _excitement_.
14. When the new girl walked into the lunchroom, I _motioned_ for her to come over to our table.

🔊 **Below-Level Practice** TE p. LR39

Advanced

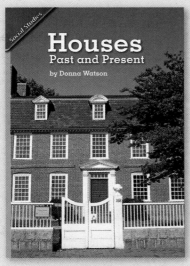

Advanced Reader

ELL Reader

ELL Poster 10

Teacher's Edition Notes

ELL notes throughout this lesson support instruction and reference additional resources at point of use.

Draw Conclusions

- When you **draw conclusions** you use what you have read and what you already know to make reasonable decisions about characters or events.

Directions Read the following passage. Then answer the questions below.

During the pioneer era of the 1800s, settlers moved west to the prairie lands. There were no forests of tall trees to cut down for lumber. So these settlers found a way to use the ground itself to make their first homes. All around them was the grass of the prairie. The grass had deep roots which held the dirt below it.

Settlers used plows to cut through the grass-covered ground, or sod. With a plow they were able to dig the grass up in long strips. Then they cut the strips of sod into sections. The pieces of sod were stacked like bricks to build the walls of the shelter.

1. Which of the following statements is a reasonable conclusion about settlers living in prairie lands?
   a. Settlers loved their sod houses.
   b. Building sod houses is easy.
   c. Settlers had to adapt to their new environment in order to survive.

2. Which of the following statements is NOT a reasonable conclusion about settlers living in prairie lands?
   a. Settlers had to work very hard to build their sod homes.
   b. Sod houses could be dirty and filled with insects.
   c. Sod houses offered a comfortable, luxurious home.

3. How do you think settlers felt about living in sod houses? Why do you think so?
   Possible response: Sod houses were not very comfortable, but
   the settlers worked well with the materials they had.

4. How might settlers have built their homes differently if there were trees? Why?
   Possible response: The trees could be used for lumber, which
   would have made stronger, wooden houses.

Advanced Practice TE p. LR44

Vocabulary
Directions Write the word from the box that matches each definition below.

Check the Words You Know

daub	kilns	mortise
pug mill	puncheon	tallow
tenon	thatch	wattle

1. thatch — grasses, leaves, or straw used to cover a roof
2. tallow — animal fat used to make candles
3. puncheon — a type of flooring made up of halved logs
4. kilns — very hot ovens used for making bricks
5. mortise — a hole in one piece of wood that helps form a joint with another wooden piece
6. wattle — sticks interwoven with twigs and branches
7. tenon — the end of a piece of wood that fits into the hole described in item 5.
8. daub — a coating of plaster, clay, mud, or any other sticky material
9. pug mill — a hollow tub with knives used for mixing and grinding clay

Directions Write a sentence about houses past and present. Use as many vocabulary words as you can.

Sentences will vary but should correctly use some vocabulary words.

Advanced Practice TE p. LR45

Teaching Guide
pp. 64–70, 230–231
- Multilingual summaries of the main selection
- Comprehension lesson
- Vocabulary strategies and word cards
- ELL Reader 3.2.5 lesson

ELL and Transition Handbook

Ten Important Sentences
- Key ideas from every selection in the Student Edition
- Activities to build sentence power

More Reading

Readers' Theater Anthology
- Fluency practice
- Five scripts to build fluency
- Poetry for oral interpretation

Leveled Trade Books

Below-Level

On-Level

Advanced

- Extended reading tied to the unit concept
- Lessons in the Trade Book Library Teaching Guide

Homework
- Family Times Newsletter
- ELL Multilingual Selection Summaries

Take-Home Books
- Leveled Readers

Cross-Curricular Centers

Listening

Listen to the Selections

MATERIALS `SINGLES`
CD player, headphones, AudioText CD, Student Edition

Listen to *William's House* and "Log Cabins" as you follow or read along in your book. As you listen, draw conclusions about each selection.

If there is anything you don't understand, you can listen again to any section.

Reading/Library

Read It *Again!*

MATERIALS `SINGLES` `PAIRS` `GROUPS`
Collection of books for self-selected reading, reading log

Select a book you have already read. Record the title of the book in your reading log. You may want to read with a partner.

You may choose to read any of the following:

• **Leveled Readers**
• **ELL Readers**
• **Stories written by classmates**
• **Books from the library**
• *William's House*

TEN IMPORTANT SENTENCES Read the Ten Important Sentences for *William's House*. Then locate the sentences in the Student Edition.

BOOK CLUB Discuss how people in different areas used available materials to build homes and establish communities.

Vocabulary

Use Context

MATERIALS `SINGLES`
Copy of sentences below, pencil, paper

1. **Read the sentences below.**
2. **One of the words or phrases in parentheses completes it correctly.**
3. **Rewrite the sentences using the correct word or words.**

• There is a big <u>basement</u> (behind/under) the house.
• Mom sells <u>real estate</u> to people hunting for a (job/home).
• <u>Steep</u> stairs are (hard to climb/easy to climb).
• <u>Construction</u> will start as soon as the (actor/builder) gets the lumber.
• A <u>bungalow</u> is a style of (house/car).

EARLY FINISHERS Draw a cartoon that illustrates the meaning of the underlined words.

Steep stairs are hard to climb.

Scott Foresman Reading Street Centers Survival Kit

Use the *William's House* materials from the Reading Street Centers Survival Kit to organize this week's centers.

Writing

Social Studies

Technology

Write a
Letter

MATERIALS `SINGLES`
Writing materials

Write a friendly letter to William and Elizabeth, the characters in *William's House.*

1. Put today's date on your letter.
2. Describe some things about homes today that are the same as they were in 1637.
3. Tell William and Elizabeth about things that are different, such as running water and electricity.
4. If you wish, tell them about things we have today that would have made their lives easier, such as washing machines and power tools.

EARLY FINISHERS Draw a picture of your "dream home" to include with the letter.

October 9, 2007
Dear William and Elizabeth,
Homes today have telephones. Telephones would have made your lives easier. With telephones, we can talk to people who live in other places.
Sincerely,
Mitch

RESEARCH
Homes

MATERIALS `SINGLES`
Books on types of homes, Internet access, writing and art materials

---

Research different kinds of homes.

1. Choose one type of home that interests you.
2. Look in a library book or online to learn about the home.
3. Draw and label a picture of the home.
4. From the information you gathered, write four facts about the home below your picture.

EARLY FINISHERS Draw pictures of furniture you would put inside the home if it belonged to you. Be creative!

Tepee

1. Native Americans of the Plains tribes lived in tepees.
2. Tepees could be moved easily.
3. Tepees were waterproof.
4. People decorated the outside of tepees.

Create a
Document

MATERIALS `SINGLES`
Computer, printer

Use lesson vocabulary to write a paragraph about the past.

1. Use what you have learned about life in 1637 to write a paragraph about the past. Use some of the lesson vocabulary words: *spoil, barrels, cellar, steep, pegs,* and *clearing.*
2. Use the grammar and spelling check features to proofread what you have written. Name and save the document.

EARLY FINISHERS Write a second paragraph using the following spelling words: *father, watch, weather,* and *catch.*

People in the past kept food in the cellar so it would not spoil. I would not want to climb down the steep stairs into the dark cellar every time I wanted something.

OBJECTIVES

- Build vocabulary by finding words related to the lesson concept.
- Listen and draw conclusions.

Concept Vocabulary

dwellings the places in which people live

gabled having a triangular section between two sloping roofs

stockade a wall made of large, strong posts stuck upright in the ground

Monitor Progress

Check Vocabulary

If... students are unable to place words on the web,	then... review the lesson concept. Place the words on the web and provide additional words for practice, such as *shutters* and *dormers*.

SUCCESS PREDICTOR

DAY 1   Grouping Options

Reading
Whole Group
Introduce and discuss the Question of the Week. Then use pp. 250l–252b.

Group Time
Differentiated Instruction
Read this week's Leveled Readers. See pp. 250f–250g for the small group lesson plan.

Whole Group
Use p. 271a.

Language Arts
Use pp. 271e–271h and 271k–271m.

Build Concepts

FLUENCY

MODEL READING SILENTLY As you read "Colonial Homes," pay careful attention and self-correct when you make a mistake or if there are parts of the text you know may be confusing for students. For example, paragraph 5 may contain some confusing information. Reread it slowly, ask yourself questions about it, then continue reading.

LISTENING COMPREHENSION

After reading "Colonial Homes," use the following questions to assess listening comprehension.

1 **Many of the older colonial homes are no longer standing. Why do you think that is?** *(Possible response: They were knocked down to make room for bigger homes as conditions improved.)* ***Draw Conclusions***

2 **What generalization about colonial homes can we make after reading the selection?** *(Possible response: Colonial homes weren't very warm or comfortable.)* ***Generalize***

BUILD CONCEPT VOCABULARY

Start a web to build concepts and vocabulary related to this week's lesson and the unit theme.

- Draw a Housing Problems Concept Web.
- Read the sentence with the word *stockade* again. Ask students to pronounce *stockade* and discuss its meaning.
- Place *stockade* in an oval attached to Protection. Explain that *stockade* is related to this concept. Read the sentences in which *dwellings* and *gabled* appear. Have students pronounce the words, place them on the web, and provide reasons.
- Brainstorm additional words and categories for the web. Keep the web on display and add words throughout the week.

Concept Vocabulary Web

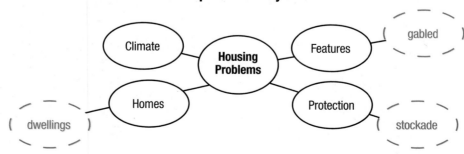

Colonial Homes

by Walter Hazen

Did you know that many of the first settlers in America lived in caves? It is true. These early arrivals—mostly men—had neither the time nor the tools to build anything better. This was especially the case in New England, where winters were harsh. Some type of immediate shelter was needed, and caves fulfilled this purpose. These hardy colonists simply dug into the side of a cliff, made a roof of bark supported by poles, and their "castle" was complete!

As conditions improved, more permanent dwellings were possible. Each section of the colonies developed its own style of house, dependent on the climate and the materials at hand.

For a while, New Englanders built wigwams similar to those of the American Indians. From these they progressed to box-shaped, wooden houses with thatched roofs. The typical New England house was about 16 feet long and 14 feet wide. It consisted of one long room with a large fireplace at one end. Beams supported a loft reached by a ladder, and this is where the children of the family slept. Floors were either dirt or wood.

Glass windows were rare in early New England houses. Those colonists who possessed such luxuries guarded them at all costs. If they left home for an extended period of time, they removed the panes and took them along. (Iron nails were just as valuable. If a home burned, the owner retrieved the nails from the ashes.) Most homes had windows covered with oiled paper or wooden shutters. This was true well into the eighteenth century in some rural areas.

Some New England colonists built what were called saltbox houses. They received this name because they resembled the boxes salt was stored in. A saltbox house was one and a half stories high in the front and one story high in the back. It was simpler and less expensive to build than the typical wooden house.

In the 1700s wealthy colonists in New England began to build large houses of brick or stone. These houses were built in the Georgian style, the style popular in England at the time. They featured gabled roofs and dormers. A dormer is a window that sticks out from a sloping roof. Many of these beautiful houses still stand today. Those built near the coast often had balustrades—railed-in areas— on the roofs called "widow's walks." From these high perches, the wives of sea captains watched and waited for their husbands' ships to come in.

The men who first came to Jamestown were more interested in looking for gold than in building permanent shelters. But the threat of Indian attacks finally led them to build a triangular stockade of upright poles. Inside the stockade they slept in tents and Indian-style wigwams. In the South, the first permanent homes were half-faced camps, which were open on only one side. Later, the typical house in the early days of Jamestown was made of thatch and mud with a hole in the roof for a chimney.

No colonial house had a bathroom. Colonists made do with outhouses

continued on TR1

SKILLS ⟷ STRATEGIES IN CONTEXT

Draw Conclusions
Ask Questions

OBJECTIVES

 Understand how to draw conclusions.

 Ask questions to draw conclusions.

Skills Trace
Draw Conclusions

Introduce/Teach	TE: 3.2 250–251, 3.3 330–331, 3.5 220–221
Practice	PB: 3.1 26, 93, 97, 106, 123, 127, 128, 136; 3.2 83, 87, 88
Reteach/Review	TE: 3.1 79; 3.2 271b, DI-56; 3.3 289, 353b, 363, DI-54; 3.5 243b, DI-55
Test	Selection Test: Unit 2 Benchmark Test: Unit 3

INTRODUCE

Write the following on the board: *Gilda always wears her red sweater on Monday. Gilda is not wearing her red sweater today.* Ask students what the information tells us about what day of the week it is (or isn't). *(It isn't Monday because Gilda isn't wearing her red sweater.)*

Have students read the information on p. 250. Explain the following:

- As you read, think about the details and facts in a selection. Use what you already know about the topic to help you draw conclusions about the selection. Then check your conclusions to see if they make sense.

- Asking yourself questions about why things happen or why characters say and do things can help you draw conclusions too.

Use Skill Transparency 10 to teach draw conclusions and ask questions.

Comprehension

Skill
Draw Conclusions

Strategy
Ask Questions

 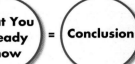 ## Draw Conclusions

- A conclusion is a decision you reach after you think about details and facts.

- As you read, think about the details and facts and use what you already know to draw conclusions about characters and the things that happen.

Fact or Detail + What You Already Know = Conclusion

Strategy: Ask Questions

Active readers ask themselves questions as they read. As you read, ask why certain things happen or why characters act as they do. The answers may not be given in a sentence, but you may be able to draw conclusions about them.

 ## Write to Read

1. Read "How to Build an Adobe House." Make a graphic organizer like the one above. Draw a conclusion about laying adobe out in the sun.

2. Use the information in "How to Build an Adobe House" and what you know to write a conclusion about the kind of weather needed to make adobe.

250

Strategic Intervention

 Draw Conclusions Work separately with students who are having trouble grasping the skill. Provide additional examples such as the one in the introduction; for example: *Martha baked a peach pie. It disappeared from the pie plate. The dog had pie crumbs on his nose.* Ask students what they can conclude about what happened to the pie. Discuss how they used the facts and their own knowledge to arrive at the conclusion.

ELL

Access Content

Beginning/Intermediate For a Picture It! lesson on drawing conclusions, see the ELL Teaching Guide, p. 65.

Advanced Before students read "How to Build an Adobe House," explain what *adobe* is, and discuss how they think a house made out of such material might look and where and why these such houses were built.

How to Build an Adobe House

Adobe is a kind of brick. Adobe bricks have been used to build desert houses for many years. You can see adobe houses in the desert southwest of our country.

To build a house of adobe, you need clay. Add water and dirt to the clay. Let it stand for a day or two. It will become soft. Then, mix in a little straw to make a paste. This will hold the brick together. Next, put the paste into molds. Each mold is made of pieces of wood put together in the shape of a brick. Then leave the bricks in the sun for about two weeks.

Once you have made the bricks, you can build your house. Add a roof, and your house is done! You will be warm in the winter and cool in the summer.

> **Strategy** This is a good place to ask a question, such as, *"Why would I leave the bricks in the sun?"*

> **Skill** Then you can use the details you have just read and what you already know about the sun to draw the conclusion that the sun will harden the bricks.

251

Available as **Skill Transparency** 10

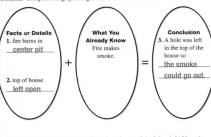

Draw Conclusions · Ask Questions

- A **conclusion** is a decision you reach after you think about details and facts. Then think about **what you already know** to help draw **conclusions**.
- As you read, **ask yourself** why certain things happen or why characters act as they do. You may be able to **draw conclusions** about them.

Directions Read the following passage.

The Chumash lived in California long before settlers came. They lived in huge round houses made from tule reeds. First, the Chumash placed willow poles around a circle. Then they bent the poles and tied them together at the top. The people covered the poles with mats made from reeds. A hole was left in the top of the house.

A house was 50 feet across. Aunts, uncles, and cousins all lived together in one house. A fire burned in the center pit. The rest of the space was divided into areas for each family.

Directions Complete the graphic organizer to draw a conclusion.

Facts or Details
1. fire burns in __center pit__
2. top of house __left open__
+
What You Already Know
Fire makes smoke.
=
Conclusion
3. A hole was left in the top of the house so __the smoke could go out.__

Home Activity Your child used a graphic organizer to draw a conclusion. Authors don't tell the reader everything. Readers draw conclusions while they read to help them understand the story. Reread or retell the story "The Three Little Pigs." Ask your child to tell you why each house except the brick house blew down. (They were not strong enough.)

Practice Book 3.1 p. 93

TEACH

1 **STRATEGY** After reading aloud the first two paragraphs, model asking questions.

 Think Aloud **MODEL** Whenever I'm reading and I don't understand something, or something sounds strange, I stop and ask myself a question about it; for example, Why would someone leave the adobe bricks in the sun?

2 **SKILL** Model using the facts and details and what you already know to draw a conclusion that answers your question.

 Think Aloud **MODEL** The facts in the selection tell me that adobe is made of clay, water, dirt, and straw. That means it's wet when it's put into the molds. I know that the sun in the desert is hot. I bet the adobe is left in the sun so it will dry and harden into bricks.

PRACTICE AND ASSESS

STRATEGY Students should stop and ask themselves questions whenever they don't understand something. They might be confused by the information at the end of paragraph 2.

SKILL Students should use facts and details in the selection and what they know about the sun to draw conclusions

WRITE Have students complete steps 1 and 2 of the Write to Read activity. You might consider using this as a whole class activity.

Monitor Progress

🎯 Draw Conclusions

If... students are unable to complete **Write to Read** on p. 250,	then... use Practice Book 3.1 p. 93 to provide additional practice.

ELL

Build Background Use ELL Poster 10 to build background and vocabulary for the lesson concept of how climate affects the way we live.

▲ **ELL Poster** 10

Build Background

ACTIVATE PRIOR KNOWLEDGE

BEGIN A KWL CHART about colonial America.

- Write "colonial America" on the board. Ask pairs of students to write as many things as they can about colonial America. Prompt them to think about where the colonists came from, why they left, where they lived once they arrived, what resources were available to them, and so on.

- Draw a KWL chart on the board. Write what students know on the chart. Then have pairs of students write two to three questions about colonial America. Add them to the chart. Include a question of your own if necessary.

- Remind students to look for answers to their questions as they read. Add their new information to the chart.

K	W	L
Many came from England.	What did they bring with them?	
They settled in the woods of New England.	How did they build homes?	

▲ **Graphic Organizer** 3

BACKGROUND BUILDING AUDIO This week's audio discusses the lives of American colonists in the 1600s. After students listen, talk about what they think would be the hardest thing about life in an early American colony.

Background Building Audio

Introduce Vocabulary

WORD RATING CHART

Create word rating charts using the categories *Know, Have Seen,* and *Don't Know.*

Word Rating Chart

Word	Know	Have Seen	Don't Know
spoil		✔	
barrels			✔
cellar			
steep			
pegs			
clearing			

▲ **Graphic Organizer** 4

Read each word to students and have them place a check in one of the three columns: *Know* (know and can use); *Have Seen* (have heard or seen the word; don't know meaning); *Don't Know* (don't know the word).

Activate Prior Knowledge

Have students share where they may have seen some of these words. Point out that some of this week's words have multiple meanings *(spoil, steep, clearing)* and students may learn new definitions for these words.

Multiple-Meaning Words

Check graphic organizers with students at the end of the week and have them make changes to their ratings.

Use the Multisyllabic Word Routine on p. DI·1 to help students read multisyllabic words.

Lesson Vocabulary

CONCEPT VOCABULARY

T **barrels** containers with round, flat tops and bottoms and sides that curve out slightly

T **cellar** an underground room or rooms

T **clearing** an open space of land in a forest

T **pegs** pins or small bolts of wood or metal used to fasten parts together

T **spoil** to become bad or not good to eat

T **steep** having a sharp slope; almost straight up and down

MORE WORDS TO KNOW

fashioned made; created

halt stop

succotash a mixture of cooked vegetables, particularly lima beans and corn

T = Tested Word

Vocabulary

Check the Words You Know
___clearing ___pegs
___steep ___cellar
___barrels ___spoil

Directions Read the sentences. Write the word from the box that fits the sentence.

1. We set up our tent in a ___clearing___ in the woods.
2. We put ___pegs___ from our tent into the ground to hold it down.
3. The hill was so ___steep___, I nearly slipped and fell.
4. We keep lots of tools downstairs in our ___cellar___.
5. You must use eggs before they ___spoil___ and make you sick.

Directions Match the word with its meaning. Draw a line from the word to its definition.

6. barrels — wooden pins
7. spoil — large containers
8. clearing — a room under a house
9. cellar — to rot or go bad
10. pegs — an open space in a forest

Write a Description

On a separate sheet of paper, write a description of your home or of any house you have been in. Describe what the home is like from the outside and inside. Describe the rooms in the home. Use as many vocabulary words as possible.
Students' writing should incorporate the lesson vocabulary in a description of their home or any other house they have been in.

Home Activity Your child identified and used vocabulary words from *William's House*. Ask your child to describe William's house using as many vocabulary words as possible.

▲ **Practice Book 3.1** p. 94

Vocabulary Strategy

OBJECTIVE

 Use context clues to determine the meaning of unfamiliar words.

INTRODUCE

Discuss the context clues strategy using the steps on p. 252.

TEACH

- Have students read "Like the Good Old Days," paying attention to how vocabulary is used.
- Model using context clues to determine the meaning of *pegs.*

Think Aloud **MODEL** *Pegs* on p. 253 are said to be made of wood and used to "hold the logs and planks together." So *pegs* must mean "small pieces of wood that hold things together."

Words to Know

clearing

pegs

steep

cellar

barrels

spoil

Remember

Try the strategy. Then, if you need more help, use your glossary or a dictionary.

Vocabulary Strategy
for Unfamiliar Words

Context Clues Sometimes when you are reading, you come across a word you don't know. How can you figure out what the word means? Look for context clues. Context clues are the words and sentences around the word. They can help you figure out the meaning of the word.

1. Read the words and sentences around the word you don't know. Sometimes the author tells you what the word means.

2. If not, use the words and sentences to predict a meaning for the word.

3. Try that meaning in the sentence. Does it make sense?

As you read "Like the Good Old Days," use context clues to help you understand the meanings of the vocabulary words.

252

DAY 2 Grouping Options

Reading
Whole Group Discuss the Question of the Day. Then use pp. 252–255.

Group Time Differentiated Instruction
Read *William's House.* See pp. 250f–250g for the small group lesson plan.

Whole Group Use pp. 271a and 271i.

Language Arts
Use pp.271e–271h and 271k–271m.

ELL

Access Content Use ELL Poster 10 to preteach vocabulary. Choose from the following to meet language proficiency levels.

Beginning Point out clues on p. 253 that describe what a *cellar* is. Have students point to the words that contain these clues.

Intermediate After reading students can create a Venn diagram to show words that belong with building, words that belong with food, and words that can belong with both.

Advanced Teach the lesson on pp. 252–253. Students can report on the names of different parts of a house in their home languages.

Resources for home-language words may include parents, bilingual staff members, bilingual dictionaries, or online translation sources.

Like the Good Old Days

Look at the photograph. These people are pretending to be colonists in the 1600s. They are called *reenactors.* They want to do things the way the colonists did. They built a house like one the colonists built.

First, the reenactors cut down trees to make a clearing, or open space. They used whole logs to make the frame of the house, and they split logs into planks, or boards, to make the walls. They carved pegs out of wood and used the pegs, instead of nails, to hold the logs and planks together. Finally, they put a very steep roof on the house so that the snow would slide off.

Behind the house the reenactors dug a cellar, or underground room. They put food into barrels and stored the barrels in the cool, dry cellar so that the food wouldn't spoil. This was one way the colonists kept their food fresh. They also salted their meat and dried their vegetables.

Words to Write

Look at the picture. Write about what you think it would be like to live in a colonial house. Use words from the Words to Know list.

253

PRACTICE AND ASSESS

- Have students determine the meanings of the remaining words and explain the context clues they used to find the meanings.
- Point out that context does not work with every word. Students may have to use the glossary or a dictionary to find the exact meaning of some words.
- Have students refine their word rating charts, reassessing their ratings if necessary.
- Have students complete Practice Book 3.1, p. 95.

WRITE Writing should include vocabulary words that describe what life in a colonial house would be like.

Monitor Progress

◎ Context Clues

| **If...** students need more practice with the lesson vocabulary, | **then...** use Tested Vocabulary Cards. |

Vocabulary • Context Clues

Sometimes in your reading you see a word you don't know. You can use **context clues**—the words and sentences around the unfamiliar word.

Directions Read the following passage. Then answer the questions.

Last summer, my family and I spent two weeks living in a log cabin. The cabin was in a clearing, where the trees had been cut down. Life in a log cabin is very different from life in the city. You hang your clothes on pegs sticking out of the wall. Even pots and pans hang on pegs in the kitchen. Under the kitchen rug was a trap door. It led downstairs to the cellar.

My brother and I loved the cellar. We had to walk down very steep stairs almost like a ladder! The cellar was filled with large, covered barrels containing dried corn and other food. Also, the cellar was very cool. Food does not spoil where it is cool. So the food in the cellar stayed fresh. The cellar was a great place to be on a hot summer day!

1. What does *clearing* mean in this passage? What clues help you determine the meaning?
   an area from which the trees have been removed; Clues: where the trees had been cut down

2. What does *pegs* mean in this passage? What clues help you determine the meaning?
   hooks on the wall; Clues: hang [things] from pegs sticking out of the wall

3. What does *cellar* mean in this passage? What clues help you determine the meaning?
   a room below a house; Clues: trap door, downstairs

4. What does *steep* mean in this passage? What clues help you determine the meaning?
   at a sharp angle or incline; Clues: almost like a ladder

5. What does *barrels* mean in this passage? What clues help you determine the meaning?
   large containers; Clues: containing dried corn and other food

Home Activity Your child identified and used context clues to understand new words in a passage. Work with your child to identify unfamiliar words in a paragraph, then have your child find context clues to help with the understanding of new words. Confirm the meaning with your child.

▲ **Practice Book 3.1** p. 95

Prereading Strategies

- Draw conclusions to improve comprehension.
- Ask questions to draw conclusions.

GENRE STUDY

Historical Fiction

William's House is historical fiction. Explain that historical fiction is realistic fiction that takes place in the past. Often, the events and/or the characters in historical fiction are based on real events or people; even when the events and people are made up, they are based on historical fact.

PREVIEW AND PREDICT

Have students preview the selection title and illustrations and discuss the topics or ideas they think this selection will cover. Encourage students to use lesson vocabulary as they talk about what they expect to learn.

Strategy Response Log

Predict Have students write their predictions in their strategy response logs. Students will check their predictions in the Strategy Response Log activity on p. 261.

WILLIAM'S HOUSE

by Ginger Howard
illustrated by Larry Day

Genre — **Historical fiction** is a story that takes place in the past. When did this story take place?

254

ELL

Activate Prior Knowledge Have students share their experiences coming to the United States. Encourage them to talk about what they expected America to be like and to compare and contrast their native country and the United States.

Consider having students read the selection summary in English or in students' home languages. See the Multilingual Summaries in the ELL Teaching Guide, pp. 68–70.

What is special about William's house?

255

SET PURPOSE

Read the first page of the selection aloud to students. Discuss with students where William is from (England) and where he is living now (New England). Brainstorm ways in which the two places are different. Read to find out how William will have to adapt to life in the new country.

Remind students to ask questions and draw conclusions as they read.

STRATEGY RECALL

Students have now used these before-reading strategies:

- preview the selection to be aware of its genre, features, and possible content;
- activate prior knowledge about that content and what to expect of that genre;
- make predictions;
- set a purpose for reading.

Remind students to be aware of and flexibly use the during-reading strategies they have learned:

- link prior knowledge to new information;
- summarize text they have read so far;
- ask clarifying questions;
- answer questions they or others pose;
- check their predictions and either refine them or make new predictions;
- recognize the text structure the author is using, and use that knowledge to make predictions and increase comprehension;
- visualize what the author is describing;
- monitor their comprehension and use fix-up strategies.

After reading, students will use these strategies:

- summarize or retell the text;
- answer questions they or others pose;
- reflect to make new information become part of their prior knowledge.

Audio CD AudioText

Guiding Comprehension

1 **Setting • Literal**
Where does the story take place?
In New England in 1637.

2 **Ask Questions • Literal**
What materials does William use to build his house?
Wood from the trees in the forest around the house.

3 **Draw Conclusions • Inferential**
William's new house is made entirely of things found in nature. Why do you think that is?
Those were the only materials available.

Monitor Progress
Draw Conclusions
If... students are unable to draw conclusions, **then...** use the skill and strategy instruction on p. 257.

ONLINE

Use the key words *New England* and *life in colonial New England* to learn more about the area William and his family moved to and the difficulties they faced.

---

1 New England, 1637

William knew just the kind of house he wanted. It would be like the house he grew up in, his father's house, in England.

William cleared an area 20 feet square. He used the felled trees for the upright posts. The saplings were used for the fence. Then he went to the woods and cut rafters to hold the thatch roof. He split planks **2** for clapboards. And he fashioned wood pegs to hold everything in place. **3**

256

ELL

Access Content Direct students' attention to the historical details on p. 256, such as saplings, rafters, the thatch roof, the clapboards, and the wood pegs. Define the terms and discuss how William had to use what was available because there were no stores where he could get supplies. Have students work in pairs to identify more historical details on p. 257.

William's wife, Elizabeth, wanted a window, but William had no glass. He scraped a piece of animal horn until it was translucent. Then he made a wide slit in the clapboards and covered the opening with the horn.

William used clay and stones from the creek bed to build a small fireplace in one corner of the room. He placed two pegs on the wall, one for his extra shirt, and one for his wife's apron. Then he made a board table with the side of a packing crate. And finally, he stuffed bags with corn husks for beds.

257

Housing

Time for SOCIAL STUDIES

The first houses built by the early settlers in New England were much like William's house—one large room that served as living room, dining room, kitchen, and bedroom for the whole family. As more people arrived and the settlements began to look like villages and small towns, people added to their homes. First, lofts were added under the rafters, serving as bedrooms. Later, houses were built with two stories, the bedrooms upstairs and living space downstairs. The wealthier citizens had large homes with many bedrooms and lots of living space. Many of these homes are still standing today, and a popular design for new houses built today is called Colonial.

SKILLS ⟷ STRATEGIES IN CONTEXT

Draw Conclusions Ask Questions

TEACH

- Explain that when we draw a conclusion, we look at the facts and details and think about what we already know to make a decision or opinion about something. Point out that *to draw*, as it is used here, means "to figure out."
- Tell students that asking questions as you read helps you understand what you are reading so you can draw conclusions about it.
- Model asking questions to draw a conclusion about the facts and details on pp. 256–257.

 Think Aloud

MODEL I wonder why William used only natural materials to build his house. He didn't even have metal nails or glass! I guess I have to remember that the story takes place in 1637. In New England, they didn't have stores that sell everything you need to build a house. William probably had to use what he had available, which was trees and rocks.

PRACTICE AND ASSESS

Have students reread p. 257, paragraph 2, and draw a conclusion about how many clothes William and his family owned. (*Possible response: They didn't have many clothes.*)

EXTEND SKILLS

Author's Language

Point out the word *clapboards* on p. 256. Tell students that this is an old word, dating from colonial times. *Clapboards* are wooden boards used as siding for a house. Discuss with students why the author may have used such a word. Remind them to consider the genre in their discussion. Have them note other old words as they read.

Guiding Comprehension

4 REVIEW **Character • Inferential**

Reread pp. 258–259. Describe the kind of person William is.

Possible response: He misses his home in England. He works hard to make a new home for his family in New England. He takes care of his family.

<table>
<tr><td colspan="2" align="center">**Monitor Progress**</td></tr>
<tr><td colspan="2" align="center">REVIEW **Character**</td></tr>
<tr><td>**If...** students have difficulty understanding William's character,</td><td>**then...** use the skill and strategy instruction on p. 259.</td></tr>
</table>

5 **Author's Purpose • Inferential**

Question the Author **Why does the author use words from colonial New England in the story?**

Possible response: to teach us about the past.

6 **Generalize • Inferential**

What is one generalization you can make about life in colonial New England?

Possible response: Life was hard.

When all was done, William and Elizabeth and their two sons sat at the board. They dipped their fingers into trenchers of pudding and bread. A noggin of cider was passed from hand to hand. After supper, they folded their long napkins and put them in the chest.

As soon as it was dark, William covered the glowing embers with ashes. William and his wife climbed into bed, and the boys climbed onto the table to sleep. William smiled. He thought of the new house, and it was just like the one he grew up in, his father's house, in England.

The days grew longer, and soon it was summer.

"It is hotter here than at home in England," said William.

258

Access Content/Build Background Point out words like *trenchers, noggin, cider, embers, barrels, spoil,* and *cellar.* Explain the use of old words like *trenchers* and *noggin* and discuss how all these words depict life in colonial New England. Have students share what they imagine life was like then.

The barrels of pork began to spoil, and the root vegetables began to sprout.

"Something must be done," said his wife, "or we'll have no food!"

So William dug a hole deep in the cool earth behind the house. He moved the barrels and the vegetables into the new cellar. **4 5 6**

SKILLS ⟷ STRATEGIES IN CONTEXT

Character (REVIEW)

TEACH

- Remind students that authors don't always tell us everything about a character; often, we have to find clues in the story that tell us what a character is like or what may cause him or her to act a certain way in the future.

- Model using clues on pp. 258–259 to understand what kind of character William is.

Think Aloud

MODEL I know William works a lot. He builds his family's house by himself, using only the materials available to him. I think he misses his home in England, though, because it says twice that he thinks about his father's house and wants a house just like it. I think he takes good care of his family too. When his wife asks him to do something, he does it right away.

PRACTICE AND ASSESS

- Have students discuss how they think William might handle future problems based on what we know about his character. (*Possible response: He would solve them as best as he could.*)

- To assess, use Practice Book 3.1, p. 96.

Develop Vocabulary

PRACTICE LESSON VOCABULARY

Have students answer each question.

1. **What did William use to hold the wood for his house in place?** (pegs)
2. **What happened to the meat that was not kept cool?** (It spoiled.)
3. **Is a *cellar* above ground or underground?** (underground)

BUILD CONCEPT VOCABULARY

Review previous concept words with students. Ask if students have met any words today in their reading or elsewhere that they would like to add to the Concept Web.

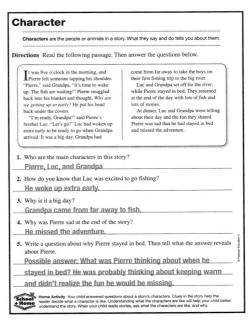

Character

Characters are the people or animals in a story. What they say and do tells you about them.

Directions Read the following passage. Then answer the questions below.

It was five o'clock in the morning, and Pierre felt someone tapping his shoulder. "Pierre," said Grandpa, "it's time to wake up. The fish are waiting!" Pierre snuggled back into his blanket and thought, *Why are we getting up so early?* He put his head back under the covers.

"I'm ready, Grandpa!" said Pierre's brother Luc. "Let's go!" Luc had woken up extra early to be ready to go when Grandpa arrived. It was a big day. Grandpa had come from far away to take the boys on their first fishing trip to the big river.

Luc and Grandpa set off for the river, while Pierre stayed in bed. They returned at the end of the day with lots of fish and lots of stories.

At dinner, Luc and Grandpa were telling about their day and the fun they shared. Pierre was sad that he had stayed in bed and missed the adventure.

1. Who are the main characters in this story?
   Pierre, Luc, and Grandpa

2. How do you know that Luc was excited to go fishing?
   He woke up extra early.

3. Why is it a big day?
   Grandpa came from far away to fish.

4. Why was Pierre sad at the end of the story?
   He missed the adventure.

5. Write a question about why Pierre stayed in bed. Then tell what the answer reveals about Pierre.
   Possible answer: What was Pierre thinking about when he stayed in bed? He was probably thinking about keeping warm and didn't realize the fun he would be missing.

School + Home **Home Activity** Your child answered questions about a story's characters. Clues like will help your child decide what a character is like. Understanding what the characters are like will help your child better understand the story. When your child reads stories, ask what the characters are like, and why.

▲ **Practice Book 3.1** p. 96

William's House **259**

Guiding Comprehension

7  **Draw Conclusions • Inferential**

How does William respond to the problems presented by the different climate? What does this tell you about William?

For every problem that comes up, William finds a solution. This shows that he is inventive, hard-working, and determined to make their lives work in the new land.

Monitor Progress	
Draw Conclusions	
If... students have difficulty drawing conclusions,	**then...** use the skill and strategy lesson on p. 261.

8 **Cause and Effect • Critical**

Text to World **The climate and the environment of New England are forcing William to change how his home looks. Think of the ways in which the environment and the climate affect the kinds of buildings we build and how we live today. In what ways have we forced the environment and the climate to change to meet our needs?**

Possible response: We use air conditioners and heating systems now.

In August, the winds started to blow.

"It is windier here than at home in England," said William.

A strong gust blew a tree down near the house. "Something must be done," said his wife, "or we'll be crushed!"

So William cut away the trees and left a large clearing all around the house.

By mid–October, the reds and oranges of autumn had turned to browns.

"It is drier here than at home in England," said William.

The sparks from the chimney landed on the dry thatch, and the roof began to smolder.

"Something must be done," said his wife, "or the house will burn!"

So William split shingles of cedar and replaced the thatch on the roof. **7** **8**

261

SKILLS ↔ STRATEGIES IN CONTEXT

Draw Conclusions

TEACH

- Tell students that when we draw conclusions, we must think about the facts and details and decide what they add up to.
- We also need to think about what we already know and use common sense to come up with information that is not stated.

Think Aloud

MODEL For every problem that comes up, William finds a solution. When he realizes it is windier in New England than he is used to and the trees could blow over on his house, he cuts down all the trees around the house. That's a lot of work! It was a smart solution too. This tells me that William is hard-working and creative. Since he doesn't give up and go back to England, I think he is also willing to do what it takes to make life work in the New World.

PRACTICE AND ASSESS

Have students find another example that tells about William and draw a conclusion. To assess, check that students' conclusions can be supported by details from the story or their own ideas.

Strategy Response Log

Check Predictions Provide the following prompt: Was your prediction accurate? Revise your old prediction or make a new prediction about the rest of the selection.

If you want to teach this selection in two sessions, stop here.

Climate

Time for SOCIAL STUDIES

In many ways, the climates of England and New England are similar. Both are described as temperate climate zones. However, New England gets both hotter in summer and colder in winter. The average summer temperature in New England is about 67°F, while in England it is closer to 60°F. The average temperature in winter in New England is 24°F, while it is warmer—about 42°F—in England. New England also gets more snow—as much as 74 inches per year—and spring is often quite windy and cool. England gets more rainfall, however, and it is typically damper.

Guiding Comprehension

If you are teaching the selection in two days, have students draw conclusions about what they have read so far and review the vocabulary.

9 🔊 **Vocabulary • Context Clues**

Use context clues to figure out the meaning of the word *steep* on p. 262.

Clues: Snow was piling up on the roof when it was not steep. Meaning: sloping

Monitor Progress	
🔊 **Context Clues**	
If... students have difficulty using context clues,	**then...** use the vocabulary strategy instruction on p. 263.

10 **Facts and Details • Literal**

Reread p. 262. Describe what you think the house looked like under all that snow.

Responses will vary; check that students understood the meaning of *sagged*.

DAY 3 Grouping Options

Reading

Whole Group Discuss the Question of the Day.

Group Time Differentiated Instruction
Read *William's House*. See pp. 250f–250g for the small group lesson plan.

Whole Group Discuss the Reader Response questions on p. 266. Then use p. 271a.

Language Arts
Use pp.271e–271h and 271k–271m.

By late November, the days were short and gray. "There is more snow here than at home in England," said William.

The snow piled higher and higher on the roof until the rafters sagged with the weight.

"Something must be done," said his wife, "or the roof will cave in!"

So William cleared the snow and removed the shingles. He built a new roof with a very steep pitch **9** and replaced the shingles. **10**

Context Clues Explain that when we come across a word we don't know, we can use context clues, or the words around the word, to figure out what the word means. Point out the word *sagged* on p. 262. Direct students' attention to the detail about the snow piling higher and higher on the roof, and William's wife's concern that the roof would cave in, or collapse. Ask students to think about what a roof with lots of heavy snow piled on top would look like. Tell students that *to sag* is to sink or bend in the middle. Have students find other words they don't know in the selection. Help them use context clues to figure out what they mean.

In January, the days were the bleakest of all.

"It is colder here than at home in England," said William.

The boys could not move their toes when they woke in the morning, and the dog could not wag his tail.

"Something must be done," said his wife, "or we'll freeze in our sleep!"

So William built a new fireplace, wider and taller, in the center of the wall.

263

 VOCABULARY STRATEGY

Context Clues

TEACH

- Tell students that when we come across a word we don't know, we can use context clues to help us figure it out.
- Context clues are the words and sentences around the word.
- Model using context clues to figure out the meaning of *steep* on p. 262.

 Think Aloud

MODEL When I come across the word *steep*, I stop to look at the words and sentences around the word. Sometimes these can help me figure out what the word means. It says William built a new roof. That doesn't tell me much, so I'll have to go back further. William's wife says the roof will cave in because of the snow piled on it. It also says the snow was piling up, so the roof must have been pretty flat. That would explain why William had to build a new roof. *Steep* must mean sloping.

PRACTICE AND ASSESS

Have students use context clues to define the word *bleakest* on p. 263. *(cold and gray)* To assess, have them use the word in a sentence of their own.

Time for SOCIAL STUDIES

Opportunity Cost

Life in seventeenth-century England was much different from life in the colonies. There were cities where people could get milk, eggs, cheese, meat, vegetables, and grains at the markets. Many homes were larger, grander, and more comfortable. People had different jobs. Friends and family were nearby, so there was always company. However, if you didn't come from a wealthy family, it was difficult to get many of the goods available, and life was hard. The New World was seen as a land of opportunity, which was why so many people, like William and his family, came here.

Guiding Comprehension

11 Sequence • Literal

William had to make several changes to his house over the course of the family's first year in the new land. In order, what were the changes, and why did he have to make them?

First, he built a cellar. Then he cleared trees. Next, he shingled the roof. Then he made the roof steeper. Finally, he built a new fireplace.

12 Draw Conclusions • Inferential

Do you think William's father would be surprised if he saw William's new house? Why or why not?

Possible response: He would probably be surprised because it does not look like the kind of house he is used to.

13 Summarize • Critical

Text to World **Write a brief summary of *William's House*. In your summary, think about how William must have felt as a newcomer to the colonies. How do you think people new to the United States today feel? What hardships do you think they face when they get here?**

Responses will vary; check students' summaries for accuracy and make sure they support their conclusions with details from the story or other stories they have read.

Strategy Response Log

Summarize When students finish reading the selection, provide this prompt: Imagine that you want to tell a friend what *William's House* is about. In four or five sentences, explain its important points.

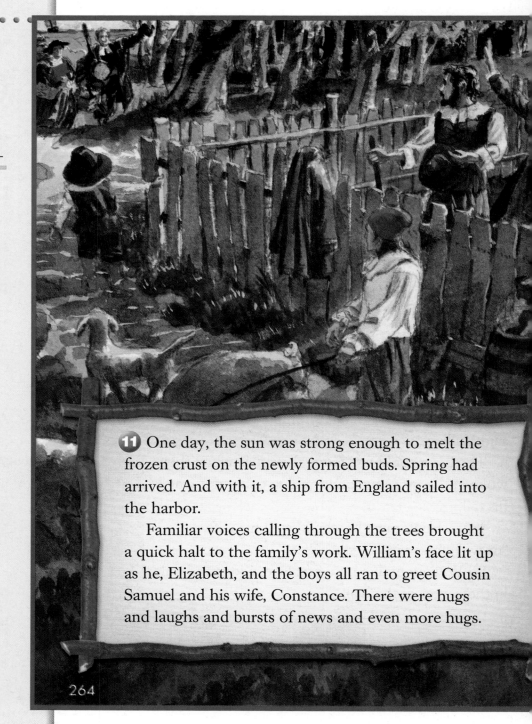

11 One day, the sun was strong enough to melt the frozen crust on the newly formed buds. Spring had arrived. And with it, a ship from England sailed into the harbor.

Familiar voices calling through the trees brought a quick halt to the family's work. William's face lit up as he, Elizabeth, and the boys all ran to greet Cousin Samuel and his wife, Constance. There were hugs and laughs and bursts of news and even more hugs.

264

And then, Cousin Samuel turned toward the clearing. "What kind of house is this?" he asked.

William turned also and took a long look at the house. The window was a piece of animal horn. The food was in a cellar. The house stood in a clearing. The roof was very steep and made of shingles. The fireplace was large and in the center of the wall. The house did not look like his father's house in England.

William looked at his wife.

Then he turned to his cousin and answered, "This is our new home. Welcome!"

They all went inside. The adults sat above the salt and the children stood below. They shared trenchers of succotash stew and passed around a noggin of cider.

265

Develop Vocabulary

PRACTICE LESSON VOCABULARY

Have students provide oral responses to each question.

1. **Where did William create a *clearing*?** (Around the house)
2. **What did William keep in the *barrels*?** (Cider)
3. **Why did William have to build a *steep* roof?** (So the snow wouldn't build up on it and cause the roof to cave in)

BUILD CONCEPT VOCABULARY

Review previous concept words with students. Ask if students have met any words today in their reading or elsewhere that they would like to add to the Concept Web.

Ask Questions

Tell students that when we have finished reading, it is a good idea to think about any questions we have about the story and go back and try to find the answers. This helps us understand what we have read.

If we can't find the answers, we can usually think about what we already know and draw our own conclusions.

Have students write at least one question they have about the story and draw a conclusion.

SELF-CHECK

Students can ask these questions to assess their ability to use the skill and strategy.

- Do my questions help me understand the story better?
- Does my conclusion make sense?
- Can I back up my conclusion with information from the selection or reasons of my own?

Monitor Progress
Draw Conclusions
If... students have difficulty drawing conclusions, / **then...** use the Reteach lesson on p. 271b.

Draw Conclusions · Ask Questions

- A **conclusion** is a decision you reach after you think about details and facts and then think about **what you already know** to help **draw conclusions.**
- As you read, ask yourself why certain things happen or why characters act as they do. You may be able to **draw conclusions** about them.

Directions Read the following passage. Then answer the questions below.

My friends and I formed a game club, but we needed a place to meet. We decided to use some leftover lumber from my backyard to build a tree house. We hauled wood up a ladder to the highest branches, and then we started to pound nails to make the floor.

"What are you doing?" screeched Mom. "Get down!" Fortunately, Dad decided to help us. He got the floorboards straight and secure, and then he put up walls and a roof. Finally, we had our game room.

1. Why do you think the club didn't meet at someone's house?
   They probably wanted to be alone or have their own place.

2. Why do you think Mom wanted the friends to get down?
   She might have been afraid they would get hurt.

3. Why might Dad have decided to help the friends?
   He wanted them to have a safe tree house.

4. Do you think the following is a valid conclusion? Explain your reasons.
   The tree house is a safe tree house.
   yes, because the dad helped to build it

5. Write a question you might ask about the friends hauling wood up the tree. Then tell how you could use the answer to draw a conclusion.
   Possible answers: Did anyone get hurt? I could conclude that what they were doing was dangerous.

Home Activity Your child answered questions that required drawing conclusions. We all draw conclusions as we read by using facts and details in the story and our own experiences. When your child reads, ask questions such as the ones above. Also ask your child to give reasons for any conclusions drawn.

▲ **Practice Book 3.1** p. 97

Reader Response

Open for Discussion Personal Response

 Think Aloud **MODEL** New England is hotter in the summer and colder and snowier in the winter than England. William had to make changes to his house in order to survive.

Comprehension Check Critical Response

1. Responses will vary, but some details include the use of dialogue, the characters' problems, and the illustrations. **Author's Purpose**

2. Possible response: They looked different from the houses in England. **Draw Conclusions**

3. Possible response: I asked questions about words I didn't know, so I understood the story better. **Ask Questions**

4. *Clearing*: so trees wouldn't fall on his house; *pegs*: hung clothes on them; *cellar*: stored food in it; *barrels*: kept food and cider in them. **Vocabulary**

 Look Back and Write For test practice, assign a 10–15 minute time limit. For assessment, see the Scoring Rubric at the right.

Retell

Have students retell *William's House.*

Monitor Progress
Check Retelling [Rubric 4 3 2 1]

If... students have difficulty retelling the story,	then... use the Retelling Cards and the Scoring Rubric for Retelling on p. 267 to assist fluent retelling.

SUCCESS PREDICTOR

Check Retelling Have students use illustrations and other text features to guide their retellings. Let students listen to other retellings before attempting their own. See the ELL and Transition Handbook.

Reader Response

Open for Discussion William's house isn't quite the way he planned it. Tell why.

1. This story happened more than 300 years ago. Still, some readers may feel as if they know William, his family, and his house. How have the author and the artist helped give that feeling? **Think Like an Author**

2. Knowing the changes that William made to his new house, what could you say about houses built in the new land? **Draw Conclusions**

3. As you read, what questions did you ask, and how did they help you better understand the selection? **Ask Questions**

4. William used a *clearing, pegs,* a *cellar,* and *barrels* to solve problems in his new home. Make a list. Write each word and tell how William used the item. **Vocabulary**

 Look Back and Write Look back at page 262. What did William do to keep the roof from caving in? Use details from the selection to write your answer. Draw a diagram if it will help your explanation.

Meet author Ginger Howard on page 412.

Scoring Rubric | Look Back and Write

Top-Score Response A top-score response will use details from p. 262 to tell what William does to keep the roof from caving in.

Example of a Top-Score Response So much snow was piled on William's roof that the rafters started to sag. William cleared the snow from the roof and took the shingles off. Then he built a new roof with steep sides. The snow would fall off the slanted roof.

For additional rubrics, see p. WA10.

Write Now

Explanatory Paragraph

Prompt

In *William's House*, special features make a house suitable for its environment. Think about the features that help your home fit into its environment. Now write an explanatory paragraph about those features.

Writing Trait

In an explanatory paragraph, **focus** on your main **idea** and support it with facts.

Student Model

Main idea is stated in first sentence.

> We live in a house built for the Arizona desert. Summer days are hot, but air conditioning keeps our house cool. We have thick walls made of stucco. This keeps warm air inside in winter and cool air inside in summer. Our floors are made of tiles. They feel cool on bare feet, even on hot summer days. We have a big patio. Fresh breezes blow across it on summer evenings, so we sit there to keep cool. Winter nights get chilly, so we have a cozy fireplace in our living room. Our house fits perfectly in the Arizona desert.

Writer stays <u>focused</u> on main <u>idea</u> and uses facts to support that idea.

Last sentence sums up main idea.

Use the model to help you write your own explanatory paragraph.

267

Write Now

Look at the Prompt Explain that each sentence in the prompt has a purpose.

- Sentence 1 presents a topic.
- Sentence 2 suggests students think about the topic.
- Sentence 3 tells what to write.

Strategies to Develop Focus/Ideas

Have students

- draw a picture of their home and discuss its features with a partner.
- list details about the environment.
- use specific details to describe a home.

NO: things to raise the house up

YES: tall stilts to keep the house from flooding

For additional suggestions and rubric, see pp. 271g–271h.

Writer's Checklist

☑ **Focus** Do all sentences stick to the topic?

☑ **Organization** Are ideas in order? Do transitions, such as so, show connections between ideas?

☑ **Support** Do details give readers information and help them picture the topic?

☑ **Conventions** Are grammar, punctuation, and spelling correct?

Scoring Rubric — Narrative Retelling

Rubric 4 3 2 1	4	3	2	1
Connections	Makes connections and generalizes beyond the text	Makes connections to other events, stories, or experiences	Makes a limited connection to another event, story, or experience	Makes no connection to another event, story, or experience
Author's Purpose	Elaborates on author's purpose	Tells author's purpose with some clarity	Makes some connection to author's purpose	Makes no connection to author's purpose
Characters	Describes the main character(s) and any character development	Identifies the main character(s) and gives some information about them	Inaccurately identifies some characters or gives little information about them	Inaccurately identifies the characters or gives no information about them
Setting	Describes the time and location	Identifies the time and location	Omits details of time or location	Is unable to identify time or location
Plot	Describes the problem, goal, events, and ending using rich detail	Tells the problem, goal, and ending with some errors that do not affect meaning	Tells parts of the problem, goal, events, and ending with gaps that affect meaning	Retelling has no sense of story

Retelling Plan

☑ **Week 1** Assess Strategic Intervention students.

☑ **Week 2** Assess Advanced students.

☑ **Week 3** Assess Strategic Intervention students.

☑ **Week 4** Assess On-Level students.

☑ **This week assess any students you have not yet checked during this unit.**

Use the Retelling Chart on p. TR16 to record retelling.

Selection Test To assess with *Williams House*, use Selection Tests, pp. 37–40.

Fresh Reads for Differentiated Test Practice For weekly leveled practice, use pp. 55–60.

Retelling

SUCCESS PREDICTOR

Social Studies in Reading

OBJECTIVES
- Examine features of expository nonfiction.
- Practice a test-taking strategy.
- Compare and contrast across texts.

PREVIEW/USE TEXT FEATURES

As students preview "Log Cabins," discuss the photographs and graphics and what they tell about the selection. After they preview, ask:

- **How do the photographs in the selection help you understand the facts?** *(Possible response: They help me visualize what the author is writing about.)*

- **What does the time line on p. 271 tell you?** *(the order in which events related to the time period in the selection occurred)*

Link to Social Studies

Help students use reference materials such as encyclopedias and the Internet. Encourage them to take notes that they can use to tell the class what they learned.

DAY 4 Grouping Options

Reading

Whole Group Discuss the Question of the Day.

Group Time Differentiated Instruction
Read "Log Cabins." See pp. 250f–250g for the small group lesson plan.

Whole Group Use pp. 271a and 271j.

Language Arts
Use pp.271e–271h and 271k–271m.

Social Studies in Reading

Expository Nonfiction

Genre
- **Expository nonfiction explains facts about objects or ideas.**
- **It often requires careful reading.**

Text Features
- **Photographs with captions are often included to help the reader understand.**
- **Graphics, such as a time line, sometimes provide additional information.**

Link to Social Studies
Use the library or the Internet to research log cabins. Find out about the inside of log cabins.

LOG Cabins
by Marlene Perez

This log cabin in Nebraska in 1886 had a sod roof.

268

Content-Area Vocabulary   Social Studies

loft	a low room under the roof of a house
logs	long pieces of wood cut from tree trunks or large branches
lumber	wood cut into boards or planks
notched	marked with a v-shaped cut

When people moved west in the 1800s, there were no houses or towns or shops. They couldn't bring many supplies along when they journeyed into the wild. They had to think of ways to build houses using what was around them.

Settlers from Europe built the first log cabins in the United States. These were square, one-room cabins. To add more room, a loft with a ladder might be added. Some cabins were made of round logs. Settlers closed the space between the logs with mud, shells from the river, or even cow manure.

Ask Questions What questions did you have as you read this page?

269

Natural Resources

Time for
SOCIAL STUDIES

The first settlers to arrive in the colonies had to use what was available to make their homes. Great forests covered much of New England, so there was plenty of wood. In fact everything, from the house to the furnishings to the plates and utensils, was made of wood. There was no glass for windows. Rather, settlers had to use paper soaked in oil. Later homes were also made of stone which was plentiful. Native vegetation, such as maize and flax, was used for bedding and clothing.

EXPOSITORY NONFICTION

Use the sidebar on p. 268 to guide discussion.

- Expository nonfiction is nonfiction writing of any length which gives information about many different topics.
- It is based on facts and often includes technical vocabulary and graphics that relate to the topic.
- Discuss how the photographs, graphics, and captions can help with understanding the selection.

Audio CD   AudioText

Ask Questions

Responses will vary; check that students' questions relate to the topic. Students' questions may or may not be answered in the selection, but encourage them to look for an answer.

ELL

Build Background Students may or may not be familiar with early American history. Explain that when the first European settlers arrived in the New World, they had very few belongings and were forced to use what was available to build homes and survive. The same was true for the early pioneers who left the colonies and headed west. Discuss with students what resources the settlers and pioneers would have had to use and how they might have used them. Review the vocabulary words on p. 268 and encourage students to use them in their discussion.

Strategies for Nonfiction

USE PHOTOGRAPHS Explain that students may be asked to read expository nonfiction and answer questions about it on standardized tests. Often, there are photographs or illustrations that go along with this kind of nonfiction. The photographs and graphics may show what something described in the selection looked like, so you can see it and better understand. Provide the following strategy.

Use the Strategy

1. Before reading, scan the photographs or illustrations and graphics and read any captions that go with them. Think about what information they give.

2. While you are reading, pay attention to what the photographs or graphics may tell you.

3. When you are finished reading, look again at the photos or illustrations and graphics and use them to help you understand what you have read.

GUIDED PRACTICE Have students discuss how they would use the strategy to answer the following question.

Explain how the log cabin in the photograph on pp. 268–269 was probably built.

INDEPENDENT PRACTICE After students answer the following test question, discuss the process they used to find information.

What is an *auger* and how was it used?

An auger like this one is used for making holes in wood.

Later, cabins were made with logs cut to fit together better. The logs were cut flat and the ends were notched. The logs were stacked in an interlocking pattern. This made the houses sturdier and easier to build.

Flat logs were notched at the ends. They fit together tightly.

Settlers made do with what they had available. Some log cabins had roofs made of grass sod or cedar planks. Log cabin floors and chimneys were

made of stone or rock, which settlers found in the wilderness. Some cabins had floors of dirt, which had been pounded flat. Other floors were made of logs that were laid flat. These log floors were called *puncheons*.

In 1862, a law was passed that gave settlers a piece of land for free if they would build a house, live there, and farm the land for five years. The log cabin was a good choice for a home. It could be built quickly. Trees from the forests could be used for logs. A log cabin didn't need nails, which were expensive and hard to find. Settlers could build a log cabin using a few simple tools, such as an ax and an auger.

When the railroad grew and pushed its way west, people could then buy lumber from mills. Wood-framed houses

270

Test Practice Look through the selection at the photographs and graphics with students. Discuss what they see and what they think each image is about. Then have them read the selection. When they are finished reading, have them look back at the photographs and graphics and tell how they relate to the selection. Have them answer the Guided and Independent Practice questions and discuss how they used the photographs and graphics.

1804
Lewis and
Clark begin
exploration.

1842
Pioneers travel
Oregon Trail
westward.

1830
Work begins
on railroads.

1869
Transcontinental
railroad
is finished.

1862
Law passed to give
settlers free land.

replaced log cabins. Often,
homeowners tore down the
cabins and reused the lumber
to build bigger houses.

Over the years, American
homes changed from
one-room cabins to larger,
sturdier buildings. But
because of the clever way
it was first made, the log
cabin will always be a symbol
of American creativity.

Reading Across Texts

When it was finished,
how was William's house
different from the early log
cabins you read about in
this article?

Writing Across Texts

Write a short paragraph
telling which house
you would rather live
in and why.

Draw Conclusions What happened to log cabins after the railroad came?

271

CONNECT TEXT TO TEXT

Reading Across Texts

Look back at *William's House* and discuss what
it looked like and how William made it. Compare
it to "Log Cabins." Jot students' ideas on the
board for reference.

Writing Across Texts Remind students to
use details from either or both texts in their
paragraphs.

Draw Conclusions

They became less common; many were probably
replaced with sturdier, larger, more comfortable
homes.

ELL

Access Content Use toy logs, craft sticks, or
branches to demonstrate the following words: *notched,
stacked, interlocking,* and *planks.* Or use the photograph
on p. 270 to make sure students understand how a
cabin could be built without nails.

Fluency Assessment Plan

☑ **Week 1** Assess Advanced students.
☑ **Week 2** Assess Strategic Intervention students.
☑ **Week 3** Assess On-Level students.
☑ **Week 4** Assess Strategic Intervention students.
☑ **This week assess any students you have not yet checked during this unit.**

Set individual goals for students to enable them to reach the year-end goal.
• Current Goal: 85–95 wcpm
• Year-End Goal: 120 wcpm

 To develop fluent readers, use Fluency Coach.

MORE READING FOR
Fluency

To practice fluency with text comprised of previously taught phonics elements and irregular words, use Decodable Reader 10.

DAY 5 Grouping Options

Reading
Whole Group
Revisit the Question of the Week.

Group Time
Differentiated Instruction
Reread this week's Leveled Readers. See pp. 250f–250g for the small group lesson plan.

Whole Group
Use pp. 271b–271c.

Language Arts
Use pp. 271d–271h and 271k–271n.

SILENTLY
Fluency

DAY 1

Model Reread "Colonial Homes" on p. 250m. Explain that you will self correct when you make a mistake or if something does not make sense as you read the selection. Model for students as you read.

DAY 2

Silent Reading Read aloud p. 258. Reread the first paragraph. Have students notice how you self correct if something does not make sense to you the first time. Have students practice reading p. 258 silently.

DAY 3

Model Read p. 261. Read two or three words incorrectly and model how to self correct. Have class read p. 261 silently three times. Encourage them to self correct if they make a mistake.

DAY 4

Choral Reading Practice choral reading "The Sure-Footed Shoe Finder," p. 273, three times.

Monitor Progress   Check Fluency WCPM

As students reread, monitor their progress toward their individual fluency goals. Current Goal: 85–95 words correct per minute. End-of-Year Goal: 120 words correct per minute.

If… students cannot read fluently at a rate of 85–95 words correct per minute,
then… make sure students practice with text at their independent level. Provide additional fluency practice, pairing nonfluent readers with fluent readers.

If… students already read at 120 words correct per minute,
then… they do not need to reread three to four times.

SUCCESS PREDICTOR

DAY 5

Assessment
Individual Reading Rate Use the Fluency Assessment Plan and do a one-minute timed reading of either selection from this week to assess students in Week 5. Pay special attention to this week's skill, reading silently. Provide corrective feedback for each student.

RETEACH

◎ Draw Conclusions

TEACH

Review the skill instruction for drawing conclusions on p. 250. Students can complete Practice Book 3.1, p. 98 on their own, or you can complete it as a class. Point out that some of the circles in the draw conclusions graphic organizer are empty. Remind students that they must fill in the circles with information from the passage.

ASSESS

Have students reread pp. 256–257. Tell them that the colonists were not able to bring many tools with them. Point out that some tools were necessary, however. Ask pairs of students to work together to draw conclusions about the kinds of tools that William must have brought with him. *(Possible response: William must have had an ax, a saw, and a knife.)*

For additional instruction of draw conclusions, see DI·56.

EXTEND SKILLS

Facts and Details

TEACH

Facts are pieces of information that can be proven true. Details are small bits of information.

- Identifying facts and details can help us answer questions about a selection.
- Details also enable us to visualize, or see, what we are reading.
- Facts and details help us draw conclusions, make generalizations, compare and contrast, recognize cause and effect, and so on.

Point out the details on pp. 256–257 that help us draw a conclusion about the things William used to build his house. *(William cut down trees and cut the trees into boards; he used clay and stones to make a fireplace; he used wooden pegs for nails, he scraped an animal horn to become a window.)*

ASSESS

Have students use details on p. 264 to draw a conclusion about how the family felt when they saw their relatives.

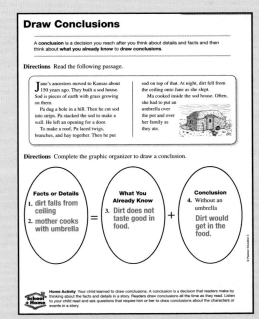

Vocabulary and Word Study

VOCABULARY STRATEGY
◎Context Clues

UNFAMILIAR WORDS Remind students that they can use context clues to determine the meaning of unfamiliar words. Have students list any unknown words they encountered as they read *William's House*. They can create a chart showing the unknown word, helpful context clues, and their definition of the word based on its context. Students can confirm word meanings using a dictionary.

Word	Context Clues	Meaning
rafters	to hold the thatch roof	the base of a roof that holds the covering material
translucent		
smolder		

House Words

House words, such as *chimney*, refer to parts of a house or things in a house. Have partners draw pictures of houses they would like to live in. Then they can use reference sources to label parts of the house.

Some House Words

roof: kitchen:

cellar: fireplace:

basement: stove:

attic: ceiling:

windows: foyer:

BUILD CONCEPT VOCABULARY
Housing Problems

LOOKING BACK Remind students of the unit theme: Smart Solutions. Discuss the unit focus question: What are smart ways that problems are solved? Ask students how the Concept Vocabulary from each week of this unit relates to the unit theme and unit focus question. Ask students whether they have any words or categories to add. If time permits, create a Unit Concept Web.

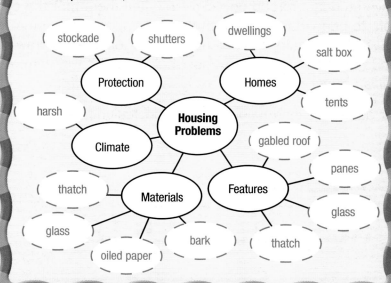

Monitor Progress

Check Vocabulary

If... students suggest words or categories that are not related to the concept,	then... review the words and categories on the Concept Web and discuss how they relate to the lesson concept.

SUCCESS PREDICTOR

Speaking and Viewing

SPEAKING

Speak to Communicate Needs

SET-UP Have students use information in *William's House* to help them talk about the needs that William's family had. Encourage students to include facts about how William met these needs.

ORGANIZATION Tell students to begin their speeches with an interesting statement about William's house. Suggest that students then identify the family's needs. Remind students to distinguish between wants and needs. Provide time for students to rehearse their speeches aloud. Share these organization suggestions:

- Open with an interesting statement.
- Share William's family's needs.
- Next, offer facts about why those needs are important.
- Use transition words and phrases, such as *but, instead, neither,* and *on the other hand.*
- Conclude with a short summary.

Listening Tips

- Identify the speaker's opinions.
- Listen for facts.
- Evaluate the speaker's message.

VIEWING

Recognize Opinion

Play a video excerpt of *Little House on the Prairie* or another dramatized work of fiction about pioneer life. Remind students to monitor their comprehension as they view the video. With partners, students can answer these questions orally or in writing.

1. **Who is the speaker?** *(Responses will vary.)*

2. **What are some facts that Laura tells us?** *(Responses will vary.)*

3. **What are some of Laura's opinions?** *(Responses will vary.)*

Support Vocabulary Use the following to review and extend vocabulary and to explore lesson concepts further:
- ELL Poster 10, Days 3–5 instruction
- Vocabulary Activities and Word Cards in ELL Teaching Guide, pp. 66–67

Assessment For information on assessing students' speaking, listening, and viewing, see the ELL and Transition Handbook.

Check Vocabulary

SUCCESS PREDICTOR

Grammar   Plural Possessive Nouns

Monitor Progress

Grammar

If... students have difficulty identifying plural possessive nouns,	then... provide additional instruction and practice in The Grammar and Writing Book pp. 104–107.

DAILY FIX-IT

This week use Daily Fix-It Transparency 10.

Spiral REVIEW

ELL

Support Grammar See the Grammar Transition lessons in the ELL and Transition Handbook.

▲ **The Grammar and Writing Book**
For more instruction and practice, use pp. 104–109.

DAY 1   Teach and Model

DAILY FIX-IT

1. The Inglish settlers had the first thanksgiving. *(English; Thanksgiving)*

2. The childrens toys were made of would. *(children's; wood)*

READING-GRAMMAR CONNECTION

Write this sentence about *William's House* on the board:

> The English families' houses were different in America.

Explain that *families'* is a **plural possessive noun.** It is used to show that two or more people share or own something. An apostrophe is added to plural nouns that end in *-s, -es,* or *-ies* to make them possessive.

Display Grammar Transparency 10. Read aloud the definitions and sample sentences. Work through the items.

Plural Possessive Nouns

To show that two or more people share or own something, use a **plural possessive noun.**

Plural Noun	The <u>trees</u> grew tall in America.
Singular Possessive Noun	That oak <u>tree's</u> wood is hard.
Plural Possessive Noun	All the <u>trees'</u> wood was strong.

Add an apostrophe (') to plural nouns that end in -s, -es, or -ies to make them possessive. To make plural nouns that do not end in -s, -es, or -ies possessive, add an apostrophe and an s.

<u>men   men's</u> boots   <u>oxen   oxen's</u> strength

Directions Write the plural possessive noun in each sentence.

1. The two towns' settlers gathered to celebrate the harvest. **towns'**
2. The settlers' tables were long boards. **settlers'**
3. The vegetables' flavors were delicious. **vegetables'**
4. The cooks' dishes smelled spicy. **cooks'**
5. Men's mouths watered at the smell. **Men's**

Directions Write the possessive form of the underlined plural noun in each sentence.

6. The <u>colonies</u> schools taught reading and arithmetic. **colonies'**
7. <u>Americans</u> roads were dusty paths. **Americans'**
8. Horses pulled <u>farmers</u> carts and wagons. **farmers'**
9. The <u>horses</u> jobs were difficult. **horses'**
10. <u>Oxen</u> size made them a better choice for the job. **Oxen's**

Unit 2 William's House   Grammar **10**

▲ **Grammar Transparency** 10

DAY 2   Develop the Concept

DAILY FIX-IT

3. The colonys had cold wether. *(colonies; weather)*

4. The two boys's cloths were not warm enough. *(boys'; clothes)*

GUIDED PRACTICE

Review the concept of plural possessive nouns.

- A **plural possessive noun** shows that two or more people share or own something.

- To make plural nouns that end in *-s, -es,* or *-ies* possessive, add an apostrophe. To make plural nouns that do not end in *-s, -es,* or *-ies* possessive, add an apostrophe and an *s.*

HOMEWORK Grammar and Writing Practice Book p. 37. Work through the first two items with the class.

Plural Possessive Nouns

To show that two or more people share or own something, use a **plural possessive noun.**

Plural Noun	The families built houses.
Singular Possessive Noun	The family's house was made of wood.
Plural Possessive Noun	Most families' houses had big fireplaces.

Add an apostrophe (') to plural nouns that end in -s, -es, or -ies to make them possessive. To make plural nouns that do not end in -s, -es, or -ies possessive, add an apostrophe and an s.

children   children's toys   women   women's books

Directions Write the plural possessive noun in each sentence.

1. With the Indians' help, colonists planted gardens. **Indians'**
2. The gardens' crops included corn and beans. **gardens'**
3. The Americans' first Thanksgiving was special. **Americans'**
4. The settlers' first winters were hard. **settlers'**
5. England's winters were cold, but the colonies' weather was harsher. **colonies'**

Directions Write the possessive form of the underlined plural noun in each sentence.

6. British <u>companies</u> ships brought settlers to America. **companies'**
7. The <u>ships</u> conditions were not good. **ships'**
8. Children illnesses were sometimes fatal. **Children's**
9. <u>Doctors</u> treatments were not very helpful. **Doctors'**
10. The <u>travelers</u> hard journey finally ended in America. **travelers'**

Home Activity Your child learned about plural possessive nouns. Name some families in your neighborhood. Have your child make up sentences using the plural possessive form of each noun, such as The Smiths' dog likes to play ball.

▲ **Grammar and Writing Practice Book** p. 37

DAY 3 — Apply to Writing

5. The children's school have onely one room. *(has (or had); only)*

6. The first Americans's fashons were very different from those of today. *(Americans'; fashions)*

USE POSSESSIVE NOUNS

Explain that using plural possessive nouns can make writing less wordy.

Wordy: The houses of the first Americans were very simple.

Not Wordy: The first Americans' houses were very simple.

- Have students review something they have written to see if they can make it less wordy by using plural possessive nouns.

HOMEWORK Grammar and Writing Practice Book p. 38.

Plural Possessive Nouns

Directions Write sentences about life in America in the 1600s. Use the plural possessive form of each noun in your sentence. **Possible answers:**

1. farm
   The farms' crops were corn and wheat.

2. tree   The trees' wood was the main building material for the colonists.

3. house
   The houses' fireplaces kept families warm.

4. settler
   The settlers' skills were needed for building houses.

5. colony
   The colonies' houses were warm and comfortable.

Directions Write a sentence about something you would have liked about colonial life. Then write a sentence about something you would not have liked. Use at least one plural possessive noun in each sentence. **Possible answers:**

6. I would have liked the early Americans' Thanksgiving.

7. I would not have liked the colonists' illnesses.

 Home Activity Your child learned how to use plural possessive nouns in writing. After watching a movie or TV program, have your child write a sentence about the show that uses at least one plural possessive noun.

▲ **Grammar and Writing Practice Book** p. 38

DAY 4 — Test Preparation

7. His fathers' house was prettyer than his house. *(father's; prettier)*

8. The family was surprised by november's sun shine. *(November's; sunshine)*

STANDARDIZED TEST PREP

Test Tip

Think about how a possessive noun is used in a sentence. Then decide whether it is singular or plural and place the apostrophe correctly.

Plural Possessive Noun: The houses' kitchens had fireplaces.

Singular Possessive Noun: The house's kitchen had a fireplace.

HOMEWORK Grammar and Writing Practice Book p. 39.

Plural Possessive Nouns

Directions Mark the letter of the correct singular or plural possessive noun to complete each sentence.

1. Most of the ____ land was full of trees.
   - A colonys'
   - B colonie's
   - C colonys's
   - (D) colonies'

2. ____ colony was the first in America.
   - A Virginias'
   - (B) Virginia's
   - C Virginias's
   - D Virginia'

3. The ____ hard work cleared the swamp.
   - (A) men's
   - B mens'
   - C mens
   - D men

4. They built their ____ homes of wood.
   - A families
   - (B) families'
   - C familys's
   - D familys'

5. Those early ____ crops saved the colony.
   - (A) farmers'
   - B farmer's
   - C farmers's
   - D farmer'

6. The ____ lives were full.
   - A colonist's
   - (B) colonists'
   - C colonists's
   - D colonist'

7. The ____ help was needed too.
   - A children'
   - B children
   - C childrens's
   - (D) children's

8. ____ colonists worked hard.
   - (A) New England's
   - B New Englands'
   - C New Englands's
   - D New England'

9. The ____ hard work made them successful.
   - A women
   - B womens'
   - (C) women's
   - D womens's

10. The ____ populations soon grew.
    - A cities
    - B citys'
    - (C) cities'
    - D city'

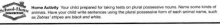 **Home Activity** Your child prepared for taking tests on plural possessive nouns. Name some kinds of animals. Have your child write sentences using the plural possessive form of each animal name, such as *Zebras'* stripes are black and white.

▲ **Grammar and Writing Practice Book** p. 39

DAY 5 — Cumulative Review

9. Is Autumn colorful in England. *(autumn; England?)*

10. Both the trees's leaves has fallen. *(trees'; have)*

ADDITIONAL PRACTICE

Assign pp. 104–107 in The Grammar and Writing Book.

EXTRA PRACTICE Grammar and Writing Practice Book p. 131.

TEST PREPARATION Grammar and Writing Practice Book pp. 153–154.

ASSESSMENT

CUMULATIVE REVIEW Grammar and Writing Practice Book p. 40.

Plural Possessive Nouns

Directions Write the correct possessive noun in ( ) to complete each sentence.

1. The early (house', houses') furniture was simple.
   houses'

2. The early (Americans, Americans') meals often included corn.
   Americans'

3. The (kitchens', kitchens's) fireplaces served many purposes.
   kitchens'

4. The (colonists, colonists') clothing was simple too.
   colonists'

Directions Write the possessive form of the underlined plural noun in each sentence.

5. The colonies fish and wildlife provided much food.
   colonies'

6. Women jobs included cooking and sewing.
   Women's

7. Children games included leapfrog and hopscotch.
   Children's

Directions How is your home like that of an American colonist? Write a sentence to answer. Use at least one plural possessive noun. **Possible answer:**

8. My home is like early Americans' homes because it has a fireplace.

 **Home Activity** Your child reviewed plural possessive nouns. Name three things you and your child saw or bought on a recent shopping trip. Have your child spell the plural possessive form of each item name.

▲ **Grammar and Writing Practice Book** p. 40

Writing for Tests. Explanatory Paragraph

OBJECTIVES

- Write an explanatory paragraph for a test.
- Identify key words in a prompt.
- Focus on focus/ideas.
- Use a rubric.

Genre Explanatory Paragraph
Writer's Craft Use Precise Words
Writing Trait Focus/Ideas

Focus/Ideas Write the following sentences on sheets of paper, one to a sheet. Work with English learners to identify the sentence that doesn't belong: Books can be about anything. Libraries have many books. We will swim after lunch. I read many books this summer.

Writing Trait

FOCUS/IDEAS Details are carefully chosen facts based on what the audience needs to know.

ORGANIZATION/PARAGRAPHS The paragraph begins with a topic sentence that communicates the paragraph's main idea. The last sentence clearly concludes the paragraph.

VOICE The writer shows knowledge of the facts.

WORD CHOICE The writer uses precise words to communicate facts clearly.

SENTENCES The paragraph includes both simple and compound sentences.

CONVENTIONS There is excellent control and accuracy.

DAY 1 — Model the Trait

READING-WRITING CONNECTION

- When you write a response for tests, remember that including only relevant details will strengthen your answer.
- Think about how the author uses words precisely in *William's House* to describe the house William built.

MODEL FOCUS/IDEAS Discuss Writing Transparency 10A. Point out underlined words in the prompt. Then discuss the model and the writing trait of focus/ideas.

 Think Aloud The writer focuses on the schedule of third-grade students during the day. All the sentences relate to third graders. A detail such as what fourth graders are doing during a particular time or how long Ms. Perez has been a teacher would take away from the focus.

Writing for Tests

Prompt Suppose you are introducing a new student to your school. What important facts about your school would you explain to him or her? Write an explanatory paragraph to a new student telling what he or she should know.

Life at McKinley School

First sentence is a topic sentence that tells what the paragraph will be about.

> The third-grade class at McKinley School is a great place to learn! At 9:00 each morning Mr. Chase, the principal, makes announcements. Then third graders have reading and spelling. Then we go to lunch. You can bring your lunch, or you can buy it. (On Wednesdays, the lunchroom serves spaghetti. It's great!) After lunch we have social studies and then physical education. Then we have math and science. In late afternoon, we work on projects, such as the science fair. Sometimes we have a field trip, like to the art museum. Finally, Ms. Perez reviews our homework assignments. It's the end of another educational day at McKinley School.

Each detail is an important fact.

Conclusion shows that the paragraph is finished.

Unit 2 William's House   Writing Model **10A**

▲ **Writing Transparency** 10A

DAY 2 — Improve Writing

WRITER'S CRAFT
Use Precise Words

Display Writing Transparency 10B. Work together to replace wordy passages with precise words.

 Think Aloud **CREATE CLEAR PICTURES WITH SPECIFIC WORDS** Tomorrow we will write an **explanatory paragraph.** What words would give new students important information? I could write, "We have art class on Tuesday afternoons. We wear big, old shirts to keep paint off our good clothes." These sentences tell the specific times for art and describe what kind of shirt is needed and why.

GUIDED WRITING Some may need more help using precise words.

- Help them find sentences in the selection that use precise words.
- Work with them to improve: Ian walked carefully and quietly on his toes.

Use Precise Words

Precise words tell a writer's exact meaning. For example, the words *hut, shack, lodge, cabin,* and *mansion* give readers a better picture than *house.* Using precise words can also help you use fewer words.
Wordy The cow made a loud, angry sound.
Precise The cow bellowed.

Directions Write the sentences. Replace the underlined words with a precise word.

1. The girls laughed in a high, happy, breathless way. Possible answers:
   The girls giggled.

2. Jane and Holly walked in a slow and relaxed way around the mall.
   Jane and Holly strolled around the mall.

3. The pig made a sharp, shrill noise.
   The pig squealed.

4. Across the street from the cabin was a body of water that was smaller and calmer than a lake.
   Across the street from the cabin was a pond.

5. For the holiday, the family had a big meal with many different dishes.
   For the holiday, the family had a feast.

Unit 2 William's House   Writer's Craft **10B**

▲ **Writing Transparency** 10B

DAY 3 Prewrite and Draft

READ THE WRITING PROMPT

on p. 267 in the Student Edition. *In William's House, special features make a house suitable for its environment.*

Think about the features that help your home fit into its environment.

Now write an explanatory paragraph about those features.

Writing Test Tips

1. Read the prompt carefully.
- Find key words.
- Consider the purpose and audience. How will they affect your writing?

2. Develop a plan. Think of what you want to say before writing. Use a graphic organizer. For example, for a story, think of a beginning, middle, and end. For a comparison/contrast essay, fill out a T-chart or a Venn diagram.

3. Support your ideas. Use facts, examples, and details to strengthen your response. Avoid making general statements that are unsupported.

4. Use a variety of sentence structures. Include compound sentences, varied sentence beginnings, and different sentence lengths and types.

5. Choose clear, precise words. Use words that create pictures and help readers understand what you mean.

6. Check your writing. If this is a timed test, you may not have time to recopy your work. However, you can neatly add, delete, or change words and make corrections. It pays to read your work again before handing it in.

DAY 4 Draft and Revise

EDITING/REVISING CHECKLIST

☑ **Focus** Do precise words create pictures for readers? Are ideas supported with details?

☑ **Organization** Is information placed in a logical order?

☑ **Support** Did I use compound sentences as well as simple sentences?

☑ **Conventions** Are words with the digraphs *sh, th, ph, ch,* and *tch* spelled correctly?

See *The Grammar and Writing Book,* pp. 104–109.

Revising Tips

Focus/Ideas
- Make sure that each detail is a key fact.
- Keep in mind that your purpose is to inform readers.
- Change vague or general words to precise ones.

ASSESSMENT Use the scoring rubric to evaluate students' work.

DAY 5 Connect to Unit Writing

How-to Report

Week 1	Summary 173g–173h
Week 2	Rules 197g–197h
Week 3	Problem/Solution 223g–223h
Week 4	Feature Story 249g–249h
Week 5	Explanatory Paragraph 271g–271h

PREVIEW THE UNIT PROMPT

Think of something you learned or figured out how to do that involves a few simple steps. Write the steps in a how-to report. Make sure you provide all the necessary information.

APPLY

- A how-to report explains the steps for making or doing something.
- Use precise words to help readers understand the process and the steps of the task.

Writing Trait Rubric

	4	3	2	1
Focus/Ideas	Excellent focus with many vivid supporting details; nothing superfluous	Clear focus with some supporting details; nothing superfluous	Limited focus with a few supporting details; some unrelated details	Unfocused with little support and many unrelated details
	Excellent paragraph with interesting, well-supported main idea	Paragraph with adequately supported main idea	Sharper focus on main idea needed in paragraph	Paragraph with no clear focus or main idea

OBJECTIVES

- Associate consonant digraphs with the letters that spell them.
- Review consonant blends.
- Blend and read words that contain consonant digraphs and consonant blends.
- Apply decoding strategies: blend longer words.

Generalization

Generalization Consonant digraphs consist of two or three consonants that stand for a single sound.

ELL

Support Phonics English language learners may need extra help understanding that there is often more than one way to spell the same sound in English, such as /f/ *cough*, *phone*, and *fast*. The *th* in *think* or *those* may be especially difficult. Let students read aloud as often as possible to give them extra practice saying words with consonant digraphs.

See the Phonics Transition Lessons in the ELL and Transition Handbook.

Consonant Digraphs

Directions Write **sh, th, ph, ch, tch,** or **ng** to complete each word. Write the whole word on the line to the left.

purchased	1. Maria's family pur_ch_ased a house.
mother	2. Her mo_th_er decided to paint it.
brushes	3. She went to the store and bought bru_sh_es and buckets.
clothing	4. When she came home she put on old clo_th_ing.
patched	5. Then she pa_tch_ed the cracks and nail holes.
going	6. Maria didn't know what color her room was goi_ng_ to be.
phoned	7. She _ph_oned her friend to talk about it.
choice	8. Her friend helped Maria make the _ch_oice.
shade	9. Maria picked a beautiful _sh_ade of peach.

Directions Say the name of each picture. Write **sh, th, wh, ph, tch,** or **ng** to complete each word.

10. tro_ph_y   11. wa_tch_   12. a_th_lete

13. _wh_ale   14. swi_ng_   15. spla_sh_

Home Activity Your child wrote words with the consonants *sh* (English), *th* (father), *wh* (wheel), *ph* (trophy), *ch* (chapter), *tch* (watch), and *ng* (wing). Have your child read the words on the page above. Ask your child to change one or more letters in some of the words to form new words. For example, substituting *t* for *p* in *peach* forms *teach*.

▲ **Practice Book 3.1** p. 99

Consonant Digraphs

TEACH

Remind students that they hear all the letters in a consonant blend. Explain that they will learn about other consonant combinations that stand for a single sound. Write the words *chat, parachute, shining, bother, white, phone, catch,* and *long*.

- How many letters do you see in *chat?* (4)
- How many sounds do you *hear?* (3)
- Which two letters stand for one sound? (*ch*)

Think Aloud

MODEL When I see the letters *ch* in *chat*, I pronounce them as a single sound, /ch/, because *ch* is a consonant digraph. But when I see the same letters in the word *parachute*, I pronounce them as /sh/. The digraph *ch* can stand for different sounds, /ch/ and /sh/. I also watch for the consonant digraphs *sh, th, wh, ph, tch,* and *ng* when I sound out words.

Model blending *parachute, shining, bother, white, phone, catch,* and *long*. Then have students blend the words with you.

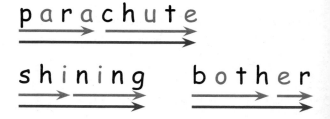

PRACTICE AND ASSESS

DECODE LONGER WORDS Write these words. Have students read them and then underline the consonant digraphs.

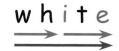 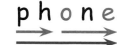

in<u>ch</u>worm   <u>ph</u>oto<u>g</u>raph   cu<u>sh</u>ion   ra<u>th</u>er

<u>th</u>imble   <u>wh</u>isper   swi<u>tch</u>   <u>ch</u>aperone

READ WORDS IN CONTEXT Write these sentences. Have individuals read them, point out words with consonant digraphs, and say the sound the letters stand for. Words with consonant digraphs are underlined.

<u>Thunder</u> scares our dog, and <u>she</u> hides under my bed.

<u>Each</u> boy let out a <u>whoop</u> of joy.

I hear a little bird <u>chirping</u> <u>beneath</u> my window.

To assess, have students identify four words on page 256 of the Student Edition that have a consonant digraph. (Possible answers: *father, thatch, fashioned, everything*.)

Review Phonics

REVIEW CONSONANT BLENDS

CONNECT Write this sentence: *Please straighten your desk.*

- We studied initial and final consonant blends.
- Read the sentence to yourself. Raise your hand when you know which words have a consonant blend. *(Please, straighten, desk)*
- What letters make up the consonant blend in please? *(pl)* In *straighten?* *(str)* In *desk?* *(sk)*

Continue in the same way with the sentence *The chi<u>ld</u> waited for the <u>tr</u>affic light to turn <u>gr</u>een before <u>cr</u>ossing the <u>str</u>eet.*

PRACTICE AND ASSESS

DECODE LONGER WORDS Have individuals read the following words. Provide help chunking and blending the words as needed.

stubborn	slightly	threaten	blend
splatter	cranberry	myself	private
classify	gratitude	stretcher	squabble

READ WORDS IN CONTEXT Have students read these sentences and write the word or words containing consonant blends on a separate sheet of paper.

I gave a <u>present</u> to my <u>brother</u> on his birthday.

<u>Practice</u> what you <u>preach</u>.

There are <u>three</u> loaves of <u>bread</u> in the <u>stove</u>.

The air was <u>crisp</u>, and <u>frost</u> <u>gleamed</u> on the <u>grass</u>.

To assess, have students read each sentence aloud. Listen to hear whether they pronounce all the consonants in the consonant blends.

Generalization

Generalization Consonant blends consist of two or more letters whose sounds are blended together when pronouncing a word.

Vocabulary TIP

You may wish to explain the meanings of these words.

stubborn	not willing to change your opinion
splatter	to splash
classify	to arrange things into groups
squabble	a noisy quarrel about nothing important

Spelling & Phonics   Digraphs *sh, th, ph, ch, tch*

OBJECTIVE

● Correctly spell words with digraphs *sh, th, ph, ch, tch.*

Generalization

Connect to Phonics Words can have two or three consonants together that are pronounced as one sound: *English, father, trophy, chapter, watch.*

Spelling Words

1. father*	9. fashion*
2. chapter	10. shrink
3. other	11. pitcher
4. alphabet	12. flash
5. watch	13. athlete
6. English	14. trophy
7. weather	15. nephew
8. catch	

Challenge Words

16. northern	19. hyphen
17. establish	20. challenge
18. emphasis	

*Words from the selection

Spelling/Phonics Support See the ELL and Transition Handbook for spelling support.

DAY 1   Pretest and Sort

PRETEST

Use the Dictation Sentences from Day 5 to administer the pretest. Read the word, read the sentence, and then read the word again. Guide students in self-correcting their pretests and correcting any misspellings.

Monitor Progress

Spelling

If... students misspell more than 4 pretest words,	then... use words 1–8 for Strategic Intervention.
If... students misspell 1–4 pretest words,	then... use words 1–15 for On-Level practice.
If... students correctly spell all pretest words,	then... use words 1–20 for Advanced Learners.

HOMEWORK Spelling Practice Book, p. 37.

Digraphs *sh, th, ph, ch, tch*

Generalization Words can have two or three consonants together that are pronounced as one sound: **English, father, trophy, chapter, watch.**

Word Sort Sort the list words by the digraphs *sh, th, ph, ch,* or *tch.*

sh
1. English
2. fashion
3. shrink
4. flash

th
5. father
6. other
7. weather
8. athlete

ph
9. alphabet
10. trophy
11. nephew

ch
12. chapter

tch
13. watch
14. catch
15. pitcher

Challenge Words

sh
16. establish

th
17. northern

ph
18. emphasis
19. hyphen

ch
20. challenge

Spelling Words
1. father
2. chapter
3. other
4. alphabet
5. watch
6. English
7. weather
8. catch
9. fashion
10. shrink
11. pitcher
12. flash
13. athlete
14. trophy
15. nephew

Challenge Words
16. northern
17. establish
18. emphasis
19. hyphen
20. challenge

School + Home Home Activity Your child is learning how to spell words with *sh, th, ph, ch,* and *tch.* To practice at home, have your child look at the word, say it, and point to the digraphs.

▲ **Spelling Practice Book** p. 37

DAY 2   Think and Practice

TEACH

Consonant digraphs can create a new sound because the letters in the digraph are pronounced together, not separately. For example, the digraph *ph* is pronounced like the letter *f*. Write each consonant digraph on the board. Have students say each digraph and then write the corresponding words underneath each digraph.

th
weather

FIND THE PATTERN Ask students to group spelling words into digraph groups, depending on the consonant digraph in each word.

HOMEWORK Spelling Practice Book, p. 38.

Digraphs *sh, th, ph, ch, tch*

Spelling Words

father	chapter	other	alphabet	watch
English	weather	catch	fashion	shrink
pitcher	flash	athlete	trophy	nephew

Rhyme Clues Read the clue. Write the list word.

1. It rhymes with patch, but starts like can.   1. catch
2. It rhymes with link, but starts like shred.   2. shrink
3. It rhymes with feather, but starts like win.   3. weather
4. It rhymes with mother, but starts like olive.   4. other
5. It rhymes with dash, but starts like flag.   5. flash
6. It rhymes with stitcher, but starts like pencil.   6. pitcher

Making Connections Write a list word to name each item.

7. It's a list of letters.   7. alphabet
8. It's something you might win.   8. trophy
9. It's a parent. It's not a mother.   9. father
10. It helps you tell the time.   10. watch
11. It's a section of a book.   11. chapter
12. It's a sister's child. It's not a girl.   12. nephew
13. It's often spoken in Australia.   13. English
14. It could be a swimmer, a boxer, or a gymnast.   14. athlete
15. It's a trend in clothing.   15. fashion

School + Home Home Activity Your child wrote words with *sh, th, ph, ch,* and *tch.* Point to a list word on this page. Ask your child to read the word and then look away and spell it correctly.

▲ **Spelling Practice Book** p. 38

DAY 3 — Connect to Writing

WRITE A NEWS REPORT

Ask students to write a news report using at least four spelling words. Have children read their reports to the class as if they were on a television news program.

Frequently Misspelled Words

they   there

their

These words are difficult for third-graders to spell because they sound alike, yet are spelled differently. Alert students to these frequently misspelled words and encourage them to think carefully before they write them.

HOMEWORK Spelling Practice Book p. 39

Digraphs sh, th, ph, ch, tch

Proofread Safety Tips Chad wrote some weather safety tips. Circle four spelling mistakes and one capitalization error. Write the words correctly.

Spelling Words: father, chapter, other, alphabet, watch, English, weather, catch, fashion, shrink, pitcher, flash, athlete, trophy, nephew

→ Don't let bad weather cach you off guard. Listen to the forecast.
→ Be ready to go to a basement if their is a tornado watch.
→ Take shelter when you hear thunder. Don't wait for a flash of lightning.
→ wear a cap, mittens, and othr warm clothes in freezing weather.

1. weather   2. catch
3. there   4. other
5. Wear

Proofread Words Circle the correctly spelled word. Write the word.

Frequently Misspelled Words: they, there, their

6. fashsun (fashion)   6. fashion
7. (pitcher) picher   7. pitcher
8. (trophy) trofy   8. trophy
9. english (English)   9. English
10. (shrink) shink   10. shrink
11. atlete (athlete)   11. athlete
12. alpabet (alphabet)   12. alphabet

Home Activity Your child identified misspelled words with sh, th, ph, ch, and tch. Have your child underline and pronounce these letter combinations in the list words.

▲ **Spelling Practice Book** p. 39

DAY 4 — Review

REVIEW DIGRAPHS sh, th, ph, ch, tch

Working in pairs, have students scramble each list word. Then have students exchange their list with another pair of students to unscramble the list words.

Spelling Strategy
Consonants Together

Consonants can create new sounds when they are put together. Encourage students to be aware of which consonants are pronounced as one sound.

HOMEWORK Spelling Practice Book p. 40

Digraphs sh, th, ph, ch, tch

Spelling Words: father, chapter, other, alphabet, watch, English, weather, catch, fashion, shrink, pitcher, flash, athlete, trophy, nephew

Missing Consonants Write the missing consonants to make a list word.

1. He is your parent.   f a t h e r
2. You put your juice in it.   p i t c h e r
3. You receive one when you win a contest. t r o p h y
4. A language spoken in the United States. E n g l i s h
5. You check this to see if you need a jacket. w e a t h e r
6. You do this to a fish.   c a t c h

Word Search Circle the words in the puzzle. Look across, down, and diagonally.

f e a l p h a b e t a s
l o t n c h a p t e r h
a l t a s h o l h c h r
s i a h a t h l e t e i
h s h r e t a n l a m n
w a t c h r i n k e r k

watch
alphabet
flash
other
chapter
athlete
shrink

Home Activity Your child has been learning to spell words with sh, th, ph, ch, and tch. Ask your child to name and spell the four most difficult list words.

▲ **Spelling Practice Book** p. 40

DAY 5 — Posttest

DICTATION SENTENCES

1. My father will be at the game.
2. Read the first chapter for homework.
3. Where is my other sock?
4. My sister knows the alphabet.
5. Dad has a new watch.
6. They are learning to speak English.
7. What will the weather be today?
8. Do you want to play catch?
9. Her mom likes the new fashion.
10. The shirt will shrink in the wash.
11. Tim is a good pitcher.
12. I saw a flash of light.
13. Who is your favorite athlete?
14. Sam won a big trophy.
15. My nephew likes to sing.

CHALLENGE

16. Patty lives in the northern part of the state.
17. We want to establish the rules.
18. Put the emphasis on the first word.
19. That word needs a hyphen.
20. These spelling words are a challenge!

OBJECTIVES

- Formulate an inquiry question that is connected to this week's lesson focus.
- Effectively and efficiently find, evaluate, and communicate information related to an inquiry question using electronic sources.

New Literacies

Day 1	**Identify Questions**
Day 2	**Navigate/Search**
Day 3	**Analyze**
Day 4	**Synthesize**
Day 5	**Communicate**

NEW LITERACIES

Internet Inquiry Activity

EXPLORE COLONIAL TIMES

Use the following 5-day plan to help students conduct this week's Internet inquiry activity about life during colonial times. Remind students to follow classroom rules when using the Internet.

DAY 1

Identify Questions Discuss the topic, colonial times. Brainstorm ideas for specific inquiry questions about life in colonial times. For example, students might want to find out what people wore or what people ate in colonial times. Have students work individually, in pairs, or in small groups to write an inquiry question they want to answer.

DAY 2

Navigate/Search Students begin an Internet search using a student-friendly search engine. Have students type in keywords related to their inquiry questions. Discuss how to use an advanced search if too many Web sites are listed. Students should use an advanced search to help narrow the number of sites shown. Students can then read the descriptions to select those sites that contain relevant information.

DAY 3

Analyze Encourage students to explore the Web sites they identified on Day 2. Tell them to scan each site for information that may help them answer their inquiry questions. Have students analyze information for credibility, reliability, and usefulness. Remind them to take notes or print out valuable information.

DAY 4

Synthesize Have students synthesize information from Day 3. Remind them that when they synthesize, they combine relevant ideas and information from different sources to develop answers to their inquiry questions.

DAY 5

Communicate Have students share their inquiry results. They can use a word processing program to create a short informational story on life in colonial times.

Diagram/Scale Drawing

TEACH

OBJECTIVES
- Review terms and ideas related to diagrams.
- Make a diagram.

Ask if students have ever made a craft item or put together a model. Explain that often diagrams are used to show how to put something together. Find diagrams in textbooks or other sources that can be used to show this.

- A **diagram** can show how something is put together.
- A diagram can show how an object's parts relate to one another; for example, it can show how computer components are attached.
- A diagram can show how something works. You might use a diagram to show the stages in the life of a butterfly.
- Sometimes you have to study a diagram in a certain order—left to right or top to bottom.
- Diagrams can use text, labels, arrows, and pictures to demonstrate an idea or process.

Have students make a diagram to show a part of the school. They might show the cafeteria, gymnasium, classroom, or even a wing or section. As a group, discuss these questions:

1. What will the school diagram show? *(how the parts of the room or building relate to one another)*

2. How will you show the parts of the diagram? *(with shapes and labels)*

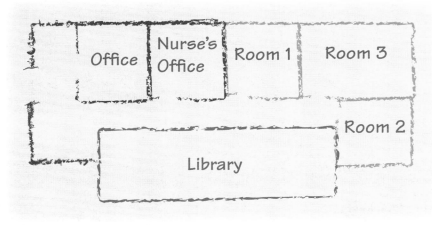

Scale: 1 inch = 50 feet

ASSESS

As students work on their diagrams, check that the components are in relative position and somewhat proportional. Make sure labels are clear and accurate.

For more practice or to assess students, use Practice Book 3.1, p. 100.

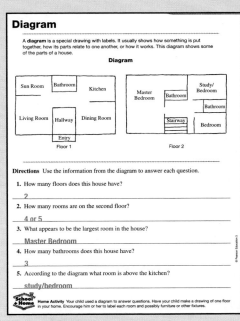

▲ **Practice Book 3.1** p. 100

Assessment Checkpoints *for the Week*

Selection Assessment

Use pp. 37–40 of Selection Tests **to check:**

   Selection Understanding

Comprehension Skill *Draw Conclusions*

Selection Vocabulary
barrels
cellar
clearing
pegs
spoil
steep

Leveled Assessment

On-Level
Strategic Intervention
Advanced

Use pp. 55–60 of Fresh Reads for Differentiated Test Practice **to check:**

   Comprehension Skill *Draw Conclusions*

REVIEW Comprehension Skill *Character*

Fluency *Words Correct Per Minute*

Managing Assessment

Use Assessment Handbook **for:**

   Observation Checklists

Record-Keeping Forms

Portfolio Assessment

Unit 2
Concept Wrap-Up

CONCEPT QUESTION

What are smart ways that problems are solved?

Students are ready to express their understanding of the unit concept question through discussion and wrap-up activities and to take the Unit 2 Benchmark Test.

Unit Poetry

Use the poetry on pp. 272–275 to help students appreciate poetry and further explore their understanding of the unit theme, Smart Solutions. It is suggested that you

- **read the poems aloud**
- **discuss and interpret the poems with students**
- **have students read the poems for fluency practice**
- **have students write interpretive responses**

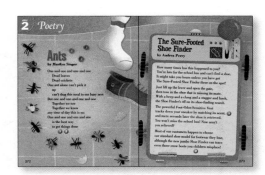

Unit Wrap-Up

Use the Unit Wrap-Up on pp. 276-277 to discuss the unit theme, Smart Solutions, and to have students show their understanding of the theme through cross-curricular activities.

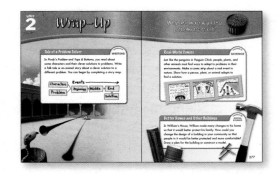

Unit Project

On p. 149, you assigned students a unit-long inquiry project, creating a Giant Book of Solutions. Students have investigated, analyzed, and synthesized information during the course of the unit as they prepared their books. Schedule time for students to present their projects. The project rubric can be found to the right.

Unit Inquiry Project Rubric

4	3	2	1
• Book of Solutions shows variety. Examples included are relevant to inquiry question. • Book of Solutions is creative and well-organized.	• Book of Solutions shows variety. Most examples included are relevant to inquiry question. • Book of Solutions is attractive but includes minor inconsistencies in organization.	• Book of Solutions shows little variety. Some items included are not relevant to inquiry question. • Book of Solutions lacks creativity and organization.	• Book of Solutions shows few examples relevant to inquiry question. • Book of Solutions is incomplete, lacks creativity, and is disorganized.

Unit 2
Reading Poetry

OBJECTIVES

- Listen and respond to poems.
- Identify how meaning is conveyed through word choice.
- Read poetry fluently.
- Connect ideas and themes across texts.

Model Fluent Reading

Tell students that often poets use line breaks to show readers where to pause. Then read "Ants" aloud, pausing at the end of each line. Have students picture in their minds what each line describes.

Discuss the Poem

1 Imagery • Critical

What does your imagination "see" as you read this poem?

Possible responses: ants marching in a line; ants working together to carry objects

2 Theme • Critical

What important lesson can people learn from ants?

Possible responses: It is best to work together; teamwork gets things done.

EXTEND SKILLS

Imagery

Explain that imagery is language that appeals to any of the five senses—sight, smell, hearing, taste, or touch. Writers use imagery to help readers feel as if they have stepped into the world of the poem. In "Ants," for example, the words *dead leaves* and *dead crickets* appeal to the reader's sense of sight. They help the reader "see" two objects that ants commonly carry.

Ants
by Marilyn Singer

One and one and one and one
  Dead leaves
  Dead crickets
One ant alone can't pick it
  up
  can't drag this meal to our busy nest
But one and one and one and one
  Together we tow
  Together we know
any time of day this is so:
One and one and one and one
  is the best way
  to get things done

1 2

272

Practice Fluent Reading

Have students practice reading aloud "The Sure-Footed Shoe Finder" in groups of four, each student reading one stanza. Point out that, like a television commercial, students' readings must communicate the "product" in a clear and convincing way. When students have finished, have them listen to the AudioText of the poem and compare and contrast their readings with the CD recording.

Audio CD AudioText

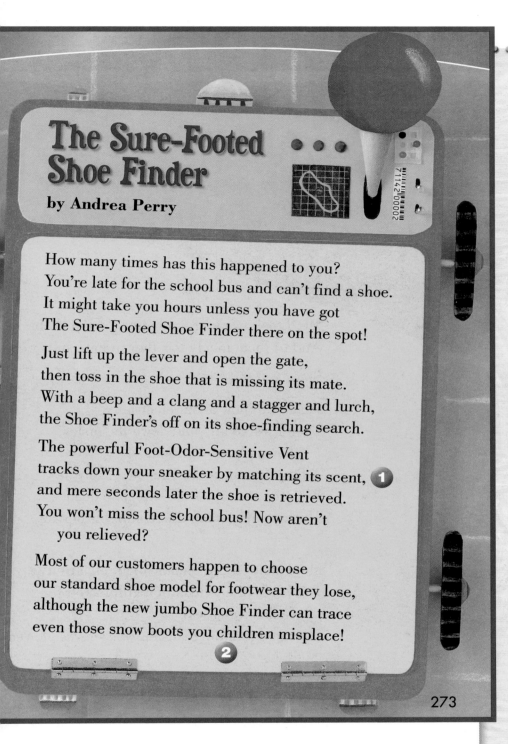

The Sure-Footed Shoe Finder
by Andrea Perry

How many times has this happened to you?
You're late for the school bus and can't find a shoe.
It might take you hours unless you have got
The Sure-Footed Shoe Finder there on the spot!

Just lift up the lever and open the gate,
then toss in the shoe that is missing its mate.
With a beep and a clang and a stagger and lurch,
the Shoe Finder's off on its shoe-finding search.

The powerful Foot-Odor-Sensitive Vent
tracks down your sneaker by matching its scent, **1**
and mere seconds later the shoe is retrieved.
You won't miss the school bus! Now aren't
    you relieved?

Most of our customers happen to choose
our standard shoe model for footwear they lose,
although the new jumbo Shoe Finder can trace
even those snow boots you children misplace! **2**

273

Model Fluent Reading

As you read "The Sure-Footed Shoe Finder" aloud, have students listen for the sense of the poem. What is it saying? How does this shoe-finder contraption actually work?

Discuss the Poem

1 **Sequence • Literal**

After you put one shoe in the shoe finder, what does the machine do?

It uses the first shoe's scent to find the missing shoe and then retrieve it.

2 **Humor • Critical**

Why is this poem funny? What human behaviors or attitudes does it poke fun at?

Possible responses: It is funny because it describes something that is impossible. It pokes fun at how people lose things and want a "quick fix."

WRITING POETRY

Have students write their own "one plus one (plus one plus one)" poems. To get students started, ask: "What things are better when they come in sets of two or more? Why?"

Reading Poetry

Model Fluent Reading

Explain that some poems tell stories, and that these stories usually involve characters. Then read "Third-Grade Genius" aloud. Have students listen for the main character's thoughts, actions, and words.

Discuss the Poem

1 **Character • Inferential**

How does the speaker feel about his invention?

Possible response: He feels proud.

2 **Simile • Literal**

To what does the poet compare the hamster's glowing eyes?

The poet compares the hamster's glowing eyes to red berries.

EXTEND SKILLS

Comparisons

Explain that poets often use comparisons to bring parts of their poems to life. Some comparisons use the words *like* or *as*. For instance, in "Third-Grade Genius," the hamster's eyes are said to glow "red *as* berries." Other comparisons say that one person or thing *is* another person or thing. In line 16 of "Third-Grade Genius," for example, the speaker calls himself "a magician." He isn't *actually* a magician—but he does think of himself as one.

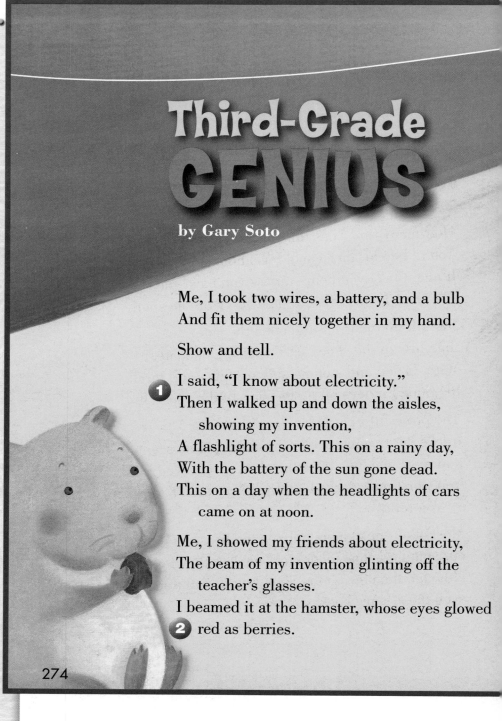

Third-Grade GENIUS

by Gary Soto

Me, I took two wires, a battery, and a bulb
And fit them nicely together in my hand.

Show and tell.

1 I said, "I know about electricity."
Then I walked up and down the aisles,
        showing my invention,
A flashlight of sorts. This on a rainy day,
With the battery of the sun gone dead.
This on a day when the headlights of cars
        came on at noon.

Me, I showed my friends about electricity,
The beam of my invention glinting off the
        teacher's glasses.
I beamed it at the hamster, whose eyes glowed
2 red as berries.

274

Practice Fluent Reading

Have partners read "Third-Grade Genius" aloud. Before they begin, have them recall a time when they felt quietly proud of themselves—not boastful, but simply "happy," like the character in this poem (line 20). Then have students take turns reading the entire poem. When they have finished, have them listen to the AudioText of the poem and compare and contrast their readings with the CD recording.

Audio CD **AudioText**

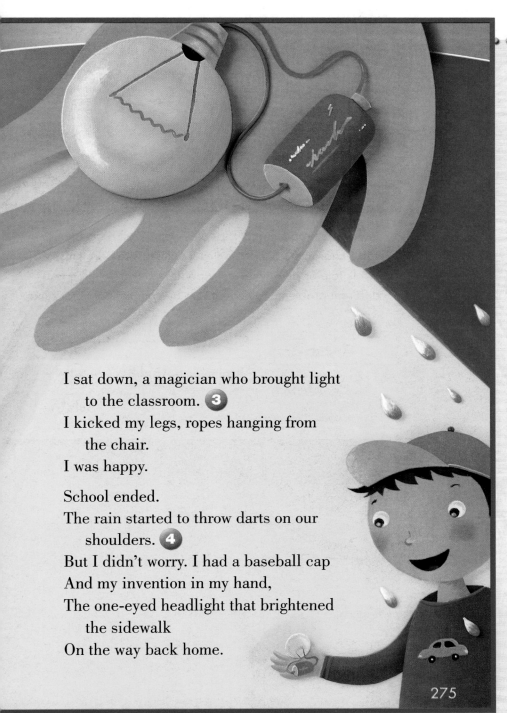

I sat down, a magician who brought light
    to the classroom. **3**
I kicked my legs, ropes hanging from
    the chair.
I was happy.

School ended.
The rain started to throw darts on our
    shoulders. **4**
But I didn't worry. I had a baseball cap
And my invention in my hand,
The one-eyed headlight that brightened
    the sidewalk
On the way back home.

275

Discuss the Poem

3 Metaphor • Inferential

Why does the speaker think of himself as a "magician"?

He thinks of himself as a magician because he has magically brought light to the classroom on a dark, rainy day.

4 Personification • Critical

In what way does the rain behave like a person?

The rain "throws darts."

Connect Ideas and Themes

Remind students that the topic of this unit is problem solving. Ask students to discuss how the creatures and people in these poems solve problems. Then have students recall times when they have solved problems in a group, tried to convince others of a certain solution, or felt particularly proud of a solution they came up with.

WRITING POETRY

Have students write a problem-solution poem—but with a catch. Explain that students' poems can describe *only* the solution, and that no mention of the problem itself should be made. Students can then exchange poems and try to guess the problem implied in each other's poems.

Unit 2

Wrap-Up

OBJECTIVES

- Critically analyze unit theme.
- Connect content across selections.
- Combine content and skills in meaningful activities that build literacy.
- Respond to unit selections through a variety of modalities.

SMART SOLUTIONS

Discuss the Big Idea

What are smart ways that problems are solved?

Write the unit theme and Big Idea question on the board. Ask students to think about the selections they have read in the unit. Discuss how each selection and lesson concept can help them answer the Big Idea question from this unit.

Model this for students by choosing a selection and explaining how the selection and lesson concept address the Big Idea.

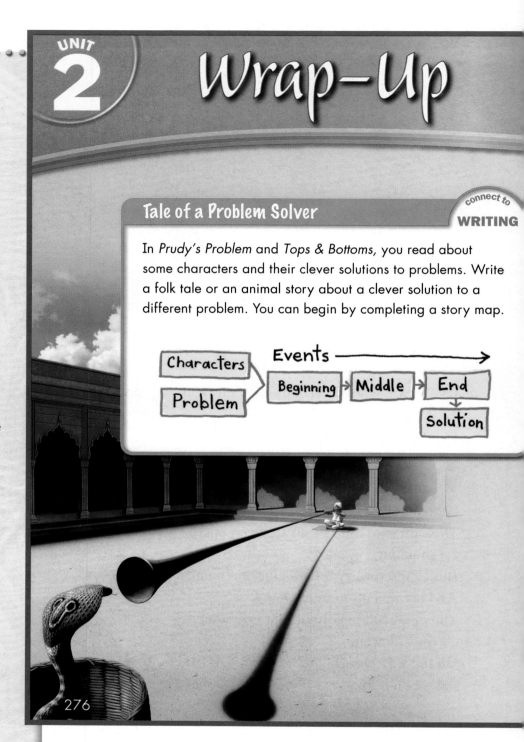

UNIT 2 Wrap-Up

Tale of a Problem Solver

connect to **WRITING**

In *Prudy's Problem* and *Tops & Bottoms*, you read about some characters and their clever solutions to problems. Write a folk tale or an animal story about a clever solution to a different problem. You can begin by completing a story map.

Characters
Problem
Events
Beginning → Middle → End
Solution

276

What are smart ways that problems are solved?

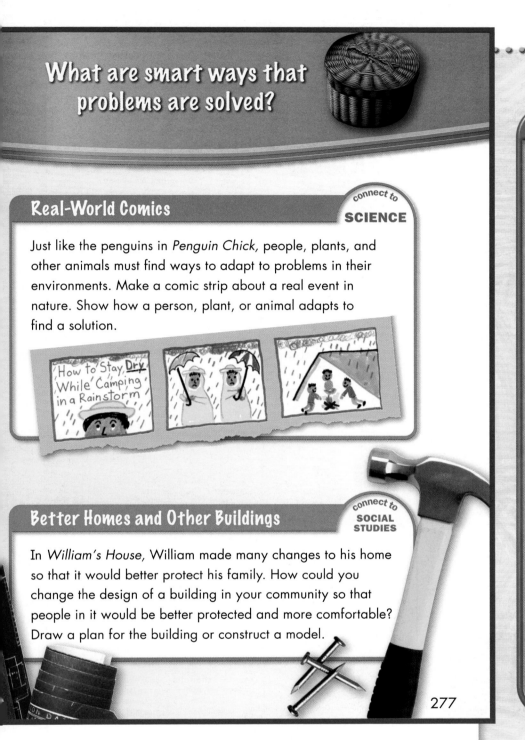

Real-World Comics

Just like the penguins in *Penguin Chick,* people, plants, and other animals must find ways to adapt to problems in their environments. Make a comic strip about a real event in nature. Show how a person, plant, or animal adapts to find a solution.

How to Stay Dry While Camping in a Rainstorm

Better Homes and Other Buildings

connect to SOCIAL STUDIES

In *William's House,* William made many changes to his home so that it would better protect his family. How could you change the design of a building in your community so that people in it would be better protected and more comfortable? Draw a plan for the building or construct a model.

277

ACTIVITIES

Tale of a Problem Solver

Write a Story Have students complete story maps. Review the story maps before writing begins. Assist students whose story maps lack a coherent plan for writing.

Real-World Comics

Make a Comic Strip Students should first decide on an event in nature and then whether they will depict people, plants, or animals in the strip. Possible events might include adapting to a sudden weather change or a different climate. You may want students to use a story map to plan their comic strips.

Better Homes and Other Buildings

Make a Drawing Have pictures or outline drawings of buildings or homes for students to use. To start students thinking of changes they could make, create a list on the board of things that would make a building safer or more comfortable.

Glossary

Glossary

How to Use This Glossary

This glossary can help you understand and pronounce some of the words in this book. The entries in this glossary are in alphabetical order. There are guide words at the top of each page to show you the first and last words on the page. A pronunciation key is at the bottom of every other page. Remember, if you can't find the word you are looking for, ask for help or check a dictionary.

The entry word is in dark type. It shows how the word is spelled and how the word is divided into syllables.

The pronunciation is in parentheses. It also shows which syllables are stressed.

Part-of-speech labels show the function or functions of an entry word and any listed form of that word.

a·dore (ə dôr′), *VERB.* to love and admire someone very greatly: *She adores her mother.* ❑ *VERB.* **a·dores, a·dored, a·dor·ing.**

Sometimes, irregular and other special forms will be shown to help you use the word correctly.

The definition and example sentence show you what the word means and how it is used.

422

Aa

ac·com·mo·date (ə kom′ə dāt), *VERB.* to hold; have room for: *The airplane is large enough to accommodate 120 passengers.* ❑ *VERB.* **ac·com·mo·dates, ac·com·mo·dat·ed, ac·com·mo·dat·ing.**

a·dore (ə dôr′), *VERB.* to love and admire someone very greatly: *She adores her mother.* ❑ *VERB.* **a·dores, a·dored, a·dor·ing.**

af·ford (ə fôrd′), *VERB.* to have the money, means, or time for: *Can we afford a new car? He cannot afford to waste time.* ❑ *VERB* **af·fords, af·ford·ed, af·ford·ing.**

a·mount (ə mount′), **1.** *NOUN.* the total sum: *What is the amount of the bill for the groceries?* **2.** *VERB.* to reach; add up: *The loss from the flood amounts to ten million dollars.* ❑ *VERB* **a·mounts, a·mount·ed, a·mount·ing.**

ant·ler (ant′lər), *NOUN.* a bony, branching growth on the head of a male deer, elk, or moose. Antlers grow in pairs and are shed once a year. ❑ *PLURAL* **ant·lers.**

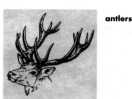

antlers

anx·ious·ly (angk′shəs lē), *ADVERB.* uneasily; with fear of what might happen: *We looked anxiously at the storm clouds.*

ar·range (ə rānj′), *VERB.* to put things in a certain order: *She arranged the books on the library shelf.* ❑ *VERB* **ar·rang·es, ar·ranged, ar·rang·ing.**

as·ton·ish·ment (ə ston′ish mənt), *NOUN.* great surprise; sudden wonder; amazement: *He stared at the Grand Canyon in astonishment.*

Bb

bar·rel (bar′əl), *NOUN.* a container with a round, flat top and bottom and sides that curve out slightly. Barrels are usually made of boards held together by hoops. ❑ *PLURAL* **bar·rels.**

bay (bā), *NOUN.* a part of a sea or lake partly surrounded by land.

beau·ty (byü′tē), *NOUN.* the quality that pleases both the mind and the senses in art or nature.

beck·on (bek′ən), *VERB.* to signal to someone by a motion of the head or hand: *She beckoned me to follow her.* ❑ *VERB* **beck·ons, beck·oned, beck·on·ing.**

a	in hat	ò	in open	sh	in she
ā	in age	ō	in all	th	in thin
â	in care	ô	in order	ᴛʜ	in then
ä	in far	oi	in oil	zh	in measure
e	in let	ou	in out	ə	= a in about
ē	in equal	u	in cup	ə	= e in taken
ėr	in term	ü	in put	ə	= i in pencil
i	in it	ü	in rule	ə	= o in lemon
ī	in ice	ch	in child	ə	= u in circus
o	in hot	ng	in long		

423

be·neath (bi nēth′), *PREPOSITION.* in a lower place; below; under: *The dog sat beneath the tree.*

blade (blād), *NOUN.* a leaf of grass.

bliz·zard (bliz′ərd), *NOUN.* a blinding snowstorm with very strong, cold winds. ❑ *PLURAL* **bliz·zards.**

bloom (blüm), *VERB.* to have flowers; open into flowers; blossom: *Many plants are blooming early this spring.* ❑ *VERB* **blooms, bloomed, bloom·ing.**

boom¹ (büm), **1.** *NOUN.* a deep hollow sound like the roar of cannon or of big waves: *We listened to the boom of the pounding surf.* **2.** *ADJECTIVE.* having a rapid growth: *The boom town grew quickly after the gold rush.*

boom² (büm), *NOUN.* a long pole or beam used to extend the bottom of a sail.

bot·tom (bot′əm), *NOUN.* the lowest part: *These berries at the bottom of the basket are crushed.*

bud (bud), *VERB.* to put forth small swellings on a plant that will grow into leaves, branches, or flowers: *The tree was budding in May.* ❑ *VERB* **buds, bud·ded, bud·ding.**

bud

bulb (bulb), *NOUN.* a round, underground part from which certain plants grow. Onions and tulips grow from bulbs. ❑ *PLURAL* **bulbs.**

bun·dle (bun′dl), *NOUN.* a number of things tied or wrapped together. ❑ *PLURAL* **bun·dles.**

bur·y (ber′ē), *VERB.* to cover up; hide: *He dug up an ancient ruin that had been buried long ago.* ❑ *VERB* **bur·ies, bur·ied, bur·y·ing.**

424

busi·ness (biz′nis), **1.** *NOUN.* work done to earn a living; occupation: *A carpenter's business is building.* **2.** *NOUN.* buying and selling; trade: *This hardware store does a lot of business in tools.*

bus·tle (bus′əl), *NOUN.* a noisy or excited activity: *There was a lot of bustle as the children got ready for the party.*

Cc

car·pen·ter (kär′pən tər), *NOUN.* someone whose work is building and repairing things made of wood.

carpenter

car·pet·mak·er (kär′pit māk ər), *NOUN.* A person who makes carpets and rugs for floors: *The carpetmaker sold us a blue carpet.*

cat·a·logue (kat′l òg), *NOUN.* a list. Many companies print catalogues showing pictures and prices of the things that they have to sell. ❑ *PLURAL* **cat·a·logues.**

cel·lar (sel′ər), *NOUN.* an underground room or rooms, usually under a building and often used for storage.

chan·nel (chan′l), *NOUN.* a body of water joining two larger bodies of water: *The small channel was too narrow for the boat's passage.*

cheat (chēt), *VERB.* to deceive or trick someone; do business or play in a way that is not honest: *I hate to play games with someone who cheats.* ❑ *VERB* **cheats, cheat·ed, cheat·ing.**

a	in hat	ò	in open	sh	in she
ā	in age	ō	in all	th	in thin
â	in care	ô	in order	ᴛʜ	in then
ä	in far	oi	in oil	zh	in measure
e	in let	ou	in out	ə	= a in about
ē	in equal	u	in cup	ə	= e in taken
ėr	in term	ü	in put	ə	= i in pencil
i	in it	ü	in rule	ə	= o in lemon
ī	in ice	ch	in child	ə	= u in circus
o	in hot	ng	in long		

425

check (chek), **1.** *VERB.* to examine something to see if it is correct, working properly, turned on, and so on: *Always check your answers.* **2.** *NOUN.* a written order directing a bank to pay money to the person named: *My parents pay most of their bills by check.* ❑ *VERB* **checks, checked, check·ing.**

chim·ney (chim′nē), *NOUN.* a tall, hollow column, usually made of brick, to carry away smoke from a fireplace or furnace.

chip (chip), *VERB.* to cut or break off a small thin piece of something: *I chipped the cup when I knocked it against the cupboard.* ❑ *VERB* **chips, chipped, chip·ping.**

clear·ing (klir′ing), *NOUN.* an open space of land in a forest.

clev·er (klev′ər), *ADJECTIVE.* bright; intelligent; having a quick mind: *She is a clever girl to have solved that math problem.*

clut·ter (klut′ər), *NOUN.* many things lying around in disorder; litter: *It was hard to find the lost pen in the clutter.*

coarse (kôrs), *ADJECTIVE.* rough: *Burlap is a coarse cloth.*

coin (koin), *NOUN.* a flat, round piece of metal used as money. Pennies, dimes, and nickels are coins. ❑ *PLURAL* **coins.**

col·lec·tion (kə lek′shən), *NOUN.* a group of things gathered from many places and belonging together: *Our library has a large collection of books.*

collection

col·lege (kol′ij), *NOUN.* a school of higher learning, where a person can study after high school, that gives degrees or diplomas: *After I finish high school, I plan to go to college to become a teacher.*

426

con·fi·dent (kon′fə dənt), *ADJECTIVE.* firmly believing; certain; sure: *I feel confident that our team will win.*

con·vince (kən vins′), *VERB.* to make someone believe something: *The mistakes she made convinced me that she had not studied her lesson.* ❑ *VERB* **con·vinc·es, con·vinced, con·vinc·ing.**

corn·stalk (kôrn′stȯk′), *NOUN.* the main stem of a corn plant.

crop (krop), *NOUN.* plants grown for food: *Wheat, corn, and cotton are major crops in the United States.* ❑ *PLURAL* **crops.**

cud·dle (kud′l), *VERB.* to lie close and comfortably; curl up: *The two puppies cuddled together in front of the fire.* ❑ *VERB* **cud·dles, cud·dled, cud·dling.**

cuddle

Dd

dan·ger·ous·ly (dān′jər əs lē), *ADVERB.* not safely: *The car drove dangerously close to the wall.*

debt (det), *NOUN.* something owed to someone else: *He paid back all his debts.*

dew (dü), *NOUN.* the moisture from the air that collects in small drops on cool surfaces during the night: *In the early morning, the grass is often wet with dew.*

dew

a in hat	ō in open	sh in she
ā in age	ȯ in all	th in thin
â in care	ô in order	ŦH in then
ä in far	oi in oil	zh in measure
e in let	ou in out	ə = a in about
ē in equal	u in cup	ə = e in taken
ėr in term	ù in put	ə = i in pencil
i in it	ü in rule	ə = o in lemon
ī in ice	ch in child	ə = u in circus
o in hot	ng in long	

427

dime (dīm), *NOUN.* a coin of the United States and Canada equal to 10 cents. Ten dimes make one dollar. ❑ *PLURAL* **dimes.**

down·town (doun′toun′), *NOUN.* the main part or business part of a town or city: *Downtown can have very bad traffic.*

doze (dōz), *VERB.* to sleep lightly; be half asleep: *After dinner, he dozed on the couch.* ❑ *VERB* **doz·es, dozed, doz·ing.**

Ee

earn (ėrn), **1.** *VERB.* to get money in return for work or service; be paid: *She earns $175 a week.* **2.** *VERB.* to get something that you deserve: *Her hard work earned her the respect of her teachers.* ❑ *VERB* **earns, earned, earn·ing.**

earth·quake (ėrth′kwāk′), *NOUN.* a violent shaking or shifting motion of the ground, caused by the sudden movement of rock far beneath the Earth's surface: *Earthquakes can cause great destruction.* ❑ *PLURAL* **earth·quakes.**

eer·ie (ir′ē), *ADJECTIVE.* causing fear because of strangeness or weirdness: *The eerie music made the movie scarier.*

e·nor·mous (i nôr′məs), *ADJECTIVE.* very, very large; huge: *Long ago, enormous animals lived on the Earth.*

enormous

er·rand (er′ənd), *NOUN.* a short trip that you take to do something: *She has errands to do downtown.* ❑ *PLURAL* **er·rands.**

e·rupt (i rupt′), *VERB.* violently to send out steam, lava, and so on: *The volcano erupted twice last year.* ❑ *VERB* **e·rupts, e·rupt·ed, e·rupt·ing.**

428

ex·cit·ed·ly (ek sī′tid lē), *ADVERB.* with strong, lively feelings: *My heart beat excitedly as I opened the old trunk.*

ex·cite·ment (ek sīt′mənt), *NOUN.* a condition of having strong, lively feelings about something that you like.

ex·pen·sive (ek spen′siv), *ADJECTIVE.* costing a lot of money; high-priced: *My uncle has an expensive car.*

Ff

feat (fēt), *NOUN.* an act that shows great skill, strength, or daring.

fetch (fech), **1.** *VERB.* to go and get something; bring: *Please fetch my glasses for me.* **2.** *VERB.* to sell for: *Those eggs fetched a good price.* ❑ *VERB* **fetch·es, fetched, fetch·ing.**

fine (fīn), *VERB.* to make someone pay money as punishment for breaking a law or regulation: *The judge fined her $50.* ❑ *VERB* **fines, fined, fin·ing.**

fire·fly (fīr′flī′), *NOUN.* a small insect that gives off flashes of light when it flies at night; lightning bug. ❑ *PLURAL* **fire·flies.**

fire·works (fīr′wėrks′), *NOUN PLURAL.* firecrackers and other things that make a loud noise or go up high in the air and burst in a shower of stars and sparks.

fireworks

flip·per (flip′ər), *NOUN.* one of the broad, flat body parts used for swimming by animals such as seals and penguins. ❑ *PLURAL* **flip·pers.**

flut·ter (flut′ər), *VERB.* to flap the wings: *The chickens fluttered excitedly when they saw the dog.* ❑ *VERB* **flut·ters, flut·tered, flut·ter·ing.**

a in hat	ō in open	sh in she
ā in age	ȯ in all	th in thin
â in care	ô in order	ŦH in then
ä in far	oi in oil	zh in measure
e in let	ou in out	ə = a in about
ē in equal	u in cup	ə = e in taken
ėr in term	ù in put	ə = i in pencil
i in it	ü in rule	ə = o in lemon
ī in ice	ch in child	ə = u in circus
o in hot	ng in long	

429

Glossary

force (fôrs), **1.** *NOUN.* power; strength: *The falling tree hit the ground with great force.* **2.** *VERB.* to make you act against your will: *His boss forced him to work on Saturdays.* □ *VERB* **for·ces, forced, for·cing.**

fro·zen (frō′zn), *ADJECTIVE.* hardened with cold; turned into ice: *frozen sherbet.*

Gg

gar·den·er (gärd′nər), *NOUN.* someone employed to take care of a garden or lawn.

Hh

har·mon·i·ca (här mon′ə kə), *NOUN.* a small musical instrument shaped like a thick candy bar, with metal reeds. It is played by breathing in and out through openings.

harmonica

hatch (hach), *VERB.* to come out of an egg: *One of the chickens hatched today.* □ *VERB* **hatch·es, hatched, hatch·ing.**

hatch

hu·mor (hyü′mər), *NOUN.* the ability to see or show the funny or amusing side of things: *Her sense of humor enabled her to joke about her problems.*

Ii

i·mag·ine (i maj′ən), *VERB.* to make a picture or idea of something in your mind: *We can hardly imagine life without cars.* □ *VERB* **i·mag·ines, i·mag·ined, i·mag·in·ing.**

in·de·scrib·a·ble (in′di skrī′bə bəl), *ADJECTIVE.* not able to be told about in words; beyond description.

430

in·for·ma·tion (in′fər mā′shən), *NOUN.* knowledge given or received of some future event; news: *We have just received information on the astronauts' safe landing.*

in·spi·ra·tion (in′spə rā′shən), *NOUN.* something that has a strong effect on what you feel or do, especially something good: *Some people get inspiration from sermons, some from nature.*

in·ter·est (in′tər ist), **1.** *NOUN.* a feeling of wanting to know, see, do, own, or take part in something: *He has an interest in collecting stamps.* **2.** *NOUN.* the money paid for the use of someone else's money: *The interest on the loan was 7 percent a year.*

Jj

jab (jab), *VERB.* to stab with something pointed: *He was jabbing his fork into the potato.* □ *VERB* **jabs, jabbed, jab·bing.**

Kk

knowl·edge (nol′ij), *NOUN.* what you know: *Gardeners have great knowledge of flowers.*

Ll

lan·guage (lan′gwij), *NOUN.* human speech, spoken or written: *Civilization would be impossible without language.* □ *PLURAL* **lan·guag·es.**

laun·dry (lȯn′drē), *NOUN.* a room or building where clothes and linens are washed and ironed.

laundry

a in hat	ȯ in open	sh in she
ā in age	ȯ in all	th in thin
â in care	ô in order	ᴛʜ in then
ä in far	oi in oil	zh in measure
e in let	ou in out	ə = a in about
ē in equal	u in cup	ə = e in taken
ėr in term	ü in put	ə = i in pencil
i in it	ü in rule	ə = o in lemon
ī in ice	ch in child	ə = u in circus
o in hot	ng in long	

431

la·va (lä′və), *NOUN.* the hot, melted rock flowing from a volcano.

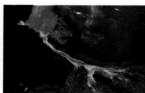

lava

la·zy (lā′zē), *ADJECTIVE.* not willing to work or move fast. *He lost his job because he was lazy.*

Mm

mag·ma (mag′mə), *NOUN.* hot melted rock beneath the surface of the Earth.

man·tle (man′tl), *NOUN.* the layer of the Earth lying beneath the crust and above the core.

mar·ket·place (mär′kət plās′), *NOUN.* a place where people meet to buy and sell things: *The marketplace was very crowded.*

mel·o·dy (mel′ə dē), *NOUN.* a pleasing or easily remembered series of musical notes; tune.

mend·ing (mend′ing), *NOUN.* sewing that repairs a hole or tear: *Mother sat down on the porch to do her mending.*

mer·chant (mėr′chənt), *NOUN.* someone who buys and sells goods for a living: *Some merchants do most of their business with foreign countries.*

mil·lion (mil′yən), *NOUN or ADJECTIVE.* one thousand thousand; 1,000,000.

mo·tion (mō′shən), *VERB.* to make a movement, as of the hand or head, to get someone to do something: *She motioned to us to come over to her side of the room.* □ *VERB* **mo·tions, mo·tioned, mo·tion·ing.**

Nn

nar·ra·tor (nar′āt ər), *NOUN.* the person who tells the story or tale: *I was the narrator in the school play.*

nec·tar (nek′tər), *NOUN.* a sweet liquid found in many flowers. Bees gather nectar and make it into honey.

432

nick·el (nik′əl), *NOUN.* a coin in the United States and Canada worth 5 cents. □ *PLURAL* **nick·els.**

note·pad (nōt′pad′), *NOUN.* a small book of blank or lined sheets of paper in which you write notes of things that you need to learn or remember.

nug·get (nug′it), *NOUN.* a small, rough piece of valuable metal ore: *gold nuggets.* □ *PLURAL* **nug·gets.**

nugget

Oo

o·ver·head (ō′vər hed′), *ADVERB.* over the head; on high; above: *The stars twinkled overhead.*

Pp

part·ner (pärt′nər), *NOUN.* a member of a company or firm who shares the risks and profits of the business. □ *PLURAL* **part·ners.**

patch (pach), *NOUN.* a small piece of ground that is different from what surrounds it: *We have a strawberry patch in our garden.*

peck (pek), *VERB.* to strike with the beak: *The baby sparrow pecks at the egg.* □ *VERB* **pecks, pecked, peck·ing.**

peg (peg), *NOUN.* a pin or small bolt of wood or metal used to fasten parts together. □ *PLURAL* **pegs.**

pick¹ (pik), *VERB.* to choose; select; take the one you want from a group: *I picked a blue shirt to wear with my jeans.* □ *VERB* **picks, picked, pick·ing.**

pick² (pik), *NOUN.* a tool with a heavy metal bar pointed at one or both ends, having a long wooden handle; pickax: *The miner used his pick to break up the hard rock.*

a in hat	ȯ in open	sh in she
ā in age	ȯ in all	th in thin
â in care	ô in order	ᴛʜ in then
ä in far	oi in oil	zh in measure
e in let	ou in out	ə = a in about
ē in equal	u in cup	ə = e in taken
ėr in term	ü in put	ə = i in pencil
i in it	ü in rule	ə = o in lemon
ī in ice	ch in child	ə = u in circus
o in hot	ng in long	

433

plenty·rich

plen·ty (plen′tē), *NOUN.* a full supply; all that you need; a large enough number or amount: *You have plenty of time to catch the train.*

poke (pōk), *VERB.* to push with force against someone or something; jab: *He poked me in the ribs with his elbow.* ❑ *VERB* **pokes, poked, pok·ing.**

pos·i·tive·ly (poz′ə tiv lē), *ADVERB.* absolutely; surely; without question or doubt.

preen (prēn), *VERB.* to smooth or arrange the feathers with the beak. ❑ *VERB* **preens, preened, preen·ing.**

pros·pec·tor (pros′pek tər), *NOUN.* someone who explores or examines a region, looking for gold, oil, uranium, or other valuable resources.

prospector

Qq

quar·ter (kwôr′tər), **1.** *NOUN.* one of four equal parts; half of a half; one fourth: *A quarter of an hour is 15 minutes.* **2.** *NOUN.* a coin of the United States and Canada equal to 25 cents; four quarters make one dollar. ❑ *PLURAL* **quar·ters.**

Rr

raft·er (raf′tər), *NOUN.* one of the slanting timbers that hold up a roof. ❑ *PLURAL* **raft·ers.**

re·al·ize (rē′ə līz), *VERB.* to understand something clearly: *I realize how hard you worked.* ❑ *VERB* **re·al·iz·es, re·al·ized, re·al·iz·ing.**

rec·og·nize (rek′əg nīz), *VERB.* to identify: *recognizing a person from a description.* ❑ *VERB* **rec·og·niz·es, rec·og·nized, rec·og·niz·ing.**

rich (rich), *ADJECTIVE.* having a great deal of money, land, goods, or other property: *That movie star is a rich man.* ❑ *ADJECTIVE* **rich·er, rich·est.**

434

rook·er·y (rùk′ər ē), *NOUN.* a breeding place or colony where other birds or animals are crowded together: *a rookery of penguins.*

rookery

Ss

sad·ness (sad′nis), *NOUN.* unhappiness, sorrow.

scat·ter (skat′ər), *VERB.* to separate and go in different directions: *The chickens scattered in fright when the truck honked at them.* ❑ *VERB* **scat·ters, scat·tered, scat·ter·ing.**

scoff (skôf), *VERB.* to make fun of something to show you do not believe or respect it; mock: *We scoffed at the idea of swimming in three inches of water.* ❑ *VERB* **scoffs, scoffed, scoff·ing.**

shin·y (shī′nē), *ADJECTIVE.* giving off or reflecting a bright light; bright: *A new penny is shiny.*

shiv·er (shiv′ər), *VERB.* to shake with cold, fear, or excitement: *I shivered in the cold wind.* ❑ *VERB* **shiv·ers, shiv·ered, shiv·er·ing.**

shiver

shock (shok), *VERB.* to cause to feel surprise, horror, or disgust: *That child's bad manners shocked everyone.* ❑ *VERB* **shocks, shocked, shock·ing.**

show·er (shou′ər), *NOUN.* rain that lasts only a short time. ❑ *PLURAL* **show·ers.**

a in hat	ò in open	sh in she
ā in age	ō in all	th in thin
â in care	ô in order	ᴛʜ in then
ä in far	oi in oil	zh in measure
e in let	ou in out	ə = a in about
ē in equal	u in cup	ə = e in taken
ėr in term	ú in put	ə = i in pencil
i in it	ü in rule	ə = o in lemon
ī in ice	ch in child	ə = u in circus
o in hot	ng in long	

435

skillet·squid

skil·let (skil′it), *NOUN.* a shallow pan with a handle, used for frying; frying pan.

slam (slam), *VERB.* to throw or hit something with great force: *That car slammed into a truck.* ❑ *VERB* **slams, slammed, slam·ming.**

snug·gle (snug′əl), *VERB.* to lie closely and comfortably together; nestle; cuddle: *The kittens snuggled together in the basket.* ❑ *VERB* **snug·gles, snug·gled, snug·gling.**

snuggle

spell¹ (spel), *VERB.* to write or say the letters of a word in order: *Some words are easy to spell.* ❑ *VERB* **spells, spelled, spel·ling.**

spell² (spel), *NOUN.* a period or time of anything: *There was a long spell of rainy weather in August.*

spoil (spoil), *VERB.* to become bad or not good to eat: *The fruit spoiled because I kept it too long.* ❑ *VERB* **spoils, spoiled, spoil·ing.**

sprout (sprout), *VERB.* to produce new leaves, shoots, or buds; begin to grow: *Tulips sprout in the spring.* ❑ *VERB* **sprouts, sprout·ed, sprout·ing.**

squid (skwid), *NOUN.* a sea animal that looks something like an octopus but having a pair of tail fins and ten arms instead of eight. It is a mollusk.

squid

436

stead·y (sted′ē), *ADJECTIVE.* firmly fixed; firm; not swaying or shaking: *This post is as steady as a rock.*

steep (stēp), *ADJECTIVE.* having a sharp slope; almost straight up and down: *The hill is steep.*

strain (strān), *VERB.* to draw tight; stretch too much: *The weight strained the rope.* ❑ *VERB* **strains, strained, strain·ing.**

stray (strā), *VERB.* to lose your way; wander; roam: *Our dog has strayed off somewhere.* ❑ *VERB* **strays, strayed, stray·ing.**

stun (stun), *VERB.* to thoroughly shock or confuse someone: *She was stunned by the news of her friend's injury.* ❑ *VERB* **stuns, stunned, stunn·ing.**

sup·plies (sə plīz′), *NOUN PLURAL.* the food and equipment necessary for an army exercise, camping trip, and so on.

sur·round (sə round′), *VERB.* to shut something in on all sides; encircle; enclose: *A high fence surrounded the field.* ❑ *VERB* **sur·rounds, sur·round·ed, sur·round·ing.**

sur·vive (sər viv′), *VERB.* to continue to live or exist; remain: *These cave paintings have survived for more than 15,000 years.* ❑ *VERB* **sur·vives, sur·vived, sur·viv·ing.**

syc·a·more (sik′ə môr), *NOUN.* a kind of shade tree with big leaves and bark that peels off in large patches.

sycamores

sym·pho·ny (sim′fə nē), *NOUN.* a long, complicated musical composition for an orchestra.

a in hat	ò in open	sh in she
ā in age	ō in all	th in thin
â in care	ô in order	ᴛʜ in then
ä in far	oi in oil	zh in measure
e in let	ou in out	ə = a in about
ē in equal	u in cup	ə = e in taken
ėr in term	ú in put	ə = i in pencil
i in it	ü in rule	ə = o in lemon
ī in ice	ch in child	ə = u in circus
o in hot	ng in long	

437

Glossary

Tt

thatch (thach), *NOUN.* made with straw, palm leaves, and so on, for a roof or covering.

thatch

thou·sand (thou′znd), *NOUN or ADJECTIVE.* ten hundred; 1,000.

thread (thred), *NOUN.* a very thin string made of strands of cotton, silk, wool, or nylon, spun and twisted together. *She sewed the sweater with cotton thread.*

to·ken (tō′kən), *NOUN.* a piece of metal shaped like a coin. Tokens are used on some buses and subways instead of money. ❑ *PLURAL* **to·kens.**

trans·lu·cent (tran slü′snt), *ADJECTIVE.* letting light through, but not easily seen through: *Frosted glass is translucent.*

trans·mit·ter (tran smit′ər), *NOUN.* a device that sends out sounds, or sounds and pictures, by radio waves or by electric current: *Radio stations and television stations have powerful transmitters.*

transmitter

trem·ble (trem′bəl), *VERB.* to move with a quick shaking motion: *The leaf trembles in the breeze.* ❑ *VERB* **trem·bles, trem·bled, trem·bling.**

438

Uu

un·wrap (un rap′), *VERB.* to open: *She unwrapped the gift.* ❑ *VERB* **un·wraps, un·wrapped, un·wrap·ping.**

Vv

val·ue (val′yü), **1.** *NOUN.* the real worth of something in money: *We bought the house for less than its value.* **2.** *VERB.* to think highly of something; regard highly: *Since he is an expert, his opinion is valued.* ❑ *VERB* **val·ues, val·ued, val·u·ing.**

vol·ca·no (vol kā′nō), *NOUN.* a cone-shaped hill or mountain built up by lava and ash around an opening in the Earth's crust. ❑ *PLURAL* **vol·ca·noes.**

volcano

Ww

wan·der·er (wän′dər ər), *NOUN.* human being or animal that moves here and there.

wealth (welth), *NOUN.* riches; many valuable possessions; property: *people of wealth, the wealth of a city.*

wob·ble (wob′əl), *VERB.* to move unsteadily from side to side; shake; tremble: *The baby wobbled when she began to walk alone.* ❑ *VERB* **wob·bles, wob·bled, wob·bling.**

worth (wėrth), **1.** *ADJECTIVE.* equal in value to: *This book is worth fifteen dollars.* **2.** *NOUN.* how much a certain amount of money will buy: *He bought a dollar's worth of stamps.*

a in hat	ö in open	sh in she
â in age	ò in all	th in thin
â in care	ô in order	ᴛʜ in then
ä in far	oi in oil	zh in measure
e in let	ou in out	ə = a in about
ē in equal	u in cup	ə = e in taken
ėr in term	ú in put	ə = i in pencil
i in it	ü in rule	ə = o in lemon
ī in ice	ch in child	ə = u in circus
o in hot	ng in long	

439

English/Spanish
Selection Vocabulary List

Unit 1

Boom Town

English	Spanish
boom	auge
business	negocio
coins	monedas
fetched	traído
laundry	lavandería
mending	coser
pick	recoger
skillet	sartén
spell	rato

What About Me?

English	Spanish
carpenter	carpintero
carpetmaker	alfombrista
knowledge	conocimiento
marketplace	mercado
merchant	comerciante
plenty	mucho
straying	descarriando
thread	hilo

440

Alexander, Who Used to Be Rich Last Sunday

English	Spanish
college	universidad
dimes	monedas de diez centavos
downtown	centro
fined	multó
nickels	monedas de cinco centavos
quarters	monedas de veinticinco centavos
rich	rico

Unit 2

If You Made a Million

English	Spanish
amount	cantidad
check	cheque
earned	ganado
expensive	caros
interest	interés
million	millón
thousand	mil
value	valor
worth	valdrá

My Rows and Piles of Coins

English	Spanish
arranged	ordené
bundles	paquetes
dangerously	peligrosamente
errands	recados
excitedly	con emoción
steady	estable
unwrapped	desenvolví
wobbled	me tambaleé

Penguin Chick

English	Spanish
cuddles	se arrima a
flippers	aletas
frozen	congelada
hatch	salir del cascarón
pecks	picotea
preen	atusa
snuggles	se acurruca

A Day's Work

English	Spanish
excitement	entusiasmo
gardener	jardinero
motioned	indicó (con un gesto)
sadness	tristeza
shivered	tiritó
shocked	sorprendido
slammed	estampó

441

Prudy's Problem and How She Solved It

English	Spanish
collection	colección
enormous	enorme
realize	darte cuenta
scattered	desparramadas
shiny	reluciente
strain	doblarse

Tops & Bottoms

English	Spanish
bottom	parte de abajo
cheated	engañaste
clever	listo
crops	cosechas
lazy	perezoso
partners	socios
wealth	riqueza

William's House

English	Spanish
barrels	barriles
cellar	sótano
clearing	claro
pegs	clavijas
spoil	estropearse
steep	empinado

442

Unit 3

The Gardener

English	Spanish
beauty	belleza
blooming	floreciendo
bulbs	bulbos
doze	me quedo dormido
humor	humor
recognizing	reconocer
showers	lluvias
sprouting	brotando

Pushing Up the Sky

English	Spanish
antlers	cuernos
imagined	imaginar
languages	idiomas
narrator	narrador
overhead	por arriba
(holes) poked	(agujeros) hechos

Night Letters

English	Spanish
blade	brizna
budding	brotando
dew	rocío
fireflies	luciérnagas
flutter	agito
notepad	libreta
patch	parcela

443

Glossary

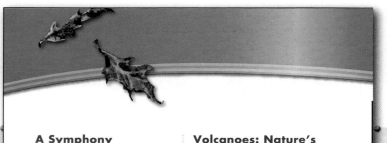

A Symphony of Whales

English	Spanish
anxiously	ansiosamente
bay	bahía
blizzards	ventiscas
channel	canal
chipped	picaron
melody	melodía
supplies	suministros
surrounded	rodeada
symphony	sinfonía

Volcanoes: Nature's Incredible Fireworks

English	Spanish
beneath	debajo de
buried	enterró
chimney	chimenea
earthquakes	terremotos
fireworks	fuegos artificiales
force	fuerza
trembles	tiembla
volcanoes	volcanes

444

Acknowledgments

Text

16: UPDATED From *Boom Town* by Sonia Levitin. Published by Orchard Books/Scholastic Inc. Copyright © 1998 by Sonia Levitin. Reprinted by permission; **38:** *The Kids' Business Book* by Arlene Erlbach. Copyright © 1998 by Arlene Erlbach. Used by permission of Lerner Publications Company, a division of Lerner Publishing Group. All rights reserved; **46:** *What About Me?* by Ed Young. Copyright © Ed Young, 2002. Published by arrangement with Philomel Books, a division of Penguin Young Readers Group, a member of Penguin Group (USA) Inc. All rights reserved; **68:** From *Alexander, Who Used to Be Rich Last Sunday.* Text copyright © 1978 by Judith Viorst. Illustrations copyright © 1978 by Ray Cruz. Reprinted with permission of Atheneum Books for Young Readers, Simon & Schuster Children's Publishing Division. All rights reserved; **90:** *If You Made a Million* by David M. Schwartz, Illustrations by Steven Kellogg, 1989. Used by permission of HarperCollins Publishers; **120:** From *My Rows and Piles of Coins* by Tololwa M. Mollel. Text copyright © 1999 by Tololwa M. Mollel. Illustrations copyright © 1999 by E. B. Lewis. Reprinted by permission of Clarion Books, a division of Houghton Mifflin Company. All rights reserved; **142:** "A Single Penny" from *The Song in My Head* by Felice Holman, 1985. Reprinted by permission of the author; **143:** "Fund-raiser" from *Almost Late to School And More School Poems* by Carol Diggory Shields, Dutton, © 2003 by Carol Diggory Shields, text. Used by permission of Dutton Children's Books, a Division of Penguin Young Readers Group, A Member of Penguin Group (USA) Inc., 345 Hudson Street, New York, NY 10014. All rights reserved. Used by permission of Ruth Cohen Inc. on behalf of the author; **144:** updated "Money" by Richard Armour from *For Partly Proud Parents: light verse about children,* with an introduction Phillis McGinley, 1950. Reprinted by permission; **145:** "coins" from *All The Small Poems and Fourteen More* by Valerie Worth. Copyright © 1987, 1994 by Valerie Worth. Reprinted by permission of Farrar, Straus & Giroux, LLC; **154:** *Penguin Chick* by Betty Tatham, illustrated by Helen K. Davie. Text copyright © 2002 Betty Tatham. Illustrations copyright © 2002 Helen Davie. Used by permission of HarperCollins Publishers; **170:** From *Seeds, Stems, and Stamens: The Ways Plants Fit into their World* by Susan E. Goodman; photographs by Michael J. Doolittle. Text copyright 2001 by Susan E. Goodman. Photographs copyright 2001 by Michael J. Doolittle. Used by permission of Millbrook Press, a division of Lerner Publishing Group. All rights reserved; **178:** *A Day's Work* by Eve Bunting, illustrated by Ronald Himler. Text copyright © 1994 by Eve Bunting. Illustrations copyright © 1994 by Ronald Himler. Reprinted by permission of Clarion Books/Houghton Mifflin Company. All rights reserved; **202:** (updated) From *Prudy's Problem and How She Solved It* by Carey Armstrong-Ellis. Published by Harry N. Abrams, Inc. Reprinted by permission; **228:** Text from *Tops And Bottoms,* copyright © 1995 by Janet Stevens, reprinted by permission of Harcourt, Inc.; **248:** "The Hare and the Tortoise" from *Aesop's Fables* selected and illustrated by Michael Hague. Specially edited text, © 1985 by Henry Holt and Company. Reprinted by permission of Henry Holt and Company, LLC.; **254:** From *William's House* by Ginger Howard, illustrated by Larry Day. Text copyright © 2001 by Ginger Howard, illustrations copyright © 2001 by Larry Day. Reprinted by permission of The Millbrook Press, Inc.; **272:** Reprinted with the permission of Atheneum Books for Young Readers, an imprint of Simon & Schuster Children's Publishing Division from *Fireflies at Midnight* by Marilyn Singer. Text copyright © 2003 Marilyn Singer; **273:** Reprinted with the permission of Atheneum Books for Young Readers, an imprint of Simon & Schuster Children's Publishing Division from *Here's What You Do When You Can't Find Your Shoe* by Andrea Perry. Text copyright © 2003 Andrea Perry; **274:** "Third-Grade Genius" from *Fearless Fernie: Hanging Out With Fernie and Me* by Gary Soto, copyright © 2002 by Gary Soto, text. Used by permission of G.P. Putnam's Sons, A Division of Penguin Young Readers Group, A Member of Penguin Group (USA) Inc., 345 Hudson Street, New York, NY 10014. All rights reserved; **284:** *The Gardener* by Sarah Stewart, pictures by David Small. Text copyright © 1997 by Sarah Stewart. Pictures copyright © 1997 by David Small. Reprinted by permission of Farrar, Straus and Giroux, LLC.; **308:** "Pushing Up the Sky," from *Pushing Up The Sky* by Joseph Bruchac, copyright © 2000 by Joseph Bruchac, text. Used by permission of Dial Books for Young Readers, A Division of Penguin Young Readers Group, A Member of Penguin Group (USA) Inc., 345 Hudson Street, New York, NY 10014. All rights reserved; **322:** Reprinted with the permission of Simon & Schuster Books for Young Readers, an imprint of Simon & Schuster Children's Publishing Division from *When The World Was Young* by Margaret Mayo, illustrated by Louise Brierley. Text copyright © 1995 Margaret Mayo. Illustrations copyright © 1995 Louise Brierley; **334:** (Updated Credit Line) From *Night Letters* by Palmyra LoMonaco, illustrations by Normand Chartier, 1996. Text © 1996 by Palmyra LoMonaco. Reprinted by permission of Palmyra LoMonaco and Normand Chartier; **352:** "dear stars" from *Dear World* by Takayo Noda, copyright © 2003 by Takayo Noda. Used by permission of Dial Books for Young Readers, A Division of Penguin Young Readers Group, A Member of Penguin Group (USA) Inc., 345 Hudson Street, New York, NY 10014. All rights reserved; **358:** Text from *A Symphony of Whales,* copyright © 1999 by Steve Schuch, reprinted by permission of Harcourt, Inc. and Steve Schuch; **376:** From "He Listens to Whales" by E. Shan Correa. Reprinted from the May 1991 issue of *Ranger Rick®* magazine, with the permission of the publisher, the National Wildlife Federation®. Copyright 1991 by the National Wildlife Federation®; **384:** Text copyright © 2002 by David L. Harrison, from *Volcanoes: Nature's Incredible Fireworks* by David L. Harrison. Published by Boyds Mill Press, Inc. Reprinted by permission; **396:** Reprinted by permission of Dr. George Pararas-Carayannis, The Tsunami Page of Dr. George PC, www.drgeorgepc.com; **396:** From "Natural Disasters," www.factmonster.com. © Pearson Education, published as Factmonster.com; **400:** "Cloud Dragons" from *Confetti Poems for Children.* Text copyright © 1996 by Pat Mora. Permission arranged with Lee & Low Books Inc., New York NY 10016; **401:** (updated) "Lemon Moon" by Beverly McLoughland, originally appeared in *Ranger Rick®*, November 1990. Reprinted by permission of the author; **402:** "springtime" from *Spin a Soft Black Song* by Nikki Giovanni. Copyright © 1971, 1985 by Nikki Giovanni. Reprinted by permission of Hill and Wang, a division of Farrar, Straus & Giroux, LLC; **403:** "Laughing Boy," original title "In the Falling Snow" by Richard Wright. Copyright © 1973 by Richard Wright. Reprinted by permission of John Hawkins & Associates, Inc.

445

Illustrations

Cover: ©Mark Buehner; **11, 16-36** John Sandford; **62-63** Ed Parker; **65** William (Bill) Cigliano; **84-85** Jim Steck; **85** Marcel Laverdet; **117, 119** Karen Blessen; **175** Chris Van Dusen; **199-201** Stephen Kroninger; **272-274** Sachiko Yoshikawa; **279, 358-372, 444** Wendell Minor; **279, 308-320, 443** Teresa Flavin; **300-303** Jeff Mangiat; **322-328** Richard Downs; **331** Susan Swann; **378** Peter Bollinger; **388-392** Patrice Rossi Calkin.

Photography

Every effort has been made to secure permission and provide appropriate credit for photographic material. The publisher deeply regrets any omission and pledges to correct errors called to its attention in subsequent editions.

Unless otherwise acknowledged, all photographs are the property of Scott Foresman, a division of Pearson Education.

Photo locators denoted as follows: Top (T), Center (C), Bottom (B), Left (L), Right (R), Background (Bkgd).

4 (CL, TC, TCR) ©Ed Honowitz/Getty Images; **6** ©Jerry Lofaro/Courtesy of Konica Minolta Business Solutions, Inc./American Artists Represents; **8** ©Tim Flach/Getty Images; **10** ©Royalty-Free/Corbis; **14** ©Michael Maslan Historic Photographs/Corbis; **15** (TR) ©Michael Maslan Historic Photographs/Corbis, (T) Corbis, (BR) ©Rex L. Stevens, X-8924/Denver Public Library, Western History Collection; **38-39** Courtesy Lerner Publishing Group; **43** Getty Images; **44** Getty Images; **45** Getty Images; **66** Getty Images; **67** Getty Images; **68** Getty Images; **73-79** Getty Images; **82** Getty Images; **89** ©HIRB/Index Stock Imagery; **112** (CR, TR, TC) Getty Images; **113** (TR, BR) Kate Warren/©Museum of Mankind/British Museum/DK Images; **114** (TL) Kate Warren/©Museum of Mankind/British Museum/DK Images, (BL) Mary Evans Picture Library, (BC) Chas Howson/©The British Museum/DK Images; **115** Kate Warren/©Museum of Mankind/British Museum/DK Images; **138** Getty Images; **143** Getty Images; **144** Getty Images; **146** (BL) ©Ed Honowitz/Getty Images, (CR, BR, BC, CL, CC) Getty Images; **147** ©Ed Honowitz/Getty Images; **148** ©Jerry Lofaro/Courtesy of Konica Minolta Business Solutions, Inc./American Artists Represents; **151** (T) Digital Stock, (BR) ©Ernest Manewal/Index Stock Imagery; **152** ©Joe McDonald/Visuals Unlimited; **153** (TC) Digital Vision, (BR) ©Volvox/Index Stock Imagery; **170-173** Michael J. Doolittle Photographer; **176** ©Jules Frazier/PhotoDisc; **177** (T, TR) Getty Images, (BR) ©Rubra/Reuters/Corbis; **194** Getty Images; **195** ©CSU/Denver County Cooperative Extension Master Gardener; **196** (BL) ©Barry Runk/Stan/Grant Heilman Photography, (BC) ©Neil Hardwick/Alamy Images, (BR) ©Peggy Heard/Frank Lane Picture Agency/Corbis; **197** (CL) ©Daniel Templeton/Alamy Images, (CR) ©Alan & Linda Detrick/Holt Studios International Ltd/Alamy Images; **221** (TL) ©Linda Nicholas/ Field Museum of Natural History, (BL) Photographer John Weinstein, A113330c/Field Museum of Natural History; **222** (TR) Photographer Ron Testa, A106506c/Field Museum of Natural History, (BR) [photographer unknown], A123T/Field Museum of Natural History; **223** Photographer John Weinstein, A112444c/Field Museum of Natural History; **225** (TC, R) Getty Images, (BC) ©Amy Neunsinger/PictureArts/Corbis; **227** (TC) Getty Images, (Bkgd) Getty Images; **251** (TR, B) ©Rick D'Elia/Corbis; **252** ©Miguel Angel Munoz/Age Fotostock; **253** (TR) ©Dana Hursey/Masterfile Corporation, (BR) ©Edward Slater/Index Stock Imagery; **254** ©Comstock, Inc.; **256** ©Dana Hursey/Masterfile Corporation; **258** Getty Images; **263** Getty Images; **266** (BC) ©Comstock, Inc., (TL) Getty Images; **268** Getty Images; **270** (TL) Brand X Pictures, (TC) Getty Images, (CL) ©Idaho State Historic Preservation Office, IHSI # 85-3697; **271** (BR) Brand X Pictures, (TL) ©Marilyn "Angel" Wynn/Native Stock, (TC) North Wind Picture Archives, (TR) Corbis, (CL) ©Minnesota Historical Society/Corbis; **277** Getty Images; **278** ©Brandon D. Cole/Corbis; **279** ©Richard Ustinich/Getty Images; **281** (T, BR) Brand X Pictures; **283** (T) ©Farrell Grehan/Corbis, (BL) Getty Images; **305** (B) ©Museum of History and Industry/Library of Congress, (TCR) ©Royalty-Free/Corbis; **307** Creatas; **332** ©Royalty-Free/Corbis; **333** (CR) ©Tony Wharton/Corbis, (BCR) ©Jim Sugar/Corbis, (BR) ©Jeff Daly/Visuals Unlimited; **355** (TR) ©Art Wolfe/Getty Images, (BL) ©David B. Fleetham/Visuals Unlimited; **356** ©David Hiser/Getty Images; **357** (T) ©Maria Stenzel/NGS Image Collection, (BR) ©Kim Westerskov/Getty Images; **376** (B) ©Joe Mobley, (C) Photo obtained under N.M.F.S. permit # 987/©Flip Nicklin/Minden Pictures; **378** ©Flip Nicklin/Minden Pictures; **379** (T) ©Royalty-Free/Corbis, (TL) Photo obtained under N.M.F.S. permit # 987/©Flip Nicklin/Minden Pictures; **381** (T) Getty Images, (B) ©Danny Lehman/Corbis; **382** Corbis; **383** ©Jim Sugar/Corbis; **384** ©Richard Ustinich/Getty Images; **386** (Bkgd, BC) Getty Images; **387** ©G. Brad Lewis/Getty Images; **388** (Bkgd) Getty Images, (C) ©Matthias Kulka/Corbis; **392** ©Jonathan Blair/Corbis; **394** ©Richard A. Cooke III/Getty Images; **396** Corbis; **398** ©Juan Carlos Munoz/AGE Fotostock; **399** (CR) ©Juan Carlos Munoz/AGE Fotostock, (TR) Corbis, (CL) ©Charles O'Rear/Corbis; **404** ©Tim Flach/Getty Images; **408** ©Hans Gutknecht; **409** Houghton Mifflin Company; **411** Photo of Judith Viorst used with permission of Simon & Schuster, Inc./©Didi Cutler; **412** ©Rose Eichenbaum/Sonia Levitin; **413** ©Michael Greenlar/Courtesy, Greenfield Review Press; **420** ©Jeff Evans; **424** ©Adam Jones/Visuals Unlimited; 427 (BL) ©Kjell B. Sandved/Visuals Unlimited, (CR) ©Myrleen Ferguson Cate/PhotoEdit; **428** ©Ann Elliott Cutting/Getty Images; **429** Getty Images; **431** ©Ranald Mackechnie/Stone/ Getty Images; **432** ©E. R. Degginger/Animals Animals/Earth Scenes; **433** ©Neal Mishler/Getty Images; **434** ©David Young-Wolff/PhotoEdit; **435** Digital Vision; **436** (CL) SuperStock, (BR) ©Mike Severns/Stone/Getty Images; **437** ©Cindy Kassab/Corbis; **438** (CL) ©C. L. Smith/Visuals Unlimited, (CR) Digital Vision; **439** ©Sally Mayman; **440** Getty Images.

Glossary

The contents of the glossary have been adapted from *Thorndike Barnhart School Dictionary,* copyright © 2001, Pearson Education, Inc.

446

Writing

Assessment

Student Tips for Making Top Scores in Writing Tests

1 **Use transitions such as those below to relate ideas, sentences, or paragraphs.**

in addition	nevertheless	finally	however
then	instead	therefore	as a result
for example	in particular	first	such as

2 **Write a good beginning. Make readers want to continue.**
- I shouldn't have opened that green box.
- Imagine being locked in a crate at the bottom of the sea.
- When I was four, I saw a purple dog.
- Have you ever heard of a talking tree?

3 **Focus on the topic.**
If a word or detail is off-topic, get rid of it. If a sentence is unrelated or loosely related to the topic, drop it or connect it more closely.

4 **Organize your ideas.**
Have a plan in mind before you start writing. Your plan can be a list, bulleted items, or a graphic organizer. Five minutes spent planning your work will make the actual writing go much faster and smoother.

5 **Support your ideas.**
- Develop your ideas with fully elaborated examples and details.
- Make ideas clear to readers by choosing vivid words that create pictures. Avoid dull (*get, go, say*), vague (*thing, stuff, lots of*), or overused (*really, very*) words.
- Use a voice that is appropriate to your audience.

6 **Make writing conventions as error-free as possible.**
Proofread your work line by line, sentence by sentence. Read for correct punctuation, then again for correct capitalization, and finally for correct spelling.

7 **Write a conclusion that wraps things up but is more than a repeating of ideas or "The end."**
- After all, he was my brother, weird or not.
- The Internet has changed our lives for better and for worse.
- It's not the largest planet but the one I'd choose to live on.
- Now tell me you don't believe in a sixth sense.

Rubric
4 | 3 | 2 | 1

Focus/Ideas

Organization/
Paragraphs

Voice

Word Choice

Sentences

Conventions

Writing Traits

- **Focus/Ideas** refers to the main purpose for writing and the details that make the subject clear and interesting. It includes development of ideas through support and elaboration.

- **Organization/Paragraphs** refers to the overall structure of a piece of writing that guides readers. Within that structure, transitions show how ideas, sentences, and paragraphs are connected.

- **Voice** shows the writer's unique personality and establishes a connection between writer and reader. Voice, which contributes to style, should be suited to the audience and the purpose for writing.

- **Word Choice** is the use of precise, vivid words to communicate effectively and naturally. It helps create style through the use of specific nouns, lively verbs and adjectives, and accurate, well-placed modifiers.

- **Sentences** covers strong, well-built sentences that vary in length and type. Skillfully written sentences have pleasing rhythms and flow fluently.

- **Conventions** refers to mechanical correctness and includes grammar, usage, spelling, punctuation, capitalization, and paragraphing.

Writing Workshop

OBJECTIVES

- Develop an understanding of a how-to report.
- Include necessary information in a how-to report.
- Use precise words and no wordiness in a how-to report.
- Establish criteria for evaluating a how-to report.

Key Features
How-to Report

In a how-to report, a writer gives a step-by-step explanation of how to perform a specific task.

- Explains a task fully
- Uses words such as *first* to show the order of steps
- Provides necessary information and details
- Has clear sentences to guide readers

Connect to Weekly Writing

Week 1	Summary 173g–173h
Week 2	Rules 197g–197h
Week 3	Problem-Solution 223g–223h
Week 4	Feature Story 249g–249h
Week 5	Explanatory Paragraph 271g–271h

Strategic Intervention

See Differentiated Instruction p. WA8.

Advanced

See Differentiated Instruction p. WA9.

E L L

See Differentiated Instruction p. WA9.

Additional Resource for Writing
Writing Rubrics and Anchor Papers, pp. 9–13.

How-to Report

Writing Prompt: Smart Solutions

Think of something you learned or figured out how to do that involves a few simple steps. Write the steps in a how-to report. Make sure you provide all the necessary information.

Purpose: Explain the steps it takes to do something

Audience: A younger child

READ LIKE A WRITER

Look back at *Penguin Chick*. Have students recall that the story describes each step the mother and father penguin take in order to help a baby penguin hatch. Point out that a writer also describes each step in a process in a **how-to report.**

EXAMINE THE MODEL AND RUBRIC

GUIDED WRITING Read the model aloud. Have students find sentences in which the writer uses time-order words to make the order of steps clear. Discuss how the model reflects traits of good writing.

How to Make a Bird Feeder

Do you like to watch birds in your yard? You can help birds and have fun too by making a bird feeder. There are many different kinds of bird feeders. Some are made especially to attract certain kinds of birds. I will tell you how to make a bird feeder that a variety of birds will like.

For this bird feeder you will need a pine cone, a long string, peanut butter, margarine, and birdseed. First, tie the string to the top of the pine cone. Second, mix some peanut butter and margarine together. Your mixture should contain one-half peanut butter and one-half margarine. Spread this sticky mixture all over the pine cone. Next put some birdseed on a plate. Roll the pine cone around so that birdseed sticks all over it. Place the pine cone in the freezer for an hour or so. Finally, hang the pine cone on a tree branch outside your house. Now you can see how many different kinds of birds live in your neighborhood.

Unit 2 How-to Report • PREWRITE **Writing Process 8**

▲ **Writing Transparency** WP8

Traits of a Good How-to Report

Focus/Ideas	How-to report is well focused and developed with necessary details.
Organization/ Paragraphs	Report begins with an introduction that states the topic and attracts interest. Instructions develop in a clear sequence.
Voice	Writer expresses enthusiasm for activity and demonstrates knowledge of the steps involved.
Word Choice	Writer uses precise verbs (*spread, roll, hang*) and time-order words (*First, Next, Finally*) to show the sequence of steps.
Sentences	Sentences are varied and of different lengths and patterns. Instructions consist of commands.
Conventions	Writer has a good control of spelling, grammar, capitalization, and usage.

Unit 2 How-to Report • PREWRITE **Writing Process 9**

▲ **Writing Transparency** WP9

FINDING A TOPIC

- With students, brainstorm simple tasks that they know how to perform. Write a list on the board.
- Have students look through books and magazines for ideas about simple tasks they know how to do.
- Have students look around a kitchen, a garage, a backyard, and a playground for ideas of activities or tasks they know how to perform.

NARROW A TOPIC

How to play the piano.   This is too difficult.

How to make fruit salad.   This might be too simple.

How to make an art rubbing.   This is a fun art project.

PREWRITING STRATEGY

GUIDED WRITING Display Writing Transparency WP10. Model how to complete a how-to chart.

Think Aloud **MODEL** This student has an interesting activity to explain. The student has listed each step in the process. Now the student can write a draft by adding details to each step.

PREWRITING ACTIVITIES

- Have students use Grammar and Writing Practice Book p. 164 to help them organize information about their chosen topic.
- Students can add details and specific language to each of the steps of the process they are describing.

How-to Chart

Directions Fill in the how-to chart with information about your project.

Task   Make an art rubbing with everyday objects.

Materials   Crayons, paper, small objects with interesting shapes such as keys and coins

Introduction   The materials for a great art project are at your fingertips.

Steps
1. Find small items.
2. Get crayons and paper.
3. Put a coin on a table.
4. Put paper over the coin.
5. Rub a crayon over the paper where the coin is.
6. Put other objects under the paper and color over them.
7. Make unusual designs by using different shapes and colors.

Conclusion   Make greeting cards for special friends. Decorate borders of stories and poems. Frame rubbing and hang it in your room. The only limit is your own creativity!

Unit 2 How-to Report • PREWRITE   Writing Process **10**

▲ **Writing Transparency** WP10

General:	Specific:
Put the coin on a table.	Put the coin on a flat table.
Place paper on top of the coin.	Place a piece of thin paper on top of the coin.

How-to Chart

Directions Fill in the graphic organizer with information about your project.

Task   **Answers should include details about**

Materials   **each part of the how-to report.**

Introduction _____

Steps _____

Conclusion _____

164 Unit 2   Grammar and Writing Practice Book

▲ **Grammar and Writing Practice Book** p. 164

Smart Solutions **WA3**

Writing Workshop

1 PREWRITE · 2 DRAFT · 3 REVISE · 4 EDIT · 5 PUBLISH

Think Like a Writer

Use Strong Verbs The focus of a how-to report is *doing* something. You will use commands to tell readers how to perform the steps. Begin each one with a strong, precise verb: *fasten, outline, paint.*

E L L

Support Writing If students include home-language words, help them find English words to replace them. Resources can include:
• conversations with you
• other home-language speakers
• bilingual dictionaries, if available
• online translation sources

Time-Order Words

Directions Add a time-order word to each of the five steps below. Write each sentence. Then add a final sentence using a time-order word. Tell what you could do with the flowers. **Possible answers:**

1. Find a pretty vase.
   First, find a pretty vase.

2. Pick some wildflowers from a field.
   Second, pick some wildflowers from a field.

3. Put water in the vase.
   Next, put water in the vase.

4. Place the flowers in the water.
   Then place the flowers in the water.

5. Arrange the flowers in an attractive pattern.
   Finally, arrange the flowers in an attractive pattern.

6. **Later, place the flowers on a table or windowsill and enjoy them.**

Grammar and Writing Practice Book   Unit 2 **165**

▲ **Grammar and Writing Practice Book** p. 165

WRITING THE FIRST DRAFT

GUIDED WRITING Use Writing Transparency WP11 to practice using time-order words.

• Have students read each step and think about its place in the process. Have them add a word that makes this step in the sequence clear.

• Point out that time-order words are especially necessary in a how-to report because readers must follow the steps in an exact order.

Think Aloud

MODEL I often follow directions for a game, project, or recipe. I know it is important to do each step in order. Otherwise, the project or recipe might not turn out right. So when I explain how to do something, I want to make sure the readers understand what has to be done first, second, next, and last. I can use each of these words to make the directions clear.

Time-Order Words

A how-to report uses time-order words that show when each step of the process should be done.

Confusing Put the coin on a flat table with a thin piece of paper on top.
Improved First put the coin on a flat table. Then place a piece of thin paper on top of the coin.

Directions Add a time-order word to each step. **Possible answers:**

1. Place a piece of thin paper on top of the coin.
   Second, place a piece of thin paper on top of the coin.

2. Rub the side of a crayon over the paper.
   Next rub the side of a crayon over the paper.

3. Try an object with a different shape.
   Then try an object with a different shape.

4. Make your design into a greeting card.
   Finally, make your design into a greeting card.

Unit 2 How-to Report · DRAFT   Writing Process **11**

▲ **Writing Transparency** WP11

WRITER'S CRAFT Use Precise Words

Here are some ways writers can use precise words:
• When using general nouns such as **objects** or **items**, give examples of them, such as **coins**.
• Use descriptive words that show what things look, sound, feel, taste, or smell like.
• Use verbs that tell exactly what to do, such as **rub**.

DRAFTING STRATEGIES

• Have students review their how-to chart before they write.

• Students should use time-order words such as *first, next,* and *then* to show the exact sequence of steps in the process.

• Remind students to keep their audiences and purposes in mind.

• Students should follow the directions above to ensure use of precise words in their reports.

• Have students use Grammar and Writing Practice Book p. 165 to choose time-order words.

WRITER'S CRAFT Elaboration

VIVID WORDS Explain that one way to elaborate is to use vivid words such as precise common nouns and proper nouns. Specific nouns help create a picture in a reader's mind.

Vague	You can form all kinds of shapes.
Improved	You can form letters, borders, and other shapes.

Use Grammar and Writing Practice Book p. 166 to practice elaboration by using precise, vivid words.

REVISING STRATEGIES

GUIDED WRITING Use Writing Transparency WP12 to model revising. Point out the Revising Marks, which students should use when they revise their work.

Think Aloud

MODEL This is part of the how-to report on art rubbings. In the fourth sentence, the vague, casual word *stuff* has been changed to a more specific word, *items*. The precise nouns *coins* and *keys* have also been added. In the next sentence, the general verb *get* has been changed to a more precise verb, *collect*. In the next sentence, the time-order word *next* has been added. This helps readers understand the exact order of the steps.

PEER REVISION Write the Revising Checklist on the board, or make copies to distribute. Students can use this checklist to revise their how-to reports. Have partners read one another's first drafts. Remind them to be courteous and specific with suggestions.

Revising Marks	
Take Out	⌐
Add	^
Small Letter	/

The materials for a great art project are at your fingertips.

All you need are some objects with interesting shapes. Check

your jangling pockets or messy desk drawer. Everyone has stuff _items_

such as paper clips and combs. Get a few of these. Get some _, coins, keys, Collect Next_

crayons and paper. I will show you the necessary steps to make

an unusual art rubbing.

Unit 2 How-to Report • REVISE   Writing Process **12**

▲ **Writing Transparency** WP12

Trait Checklist
REVISING

Focus/Ideas
- ✔ Is the how-to report focused?
- ✔ Are there enough details?

Organization/Paragraphs
- ✔ Do time-order words help make the sequence of steps clear?

Voice
- ✔ Does the writer show enthusiasm and knowledge?

Word Choice
- ✔ Do vivid, precise words make the process clear?

Sentences
- ✔ Are commands with strong verbs used to explain the steps?

Elaboration
Vivid Words

When you write, you can elaborate by using vivid, precise words. For example, you can use specific common nouns and proper nouns.
General Words   Watch that kite go in the air.
Precise Words   Watch that kite soar up in the clouds.

Directions Replace each underlined word with a vivid, precise word. Write each sentence. Possible answers:

1. Cut paper for your kite in a shape.
   Cut paper for your kite in a triangle.

2. Make your kite a good color.
   Paint your kite a brilliant red.

3. Put some sticks on your kite.
   Glue some sticks on your kite.

4. Put your kite high in the air.
   Float your kite high in the air.

5. Use your kite with some people.
   Fly your kite with some good friends.

166 Unit 2   Grammar and Writing Practice Book

▲ **Grammar and Writing Practice Book** p. 166

Writing Workshop

1 PREWRITE 2 DRAFT 3 REVISE **4 EDIT** 5 PUBLISH

Editing Checklist

✔ Did I spell words ending in -le correctly?

✔ Did I use the correct form for possessive nouns?

✔ Did I spell irregular plurals correctly?

✔ Did I indent each paragraph?

Support Writing Invite students to read their drafts aloud to you. Observe whether they seem to note any spelling or grammatical errors by stumbling or self-correcting. Return to those errors and how to correct them. Use the appropriate Grammar Transition Lessons in the ELL Resource Handbook to explicitly teach the English conventions.

EDITING STRATEGY

KEEP A DICTIONARY HANDY Suggest that students use an editing strategy. They can check their spelling by looking up words they are unsure of in a dictionary.

GUIDED WRITING Use Writing Transparency WP13 to model the process of keeping a dictionary handy. Indicate the Proofreading Marks, which students should use when they edit their work. Write the Editing Checklist on the board, or make copies to distribute. Students can use this checklist to edit their work.

 Think Aloud

MODEL First, I'll check spelling. I notice that a word with the ending -le, table, was misspelled. The writer has corrected it. In the next sentence, the word *peice* does not look right. By keeping a dictionary nearby, you can look up words that you are unsure of. The dictionary shows that the spelling is *piece,* and the writer has corrected it. Further down in the paragraph, the phrase *papers edges* should have a possessive noun. *Papers* needs an apostrophe. The writer has added one.

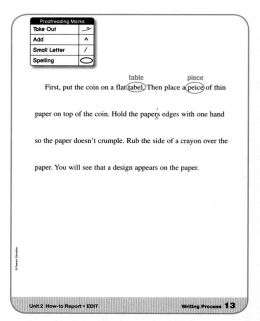

▲ **Writing Transparency** WP13

If time permits, conference with students to see that they understand how to edit their writing.

Tech Talk
OFFLINE

USING TECHNOLOGY Students who have written or revised their how-to reports on computers should keep these points in mind as they edit:

- A computer spell checker is useful, but it should not be relied on exclusively. A dictionary is the best source for accurate information.

- If your work is more than a single page, you may wish to use the header or footer feature in the menu to include a page number.

- When unsure about how to use a computer feature correctly, don't guess. Ask a friend or use the *help* menu item.

SELF-EVALUATION

Prepare students to fill out a Self-Evaluation Guide. Display Writing Transparency WP14 to model the self-evaluation process.

Think Aloud **MODEL** I would give the how-to report a 4.

Focus/Ideas This how-to report focuses on making an art rubbing. All the sentences contribute to this main idea.

Organization/Paragraphs The steps of the process are described in order.

Voice The narrator has a unique voice. It is enthusiastic and shows knowledge about the process.

Word Choice Time-order words make the order of steps clear. Vivid words such as *jangling* and *crumple* make the report lively.

Sentences Sentences that tell readers what to do are commands.

Conventions Grammar, capitalization, and handwriting are excellent.

EVALUATION Assign Grammar and Writing Practice Book p. 167. Tell students that when they evaluate their own narratives, assigning a score of 3, 2, or even 1 does not necessarily indicate a bad paper. The ability to identify areas for improvement in future writing is a valuable skill.

How to Make an Art Rubbing

The materials for a great art project are at your fingertips. All you need are some objects with interesting shapes. Check your jangling pockets or messy desk drawer. Everyone has items such as paper clips, coins, keys, and combs. Collect a few of these. Next get some crayons and paper. I will show you the necessary steps to make an unusual art rubbing.

First, put the coin on a flat table. Then place a piece of thin paper on top of the coin. Hold the paper's edges with one hand so the paper doesn't crumple. Rub the side of a crayon over the paper. You will see that a design appears on the paper. Next, try an object with a different shape, such as a key. You can rub each object on several different areas of the page. Repeat these steps to form letters, borders, and other shapes. Use additional colors, and soon your paper will be decorated with bright patterns.

Use your artwork to make different items, such as greeting cards for special friends. Decorate the borders of stories and poems that you write. You can even frame an especially interesting rubbing and hang it in your room. The only limit is your own creativity!

Unit 2 How-to Report • PUBLISH — Writing Process **14**

▲ **Writing Transparency** WP14

Self-Evaluation Guide
How-to Report

Directions Think about the final draft of your how-to report. Then rate yourself on a scale of from 4 to 1 (4 is the highest) on each writing trait. After you fill out the chart, answer the questions.

Writing Traits	4	3	2	1
Focus/Ideas				
Organization/Paragraphs				
Voice				
Word Choice				
Sentences				
Conventions				

1. What is the best part of your how-to report?
   Students' responses should show that they have given thought to the how-to reports they have written.

2. Write one thing you would change about this how-to report if you had the chance to write it again.
   Students' responses should show that they have given thought to the how-to reports they have written.

Grammar and Writing Practice Book — Unit 2 **167**

▲ **Grammar and Writing Practice Book** p. 167

Scoring Rubric — How-to Report

Rubric 4 3 2 1	4	3	2	1
Focus/Ideas	How-to report well focused and fully developed	How-to report generally focused and developed	How-to report that strays from subject or lacks necessary details	How-to report that lacks focus or has insufficient information
Organization/ Paragraphs	Sequence of events entirely clear	Sequence fairly clear	Confused sequence of events	No sequence, or sequence is incoherent
Voice	Knowledgeable, enthusiastic voice	Voice trustworthy but not compelling or unique	No clear, original voice	Uninvolved or indifferent
Word Choice	Vivid descriptive words; time-order words used to clarify	Some vivid words; some use of time-order words	Few vivid words; few or no time-order words	Incorrect or limited word choice
Sentences	Clear sentences; use of commands	Mostly clear sentences some commands	Little or no variety; no commands	Incoherent sentences, or short, choppy sentences
Conventions	Few, if any, errors	Few errors	Errors that detract from writing and may interfere with understanding	Errors that seriously detract from writing and may prevent understanding

For 6-, 5-, and 3-point Scoring Rubrics, see pp. WA11–WA14.

Writing Workshop

How-to Report
Differentiated Instruction

WRITING PROMPT: Smart Solutions

Think of something you learned or figured out how to do that involves a few simple steps. Write the steps in a how-to report. Make sure you provide all the necessary information

Purpose: Explain the steps it takes to do something

Audience: A younger child

MODIFY INSTRUCTION

Pick One

ALTERNATIVE PROMPTS

ALTERNATIVE PROMPTS: Expository Writing

Strategic Intervention What kind of sandwich do you like to eat? Write a paragraph that tells someone younger than you how to make the sandwich.

On-Level You are writing instructions to go with your favorite board game. Write a paragraph or two to tell younger people how to play the game. Accompany your how-to explanation with an illustration.

Advanced Think of something you have made on your own. Write two or three paragraphs that explain to adults the steps for making it. Give vivid details about each step that help readers picture how it is done. Provide an introduction and a conclusion.

Strategic Intervention

MODIFY THE PROMPT

Help emerging writers collaborate on a how-to paragraph. Help them decide on a topic. Call on students to describe each step of the activity. Help them express each step in writing.

PREWRITING SUPPORT

- Describe an experience in which how-to steps were necessary in order to complete a project or enjoy the experience. Discuss the importance of writing clear steps to give readers the help they need.

- Bring several examples of how-to writing, such as game directions, craft instructions, and a recipe, to class. Read them aloud and then have students summarize the steps involved.

- Interview students about the steps involved in the activity. Help them write a numbered list of steps. Circle verbs to indicate the focus for each step.

OPTIONS

- Give students the option of writing a group how-to paragraph under your supervision.

CHECK PROGRESS Segment the assignment into manageable pieces. Check work at intervals, such as graphic organizers and first drafts, to make sure writing is on track.

MODIFY THE PROMPT

Expect advanced writers to produce a report that explains how to do an activity of at least five steps. They should use interesting verbs and include details that create a unique voice. Students should provide an introduction and a conclusion to their how-to explanation.

APPLY SKILLS

- As students revise their work, have them consider ways to improve it.
- Use strong, precise verbs in each command to make each step clearer.
- Eliminate wordiness to help readers focus on the necessary information.
- Use interesting nouns and make sure their plurals are spelled correctly.

OPTIONS

- Students can follow these steps to create their own class rubrics.

  1. Read examples of class how-to reports and rank them 1–4, with 4 the highest.
  2. Discuss how they arrived at each rank.
  3. Isolate the six traits and make a rubric based on them.

CHECK PROGRESS Discuss the students' Self-Evaluation Guides. Work with students to monitor their growth and identify their strengths and weaknesses as writers.

MODIFY THE PROMPT

Have beginning speakers dictate their reports to you or to another proficient speaker to record. Help them restate their ideas as complete sentences. Record the sentences and have students copy them.

BUILD BACKGROUND

- Write the word *how-to* on the board. Explain that it describes the way something is done. Discuss the fact that a how-to report always involves a number of steps. Each step explains how to do one part of the activity. Discuss the list of Key Features of a how-to report that appears in the left column of p. WA2.

OPTIONS

- As students write their how-to reports, guide them toward books, magazines, or Web sites that provide comprehension support through features such as the following:

  step-by-step instructions with illustrations or diagrams

  text in the home-language

- For more suggestions on scaffolding the Writing Workshop, see the ELL and Transition Handbook.

CHECK PROGRESS You may need to explain certain traits and help students fill out their Self-Evaluation Guides. Downplay conventions and focus more on ideas. Recognize examples of vocabulary growth and efforts to use language in more complex ways.

Scoring Rubric **Look Back and Write**

2 points The response indicates that the student has a complete understanding of the reading concept embodied in the task. The response is accurate, complete, and fulfills all the requirements of the task. Necessary support and/or examples are included, and the information given is clearly text-based.

1 point The response indicates that the student has a partial understanding of the reading concept embodied in the task. The response includes information that is essentially correct and text-based, but the information is too general or too simplistic. Some of the support and/or examples may be incomplete or omitted.

0 points The response indicates that the student does not demonstrate an understanding of the reading concept embodied in the task. The student has either failed to respond or has provided a response that is inaccurate or has insufficient information.

Scoring Rubric **Look Back and Write**

4 points The response indicates that the student has a thorough understanding of the reading concept embodied in the task. The response is accurate, complete, and fulfills all the requirements of the task. Necessary support and/or examples are included, and the information is clearly text-based.

3 points The response indicates that the student has an understanding of the reading concept embodied in the task. The response is accurate and fulfills all the requirements of the task, but the required support and/or details are not complete or clearly text-based.

2 points The response indicates that the student has a partial understanding of the reading concept embodied in the task. The response that includes information is essentially correct and text-based, but the information is too general or too simplistic. Some of the support and/or examples and requirements of the task may be incomplete or omitted.

1 point The response indicates that the student has a very limited understanding of the reading concept embodied in the task. The response is incomplete, may exhibit many flaws, and may not address all requirements of the task.

0 points The response indicates that the student does not demonstrate an understanding of the reading concept embodied in the task. The student has either failed to respond or has provided a response that is inaccurate or has insufficient information.

Scoring Rubric — Narrative Writing

Rubric 4 3 2 1

	6	5	4	3	2	1
Focus/Ideas	Excellent, focused narrative; well elaborated with quality details	Good, focused narrative; elaborated with telling details	Narrative focused; adequate elaboration	Generally focused narrative; some supporting details	Sometimes unfocused narrative; needs more supporting details	Rambling narrative; lacks development and detail
Organization/ Paragraphs	Strong beginning, middle, and end; appropriate order words	Coherent beginning, middle, and end; some order words	Beginning, middle, and end easily identifiable	Recognizable beginning, middle, and end; some order words	Little direction from beginning to end; few order words	Lacks beginning, middle, end; incorrect or no order words
Voice	Writer closely involved; engaging personality	Reveals personality	Pleasant but not compelling voice	Sincere voice but not fully engaged	Little writer involvement, personality	Careless writing with no feeling
Word Choice	Vivid, precise words that bring story to life	Clear words to bring story to life	Some specific word pictures	Language adequate but lacks color	Generally limited or redundant language	Vague, dull, or misused words
Sentences	Excellent variety of sentences; natural rhythm	Varied lengths, styles; generally smooth	Correct sentences with some variations in style	Correctly constructed sentences; some variety	May have simple, awkward, or wordy sentences; little variety	Choppy; many incomplete or run-on sentences
Conventions	Excellent control; few or no errors	No serious errors to affect understanding	General mastery of conventions but some errors	Reasonable control; few distracting errors	Weak control; enough errors to affect understanding	Many errors that prevent understanding

Scoring Rubric — Narrative Writing

Rubric 4 3 2 1

	5	4	3	2	1
Focus/Ideas	Excellent, focused narrative; well elaborated with quality details	Good, focused narrative; elaborated with telling details	Generally focused narrative; some supporting details	Sometimes unfocused narrative; needs more supporting details	Rambling narrative; lacks development and detail
Organization/ Paragraphs	Strong beginning, middle, and end; appropriate order words	Coherent beginning, middle, and end; some order words	Recognizable beginning, middle, and end; some order words	Little direction from beginning to end; few order words	Lacks beginning, middle, end; incorrect or no order words
Voice	Writer closely involved; engaging personality	Reveals personality	Sincere voice but not fully engaged	Little writer involvement, personality	Careless writing with no feeling
Word Choice	Vivid, precise words that bring story to life	Clear words to bring story to life	Language adequate but lacks color	Generally limited or redundant language	Vague, dull, or misused words
Sentences	Excellent variety of sentences; natural rhythm	Varied lengths, styles; generally smooth	Correctly constructed sentences; some variety	May have simple, awkward, or wordy sentences; little variety	Choppy; many incomplete or run-on sentences
Conventions	Excellent control; few or no errors	No serious errors to affect understanding	Reasonable control; few distracting errors	Weak control; enough errors to affect understanding	Many errors that prevent understanding

Scoring Rubric — Narrative Writing

Rubric 4 3 2 1

	3	2	1
Focus/Ideas	Excellent, focused narrative; well elaborated with quality details	Generally focused narrative; some supporting details	Rambling narrative; lacks development and detail
Organization/ Paragraphs	Strong beginning, middle, and end; appropriate order words	Recognizable beginning, middle, and end; some order words	Lacks beginning, middle, end; incorrect or no order words
Voice	Writer closely involved; engaging personality	Sincere voice but not fully engaged	Careless writing with no feeling
Word Choice	Vivid, precise words that bring story to life	Language adequate but lacks color	Vague, dull, or misused words
Sentences	Excellent variety of sentences; natural rhythm	Correctly constructed sentences; some variety	Choppy; many incomplete or run-on sentences
Conventions	Excellent control; few or no errors	Reasonable control; few distracting errors	Many errors that prevent understanding

Scoring Rubric — Descriptive Writing

Rubric 4 3 2 1

	6	5	4	3	2	1
Focus/Ideas	Excellent, focused description; well elaborated with quality details	Good, focused description; elaborated with telling details	Description focused; good elaboration	Generally focused description; some supporting details	Sometimes unfocused description; needs more supporting details	Rambling description; lacks development and detail
Organization/ Paragraphs	Compelling ideas enhanced by order, structure, and transitions	Appealing order, structure, and transitions	Structure identifiable and suitable; transitions used	Adequate order, structure, and transitions to guide reader	Little direction from beginning to end; few transitions	Lacks direction and identifiable structure; no transitions
Voice	Writer closely involved; engaging personality	Reveals personality	Pleasant but not compelling voice	Sincere voice but not fully engaged	Little writer involvement, personality	Careless writing with no feeling
Word Choice	Vivid, precise words that create memorable pictures	Clear, interesting words to bring description to life	Some specific word pictures	Language adequate; appeals to senses	Generally limited or redundant language	Vague, dull, or misused words
Sentences	Excellent variety of sentences; natural rhythm	Varied lengths, styles; generally smooth	Correct sentences with variations in style	Correctly constructed sentences; some variety	May have simple, awkward, or wordy sentences; little variety	Choppy; many incomplete run-on sentences
Conventions	Excellent control; few or no errors	No serious errors to affect understanding	General mastery of conventions but some errors	Reasonable control; few distracting errors	Weak control; enough errors to affect understanding	Many errors that prevent understanding

Scoring Rubric — Descriptive Writing

Rubric 4 3 2 1

	5	4	3	2	1
Focus/Ideas	Excellent, focused description; well elaborated with quality details	Good, focused description; elaborated with telling details	Generally focused description; some supporting details	Sometimes unfocused description; needs more supporting details	Rambling description; lacks development and detail
Organization/ Paragraphs	Compelling ideas enhanced by order, structure, and transitions	Appealing order, structure, and transitions	Adequate order, structure, and some transitions to guide reader	Little direction from beginning to end; few transitions	Lacks direction and identifiable structure; no transitions
Voice	Writer closely involved; engaging personality	Reveals personality	Sincere voice but not fully engaged	Little writer involvement, personality	Careless writing with no feeling
Word Choice	Vivid, precise words that create memorable pictures	Clear, interesting words to bring description to life	Language adequate; appeals to senses	Generally limited or redundant language	Vague, dull, or misused words
Sentences	Excellent variety of sentences; natural rhythm	Varied lengths, styles; generally smooth	Correctly constructed sentences; some variety	May have simple, awkward, or wordy sentences; little variety	Choppy; many incomplete or run-on sentences
Conventions	Excellent control; few or no errors	No serious errors to affect understanding	Reasonable control; few distracting errors	Weak control; enough errors to affect understanding	Many errors that prevent understanding

Scoring Rubric — Descriptive Writing

Rubric 4 3 2 1

	3	2	1
Focus/Ideas	Excellent, focused description; well elaborated with quality details	Generally focused description; some supporting details	Rambling description; lacks development and detail
Organization/ Paragraphs	Compelling ideas enhanced by order, structure, and transitions	Adequate order, structure, and some transitions to guide reader	Lacks direction and identifiable structure; no transitions
Voice	Writer closely involved; engaging personality	Sincere voice but not fully engaged	Careless writing with no feeling
Word Choice	Vivid, precise words that create memorable pictures	Language adequate; appeals to senses	Vague, dull, or misused words
Sentences	Excellent variety of sentences; natural rhythm	Correctly constructed sentences; some variety	Choppy; many incomplete or run-on sentences
Conventions	Excellent control; few or no errors	Reasonable control; few distracting errors	Many errors that prevent understanding

Scoring Rubric — Persuasive Writing

Rubric 4 3 2 1	6	5	4	3	2	1
Focus/Ideas	Persuasive argument carefully built with quality details	Persuasive argument well supported with details	Persuasive argument focused; good elaboration	Persuasive argument with one or two convincing details	Persuasive piece sometimes unfocused; needs more support	Rambling persuasive argument; lacks development and detail
Organization/ Paragraphs	Information chosen and arranged for maximum effect	Evident progression of persuasive ideas	Progression and structure evident	Information arranged in a logical way with some lapses	Little structure or direction	No identifiable structure
Voice	Writer closely involved; persuasive but not overbearing	Maintains persuasive tone	Persuasive but not compelling voice	Sometimes uses persuasive voice	Little writer involvement, personality	Shows little conviction
Word Choice	Persuasive words carefully chosen for impact	Argument supported by persuasive language	Uses some persuasive words	Occasional persuasive language	Generally limited or redundant language	Vague, dull, or misused words; no persuasive words
Sentences	Excellent variety of sentences; natural rhythm	Varied lengths, styles; generally smooth	Correct sentences with variations in style	Carefully constructed sentences; some variety	Simple, awkward, or wordy sentences; little variety	Choppy; many incomplete or run-on sentences
Conventions	Excellent control; few or no errors	No serious errors to affect understanding	General mastery of conventions but some errors	Reasonable control; few distracting errors	Weak control; enough errors to affect understanding	Many errors that prevent understanding

Scoring Rubric — Persuasive Writing

Rubric 4 3 2 1	5	4	3	2	1
Focus/Ideas	Persuasive argument carefully built with quality details	Persuasive argument well supported with details	Persuasive argument with one or two convincing details	Persuasive piece sometimes unfocused; needs more support	Rambling persuasive argument; lacks development and detail
Organization/ Paragraphs	Information chosen and arranged for maximum effect	Evident progression of persuasive ideas	Information arranged in a logical way with some lapses	Little structure or direction	No identifiable structure
Voice	Writer closely involved; persuasive but not overbearing	Maintains persuasive tone	Sometimes uses persuasive voice	Little writer involvement, personality	Shows little conviction
Word Choice	Persuasive words carefully chosen for impact	Argument supported by persuasive language	Occasional persuasive language	Generally limited or redundant language	Vague, dull, or misused words; no persuasive words
Sentences	Excellent variety of sentences; natural rhythm	Varied lengths, styles; generally smooth	Carefully constructed sentences; some variety	Simple, awkward, or wordy sentences; little variety	Choppy; many incomplete or run-on sentences
Conventions	Excellent control; few or no errors	No serious errors to affect understanding	Reasonable control; few distracting errors	Weak control; enough errors to affect understanding	Many errors that prevent understanding

Scoring Rubric — Persuasive Writing

Rubric 4 3 2 1	3	2	1
Focus/Ideas	Persuasive argument carefully built with quality details	Persuasive argument with one or two convincing details	Rambling persuasive argument; lacks development and detail
Organization/ Paragraphs	Information chosen and arranged for maximum effect	Information arranged in a logical way with some lapses	No identifiable structure
Voice	Writer closely involved; persuasive but not overbearing	Sometimes uses persuasive voice	Shows little conviction
Word Choice	Persuasive words carefully chosen for impact	Occasional persuasive language	Vague, dull, or misused words; no persuasive words
Sentences	Excellent variety of sentences; natural rhythm	Carefully constructed sentences; some variety	Choppy; many incomplete or run-on sentences
Conventions	Excellent control; few or no errors	Reasonable control; few distracting errors	Many errors that prevent understanding

Scoring Rubric — Expository Writing

Rubric 4 3 2 1	6	5	4	3	2	1
Focus/Ideas	Insightful, focused exposition; well elaborated with quality details	Informed, focused exposition; elaborated with telling details	Exposition focused, good elaboration	Generally focused exposition; some supporting details	Sometimes unfocused exposition needs more supporting details	Rambling exposition; lacks development and detail
Organization/ Paragraphs	Logical, consistent flow of ideas; good transitions	Logical sequencing of ideas; uses transitions	Ideas sequenced with some transitions	Sequenced ideas with some transitions	Little direction from beginning to end; few order words	Lacks structure and transitions
Voice	Writer closely involved; informative voice well suited to topic	Reveals personality; voice suited to topic	Pleasant but not compelling voice	Sincere voice suited to topic	Little writer involvement, personality	Careless writing with no feeling
Word Choice	Vivid, precise words to express ideas	Clear words to express ideas	Words correct and adequate	Language adequate but may lack precision	Generally limited or redundant language	Vague, dull, or misused words
Sentences	Strong topic sentence; fluent, varied structures	Good topic sentence; smooth sentence structure	Correct sentences that are sometimes fluent	Topic sentence correctly constructed; some sentence variety	Topic sentence unclear or missing; wordy, awkward sentences	No topic sentence; many incomplete or run-on sentences
Conventions	Excellent control; few or no errors	No serious errors to affect understanding	General mastery of conventions but some errors	Reasonable control; few distracting errors	Weak control; enough errors to affect understanding	Many errors that prevent understanding

Scoring Rubric — Expository Writing

Rubric 4 3 2 1	5	4	3	2	1
Focus/Ideas	Insightful, focused exposition; well elaborated with quality details	Informed, focused exposition; elaborated with telling details	Generally focused exposition; some supporting details	Sometimes unfocused exposition needs more supporting details	Rambling exposition; lacks development and detail
Organization/ Paragraphs	Logical, consistent flow of ideas; good transitions	Logical sequencing of ideas; uses transitions	Sequenced ideas with some transitions	Little direction from beginning to end; few order words	Lacks structure and transitions
Voice	Writer closely involved; informative voice well suited to topic	Reveals personality; voice suited to topic	Sincere voice suited to topic	Little writer involvement, personality	Careless writing with no feeling
Word Choice	Vivid, precise words to express ideas	Clear words to express ideas	Language adequate but may lack precision	Generally limited or redundant language	Vague, dull, or misused words
Sentences	Strong topic sentence; fluent, varied structures	Good topic sentence; smooth sentence structure	Topic sentence correctly constructed; some sentence variety	Topic sentence unclear or missing; wordy, awkward sentences	No topic sentence; many incomplete or run-on sentences
Conventions	Excellent control; few or no errors	No serious errors to affect understanding	Reasonable control; few distracting errors	Weak control; enough errors to affect understanding	Many errors that prevent understanding

Scoring Rubric — Expository Writing

Rubric 4 3 2 1	3	2	1
Focus/Ideas	Insightful, focused exposition; well elaborated with quality details	Generally focused exposition; some supporting details	Rambling exposition; lacks development and detail
Organization/ Paragraphs	Logical, consistent flow of ideas; good transitions	Sequenced ideas with some transitions	Lacks structure and transitions
Voice	Writer closely involved; informative voice well suited to topic	Sincere voice suited to topic	Careless writing with no feeling
Word Choice	Vivid, precise words to express ideas	Language adequate but may lack precision	Vague, dull, or misused words
Sentences	Strong topic sentence; fluent, varied structures	Topic sentence correctly constructed; some sentence variety	No topic sentence; many incomplete or run-on sentences
Conventions	Excellent control; few or no errors	Reasonable control; few distracting errors	Many errors that prevent understanding

Unit 2
Monitoring Fluency

Ongoing assessment of student reading fluency is one of the most valuable measures we have of students' reading skills. One of the most effective ways to assess fluency is taking timed samples of students' oral reading and measuring the number of words correct per minute (WCPM).

How to Measure Words Correct Per Minute—WCPM

Choose a Text
Start by choosing a text for the student to read. The text should be:

- narrative
- unfamiliar
- on grade level

Make a copy of the text for yourself and have one for the student.

Timed Reading of the Text
Tell the student: As you read this aloud, I want you to do your best reading and to read as quickly as you can. That doesn't mean it's a race. Just do your best, fast reading. When I say begin, start reading.

As the student reads, follow along in your copy. Mark words that are read incorrectly.

Incorrect	Correct
• omissions	• self-corrections within 3 seconds
• substitutions	• repeated words
• mispronunciations	
• reversals	

After One Minute
At the end of one minute, draw a line after the last word that was read. Have the student finish reading but don't count any words beyond one minute. Arrive at the words correct per minute—WCPM—by counting the total number of words that the student read correctly in one minute.

Fluency Goals
Grade 3 End-of-Year Goal = 120 WCPM

Target goals by unit

Unit 1 80 to 90 WCPM	**Unit 4** 95 to 105 WCPM
Unit 2 85 to 95 WCPM	**Unit 5** 102 to 112 WCPM
Unit 3 90 to 100 WCPM	**Unit 6** 110 to 120 WCPM

More Frequent Monitoring
You may want to monitor some students more frequently because they are falling far below grade-level benchmarks or they have a result that doesn't seem to align with their previous performance. Follow the same steps above, but choose 2 or 3 additional texts.

Fluency Progress Chart Copy the chart on the next page. Use it to record each student's progress across the year.

WCPM

Fluency Progress Chart, Grade 3

Name ————————————

	1	2	3	4	5	6	7	8	9	10	11	12	13	14	15	16	17	18	19	20	21	22	23	24	25	26	27	28	29	30
145																														
140																														
135																														
130																														
125																														
120																														
115																														
110																														
105																														
100																														
95																														
90																														
85																														
80																														
75																														
70																														
65																														
60																														
55																														
50																														

Timed Reading

See also Assessment Handbook, p. 158

Name

Date

Assessment and Regrouping Chart

Unit 2

Day 3 Retelling Assessment			Day 5 Fluency Assessment			Reteach	Teacher's Comments	Grouping
The assessed group is highlighted for each week.	Benchmark Score	Actual Score	The assessed group is highlighted for each week.	Benchmark WCPM	Actual Score	✓		
Penguin Chick Main Idea and Details								
Strategic	1–2		Strategic	Less than 85				
On-Level	3		On-Level	85–95				
Advanced	4		Advanced*	85–95				
A Day's Work Character								
Strategic	1–2		Strategic	Less than 85				
On-Level	3		On-Level	85–95				
Advanced	4		Advanced*	85–95				
Prudy's Problem Main Idea								
Strategic	1–2		Strategic	Less than 85				
On-Level	3		On-Level	85–95				
Advanced	4		Advanced*	85–95				
Tops & Bottoms Author's Purpose								
Strategic	1–2		Strategic	Less than 85				
On-Level	3		On-Level	85–95				
Advanced	4		Advanced*	85–95				
William's House Draw Conclusions								
Strategic	1–2		Strategic	Less than 85				
On-Level	3		On-Level	85–95				
Advanced	4		Advanced*	85–95				
Unit 2 Benchmark Test Score								

WEEK 1 · WEEK 2 · WEEK 3 · WEEK 4 · WEEK 5

© Pearson Education

• **RECORD SCORES** Use this chart to record scores for the Day 3 Retelling, Day 5 Fluency, and Unit Benchmark Test Assessments.

*Students in the advanced group should read above grade-level materials.

• **REGROUPING** Compare the student's actual score to the benchmark score for each group level and review the Questions to Consider. Students may move to a higher or lower group level, or they may remain in the same group.

• **RETEACH** If a student is unable to complete any part of the assessment process, use the weekly Reteach lessons for additional support. Record the lesson information in the space provided on the chart. After reteaching, you may want to reassess using the Unit Benchmark Test.

Unit 2
Assess and Regroup

FYI In Grade 3 there are opportunities for regrouping every five weeks—at the end of Units 2, 3, 4, and 5. These options offer sensitivity to each student's progress although some teachers may prefer to regroup less frequently.

Regroup at the End of Unit 2

To make regrouping decisions at the end of Unit 2, consider student's end-of-unit scores for

- Units 1 and 2 Retelling
- Fluency (WCPM)
- Units 1 and 2 Benchmark Tests

Group Time

On-Level	Strategic Intervention	Advanced
To continue On-Level or to move into the On-Level group, students should	**Students would benefit from Strategic Intervention if they**	**To move to the Advanced group, students should**
• score 3 or better on their cumulative unit rubric scores for Retelling	• score 2 or lower on their cumulative unit rubric scores for Retelling	• score 4 on their cumulative unit rubric scores for Retelling
• meet the current benchmark for fluency (85–95 WCPM), reading On-Level text such as Student Edition selections	• do not meet the current benchmark for fluency (85–95 WCPM)	• read fluently at the rate of 140 WCPM
• score 80% or better on the Units 1 and 2 Benchmark Tests	• score below 60% on the Units 1 and 2 Benchmark Tests	• score 95% on the Units 1 and 2 Benchmark Tests
• are capable of working in the On-Level group based on teacher judgment	• are struggling to keep up with the On-Level group based on teacher judgment	• read above grade-level material (85–95 WCPM) with speed, accuracy, and expression. You may try them out on one of the Advanced leveled readers.
		• use expansive vocabulary and ease of language in retelling.
		• be capable of handling the problem solving and investigative work of the Advanced group based on teacher judgment

QUESTIONS TO CONSIDER

- What types of test questions did the student miss? Are they specific to a particular skill or strategy?
- Does the student have adequate background knowledge to understand the test passages or selections for retelling?

- Has the student's performance met expectations for daily lessons and assessments with little or no reteaching?
- Is the student performing more like students in another group?
- Does the student read for enjoyment, different purposes, and with varied interests?

Benchmark Fluency Scores

Current Goal: **85–95 WCPM**

End-of-Year Goal: **120 WCPM**

Leveled Readers

Table of Contents

Antarctica: The Frozen Continent

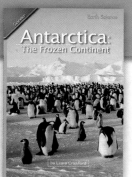

Unit 2 Week 1

◎ **MAIN IDEA**

◎ **GRAPHIC ORGANIZERS**

LESSON VOCABULARY cuddles, flippers, frozen, hatch, pecks, preen, snuggles

SUMMARY Though Antarctica is the coldest place on Earth, it is home to penguins, seals, and other animals. Antarctica is also a fascinating place for scientists who study weather. They measure its temperature changes to understand effects of air pollution on global climates.

INTRODUCE THE BOOK

BUILD BACKGROUND Invite students to discuss what they know about Antarctica from movies, TV, books, or magazines. Ask: What might you see if you traveled to Antarctica?

ELL Ask students to sketch small Antarctic images as they skim the book. Then have them write in details beneath each picture as they read.

PREVIEW/USE TEXT FEATURES Have students find clues about the topic of the book by looking at the title, pictures, captions, and diagrams. Point out that certain images, such as snow and penguins, appear often in the pictures.

TEACH/REVIEW VOCABULARY Discuss the vocabulary words and reinforce meaning by asking: *What are some animals that have* flippers? Repeat this type of questioning with the rest of the words.

TARGET SKILL AND STRATEGY

◎ **MAIN IDEA** The *main idea* is the most important idea about a topic. *Supporting details* are pieces of information that tell more about the main idea. Model how to ask questions to find the main idea. Point out details supporting it. Ask students to look for the main idea as they read.

◎ **GRAPHIC ORGANIZERS** *Graphic organizers* are pictorial devices that help students view and construct relationships among concepts. Guide students through the completion of a main idea graphic organizer. Then invite them to fill one out during an independent reading period.

READ THE BOOK

Use the following questions to support comprehension.

PAGE 5 What types of animals live in Antarctica? *(penguins, fish, seals, and whales)*

PAGE 9 How is Antarctica helping scientists learn about climate change? *(Its changes in temperature tell about the effects of global warming.)*

PAGE 12 What might happen to Antarctica if there is a great deal of climate change? *(Ice might melt. Animal habitats might disappear.)*

TALK ABOUT THE BOOK

READER RESPONSE

1. Possible response: Scientists study the climate in Antarctica as a way to protect animals living there.

2. Possible response: *acoustic sounders*—send out beeps whose echoes tell scientists about wind; *satellites*—send information to weather stations in Antarctica; *weather balloons*—radio information about air to weather stations in Antarctica

3. The words that follow—"or clean and smooth their feathers"—show what *preen* means.

4. Possible response: The Earth receives heat from the Sun. Most of this heat is released into space, but some of it is trapped inside Earth's atmosphere.

RESPONSE OPTIONS

WRITING Ask students to pretend they are writing home to a friend from an Antarctic station. Have them write one or two paragraphs that describe their visit.

CONTENT CONNECTIONS

SCIENCE Scientists in Antarctica use special equipment to gather information. Invite students to learn about how scientists in other environments use special tools and technology to gather information.

TIME FOR Science

Main Idea

- The **main idea** is the most important idea about a paragraph, passage, article, or book.
- **Details** are pieces of information that support, or tell more about, the main idea.

Directions Read the following passage. What is the main idea of the paragraph? Write it in the box at the top. Then find three details that tell about the main idea. Write one detail in each smaller box.

> Antarctica is very windy and dry. Antarctica is so dry that scientists call it a desert. The small amount of snow that falls there never melts. It is moved around by the wind until it freezes into ice.

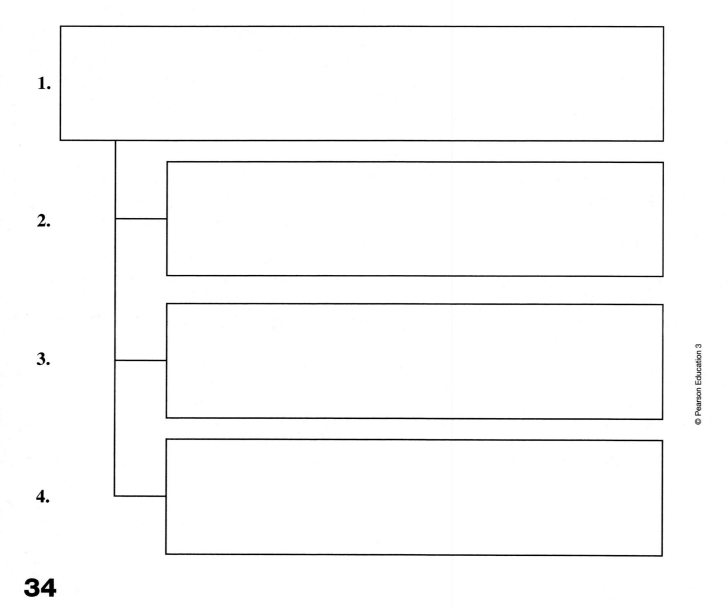

1.

2.

3.

4.

© Pearson Education 3

34

Vocabulary

Directions For each vocabulary word, write the letter of the definition that matches it.

Check the Words You Know
___cuddles   ___flippers   ___frozen   ___hatch ___pecks   ___preen   ___snuggles

1. _____ cuddles   **a.** strikes at with the beak

2. _____ flippers   **b.** presses closely against, as for comfort

3. _____ frozen   **c.** to come out of an egg

4. _____ hatch   **d.** hugs closely

5. _____ pecks   **e.** flat body parts that are used for swimming

6. _____ preen   **f.** turned into ice

7. _____ snuggles   **g.** to clean and smooth feathers

Directions Write the vocabulary word or words that go best with each clue.

8. This word describes Antarctica. _____

9. Penguins use these to swim well. _____

10. A penguin chick does this to its eggshell. _____

11. This is another word for how a penguin chick is born. _____

Directions Write a short paragraph. Use at least three of the vocabulary words.

_____

_____

_____

_____

_____

_____

35

Birds That Can't Fly!

Unit 2 Week 1

MAIN IDEA

GRAPHIC ORGANIZERS

LESSON VOCABULARY cuddles, flippers, frozen, hatch, pecks, preen, snuggles

SUMMARY Birds that cannot fly can still thrive in different environments. This book introduces the reader to flightless birds from around the world. It explains how key characteristics help the emu, flightless cormorant, and others meet their survival needs.

INTRODUCE THE BOOK

BUILD BACKGROUND Have students think about birds with which they are familiar—from outdoors, TV, or the zoo. Ask them if they think there are skills other than flying that can help birds move around and survive.

PREVIEW/USE TEXT FEATURES Point out that photographs are paired together on pages 3, 5, and, 14 for specific reasons. Ask students how pairing photos helps illustrate important ideas on each page.

TEACH/REVIEW VOCABULARY Have volunteers demonstrate their knowledge of vocabulary words through the use of pantomime and/or incorporating them into sentences.

ELL Invite students to draw pictures of flightless birds and write bilingual labels or captions for the birds' body parts.

TARGET SKILL AND STRATEGY

MAIN IDEA The *main idea* is the most important idea about a topic. Supporting *details* are pieces of information that tell more about the main idea. Model how to ask questions to find the main idea, starting with identifying the topic. Point out details that support the main idea. Tell students to look for the main idea of the book as they read.

GRAPHIC ORGANIZERS *Graphic organizers* are pictorial devices that help students view and construct relationships among concepts. Create a *KWL* chart and use it to discuss what students *K*now, *W*ant to know, and *L*earned about flightless birds.

READ THE BOOK

Use the following questions to support comprehension.

PAGE 3 Contrast flightless birds with flying birds. *(Their bones are heavier and their feathers are different from those of flying birds.)*

PAGES 6, 11 How do birds such as the emu and flightless cormorant meet their needs without the ability to fly? *(Emus have powerful legs and flightless cormorants can swim well. This allows them to move quickly and survive.)*

PAGES 8–9 What does the map on pages 8 and 9 tell you about flightless birds? *(Different varieties live all over the world.)*

TALK ABOUT THE BOOK

READER RESPONSE

1. Possible response: There are many different kinds of flightless birds.
2. In descending order of weight: male ostriches: 300 pounds; cassowaries: 130 pounds; flightless cormorants: 9 pounds
3. Possible response: He climbed through the ship's hatch to get on deck. He decided to hatch a plan to get the money.
4. the flightless cormorant of the Galápagos Islands

RESPONSE OPTIONS

WRITING Ask students: If you could be any flightless bird, which one would you be and why? Have them answer this question in one or two paragraphs.

CONTENT CONNECTIONS

TIME FOR Science

SCIENCE Invite students to use reference sources to learn more about what characteristics help flightless birds thrive without the ability to fly.

Main Idea

- The **main idea** is the most important idea about a paragraph, passage, or story.
- **Details** are pieces of information that tell more about the main idea.

Directions Read the following passage. Then answer the questions below.

Birds that cannot fly are called flightless birds. They differ from flying birds in many ways. The bones of flightless birds are heavier than those of flying birds. Flightless birds' feathers are also different from those of flying birds. Like humans, all birds have a breastbone. However, a flightless bird's breastbone is different from that of a flying bird since it has no flight muscles attached.

1. In one or two words, what is this paragraph about?

_____

2. What is the main idea of the paragraph?

_____

_____

3. What is one important detail that tells more about the main idea?

_____

_____

4. What is another important detail about the main idea?

_____

_____

5. What is a third detail about the main idea?

_____

_____

34

Name _____

Vocabulary

Directions Read each vocabulary word. Find two other words that have almost the same meaning and circle them.

Check the Words You Know

___cuddles   ___flippers   ___frozen   ___hatch
___pecks   ___preen   ___snuggles

1. cuddles

   slaps   hugs   throws   snuggles

2. flippers

   eyes   paddles   fins   noses

3. frozen

   chilly   icy   melted   burned

4. hatch

   fall   fly   produce   cause

5. pecks

   strikes   walks   swims   hits

6. preen

   see   dress   groom   laugh

7. snuggles

   nestles   avoids   holds   kicks

Directions Write a paragraph about penguins using at least four vocabulary words.

_____

_____

_____

_____

_____

© Pearson Education 3

35

Advanced-Level Reader

Penguins On Parade

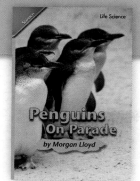

Unit 2 Week 1

◎ **MAIN IDEA**

◎ **GRAPHIC ORGANIZERS**

LESSON VOCABULARY blubber, brood patch, crest, down, incubate, molt, rookery

---

SUMMARY Though Antarctica's emperor penguins are perhaps the best known birds of their kind, many other varieties of penguins are just as interesting. The book describes how these birds are equipped to thrive in some of the coldest and most isolated places on Earth.

INTRODUCE THE BOOK

BUILD BACKGROUND Have students discuss what comes to mind when they think of penguins. Where do their ideas about penguins come from?

ELL Ask students to name some birds with which they are familiar. Discuss features and traits most birds have in common, such as wings, beaks, egg laying.

PREVIEW/USE TEXT FEATURES Have students preview the book by skimming over the heads, photographs, and captions. Ask what they can predict about penguins based on these text features.

TEACH/REVIEW VOCABULARY Have students look at the glossary. Ask volunteers to point out familiar terms and explain, in their own words, what they mean.

TARGET SKILL AND STRATEGY

◎ **MAIN IDEA** The *main idea* is the most important idea about the topic. To find it, students must determine the relative importance of information as they read. Invite students to find the main idea of the book while they are reading. *Supporting details* are pieces of information that tell more about the main idea and expand upon it. Ask students to point out supporting details for their main idea.

◎ **GRAPHIC ORGANIZERS** *Graphic organizers* are pictorial devices that help students view and construct relationships among concepts. Have students create a *KWL* chart about penguins: Direct them to write, in the appropriate columns, what they know about these birds, questions about what they would like to know, and what they learn as they read.

READ THE BOOK

Use the following questions to support comprehension.

PAGE 3 All penguins live in what part of the world? *(the Southern Hemisphere)*

PAGES 6–8 What is the topic of this section? What is the main idea? *(emperor penguins; Emperor penguins are well equipped for surviving in the cold.)*

TALK ABOUT THE BOOK

READER RESPONSE

1. Possible response: There are many different varieties of penguins around the world, but they all have ways to survive in cold weather.

2. Possible response: Differences: Emperor Penguins— the world's largest penguins, live in Antarctica; Little Blue Penguins—the world's smallest penguins, live in Australia, New Zealand, and Tasmania; Similarities: cannot fly, have dark feathers on their backs and white feathers on their bellies

3. Possible answer: My friend waved from the crest of the hill.

4. calcium

RESPONSE OPTIONS

WRITING Ask students what people do to stay warm in cold environments. How are their ways similar to or different from those of penguins? Have them answer this question in one or two paragraphs.

CONTENT CONNECTIONS

SCIENCE Remind students that penguins have special characteristics that enable them to survive in specific types of environments. Discuss how other animals have characteristics that make them well-suited for where they live.

Time for Science

Main Idea

- The **main idea** is the most important idea about a paragraph, passage, or story.
- **Supporting details** are pieces of information that tell more about the main idea.

Directions Read each passage. Then answer the questions that follow.

> The Southern Hemisphere is the natural home to the world's penguins. Penguins live on the Galápagos Islands and in Australia, New Zealand, Africa, South America, and the islands that surround Antarctica. They also live on Antarctica itself. All penguins share lives that are tied to the sea and the Southern Hemisphere's marine ecosystems.

1. In a few words, what is this paragraph about?

_____

2. What is the main idea of the paragraph?

_____

3. What is an important detail that tells more about the main idea?

_____

_____

> Emperor penguins reduce heat loss through their feet by standing on their heels. This keeps the rest of the foot from touching cold ice.
> Male emperor penguins also huddle to help conserve heat. The temperature in the middle of an emperor penguin huddle can be 95°F! Of course, some penguins must stand on the outside of the huddle. So what do they do to stay warm? They rotate. The penguins on the outside gradually push their way into the middle of the huddle. This way, each penguin gets a chance to become warmed.

4. What is the main idea of the passage?

_____

5. What is one detail that tells more about the main idea?

_____

34

Vocabulary

Directions Choose the word from the box that best completes each sentence. Write the word on the line.

Check the Words You Know
___blubber ___brood patch ___crest ___down
___incubate ___molt ___rookery

1. Emperor penguins choose to _____ their eggs during the winter.

2. Large groups of penguins gather in a _____ to raise their young.

3. A penguin's _____ stores energy and helps protect the penguin from cold weather.

4. Fluffy inner feathers known as _____ trap air to keep penguins warm.

5. Penguins _____ when their old feathers get worn out.

6. Male penguins have a featherless area of skin known as a

   _____, which warms their eggs.

7. Some penguins have a _____ that sticks up from their heads.

Directions Use the context clues in the above sentences to define these words.

8. molt _____

_____

9. rookery _____

_____

10. blubber _____

_____

35

Sarah's Choice

SUMMARY While playing with a friend, Sarah ignores her mother's directions and decides to have a snack of blueberries without asking if it's okay. This decision has consequences later in the day.

INTRODUCE THE BOOK

BUILD BACKGROUND Ask volunteers to talk about a time when they ignored instructions from a parent or teacher. What happened? What did they learn from the experience?

PREVIEW/USE ILLUSTRATIONS Have students preview the book by looking at the title and illustrations. How might the title tell what the pictures and story describe?

ELL Encourage students to work in pairs as they preview the book. Have them talk about what the illustrations make them think about in their own lives.

TEACH/REVIEW VOCABULARY Ask students how each vocabulary word helps them better understand the story and its characters.

TARGET SKILL AND STRATEGY

◎ **CHARACTER** Remind students that a *character* is a person or animal who takes part in the events of a story. Ask them to identify the three main characters in the book. Then explain that the qualities of a character are known as *character traits* and that they usually relate to his or her personality. While students are reading, have them identify the character traits of Sarah, Julia, and Sarah's mother.

◎ **VISUALIZE** *Visualizing* lets students create pictures in their minds by using their senses and prior knowledge. A reader's mental images come not from just seeing, but from all five senses. Point out specific instances in the book that offer strong opportunities for visualizing. What does a warm summer day feel like? How might it feel to run through sprinklers? How might the lemonade taste?

READ THE BOOK

Use the following questions to support comprehension.

PAGE 8 How is Sarah different from Julia when making decisions? Explain. *(Sarah does not ask her mother for permission when making decisions.)*

PAGE 10 What happened as a result of Sarah's choice? *(They couldn't bake the cake, which made Sarah sad.)*

PAGE 11 What do you think Sarah will do the next time she gets directions from her mother? *(She is likely to follow the directions.)*

TALK ABOUT THE BOOK

READER RESPONSE
1. Possible response: Sarah does not always follow other people's directions.
2. Responses will vary.
3. Possible response: 1. surprised—*I was shocked by the loud, sudden noise.* 2. to have received an electric shock—*You can get shocked if you rub your feet on a carpet and touch something metal.*
4. Students should indicate how they would change their behavior to make a better choice in a specific situation.

RESPONSE OPTIONS

WRITING Ask students to write about the kinds of decisions that Sarah and Julia made in the story. Which choices were right? Which were wrong? Have them offer advice for both girls on what they should do in future situations where they may be tempted to ignore other people's directions.

CONTENT CONNECTIONS

SOCIAL STUDIES Discuss why it is important to follow rules and directions at home and in school. Identify situations where it could be dangerous to ignore rules, such as a fire drill.

Time for SOCIAL STUDIES

Character

- A **character** is a person who takes part in the events of a story.
- The qualities of a character are known as **character traits** and usually tell about his or her personality.

Directions How are Sarah and Julia alike? How are they different? Use the Venn Diagram below to compare the two characters.

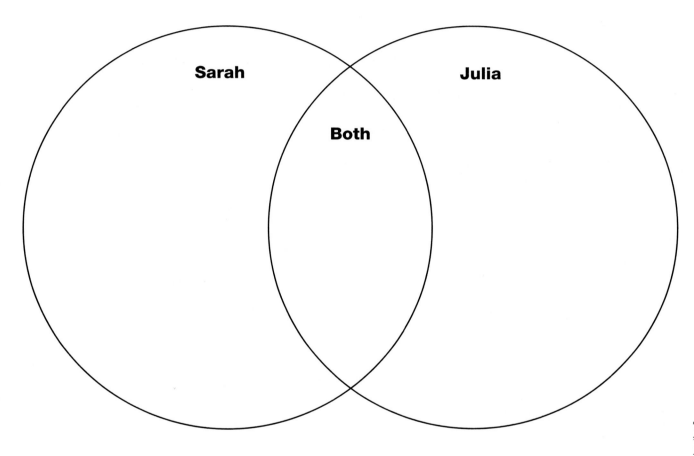

Sarah   **Julia**

Both

38

Vocabulary

Directions Draw a line to match each vocabulary word with its definition.

> ## Check the Words You Know
>
> ___excitement   ___gardener   ___motioned   ___sadness
> ___shivered   ___shocked   ___slammed

1. shivered
2. slammed
3. excitement
4. motioned
5. shocked
6. gardener
7. sadness

a. thrill
b. signaled
c. a person who works outdoors with plants
d. trembled
e. a feeling of unhappiness
f. to be surprised
g. closed with a bang

Directions Write the vocabulary word that completes each sentence.

8. I was _____ when I heard he was joining the circus.

9. The fact that we might never see each other again filled me with

   _____.

10. She _____ as she stepped out into the cold.

11. He stomped angrily out of the room and _____ the door
    behind him.

12. I wondered why the _____ planted the bushes so close
    to the house.

13. When our team won the big game, everyone at school shared the

    _____.

14. When the new girl walked into the lunchroom, I _____ for
    her to come over to our table.

39

THE BOY WHO CRIED WOLF
retold by Linda B. Ross
illustrated by Mark Weber

🔄 **CHARACTER**

🔄 **VISUALIZE**

LESSON VOCABULARY excitement, gardener, motioned, sadness, shivered, shocked, slammed

The Boy Who Cried Wolf

SUMMARY In a retelling of the classic tale, a young shepherd enjoys getting attention by crying "wolf" even though no wolf threatens his sheep. He learns a lesson about being trustworthy when a real wolf appears and the villagers ignore his cries.

INTRODUCE THE BOOK

BUILD BACKGROUND Have students discuss what it means to be trustworthy. Ask volunteers to talk about instances where someone had trust in them and why it was important to maintain that trust.

PREVIEW/USE ILLUSTRATIONS Suggest students skim the text and look at the illustrations. Ask what the characters' poses and facial expressions suggest about them.

ELL Ask a volunteer to explain the idiom "crying wolf" for the benefit of less-proficient English speakers. Encourage a discussion of its meaning.

TEACH/REVIEW VOCABULARY Have volunteers help the rest of the class to better understand the vocabulary words by defining them in their own words or using pantomime.

TARGET SKILL AND STRATEGY

🔄 **CHARACTER** Tell students that a *character* is a person or animal who takes part in the events of a story. Ask them to identify the main characters in the book. Explain that the qualities of a character are known as *character traits* and that these traits usually relate to personalities. While students read, have them identify details that reveal traits of the different characters. Ask them to predict what the characters will do based on those traits.

🔄 **VISUALIZE** *Visualizing* is useful when exploring characters in greater depth. To create meaningful mental pictures of characters, students should use their own experiences and knowledge when they visualize. Have them relate details of characters to details of real people they can recall.

READ THE BOOK

Use the following questions to support comprehension.

PAGE 5 What do Daniel's actions tell you about his character? *(He is restless and easily bored.)*

PAGE 12 When did the villagers start ignoring Daniel's cries for help? *(after he had tricked them twice)*

PAGE 15 If you were the farmer, would you have trusted Daniel to work for you? Why or why not? *(Possible response: Yes; because everyone deserves a second chance)*

TALK ABOUT THE BOOK

READER RESPONSE
1. Possible response: Daniel may be happy knowing that he has a chance to win back the villagers' trust.
2. Possible response: The village might be a good place to live because it is peaceful and pretty. It might not be such a good place because there would not be many things to do there.
3. Possible response: *sadness*—unhappiness, *shivered*—shook, *shocked*—surprised, *slammed*—smashed, *motioned*—pointed
4. Responses will vary.

RESPONSE OPTIONS

WRITING Have students pretend they are either Daniel or the farmer. Ask those who are Daniel to write letters to the farmer explaining how Daniel feels about him and what he plans to do as his worker. Those who are the farmer should write letters to Daniel stating what he expects from his new worker.

CONTENT CONNECTIONS

SOCIAL STUDIES Have students discuss people in their community with jobs that are based on trust, such as police officers and guards. Talk about why trust is an important part of their work.

Time for SOCIAL STUDIES

Character

- A **character** is a person who takes part in the events of a story.
- The qualities of a character are known as **character traits** and usually tell about his or her personality.

Directions Follow the directions below to describe the boy who cried "Wolf!"

1. Name the main character.

_____

2. Write two sentences about Daniel's character traits.

_____

_____

_____

3. Write three sentences about what Daniel wants.

_____

_____

_____

_____

_____

Directions Write four sentences about what Daniel does and feels during the story.

4. _____

_____

5. _____

_____

6. _____

_____

7. _____

_____

38

© Pearson Education 3

Vocabulary

Directions Below each vocabulary word is a list of four words. Find two other words that have almost the same meaning as the vocabulary word. Circle them.

Check the Words You Know

| ___excitement | ___gardener | ___motioned | ___sadness |
| ___shivered | ___shocked | ___slammed | |

1. sadness

   unhappiness   sorrow   delight   joy

2. slammed

   smashed   petted   smacked   touched

3. shivered

   sat   trembled   shook   stood

4. excitement

   boredom   action   dullness   adventure

5. gardener

   grower   fisherman   shepherd   farmer

6. motioned

   fell   pointed   stared   signaled

7. shocked

   surprised   jolted   certain   confident

Directions What do you think happened after the story ended? Write a paragraph about how Daniel and the farmer worked together. Use as many vocabulary words as you can.

_____

_____

_____

_____

The Song Makers Go to Salem

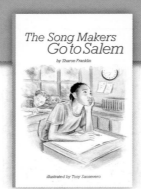

The Song Makers Go to Salem
by Sharon Franklin

illustrated by Tony Sansevero

Unit 2 Week 2

⊙ **CHARACTER**

⊙ **VISUALIZE**

LESSON VOCABULARY anxious, concentrate, erupted, frantically, relieved, solution, suspect

---

SUMMARY Tabitha struggles with her conscience after witnessing her friend Abbey steal money from a school fund-raising drive. Unsure of whether to tell on her friend, Tabitha finally confronts Abbey and discovers the reason behind the theft, and works out a constructive solution where Abbey takes responsibility for what she did.

INTRODUCE THE BOOK

BUILD BACKGROUND Have students discuss real-life conflicts where they or someone they know struggled to make the right decision in an uncertain situation. What made the decision so difficult?

PREVIEW/USE ILLUSTRATIONS Have students look at the illustrations and focus on the characters' poses and facial expressions. Discuss what they think the characters are doing and feeling in these pictures.

ELL Have students use a t-chart to list characteristics of the two girls and their situations.

TEACH/REVIEW VOCABULARY Have students make a word chart to use with this book. Have them add the vocabulary words to the chart as they read.

Word	Context Clues	Definitions

TARGET SKILL AND STRATEGY

⊙ **CHARACTER** A *character* is a person or animal who takes part in the events of a story. *Character traits* are qualities that usually relate to the character's personality. Have students analyze the character traits of Tabitha and Abbey while they are reading. How are they alike? How are they different? Students should back up their statements with details.

⊙ **VISUALIZE** When we *visualize* a scene we create pictures in our minds. These images come from not just our ability to see but from prior knowledge and all five senses. Suggest that, as students form mental images of what is happening, they look for sensory clues.

READ THE BOOK

Use the following questions to support comprehension.

PAGE 3 Why is Tabitha's school chorus raising money? *(They will travel to Salem for their spring performance.)*

PAGE 12 What does Abbey's confession tell you about her character? *(Possible response: Abbey can make wrong decisions, but she is not greedy.)*

PAGE 20 What might Tabitha have done if Abbey had refused to admit her mistake? *(Possible responses: Tabitha might have told on her. Tabitha might not trust Abbey again.)*

TALK ABOUT THE BOOK

1. Possible response: She is thoughtful and honest.
2. Possible response: "Tears were running down Abbey's cheeks, but she had a big smile on her face, too."
3. Possible response: simple, clear
4. Responses will vary.

RESPONSE OPTIONS

WRITING Ask students to write a letter to either Tabitha or Abbey with comments on their actions and advice on how to make good choices in the future.

CONTENT CONNECTIONS

SOCIAL STUDIES Discuss recent or historic events where people struggled to do the right thing in the midst of uncertainty. What factors made their decisions so difficult? How did their choices affect your community or the world?

Time for SOCIAL STUDIES

Name _____

Character

- A **character** is a person who takes part in the events of a story.
- The qualities of a character are known as **character traits** and usually relate to his or her personality.

Directions Fill in the graphic organizers below using details from your reading.

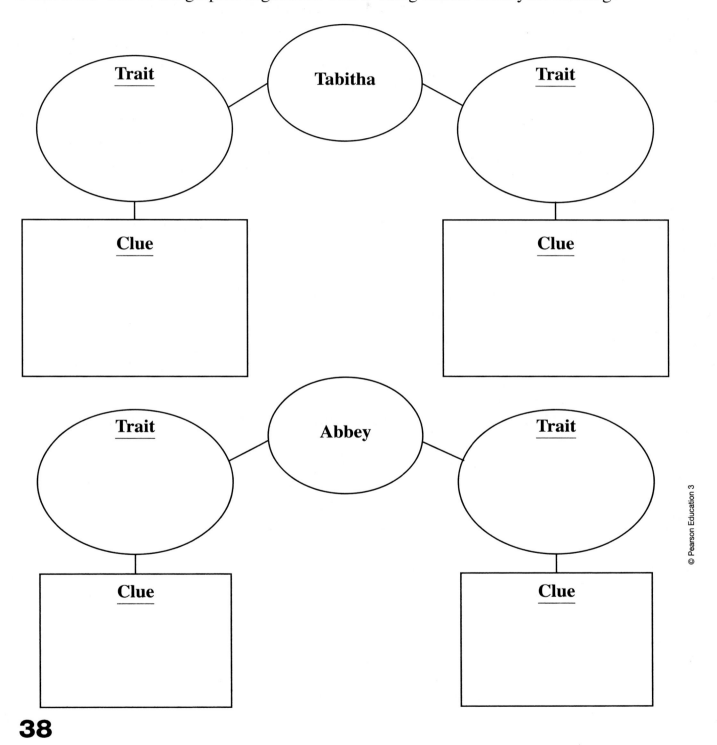

38

© Pearson Education 3

Vocabulary

Directions Choose the word from the box that best completes each sentence.
Write the word on the line.

Check the Words You Know
___anxious   ___concentrate   ___erupted   ___frantically
___relieved   ___solution   ___suspect

1. Tabitha fought hard to find a _____ to the problem.

2. Zoe _____ waved her hands at Tabitha.

3. People often _____ too much on what others will think.

4. Tabitha didn't just _____ that Abbey had taken money—
   she knew it.

5. Tabitha was _____ because she wasn't sure how Abbey
   would react.

6. Abbey felt _____ after she admitted she had taken the money.

7. The crowd _____ with applause as Abbey arrived with
   her delicious cookies.

Directions What do you think happened after the story ended? Write a paragraph
about the Song Makers' trip to Salem. Use as many vocabulary words as you can.

_____

_____

_____

_____

_____

_____

_____

_____

_____

© Pearson Education 3

39

Metal Detector Detective

Metal Detector Detective

by Linda Lott
illustrated by Nicole Wong

Unit 2 Week 3

◉ **MAIN IDEA**

◉ **MONITOR AND FIX UP**

LESSON VOCABULARY collection, enormous, realize, scattered, shiny, strain

---

SUMMARY A boy named Joe is bored until his grandmother teaches him how to use a metal detector. Joe has a chance to use the device to find a gold ring that was lost by his grandmother's neighbor. He decides that using the metal detector will be a fun way to stay busy during the summer.

INTRODUCE THE BOOK

BUILD BACKGROUND Have students discuss times when they or someone they know helped others by coming up with a creative solution to a problem. What was the solution and how did it solve the problem? How did everyone feel afterward?

PREVIEW/USE ILLUSTRATIONS Read aloud the title and have students glance through the illustrations. Ask students to predict what type of story they will read and what will happen in it.

TEACH/REVIEW VOCABULARY Ask volunteers to define the vocabulary words and use them in sentences that help classmates improve their understanding of them.

ELL In pairs, have students make up a riddle game using vocabulary words. Suggest an example such as "I have a penny and it is very _____."

TARGET SKILL AND STRATEGY

◉ **MAIN IDEA** Explain to students that the *main idea* in fiction explains what a story is about and identifies its most important ideas. Ask students to tell what the book is about in their own words and then provide reasons to support their answers.

◉ **MONITOR AND FIX UP** When students *monitor* comprehension they know when they understand what they read and when they do not. They also have strategies to restore their understanding when problems arise, such as summarizing facts and details to clarify and organize ideas. Tell students to use this strategy when they are unsure of meaning. Encourage them to write down these facts and details in a main idea chart.

READ THE BOOK

Use the following questions to support comprehension.

PAGE 7 How did Ms. Choi lose her gold ring? *(It most likely slipped from her finger while she was working in her garden.)*

PAGE 9 What solution did Joe and Grandma come up with for finding Ms. Choi's ring? Why did it make sense? *(They decided to use the metal detector to find the ring, because the ring was made of metal.)*

PAGE 11 What might Joe do with the metal detector later in the summer? *(Possible response: He might find coins for his coin collection or metal cans for recycling.*

TALK ABOUT THE BOOK

READER RESPONSE
1. Possible response: You can solve problems more easily if you think creatively and use the right tools.
2. Joe searches the flower beds, the bushes, and the ivy.
3. Possible responses: *colossal, gigantic, huge, massive, titanic, big*
4. Possible responses: They can find sharp objects on lawns before they can harm people. They can help police find evidence in crimes.

RESPONSE OPTIONS

WRITING How should Joe spread the word about being a metal detector detective? Ask students to write an advertisement that promotes his services.

CONTENT CONNECTIONS

SCIENCE Remind students that a metal detector was used to search for a lost metal object in the story. Have students come up with other examples of how specific tools and devices are designed to solve specific problems.

TIME FOR Science

Main Idea

- The **main idea** is the most important idea about a paragraph, passage, or article.
- **Details** are small pieces of information that tell more about the main idea.

Directions Read the following passage. What is the main idea of the paragraph? Write it in the box on the left. Then find three details that tell about the main idea. Write them in the boxes on the right.

> Using a metal detector can be a fun hobby. But there are rules you must follow before using a metal detector. Metal detectors are not allowed on National Park Service lands. There are also many places, such as public schools, churches, and private lands, where you must ask permission before you use a metal detector. If you are not sure of whether you can use a metal detector, just ask!

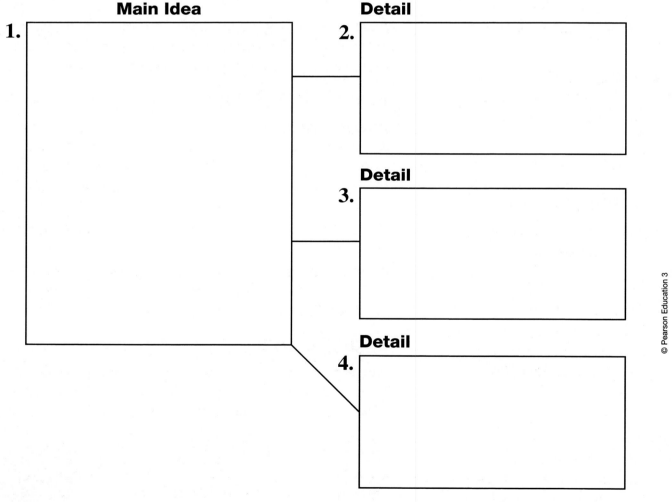

Main Idea

1.

Detail

2.

Detail

3.

Detail

4.

© Pearson Education 3

42

Vocabulary

Directions Draw a line to connect each vocabulary word with the correct description.

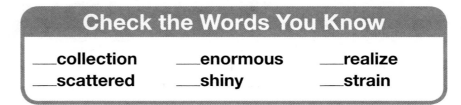

Check the Words You Know

___collection   ___enormous   ___realize
___scattered   ___shiny   ___strain

1. collection   **a.** sprinkled

2. enormous   **b.** giant

3. realize   **c.** glossy

4. scattered   **d.** struggle

5. shiny   **e.** group

6. strain   **f.** understand

Directions Write the vocabulary word that completes each clue.

7. This word describes the size of something.

_____

8. When you try hard, you do this.

_____

9. If you sprinkle seeds over a flower bed, you might describe the seeds this way.

_____

10. You often use this word to describe a new car.

_____

11. People organize seashells, stamps, dolls, and baseball cards into one of these.

_____

43

Katy's Last-Minute Book Report

MAIN IDEA

MONITOR AND FIX UP

LESSON VOCABULARY collection, enormous, realize, scattered, shiny, strai

SUMMARY Katy puts off reading a book for an assigned book report. When she is forced to finish her book and write about it during one very stressful weekend, Katy vows to never again leave any assignment until the last minute.

INTRODUCE THE BOOK

BUILD BACKGROUND Have students discuss situations in which they put off assignments or tasks until the last minute. What challenges did they face while trying to meet their deadlines?

PREVIEW/USE ILLUSTRATIONS As students look through the illustrations, have them focus on the characters' poses and facial expressions. Then discuss what they think the characters are doing.

TEACH/REVIEW VOCABULARY Ask students to find how each vocabulary word is used in the book. Encourage them to use the illustrations for clues of ways to define the vocabulary in their own words.

ELL Show students how to make a simple cause-and-effect diagram charting the cause of Katy's situation and the effect.

TARGET SKILL AND STRATEGY

MAIN IDEA Explain to students that the *main idea* in fiction tells what a story is about and identifies its most important ideas. Ask students to identify important ideas and details while they are reading and explain what the story is about in their own words.

MONITOR AND FIX UP When students *monitor* comprehension, they know when they understand what they read and when they do not. They also use strategies to restore their understanding when problems arise, such as rereading and reviewing. Encourage students to use these strategies when their understanding of the text breaks down. They may also reread if they have a question after reading.

READ THE BOOK

Use the following questions to support comprehension.

PAGE 3 How much time does Katy's teacher give his class to finish their book reports? *(He gives them one week to do their reports.)*

PAGES 6–10 What drew Katy's attention away from writing her report? *(Katy was distracted by soccer practice, TV, her coin collection, cleaning up her room, and a soccer game.)*

PAGE 15 What did Katy promise to do after she handed in her book report? Why? *(Katy promised to never leave anything until the last minute again, because cramming for her book report was so stressful.)*

TALK ABOUT THE BOOK

READER RESPONSE

1. Possible response: Katy did a poor job on her book report because she rushed to finish it.
2. Katy was unable to watch a video, enjoy the soccer game, go out for ice cream, and go with Pam for pizza and a movie.
3. The base words are *inform* and *collect*. Possible sentences: When are you going to inform your teacher of your book selection? Chris decided to collect baseball cards.
4. Possible response: Start my homework earlier.

RESPONSE OPTIONS

WRITING Invite students to select a real-life assignment with a deadline and then create a timetable of things they must do to meet the deadline.

CONTENT CONNECTIONS

SOCIAL STUDIES Many people face deadlines as part of their daily routines. Discuss what kinds of jobs involve deadlines and why it is important for people with those jobs to manage their time carefully.

Main Idea

- The **main idea** is the most important idea about a paragraph, passage, or story.
- **Details** are small pieces of information that tell more about the main idea.

Directions Read the following passage. Then answer the questions below.

Third-grade students have many things to do each day. Homework, sports, and family activities take up a lot of time.
It can be hard to decide what to do when. If you don't plan your time well, you might forget to do something important. Sometimes people put off doing things until the last minute. Then they don't have enough time left to do a good job.

1. Use one to three words to tell what this paragraph is about.

_____

2. What is the main idea of the paragraph?

_____

3. What is one detail that tells more about the main idea?

_____

_____

4. What is another detail about the main idea?

_____

_____

5. What is a third detail about the main idea?

_____

_____

42

Vocabulary

Directions Read each vocabulary word and the four words that follow it. Find two other words that have almost the same meaning and circle them.

Check the Words You Know

| ___collection | ___enormous | ___realize |
| ___scattered | ___shiny | ___strain |

1. collection

   group   set   scattering   book

2. enormous

   huge   tiny   medium   giant

3. realize

   forget   overlook   recognize   understand

4. scattered

   grouped   separated   sprinkled   sorted

5. shiny

   glossy   dull   sparkly   cloudy

6. strain

   achieve   try   strive   complete

Directions Write a paragraph that includes at least four of the vocabulary words.

_____

_____

_____

_____

_____

_____

43

Collecting Dreams

Collecting Dreams
by Joanna Korba
Illustrated by Bradley Clark

◎ **MAIN IDEA**

◎ **MONITOR AND FIX UP**

LESSON VOCABULARY collectibles, credit, fond, kaleidoscope, porcelain, propped, rim, specialize, suspiciously

SUMMARY At first, a girl named Tina cannot understand why her mother loves collecting teacups. Tina later discovers the joy of collecting for herself while searching for a birthday gift for her mother. She sees her mother's teacups in a whole new light.

INTRODUCE THE BOOK

BUILD BACKGROUND Ask students if they collect objects such as dolls or baseball cards. What makes those objects so special? Discuss why people collect things in general.

PREVIEW/USE ILLUSTRATIONS Have students preview the book by looking at the title and illustrations. What predictions can they make about the story based on these features?

TEACH/REVIEW VOCABULARY Have volunteers show how the vocabulary words are used in the book. Then ask them how each word helped them better understand the story and its characters.

ELL Ask students to speak about, or present in photographs or drawings, examples of things collected by a family member.

TARGET SKILL AND STRATEGY

◎ **MAIN IDEA** The *main idea* in fiction tells what a story is about and identifies its most important ideas. Invite students to tell what the story is about and then provide reasons to support their answers. Suggest that they create an outline of the story to determine or keep track of its key ideas and details.

◎ **MONITOR AND FIX UP** Students who *monitor* their comprehension are constantly aware of their understanding of the text. They know when the text is making sense to them or if their understanding of it has broken down. Self-questioning is a strategy that can be used to restore understanding. It involves asking oneself key questions while reading, such as, "Who is the story about? Where and when does it take place?"

READ THE BOOK

Use the following questions to support comprehension.

PAGE 6 At first, how does Tina feel about the teacups? *(Tina does not understand why her mother likes them.)*

PAGE 8 How does Tina's father feel about his wife's teacups? *(He supports her hobby, as seen in the trip to the collectibles fair.)*

PAGE 23 How did Tina's feelings about teacups change? *(When Tina bought a kaleidoscope, she understood why her mother loved collecting pretty objects.)*

TALK ABOUT THE BOOK

READER RESPONSE

1. Possible response: It is easier to understand someone's feelings once you've experienced similar feelings.
2. Possible response: The Chinese developed porcelain hundreds of years ago. Later, the English added ash made from animal bones. This led to the name English bone china.
3. Possible response: Invented by Sir David Brewster. Patented in 1817. Designers use them to find patterns. Most are about 10 inches long.
4. Possible response: Buy the kaleidoscope sooner.

RESPONSE OPTIONS

WRITING Remind students of the care Tina's father took in selecting a gift. Invite students to write about a time when they faced a similar challenge (gift-related or not) and what strategies they used to tackle it.

CONTENT CONNECTIONS

TIME FOR Science

SCIENCE Tell students that scientists must often collect objects and/or living things in order to explore their fields of study. Ask why it might be helpful for scientists to have such collections on hand.

Main Idea

- The **main idea** is the most important idea about a paragraph, passage, or story.
- **Supporting details** are small pieces of information that tell more about the main idea.

Directions Read the following passage. Then answer the questions below.

Tina's mother collects teacups made of English bone china. China is another name for porcelain. Porcelain was first made in China, hundreds of years ago. That is why people often call it china. For a long time the Chinese guarded the secret of how porcelain is made. But after a while their secret began to spread to other countries. Then, about two hundred years ago, the English added ash, made from animal bones, to make a special kind of porcelain called bone china.

1. In one or two words, what is this paragraph about?

_____

2. What is the main idea of the paragraph?

_____

3–4. What are the two details that tell more about the main idea?

_____

_____

_____

_____

5–7. Imagine you are writing a paragraph about one of the characters in *Collecting Dreams*. Write the main idea of your paragraph and two details to support that main idea.

Main idea _____

Detail _____

Detail _____

42

Vocabulary

Directions Choose the word from the box that best completes each sentence.
Write the word on the line.

Check the Words You Know

___collectibles ___credit ___fond
___kaleidoscope ___porcelain ___propped
___rim ___specialize ___suspiciously

1. The spoon was resting on the _____ of the teacup.

2. Tina worked hard to find the perfect present, so she deserves
   the _____ for finding such a nice gift.

3. You can see beautiful colors and patterns if you look through
   a _____.

4. An antiques market is a great place for buyers to find _____.

5. The teacher looked at the boy _____ when he tried
   to hide candy in his desk.

6. She was especially _____ of long walks on warm
   summer nights.

7. Please handle the _____ dishes carefully, because they
   break easily.

8. The broom is _____ against the closet door.

9. I brought my broken antique doll to people who_____
   in repairing toys.

43

Growing Vegetables

Growing Vegetables
by Kim Borland

Life Science

Unit 2 Week 4

illustrated by Chad Thompson

AUTHOR'S PURPOSE

PREDICT

LESSON VOCABULARY bottom, cheated, clever, crops, lazy, partners, wealth

SUMMARY This is a story about working together for a common goal: creating a vegetable garden. By taking readers through a busy day in the garden, the story shows how much work goes into making a garden and how sharing the work makes it more fun for all.

INTRODUCE THE BOOK

BUILD BACKGROUND Ask students if they have ever grown any plants. What kind of plants did they grow? How did they care for the plants?

PREVIEW/USE ILLUSTRATIONS As students preview the book, point out that illustrations may help them when they encounter unfamiliar words, terms, or ideas. For example, on page 8, students can see a picture of the kind of plant the boy is growing. That can help them figure out what the words *bean plants* mean.

ELL Ask students who have had some experience tending a garden to describe or draw pictures of the tools they used or things they grew.

TEACH/REVIEW VOCABULARY To reinforce the meaning of the words, ask volunteers to think of a synonym for each word, such as *smart* for *clever*, and so on. Then have them think of an antonym for each word.

TARGET SKILL AND STRATEGY

AUTHOR'S PURPOSE Remind students that every author has a purpose, or reason, for writing a story. An author may want to entertain, inform, or persuade. Ask: Why do you think the author wrote this story? What does the author want you to learn?

PREDICT Remind students that *predicting* is when you guess what will happen next in a story based on what has already happened. As students read, ask: What events help you to predict what is going to happen next? Then have students read ahead and see if their predictions are correct.

READ THE BOOK

Use the following questions to support comprehension.

PAGE 4 Why did the Garden Bunch plant their garden in a sunny spot? *(Vegetables need lots of sunlight to grow.)*

PAGE 7 Can you predict what will happen if Miranda forgets to water the carrots again? *(The carrots will wilt even more.)*

PAGE 10 Using clues in the text, explain what *harvest* means. *(It means to pick or gather.)*

TALK ABOUT THE BOOK

READER RESPONSE
1. Possible response: to inform readers about growing vegetables
2. Possible response: They will plant a new garden. One clue in the story is that the kids also planted a vegetable garden last summer.
3. Possible response: *busy, lively*
4. Possible response: The plants were planted in rows; the vegetables were planted in separate areas; markers identified each crop.

RESPONSE OPTIONS

WRITING Instruct students to look at the illustration of the Garden Bunch's vegetable stand on page 12. Ask students to write a short radio commercial for the stand.

CONTENT CONNECTIONS

TIME FOR Science

SCIENCE Students can learn more about measuring by planting a fast-growing flower, such as a sunflower, in the classroom. Invite students to measure the height of their flowers every day and track the growth on a weekly chart posted in the classroom.

Author's Purpose

- The **author's purpose** is the reason or reasons the author has for writing.
- An author may have one or more reasons for writing. To *inform, persuade, entertain,* or *express* are common reasons.

Directions Answer the questions.

1. Why do you think the author wrote about the time Miranda forgot to water the plants?

_____

_____

_____

2. Why do you think the author told about the special job each person had?

_____

_____

_____

3. Why do you think the author wrote a book about growing vegetables?

_____

_____

_____

4. What do you think the author wanted you to learn about plants?

_____

_____

_____

5. What do you think the author wanted you to learn about working together?

_____

_____

_____

46

Name _____

Vocabulary

Directions Circle the letter of the correct definition below each vocabulary word.

Check the Words You Know

___bottom   ___cheated   ___clever   ___crops
___lazy   ___partners   ___wealth

1. lazy
   a. quick   b. not wanting to do any work   c. simple to do

2. crops
   a. big hairy dogs   b. clothing   c. plants or fruits

3. partners
   a. wooden fences   b. people who work together   c. enemies

4. cheated
   a. not playing fairly   b. dressed for dinner   c. destroyed

5. clever
   a. hungry   b. silly   c. smart

6. wealth
   a. dirt   b. money   c. talent

7. bottom
   a. lowest part   b. highest part   c. middle

Directions Unscramble the letters to form a vocabulary word.

8. TAEEHCD _____

9. CREVEL _____

10. TOMBOT _____

11. PRCOS _____

12. PTNSERAR _____

13. ZALY _____

14. HTWEAL _____

© Pearson Education 3

47

Our Garden

AUTHOR'S PURPOSE

PREDICT

LESSON VOCABULARY bottom, cheat, clever, crops, lazy, partners, wealth

SUMMARY This is a story about how a group of children transforms an empty urban lot into a beautiful garden and gets the entire community involved.

INTRODUCE THE BOOK

BUILD BACKGROUND Discuss what students know about planting. Ask students if they understand what is involved in growing plants. Discuss any gardening projects students have done.

PREVIEW/USE ILLUSTRATIONS As students preview the book, suggest that they notice how the artwork shows groups of people, rather than showing individuals. Then ask students to read the title of the story, *Our Garden*, and discuss the connection they see between the title and the illustrations.

TEACH/REVIEW VOCABULARY Ask students to write sentences that use each vocabulary word. Then invite students to build a *word wall* of other words they can think of that have to do with plants.

ELL Make a list of words for the word wall that the students may use in a more formal conversation with the mayor. Ask them to contrast these words with informal words they use with one another.

TARGET SKILL AND STRATEGY

AUTHOR'S PURPOSE Remind students that every author writes a story for a *purpose*, or reason. Ask: Why do you think this author wrote this story? Suggest that students track story details that might support their answers.

PREDICT Remind students that to *predict* means to tell what you think might happen next in a story based on what has already happened. Suggest that students pause once or twice while they read the story to make a prediction. Then they can see whether their predictions are accurate, as they continue to read.

READ THE BOOK

Use the following questions to support comprehension.

PAGE 4 Why would a garden give the old lot new life? *(Possible response: A garden is full of growing, living things.)*

PAGE 5 Why do you think Mayor Smith was so excited about the garden? *(He knew the children's garden would benefit the whole community.)*

PAGE 15 What was the author's purpose in writing a story about a whole community getting involved in a project? *(to show that everyone had fun and built something beautiful by working together)*

TALK ABOUT THE BOOK

READER RESPONSE
1. Possible response: to show how rundown the lot had become and how much work the kids needed to do
2. Possible response: People will see what a lovely spot the lot has become and will help care for the garden.
3. Possible response: *Crops* as a verb means "to shorten." Possible sentence: The haircutter crops five inches off the girl's hair.
4. Possible response: don't litter, no loud music, no fighting, no dogs allowed in the garden

RESPONSE OPTIONS

WRITING Suggest that students write about their own perfect garden spot. What kind of garden would it be? How would they share the beauty and bounty of their garden with others?

CONTENT CONNECTIONS

SCIENCE Students can learn more about how plants grow by growing their own bean plants from seeds in the classroom. Suggest that students keep a plant diary to keep track of watering, sunlight, and the rate of growth.

TIME FOR Science

Author's Purpose

- The **author's purpose** is the reason or reasons the author has for writing.
- To *inform, persuade, entertain,* or *express* are common reasons for writing.

Directions Answer the questions.

1. Why do you think the author gave so many details about how everyone cleaned up the empty lot?

_____

_____

_____

2. Why do you think the author wrote a book about a group of people building a garden rather than just one person?

_____

_____

_____

3. Explain why one of the purposes the author may have had was to inform.

_____

_____

_____

4. How did the author show she also wanted to entertain?

_____

_____

_____

5. In what way did the author try to persuade?

_____

_____

_____

© Pearson Education 3

46

Name _____

Vocabulary

Directions Find the vocabulary word that matches each clue below.

Check the Words You Know

___bottom   ___cheat
___clever   ___crops
___lazy   ___partners
___wealth

1. It means a large amount of something, usually money. _____

2. It means the opposite of hardworking. _____

3. It means the opposite of top. _____

4. If someone is dishonest, he or she might do this. _____

5. We use this word to describe a person who likes to lie around all day. _____

6. We use this word to describe kinds of plants you grow to eat. _____

7. This word is used to describe someone who is smart. _____

8. If you and somebody else are these, you work together toward a goal. _____

Directions Write a sentence that uses two of the vocabulary words.

_____

_____

_____

_____

_____

47

The Magic of Coyote

The Magic of Coyote

by Joyce A. Churchill
illustrated by David Sheldon

◉ **AUTHOR'S PURPOSE**

◉ **PREDICT**

LESSON VOCABULARY artifacts, breakthrough, cunning, descendant, retreated, scampered, yelping

SUMMARY A Navajo storyteller and a dog that is part coyote help a boy conquer his fear of dogs.

INTRODUCE THE BOOK

BUILD BACKGROUND Within this story, a Navajo storyteller shares a tradtional Navajo tale about a clever coyote who teaches humans to use fire. Discuss with students other fictional tales they've encountered in which animals are smart, can talk, or otherwise behave like people.

PREVIEW/USE TEXT FEATURES As students preview the book, draw their attention to the thought bubbles in the illustrations on pages 4 and 17. Ask: What do you think is shown in these clouds above the character's head?

TEACH/REVIEW VOCABULARY Write the vocabulary words on the board. Have volunteers look up their definitions and share them with the class. Invite discussion as to how each word contributes to the story. For example, if a character is described as *cunning,* what might you expect from that character?

ELL Word studies can often make vocabulary more memorable. Demonstrate how *breakthrough* divides into *break* and *through.* Discuss the meanings of the separate words and then what they mean together. Show that *descendant* is related to *descend,* which means "to come down." Use a diagram with *grandparents* on top, then *parents,* then *children,* to show how *descend* means going down. Review that the *-ed* at the end of several words makes them past tense.

TARGET SKILL AND STRATEGY

◉ **AUTHOR'S PURPOSE** Remind students that an *author's purpose* is the reason she or he writes a story. Point out that this is a story about fear and ask: What lesson do you think the author wants to teach about facing your fears?

◉ **PREDICT** Tell students that to *predict* means to tell what you think happens next in a story based on what has happened before. Ask: What events might make Henry even more comfortable with dogs in the future?

READ THE BOOK

Use the following questions to support comprehension.

PAGE 3 What details show you why Henry is afraid of dogs? *(They yelp and have sharp teeth and unpleasant smells.)*

PAGE 10 What clues show that Mr. Gordon's story is fiction? *(Coyote understands human conversation; coyote feels sympathy; fire beings do not exist.)*

PAGES 21–22 What do you think the author's purpose was in having Henry pet Ranger? *(The author wanted to show that when Henry faced his fear and touched the dog, he started to get over his fear.)*

TALK ABOUT THE BOOK

READER RESPONSE
1. Possible response: to give information about Navajo culture and to show how a story can help you get over your fear
2. Possible response: Henry will probably be less fearful around dogs in the future.
3. brunch=breakfast+lunch; motel=motor+hotel; moped=motor+pedal; paratroops=parachute+troops; Skylab=sky+laboratory; smog=smoke+fog; telethon=telephone+marathon
4. Answers will vary.

RESPONSE OPTIONS

WRITING Suggest that students write a fable. Suggest topics such as how the sky got its blue color or why leopards have spots.

CONTENT CONNECTIONS

SOCIAL STUDIES Invite students to learn more about the lives of Navajo children. Encourage them to use research books or the Internet. Ask them to present short reports on their findings.

Time for
SOCIAL
STUDIES

Author's Purpose

- The **author's purpose** is the reason or reasons the author has for writing.
- An author may have one or more reasons for writing. Common reasons are to *inform, persuade, entertain,* or *express.*

Directions Answer the questions.

1. What do you think is the author's purpose for writing this story?

_____

_____

_____

2. What do you think is the author's purpose for including the story about Coyote?

_____

_____

_____

3. How does the story about Coyote stealing fire help Henry?

_____

_____

_____

4. What do you think the author wants you to learn about Navajo culture?

_____

_____

_____

5. Why do you think the author had Henry meet a coydog?

_____

_____

_____

46

Vocabulary

Directions Complete each sentence in the story with one of the vocabulary words.

Check the Words You Know
___artifacts   ___breakthrough   ___cunning   ___descendant   ___retreated   ___scampered   ___yelping

Henry was afraid of the (**1**) _____ dogs. Every time he saw

them, he (**2**) _____ to the back of the room.

One day, Henry and his class visited a Native American museum. First they

studied ancient (**3**) _____, such as pieces of pottery. Then it was time

for a story.

The story was told by Mr. Gordon, who was a (**4**) _____ of a

Navajo storyteller. Mr. Gordon told tales about the coyote, a (**5**) _____

creature who often played tricks on the Navajo people. Henry discovered that his

interest in coyotes made him feel less afraid about dogs. When Mr. Gordon's coydog,

Ranger, (**6**) _____ over to Henry, Henry actually petted Ranger. Henry

was excited, because he knew this was a real (**7**) _____.

Directions Write the definition of each word based on its context above.
Use a dictionary if necessary.

8. retreated _____

_____

9. breakthrough _____

_____

10. yelping _____

_____

47

Colonial New England

Unit 2 Week 5

🔊 **DRAW CONCLUSIONS**

🔊 **ASK QUESTIONS**

LESSON VOCABULARY barrels, cellar, clearing, peg, spoil, steep

SUMMARY The author describes how early colonists met basic needs of food, clothing, and shelter. The work habits and education of children reveal the demands of life at that time.

INTRODUCE THE BOOK

BUILD BACKGROUND Ask students to discuss how they would feel if they did not have modern conveniences such as refrigerators, supermarkets, ready-to-wear clothing, and video games. What could they do to meet their needs?

PREVIEW/USE TEXT FEATURES Tell students to look at the pictures and read the captions while flipping through the book. Ask them to share any impressions or questions they may have about colonial life.

TEACH/REVIEW VOCABULARY Before reading, ask if students recognize the vocabulary words. Have volunteers use the words in sentences.

ELL Help students sort words related to colonial New England by creating categories such as food, clothing, and homes.

TARGET SKILL AND STRATEGY

🔊 **DRAW CONCLUSIONS** Tell students that a *conclusion* is a decision you reach after you think about what you have read. Model how to draw conclusions by using a web or a blank chart with spaces to write facts from the book, what one already knows, and the conclusions that result.

🔊 **ASK QUESTIONS** This strategy involves *asking questions* about important text information. Good questions often start with *who, what, when, where, why,* or *how.* They are about important details in the story and are usually answered by information in the story. Ask students to write down questions they have while reading about colonial New England. Students who ask questions and find answers during reading are better able to draw conclusions.

READ THE BOOK

Use the following questions to support comprehension.

PAGE 3 Why was colonial America called New England by settlers? *(Most settlers came to America from England, so their new home was like a "new" England.)*

PAGE 4 Was it easy for colonists to get clothing to wear? *(No. They had to make things themselves, from spinning yarn using sheep's wool to sewing wool cloth into clothing.)*

PAGE 9 Why was food salted, smoked, dried, and stored in cool places? *(These methods prevented food from spoiling during a time when there were no refrigerators.)*

TALK ABOUT THE BOOK

READER RESPONSE
1. Responses will vary.
2. Responses will vary but may include questions about playtime, chores, learning, and family life.
3. *Clearing* means to remove things such as trees, rocks, branches, and weeds. Fields need to be cleared for planting crops.
4. Responses will vary, but will probably include mud walls, small size, furniture, and dirt floor.

RESPONSE OPTIONS

WRITING Ask students to pretend they are children in colonial New England in 1650. Tell them to write journal entries about a typical day in their lives.

CONTENT CONNECTIONS

SOCIAL STUDIES Provide reference materials that will help students learn more about different roles that colonists played in their communities. Then ask them to work in pairs and interview each other about what they did and needed to know to do their jobs.

Time for SOCIAL STUDIES

Draw Conclusions

- **Drawing conclusions** means using what you already know and what you read to make reasonable decisions about characters or events.

Directions Read the following passage. Then fill in the charts with facts from the passage and things you know that are related to the facts. Finally, write conclusions based on the facts and what you know.

There are no shopping malls in 1650. New England colonists have to make almost everything themselves. When they need clothes, they make yarn from sheep's wool. Then they weave the yarn into wool cloth. Finally, they sew the cloth into clothing.

Men and boys in colonial New England wear shirts with long sleeves. Their pants, called breeches, go to their knees. They wear long stockings.

Girls dress like their mothers. They wear long wool dresses and aprons. Outdoors and indoors, they wear caps called coifs.

1.

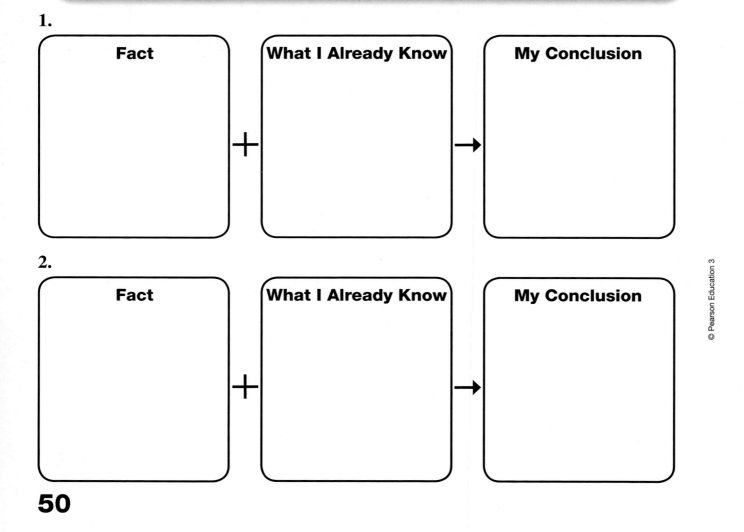

Fact		What I Already Know		My Conclusion

2.

Fact		What I Already Know		My Conclusion

50

Name _____

Vocabulary

Directions Write the word that best completes each sentence.

> ## Check the Words You Know
>
> ___barrels ___cellar ___clearing
> ___peg ___spoil ___steep

1. Your food will _____ unless you put it in the refrigerator.

2. My coat is hanging from a _____ on the wall.

3. The mountain was hard to climb because it was very _____.

4. The man sells pickles in large _____ at the market.

5. The underground _____ is a good place to store things.

6. There is a _____ in the middle of the forest where you can have a picnic.

Directions Write a paragraph about life in colonial New England. Use at least four vocabulary words.

_____

_____

_____

_____

_____

_____

_____

_____

_____

© Pearson Education 3

51

The Colonial Adventure

The Colonial Adventure
by J. Matteson Claus • illustrated by Burgandy Beam

- **DRAW CONCLUSIONS**
- **ASK QUESTIONS**

LESSON VOCABULARY barrels, cellar, clearing, peg, spoil, steep

SUMMARY This book recounts life in colonial America from the perspectives of two young cousins whose families settle in Massachusetts and Virginia. Their stories reveal the challenges of colonial living and how it differed from the lives they left behind in England.

INTRODUCE THE BOOK

BUILD BACKGROUND Point out the locations of England, Virginia, and Massachusetts on a large map. Ask students to discuss what traveling between these places must have been like in a time when only slower forms of transportation existed.

PREVIEW/USE TEXT FEATURES Tell students to look at the sketches on pages 6, 7, and 12. Ask them how the labels on the sketches further their understanding.

TEACH/REVIEW VOCABULARY Before reading, ask students if they recognize the vocabulary words. Have volunteers use the words in sentences.

ELL Look over the book's illustrations with students. Have them point to items and then name them in English and their home languages.

TARGET SKILL AND STRATEGY

DRAW CONCLUSIONS A *conclusion* is a decision you reach after you think about details in what you have read. Ask students to use what they have read plus common sense and past experiences to *draw conclusions* about Elizabeth and Sarah's lives. Suggest that they use a simple web or other graphic organizer to write facts that support a conclusion.

ASK QUESTIONS Readers who use this strategy *ask questions* and look for answers as they read. Ask students to write questions they think of while reading. Invite volunteers to share questions and tell if they were answered by the book.

READ THE BOOK

Use the following questions to support comprehension.

PAGES 4–5 How did Elizabeth travel to New England with her family? *(They sailed from England on board a crowded ship for two months.)*

PAGE 11 Do you think Elizabeth's first winter in Massachusetts was a happy time? *(No, because there was not enough food to eat, and colonists got sick)*

PAGE 14 From whom did colonists get valuable advice on farming? *(New England's native peoples taught the colonists how to plant pumpkin, squash, and corn.)*

TALK ABOUT THE BOOK

READER RESPONSE

1. The weather in Massachusetts was cold and its land was rocky, while the weather in Virginia was hot and its land was swampy. People in Massachusetts grew corn, and those in Virginia grew wheat and tobacco. Possible conclusion: Life in the colonies was difficult.
2. Responses will vary.
3. Possible response: Food spoils if you leave it out. The mother spoils her son by giving him everything he wants. My sister spoils our card games by talking.
4. Responses will vary.

RESPONSE OPTIONS

WRITING Invite students to write and act out a skit about life in colonial America based on what they have read. The skit should be written from either Elizabeth's or Sarah's perspective.

CONTENT CONNECTIONS

SOCIAL STUDIES Provide reference materials to help students explore colonists' diverse experiences. Then have them each choose a colony and write a letter from the perspective of a colonist.

Time for **SOCIAL STUDIES**

Draw Conclusions

- To **draw a conclusion** means to use what you already know and what you have read to make reasonable decisions about characters or events.

Directions Read the following message written by a fictional person from England who has settled in colonial Jamestown. Then fill in the charts with facts from the passage and things you know that are related to the facts. Finally, write conclusions based on the facts and what you know.

Sometimes life in New World can be difficult. The land here is very different from England. Jamestown is filled with swamps. Because the land is swampy, the water that we drink is brown, muddy, and not at all fresh. Also, the people of our settlement are trying to make friends with the native people. But there is little that they understand about us or that we understand about them. Papa says that we should still try to work with them and respect their ways.

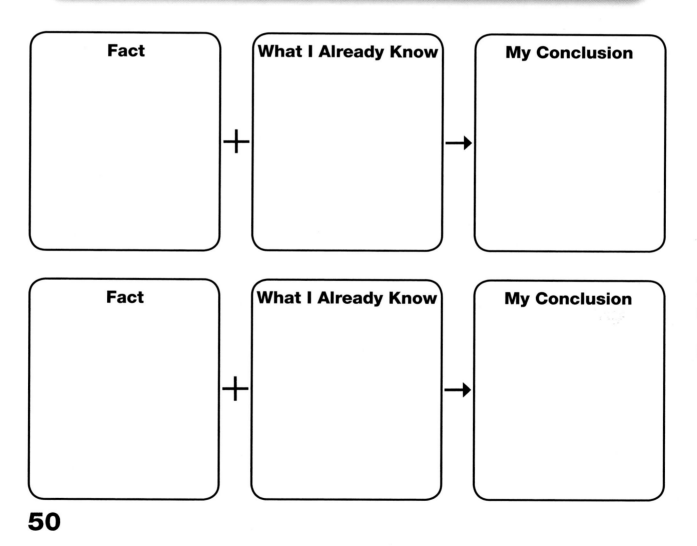

Fact		What I Already Know		My Conclusion
	+		→	
	+		→	

50

Vocabulary

Directions Read each list of words. Write a vocabulary word that relates to each group.

Check the Words You Know

___barrels   ___cellar   ___clearing

___peg   ___spoil   ___steep

1. _____

hanger

hook

rod

2. _____

sharp

sudden

raised

3. _____

ruin

rot

decay

4. _____

cans

buckets

containers

5. _____

empty space

gap

opening

6. _____

basement

underground room

vault

Directions Write a paragraph about life in colonial New England. Use as many vocabulary words as you can.

_____

_____

_____

_____

_____

© Pearson Education 3

Houses Past and Present

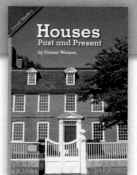

Houses Past and Present by Donna Watson

🔵 **DRAW CONCLUSIONS**

🔵 **ASK QUESTIONS**

LESSON VOCABULARY daub, kilns, mortise, pug mill, puncheon, tallow, tenon, thatch, wattle

SUMMARY The author traces the evolution of building materials and styles from the thatched-roof wooden homes of America's early colonists to today's modern fire-proof structures.

INTRODUCE THE BOOK

BUILD BACKGROUND Invite students to think about how different kinds of shelters protect people from the weather. For example, the sloping sides and waterproof fabric of a tent repel water.

PREVIEW/USE TEXT FEATURES Ask students to flip through the pages and look at the photographs. Based on these images, have them tell about how the size, shape, materials, and construction of houses have changed over the years.

TEACH/REVIEW VOCABULARY Have students create bookmarks where they can write down new and unusual words they discover while reading.

ELL Have students draw pictures of houses from the past or present and then write bilingual labels or captions for the parts.

TARGET SKILL AND STRATEGY

🔵 **DRAW CONCLUSIONS** When students use details to make reasonable decisions about characters or events, they are *drawing conclusions*. Ask students to use what they read plus common sense and experience to draw conclusions about houses past and present.

🔵 **ASK QUESTIONS** It's important to *ask questions* about text information before, during and after reading. Remind students that good questions often start with *who, what, when, where, why,* and *how*. Good questions also ask about important details of the story and can usually be answered by the story they read.

READ THE BOOK

Use the following questions to support comprehension.

PAGE 8 Why did colonists use moss, leaves, and mud while building log cabins? *(They stuffed these materials between logs to keep out the cold and wind.)*

PAGE 11 By the 1700s, how did colonists build strong homes without using nails or pegs? *(They cut slots, or mortises, in one slab of wood, placed a peg-like piece, or tenon, on a connecting slab of wood, and then fit the two sides of the wooden slabs together.)*

PAGE 16 Why did settlers in prairie lands build homes out of sod instead of lumber? *(Prairie lands had no forests for lumber, so settlers used materials that were there.)*

TALK ABOUT THE BOOK

READER RESPONSE

1. Possible responses: The stone chimney, shake shingle roofs, and tile roofs were the most important improvements, because they did not catch fire, thus preventing homes from burning down.

2. Possible responses: "How was your home built? Where did you learn your building skills?"

3. Responses will vary.

4. It shows what a mortise and a tenon look like, and you can see how they would fit together.

RESPONSE OPTIONS

WRITING Ask students to pretend they are home builders from the 1700s. Tell them to write a "how-to" manual on building or maintaining a colonial home.

CONTENT CONNECTIONS

SOCIAL STUDIES Invite students to consult books and other reference materials for information on different types of shelters and homes around the world.

Time for SOCIAL STUDIES

Draw Conclusions

- When you **draw conclusions** you use what you have read what you already know to make reasonable decisions about characters or events.

Directions Read the following passage. Then answer the questions below.

> During the pioneer era of the 1800s, settlers moved west to the prairie lands. There were no forests of tall trees to cut down for lumber. So these settlers found a way to use the ground itself to make their first homes. All around them was the grass of the prairie. The grass had deep roots which held the dirt below it.
>
> Settlers used plows to cut through the grass-covered ground, or sod. With a plow they were able to dig the grass up in long strips. Then they cut the strips of sod into sections. The pieces of sod were stacked like bricks to build the walls of the shelter.

1. Which of the following statements is a reasonable conclusion about settlers living in prairie lands?

   a. Settlers loved their sod houses.

   b. Building sod houses is easy.

   c. Settlers had to adapt to their new environment in order to survive.

2. Which of the following statements is NOT a reasonable conclusion about settlers living in prairie lands?

   a. Settlers had to work very hard to build their sod homes.

   b. Sod houses could be dirty and filled with insects.

   c. Sod houses offered a comfortable, luxurious home.

3. How do you think settlers felt about living in sod houses? Why do you think so?

   _____

   _____

4. How might settlers have built their homes differently if there were trees? Why?

   _____

© Pearson Education 3

50

Name _____

Vocabulary

Directions Write the word from the box that matches each definition below.

Check the Words You Know

___daub   ___kilns   ___mortise
___pug mill   ___puncheon   ___tallow
___tenon   ___thatch   ___wattle

1. _____ grasses, leaves, or straw used to cover a roof

2. _____ animal fat used to make candles

3. _____ a type of flooring made up of halved logs

4. _____ very hot ovens used for making bricks

5. _____ a hole in one piece of wood that helps form a joint with another wooden piece

6. _____ sticks interwoven with twigs and branches

7. _____ the end of a piece of wood that fits into the hole described in item 5.

8. _____ a coating of plaster, clay, mud, or any other sticky material

9. _____ a hollow tub with knives used for mixing and grinding clay

Directions Write a sentence about houses past and present. Use as many vocabulary words as you can.

_____

_____

_____

51

Antarctica: The Frozen Continent LR1

 Main Idea, LR2

Possible responses are given. **1.** Antarctica is very windy and dry. **2.** Scientists call Antarctica a desert. **3.** The small amount of snow that falls in Antarctica never melts. **4.** Snow is moved around by the wind until it freezes into ice.

Vocabulary, LR3

1. d **2.** e **3.** f **4.** c **5.** a **6.** g **7.** b **8.** frozen **9.** flippers **10.** pecks **11.** hatch
Paragraphs will vary.

Sarah's Choice LR10

 Character, LR11

Possible responses given. Sarah: didn't listen to her mother; didn't ask permission. Julia: just moved in; asked permission. Both: friendly; like blueberries

Vocabulary, LR12

1. d **2.** g **3.** a **4.** b **5.** f **6.** c **7.** e **8.** shocked **9.** sadness **10.** shivered **11.** slammed **12.** gardener **13.** excitement **14.** motioned

Metal Detector Detective LR19

 Main Idea, LR20

Possible responses given. **1.** Main Idea: There are rules you must follow before using a metal detector. **2.** Detail: Metal detectors are not allowed on National Park Service lands. **3.** Detail: Ask permission before you use a metal detector in public places. **4.** Detail: If you are not sure whether you can use a metal detector, just ask.

Vocabulary, LR21

1. e **2.** b **3.** f **4.** a **5.** c **6.** d **7.** enormous **8.** strain **9.** scattered **10.** shiny **11.** collection

Growing Vegetables LR28

 Author's Purpose, LR29

Possible responses given. **1.** to show that when you don't water plants, they wilt **2.** to tell about the different things you need to do to grow vegetables **3.** to inform the reader how to grow a vegetable garden **4.** They need water, weeding, and sunlight. **5.** It's more fun for everyone, and the end result is better.

Vocabulary, LR30

1. b **2.** c **3.** b **4.** a **5.** c **6.** b **7.** a **8.** cheated **9.** clever **10.** bottom **11.** crops **12.** partners **13.** lazy **14.** wealthy

Colonial New England LR37

 Draw Conclusions, LR38

Possible responses given. **1.** New England colonists had to make their own clothing. + Making your own clothing takes a lot of time and energy. → New England colonists had to work very hard to dress themselves. **2.** Colonial girls wore long wool dresses and aprons. + Today most girls wear pants. → Colonial girls dressed differently from girls of today.

Vocabulary, LR39

1. spoil **2.** peg **3.** steep **4.** barrel **5.** cellar **6.** clearing
Paragraphs will vary but should use four vocabulary words correctly in context.

Birds That Can't Fly! LR4

 Main Idea, LR5

Possible responses given. **1.** flightless birds **2.** Flightless birds differ from flying birds in many ways. **3.** The bones of flightless birds are heavier than those of flying birds. **4.** The feathers of flightless birds are different from those of flying birds. **5.** A flightless bird's breastbone is different from that of a flying bird.

Vocabulary, LR6

1. hugs, snuggles **2.** paddles, fins **3.** chilly, icy **4.** produce, cause **5.** strikes, hits **6.** dress, groom **7.** nestles, holds
Responses will vary.

The Boy Who Cried Wolf LR13

 Character, LR14

1. Daniel **2.** He is easily bored. He is mischievous. **3.** He wants excitement. He wants more responsibility. He wants the villagers to notice him. **4–7.** Daniel starts out feeling bored. He acts mischievously and cries "wolf" to get the villagers' attention. He gets scared when a real wolf shows up near his sheep. He promises never to lie again.

Vocabulary, LR15

1. unhappiness, sorrow **2.** smashed, smacked **3.** trembled, shook **4.** action, adventure **5.** grower, farmer **6.** pointed, signaled **7.** surprised, jolted
Responses will vary.

Katy's Last-Minute Book Report LR22

 Main Idea, LR23

Possible responses given. **1.** planning time well **2.** It is important to plan your time well. **3.** Homework, sports, and family activities take up a lot of time. **4.** If you don't plan your time well, you might forget to do something important. **5.** You need to plan enough time to do a good job.

Vocabulary, LR24

1. group, set **2.** huge, giant **3.** recognize, understand **4.** separated, sprinkled **5.** glossy, sparkly **6.** try, strive
Paragraphs will vary but should use vocabulary words correctly.

Our Garden LR31

 Author's Purpose, LR32

Possible responses given. **1.** to show how much work is involved **2.** to show that people working together can do great things **3.** The author tells what they can accomplish by working together. **4.** the heartwarming way the author shows how people improve their community **5.** by trying to convince people that good things come from working together

Vocabulary, LR33

1. wealth **2.** lazy **3.** bottom **4.** cheat **5.** lazy **6.** crops **7.** clever **8.** partners
Sentences will vary but should use vocabulary words correctly.

The Colonial Adventure LR40

 Draw Conclusions, LR41

Possible responses given. Fact: Colonists are drinking brown, muddy water that is not fresh. What I Know: Drinking water that is not fresh can make you sick. Conclusion: The brown, muddy water may be making the colonists sick. Fact: Colonists try to make friends with native people, but they do not understand each other. What I Know: Making friends with other people is hard when you do not understand them. Conclusion: The colonists may find it hard to make friends with the native people.

Vocabulary, LR42

1. peg **2.** steep **3.** spoil **4.** barrels **5.** clearing **6.** cellar
Paragraphs will vary but should include some correctly used vocabulary words.

Answer Key for Advanced-Level Reader Practice

Penguins On Parade — LR7

 Main Idea, LR8

Possible responses given. **1.** penguins and the Southern Hemisphere **2.** The Southern Hemisphere is home to the world's penguins. **3.** Penguins live on the Galápagos Islands, in Australia, New Zealand, Africa, South America, and islands that surround Antarctica. **4.** There are many things emperor penguins do to stay warm. **5.** They stand on heels; they huddle together.

Vocabulary, LR9

1. incubate **2.** rookery **3.** blubber **4.** down **5.** molt **6.** brood patch **7.** crest **8.** grow new feathers **9.** a place where groups of birds gather to raise their young **10.** a layer that protects animals from the cold

The Song Makers Go to Salem — LR16

 Character, LR17

Possible responses given.

Tabitha—Trait: honest; Clue: told Abbey that she saw her take money; Trait: thoughtful; Clue: gently convinced Abbey to admit her theft

Abbey—Trait: trusting; Clue: believed that Tabitha gave her good advice; Trait: strong; Clue: stood up and admitted she stole money

Vocabulary, LR18

1. solution **2.** frantically **3.** concentrate **4.** suspect **5.** anxious **6.** relieved **7.** erupted
Paragraphs will vary.

Collecting Dreams — LR25

 Main Idea, LR26

Possible responses given. **1.** china; porcelain **2.** English bone china is a special kind of porcelain. **3–4.** Porcelain was first made in China, hundreds of years ago. About two hundred years ago, the English added ash to make a special kind of porcelain called bone china. **5–7.** Responses will vary.

Vocabulary, LR27

1. rim **2.** credit **3.** kaleidoscope **4.** collectibles **5.** suspiciously **6.** fond **7.** porcelain **8.** propped **9.** specialize

The Magic of Coyote — LR34

 Author's Purpose, LR35

Possible responses given. **1.** to entertain with a story of how a boy conquered his fear of dogs **2.** This story informs, or explains, how humans got fire. **3.** Henry likes the story about the coyote, which is similar to a dog, and it makes him less afraid of dogs. **4.** She wants to inform readers about their rich tradition of storytelling. **5.** Henry already liked coyotes, so it was easier to like the dog part of the coydog.

Vocabulary, LR36

1. yelping **2.** retreated **3.** artifacts **4.** descendant **5.** cunning **6.** scampered **7.** breakthrough
Possible responses given. **8.** withdrew **9.** a significant advance **10.** making sharp, shrill cries or barks

Houses Past and Present — LR43

 **Draw Conclusions, LR44**

1. c **2.** c **3.** Possible response: Sod houses were not very comfortable, but the settlers worked well with the materials they had. **4.** Possible response: The trees could be used for lumber, which would have made stronger, wooden houses.

Vocabulary, LR45

1. thatch **2.** tallow **3.** puncheon **4.** kilns **5.** mortise **6.** wattle **7.** tenon **8.** daub **9.** pug mill
Sentences will vary but should correctly use vocabulary words.

Differentiated Instruction

Table of Contents

Routine Cards

Oral Rereading Routine

Use this Routine when students read orally.

1 Read Have students read the entire book orally.

2 Reread For optimal fluency, students should reread the text three or four times.

3 Provide Feedback Listen as students read and provide corrective feedback regarding their oral reading and their use of decoding strategies.

Choral Reading Routine

Use this Routine when students read chorally.

1 Select a Passage Choose an appropriate passage from the selection.

2 Divide into Groups Assign each group a part to read.

3 Model Have students track the print as you read.

4 Read Together Have students read along with you.

5 Independent Reading Have the groups read aloud without you. Monitor progress and provide feedback. For optimal fluency, students should reread three to four times.

Fluent Word Reading Routine

Teach students to read words fluently using this Routine.

1 Connect Write an example word. Isolate the sound-spelling or word structure element you will focus on and ask students to demonstrate their understanding.

2 Model When you come to a new word, look at all the letters in the word and think about its vowel sound. Say the sounds in the word to yourself and then read the word. Model reading the example words in this way. When you come to a new word, what are you going to do?

3 Group Practice Write other similar words. Let's read these words. Look at the letters, think about the vowel sounds, and say the sounds to yourself. When I point to the word, let's read it together. Allow 2-3 seconds previewing time for each word.

Paired Reading Routine

Use this Routine when students read in pairs.

1 Reader 1 Begins Students read the entire book, switching readers at the end of each page.

2 Reader 2 Begins Have partners reread; now the other partner begins.

3 Reread For optimal fluency, students should reread three or four times.

4 Provide Feedback Listen as students read. Provide corrective feedback regarding their oral reading and their use of decoding strategies.

Routine Cards

Routine Card

Multisyllabic Word Routine

Teach students this Routine to read long words with meaningful parts.

1 Teach Tell students to look for meaningful parts and to think about the meaning of each part. They should use the parts to read the word and determine meaning.

2 Model Think aloud to analyze a long word for the base word, ending, prefix, and/or suffix and to identify the word and determine its meaning.

3 Guide Practice Provide examples of long words with endings (-ing, -ed, -s), prefixes (un-, re-, dis-, mis-, non-), and/or suffixes (-ly, -ness, -less, -ful, and so on). Help students analyze base words and parts.

4 Provide Feedback Encourage students to circle parts of the words to help identify parts and determine meaning.

Routine Card

Picture Walk Routine

To build concepts and vocabulary, conduct a structured picture walk before reading.

1 Prepare Preview the selection and list key concepts and vocabulary you wish to develop.

2 Discuss As students look at the pages, discuss illustrations, have students point to pictured items, and/or ask questions that target key concepts and vocabulary.

3 Elaborate Elaborate on students' responses to reinforce correct use of the vocabulary and to provide additional exposure to key concepts.

4 Practice For more practice with key concepts, have each student turn to a partner and do the picture walk using the key concept vocabulary.

Routine Card

Multisyllabic Word Routine

Teach students this Routine to chunk words with no recognizable parts.

1 Teach Tell students to look for chunks in words with no meaningful parts. They should say each chunk slowly and then say the chunks fast to make a whole word.

2 Model Think aloud to demonstrate breaking a word into chunks, saying each chunk slowly, and then saying the chunks fast to make a word.

3 Guide Practice Provide examples of long words with no meaningful parts. Help students chunk the words.

4 Provide Feedback If necessary, reteach by modeling how to break words into chunks.

Routine Card

Concept Vocabulary

Use this Routine to teach concept vocabulary.

1 Introduce the Word Relate the word to the week's concept. Supply a student-friendly definition.

2 Demonstrate Provide several familiar examples to demonstrate meaning.

3 Apply Have students demonstrate understanding with a simple activity.

4 Display the Word Relate the word to the concept by displaying it on a concept web. Have students identify word parts and practice reading the word.

5 Use the Word Often Encourage students to use the word often in their writing and speaking. Ask questions that require students to use the word.

Group Time

DAY 1

Leveled Reader Database ONLINE

PearsonSuccessNet.com

❶ Preteach Phonics

SYLLABLE PATTERNS V/CV AND VC/V Write *silent*. If a syllable ends with a vowel, the vowel sound is usually long. If a syllable ends with a consonant, the vowel sound is usually short. If you don't know with which syllable the consonant goes, you can read the word both ways. Cover *ent*. If the consonant ends the first syllable, I would say the word with a short *i*: **sil ent**. That doesn't sound right. I'll try putting *l* with the second syllable. Cover *lent*. Now I'll say the first syllable with a long *i*: **sī lent**. That's it! That's a word I know. Write and repeat this procedure with *solid: sō lid; sol id.* Have students blend *melon* and *human* with you in this way: *mē lon, mel on; hum an, hū man.*

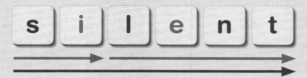

❷ Preview Decodable Reader 6

BEFORE READING Review the words on Decodable Reader p. 41. Then have students blend these story words: *pounded, borrowed, worried, suggested.* Be sure students understand the meanings of words such as *pounded.*

Use the Picture Walk Routine on p. DI·1 to guide students through the text.

❸ Read Leveled Reader *Antarctica: The Frozen Continent*

REINFORCE CONCEPTS This week's concept is *animal adaptation.* Animals have certain body parts or ways of behaving that help them live in their environments. For example, how do you think a zebra's stripes help it survive?

BEFORE READING Using the Picture Walk routine on p. DI·1, guide students through the text focusing on key concepts and vocabulary. Ask questions such as:

p. 3 What can you tell about the weather in Antarctica?

p. 4 How do you think these animals can survive in Antarctica?

Read pp. 3–4 aloud. Then do a choral reading of pp. 5–8. Have students read and discuss the remainder of the book with a partner.

Monitor Progress

Word and Selection Reading

If... students have difficulty reading story words from the Decodable Reader,	then... reteach them by modeling blending or reading multisyllabic words.
If... partners have difficulty reading the Leveled Reader on their own,	then... have them follow along as they listen to the Online Leveled Reader Audio.

For alternate Leveled Reader lesson plans that teach ⟳ **Main Idea,** ⟳ **Graphic Organizers,** and **Lesson Vocabulary,** see pp. LR1–LR9.

On-Level

ROUTINE

1 Build Background

DEVELOP VOCABULARY Write the word *refuge* and explain that it means "shelter or protection from danger or trouble or worry." Ask: What place might you, or someone you know, think of as a refuge? *(a bedroom or other part of their home, a relative's house, school)* Repeat this activity with the word *flightless* and other words from the Leveled Reader *Birds That Can't Fly!* Use the Concept Vocabulary routine on p. DI·1 as needed.

2 Read Leveled Reader *Birds That Can't Fly!*

BEFORE READING Have students create a four-column chart with the headings *Bird, Home, Diet, Special Body Parts.* This book gives many facts about different kinds of flightless birds. As you read, record information about each bird—such as its name, where it lives, what it eats, and any special features about its body—on your chart.

DURING READING Have students follow along as you read pp. 3–7. Then let them complete the book on their own. Remind students to add information to their charts as they read.

AFTER READING Have students compare the information on their charts. Point out that information they learned about penguins will help them as they read tomorrow's selection, *Penguin Chick.*

Advanced

ROUTINE

1 Read Leveled Reader *Penguins on Parade*

BEFORE READING Recall the Read Aloud "Swamp Scramblers." How do the body features of mudskippers help them survive in their environment? *(Strong front fins help them move on ground. Back fins help them climb. Pockets help them keep gills moist so they can get oxygen.)* Today you will read how the body parts of penguins help them survive in a very different environment.

CRITICAL THINKING Have students read the Leveled Reader independently. Encourage them to think critically. For example, ask:

- How do you think some of the penguins you read about got their names?
- How are all penguins alike? What are some of the key differences among them?
- Why do you think penguins balance their eggs on their feet instead of building nests?

AFTER READING Have students review the book to select four or more unfamiliar or interesting words and determine their meanings by using context or the dictionary. Then have students write True or False statements about penguins using the words and exchange papers with partners. Have students meet with you to discuss the selection and the statements they wrote.

2 Independent Extension Activity

NOW TRY THIS Assign "Now Try This" on pp. 18–19 of *Penguins on Parade* for students to work on throughout the week. Ask them to write down what they discovered.

Penguin Chick
Group Time

ROUTINE

DAY 2

Audio CD AudioText

Monitor Progress

Word and Selection Reading

If... students have difficulty reading multisyllabic words in the selection,	then... have them look for and read meaningful parts in the words or have them chunk words with no recognizable parts.
If... students have difficulty reading along with the group,	then... have them follow along as they listen to the AudioText.

① Reread for Fluency

Use Decodable Reader 6.

② Word Study/Phonics

LESSON VOCABULARY Use p. 152b to review the meanings of *cuddles, flippers, frozen, hatch, pecks, preen,* and *snuggles.* Students can blend all of the words. Have individuals practice reading the words from word cards.

DECODING MULTISYLLABIC WORDS Write *toboggan* and model how to decode when there are no meaningful word parts. *I see a chunk at the beginning of the word: to. I'll split the rest of the word into two chunks, between the two g's. In the middle I see bog. At the end I see gan. I say each chunk slowly: to bog gan. I say the chunk fast to make a whole word: toboggan. If I change the vowel sound in the first and last chunks a little, I can see the word is toboggan.*

Use the Multisyllabic Word routine on p. DI·1 to help students read these other words from *Penguin Chick: webbed, rookery, shuffles, nursery, slippery, waterproof,* and *headfirst.* Be sure students understand the meanings of words such as *rookery* and *shuffles.*

③ Read *Penguin Chick,* pp. 154–161

BEFORE READING Yesterday we read about Antarctica and learned about the animals that live there. Today we will read about how the emperor penguins are able to live in the coldest place on earth.

Using the Picture Walk routine on p. DI·1, guide students through the text, asking questions such as those listed below. Then read the question on p. 155. Together, set a purpose for reading.

p. 157 What is the penguin doing with the egg? *(putting it under its body on top of its feet)* Why do you think it is doing that?

p. 160 What are the penguins doing? *(standing close together in a large group)* They are huddling together to keep warm. As we read, let's pay attention to other ways the penguins have of surviving.

DURING READING Follow the Guiding Comprehension routine on pp. 156–161. Have students read along with you while tracking the print or do a choral reading. Stop every two pages to ask what students have learned so far. Prompt as necessary.

• What was p. 157 about?
• What does the mother penguin do after she leaves the rookery?

AFTER READING What have you learned so far? What do you think you will learn about tomorrow? Reread passages as needed.

Advanced

ROUTINE

1 Extend Vocabulary

⊙ **CONTEXT CLUES** Choose and read a sentence or passage containing a difficult word with a synonym as a context clue, such as this sentence from p. 11 of *Penguins on Parade:* "All penguin tongues have tiny barbs or spines for keeping a firm grip on prey they have caught." What does the word *barbs* mean? *(spines, or sharp things)* How did you figure out the word's meaning? *(I looked at the words around it and saw "or spines," so I thought that* spines *must be a synonym for* barbs.) A context clue that is a synonym can help you figure out the meaning of an unknown word. Remind students to use the strategy as they read *Penguin Chick.*

2 Read *Penguin Chick,* pp. 154–161

BEFORE READING In "Penguins on Parade," you read about many different kinds of penguins. Today you will read a selection that explains the life cycle of one particular penguin—the emperor penguin. As you read, think about how emperor penguins manage to survive in the cold Antarctic environment.

Have students write their predictions about what topics or ideas they think the selection will cover in their Strategy Response Logs (p. 154). Have them revise their predictions as they read.

CRITICAL THINKING/PROBLEM SOLVING Have students read pp. 154–161 independently. Encourage them to think critically and creatively. For example, ask:

- What special ways of behaving do the mother and father penguins have that help them protect their eggs?
- How is the emperor penguin different from birds you might see near your home?
- What sort of environment would you need to make for emperor penguins in a zoo?

AFTER READING Meet with students to discuss the selection and have them share their Strategy Response Log entries. Then have them imagine they are zookeepers expecting several emperor penguins and write a description of the environment they would create for the birds.

DAY 2

AudioText

Penguin Chick
Group Time

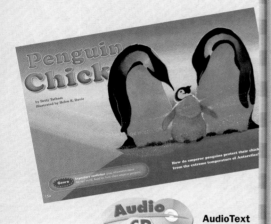

DAY 3

Audio CD AudioText

ROUTINE

1 Reinforce Comprehension

SKILL MAIN IDEA AND DETAILS Have students tell what the main idea of a piece of writing is *(the most important idea)* and what supporting details are *(little bits of information that support the main idea)*. If necessary, review the meanings and provide a model. The main idea of a piece of writing is the most important idea. Details tell about the main idea. Suppose I read this paragraph: "The mother penguin moves by tobogganing. She walks or slides on her belly. She uses her flippers to push herself forward." The main idea is "The mother penguin moves by tobogganing." I know that because it's the most important idea. The other two sentences help explain or give more information about it.

Have students find the main idea *(Emperor penguins are the largest of all penguins)* and details in the paragraph below.

> **Emperor penguins are the largest of all penguins. They grow up to 40 inches tall, and they weigh about 90 pounds. They have big heads and short, thick necks.**

2 Read *Penguin Chick,* pp. 162–167

BEFORE READING Have students retell what they have learned so far from the selection. Reread the last two paragraphs on p. 157 and model how to use a main ideas graphic organizer, such as the one shown on p. 150. These paragraphs are about staying with the egg to keep it warm. That's the topic. I ask myself, "What's the most important idea about staying with the egg?" It's that the father stays with it. That's the main idea. Some details that support or explain that idea are (1) the father is bigger and fatter, (2) he can live longer without food, and (3) the mother needs to go to the sea for food. Remind students to look for main ideas and details as they read the rest of *Penguin Chick.* **STRATEGY Graphic Organizers**

DURING READING Follow the Guiding Comprehension routine on pp. 162–167. Have students read along with you while tracking print or do a choral reading. Stop every two pages to ask students what they have learned so far. Prompt as necessary.

- What did you learn about how penguin chicks get food?
- What is p. 164 about?

AFTER READING How does this selection show that penguins can survive in their environment? Reread with students for comprehension as needed. Tell them that tomorrow they will read "Plants: Fitting into Their World," a photo essay that tells how some plants survive in their environments.

Monitor Progress

Word and Selection Reading

If... students have difficulty reading multisyllabic words in the selection,	**then...** have them look for and read meaningful parts in the words or have them chunk words with no recognizable parts.
If... students have difficulty reading along with the group,	**then...** have them follow along as they listen to the AudioText.

Advanced

1 Extend Comprehension

SKILL MAIN IDEA AND DETAILS Discuss with students how sometimes the main idea of a paragraph or section does not appear at the beginning; it may be in the middle or end of a paragraph or section. Also, the main idea may not even be stated outright; you might need to infer it from the details. Have students read the following paragraph and identify the main idea from the details: Like the emperor penguin, the king penguin is large. In fact, it is the second largest species of penguin. Also like the emperor penguin, the king penguin doesn't build a nest; rather, it tucks the egg into a brood patch. Finally, the parents of king penguins take turns caring for their egg and feeding their chick just as emperor penguins do.

(Main idea: The emperor and king penguin are similar in many ways.)

STRATEGY GRAPHIC ORGANIZERS Have students write a paragraph about penguins that includes a main idea and details that support the main idea. Review their paragraphs with them. Then have partners exchange paragraphs and use graphic organizers to identify each other's main idea and supporting details. Encourage students to discuss their graphic organizers with their partners.

AudioText

2 Read *Penguin Chick,* pp. 162–167

BEFORE READING Have students recall what they have learned from the selection so far. Remind them to look for main ideas and supporting details and to use graphic organizers to help them as they read the remainder of *Penguin Chick.*

CRITICAL THINKING/CREATIVE THINKING Have students read pp. 162–167 independently. Encourage them to think critically and creatively. For example, ask:

• How do you know the author has done a lot of research for this selection?

AFTER READING Have students complete the Strategy Response Log activity (p. 166). Then discuss *pourquoi,* or "why," tales with students. Help students use the library or Internet to find and read a *pourquoi* tale. Then encourage them to write a *pourquoi* tale about the emperor penguin, explaining why it doesn't have wings or why it slides on its belly. Give students an opportunity to meet with you as they plan their writing.

Group Time

DAY 4

AudioText

Strategic Intervention

ROUTINE

1 Practice Retelling

REVIEW MAIN IDEAS Help students identify the main ideas in *Penguin Chick*. List the ideas students mention. Then ask questions to help students differentiate between essential and nonessential information.

RETELL Using the Retelling Cards, have students work with partners to retell the important ideas. Show partners how to summarize in as few words as possible. Monitor retelling and prompt students as needed. For example, ask:

- What did you learn from reading this selection?
- Tell me in order the major events from the time a mother penguin lays an egg to the time the young penguin is about five years old.

If students struggle, model a fluent retelling.

2 Read "Plants: Fitting into Their World"

BEFORE READING Read the genre information on p. 170. Point out that students can use photo essays to find information and learn new things. As we read "Plants: Fitting into Their World," study the photos and look for interesting facts in the text about how plants survive in their environments.

Read the rest of the panel on p. 170. Have students read the title and main headings in the selection. Then have them use their fingers to move from each arrow/text section to the photo that accompanies it. Look at each photo. Is it a close-up view? Then ask: How do reading the headings and studying the photos help you prepare for reading the text?

DURING READING Have students read along with you while tracking the print or do a choral reading of the selection. Stop to discuss difficult vocabulary, such as *photosynthesis, bromeliad,* and *nutrients.*

AFTER READING Have students share their reactions to the selection. Then guide them through the Reading Across Texts and Writing Across Texts activities, prompting if necessary.

- What do penguin chicks depend on for food and shelter?
- How do the plants in this selection get what they need to survive?
- What kinds of dangers do the penguin chicks face? How do these dangers compare with dangers the plants in this selection face?

Monitor Progress

Word and Selection Reading

If... students have difficulty reading multisyllabic words in the selection,	then... have them look for and read meaningful parts in the words or have them chunk words with no recognizable parts.
If... students have difficulty reading along with the group,	then... have them follow along as they listen to the AudioText.

Advanced

1 **Read** "Plants: Fitting into Their World"

CRITICAL THINKING Have students read pp. 170–173 independently. Encourage them to think critically. For example, ask:

- Compare and contrast the ways in which plants get as much sunlight as possible.
- The terminalia tree and the floss-silk tree have physical features that protect them from harmful plants and animals. What other plants can you think of that have physical features that protect them?

AFTER READING Have students meet with you to discuss the selection and Reading Across Texts. Have students do Writing Across Texts independently.

2 **Extend Genre Study**

RESEARCH Have students locate other photo essays about plants or animals and how they survive. They should look in children's science magazines, their own textbooks, and library books, as well as on the Internet. Have them list the titles and subjects of the photo essays.

WRITE Have students choose a plant or an animal that interests them and create a photo essay about it. They may photocopy photos they find in print, download images from online sources, or draw their own illustrations. Ask them to focus on how the plant or animal survives. Remind them to write headings and text to go with the photos. Encourage them to present their photo essays in an eye-catching manner, using this selection as an example. Invite them to share their work.

AudioText

Penguin Chick

Group Time

Leveled Reader
Database
ONLINE
PearsonSuccessNet.com

1 Reread for Fluency

MODEL Read aloud pp. 6–7 of the Leveled Reader *Antarctica: The Frozen Continent* accurately and at an appropriate pace. Have students note how you read each word correctly (self-correct if necessary) and how the speed at which you read helped them follow and understand. Next, read a few sentences very quickly, mispronouncing a word or two. Then read a few sentences very slowly, pausing after each word. Ask which pace sounded best to students. Discuss how reading at an appropriate pace will help students understand and remember what they read.

PRACTICE Have individuals reread passages from *Antarctica: The Frozen Continent* with a partner or individually. For optimal fluency, they should reread three or four times. As students read, monitor fluency and provide corrective feedback. Students in this group are assessed in Weeks 2 and 4.

2 Retell Leveled Reader *Antarctica: The Frozen Continent*

Model how to use the photos and captions to retell the book. Then ask students to retell *Antarctica: The Frozen Continent,* photo by photo. Prompt them as needed.

• What is this photo mostly about?
• Why do you think the author included this photo?

Monitor Progress

Fluency

If... students have difficulty reading fluently,	then... provide additional fluency practice by pairing nonfluent readers with fluent ones.

For alternate Leveled Reader lesson plans that teach
 **Main Idea** and **Details,**  **Graphic Organizers,**
and **Lesson Vocabulary,** see pp. LR1–LR9.

On-Level

① Reread for Fluency   ROUTINE

MODEL Read aloud p. 3 of the Leveled Reader *Birds That Can't Fly!* accurately and at an appropriate pace. Have students note how you read each word correctly and how the speed at which you read helped them follow and understand. Point out that it's often helpful to read nonfiction such as this selection at a slower pace than fiction. Discuss how reading at an appropriate pace will help them understand and remember what they read.

PRACTICE Have individuals reread passages from *Birds That Can't Fly!* with a partner or individually. For optimal fluency, students should reread three or four times. As students read, monitor fluency and provide corrective feedback. Students in this group are assessed in Week 3.

② Retell Leveled Reader *Birds That Can't Fly!*

Have students skim the text as a guide to summarize important facts they learned from the book. Prompt as needed.

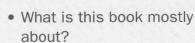

- What is this book mostly about?
- What did you learn from reading this book?
- Why do you think the author wrote this book?

Advanced

① Reread for Fluency   ROUTINE

PRACTICE Have students reread passages from the Leveled Reader *Penguins on Parade* with a partner or individually. As students read, monitor fluency and provide corrective feedback. If students read fluently on the first reading, they do not need to reread three to four times. Assess the fluency of students in this group using p. 173a.

② Revisit Leveled Reader *Penguins on Parade*

RETELL Have students retell the Leveled Reader *Penguins on Parade.*

NOW TRY THIS Discuss with students the results of their experiments. Then have them share their findings with classmates.

A Day's Work

Group Time

DAY 1

ROUTINE

① Preteach Phonics

SYLLABLE PATTERN C + le Write *little*. If a word ends in a consonant plus *-le*, those three letters usually make up the last syllable. Which is the first syllable in this word? *(lit)* Which is the second syllable? *(tle)* Blend the word: *lit tle, little.* Have students blend it with you.

Repeat this process with these words: *cuddle, poodle,* and *grumble.*

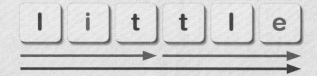

② Preview Decodable Reader 7

BEFORE READING Review the words on Decodable Reader p. 49. Then have students blend these story words: *supermarkets, cider, sorting, loaded,* and *jelly.* Be sure students understand the meanings of words such as *cider.*

Use the Picture Walk Routine on p. DI·1 to guide students through the text.

③ **Read** Leveled Reader *Sarah's Choice*

REINFORCE CONCEPTS This week's concept is *right and wrong.* People can choose to do the right thing or the wrong thing. What kinds of right choices have you seen people make? What kinds of wrong choices have you seen?

BEFORE READING Using the Picture Walk routine on p. DI·1, guide students through the text focusing on key concepts and vocabulary. Ask questions such as:

p. 4 This story is about two girls who are friends. Who do you think is talking with the girls in this picture?

pp. 8–9 What are the girls doing in this picture?

Read pp. 3–4 aloud. Then do a choral reading of pp. 5–7. Have students read and discuss the remainder of the book with a partner. Ask: What was Sarah's choice? *(to eat the blueberries without asking)* Was it the right choice or the wrong choice? Why? *(wrong, because she should have asked her mother first)*

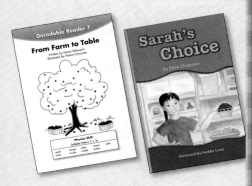

Leveled Reader Database

ONLINE

PearsonSuccessNet.com

Monitor Progress

Word and Selection Reading

If... students have difficulty reading story words from the Decodable Reader,	then... reteach them by modeling blending or reading multisyllabic words.
If... partners have difficulty reading the Leveled Reader on their own,	then... have them follow along as they listen to the Online Leveled Reader Audio.

For alternate Leveled Reader lesson plans that teach ⟳**Character,** ⟳**Visualize,** and **Lesson Vocabulary,** see pp. LR10–LR18.

On-Level

ROUTINE

1 Build Background

DEVELOP VOCABULARY Write the word *victims* and ask students to define it in their own words. *(people who are treated badly or who have bad things happen to them)* What are some examples of victims? *(people in a car crash, or who have had a crime committed against them)* Repeat this activity with the word *trust* and other words from the Leveled Reader *The Boy Who Cried Wolf.* Use the Concept Vocabulary routine on p. DI·1 as needed.

2 Read Leveled Reader
The Boy Who Cried Wolf

THE BOY WHO CRIED WOLF
retold by Linda B. Ross
Illustrated by Mark Weber

BEFORE READING Have students create T-charts with the labels "Actions" and "Consequences." This book tells about the actions of a boy named Daniel. As you read, look for the actions Daniel takes and the consequences, or what happens as a result, of each action. Record these events on your T-charts.

DURING READING Have students follow along as you read pp. 3–7. Then let them complete the book on their own. Remind students to add actions and consequences to their T-charts as they read.

AFTER READING Have students compare the ideas on their T-charts. Point out that looking for actions and their consequences will help them as they read tomorrow's story, *A Day's Work.*

Advanced

ROUTINE

1 Read Leveled Reader
The Song Makers Go to Salem

The Song Makers Go to Salem
by Sharon Franklin

Illustrated by Troy Saunveero

BEFORE READING Recall the Read Aloud "The Honest-to-Goodness Truth." What did Libby learn about telling the truth? *(It's important to tell the truth in the right way and for the right reasons.)* Today you will read about some friends who also must wrestle with the best way to tell the truth.

CRITICAL THINKING/PROBLEM SOLVING Have students read the Leveled Reader independently. Encourage them to think critically and in terms of problems and solutions. For example, ask:

- Do you think Tabitha and Abbey made the right decision to have Abbey admit what she had done? Explain.
- What do Tabitha's actions tell you about the kind of friend she is?

AFTER READING Have students review the selection to find five or more unfamiliar words and determine their meanings. Then ask them to use the words in statements that deal with doing the right thing or the wrong thing. For example, *John was **relieved** when he discovered someone had returned his wallet.* Have students meet with you to discuss the selection and the statements they wrote.

2 Independent Extension Activity

WRITE A SONG Assign the article on p. 24 of *The Song Makers Go to Salem.* Have students collaborate to write a song. Encourage them to write lyrics about telling the truth or choosing between right and wrong.

Group Time

AudioText

Monitor Progress

Word and Selection Reading

If... students have difficulty reading multisyllabic words in the selection,	then... have them look for and read meaningful parts in the words or have them chunk words with no recognizable parts.
If... students have difficulty reading along with the group,	then... have them follow along as they listen to the AudioText.

Strategic Intervention

ROUTINE

1 Reread for Fluency

Use Decodable Reader 7.

2 Word Study/Phonics

LESSON VOCABULARY Use p. 176b to review the meanings of *excitement, gardener, motioned, sadness, shivered, shocked,* and *slammed*. Students can blend all of the words. Have individuals practice reading the words from word cards.

DECODING MULTISYLLABIC WORDS Write *replanted* and model how to decode a word with meaningful word parts—in this case, a base word with both a prefix and an ending. First I look for meaningful parts. I see the prefix *re-*. I cover that up and see the word *planted*. Now I see the ending *-ed*. So I look for the base word: *plant*. I say the parts of the word: *re plant ed*. Then I say the whole word: *replanted*. The prefix *re-* means "again," so I can tell that *replanted* means "planted again."

Use the Multisyllabic Word routine on p. DI·1 to help students read these other words from *A Day's Work: cruised, shuffled, swallowed, urgently, politely, freeway, rooftops, overgrown, spiky, chickweed, appreciate,* and *wrappings*. Be sure students understand the meanings of words such as *urgently, overgrown,* and *chickweed*.

3 Read *A Day's Work*, pp. 178–185

BEFORE READING Yesterday we read about a girl who learned a lesson about doing the right thing. Today we will read about a boy who learns the value of doing the right thing. Using the Picture Walk routine on p. DI·1, guide students through the text, asking questions such as those listed below. Then read the question on p. 179. Together, set a purpose for reading.

pp. 180–181 What do you see in this picture? *(a group of men and a boy watching other men climb into a pickup)* The boy is with his *abuelo*, or grandfather, and they are all looking for jobs. People who need work come to this lot and wait for people to hire them.

p. 185 What kind of work are the boy and his grandfather doing?

DURING READING Follow the Guiding Comprehension routine on pp. 180–185. Have students read along with you while tracking print or do a choral reading of the selection. Stop every two pages to ask what has happened so far. Prompt as necessary.

- Where and when did this story begin?
- What did Francisco do to get Ben to hire them?

AFTER READING What has happened in the story so far? What do you think will happen next? **Reread passages as needed.**

Advanced

ROUTINE

① Extend Vocabulary

CONTEXT CLUES Choose and read a sentence or passage containing a difficult word, such as these sentences from the Read Aloud "The Honest-to-Goodness Truth": "Her eyes commenced to fill with water, and her bottom lip quivered. Then, taking a deep breath and gulping hard, she owned up to her lie." What does the word *commenced* mean? *(began, started)* How did you figure out the word's meaning? *(I looked at the rest of the sentence and the sentence after it. I could tell she was sad and scared about admitting her lie, so it makes sense that she started to cry.)* Discuss how surrounding details can provide a context that gives clues to a word's meaning. Remind students to use context clues to figure out the meanings of unfamiliar words as they read *A Day's Work*.

② Read *A Day's Work*, pp. 178–185

BEFORE READING In *The Song Makers Go to Salem*, you read about the importance of doing the right thing—even in a difficult situation. Today you will read a story about a boy who discovers that doing the wrong thing—even for the "right" reason—can have consequences. As you read, think about how the choices a person makes to do the right thing or the wrong thing tell you about his or her character.

Have students write questions about the selection in their Strategy Response Logs (p. 178). Remind them to think about the answers to their questions and any other questions that arise as they read.

CRITICAL THINKING/PROBLEM SOLVING Have students read pp. 178–185 independently. Encourage them to think critically and in terms of problems and solutions. For example, ask:

- Do you think it was okay for Francisco to lie in this situation? Why or why not?
- How else might Francisco have gotten work for his grandfather without lying?
- What do you think of Francisco? Would you want him for a friend?

AFTER READING Meet with students to discuss the selection. Have them share their Strategy Response Log questions and answers. Then ask students to write a short skit in which Francisco does not lie about his grandfather's gardening skills. Have students write lines for Francisco, his grandfather, and Ben. Invite them to share their skit with the class.

DAY 2

AudioText

A Day's Work
Group Time

AudioText

DAY
3

Strategic Intervention

ROUTINE

1 **Reinforce Comprehension**

SKILL CHARACTER Have students tell what characters are. *(people in a story)* How can you tell what a character is like? *(by what he or she says and does)* If necessary, review the meaning and provide a model. A character is a person in a story. I can tell what kind of person a character is by what he or she says and does. For example, if I read that a character takes the last three cookies from a plate at a party even though others haven't had any, I can tell the character probably is selfish and thinks only of himself or herself.

Ask students what they can learn about Ben from these details:

> The man grinned. "OK. I'm convinced. But I'm not Mr. Benjamin. Call me Ben."
> "It will be hot. Your grandfather will need a hat." He took a straw one from the van.

(Ben is friendly and caring.)

2 **Read** *A Day's Work,* pp. 186–191

BEFORE READING Have students retell what has happened in the story so far. Ask: How do you think Francisco looked and sounded when he was trying to persuade Ben to hire them? Reread p. 182 and model how to visualize Francisco. As I read, I try to picture Francisco in my mind. I can see him pointing to his grandfather, showing Ben his Lakers hat, and waving at his grandfather to come. I can hear the determination in his voice. These things tell me he is determined and a good salesman. Remind students to visualize as they read the rest of *A Day's Work*. **STRATEGY Visualize**

DURING READING Follow the Guiding Comprehension routine on pp. 186–191. Have students read along with you while tracking the print or do a choral reading. Stop every two pages to ask students what has happened so far. Prompt as necessary.

- What mistake did Francisco and his grandfather make?
- What did Ben do when he looked at the work Francisco and his grandfather did? Why did he react this way?
- What did Francisco's grandfather offer to do when he found out they had made a mistake?

AFTER READING How does this selection show the importance of doing the right thing? Reread with students for comprehension as needed. Tell them that tomorrow they will read "What Is a Weed?", an e-mail that will help Francisco and his grandfather the next time they go on a gardening job.

Monitor Progress

Word and Selection Reading

If... students have difficulty reading multisyllabic words in the selection,	**then...** have them look for and read meaningful parts in the words or have them chunk words with no recognizable parts.
If... students have difficulty reading along with the group,	**then...** have them follow along as they listen to the AudioText.

ROUTINE

1 Extend Comprehension

SKILL CHARACTER Have students summarize what they know about Francisco's character from reading *A Day's Work*. To gain an even better understanding of his character, have them imagine, based on their summaries, what Francisco will be doing in ten or fifteen years. What kind of person is he? Have students support their ideas with examples from the selection.

STRATEGY VISUALIZE Have a volunteer reread p. 183 while others close their eyes. Ask students which words or phrases help them visualize Francisco, what he is doing, and how he is speaking. Ask questions such as:

- How does Francisco look pushing the "big, tough guy" out of the van and thinking that *he* is tough?
- How do you think Francisco says, "It is easy. . . . Flowers, roses, things like that"?

2 Read *A Day's Work,* pp. 186–191

BEFORE READING Have students recall what has happened in the story so far. Remind them to think about the characters' actions and words and to visualize as they read the remainder of *A Day's Work*.

CRITICAL THINKING Have students read pp. 186–191 independently. Encourage them to think creatively. For example, ask:

- How do the text and illustrations go together? Why do you think the author wanted artwork on certain pages? What art would you add?

AFTER READING Have students complete the Strategy Response Log activity (p. 190). Meet with them to discuss their reaction to the story. Then have students analyze the art in the story and find parts of the text they wish had been illustrated. Have them write the page number and a brief description of the art they feel is needed. Suggest they draw the appropriate art if they like.

DAY
3

AudioText

A Day's Work

Group Time

Audio CD AudioText

Monitor Progress

Word and Selection Reading

If... students have difficulty reading multisyllabic words in the selection,	**then...** have them look for and read meaningful parts in the words or have them chunk words with no recognizable parts.
If... students have difficulty reading along with the group,	**then...** have them follow along as they listen to the AudioText.

Strategic Intervention

ROUTINE

1 Practice Retelling

REVIEW STORY ELEMENTS Help students identify the main characters and the setting of *A Day's Work*. Then guide them in using the Retelling Cards to list story events in sequence. Prompt students to include important details.

RETELL Using the Retelling Cards, have students work in pairs to retell *A Day's Work*. Monitor retelling and prompt students as needed. For example, ask:

- What else happened in this story?
- How was the problem solved?
- What is the author trying to tell us or teach us?

If students struggle, model a fluent retelling.

2 Read "What Is a Weed?"

BEFORE READING Read the genre information on p. 194. Point out that students can use e-mail to communicate with friends and family members. They can also use e-mail to ask questions about things they want to know more about. Ask students about their experiences with e-mail.

Read the rest of the panel on p. 194. Have students identify the *To:* box and the message in the e-mail. *What do you see two lines below the To: box? (the Subject: box) How is the message like a regular letter? (It has a greeting, a body, and the writer's name.)* Discuss with students the reply e-mail on p. 196 and the Web pages on pp. 196–197.

DURING READING Have students read along with you while tracking the print or do a choral reading of the selection. Stop to discuss difficult vocabulary, such as *foliage, spiny,* and *purslane.*

AFTER READING Have students share their reactions to the selection. Then guide them through the Reading Across Texts and Writing Across Texts activities, prompting if necessary.

- What kinds of information did Francisco learn about gardening?
- How can Francisco use the information he learned in his next job as a gardener?

Advanced

1 Read "What Is a Weed?"

CRITICAL THINKING/SOLVE PROBLEMS Have students read pp. 194–197 independently. Encourage them to think critically and in terms of problems and solutions. For example, say:

- The title of the selection is "What Is a Weed?" Is this question really answered?
- How could you find the answer to that question?

AFTER READING Have students meet with you to discuss Reading Across Texts. Have students do Writing Across Texts independently.

2 Extend Genre Study

RESEARCH Have students use e-mail to do more research about weeds. Provide them with e-mail addresses of science teachers at your school or your local middle or high school who are willing to receive and respond to such e-mails. Have them do research to find the e-mail addresses of others in the field, such as owners of nurseries, radio hosts of gardening shows, or newspaper gardening columnists.

WRITE Have students write short reports on the results of their e-mail research. Ask them to include a list of the e-mail addresses they wrote to, the questions they asked, and a summary of the information they learned. Encourage them to share their reports with the class.

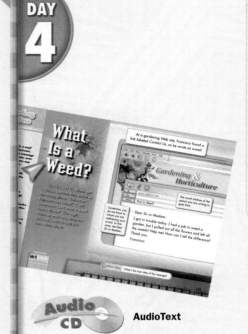

AudioText

Group Time

ROUTINE

DAY 5

ONLINE

PearsonSuccessNet.com

1 Reread for Fluency

MODEL Read aloud pp. 4–5 of the Leveled Reader *Sarah's Choice* with characterization in mind. Have students note how your voice shows emotion and changes when you read lines of dialogue of the various characters. Then read p. 10 with no variation in your voice. Discuss how reading with characterization in mind makes the story more interesting and enjoyable.

PRACTICE Have individuals reread passages from *Sarah's Choice* with a partner or individually. For optimal fluency, they should reread three or four times. As students read, monitor fluency and provide corrective feedback. Assess the fluency of students in this group using p. 197a.

2 Retell Leveled Reader *Sarah's Choice*

Model how to retell the story using the illustrations. Then ask students to retell *Sarah's Choice*, illustration by illustration. Prompt them as needed.

- What does this illustration show?
- Has anything like this happened to you?

Monitor Progress

Fluency

If... students have difficulty reading fluently,	then... provide additional fluency practice by pairing nonfluent readers with fluent ones.

For alternate Leveled Reader lesson plans that teach 🔄 **Character,** 🔄 **Visualize,** and **Lesson Vocabulary,** see pp. LR10–LR18.

On-Level

1 Reread for Fluency — ROUTINE

MODEL Read aloud pp. 5–7 of the Leveled Reader *The Boy Who Cried Wolf,* emphasizing characterization. Have students note how your voice shows emotion and changes when you read lines of dialogue for the various characters. Discuss how reading with characterization in mind makes the story more interesting and enjoyable.

PRACTICE Have students reread passages from *The Boy Who Cried Wolf* with a partner or individually. For optimal fluency, they should reread three or four times. As students read, monitor fluency and provide corrective feedback. Students in this group are assessed in Week 3.

2 Retell Leveled Reader *The Boy Who Cried Wolf*

Have students use the illustrations as a guide to retell *The Boy Who Cried Wolf.* Prompt as needed.

- Tell me what this story is about in a few sentences.
- Why do you think the author wrote this story?
- How does this story remind you of other stories?

Advanced

1 Reread for Fluency — ROUTINE

PRACTICE Have students reread passages from the Leveled Reader *The Song Makers Go to Salem* with a partner or individually. As students read, monitor fluency and provide corrective feedback. If students read fluently on the first reading, they do not need to reread three to four times. Students in this group were assessed in Week 1.

2 Revisit Leveled Reader *The Song Makers Go to Salem*

RETELL Have students retell the Leveled Reader *The Song Makers Go to Salem.*

WRITE A SONG Have students complete the songs they have been collaborating on throughout the week. Ask them to either read the lyrics or sing their songs to you. Then invite them to present their songs to the class.

Group Time

ROUTINE

DAY 1

Leveled Reader
Database
ONLINE
PearsonSuccessNet.com

① Preteach Phonics

COMPOUND WORDS Write and say the word *fireplace*. This is a compound word. A compound word is made up of two words put together. Cover the second word and read the first: fire. Cover the first word and read the second: place. Model blending *fireplace*: fire place, fireplace. Then have students blend the word with you. Each word in a compound word adds to its meaning. Fire is something that is hot and burns. The word *place* means "a spot, an area." So a fireplace is an area where a fire can burn. Repeat this process with the compound word *fingertip*. Blend and read the word and have students blend with you. Then ask them to define each word and the compound word.

② Preview Decodable Reader 8

BEFORE READING Review the words on Decodable Reader p. 57. Then have students blend these story words: *campgrounds, tremble, farmhouse, spied, mumbled, stumbled,* and *sunset.* Be sure students understand the meanings of words such as *campgrounds* and *tremble.*

Use the Picture Walk Routine on p. DI·1 to guide students through the text.

③ Read Leveled Reader *Metal Detector Detective*

REINFORCE CONCEPTS This week's concept is *ideas and inventions.* What idea or invention has helped you solve a problem or do something you needed to do? Did you think of it yourself?

BEFORE READING Using the Picture Walk routine on p. DI·1, guide students through the text focusing on key concepts and vocabulary. Ask questions such as:

p. 4 This picture shows a woman holding a metal detector. What do you think this tool does?

p. 9 What idea does the boy have in this picture? Read pp. 3–4 aloud. Then do a choral reading of pp. 5–8. Have students read and discuss the remainder of the book with a partner. What idea did Joe have? Was it a good idea? Why or why not?

Monitor Progress

Word and Selection Reading

If... students have difficulty reading story words from the Decodable Reader,	**then...** reteach them by modeling blending or reading multisyllabic words.
If... partners have difficulty reading the Leveled Reader on their own,	**then...** have them follow along as they listen to the Online Leveled Reader Audio.

For alternate Leveled Reader lesson plans that teach 🔄 **Main Idea,** 🔄 **Monitor and Fix Up,** and **Lesson Vocabulary,** see pp. LR19–LR27.

On-Level

1 Build Background

DEVELOP VOCABULARY Write the word *portable* and ask students to define it in their own words. *(able to be carried or moved.)* What are some examples of things that are portable? *(mobile phones, purses, wallets, small CD players, MP3 players)* Repeat this activity with the word *colorful* and other words from the Leveled Reader *Katy's Last-Minute Book Report.* Use the Concept Vocabulary routine on p. DI·1 as needed.

2 Read Leveled Reader *Katy's Last-Minute Book Report*

BEFORE READING Have students create a time line for the week before Katy's book report was due. This book tells how a girl named Katy prepared her book report. As you read, record what she did each day on your time lines.

DURING READING Have students follow along as you read pp. 3–7. Then let them complete the book on their own. Remind students to add events to their time lines as they read.

AFTER READING Have students compare the events they noted on their time lines. Point out that seeing how Katy had a problem and decided how to avoid it in the future will help them as they read tomorrow's story, *Prudy's Problem and How She Solved It.*

Advanced

1 Read Leveled Reader *Collecting Dreams*

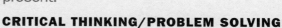

BEFORE READING Recall the Read Aloud "The Rampanion." What idea did Alison have to help people in wheelchairs? *(to build a portable ramp)* Today you will read about a father and daughter who come up with good ideas for choosing the perfect birthday present.

CRITICAL THINKING/PROBLEM SOLVING Have students read the Leveled Reader independently. Encourage them to think critically and in terms of problems and solutions. For example, ask:

- What are some problems Tina and her father encountered? How did they solve them?
- What kind of collection would you consider starting?

AFTER READING Have students review the selection to find five or more unfamiliar words and determine their meanings. Ask them to write a sentence with each word that explains how the word helped them better understand the story or the characters. Meet with students to discuss their sentences and their reactions to the selection.

2 Independent Extension Activity

Assign the article on page 24 of *Collecting Dreams.* Have students choose toys they would like to collect and use online or print resources to find out more about the toys. Ask them to make posters that include the name of each toy and, an illustration, and any other information they discovered.

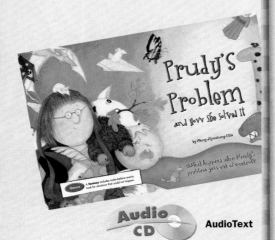

Group Time

ROUTINE

DAY 2

1 Reread for Fluency

Use Decodable Reader 8.

2 Word Study/Phonics

LESSON VOCABULARY Use p. 200b to review the meanings of *collection, enormous, realize, scattered, shiny,* and *strain.* Students can blend all of the words. Have individuals practice reading the words from word cards.

DECODING MULTISYLLABIC WORDS Write *valentine* and model how to chunk a word to read it when there are no meaningful word parts. I see a chunk at the beginning: *val.* I see a chunk in the middle: *en.* I see a chunk at the end: *tine.* I say each chunk slowly: *val en tine.* I say the chunks fast to make the word: *valentine.* I know that word.

Use the Multisyllabic Word routine on p. DI·1 to help students read these other words from *Prudy's Problem: fungi, souvenir, erasers, distraction, navigate, avalanche, inspiration, scrutinizing, whirring, indescribable, wonderment, orderly,* and *appreciated.* Be sure students understand the meanings of words such as *fungi, navigate, avalanche,* and *scrutinizing.*

3 Read *Prudy's Problem,* pp. 202–209

BEFORE READING Yesterday we read about a boy who came up with a good idea for solving a problem. Today we will read about a big problem that a girl named Prudy has. Think about how she might solve her problem as you read.

Using the Picture Walk routine on p. DI·1, guide students through the text, asking questions such as those listed below. Then read the question on p. 203. Together, set a purpose for reading.

p. 206 This is Prudy's room. What does it look like? *(very messy, full of things)* Yes, maybe it is the problem mentioned in the title.

p. 207 What is on the lawn? *(pink flamingos, elves, mushrooms)* Why do you think the man seems angry? *(He is tripping over a flamingo.)* Prudy's problem might be bigger than we realized.

DURING READING Follow the Guiding Comprehension routine on pp. 204–209. Have students read along with you while tracking the print or do a choral reading of the selection. Stop every two pages to ask what has happened so far. Prompt as necessary.

• What was Prudy's main problem?
• What happened as a result of Prudy's collecting?

AFTER READING What has happened so far? What do you think will happen next? Reread passages for comprehension as needed.

Monitor Progress

Word and Story Reading

If... students have difficulty reading multisyllabic words in the selection,	then... have them look for and read meaningful parts in the words or have them chunk words with no recognizable parts.
If... students have difficulty reading along with the group,	then... have them follow along as they listen to the AudioText.

Audio CD AudioText

Advanced

1 Extend Vocabulary

⊙ DICTIONARY Choose and read a sentence containing a difficult word, such as this passage from p. 11 of *Collecting Dreams* "'Most sellers specialize,' Dad explained." Suppose you break *specialize* into word parts and come up with the meaning "to make special." Does that meaning make sense in the sentence? *(no)* What's another way that you can find out the meaning of *specialize*? *(look it up in the dictionary)* Ask a student to look up the word, explaining the steps to take. *(First go to the S section, then use guide words at the top to locate the page, then use the second letter, third letter, and so on to find* specialize.*)* Have the volunteer read the definitions and ask students to decide which meaning fits the sentence. *(to concentrate on a certain product, activity, or field of study)* Remind students to use a dictionary to find out the meanings of unfamiliar words as they read *Prudy's Problem.*

DAY
2

2 Read *Prudy's Problem,* pp. 202–209

BEFORE READING In *Collecting Dreams,* you read how Tina and her father came up with a good idea to solve the problem of finding a birthday present. Today you will read a story in which a girl named Prudy has a problem. As you read, try to come up with your own ideas for solving Prudy's problem.

Have students write their predictions about the story in their Strategy Response Logs (p. 202). Remind them to check their predictions as they read, and then revise their predictions or make new ones.

CRITICAL THINKING/PROBLEM SOLVING Have students read pp. 202–209 independently. Encourage them to think critically and in terms of problem solving. For example, ask:

- Why do you think Prudy keeps saying she doesn't have a problem?
- Do you think Prudy will admit that she does have a problem? What in the story tells you this?
- How would you solve her problem?

AFTER READING Meet with students to discuss the selection and their Strategy Response Log entries. Then have students write a conversation between themselves and Prudy. Encourage them to include advice they would give Prudy.

Audio
CD   AudioText

Prudy's Problem

Group Time

Audio CD AudioText

Monitor Progress

Word and Story Reading

If... students have difficulty reading multisyllabic words in the selection,	then... have them look for and read meaningful parts in the words or have them chunk words with no recognizable parts.
If... students have difficulty reading along with the group,	then... have them follow along as they listen to the AudioText.

1 Reinforce Comprehension

SKILL MAIN IDEA AND DETAILS Have students tell what main idea and details are. *(the most important idea and small pieces of information that tell more)* The main idea of a story is what the story is all about. Details are small pieces of information that tell more about the main idea. On the board draw a main idea/supporting details chart as on p. 198. Write the following details and main idea in the chart as you say them: In the story *Metal Detector Detective*, one detail is that Joe was bored. Another is that Ms. Choi lost her ring. A third detail is that Joe had a good time using a metal detector to find the ring. The main idea is that Joe realized the metal detector gave him something to do.

Have students complete a main idea/details chart for the first part of *Prudy's Problem*. Have them decide which of the following are details and which is the main idea:

Prudy collected everything her friends did. *(detail)*

Prudy had a problem because she collected everything. *(main idea)*

Prudy's mother couldn't walk through the living room. *(detail)*

2 Read *Prudy's Problem* pp. 210–217

BEFORE READING Have students retell what happened in the story so far. Ask: Why did Prudy have a problem? Reread pp. 204–205 and model how to look for details to check your understanding of the story. As I reread, I see that each of her friends collected one thing, but Prudy collected those things and everything else. On p. 205 I read about some of the useless things Prudy collected. That helps me understand that the story is about her problem of collecting everything. Remind students to monitor their understanding and use fix-up strategies if necessary as they read the rest of *Prudy's Problem*.
STRATEGY Monitor and Fix Up

DURING READING Follow the Guiding Comprehension routine on pp. 210–217. Have students read along with you while tracking the print or do a choral reading. Stop every two pages to ask students what has happened so far. Prompt as necessary.

AFTER READING How does this story show that a good idea can solve a problem? Reread with students for comprehension as needed. Tell them that tomorrow they will read "Meeting the Challenge of Collecting," an interview about organizing collections.

Advanced

1 Extend Comprehension

⊙ **SKILL MAIN IDEA AND DETAILS** Ask students to create a graphic organizer that shows the main idea and details of the first part of the story *Prudy's Problem*.

⊙ **STRATEGY MONITOR AND FIX UP** Ask students what they do if they are confused about the main idea of a story. Ask:

• What page would you reread if you realized you didn't understand why Prudy's mother thought she had a problem?

2 Read *Prudy's Problem*, pp. 210–217

BEFORE READING Have students recall what has happened in the story so far. Remind them to try to identify the main idea and details and to use a fix-up strategy such as rereading if they realize they are unclear about the story.

CREATIVE THINKING/CRITICAL THINKING Have students read pp. 210–217 independently. Encourage them to think creatively. For example, ask:

• How would the story be different if there were no illustrations? How do the illustrations add to your understanding and enjoyment of the story?

• What do you think of Prudy's solution to her problem?

AFTER READING Have students complete the Strategy Response Log activity (p. 216). Then meet with students to discuss the story. Point out that the author of the story is also the illustrator. Ask: What advantage does a writer who is also an illustrator have when creating a book? Have students write a letter to the author telling how they feel about her story and her illustrations.

DAY 3

AudioText

Group Time

DAY 4

1 Practice Retelling

REVIEW STORY ELEMENTS Help students identify the main characters and setting of *Prudy's Problem*. Then guide them in using the Retelling Cards to list story events in sequence. Prompt students to include important details.

RETELL Using the Retelling Cards, have students work in pairs to retell *Prudy's Problem.* Monitor retelling and prompt students as needed. For example, ask:

* Tell me what this story is about in a few sentences.
* What else happened in this story?
* What is the character in this story like?

If students struggle, model a fluent retelling.

2 Read "Meeting the Challenge of Collecting"

BEFORE READING Read the genre information on p. 220. Point out that in an interview, one person asks questions of another person to gain information. Often the person being interviewed is an expert on a topic. As we read "Meeting the Challenge of Collecting," look for expert information about a museum's collections that the person being interviewed provides.

Read the rest of the panel on p. 220. Have students study the photographs and their captions. Call attention to the boldfaced names of the interviewer and interviewee. Point out that these tell which person is speaking and that, after the first mention, only initials are used. Ask: What else is in bold type in the interview?

DURING READING Have students read along with you while tracking the print or do a choral reading of the selection. Stop to discuss difficult vocabulary, such as *anthropology, tapestries,* and *sculpture.*

AFTER READING Have students share their reactions to the selection. Then guide them through the Reading Across Texts and Writing Across Texts activities, prompting if necessary.

* What kinds of things are displayed at the Field Museum of Natural History? Where did they come from? What were they used for?
* What kinds of things did Prudy display in her museum?
* How are the objects in the Field Museum organized?
* How are the objects in Prudy's museum organized?
* What kind of a chart do you think would best help you to compare the two museums? Explain.

AudioText

Monitor Progress

Word and Selection Reading

If... students have difficulty reading multisyllabic words in the selection,	**then...** have them look for and read meaningful parts in the words or have them chunk words with no recognizable parts.
If... students have difficulty reading along with the group,	**then...** have them follow along as they listen to the AudioText.

Advanced

① Read "Meeting the Challenge of Collecting"

CREATIVE THINKING/PROBLEM SOLVING Have students read pp. 220–223 independently. Encourage them to think creatively and in terms of problems and solutions. For example, ask:

- Can you think of a way that the museum might be able to display more of the items it has?
- What other questions would you like to ask Dr. Feinman?

AFTER READING Have students meet with you to discuss Reading Across Texts. Have students do Writing Across Texts independently.

② Extend Genre Study

RESEARCH Have students choose someone to interview who works with a collection, such as the school or local librarian or an employee of a local museum. Ask students to write questions they would like to ask the person. Then help students interview the person they chose, either in person, on the telephone, or through e-mail. Explain that they should take notes on the person's answers.

WRITE Have students write their interviews in a question-and-answer format. Encourage them to draw pictures to accompany their interviews.

 **AudioText**

Group Time

ROUTINE

DAY 5

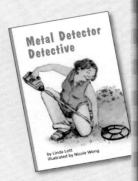

Metal Detector Detective

by Linda Lott
illustrated by Nicole Wong

Leveled Reader Database

ONLINE

PearsonSuccessNet.com

① Reread for Fluency

MODEL Read aloud pp. 3–4 of the Leveled Reader *Metal Detector Detective,* using appropriate expression and intonation. Have students note how your voice changes to express boredom, curiosity, and friendliness. Then read pp. 5–6 with no expression or intonation. Ask students which reading sounded better. Discuss how reading with expression and intonation helps make the story more understandable and enjoyable.

PRACTICE Have individuals reread passages from *Metal Detector Detective* with a partner or individually. For optimal fluency, they should reread three or four times. As students read, monitor fluency and provide corrective feedback. Students in this group are assessed in Weeks 2 and 4.

② Retell Leveled Reader *Metal Detector Detective*

Model how to use the illustrations to retell. Then ask students to retell *Metal Detector Detective,* illustration by illustration. Prompt them as needed.

- Tell me about the major events in order.
- What was this selection mostly about?
- Why do you think the author wrote this selection?

Monitor Progress

Fluency

If... students have difficulty reading fluently,	then... provide additional fluency practice by pairing nonfluent readers with fluent ones.

For alternate Leveled Reader lesson plans that teach
⟳**Main Idea and Details,** ⟳**Monitor and Fix Up,**
and **Lesson Vocabulary,** see pp. LR19–LR27.

On-Level

1 ReRead for Fluency — ROUTINE

MODEL Read pp. 3–4 of the Leveled Reader *Katy's Last-Minute Book Report,* emphasizing appropriate expression and intonation. Have students note how your voice changes to convey expression and tone. Discuss how reading with appropriate expression and intonation makes the story and characters more understandable and enjoyable.

PRACTICE Have individuals reread passages from *Katy's Last-Minute Book Report* with a partner or individually. For optimal fluency, they should reread three or four times. As students read, monitor fluency and provide corrective feedback. Assess the fluency of students in this group using p. 223a.

2 Retell Leveled Reader *Katy's Last-Minute Book Report*

Have students use the illustrations as a guide to retell *Katy's Last-Minute Book Report.* Prompt as needed.

- What is Katy like?
- What is the problem in this story?
- Has anything like this ever happened to you?

Advanced

1 ReRead for Fluency — ROUTINE

PRACTICE Have students reread passages from the Leveled Reader *Collecting Dreams* with a partner or individually. As students read, monitor fluency and provide corrective feedback. If students read fluently on the first reading, they do not need to reread three to four times. Students in this group were assessed in Week 1.

2 Revisit Leveled Reader *Collecting Dreams*

RETELL Have students retell the Leveled Reader *Collecting Dreams.*

INDEPENDENT EXTENSION ACTIVITY Have students complete the posters about toy collecting that they have been working on throughout the week. You may wish to review their sources and see whether they need additional resources. Have them share their posters.

Group Time

ROUTINE

DAY 1

Leveled Reader Database
ONLINE
PearsonSuccessNet.com

Monitor Progress

Word and Selection Reading

If... students have difficulty reading story words from the Decodable Reader,	**then...** reteach them by modeling blending or reading multisyllabic words.
If... partners have difficulty reading the Leveled Reader on their own,	**then...** have them follow along as they listen to the Online Leveled Reader Audio.

① Preteach Phonics

CONSONANT BLENDS Write and say the word *smart*. What two consonants begin this word? (s and m) When a word begins with two consonants, their sounds are usually blended together. I don't say /s/ /m/; I say /sm/. Blend the word *smart*. Then have students blend it with you. Repeat this process with the word *plan*.

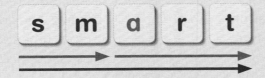

② Preview Decodable Reader 9

BEFORE READING Review the words on Decodable Reader p. 65. Then have students blend these story words: *sports, greeted, squinted, squiggle,* and *squeak.* Be sure students understand the meanings of words such as *squinted* and *squiggle.*

Use the Picture Walk Routine on p. DI·1 to guide students through the text.

③ **Read** Leveled Reader *Growing Vegetables*

REINFORCE CONCEPTS This week's concept is *personal responsibility.* When we take personal responsibility, we work hard, we do what we're supposed to do, and we don't blame others for our actions or our problems. In what ways do you take personal responsibility?

BEFORE READING Using the Picture Walk routine on p. DI·1, guide students through the text focusing on key concepts and vocabulary. Ask questions such as:

p. 3 What do you think the children in this picture are going to do? *(plant a garden)* What makes you think that? *(They're wearing shirts that say "The Garden Bunch," and they're holding gardening tools.)*

p. 8 What is this boy doing? *(putting sticks or poles in the ground so that the plants can grow up them)*

Read pp. 3–4 aloud. Then do a choral reading of pp. 5–8. Have students read and discuss the remainder of the book with a partner. Ask: How did the hard work of The Garden Bunch pay off? *(They harvested a lot of vegetables that they can sell.)*

For alternate Leveled Reader lesson plans that teach **Author's Purpose,** **Predict,** and **Lesson Vocabulary,** see pp. LR28–LR36.

On-Level

1 Build Background

DEVELOP VOCABULARY Write the word *vain* and ask students to define it in their own words. *(thinking you look good)* What might a vain person say? *("I am so beautiful!")* Repeat this activity with the word *thrilled* and other words from the Leveled Reader *Our Garden*. Use the Concept Vocabulary routine on p. DI·1 as needed.

2 Read Leveled Reader *Our Garden*

BEFORE READING Have students make three-column charts with the following headings: Cleaning Up, Planting, and Harvesting. This book tells about a community garden started by some children. As you read, record on your charts what the characters did during each stage of the garden.

DURING READING Have students follow along as you read pp. 3–7. Then let them complete the book on their own. Remind students to add garden activities to their charts as they read.

AFTER READING Have students compare the activities on their charts. Point out that they will read about two other characters who try to share a garden in tomorrow's story, *Tops & Bottoms.*

Advanced

1 Read Leveled Reader *The Magic of Coyote*

BEFORE READING Recall the Read Aloud "Why Possum's Tail Is Bare." Today you will read a story that includes another Native American tale. This one tells how Coyote takes responsibility for helping people.

CRITICAL THINKING/ PROBLEM SOLVING

Have students read the Leveled Reader independently. Encourage them to think critically and in terms of problems and solutions. For example, ask:

- How does Coyote in this story compare with Rabbit in "Why Possum's Tail Is Bare"?
- Why do you think the author interrupted the Coyote story and told it in two parts?
- Do you or does someone you know fear something, as Henry does? How can this fear be overcome?

AFTER READING Have students review the selection to find five or more unfamiliar words and determine their meanings with context clues or the dictionary. Have them write the words in sentences that convey the words' meanings. Meet with students to discuss the story. Have them share their sentences.

2 Independent Extension Activity

MAKE A TRAVEL BROCHURE Assign the article on p. 24 of *The Magic of Coyote*. Then have students use online or print resources to find out more about Mesa Verde or other national parks and monuments of Anasazi or Pueblo ruins. Encourage students to find out about the park itself and about the ancient people who once lived there. Have them create a travel brochure or poster about the park.

Tops & Bottoms
Group Time

Audio CD   AudioText

ROUTINE

1 Reread for Fluency

Use Decodable Reader 9.

2 Word Study/Phonics

LESSON VOCABULARY Use p. 226b to review the meanings of *bottom, cheated, clever, crops, lazy, partners,* and *wealth.* Students can blend all of the words. Have individuals practice reading the words from word cards.

DECODING MULTISYLLABIC WORDS Write *harvesting* and model how to decode a word with a verb ending. First I look for meaningful parts. I see the verb ending *-ing,* so I look for a base word. I see *harvest.* I can break that into the chunk *har* and the chunk *vest.* I say all the parts of the word: *har vest ing.* Then I read the word: *harvesting.*

Use the Multisyllabic Word routine on p. DI·1 to help students read these other words from *Tops & Bottoms: risky, grunted, profit, radishes, celery, cornstalk,* and *tassels.* Be sure students understand the meanings of words such as *risky* and *tassels.*

3 Read *Tops & Bottoms,* pp. 228–237

BEFORE READING Yesterday we read about children who worked together to make a vegetable garden. Today we will read about two funny animal characters that plant vegetables.

Using the Picture Walk routine on p. DI·1, guide students through the text, asking questions such as those listed below. Then read the question on p. 229. Together, set a purpose for reading.

p. 230 What can you tell about Bear, just by looking at this picture? *(He is lazy and messy.)* Yes, I think you'll find that Bear's laziness will cause a problem.

p. 234 What are the characters doing in this picture? *(The Hare family is busy gardening, while Bear is sleeping.)* The Hare and his family seem to be taking responsibility for growing their food.

DURING READING Follow the Guiding Comprehension routine on pp. 230–237. Have students read along with you while tracking the print or do a choral reading of the selection. Stop every two pages to ask students what has happened so far. Prompt as necessary.

• What plan did Hare share with Bear? Why?
• How did Hare end up with the best part of the carrots?

AFTER READING What has happened so far? What do you think will happen next? **Reread passages with students for comprehension as needed.**

Monitor Progress

Word and Story Reading

If... students have difficulty reading multisyllabic words in the selection,	then... have them look for and read meaningful parts in the words or have them chunk words with no recognizable parts.
If... students have difficulty reading along with the group,	then... have them follow along as they listen to the AudioText.

Advanced

ROUTINE

1 Extend Vocabulary

CONTEXT CLUES Write a sentence containing a difficult word with an antonym as a context clue, such as the following: "Squirrel's back was scorched, but her tail was unburned." What does the word *scorched* mean? *(burned)* How did you figure out the word's meaning? *(I looked at the words around it and noticed* unburned. *It probably means the opposite of* scorched *because the word* but *usually signals an opposite.)* A context clue that is an antonym can help you figure out the meaning of an unknown word. Remind students to use this strategy as they read *Tops & Bottoms*.

2 Read *Tops & Bottoms*, pp. 228–237

BEFORE READING In "Why Possum's Tail Is Bare," you read how Rabbit tricked Possum because Possum was vain. Today you will read a story in which a hare tricks a bear because he is lazy. As you read, think about how each character is responsible for what happens to him.

Have students write questions about the story in their Strategy Response Logs (p. 228). Tell them to look for answers to their questions as they read.

CRITICAL THINKING Have students read pp. 228–237 independently. Encourage them to think critically. For example, ask:

- What do you think of Hare? What do you think of Bear?
- What do you think Hare will plant next?

AFTER READING Have partners discuss the story and share their Strategy Response Log entries. Ask students to write a paragraph contrasting Hare and Bear using antonyms whenever possible. For example: "Hare is clever, but Bear is dumb. Hare is hard-working, but Bear is lazy."

DAY 2

Audio CD **AudioText**

Tops & Bottoms

Group Time

AudioText

Monitor Progress

Word and Story Reading

If... students have difficulty reading multisyllabic words in the selection,	then... have them look for and read meaningful parts in the words or have them chunk words with no recognizable parts.
If... students have difficulty reading along with the group,	then... have them follow along as they listen to the AudioText.

Strategic Intervention

ROUTINE

1 Reinforce Comprehension

◎ SKILL AUTHOR'S PURPOSE Have students tell what the author's purpose is. *(the reason an author writes something)* If necessary, review the meaning of *author's purpose* and provide a model. An author writes for a reason. This reason is the author's purpose. The purpose may be to persuade you, inform you, entertain you, or tell you the author's ideas or feelings. **Recall the Leveled Reader *Growing Vegetables.*** That story told about a group of kids who worked to make a vegetable garden. The kids divided the work, sold the vegetables, and had a lot of fun. I think the author's purpose was to inform us about the hard work and rewards of a garden.

Read aloud the article "Farming" on p. 227. Ask students to choose the author's purpose from the following: The author wanted to entertain us with a funny story about farmers.
The author wanted to persuade us to become farmers.
The author wanted to inform us about how hard farmers work.

2 Read *Tops & Bottoms*, pp. 238–245

BEFORE READING Have students retell what happened in the story so far. Ask: Based on what you have read, would you predict the author's purpose in writing this story was to persuade or entertain us? Remind students to check this prediction about author's purpose and to make other predictions as they read the rest of *Tops & Bottoms*. **◎ STRATEGY Predict**

DURING READING Follow the Guiding Comprehension routine on pp. 238–245. Have students read along with you while tracking the print or do a choral reading. Stop every two pages to ask students what has happened so far. Prompt as necessary.

- What happened when Hare gave Bear the bottom parts of the second crop? Why?
- What happened when Hare gave Bear the tops & bottoms of the last crop? Why?

AFTER READING How does this story show the importance of taking responsibility for your own life? Reread with students for comprehension as needed. Tell them that tomorrow they will read "The Hare and the Tortoise," a fable that also teaches a lesson.

Advanced

1 **Extend Comprehension**

SKILL **AUTHOR'S PURPOSE** Discuss with students how an author often has more than one purpose in mind for a piece of writing. Recall the Leveled Reader *The Magic of Coyote.* Have students note details, events, and sections of the book and tell whether the author's purpose for each was to persuade, to inform, to entertain, to tell ideas or feelings, or some other purpose.

STRATEGY **PREDICT** Point out that students can predict what an author's purpose will be, but they can also use their knowledge of author's purpose to predict what will happen next. Ask questions such as:

• Based on what you have read so far, what kinds of events do you think will happen in the rest of the story—funny? serious? informative?

2 **Read** *Tops & Bottoms,* pp. 238–245

BEFORE READING Have students recall what has happened in the story so far. Remind them to identify the author's purpose or purposes and to make predictions as they read the remainder of the story.

CREATIVE THINKING Have students read pp. 238–245 independently. Encourage them to think creatively. For example, ask:

• Why do you think the author chose the animals that she did for the characters?

• Would the story have worked if Bear were the hardworking trickster and Hare were the lazy one?

AFTER READING Have students complete the Strategy Response Log activity (p. 244). Then have students think about what kinds of animals they would choose for certain types of characters. For example, what kind of character might be represented by a lion? Why? What about a monkey? Have students list five different animals and, next to each one, several personality traits. Give students an opportunity to meet with you to discuss their lists.

DAY
3

Audio CD   **AudioText**

Group Time

DAY 4

① Practice Retelling

REVIEW STORY ELEMENTS Help students identify the main characters and the setting of *Tops & Bottoms*. Then guide them in using the Retelling Cards to list story events in sequence. Prompt students to include important details.

RETELL Using the Retelling Cards, have students work in pairs to retell *Tops & Bottoms*. Monitor retelling and prompt students as needed. For example, ask:

- What are Hare and Bear like?
- What is the author trying to tell us or teach us?
- How does this story remind you of other stories?

If students struggle, model a fluent retelling.

② Read "The Hare and the Tortoise"

BEFORE READING Read the genre information on p. 248. Explain that a fable is different from an animal fantasy such as *Tops & Bottoms* because a fable is much shorter and states the moral of the story at the end. Have students identify the moral at the end of the story. As we read "The Hare and the Tortoise," think about how the behavior of the characters helps you understand the moral.

Read the rest of the panel on p. 248. Ask if students can name other fables and their morals.

DURING READING Have students read along with you while tracking the print or do a choral reading of the selection. Stop to discuss difficult vocabulary, such as *challenge, plodded,* and *course.*

AFTER READING Have students share their reactions to the selection. Then guide them through the Reading Across Texts and Writing Across Texts activities, prompting if necessary.

- Why was Hare able to trick Bear in *Tops & Bottoms*?
- Why did the slow Tortoise beat the speedy Hare in "The Hare and the Tortoise?"

Audio CD AudioText

Monitor Progress

Word and Selection Reading

If... students have difficulty reading multisyllabic words in the selection,	then... have them look for and read meaningful parts in the words or have them chunk words with no recognizable parts.
If... students have difficulty reading along with the group,	then... have them follow along as they listen to the AudioText.

Advanced

ROUTINE

1 Read "The Hare and the Tortoise"

CREATIVE THINKING Have students read pp. 248–249 independently. Encourage them to think critically. For example, ask:

- How do you think the Tortoise knew he would win the race?
- Do you think the Hare will make fun of Tortoise or other animals again? Why or why not?

AFTER READING Have students meet with you to discuss Reading Across Texts. Have students do Writing Across Texts independently.

2 Extend Genre Study

RESEARCH Have students use online or print resources to find other fables. Have them list the titles of the fables and their morals.

WRITE Have students write a new fable that teaches one of the same morals they found during their research. Remind them to use animals as characters and to keep their fables short. Encourage them to illustrate and then share their fables with the class.

DAY 4

Audio CD **AudioText**

Tops & Bottoms
Group Time

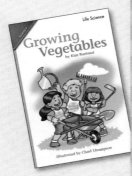

ONLINE

PearsonSuccessNet.com

Strategic Intervention

1 Reread for Fluency

MODEL Read aloud pp. 3–5 of the Leveled Reader *Growing Vegetables,* emphasizing appropriate phrasing. Have students note how you read words in meaningful groups together. Then read aloud pp. 6–7 word by word, with no phrasing. Have students tell you which model sounded better. Discuss how reading in phrases creates a pleasing rhythm and makes the text easier to understand.

PRACTICE Have students reread passages from *Growing Vegetables* with a partner or individually. For optimal fluency, they should reread three or four times. As students read, monitor fluency and provide corrective feedback. Assess the fluency of students in this group using p. 249a.

2 Retell Leveled Reader *Growing Vegetables*

Model how to use the illustrations to retell. Then ask students to retell *Growing Vegetables,* illustration by illustration. Prompt them as needed.

- Tell me what this story is about in a few sentences.
- What else happened in this story?
- Why do you think the author wrote this story?

Monitor Progress

Fluency

If... students have difficulty reading fluently,	then... provide additional fluency practice by pairing nonfluent readers with fluent ones.

For alternate Leveled Reader lesson plans that teach 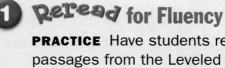 **Author's Purpose,** **Predict,** and **Lesson Vocabulary,** see pp. LR28–LR36.

On-Level

1 Reread for Fluency
ROUTINE

MODEL Read aloud p. 3 of the Leveled Reader *Our Garden,* emphasizing appropriate phrasing. Have students note how you read words in meaningful groups together. Discuss how reading in phrases creates a pleasing rhythm and makes the text easier to understand.

PRACTICE Have students reread passages from *Our Garden* with a partner or individually. For optimal fluency, students should reread three or four times. As students read, monitor fluency and provide corrective feedback. Students in this group were assessed in Week 3.

2 Retell Leveled Reader *Our Garden*

Have students use the illustrations and skimming as a guide to retell *Our Garden*. Prompt as needed.

- What else happened in this story?
- Why do you think the author wrote this story?
- How does this story remind you of other stories?

Advanced

1 Reread for Fluency
ROUTINE

PRACTICE Have students reread passages from the Leveled Reader *The Magic of Coyote* with a partner or individually. As students read, monitor fluency and provide corrective feedback. If students read fluently on the first reading, they do not need to reread three to four times. Students in this group were assessed in Week 1.

2 Revisit Leveled Reader *The Magic of Coyote*

RETELL Have students retell the Leveled Reader *The Magic of Coyote.*

MAKE A TRAVEL BROCHURE Have students complete their projects. You may wish to review their sources and see whether they need any additional supplies or resources. Ask them to explain their brochures or posters to you, and then invite them to display their work.

Group Time

DAY 1

ROUTINE

1 Preteach Phonics

CONSONANT DIGRAPHS Write and say the word *ship*. What two consonants begin this word? *(s and h)* These two consonants form a consonant digraph. The consonants in a consonant digraph make just one sound. I read *s-h* as /sh/. Blend the word *ship*. Then have students blend it with you. Review the sounds of these consonant digraphs: *ch* as in *chip* and as in *machine*, *th* as in *thin*, *wh* as in *when*, *ph* as in *elephant*, *tch* as in *pitch*, and *ng* as in *ring*.

2 Preview Decodable Reader 10

BEFORE READING Review the words on Decodable Reader p. 73. Then have students blend these story words: *Shasta, Cher, relay, sprints, nonstop, gentle, rushes,* and *goal.* Be sure students understand the meanings of words such as *relay, sprints, nonstop,* and *goal.*

Use the Picture Walk Routine on p. DI·1 to guide students through the text.

3 Read Leveled Reader *Colonial New England*

REINFORCE CONCEPTS This week's concept is *housing problems*. Deciding how to build a house and what materials to use can be a problem. The best solution depends on where you live. What is the building you live in like? What is it made of?

BEFORE READING Using the Picture Walk routine on p. DI·1, guide students through the text focusing on key concepts and vocabulary. Ask questions such as:

p. 6 This picture shows a cottage like the ones many New England colonists built.

p. 7 This picture shows the inside of the cottage. How many rooms do you see?

Read pp. 3–5 aloud. Then do a choral reading of pp. 6–7. Have students read and discuss the remainder of the book with a partner. Ask: Do you think it would be hard to live in a cottage house in colonial times? Why or why not?

Leveled Reader Database
ONLINE
PearsonSuccessNet.com

Monitor Progress

Word and Selection Reading

If... students have difficulty reading story words from the Decodable Reader,	then... reteach them by modeling blending or reading multisyllabic words.
If... partners have difficulty reading the Leveled Reader on their own,	then... have them follow along as they listen to the Online Leveled Reader Audio.

For alternate Leveled Reader lesson plans that teach

🔄 **Draw Conclusions,** 🔄 **Ask Questions,** and **Lesson Vocabulary,** see pp. LR37–LR45.

On-Level

ROUTINE

1 Build Background

DEVELOP VOCABULARY Write the word *dwellings* and ask students to define it in their own words. *(places that people live in)* What kinds of things do you find in a dwelling? *(tables, chairs, beds, dishes)* Repeat this activity with the words *swamps, chores,* and other words from the Leveled Reader *The Colonial Adventure.* Use the Concept Vocabulary routine on p. DI·1 as needed.

2 Read Leveled Reader *The Colonial Adventure*

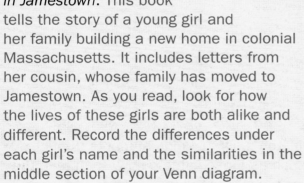

BEFORE READING Have students make a Venn diagram with the left circle labeled *Elizabeth in Massachusetts* and the right circle labeled *Sarah in Jamestown.* This book tells the story of a young girl and her family building a new home in colonial Massachusetts. It includes letters from her cousin, whose family has moved to Jamestown. As you read, look for how the lives of these girls are both alike and different. Record the differences under each girl's name and the similarities in the middle section of your Venn diagram.

DURING READING Have students follow along as you read pp. 3–7. Then let them complete the book on their own. Remind students to add similarities and differences to their Venn diagrams as they read.

AFTER READING Have students compare the similarities and differences in their Venn diagrams. Discuss how the surroundings had some effect on how Elizabeth's and Sarah's families lived. Point out that recognizing the problems colonists faced in building their new homes will help students as they read tomorrow's story *William's House.*

Advanced

ROUTINE

1 Read Leveled Reader Houses: *Past and Present*

BEFORE READING Recall the Read Aloud "Colonial Homes." In what ways did the surroundings affect the kinds of houses that were built in colonial America? *(In New England winters are harsh. Colonists built homes of wood with big fireplaces. Later they used brick or stone. In Jamestown the first homes were open on one side. Later colonists used thatch and mud.)* Today you will read how climate and surroundings affected the kinds of homes people have built throughout our history.

CRITICAL THINKING/CREATIVE THINKING Have students read the Leveled Reader independently. Encourage them to think critically and creatively. For example, ask:

- How did the kinds of housing develop differently from one area to another and over time?
- What must it have been like living in a colonial log house? a sod house?

AFTER READING Have students review the selection to find five or more unfamiliar words and determine their meanings with context clues or the dictionary. Ask them to write a sentence with each word explaining how it helps them understand houses better. Have students meet with you to discuss the selection and their words and sentences.

2 Independent Extension Activity

NOW TRY THIS Assign "Now Try This" on pp. 22–23 of *Houses: Past and Present* for students to work on throughout the week.

Group Time

DAY 2

AudioText

1 Reread for Fluency

Use Decodable Reader 10.

2 Word Study/Phonics

LESSON VOCABULARY Use p. 252b to review the meanings of *barrels, cellar, cleaning, pegs, spoil,* and *steep.* Students can blend all of the words. Have individuals practice reading word cards.

DECODING MULTISYLLABIC WORDS Write and say the word *windier.* Then model how to decode a word with a suffix when the spelling of the base word has changed. I see the suffix *-er* at the end of the word. So I cover the suffix and see the base: *windi.* I know that the spelling of a base word can change when a suffix is added. The base was *windy,* and the *y* changed to *i,* but it still has the same long *e* sound. So I can blend the whole word: *win di er; windier.* It means "more windy."

Use the Multisyllabic Word routine on p. DI·1 to help students read these other words from *William's House: upright, clapboards, fashioned, translucent, embers, smolder, shingles,* and *bleakest.* Be sure students understand the meanings of words such as *fashioned, translucent, smolder,* and *bleakest.*

3 Read *William's House,* pp. 254–261

BEFORE READING Yesterday we read about how people built houses, farmed, and lived in colonial New England. Today we will read about one man who built a house that was just right for New England.

Using the Picture Walk routine on p. DI·1, guide students through the text, asking questions such as those listed below. Then read the question on p. 255. Together, set a purpose for reading.

p. 256 This picture shows a family building a house. What material is it being made of? *(wood)* Why do you think they are using wood?

p. 259 What is the man doing in this picture? *(carrying barrels underground.)*

DURING READING Follow the Guiding Comprehension routine on pp. 256–261. Have students read along with you while tracking the print or do a choral reading of the selection. Stop every two pages to ask what has happened so far. Prompt as necessary.

- Where and when did this story take place?
- What problem happened during the hot summer?

AFTER READING What has happened in the story so far? What do you think may happen next? **Reread passages as needed.**

Monitor Progress

Word and Selection Reading

If... students have difficulty reading multisyllabic words in the selection,	then... have them look for and read meaningful parts in the words or have them chunk words with no recognizable parts.
If... students have difficulty reading along with the group,	then... have them follow along as they listen to the AudioText.

Advanced

ROUTINE

1 Extend Vocabulary

CONTEXT CLUES Choose and read a sentence or passage containing a difficult word defined in context, such as this passage on p. 16 of the Leveled Reader *Houses: Past and Present:* ". . . these homes were sturdy. They lasted until the settlers could have lumber shipped to them to build a log cabin." What does the word *sturdy* mean? *(strong)* How did you figure out the word's meaning? *(I looked at the sentences around it. In the next sentence, it says that the homes lasted, so I figured they must have been strong.)* Discuss how using context clues like this can be helpful, and remind students to use context clues to figure out the meanings of unfamiliar words as they read *William's House.*

2 Read *William's House,* pp. 254–261

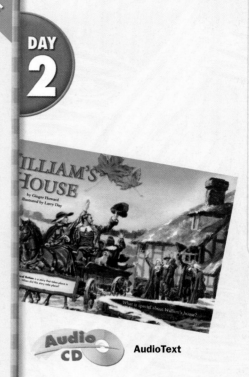

Audio CD **AudioText**

BEFORE READING In *Houses: Past and Present,* you read how colonists in America built houses using the materials at hand. Today you will read a story about one colonial family in particular and the house that they built. As you read, think about how the characters adapted their house to their surroundings.

Have students write their predictions about the selection in their Strategy Response Logs (p. 254). Remind them to check and revise their predictions as they read.

CRITICAL THINKING/CREATIVE THINKING Have students read pp. 254–261 independently. Encourage them to think critically and creatively. For example, ask:

- How do the climate and environment affect how William builds his house?
- What words would you use to describe William?
- What do you predict will happen in the fall and winter?

AFTER READING Have partners discuss the selection and share their Strategy Response Log entries. Then ask them to imagine they are William and write a journal entry for a day he spent building his house. Encourage them to add details about what William did and how he felt.

William's House
Group Time

DAY 3

Audio CD — **AudioText**

Strategic Intervention

ROUTINE

1 Reinforce Comprehension

SKILL DRAW CONCLUSIONS Have students explain what we do when we draw conclusions. *(use details in a story along with what we already know to make a decision about something)* If necessary, review the process and provide a model. When we draw a conclusion, we look at story details and think about what we already know to make a decision. For example, I read that William wanted a house just like his father's house in England. I know he wouldn't want that if he had an unhappy childhood in that home. So I can draw the conclusion that William liked his childhood home and had a happy life there.

Ask students to draw a conclusion from this story detail and fact:

> **The family dipped their fingers into pudding and bread.**

> **We use spoons and forks to eat.**

(Conclusion: Colonial families like William's didn't use utensils to eat.)

2 Read *William's House*, pp. 262–265

BEFORE READING Have students retell what happened in the story so far. Ask: Why did their pork begin to spoil? Reread the last sentence on p. 258 and the first sentence on p. 259 and model how to ask questions as you read. As I read these story details, I ask myself, "Why did the pork begin to spoil and the vegetables begin to sprout?" I read on to see if I can find the answer. Read the rest of p. 259. William is putting the food down in a cool cellar, so I can draw the conclusion that food can spoil in the summer heat. Now I understand. Remind students to ask questions to guide their reading as they read the rest of *William's House*. **STRATEGY Ask Questions**

DURING READING Follow the Guiding Comprehension routine on pp. 262–265. Have students read along with you while tracking the print or do a choral reading. Stop every two pages to ask students what has happened so far. Prompt as necessary.

- What problem happened when the snow fell?
- What happened in January?
- How did the story end?

AFTER READING How did William come up with smart solutions to problems with his New England home? Reread with students for comprehension as needed. Tell them that tomorrow they will read "Log Cabins," an article that describes another kind of early American house.

Advanced

ROUTINE

1 Extend Comprehension

SKILL DRAW CONCLUSIONS Have students give two conclusions about William, his family, or their home that they can draw from reading the selection so far. Ask them to support their conclusions with details from the story.

STRATEGY ASK QUESTIONS Have students share at least one question they asked themselves as they were reading pp. 256–261. Ask them to explain whether they found the answer by reading ahead or by drawing a conclusion. If they have not yet answered their question, discuss how they might find the answer.

2 Read *William's House,* pp. 262–265

BEFORE READING Have students recall what has happened in the story so far. Remind them to draw conclusions and to ask questions about things that puzzle them as they read the remainder of the story.

PROBLEM SOLVING Have students read pp. 262–265 independently. Encourage them to think in terms of problems and solutions. For example, ask:

• Do you agree with William's solutions for making his house better? If so, why? If not, what would you have done differently?

AFTER READING Have students complete the Strategy Response Log activity (p. 264). Meet with students to discuss their reactions to the story. Then tell students to write down any additional questions they have about it and discuss how they can find the answers to those questions.

DAY 3

Audio CD AudioText

Group Time

DAY 4

1 Practice Retelling

REVIEW STORY ELEMENTS Help students identify the main characters and the setting of *William's House*. Then guide them in using the Retelling Cards to list story events in sequence. Prompt students to include important details.

RETELL Using the Retelling Cards, have students work in pairs to retell *William's House*. Monitor retelling and prompt students as needed. For example, ask:

- Where and when does this story take place?
- What else happened in this story?
- Why do you think the author wrote this story?

If students struggle, model a fluent retelling.

2 Read "Log Cabins"

BEFORE READING Read the genre information on p. 268. Recall the Leveled Reader *Colonial New England*. Reread a page or two to refresh students' memories. Point out that this selection is expository nonfiction. What does this book explain? *(how people in colonial New England built homes and lived)* As we read "Log Cabins," think about what it explains.

Read the rest of the panel on p. 268. Have students scan the article for the photographs, captions, and illustrated time line. Discuss how those features might be helpful as they read.

DURING READING Have students read along with you while tracking the print or do a choral reading of the selection. Stop to discuss difficult vocabulary, such as *manure, augur,* and *creativity.*

AFTER READING Have students share their reactions to the selection. Then guide them through the Reading Across Texts and Writing Across Texts activities, prompting if necessary.

- What did William's house look like after he was through changing it?
- How would you describe the log cabin pictured on p. 268?
- Which house seems like it would be more comfortable to live in?

AudioText

Monitor Progress

Word and Selection Reading

If... students have difficulty reading multisyllabic words in the selection,	**then...** have them look for and read meaningful parts in the words or have them chunk words with no recognizable parts.
If... students have difficulty reading along with the group,	**then...** have them follow along as they listen to the AudioText.

Advanced

① Read "Log Cabins"

CRITICAL THINKING/CREATIVE THINKING Have students read pp. 268–271 independently. Encourage them to think critically and creatively. For example, ask:

- How would your life change if you lived in the log cabin pictured on p. 268 and 269?
- What would be some advantages and disadvantages of the different types of floors?
- How does the log cabin show the cleverness of American settlers?

AFTER READING Have students meet with you to discuss Reading Across Texts. Have students do Writing Across Texts independently.

② Extend Genre Study

RESEARCH Have students use Web sites and print resources (magazines, books, and textbooks) to locate expository nonfiction about other kinds of early houses, such as Southwest adobe homes and various kinds of Native American housing. Have students note the Web site URLs and print titles and list the types of housing they learned about.

WRITE Have students select one kind of early housing they found during their research and use that source to gather detailed information. Tell them to write a piece of expository nonfiction that describes the house and how it was built. Encourage students to include drawings or photographs as well as graphics such as time lines or maps, if appropriate.

DAY 4

AudioText

Group Time

DAY 5

ONLINE

PearsonSuccessNet.com

Strategic Intervention

ROUTINE

1 Reread for Fluency

MODEL Tell students that good silent readers block out other noises and pay attention to what they are reading. They also self-correct when they misread or skip a word. Then model, reading aloud pp. 6–7 of the Leveled Reader *Colonial New England*. Misread a word or two. Have students notice how you self-correct. Discuss how being good silent readers will help students understand and remember what they read.

PRACTICE Have individuals find a comfortable place to silently reread passages from *Colonial New England*. Encourage students to self-correct. Then have partners reread passages aloud. For optimal fluency, they should reread three or four times. As students read, monitor fluency and provide corrective feedback. Assess any students you have not yet checked during this unit.

2 Retell Leveled Reader *Colonial New England*

Model how to use photographs to retell pp. 3–5. Then ask students to retell *Colonial New England,* one photograph or illustration at a time. Prompt them as needed.

- What did you learn from reading this selection?
- Why do you think the author wrote this selection?

Monitor Progress

Fluency

If... students have difficulty reading fluently,	then... provide additional fluency practice by pairing nonfluent readers with fluent ones.

For alternate Leveled Reader lesson plans that teach
🔖 **Draw Conclusions,** 🔖 **Ask Questions,** and
Lesson Vocabulary, see pp. LR37–LR45.

On-Level

1 Reread for Fluency ROUTINE

MODEL Tell students that good silent readers block out other noises and concentrate on what they are reading. Point out that they also self-correct when they misread or skip a word. Then model, reading p. 3 of the Leveled Reader *The Colonial Adventure*. Discuss how being a good silent reader will help students understand and remember what they read.

PRACTICE Have individuals find a comfortable place to silently reread passages from *The Colonial Adventure*. Remind them to self-correct if they misread or skip a word. Then have partners reread passages aloud. For optimal fluency, students should reread three or four times. As students read, monitor fluency and provide corrective feedback. Assess any students you have not yet checked during this unit.

2 Retell Leveled Reader *The Colonial Adventure*

Have students use the illustrations as a guide to retell *The Colonial Adventure*. Prompt as needed.

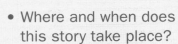

- Where and when does this story take place?
- Tell me what this story is about in a few sentences.
- How does this story remind you of other stories?

Advanced

1 Reread for Fluency ROUTINE

PRACTICE Have students silently reread passages from the Leveled Reader *Houses: Past and Present*. Then have them reread aloud with a partner or individually. As students read, monitor fluency and provide corrective feedback. If students read fluently on the first reading, they do not need to reread three to four times. Assess any students you have not yet checked during this unit.

2 Revisit Leveled Reader *Houses: Past and Present*

RETELL Have students retell the Leveled Reader *Houses: Past and Present*.

NOW TRY THIS Have students complete their projects. You may wish to review their drawings and models to see whether they should do more research or need additional supplies. Have them share their projects with their classmates.

Main Idea/Details

Determining the main idea in a text helps readers distinguish between important and less important information. When students can correctly identify the main idea, they understand the gist of what they read. Use this routine to teach main idea.

1 EXPLAIN ITS USE

Explain that finding the main idea is an important tool in helping students understand and remember what they read.

2 DEFINE THE TERMS

Explain that the topic is the subject, what the selection is all about. The main idea is the most important idea about the topic. The main idea can be stated in a sentence.

3 MODEL FINDING THE MAIN IDEA

Read a nonfiction paragraph with a stated main idea. Have students identify the topic by asking: *What is this paragraph about?* Then model how you determine the main idea.

4 FINDING SUPPORTING DETAILS

Explain that supporting details are small pieces of information that tell more about the main idea. Model how to identify supporting details.

5 USE A GRAPHIC ORGANIZER

Have students find the main idea and supporting details in a nonfiction selection. Use a main idea chart to help students organize their thoughts.

Choose passages carefully to practice this succession of skills:

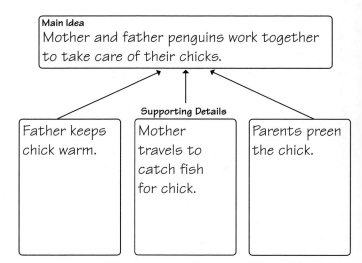

▲ **Graphic Organizer** 16

Research on Main Idea/Details

"When great readers are reading this stuff that has so many ideas in it, they have to listen to that mental voice tell them which words, which sentences or paragraphs, and which ideas are most important. Otherwise they won't get it."

Ellin Oliver Keene and Susan Zimmermann,
Mosaic of Thought

Keene, Ellin Oliver, and Susan Zimmermann. *Mosaic of Thought: Teaching Comprehension in a Reader's Workshop.* Heinemann, 1997, p. 86.

Character

Understanding characters helps readers comprehend a story and make good predictions about what will happen next. Use this routine to help students understand characters.

1 REVIEW CHARACTER TRAITS

Remind students that readers learn about characters by thinking about what they do, say, and think and how they interact with other characters. Readers infer character traits by thinking about these clues and their own experiences.

2 TEACH CHARACTER DEVELOPMENT

Explain that events in a story often cause a character to change in a significant way, such as in attitudes or beliefs. Students should read to see if this happens to the main character.

3 MODEL INFERRING TRAITS

Provide an example from a story you have read. Model inferring character traits from the character's words and actions. Point out how and why the character changes. Compare characters with each other and with real people.

4 APPLY TO A SELECTION

Read with students a story in which there are well-developed characters. Have students draw conclusions about character traits from clues in the story and their own experiences.

5 USE A GRAPHIC ORGANIZER

Have students record clues about a character in a web. They can record details about what the character said and did and how characters interacted.

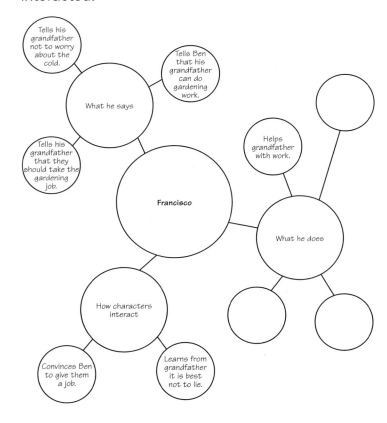

▲ **Graphic Organizer** 15

Research on Author's Purpose

"In life and in books, children can sense differences in human beings and are capable of recognizing and responding to well-developed characters. Even in the simplest stories it is possible to find characters that verify truths about human nature."

Rebecca J. Lukens,
A Critical Handbook of Children's Literature

Lukens, Rebecca J. *A Critical Handbook of Children's Literature.* Pearson Education, 2003, p. 94.

Main Idea/Details

Determining the main idea in a text helps readers distinguish between important and less important information. When students can correctly identify the main idea, they understand the gist of what they read. Use this routine to teach main idea.

1 EXPLAIN ITS USE

Explain that finding the main idea is an important tool in helping students understand and remember what they read.

2 DEFINE THE TERMS

Explain that the topic is the subject, what the selection is all about. The main idea is the most important idea about the topic. The main idea can be stated in a sentence.

3 MODEL FINDING THE MAIN IDEA

Read a nonfiction paragraph with a stated main idea. Have students identify the topic by asking: *What is this paragraph about?* Then model how you determine the main idea.

4 FINDING SUPPORTING DETAILS

Explain that supporting details are small pieces of information that tell more about the main idea. Model how to identify supporting details.

5 USE A GRAPHIC ORGANIZER

Have students find the main idea and supporting details in a nonfiction selection. Use a main idea chart to help students organize their thoughts.

Choose passages carefully to practice this succession of skills:

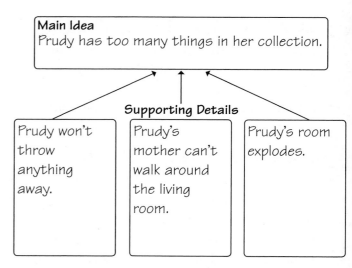

▲ **Graphic Organizer** 16

Research on Main Idea/Details

"When great readers are reading this stuff that has so many ideas in it, they have to listen to that mental voice tell them which words, which sentences or paragraphs, and which ideas are most important. Otherwise they won't get it."

Ellin Oliver Keene and Susan Zimmermann,
Mosaic of Thought

Keene, Ellin Oliver, and Susan Zimmermann. *Mosaic of Thought: Teaching Comprehension in a Reader's Workshop.* Heinemann, 1997, p. 86.

Author's Purpose

Evaluating the author's purpose for writing helps students decide how quickly or slowly and carefully to read. Use this routine to teach author's purpose.

1 DISCUSS AUTHOR'S PURPOSE

Explain that the author's purpose is the author's reason or reasons for writing. Four common reasons for writing are to persuade, to inform, to entertain, or to express ideas or feelings.

2 EXPLAIN ITS USE

Tell students that one reason they need to consider the author's purpose is to adjust their reading rate. If a story is meant to be fun, they may decide to read quickly. If the author wants to explain how something works, they may need to read slowly and carefully.

3 ASK QUESTIONS

Authors don't usually state their purposes for writing, and they often have more than one purpose. Before, during, and after reading a selection, ask questions to help students draw conclusions about the author's purposes: *Why do you think the author wrote this story? What reasons might the author have for writing the story this way? What is the author trying to tell you? Why is the author telling you that?*

4 USE A GRAPHIC ORGANIZER

Have students predict the author's purpose before reading by previewing the title, illustrations, and graphics. During and after reading, students should check and confirm their predictions. Have them record ideas and evidence in a Three-column chart.

	Author's Purpose	Why Do You Think So?
Before you read: What do you think it will be?	to entertain	The pictures are funny.
As you read: What do you think it is?	to entertain	The characters are animals, but they act like people.
After you read: What was it?	to entertain and to teach a lesson	The story was fun to read, and the animals learned a lesson at the end.

▲ **Graphic Organizer** 26

Research on Author's Purpose

"Younger and less proficient readers are unlikely to differentiate between 'study' reading and 'fun' reading."

Ruth Garner,
"Metacognition and Self-Monitoring Strategies"

Garner, Ruth. "Metacognition and Self-Monitoring Strategies." In *What Research Has to Say About Reading Instruction,* edited by S. J. Samuels and A. E. Farstrup. Second Edition. International Reading Association, 1992, p. 238.

Draw Conclusions

When students move beyond the literal meaning of a text to draw conclusions, they get more ideas from what they read and understand better the points an author is trying to make. Use the following routine to guide students in drawing conclusions.

① DISCUSS DRAWING CONCLUSIONS

Tell students a conclusion is a sensible decision they reach based on details or facts in a story or an article. Explain when they draw conclusions, they think about information in the text and what they already know.

② MODEL DRAWING A CONCLUSION

Model using your own experiences to draw a conclusion.

 Think Aloud **MODEL** The smell of peanuts and cotton candy filled the air. I heard clapping, I even heard loud bellows that sounded like elephants. I knew a circus was going on.

Discuss how you combined what you already knew with details (smell of peanuts and cotton candy, clapping, loud bellows) to draw a conclusion.

③ ASK QUESTIONS

Read aloud a passage and ask questions that foster drawing conclusions. For example: *What kind of person is the main character? How can you tell? Why do you think the character acts this way?*

④ USE A GRAPHIC ORGANIZER

Have partners read both fiction and nonfiction passages. Students can ask each other questions that lead to drawing conclusions. Suggest that they use webs or charts to show the facts or details that support their conclusions.

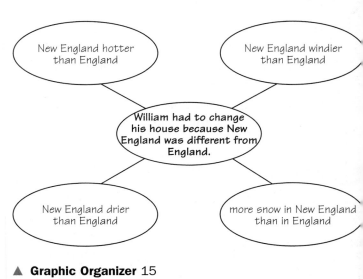

▲ **Graphic Organizer** 15

Research on Main Idea/Details

"Inference is a mosaic, a dazzling constellation of thinking processes, but the tiles available to form each mosaic are limited, circumscribed. There must be a fusion of words on a page—and constraints of meaning they impose—and the experience and knowledge of the reader."

Ellin Oliver Keene and Susan Zimmermann,
Mosaic of Thought

Keene, Ellin Oliver, and Susan Zimmermann. *Mosaic of Thought: Teaching Comprehension in a Reader's Workshop.* Heinemann, 1997, p. 154. 1992, p. 238.

Providing students with reading materials they can and want to read is an important step toward developing fluent readers. A running record allows you to determine each student's instructional and independent reading level. Information on how to take a running record is provided on pp. DI•59–DI•60.

Instructional Reading Level

Only approximately 1 in 10 words will be difficult when reading a selection from the Student Edition for students who are at grade level. (A typical third-grader reads approximately 105–120 words correct per minute.)

- Students reading at grade level should read regularly from the Student Edition and On-Level Leveled Readers, with teacher support as suggested in the Teacher's Editions.
- Students reading below grade level can read the Strategic Intervention Leveled Readers. Instructional plans can be found in the Teacher's Edition and the Leveled Reader Teaching Guide.
- Students who are reading above grade level can read the Advanced Leveled Readers. Instructional plans can be found in the Teacher's Edition and the Leveled Reader Teaching Guide.

Independent Reading Level

Students should read regularly in independent-level texts in which no more than approximately 1 in 20 words is difficult for the reader. Other factors that make a book easy to read include the student's interest in the topic, the amount of text on a page, how well illustrations support meaning, and the complexity and familiarity of the concepts. Suggested books for self-selected reading are provided for each lesson on p. TR14 in this Teacher's Edition.

Guide students in learning how to self-select books at their independent reading level. As you talk about a book with students, discuss the challenging concepts in it, list new words students find in sampling the book, and ask students about their familiarity with the topic. A blackline master to help students evaluate books for independent reading is provided on p. DI•58.

Self-Selected/Independent Reading

While oral reading allows you to assess students' reading level and fluency, independent reading is of crucial importance to students' futures as readers and learners. Students need to develop their ability to read independently for increasing amounts of time.

- Schedule a regular time for sustained independent reading in your classroom. During the year, gradually increase the amount of time devoted to independent reading.
- Encourage students to track the amount of time they read independently and the number of pages they read in a given amount of time. Tracking will help motivate them to gradually increase their duration and speed. Blackline masters for tracking independent reading are provided on pp. DI•58 and TR15.

Choosing a Book for Independent Reading

When choosing a book, story, or article for independent reading, consider these questions:

_____ 1. Do I know something about this topic?

_____ 2. Am I interested in this topic?

_____ 3. Do I like reading this kind of book (fiction, fantasy, biography, or whatever)?

_____ 4. Have I read other things by this author? Do I like this author?

If you say "yes" to at least one of the questions above, continue:

_____ 5. In reading the first page, was only about 1 of every 20 words hard?

If you say "yes," continue:

_____ 6. Does the number of words on a page look about right to me?

If you say "yes," the book or article is probably at the right level for you.

Silent Reading

Record the date, the title of the book or article you read, the amount of time you spent reading, and the number of pages you read during that time. Remember to capitalize the first word, last word, and every important word in a book title.

Date	Title	Minutes	Pages

Taking a Running Record

A running record is an assessment of a student's oral reading accuracy and oral reading fluency. Reading accuracy is based on the number of words read correctly. Reading fluency is based on the reading rate (the number of words correct per minute) and the degree to which a student reads with a "natural flow."

How to Measure Reading Accuracy

1. Choose a grade-level text of about 80 to 120 words that is unfamiliar to the student.
2. Make a copy of the text for yourself. Make a copy for the student or have the student read aloud from a book.
3. Give the student the text and have the student read aloud. (You may wish to record the student's reading for later evaluation.)
4. On your copy of the text, mark any miscues or errors the student makes while reading. See the running record sample on page DI·60, which shows how to identify and mark miscues.
5. Count the total number of words in the text and the total number of errors made by the student. Note: If a student makes the same error more than once, such as mispronouncing the same word multiple times, count it as one error. Self-corrections do not count as actual errors. Use the following formula to calculate the percentage score, or accuracy rate:

$$\frac{\text{Total Number of Words} - \text{Total Number of Errors}}{\text{Total Number of Words}} \times 100 = \text{percentage score}$$

Interpreting the Results

- A student who reads **95–100%** of the words correctly is reading at an **independent level** and may need more challenging text.
- A student who reads **90–94%** of the words correctly is reading at an **instructional level** and will likely benefit from guided instruction.
- A student who reads **89%** or fewer of the words correctly is reading at a **frustrational level** and may benefit most from targeted instruction with lower-level texts and intervention.

How to Measure Reading Rate (WCPM)

1. Follow Steps 1–3 above.
2. Note the exact times when the student begins and finishes reading.
3. Use the following formula to calculate the number of words correct per minute (WCPM):

$$\frac{\text{Total Number of Words Read Correctly}}{\text{Total Number of Seconds}} \times 60 = \text{words correct per minute}$$

Interpreting the Results

An appropriate reading rate for a third-grader is 105–120 (WCPM).

Running Record Sample

Running Record Sample

Dana had recently begun volunteering at the animal rescue shelter where her mom worked as a veterinarian. The shelter was (just) across the bay from their house.

Dana was learning many different jobs at the shelter. She fed the dogs and cleaned their cages. She played catch with the dogs in the shelter's backyard. Dana's favorite job, however, was introducing people to the dogs waiting for adoption. Whenever a dog found a new home, Dana was especially pleased!

The road to the shelter crossed over the bay. Dana looked for boats in the channel, but there were none. Dana's mom turned on the radio to listen to the news as they drove. The weather reporter announced that a blizzard might hit some parts of the state.

—From *A Day with the Dogs*
On-Level Reader 3.3.4

Symbols

Accurate Reading
The student reads a word correctly.

Omission
The student omits words or word parts.

Hesitation
The student hesitates over a word, and the teacher provides the word. Wait several seconds before telling the student what the word is.

Mispronunciation/Misreading
The student pronounces or reads a word incorrectly.

Self-Correction
The student reads a word incorrectly but then corrects the error. Do not count self-corrections as actual errors. However, noting self-corrections will help you identify words the student finds difficult.

Insertion
The student inserts words or parts of words that are not in the text.

Substitution
The student substitutes words or parts of words for the words in the text.

Running Record Results ▶	**Reading Accuracy** ▶	**Reading Rate—WCPM**
Total Number of Words: **126**	$\dfrac{126-5}{126} = \dfrac{121}{126} = .9603 = 96\%$	$\dfrac{121}{64} \times 60 = 113.43 = 113$ words correct per minute
Number of Errors: **5**		
Reading Time: **64 seconds**	Accuracy Percentage Score: **96%**	Reading Rate: **113 WCPM**

Teacher Resources

Table of Contents

The Honest-to-Goodness Truth
from p. 174m

Libby jumped right in with what was bothering her. "Can the truth be wrong?"

"Oh, no," Miz Tusselbury said, fanning faster. "The truth is never wrong. Always, always tell the truth!"

"That's what I thought," Libby said, a smile of relief lighting up her face.

Miz Tusselbury leaned over the railing to pluck a bloom from one of the vines that grew all over her yard and up her house. "Don't you think my garden is lovely?"

Libby thought on it. Ordinarily she would have just said yes, for fear of sounding sassy. But that wasn't the truth. So polite as you please, she answered, "Miz Tusselbury, truly and honestly, your yard looks like a . . . a . . . a jungle."

"Well, I declare!" Miz Tusselbury gasped.

"Don't be mad!" Libby pleaded.

But it was too late. Miz Tusselbury rushed inside her house and slammed the door.

Even though Mama was busy putting the finishing touches on Virginia Washington's wedding dress, she still took time to listen to Libby's problem.

"I feel something awful. My friends don't like me no more."

"Any more," repeated her mother.

"No, they don't—and just 'cause I told the truth." The girl sighed deeply.

Handing her a needle to thread, Mama asked gently, "Are you sure they're mad at you for telling the truth?"

"I think so," said Libby. "Willie was mad as a hornet when I told Miz Jackson he didn't have his homework. And Miz Tusselbury got plenty upset when I said her garden looked like a jungle."

Mama smiled. "Oh, I see." Then, putting down her work, she took Libby's hands, saying, "Sometimes the truth is told at the wrong time or in the wrong way, or for the wrong reasons. And that can be harmful. But the honest-to-goodness truth is never wrong." Then Mama went back to stitching and pulling, stitching and pulling.

Now Libby thought back on her own truth-telling, and Mama's words suddenly became crystal clear.

The next day, Libby caught up with her friends on the way to school. Libby apologized to Willie. "I should have let you tell Miz Jackson 'bout your own homework. It was unfair. Besides, nobody asked me in the first place."

"That's all right. But, hey," he added, "do you think you could help me with my geography homework?"

"No problem," said Libby.

Later, Libby talked to all the other victims of her truth-telling.

But there was one more person she had to see. On the way home, she headed straight for Miz Tusselbury's house.

Libby found her neighbor out front, down on all fours, pulling up flowers and snatching up vines by the roots. When Miz Tusselbury saw her, she wiped her brow with the back of her hand and flashed a full smile.

"I'm sorry if I hurt your feelings yesterday," Libby said.

"Libby Louise, you were right," Miz Tusselbury replied. "This place had gone completely and uncontrollably wild!"

"But you were so mad at me."

Miz Tusselbury waved a dismissing hand. "The truth is often hard to chew. But if it is sweetened with love, then it is a little easier to swallow."

Libby really did understand. She picked up a hoe and began helping. "Things are really looking pretty good around here," she said. And that was the honest-to-goodness truth.

Why Possum's Tail Is Bare
from p. 224m

Soon the other animals began to call, "Possum dance! Possum, dance!" So Possum reached around behind him and pulled off the red string. With that, every hair on his tail fell off, but Possum didn't know it. He leaped into the circle of firelight and began to dance, singing, "See my beautiful bushy, furry tail!" The animals began to laugh. Possum sang, "See how it sweeps the ground!" And the animals laughed louder.

Possum decided maybe they hadn't heard him right, and so he sang louder, and the animals laughed harder. Finally, Possum realized that something must be wrong. He looked around behind him, and instead of the beautiful bushy, furry tail that he had always known, there was a long, red, skinny, hairless tail. Possum was so surprised and humiliated, all he could do was fall to the ground and grin helplessly, which Possum still does whenever you take him by surprise. And Possum's grandchildren all have red, skinny, hairless tails to this very day.

Colonial Homes
from p. 250m

located in barns or sheds some distance from the house. In the winter months they used chamber pots that were emptied daily. Bathing was infrequent, probably done no more than once a month. Often this consisted of washing the hands and face only. Many people thought bathing opened the skin's pores to disease. Submersing the body in water was considered by some to be improper. Several states even tried to pass laws making bathing illegal!

Many homes built during colonial times are still standing today. You can see and visit these houses throughout what used to be the thirteen original colonies. They are a testimony to the skill and craftsmanship of those who built them.

Unit 1

Vocabulary Words		Spelling Words		

Boom Town

boom	mending
business	pick
coins	skillet
fetched	spell
laundry	

Short vowels VCCV

happen	supper	traffic
lettuce	subject	suggest
basket	lesson	puppet
winter	spelling	
sister	napkin	
monster	collar	

What About Me?

carpenter	merchant
carpetmaker	plenty
knowledge	straying
marketplace	thread

Plurals -s, -es

pennies	wishes	crashes
inches	pockets	supplies
plants	lists	pencils
families	copies	
bodies	parties	
glasses	bunches	

Alexander, Who Used to Be Rich Last Sunday

college	nickels
dimes	quarters
downtown	rich
fined	

Adding -ed, -ing, -er, -est

using	pleased	funniest
getting	emptied	angrier
easiest	leaving	shopped
swimming	worried	
heavier	strangest	
greatest	freezing	

If You Made a Million

amount	million
check	thousand
earned	value
expensive	worth
interest	

Long vowel digraphs

clean	display	Sunday
agree	window	float
teeth	shadow	thrown
dream	cheese	
grain	peach	
coach	braid	

My Rows and Piles of Coins

arranged
bundles
dangerously
errands
excitedly
steady
unwrapped
wobbled

Vowel sounds in *out* and *toy*

proud	avoid	annoy
shower	thousand	appoint
hour	prowl	broil
amount	employ	
voyage	bounce	
choice	poison	

Unit 2   Vocabulary Words   Spelling Words

Penguin Chick

Vocabulary Words
- cuddles
- flippers
- frozen
- hatch
- pecks
- preen
- snuggles

Syllable pattern V/CV, VC/V

finish	rapid	tulip
pilot	female	camel
even	lemon	salad
wagon	pupil	
music	focus	
silent	robot	

A Day's Work

Vocabulary Words
- excitement
- gardener
- motioned
- sadness
- shivered
- shocked
- slammed

Words ending in -le

handle	little	juggle
trouble	gentle	uncle
simple	poodle	riddle
people	pickle	
middle	noodle	
table	saddle	

Prudy's Problem and How She Solved It

Vocabulary Words
- collection
- enormous
- realize
- scattered
- shiny
- strain

Compound words

sunglasses	snowstorm	campground
football	earring	sandbox
homework	scarecrow	toothbrush
haircut	blueberry	
popcorn	butterflies	
railroad	lawnmower	

Tops & Bottoms

Vocabulary Words
- bottom
- cheated
- clever
- crops
- lazy
- partners
- wealth

Consonant blends spl, thr, squ, str

splash	street	throne
throw	split	strawberry
three	splurge	squeeze
square	thrill	
throat	strength	
strike	squeak	

William's House

Vocabulary Words
- barrels
- cellar
- clearing
- pegs
- spoil
- steep

Digraphs sh, th, ph, ch, tch

father	weather	athlete
chapter	catch	trophy
other	fashion	nephew
alphabet	shrink	
watch	pitcher	
English	flash	

Unit 3   Vocabulary Words   Spelling Words

The Gardener

Vocabulary Words

beauty	humor
blooming	recognizing
bulbs	showers
doze	sprouting

Contractions

let's	haven't	they'd
he'd	hasn't	wasn't
you'll	she'd	didn't
can't	they'll	
I'd	when's	
you'd	we'd	

Pushing Up the Sky

Vocabulary Words

antlers
imagined
languages
narrator
overhead
poked

Prefixes un-, re-, mis-, dis-

unhappy	dislike	unknown
recall	replace	dishonest
disappear	mislead	react
unload	disagree	
mistake	rewrite	
misspell	unroll	

Night Letters

Vocabulary Words

blade
budding
dew
fireflies
flutter
notepad
patch

Consonant sounds /j/ and /k/

clock	crack	jacket
large	edge	budge
page	pocket	orange
mark	brake	
kitten	change	
judge	ridge	

A Symphony of Whales

Vocabulary Words

anxiously	melody
bay	supplies
blizzards	surrounded
channel	symphony
chipped	

Suffixes -ly, -ful, -ness, -less

beautiful	illness	fairness
safely	helpful	cheerful
kindness	daily	painful
finally	suddenly	
spotless	wireless	
worthless	quietly	

Volcanoes: Nature's Incredible Fireworks

Vocabulary Words

beneath
buried
chimney
earthquakes
fireworks
force
trembles
volcanoes

Words with wr, kn, mb, gn

thumb	wrist	lamb
gnaw	crumb	knob
written	assign	knit
know	wrench	
climb	knot	
design	wrinkle	

Unit 4	Vocabulary Words		Spelling Words

Wings

Vocabulary Words:
attention, complained, drifting, giggle, glaring, looping, struggled, swooping

Irregular Plurals

wolves	sheep	elves
knives	heroes	banjos
feet	scarves	halves
men	mice	
children	geese	
women	cuffs	

Hottest, Coldest, Highest, Deepest

Vocabulary Words:
average, depth, deserts, outrun, peak, tides, waterfalls

Vowels with *r*

third	earth	thirsty
early	word	workout
world	perfect	earn
certain	verb	
dirty	nerve	
herself	worm	

Rocks in His Head

Vocabulary Words:
attic, board, chores, customer, labeled, spare, stamps

Prefixes *pre-, mid-, over-, out-*

prepaid	prefix	overdue
midnight	Midwest	outside
overflow	pretest	outfield
outdoors	midpoint	
outline	outgoing	
overgrown	overtime	

America's Champion Swimmer: Gertrude Ederle

Vocabulary Words:
celebrate, continued, current, drowned, medals, stirred, strokes

Suffixes *-er, -or, -ess, -ist*

dentist	seller	chemist
editor	tutor	investor
artist	tourist	conductor
hostess	organist	
actress	lioness	
swimmer	shipper	

Fly, Eagle, Fly!

Vocabulary Words:
clutched, echoed, gully, reeds, scrambled, valley

Syllable pattern VCCCV

monster	instant	address
surprise	inspect	substance
hundred	pilgrim	children
complete	contrast	
control	explode	
sample	district	

Unit 5	Vocabulary Words		Spelling Words

Suki's Kimono

Vocabulary Words: cotton, festival, graceful, handkerchief, paces, pale, rhythm, snug

Syllable patterns CVVC, CVV

create, studio, trio, medium, violin, stadium, piano, duo, audio, idea, patio, radio, rodeo, video, pioneer

How My Family Lives in America

Vocabulary Words: admire, custom, famous, mention, overnight, popular, public, twist

Homophones

to, hour, right, too, stair, new, two, stare, knew, week, flour, weak, flower, our, write

Good-Bye, 382 Shin Dang Dong

Vocabulary Words: airport, curious, delicious, described, farewell, homesick, memories, raindrops

Vowel sound in ball

small, also, applause, almost, author, walnut, always, false, lawn, because, already, straw, flaw, drawn, sausage

Jalapeño Bagels

Vocabulary Words: bakery, batch, boils, braided, dough, ingredients, knead, mixture

More vowel sound in ball

thought, cough, trough, fought, talk, chalk, bought, daughter, stalk, taught, ought, caught, sought, walk, brought

Me and Uncle Romie

Vocabulary Words: cardboard, feast, fierce, flights, pitcher, ruined, stoops, treasure

Suffixes -y, -ish, -hood, -ment

rocky, movement, bumpy, foolish, neighborhood, payment, rainy, sleepy, childhood, childish, shipment, selfish, parenthood, treatment, crunchy

Unit 6	Vocabulary Words		Spelling Words

The Story of the Statue of Liberty

Vocabulary Words: crown, liberty, models, symbol, tablet, torch, unforgettable, unveiled

Spelling Words — Vowel Sounds in *tooth* and *cook*:
few, school, true, goose, fruit, cookie, cushion, noodle, bookmark, balloon, suit, chew, glue, Tuesday, bushel

Happy Birthday Mr. Kang

Vocabulary Words: bows, chilly, foolish, foreign, narrow, perches, recipe

Spelling Words — Schwa:
above, another, upon, animal, paper, open, family, travel, afraid, nickel, sugar, circus, item, gallon, melon

Talking Walls: Art for the People

Vocabulary Words: encourages, expression, local, native, settled, social, support

Spelling Words — Words with -tion, -sion, -ture:
question, creature, furniture, division, action, collision, direction, culture, vacation, mansion, fiction, feature, sculpture, vision, celebration

Two Bad Ants

Vocabulary Words: crystal, disappeared, discovery, goal, journey, joyful, scoop, unaware

Spelling Words — Multisyllabic Words:
leadership, gracefully, refreshment, uncomfortable, overdoing, remarkable, carefully, unbearably, ownership, unacceptable, impossibly, reappeared, unprepared, oncoming, misbehaving

Elena's Serenade

Vocabulary Words: burro, bursts, factory, glassblower, puffs, reply, tune

Spelling Words — Related Words:
cloth, clothes, nature, natural, able, ability, mean, meant, deal, dealt, please, pleasant, sign, signal, signature

Grade 2 Vocabulary

Use this list of second grade tested vocabulary words for leveled activities.

A
above
adventure
afternoon
ago
alone
America
angry
animals
answer
aunt

B
bank
bases
basket
bear
beautiful
been
behind
believe
birthday
blame
blankets
block
borrow
bought
branches
break
brought
build
building
bumpy
burning
buy

C
campfire
cattle
caught
certainly
chased
cheers

chewing
chuckle
clattering
climbed
clothes
clubhouse
clung
collects
company
couldn't
country
cowboy
crawls

D
daughters
door
dripping
drum

E
early
either
enough
everybody
everywhere
exploring
eyes

F
fair
family
faraway
father
favorite
field
finally
fingers
flag
flashes
freedom
friend
front

fruit
full

G
galloped
giant
gone
grabbed
great
greatest
guess

H
half
harvest
heard
herd
hours

I
idea
important
insects

J
jingle

L
laugh
learn
lightning
listen
live
love

M
machines
many
masks
minute
money
mother
move

N
neighbor
nicknames

O
often
once
only

P
parents
people
picnic
picture
pieces
plate
pleasant
pond
pounds
pours
powerful
practice
present
pressing
pretended
pretty
probably
promise
pull

Q
question
quickly
quilt

R
railroad
roar
rolling
root

S
sailed
scared
school
science
second
shall
shed
shoe
sign
signmaker
silver
skin
smooth
soil
someone
somewhere
sorry
special
stars
station
storm
straight
stripes
strong
stuffing

T
taught
tears
their
though
threw
thunder
tightly
today
together
tomorrow
toward
townspeople
trails

treat
trouble
truest
trunks

U
unpacked

V
very
village
vine
voice

W
wagged
warm
wash
watch
water
whatever
whole
woman
won
wondered
wonderful
word
work
world
worst
wrapped

Y
you're
youngest

Grade 4 Vocabulary

Use this list of fourth grade tested vocabulary words for leveled activities.

A

aboard
affords
amazed
amphibians
ancestors
ancient
anticipation
appeared
aquarium
astronauts
atlas
aviator
avoided
awkward

B

bargain
bawling
bewildered
biologist
bluff
boarding school
bow
brilliant
brisk
bustling

C

canopy
capable
capsule
cargo
celestial
chant
chorus
cockpit
colonel
conducted
Constitution
continent
convergence
cord

coward
coyote
cradle
crime
crumbled
curiosity

D

dangle
dappled
daring
depart
destruction
dignified
dismay
docks
dolphins
dormitory
draft
drag
dudes
duke
dungeon

E

elegant
enchanted
endurance
escape
etched
exhibit
expected

F

fascinated
favor
flex
flexible
forbidding
forecasts
fouled
fragrant
frost
furiously

G

generations
genius
glacier
gleamed
glider
glimpses
glint
glorious
grand
granite
grizzly

H

hangars
hatch
heaves
homeland
hoop
horizon
howling
humble

I

icebergs
immense
impressive
inland

J

jersey

L

lagoon
lassoed
link
lizards
longed
loomed
lunar
lurking

M

magician
majesty
manual
marveled
massive
mechanical
memorial
migrating
minister
miracle
module
monument

N

naturalist
navigation
noble
numerous

O

offended
outspoken

P

palettes
parlor
payroll
peasant
peculiar
politics
pollen
pollinate
porridge
positive
prairie
preserve
prideful
pulpit
pulses

Q

quaint
quarantine
quivered

R

recalls
reference
reptiles
resemblance
reservation
responsibility
rille
rim
riverbed
roundup
rudder
ruins
rumbling
runt

S

salamanders
scan
scent
scholars
sculptures
seeker
selecting
shatter
shielding
shimmering
shrieked
slithered
slopes
society
solemnly
solo
species
speechless
spurs
staggered

stalled
stern
still
stumped
summoning
surface
surge
swatted

T

taunted
temple
terraced
terror
thickets
timid
torrent
towering
translate
trench
triumph
tropical
trudged

U

unbelievable
uncover

V

vain
vanished
vehicle

W

wharf
wilderness
wondrous

Y

yearned

Legibility

When handwriting is legible, letters, words and numbers can be read easily. Handwriting that is not legible can cause problems for the reader and make communication difficult. Legibility can be improved if students are able to identify what is causing legibility problems in their handwriting. Focus instruction on the following five elements of legible handwriting.

Size

Letters need to be a consistent size. Students should focus on three things related to size: letters that reach to the top line, letters that reach halfway between the top and bottom line, and letters that extend below the bottom line. Writing letters the correct size can improve legibility. Often the letters that sit halfway between the top and bottom line cause the most problems. When students are writing on notebook paper, there is no middle line to help them size letters such as *m, a, i,* and *r* correctly. If students are having trouble, have them draw middle lines on their notebook paper.

Shape

Some of the most common handwriting problems are caused by forming letters incorrectly. These are the most common types of handwriting problems:

- round letters such as *a, o,* and *g* are not closed
- looped letters such as *i, e,* and *b* have no loops
- letters such as *i, t,* and *d* have loops that shouldn't be there

Have students examine one another's writing to indicate which words are hard to read, and then discuss which letters aren't formed correctly. They can then practice those particular letters.

Spacing

Letters within words should be evenly spaced. Too much or too little space can make writing difficult to read. A consistent amount of space should also be used between words in a sentence and between sentences. Suggest that students use the tip of their pencil to check the spacing between words and the width of their pencil to check the spacing between sentences.

Slant

Correct writing slant can be to the right or to the left, or there may be no slant at all. Slant becomes a legibility problem when letters are slanted in different directions. Suggest that students use a ruler to draw lines to determine if their slant is consistent.

Smoothness

Written letters should be produced with a line weight that is not too dark and not too light. The line should be smooth without any shaky or jagged edges. If students' writing is too dark, they are pressing too hard. If the writing is too light, they are not pressing hard enough. Usually shaky or jagged lines occur if students are unsure of how to form letters or if they are trying to draw letters rather than using a flowing motion.

D'Nealian™ Cursive Alphabet

a b c d e f g
h i j k l m n
o p q r s t u
v w x y z

A B C D E F G
H I J K L M N
O P Q R S T U
V W X Y Z . , ' ?

1 2 3 4 5 6
7 8 9 10

D'Nealian™ Alphabet

a b c d e f g h i

j k l m n o p q r s t

u v w x y z

A B C D E F G

H I J K L M N O

P Q R S T U V

W X Y Z . , ' ?

1 2 3 4 5 6

7 8 9 10

Manuscript Alphabet

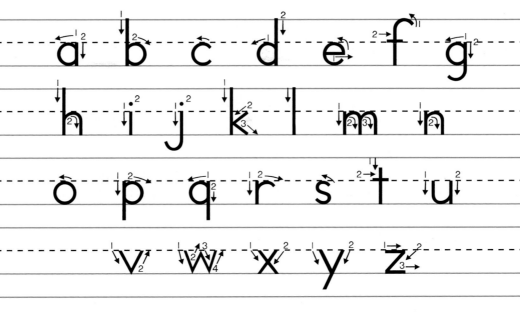

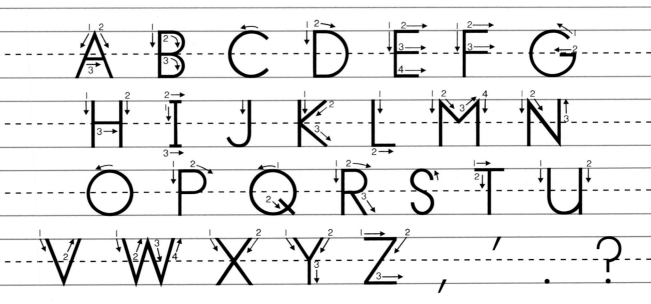

Unit 2 *Smart Solutions*

	Below-Level	On-Level	Advanced

Penguin Chick

To Read Aloud!
My Season With Penguins: An Antarctic Journal
by Sophie Webb (Houghton Mifflin, 2000) The author describes her two-month stay in Antarctica to study and draw penguins.

Antarctic Antics: A Book of Penguin Poems
by Judy Sierra (Harcourt Brace, 1998) This is a collection of poems celebrating the habits and habitat of Emperor penguins.

Growing Up Wild: Penguins
by Sandra Markle (Scholastic, 2002) This book depicts the hatching, care, growth, and education of baby Adelie penguins.

Arctic Lights, Arctic Nights
by Debbie S. Miller (Walker & Company, 2003) This book describes the unique light phenomena of the Alaskan Arctic and how animals adapt to the temperature and daylight changes.

A Day's Work

To Read Aloud!
Winners Take All
by Fred Bowen (Peachtree Publishers, 2000) During an important baseball game, Kyle pretends he caught the ball, leading his team to victory. Soon, though, his lie catches up with him.

Honest Tulio
by John Himmelman (Bridgewater, 1997) When honest Tulio sees a man drop a copper coin in the bustling marketplace, he sets off to find him and return it.

The Empty Pot
by Demi (Henry Holt, 1990) When the emperor needs to find an heir to his throne, he rewards a young boy's honesty.

The Donkey and the Rock
by Demi (Henry Holt, 1999) A man's donkey knocks over another man's jar of oil. The two men ask their king to decide whom to blame. The king holds a trial between the donkey and the rock.

Prudy's Problem

To Read Aloud!
Hello, Mrs. Piggle Wiggle
by Betty MacDonald (Scholastic, 1957) Mrs. Piggle-Wiggle loves healthy children, and she has the cure for any bad habit.

Owen
by Kevin Henkes (Greenwillow, 1993) Owen's parents want him to give up his favorite blanket before he starts school, so they come up with a solution that makes everyone happy.

The Library
by Sarah Stewart (Farrar, Straus & Giroux, 1995) Elizabeth Bowen loves to read so much that her house is overrun with books.

Every Dog Has His Day
by John Erickson (Maverick Books, 1988) Hank the Cowdog gets into more and more trouble before he is able to find a happy solution to his problems.

Tops and Bottoms

To Read Aloud!
Jump!: The Adventures of Brer Rabbit
by Joel Harris, Joel Chandler, and Van Dyke Parks (Harcourt Brace, 1986) This book contains five adventures of Brer Rabbit, the classic underdog who outsmarts all the other folks in Hominy Grove.

Anansi and the Magic Stick
by Eric Kimmel (Holiday House, 2002) When Anansi, the lazy but clever spider, discovers that Hyena has a magic stick, he sets out to steal it.

Anansi Does the Impossible
by Verna Aardema (Atheneum Book, 1997) Anansi and his wife outsmart the Sky God and win back the beloved folktales of their people.

The Barefoot Book of Trickster Tales
by Richard Walker (Barefoot Books, 1998) This colorful collection of trickster tales from around the world features the exploits of characters such as Anansi and Brer Rabbit.

William's House

To Read Aloud!
Stranded at Plimoth Plantation
by Gary Bowen (HarperCollins, 1994) This fictional diary of a young settler documents a year at Plimoth Colony in New England.

A House Is a House For Me
by Mary Ann Hoberman (Puffin, 1982) In a rollicking rhyme, the author introduces us to all types of homes for both people and animals.

Pilgrim Cat
by Carol Antoinette Peacock (Albert Whitman & Company, 2004) This book tells the story of the pilgrim journey to New England and the building of a new colony through the eyes of a cat.

Little House in the Big Woods
by Laura Ingalls Wilder (Scholastic, 1960) This is the story of four-year-old Laura and her family's pioneer life on the edge of the Big Woods of Wisconsin.

Unit 2 Reading Log

Name _____

Dates Read	Title and Author	What is it about?	How would you rate it?	Explain your rating.
From _____ to _____			Great 5 4 3 2 1 Awful	
From _____ to _____			Great 5 4 3 2 1 Awful	
From _____ to _____			Great 5 4 3 2 1 Awful	
From _____ to _____			Great 5 4 3 2 1 Awful	
From _____ to _____			Great 5 4 3 2 1 Awful	

Unit 2 Narrative Retelling Chart

Selection Title _____

Name _____

Date _____

Retelling Criteria/Teacher Prompt	Teacher-Aided Response	Student-Generated Response	Rubric Score (Circle one.)
Connections Has anything like this happened to you? How does this story remind you of other stories?			4 3 2 1
Author's Purpose Why do you think the author wrote this story? What was the author trying to tell us?			4 3 2 1
Characters Describe _____ (character's name) at the beginning and end of the story.			4 3 2 1
Setting Where and when did the story happen?			4 3 2 1
Plot Tell me what the story was about in a few sentences.			4 3 2 1

Summative Retelling Score   4   3   2   1

Comments _____

_____

_____

Unit 2 Expository Retelling Chart

Selection Title _____ **Name** _____ **Date** _____

Retelling Criteria/Teacher Prompt	Teacher-Aided Response	Student-Generated Response	Rubric Score (Circle one.)
Connections Did this selection make you think about something else you have read? What did you learn about as you read this selection?			4 3 2 1
Author's Purpose Why do you think the author wrote this selection?			4 3 2 1
Topic What was the selection mostly about?			4 3 2 1
Important Ideas What is important for me to know about _____ (topic)?			4 3 2 1
Conclusions What did you learn from reading this selection?			4 3 2 1

Summative Retelling Score   4   3   2   1

Comments _____

_____

Reading

Concepts of Print and Print Awareness

	Pre-K	K	1	2	3	4	5
Develop awareness that print represents spoken language and conveys and preserves meaning	•	•	•				
Recognize familiar books by their covers; hold book right side up	•	•					
Identify parts of a book and their functions (front cover, title page/title, back cover, page numbers)	•	•	•				
Understand the concepts of letter, word, sentence, paragraph, and story	•	•	•				
Track print (front to back of book, top to bottom of page, left to right on line, sweep back left for next line)	•	•	•				
Match spoken to printed words	•	•	•				
Know capital and lowercase letter names and match them	•	• T	•				
Know the order of the alphabet	•	•	•				
Recognize first name in print	•	•	•				
Recognize the uses of capitalization and punctuation		•	•				
Value print as a means of gaining information	•	•	•				

Phonological and Phonemic Awareness

	Pre-K	K	1	2	3	4	5
Phonological Awareness							
Recognize and produce rhyming words	•	•	•				
Track and count each word in a spoken sentence and each syllable in a spoken word	•	•	•				
Segment and blend syllables in spoken words			•				
Segment and blend onset and rime in one-syllable words			•				
Recognize and produce words beginning with the same sound	•	•	•				
Identify beginning, middle, and/or ending sounds that are the same or different	•	•	•				
Understand that spoken words are made of sequences of sounds	•	•	•				
Phonemic Awareness							
Identify the position of sounds in words		•	•				
Identify and isolate initial, final, and medial sounds in spoken words	•	•	•				
Blend sounds orally to make words or syllables		•	•				
Segment a word or syllable into sounds; count phonemes in spoken words or syllables		•	•				
Manipulate sounds in words (add, delete, and/or substitute phonemes)	•	•	•				

Phonics and Decoding

	Pre-K	K	1	2	3	4	5
Phonics							
Understand and apply the *alphabetic principle* that spoken words are composed of sounds that are represented by letters	•	•	•				
Know letter-sound relationships	•	• T	• T	• T			
Blend sounds of letters to decode		•	• T	• T	• T		
Consonants, consonant blends, and consonant digraphs		•	• T	• T	• T		
Short, long, and r-controlled vowels; vowel digraphs; diphthongs; common vowel patterns			• T	• T	• T		
Phonograms/word families		•	•	•	•		
Word Structure							
Decode words with common word parts		•	• T	• T	• T	•	•
Base words and inflected endings			• T	• T	•	•	•
Contractions and compound words			• T	• T	• T	•	•
Suffixes and prefixes			• T	• T	• T	•	•
Greek and Latin roots						•	•
Blend syllables to decode words			• T	• T	• T	•	•
Decoding Strategies							
Blending strategy: Apply knowledge of letter-sound relationships to decode unfamiliar words		•	•	•	•		
Apply knowledge of word structure to decode unfamiliar words		•	•	•	•	•	•
Use context and syntax along with letter-sound relationships and word structure to decode		•	•	•	•	•	•
Self-correct			•	•	•	•	•

Fluency

	Pre-K	K	1	2	3	4	5
Read aloud fluently with accuracy, comprehension, appropriate pace/rate; with expression/intonation (prosody); with attention to punctuation and appropriate phrasing			• T	• T	• T	• T	• T
Practice fluency in a variety of ways, including choral reading, partner/paired reading, Readers' Theater, repeated oral reading, and tape-assisted reading		•	•	•	•	•	•

• instructional opportunity   **T** tested in standardized test